Ajax in Action

DAVE CRANE
ERIC PASCARELLO
WITH DARREN JAMES

MANNING
Greenwich
(74° w. long.)

For online information and ordering of this and other Manning books, please go to
www.manning.com. The publisher offers discounts on this book when ordered in quantity.
For more information, please contact:

Special Sales Department
Manning Publications Co.
209 Bruce Park Avenue
Greenwich, CT 06830

Fax: (203) 661-9018
email: orders@manning.com

Manning Publications Co.
209 Bruce Park Avenue
Greenwich, CT 06830

Copyeditor: Liz Welch
Typesetter: Denis Dalinnik
Cover designer: Leslie Haimes

ISBN 1-932394-61-3

Printed in the United States of America
2 3 4 5 6 7 8 9 10 – VHG – 09 08 07 06 05

To Hermes, Apollo, Athena, and my cats, for their wisdom
—D.C.

To my wife; I'm surprised you said yes
—E.P.

To my red-headed wife
—D.J.

brief contents

contents

ix

preface

Sometimes your destiny will follow you around for years before you notice it. Amidst the medley of fascinating new technologies that I was playing—I mean *working*—with in the early 1990s was a stunted little scripting language called JavaScript. I soon realized that, despite its name, it didn't really have anything to do with my beloved Java, but it persistently dogged my every step.

By the late 90s, I had decided to cut my hair and get a proper job, and found myself working with the early adopters of digital set-top box technology. The user interface for this substantial piece of software was written entirely in JavaScript and I found myself the technical lead of a small team of developers writing window-management code, schedulers, and all kinds of clever stuff in this language. "How curious," I thought. "It'll never catch on."

With time I moved on to more demanding work, developing the enterprise messaging backbone and various user interface components for an "intelligent," talking "House of the Future." I was hired for my Java skills, but I was soon writing fancy JavaScript user interfaces again. It was astonishing to find that some people were now taking this scripting language seriously enough to write frameworks for it. I quickly picked up the early versions of Mike Foster's x library (which you'll find put into occasional action in this book). One afternoon, while working on an email and text message bulletin board, I had the weird, exciting idea of checking for new messages in a hidden frame and adding them to the user interface *without refreshing the screen*.

After a few hours of frenzied hacking, I had it working, and I'd even figured out how to render the new messages in color to make them noticeable to the user. "What a laugh," I thought, and turned back to some serious code. Meantime, unbeknownst to me, Eric Costello, Erik Hatcher, Brent Ashley, and others were thinking along similar lines, and Microsoft was cooking up the XMLHttpRequest for its Outlook Web Access.

Destiny was sniffing at my heels. My next job landed me in a heavy-duty development role, building software for big Tier 1 banks. We use a mixture of Java and JavaScript and employ tricks with hidden frames and other things. My team currently looks after more than 1.5 million bytes of such code—that's static JavaScript, in addition to code we generate from JSPs. No, I'm not counting any image resources in there either. We use it to develop applications for hundreds of operators managing millions of dollars' worth of accounts. Your bank account may well be managed by this software.

Somewhere along the way, JavaScript had grown up without my quite realizing it. In February 2005, Jesse James Garrett provided the missing piece of the jigsaw puzzle. He gave a short, snappy name to the cross-browser-asynchronous-rich-client-dynamic-HTML-client-server technology that had been sneaking up on us all for the last few years: *Ajax*.

And the rest, as they say, is history. Ajax is generating a lot of interest now, and a lot of good code is getting written by the people behind Prototype, Rico, Dojo, qooxdoo, Sarissa, and numerous other frameworks, too plentiful to count. Actually, we do try to count them, in appendix C. We think we've rounded up most of the suspects. And I've never had so much fun playing—I mean *working*—with computers.

We have not arrived yet. The field is still evolving. I was amazed to see just how much when I did the final edits in September on the first chapter that I wrote back in May! There's still a lot of thinking to be done on this subject, and the next year or two will be exciting. I've been very lucky to have Eric and Darren on the book piece of the journey with me so far.

We hope you will join us—and enjoy the ride.

DAVE CRANE

acknowledgments

Although there are only three names on the cover of this book, a legion of talented, hardworking, and just plain crazy people supported us behind the scenes. We'd like to thank everyone at Manning, especially our publisher, Marjan Bace, and our development editors, Jackie Carter and Doug Bennett, for their continuous support and help on so many aspects of the manuscript. To the others at Manning who worked with us in different stages of the project—Blaise Bace, review editor Karen Tegtmayer, webmaster Iain Shigeoka, publicist Helen Trimes, and not least of all project editor Mary Piergies—thanks for helping to steer us along so smoothly. Our copyeditors, Linda Recktenwald and Liz Welch, and proofreaders Barbara Mirecki and Tiffany Taylor, proved to be indispensable, and design editor Dottie Marsico and typesetter Denis Dalinnik did a marvelous job of converting our scribbles into pictures and our text into a real book!

Many talented coders gave their time unflinchingly to our cause, as technical proofreaders and reviewers. Leading the charge were Phil McCarthy (who not only corrected our code, but also our grammar and style, even setting us straight on the rules of Battleship) and Bear Bibeault, who bravely advised on server architecture, client-side code, and Mac compatibility, in the face of Hurricane Rita. Joe Mayo, Valentin Crettaz, James Tikalsky, Shane Witbeck, Frank Zammetti, Joel Webber, Jonathan Esterhazy, Garret Wilson, Joe Walker, and

J.B. Rainsberger provided first-rate technical support at very short notice. We are truly grateful to them.

We also thank the many reviewers of the manuscript, in its various stages, for their thoughtful feedback: Ernest Friedman-Hill, Craig Walls, Patrick Peak, J. B. Rainsberger, Jack Herrington, Erik Hatcher, Oliver Zeigermann, Suresh Kumar, Mark Chaimungkalanont, Doug Warren, Deiveehan Nallazhagappan, Norman Richards, Mark Eagle, Christophe Avare, Bill Lynch, Wayland Chan, Shane Witbeck, Mike Stenhouse, Frank Zammetti, Brendan Murray, Ryan Cox, Valentin Crettaz, Thomas Baekdal, Peter-Paul Koch, Venkatt Guhesan, Frank Jania, Mike Foster, Bear Bibeault, Peter George, Joel Webber, Nikhil Narayana, Harshad Oak, and Bas Vodde.

Thanks to Paul Hobbs, Bill Gathen, and Charlie Arehart for spotting typos in the code in the Manning Early Access Program chapters (MEAP). Finally, special thanks are due to Brian J. Sletten, Ben Galbraith, and Kito Mann for helping to get the ball rolling in the first place. Our thanks also go to the authors of the many Ajax frameworks that we have used in the book, and to Jesse James Garrett for providing us with a short, snappy acronym to grace the cover of our book. (We feel that "Those Rich Client JavaScript Network Things in Action" wouldn't have been quite as effective.)

We're standing on the shoulders of a whole group of giants here. The view is fantastic.

DAVE CRANE

I'd like to thank Chia, Ben, and Sophie for their support, wisdom, and enthusiasm, and for putting up with me through all the late nights and early mornings. I'm finished now and I promise to behave. Thanks too to my parents for listening to the book-writing saga unfold and for instilling in me the strength and foolishness to undertake such a project in the first place.

Eric and Darren have been excellent co-authors to work with, and I'd like to extend my thanks to them too, for their invaluable contributions to the book.

My thanks to my colleagues at Smartstream Technologies for exploring the world of Ajax with me before it was christened—Tony Coombes, John Kellett, Phil McCarthy, Anthony Warner, Jon Green, Rob Golder, David Higgins, Owen Rees-Hayward, Greg Nwosu, Hristo Gramatikov, and Stuart Martin, and to my managers Colin Reid and Andrew Elmore. Thanks too to our colleagues overseas: Bhupendra, Pooja, Rahul, Dhiraj, Josef, Vjeko and Ted, and to the many other talented people with whom I've had the pleasure to work over the years. Special thanks are due to Rodrigo Barnes for introducing me to this new programming language called "Java" ten years ago, and to my brother Mike for figuring out how to drive our BBC microcomputer.

ERIC PASCARELLO

I would like to thank Shona, my wife, for putting up with the late nights and for planning our wedding without my help, while I wrote this book. Thanks to my parents for letting me become a computer nerd. Thanks to my co-workers Fred Grau, Paul Fuseyamore, Tim Stanton, Tracey Baker, Adrienne Cantler, and Kelly Singleton for putting up with my early morning grumpiness after the long nights of writing. Thanks to the people at www.JavaRanch.com for their support and many great ideas. And I cannot forget to thank the aliens who abducted me and taught me to program.

DARREN JAMES

I would like to thank my wife, Alana, and my children, Hannah and Paul, for being my life's inspiration. Thanks to my parents for encouraging me to do well in school; to my colleague and friend, Bill Scott, for his ideas and support; to Richard Cowin and the contributors to Rico; to Butch Clarke for being an anchor in the storm; and to Gordon, Junior, and Jub-Jub for making me laugh.

about this book

Ajax is a growing new technology at the time of this writing and we're delighted to bring you the lowdown on it, in the inimitable style of Manning's *In Action* series. In doing so, though, we faced an interesting problem. Although Ajax is indisputably hot, it isn't really new. It isn't really a technology, either.

Let us explain. Ajax brings together several well-established web technologies and uses them in new and interesting ways. Learning to use a completely new technology for the first time is in some ways simpler because you start with a blank slate. Ajax is different: there is also much to unlearn. Because of this, our book is organized somewhat differently from most Manning *In Action* books. You may notice this when reading and should know that we feel the way it is organized best suits this subject.

And, as you will see, although the Ajax technologies themselves are all client side, the differences extend all the way down to the server. This book is mainly about client-side programming, and most of the code examples that you'll find in here are JavaScript. The principles of Ajax decouple the client from the server beautifully, and can be used with any server-side language. We've therefore got a broad audience to address and have opted to present our server-side code in a mixture of languages: PHP, Java, C#, and Visual Basic .NET. More importantly, though, we've tried to keep the server-side code relatively simple and implementation-agnostic, so that you can port it to whatever environment you choose. Where we do use language-specific features, we explain them in enough detail for those unfamiliar with that particular environment to figure out what we're doing.

Who should read this book?

Ajax is at the crossroads of a number of disciplines; readers will approach it from a number of directions. On the one hand there are professional enterprise developers with computer science degrees and several years of hands-on experience with large software projects, who need to sometimes pop their heads above the battlements and work with the presentation tier. On the other hand are creative professionals who have moved from graphic design to web design and "new media," and taught themselves how to program using scripting languages such as PHP, Visual Basic, or JavaScript/ActionScript. In between there are desktop app developers retraining for the Web and sysadmins called upon to put together web-based management tools, as well as many others.

All of these possible readers have a real interest in Ajax. We've tried to address the needs of all of them, at least to some extent, in this book. We provide pointers to the basic web technologies for the server-side developer used to treating the web browser as a dumb terminal. We also give a grounding in software design and organization for the new media developer who may be more used to ad hoc coding styles. Wherever you come from, Ajax is a cross-disciplinary technology and will lead you into some unfamiliar areas. We're going to stretch you a bit, and ask you to pick up a few new skills along the way. We've done the same in our own use of Ajax, even while writing this book. We have found it to be a very rewarding and enjoyable experience, with benefits extending to other aspects of our professional lives.

Roadmap

This book is divided into four parts. Part 1 will tell you what Ajax is, explain why it is a useful addition to your development toolbox, and introduce the tools that can make you successful. Part 2 covers the core techniques that make an Ajax application work, and part 3 builds on these to discuss what is needed to go from proof of concept to production-ready software. In part 4 we take a direct hands-on approach, and build five Ajax projects step by step; we then refactor them into drop-in components that you can use in your own web applications.

As we have said, Ajax is not a technology but a process. We've therefore dedicated chapter 1 to reorienting developers familiar with pre-Ajax web development. We discuss the fundamental differences between Ajax and the classic web application, how to think about usability, and other conceptual goodies. If you want to find out what the buzz around Ajax is, we suggest you start here. If you just want to eat, drink, and sleep code, then you'd best move on to chapter 2.

The Ajax technologies are all reasonably well documented in their own right already. We've provided a whistle-stop, example-driven run through these technologies in chapter 2, but we haven't aimed at being comprehensive. What we have done is emphasize where the technology is used differently, or behaves differently, as a result of being part of Ajax.

Chapter 3 introduces the third main theme for this book, managing the Ajax codebase. Having watched a JavaScript codebase grow to over 1.5 MB of source code, we can attest to the fact that writing JavaScript for Ajax is a different ball game. We talk design patterns and refactoring here, not because we think they're cool, but because we've found them to be invaluable, practical tools in working with Ajax. And we think you will too as you start to pick up speed.

In chapters 4 and 5, we turn our sights on the core components of Ajax, and apply our design pattern knowledge to find the best practices. Chapter 4 looks at ways of keeping your code clean on the client itself, applying the old web workhorse, Model-View-Controller, in a new way. Chapter 5 looks at the different ways of communicating between the client and the server and how various types of frameworks can be adapted to work with Ajax. By this point, we have covered all the basic plumbing and you'll know how Ajax operates end to end.

Chapters 6 through 8 build on the fundamental knowledge that we've acquired to look at how to add polish to your application and go beyond a proof of concept to something that's fun, and safe, to usable in the real world. Chapter 6 addresses the user experience, and takes an in-depth look at ways of keeping the user informed while asynchronous tasks are executing. There's a balance to be struck between keeping out of the user's way and keeping him in the dark, and we show you how to find that happy middle ground here.

Chapter 7 looks at the issue of security in Ajax from a number of angles. Ajax is a web technology and many of the issues that it faces are no different from any other web app. We cover the basic ground, concentrating on Ajax-specific issues here, such as securely importing generated JavaScript from the server, and protecting your web service entry points from unwanted direct manipulation. Security can be a showstopper for serious applications, and we give the basic steps needed to keep it under control here.

Chapter 8 discusses that other showstopper, performance (or rather, lack of it!). We show how to monitor the performance of your application and how to analyze code in order to improve it and keep those improvements consistent across an application.

In part 4, which consists of chapters 9 through 13, we switch gears to look at a number of Ajax projects. In each case, we code the functionality up in a straight-forward way and then refactor it into something robust that you can drop into your own projects with no more than a few lines of code. This gives you the bene-fit of understanding the principles, the benefits of reuse, as well as showing Ajax refactoring in action.

In chapter 9, we look at a simple way to give the user a richer experience by enhancing HTML forms with Ajax: we use data entered in one field to pre-populate a second drop-down list by making a background request to the server. We continue the theme of form enhancement in chapter 10 with an implementation of type-ahead suggest, fetching data from the server in response to user keystrokes.

Chapter 11 moves on to the wider possibilities of Ajax user interfaces. We develop a complete portal application that resembles a workstation desktop more than a web page, complete with its own draggable, resizable windows. Ajax processes track window movements in the background, so that the desktop is always in the same state you left it, even if you log back in on a different machine.

Chapter 12 develops an Ajax-based search system and demonstrates the power of client-side XSLT as a way of turning raw XML data into formatted, styled content.

In chapter 13, we present an Ajax client without a back-end implementation. It still talks to server processes, but in this case, does so directly to blog and news syndication feeds, using the Internet standard RSS protocol.

Finally, we include three appendices that we hope you'll find useful. The body of the book discusses the technology itself. With a new, cross-disciplinary tech-nology, assembling the tools to use it effectively is more of a challenge than with a mature technology stack such as J2EE or .NET. The vendors haven't started offering Ajax tools yet, but we're sure that they will! In the meantime, we provide in appendix A an overview of the tools and tricks that we've used to develop our Ajax projects and to keep our house in order.

Appendix B is for enterprise programmers who understand software design principles but aren't quite sure how to apply them in such a flexible, unstructured, and well, downright odd language as JavaScript. We walk through what the lan-guage can do, and point out where the main divergences from Java and C# lie.

If the tool vendors haven't quite caught up with Ajax yet, neither have the framework developers. The Ajax framework scene is a hotbed of innovation, intrigue (and often re-invention) right now. Appendix C rounds up the Ajax frameworks and toolkits that we know of at the moment, and provides a short overview and link for each.

Code conventions

All source code in listings or in text is in a `fixed-width font like this` to separate it from ordinary text. We make use of many languages and markups in this book—JavaScript, HTML, CSS, XML, Java, C#, Visual Basic .NET, and PHP—but we try to adopt a consistent approach. Method and function names, object properties, XML elements, and attributes in text are presented using this same font.

In many cases, the original source code has been reformatted: we've added line breaks and reworked indentation to accommodate the available page space in the book. In rare cases even this was not enough, and listings include line-continuation markers. Additionally, many comments have been removed from the listings. Where appropriate, we've also cut implementation details that distract rather than help tell the story, such as JavaBean setters and getters, import and include statements, and namespace declarations.

Code annotations accompany many of the listings, highlighting important concepts. In some cases, numbered bullets link to explanations that follow the listing.

Code downloads

Source code for all of the working examples in this book is available for download from http://www.manning.com/crane.

We realize that not all of you will have a .NET server, J2EE app server, and a Linux, Apache, MySQL, PHP/Python/Perl (LAMP) setup sitting on your desk, and that your principal interest in this book is in the client technology. As a result, we've tried to include "mock"-based versions of the example code that can be run with static dummy data from any web server, including Apache, Tomcat, and IIS. These are in addition to the full working examples, so that if you do enjoy wrestling with databases and app servers, you can dig in. Some basic setup documentation is provided with the download.

Author Online

Purchase of *Ajax in Action* includes free access to a private web forum run by Manning Publications where you can make comments about the book, ask technical questions, and receive help from the authors and from other users. To access the forum and subscribe to it, point your web browser to http://www.manning.com/crane. This page provides information on how to get on the forum once you are registered, what kind of help is available, and the rules of conduct on the forum.

Manning's commitment to our readers is to provide a venue where a meaningful dialogue between individual readers and between readers and the authors can take place. It is not a commitment to any specific amount of participation on the part of the authors, whose contribution to the book's forum remains voluntary (and unpaid). We suggest you try asking the authors some challenging questions, lest their interest stray!

The Author Online forum and the archives of previous discussions will be accessible from the publisher's website as long as the book is in print.

About the title

By combining introductions, overviews, and how-to examples, the *In Action* books are designed to help learning and remembering. According to research in cognitive science, the things people best remember are things they discover during self-motivated exploration.

Although no one at Manning is a cognitive scientist, we are convinced that in order for learning to become permanent it must pass through stages of exploration, play, and, interestingly, retelling of what was learned. People understand and remember new things, which is to say they master them, only after actively exploring them. Humans learn in action. An essential part of all *In Action* guides is that they are example-driven. This encourages readers to try things out, to play with new code, and explore new ideas.

There is another, more mundane, reason for the title of this book: our readers are busy. They use books to do a job or to solve a problem. They need books that allow them to jump in and jump out easily and learn just what they want just when they want it. They need books that aid them "in action." The books in this series are designed for such readers.

About the cover illustration

The figure on the cover of *Ajax in Action* is a "Sultana," a female member of a sultan's family; both his wife and his mother could be addressed by that name. The illustration is taken from a collection of costumes of the Ottoman Empire published on January 1, 1802, by William Miller of Old Bond Street, London. The title page is missing from the collection and we have been unable to track it down to date. The book's table of contents identifies the figures in both English and French, and each illustration bears the names of two artists who worked on it, both of whom would no doubt be surprised to find their art gracing the front cover of a computer programming book...two hundred years later.

The collection was purchased by a Manning editor at an antiquarian flea market in the "Garage" on West 26th Street in Manhattan. The seller was an American based in Ankara, Turkey, and the transaction took place just as he was packing up his stand for the day. The Manning editor did not have on his person the substantial amount of cash that was required for the purchase, and a credit card and check were both politely turned down. With the seller flying back to Ankara that evening the situation was getting hopeless. What was the solution? It turned out to be nothing more than an old-fashioned verbal agreement sealed with a handshake. The seller simply proposed that the money be transferred to him by wire and the editor walked out with the bank information on a piece of paper and the portfolio of images under his arm. Needless to say, we transferred the funds the next day, and we remain grateful and impressed by this unknown person's trust in one of us. It recalls something that might have happened a long time ago.

The pictures from the Ottoman collection, like the other illustrations that appear on our covers, bring to life the richness and variety of dress customs of two centuries ago. They recall the sense of isolation and distance of that period—and of every other historic period except our own hyperkinetic present.

Dress codes have changed since then and the diversity by region, so rich at the time, has faded away. It is now often hard to tell the inhabitant of one continent from another. Perhaps, trying to view it optimistically, we have traded a cultural and visual diversity for a more varied personal life. Or a more varied and interesting intellectual and technical life.

We at Manning celebrate the inventiveness, the initiative, and, yes, the fun of the computer business with book covers based on the rich diversity of regional life of two centuries ago—brought back to life by the pictures from this collection.

Part 1

Rethinking
the web application

This part of the book introduces the main concepts of Ajax. Chapter 1 presents Ajax and reasons to use it. Chapter 2 covers the technical fundamentals, and shows how they fit together. The aim is that, by the end of the book, you'll be able to tackle real-world projects bigger than a "hello world." Chapter 3 introduces the software development tools that we've used to manage large projects, and shows you how to use them with Ajax.

A new design for the Web

This chapter covers

- Asynchronous network interactions and usage patterns
- The key differences between Ajax and classic web applications
- The four fundamental principles of Ajax
- Ajax in the real world

Ideally, a user interface (UI) will be invisible to users, providing them with the options they need when they need them but otherwise staying out of their way, leaving users free to focus on the problem at hand. Unfortunately, this is a very hard thing to get right, and we become accustomed, or resigned, to working with suboptimal UIs on a daily basis—until someone shows us a better way, and we realize how frustrating our current method of doing things can be.

The Internet is currently undergoing such a realization, as the basic web browser technologies used to display document content have been pushed beyond the limits of what they can sanely accomplish.

Ajax (Asynchronous JavaScript + XML) is a relatively recent name, coined by Jesse James Garrett of Adaptive Path. Some parts of Ajax have been previously described as *Dynamic HTML* and *remote scripting*. Ajax is a snappier name, evoking images of cleaning powder, Dutch football teams, and Greek heroes suffering the throes of madness.

It's more than just a name, though. There is plenty of excitement surrounding Ajax, and quite a lot to get excited about, from both a technological and a business perspective. Technologically, Ajax gives expression to a lot of unrealized potential in the web browser technologies. Google and a few other major players are using Ajax to raise the expectations of the general public as to what a web application can do.

The classical "web application" that we have become used to is beginning to creak under the strain that increasingly sophisticated web-based services are placing on it. A variety of technologies are lining up to fill the gap with richer, smarter, or otherwise improved clients. Ajax is able to deliver this better, smarter richness using only technologies that are already installed on the majority of modern computers.

With Ajax, we are taking a bunch of dusty old technologies and stretching them well beyond their original scope. We need to be able to manage the complexity that we have introduced. This book will discuss the how-tos of the individual technologies but will also look at the bigger picture of managing large Ajax projects. We'll introduce Ajax *design patterns* throughout the book as well to help us get this job done. Design patterns help us to capture our knowledge and experience with a technology as we acquire it and to communicate it with others. By introducing regularity to a codebase, they can facilitate creating applications that are easy to modify and extend as requirements change. Design patterns are even a joy to work with!

1.1 Why Ajax rich clients?

Building a rich client interface is a bit more complicated than designing a web page. What is the incentive, then, for going this extra mile? What's the payoff? What is a rich client, anyway?

Two key features characterize a rich client: it's rich, and it's a client.

Let me explain a little more. *Rich* refers here to the interaction model of the client. A rich user interaction model is one that can support a variety of input methods and that responds intuitively and in a timely fashion. We could set a rather unambitious yardstick for this by saying that for user interaction to be rich, it must be as good as the current generation of desktop applications, such as word processors and spreadsheets. Let's take a look at what that would entail.

1.1.1 Comparing the user experiences

Take a few minutes to play with an application of your choice (other than a web browser), and count the types of user interaction that it offers. Come back here when you've finished. I'm going to discuss a spreadsheet as an example shortly, but the points I'll make are sufficiently generic that anything from a text editor up will do.

Finished? I am. While typing a few simple equations into my spreadsheet, I found that I could interact with it in a number of ways, editing data in situ, navigating the data with keyboard and mouse, and reorganizing data using drag and drop.

As I did these things, the program gave me feedback. The cursor changed shape, buttons lit up as I hovered over them, selected text changed color, highlighted windows and dialogs were represented differently, and so on (figure 1.1). That's what passes for rich interactivity these days. Arguably there's still some way to go, but it's a start.

So is the spreadsheet application a rich *client*? I would say that it isn't.

In a spreadsheet or similar desktop application, the logic and the data model are both executed in a closed environment, in which they can see each other very clearly but shut the rest of the world out (figure 1.2). My definition of a *client* is a program that communicates to a different, independent process, typically running on a server. Traditionally, the server is bigger, stronger, and better than the client, and it stores monstrously huge amounts of information. The client allows end users to view and modify this information, and if several clients are connected to the same server, it allows them to share that data. Figure 1.3 shows a simple schematic of a client/server architecture.

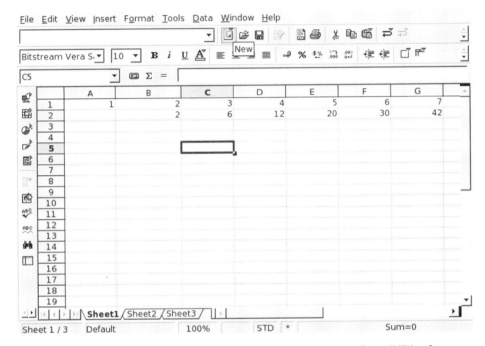

Figure 1.1 This desktop spreadsheet application illustrates a variety of possibilities for user interaction. The headers for the selected rows and columns are highlighted; buttons offer tooltips on mouseover; toolbars contain a variety of rich widget types; and the cells can be interactively inspected and edited.

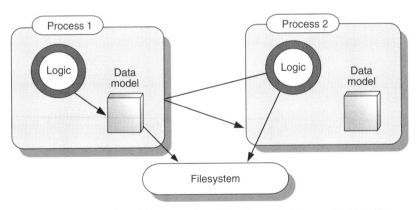

Figure 1.2 Schematic architectures for a standalone desktop application. The application runs in a process of its own, within which the data model and the program logic can "see" one another. A second running instance of the application on the same computer has no access to the data model of the first, except via the filesystem. Typically, the entire program state is stored in a single file, which is locked while the application is running, preventing any simultaneous exchange of information.

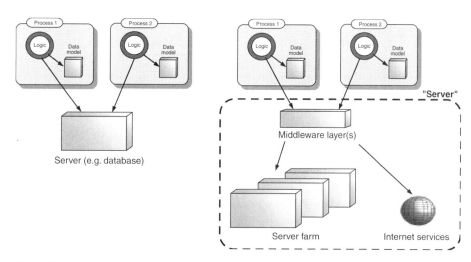

Figure 1.3 Schematic architectures for client/server systems and n-tier architectures. The server offers a shared data model, with which clients can interact. The clients still maintain their own partial data models, for rapid access, but these defer to the server model as the definitive representation of the business domain objects. Several clients can interact with the same server, with locking of resources handled at a fine-grain level of individual objects or database rows. The server may be a single process, as in the traditional client/server model of the early- to mid-1990s, or consist of several middleware tiers, external web services, and so on. In any case, from the client's perspective, the server has a single entry point and can be considered a black box.

In a modern n-tier architecture, of course, the server will communicate to further back-end servers such as databases, giving rise to middleware layers that act as both client and server. Our Ajax applications typically sit at the end of this chain, acting as client only, so we can treat the entire n-tier system as a single black box labeled "server" for the purposes of our current discussion.

My spreadsheet sits on its own little pile of data, stored locally in memory and on the local filesystem. If it is well architected, the coupling between data and presentation may be admirably loose, but I can't split it across the network or share it as such. And so, for our present purposes, it isn't a client.

Web browsers are clients, of course, contacting the web servers from which they request pages. The browser has some rich functionality for the purpose of managing the user's web browsing, such as back buttons, history lists, and tabs for storing several documents. But if we consider the web pages for a particular site as an application, then these generic browser controls are not related to the application any more than the Windows Start menu or window list are related to my spreadsheet.

Let's have a look at a modern web application. Simply because everyone has heard of it, we'll pick on Amazon, the bookseller (figure 1.4). I point my browser to the Amazon site, and, because it remembers who I am from my last visit, it shows me a friendly greeting, a list of recommended books, and information about my purchasing history.

Clicking on a title from the recommendations list leads me to a separate page (that is, the screen flickers and I lose sight of all the lists that I was viewing a few seconds earlier). This, too, is stuffed full of contextual information: reviews, second-hand prices for the book, links to similar authors, and titles of other books that I've recently checked out (figure 1.5).

In short, I'm presented with very rich, tightly interwoven information. And yet my only way of interacting with this information is through clicking hyperlinks and filling in text forms. If I fell asleep at the keyboard while browsing the site and awoke the next day, I wouldn't know that the new Harry Potter book had been released until I refreshed the entire page. I can't take my lists with me from one

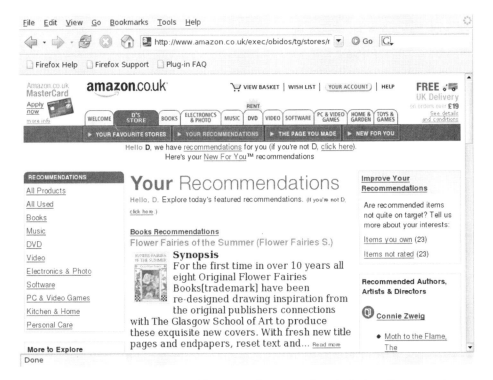

Figure 1.4 Amazon.com home page. The system has remembered who I am from a previous visit, and the navigational links are a mixture of generic boilerplate and personal information.

Figure 1.5 Amazon.com book details page. Again, a dense set of hyperlinks combines generic and personal information. Nonetheless, a significant amount of detail is identical to that shown in figure 1.4, which must, owing to the document-based operation of the web browser, be retransmitted with every page.

page to another, and I can't resize portions of the document to see several bits of content at once.

This is not to knock Amazon. It's doing a good job at working within some very tight bounds. But compared to the spreadsheet, the interaction model it relies on is unquestionably limiting.

So why are those limits present in modern web applications? There are sound technical reasons for the current situation, so let's take a look at them now.

1.1.2 *Network latency*

The grand vision of the Internet age is that all computers in the world interconnect as one very large computing resource. Remote and local procedure calls become indistinguishable, and issuers are no longer even aware of which physical machine (or machines) they are working on, as they happily compute the folds in their proteins or decode extraterrestrial signals.

Remote and local procedure calls are not the same thing at all, unfortunately. Communications over a network are expensive (that is, they are slow and unreliable). When a non-networked piece of code is compiled or interpreted, the various methods and functions are coded as instructions stored in the same local memory as the data on which the methods operate (figure 1.6). Thus, passing data to a method and returning a result is pretty straightforward.

Under the hood, a lot of computation is going on at both ends of a network connection in order to send and receive data (figure 1.7). It's this computation that slows things down, more than the physical journey along the wire. The various stages of encoding and decoding cover aspects of the communication ranging from physical signals passing along the wire (or airwaves), translation of these signals as the 1s and 0s of binary data, error checking and re-sending, to the reassembling of the sequence, and ultimately the meaning, of the binary information.

The calling function's request must be encoded as an object, which is then serialized (that is, converted into a linear set of bytes). The serialized data is then passed to the application protocol (usually HTTP these days) and sent across the physical transport (a copper or fiber-optic cable, or a wireless connection of some sort).

On the remote machine, the application protocol is decoded, and the bytes of data deserialized, to create a copy of the request object. This object can then be applied to the data model and a response object generated. To communicate the response to the calling function, the serialization and transport layers must be navigated once more, eventually resulting in a response object being returned to the calling function.

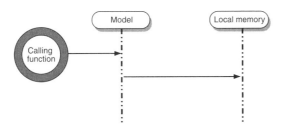

Figure 1.6   Sequence diagram of a local procedure call. Very few actors are involved here, as the program logic and the data model are both stored in local memory and can see each other directly.

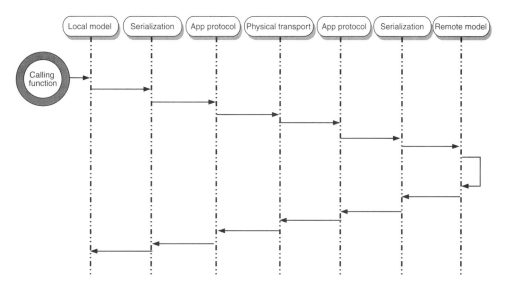

Figure 1.7   Sequence diagram of a remote procedure call. The program logic on one machine attempts to manipulate a data model on another machine.

These interactions are complex but amenable to automation. Modern program-ming environments such as Java and the Microsoft .NET Framework offer this functionality for free. Nonetheless, internally a lot of activity is going on when a remote procedure call (RPC) is made, and if such calls are made too freely, perfor-mance will suffer.

So, making a call over a network will never be as efficient as calling a local method in memory. Furthermore, the unreliability of the network (and hence the need to resend lost packets of information) makes this inefficiency variable and hard to predict. The responsiveness of the memory bus on your local machine is not only better but also very well defined in comparison.

But what does that have to do with usability? Quite a lot, as it turns out.

A successful computer UI does need to mimic our expectations of the real world *at the very basic level*. One of the most basic ground rules for interaction is that when we push, prod, or poke at something, it responds immediately. Slight delays between prodding something and the response can be disorienting and distracting, moving the user's attention from the task at hand to the UI itself.

Having to do all that extra work to traverse the network is often enough to slow down a system such that the delay becomes noticeable. In a desktop application, we need to make bad usability design decisions to make the application feel buggy or unresponsive, but in a networked application, we can get all that for free!

Because of the unpredictability of network latency, this perceived bugginess will come and go, and testing the responsiveness of the application can be harder, too. Hence, network latency is a common cause of poor interactivity in real-world applications.

1.1.3 Asynchronous interactions

There is only one sane response to the network latency problem available to the UI developer—assume the worst. In practical terms, we must try to make UI responses independent of network activity. Fortunately, a holding response is often sufficient, as long as it is timely. Let's take a trip to the physical world again. A key part of my morning routine is to wake my children up for school. I could stand over them prodding them until they are out of bed and dressed, but this is a time-consuming approach, leaving a long period of time in which I have very little to do (figure 1.8).

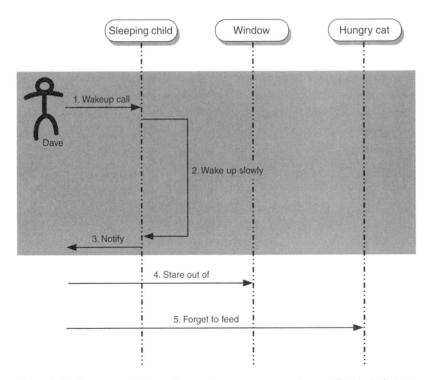

Figure 1.8 Sequence diagram of a synchronous response to user input, during my morning routine. In a sequence diagram, the passage of time is vertical. The height of the shaded area indicates the length of time for which I am blocked from further input.

I need to wake up my children, stare out the window, and ignore the cat. The children will notify me when they are properly awake by asking for breakfast. Like server-side processes, children are slow to wake. If I follow a synchronous interaction model, I will spend a long time waiting. As long as they are able to mutter a basic "Yes, I'm awake," I can happily move on to something else and check up on them later if need be.

In computer terms, what I'm doing here is spawning an asynchronous process, in a separate thread. Once they're started, my children will wake up by themselves in their own thread, and I, the parent thread, don't need to synchronize with them until they notify me (usually with a request to be fed). While they're waking up, I can't interact with them as if they were already up and dressed, but I can be confident that it will happen in due course (figure 1.9).

With any UI, it's a well-established practice to spawn an asynchronous thread to handle any lengthy piece of computation and let it run in the background while the user gets on with other things. The user is necessarily blocked while that thread is launched, but this can be done in an acceptably short span of time.

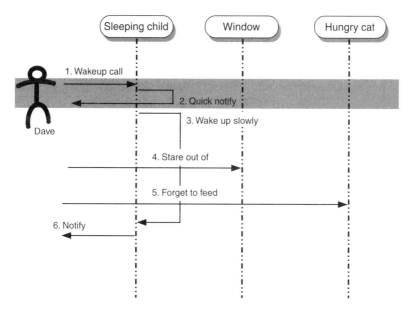

Figure 1.9   Sequence diagram of an asynchronous response to user input. If I follow an asynchronous input model, I can let the children notify me that they are starting to wake up. I can then continue with my other activities while the wakeup happens and remain blocked for a much shorter period of time.

Because of network latency, it is good practice to treat any RPC as potentially lengthy and handle it asynchronously.

This problem, and the solution, are both well established. Network latency was present in the old client/server model, causing poorly designed clients to freeze up inexplicably as they tried to reach an overloaded server. And now, in the Internet age, network latency causes your browser to "chug" frustratingly while moving between web pages. We can't get rid of latency, but we know how to deal with it—by processing the remote calls asynchronously, right?

Unfortunately for us web app developers, there's a catch. HTTP is a request-response protocol. That is, the client issues a request for a document, and the server responds, either by delivering the document, saying that it can't find it, offering an alternative location, or telling the client to use its cached copy, and so on. A request-response protocol is one-way. The client can make contact with the server, but the server cannot initiate a communication with the client. Indeed, the server doesn't remember the client from one request to the next.

The majority of web developers using modern languages such as Java, PHP, or .NET will be familiar with the concept of user sessions. These are an after-thought, bolted onto application servers to provide the missing server-side state in the HTTP protocol. HTTP does what it was originally designed for very well, and it has been adapted to reach far beyond that with considerable ingenuity. However, the key feature of our asynchronous callback solution is that the client gets notified twice: once when the thread is spawned and again when the thread is completed. Straightforward HTTP and the classic web application model can't do this for us.

The classic web app model, as used by Amazon, for example, is still built around the notion of pages. A document is displayed to the user, containing lists of links and/or form elements that allow them to drill down to further documents. Complex datasets can be interacted with in this way on a large scale, and as Amazon and others have demonstrated, the experience of doing so can be compelling enough to build a business on.

This model of interaction has become quite deeply ingrained in our way of thinking over the ten years or so of the commercial, everyday Internet. Friendly WYSIWYG web-authoring tools visualize our site as a collection of pages. Server-side web frameworks model the transition between pages as state transition diagrams. The classic web application is firmly wedded to the unavoidable lack of responsiveness when the page refreshes, without an easy recourse to the asynchronous handler solution.

But Amazon has built a successful business on top of its website. Surely the classic web application can't be that unusable? To understand why the web page works for Amazon but not for everyone, we ought to consider usage patterns.

1.1.4 Sovereign and transient usage patterns

It's futile to argue whether a bicycle is better than a sports utility vehicle. Each has its own advantages and disadvantages—comfort, speed, fuel consumption, vague psychological notions about what your mode of transport "says" about you as a person. When we look at particular use patterns, such as getting through the rush hour of a compact city center, taking a large family on vacation, or seeking shelter from the rain, we may arrive at a clear winner. The same is true for computer UIs.

Software usability expert Alan Cooper has written some useful words about usage patterns and defines two key usage modes: transient and sovereign. A *transient* application might be used every day, but only in short bursts and usually as a secondary activity. A *sovereign* application, in contrast, must cope with the user's full attention for several hours at a time.

Many applications are inherently transient or sovereign. A writer's word processor is a sovereign application, for example, around which a number of transient functions will revolve, such as the file manager (often embedded into the word processor as a file save or open dialog), a dictionary or spellchecker (again, often embedded), and an email or messenger program for communicating with colleagues. To a software developer, the text editor or Integrated Development Environment (IDE) is sovereign, as is the debugger.

Sovereign applications are also often used more intensely. Remember, a well-behaved UI should be invisible. A good yardstick for the intensity of work is the effect on the user's workflow of the UI stalling, thus reminding the user that it exists. If I'm simply moving files from one folder to another and hit a two-second delay, I can cope quite happily. If I encounter the same two-second delay while composing a visual masterpiece in a paint program, or in the middle of a heavy debugging session with some tricky code, I might get a bit upset.

Amazon is a transient application. So are eBay and Google—and most of the very large, public web-based applications out there. Since the dawn of the Internet, pundits have been predicting the demise of the traditional desktop office suite under the onslaught of web-based solutions. Ten years later, it hasn't happened. Web page–based solutions are good enough for transient use but not for sovereign use.

1.1.5 *Unlearning the Web*

Fortunately, modern web browsers resemble the original ideal of a client for remote document servers about as closely as a Swiss army knife resembles a neolithic flint hunting tool. Interactive gizmos, scripting languages, and plug-ins have been bolted on willy-nilly over the years in a race to create the most compelling browsing experience. (Have a look at www.webhistory.org/www.lists/www-talk.1993q1/0182.html to get a perspective on how far we've come. In 1993, a pre-Netscape Marc Andreessen tentatively suggested to Tim Berners-Lee and others that HTML might benefit from an image tag.)

A few intrepid souls have been looking at JavaScript as a serious programming language for several years, but on the whole, it is associated with faked-up alert dialogs and "click the monkey to win" banners.

Think of Ajax as a rehabilitation center for this misunderstood, ill-behaved child of the browser wars. By providing some guidance and a framework within which to operate, we can turn JavaScript into a helpful model citizen of the Internet, capable of enhancing the real usability of a web application—and without enraging the user or trashing the browser in the process. Mature, well-understood tools are available to help us do this. Design patterns are one such tool that we make frequent use of in our work and will refer to frequently in this book.

Introducing a new technology is a technical and social process. Once the technology is there, people need to figure out what to do with it, and a first step is often to use it as if it were something older and more familiar. Hence, early bicycles were referred to as "hobbyhorses" or "dandy horses" and were ridden by pushing one's feet along the ground. As the technology was exposed to a wider audience, a second wave of innovators would discover new ways of using the technology, adding improvements such as pedals, brakes, gears, and pneumatic tires. With each incremental improvement, the bicycle became less horse-like (figure 1.10).

Figure 1.10   Development of the modern bicycle

The same processes are at work in web development today. The technologies behind Ajax have the ability to transform web pages into something radically new. Early attempts to use the Ajax technologies resembled the traditional web page document and have that neither-one-thing-nor-the-other flavor of the hobbyhorse. To grasp the potential of Ajax, we must let go of the concept of the web page and, in doing so, unlearn a lot of the assumptions that we have been making for the last few years. In the short few months since Ajax was christened, a lot of unlearning has been taking place.

1.2 The four defining principles of Ajax

The classic page-based application model is hard-wired into many of the frameworks that we use, and also into our ways of thinking. Let's take a few minutes to discover what these core assumptions are and how we need to rethink them to get the most out of Ajax.

1.2.1 The browser hosts an application, not content

In the classic page-based web application, the browser is effectively a dumb terminal. It doesn't know anything about where the user is in the greater workflow. All of that information is held on the web server, typically in the user's session. Server-side user sessions are commonplace these days. If you're working in Java or .NET, the server-side session is a part of the standard API, along with requests, responses, and Multipurpose Internet Mail Extensions (MIME) types. Figure 1.11 illustrates the typical lifecycle of a classic web application.

When the user logs in or otherwise initializes a session, several server-side objects are created, representing, say, the shopping basket and the customer credentials if this is an e-commerce site. At the same time, the home page is dished up to the browser, in a stream of HTML markup that mixes together standard boilerplate presentation and user-specific data and content such as a list of recently viewed items.

Every time the user interacts with the site, another document is sent to the browser, containing the same mixture of boilerplate and data. The browser dutifully throws the old document away and displays the new one, because it is dumb and doesn't know what else to do.

When the user hits the logout link or closes the browser, the application exits and the session is destroyed. Any information that the user needs to see the next time she or he logs on will have been handed to the persistence tier by

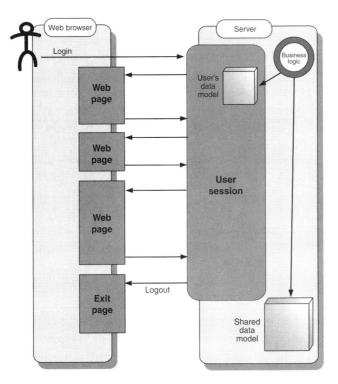

Figure 1.11 Lifecycle of a classic web application. All the state of the user's "conversation" with the application is held on the web server. The user sees a succession of pages, none of which can advance the broader conversation without going back to the server.

now. An Ajax application moves some of the application logic to the browser, as figure 1.12 illustrates.

When the user logs in, a more complex document is delivered to the browser, a large proportion of which is JavaScript code. This document will stay with the user throughout the session, although it will probably alter its appearance considerably while the user is interacting with it. It knows how to respond to user input and is able to decide whether to handle the user input itself or to pass a request on to the web server (which has access to the system database and other resources), or to do a combination of both.

Because the document persists over the entire user session, it can store state. A shopping basket's contents may be stored in the browser, for example, rather than in the server session.

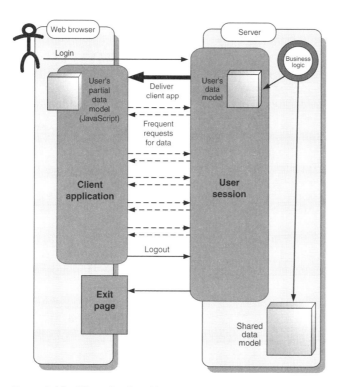

Figure 1.12 Lifecycle of an Ajax application. When the user logs in, a client application is delivered to the browser. This application can field many user interactions independently, or else send requests to the server behind the scenes, without interrupting the user's workflow.

1.2.2 *The server delivers data, not content*

As we noted, the classic web app serves up the same mixture of boilerplate, content, and data at every step. When our user adds an item to a shopping basket, all that we really need to respond with is the updated price of the basket or whether anything went wrong. As illustrated in figure 1.13, this will be a very small part of the overall document.

An Ajax-based shopping cart could behave somewhat smarter than that, by sending out asynchronous requests to the server. The boilerplate, the navigation lists, and other features of the page layout are all there already, so the server needs to send back only the relevant data.

The Ajax application might do this in a number of ways, such as returning a fragment of JavaScript, a stream of plain text, or a small XML document. We'll

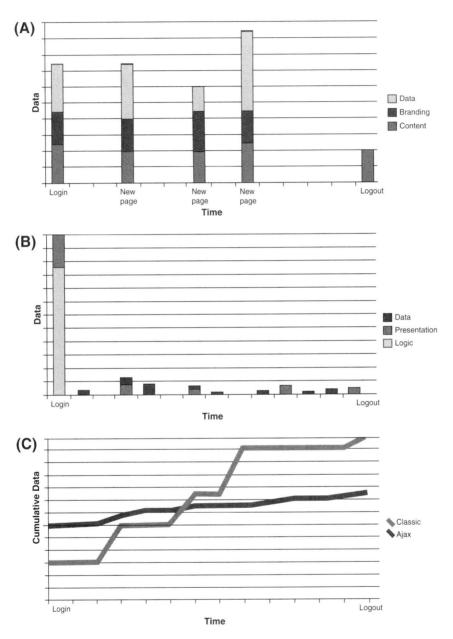

Figure 1.13 **Breakdown of the content delivered (A) to a classic web application and (B) to an Ajax application. As the application continues to be used, cumulative traffic (C) increases.**

look at the pros and cons of each in detail in chapter 5. Suffice it to say for now that any one of these formats will be much smaller than the mish-mash returned by the classic web application.

In an Ajax application, the traffic is heavily front-loaded, with a large and complex client being delivered in a single burst when the user logs in. Subsequent communications with the server are far more efficient, however. For a transient application, the cumulative traffic may be less for a conventional web page application, but as the average length of interaction time increases, the bandwidth cost of the Ajax application becomes less than that of its classic counterpart.

1.2.3 *User interaction with the application can be fluid and continuous*

A web browser provides two input mechanisms out of the box: hyperlinks and HTML forms.

Hyperlinks can be constructed on the server and preloaded with Common Gateway Interface (CGI) parameters pointed at dynamic server pages or servlets. They can be dressed up with images and Cascading Style Sheets (CSS) to provide rudimentary feedback when the mouse hovers over them. Given a good web designer, hyperlinks can be made to look like quite fancy UI components.

Form controls offer a basic subset of the standard desktop UI components: input textboxes, checkboxes and radio buttons, and drop-down lists. Several likely candidates are missing, though. There are no out-of-the-box tree controls, editable grids, or combo-boxes provided. Forms, like hyperlinks, point at server-side URLs.

Alternatively, hyperlinks and form controls can be pointed at JavaScript functions. It's a common technique in web pages to provide rudimentary form validation in JavaScript, checking for empty fields, out-of-range numbers, and so on, before submitting data to the server. These JavaScript functions persist only as long as the page itself and are replaced when the page submits.

While the page is submitting, the user is effectively in limbo. The old page may still be visible for a while, and the browser may even allow the user to click on any visible links, but doing so will produce unpredictable results and may wreak havoc with the server-side session. The user is generally expected to wait until the page is refreshed, often with a set of choices similar to those that were snatched away from them seconds earlier. After all, adding a pair of trousers to the shopping basket is unlikely to modify the top-level categories from "menswear," "women's wear," "children's," and "accessories."

Let's take the shopping cart example again. Because our Ajax shopping cart sends data asynchronously, users can drop things into it as fast as they can click. If the cart's client-side code is robust, it will handle this load easily, and the users can get on with what they're doing.

There is no cart to drop things into, of course, just an object in session on the server. Users don't want to know about session objects while shopping, and the cart metaphor provides a more comfortable real-world description of what's taking place. Switching contexts between the metaphor and direct access to the computer is distracting to users. Waiting for a page to refresh will jerk them back to the reality of sitting at a computer for a short time (figure 1.14), and our Ajax implementation avoids doing this. Shopping is a transient activity, but if we consider a different business domain, for example, a high-pressure help desk scenario or a complex engineering task, then the cost of disrupting the workflow every few seconds with a page refresh is prohibitive.

The second advantage of Ajax is that we can hook events to a wider range of user actions. More sophisticated UI concepts such as drag-and-drop become feasible, bringing the UI experience fully up to par with the desktop application widget sets. From a usability perspective, this freedom is important not so much because it allows us to exercise our imagination, but because it allows us to blend the user interaction and server-side requests more fully.

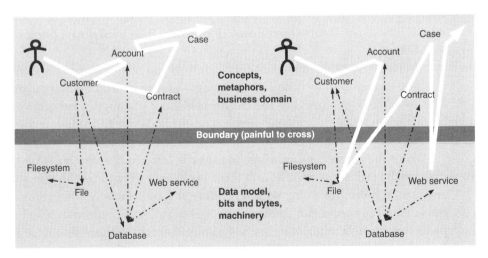

Figure 1.14 Interrupting the user's workflow to process events. The user deals with two types of object: those relating to their business, and those relating to the computer system. Where the user is forced to switch between the two frequently, disorientation and lack of productivity may occur.

To contact the server in a classic web application, we need to click a hyperlink or submit a form, and then wait. This interrupts the user's workflow. In contrast, contacting the server in response to a mouse movement or drag, or a keystroke, allows the server to work alongside the user. Google Suggest (www.google.com/webhp?complete=1) is a very simple but effective example of this: responding to users keystrokes as they type into the search box and contacting the server to retrieve and display a list of likely completions for the phrases, based on searches made by other users of the search engine worldwide. We provide a simple implementation of a similar service in chapter 8.

1.2.4 *This is real coding and requires discipline*

Classic web applications have been making use of JavaScript for some time now, to add bells and whistles around the edge of their pages. The page-based model prevents any of these enhancements from staying around for too long, which limits the uses to which they can be put. This catch-22 situation has led, unfairly, to JavaScript getting a reputation as a trivial, hacky sort of language, looked down upon by the serious developers.

Coding an Ajax application is a different matter entirely. The code that you deliver when users launch the application must run until they close it, without breaking, without slowing down, and without generating memory leaks. If we're aiming at the sovereign application market, then this means several hours of heavy usage. To meet this goal, we must write high-performance, maintainable code, using the same discipline and understanding that is successfully applied to the server tiers.

The codebase will also typically be larger than anything written for a classic web application. Good practices in structuring the codebase become important. The code may become the responsibility of a team rather than an individual, bringing up issues of maintainability, separation of concerns, and common coding styles and patterns.

An Ajax application, then, is a complex functional piece of code that communicates efficiently with the server while the user gets on with work. It is clearly a descendent of the classic page-based application, but the similarity is no stronger than that between the early hobbyhorse and a modern touring bike. Bearing these differences in mind will help you to create truly compelling web applications.

1.3 Ajax rich clients in the real world

So much for the theory. Ajax is already being used to create real applications, and the benefit of the Ajax approach can already be seen. It's still very much early days—the bicycles of a few far-sighted individuals have pedals and solid rubber tires, and some are starting to build disc brakes and gearboxes, so to speak. The following section surveys the current state of the art and then looks in detail at one of the prominent early adopters to see where the payoff in using Ajax lies.

1.3.1 Surveying the field

Google has done more than any other company to raise the profile of Ajax applications (and it, like the majority of adopters, was doing so before the name Ajax was coined). Its GMail service was launched in beta form in early 2004. Along with the extremely generous mailbox size, the main buzz around GMail was the UI, which allowed users to open several mail messages at once and which updated mailbox lists automatically, even while the user was typing in a message. Compared with the average web mail system offered by most Internet service providers (ISPs) at the time, this was a major step forward. Compared with the corporate mail server web interfaces of the likes of Microsoft Outlook and Lotus Notes, GMail offered most of the functionality without resorting to heavy, troublesome ActiveX controls or Java applets, making it available across most platforms and locations, rather than the corporate user's carefully preinstalled machine.

Google has followed this up with further interactive features, such as Google Suggest, which searches the server for likely completions for your query as you type, and Google Maps, an interactive zoomable map used to perform location-based searches. At the same time, other companies have begun to experiment with the technology, such as Flickr's online photo-sharing system, now part of Yahoo!

The applications we have discussed so far are testing the water. They are still transient applications, designed for occasional use. There are signs of an emerging market for sovereign Ajax applications, most notably the proliferation of frameworks in recent months. We look at a few of these in detail in chapter 3, and attempt to summarize the current state of the field in appendix C.

There are, then, sufficient signals to suggest that Ajax is taking hold of the market in a significant way. We developers will play with any new technology for its own sake, but businesses like Google and Yahoo! will join in only if there are compelling business reasons. We've already outlined many of the theoretical advantages of Ajax. In the following section, we'll take apart Google Maps, in order to see how the theory stacks up.

1.3.2 Google Maps

Google Maps is a cross between a map viewer and a search engine. Initially, the map shows the entire United States (figure 1.15). The map can be queried using free text, allowing drill-down to specific street addresses or types of amenity such as hotels and restaurants (figure 1.16).

The search feature functions as a classic web app, refreshing the entire page, but the map itself is powered by Ajax. Clicking on individual links from a hotel search will cause additional pop-ups to be displayed on the fly, possibly even scrolling the map slightly to accommodate them. The scrolling of the map itself is

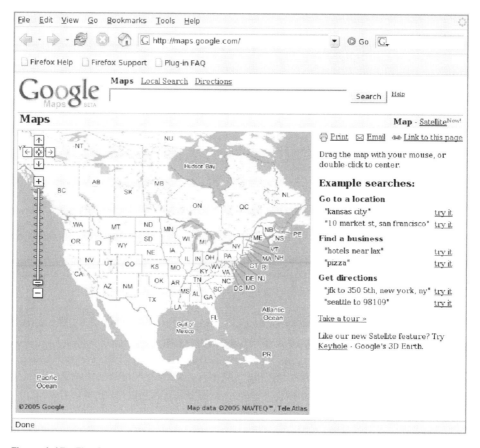

Figure 1.15 The Google Maps home page offers a scrolling window on a zoomable map of the United States, alongside the familiar Google search bar. Note that the zoom control is positioned on top of the map rather than next to it, allowing the user to zoom without taking his eyes off the map.

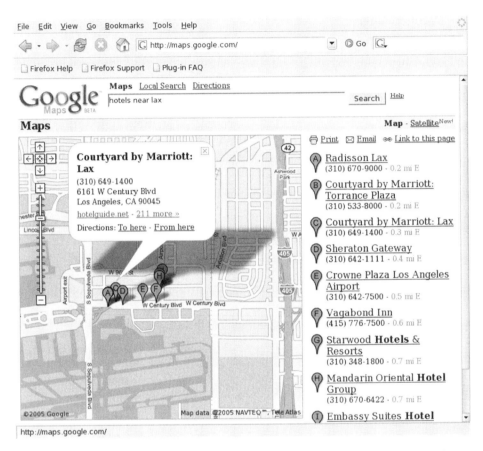

Figure 1.16 Google Maps hotel search. Note the traditional use of the DHTML technologies to create shadows and rich tooltip balloons. Adding Ajax requests makes these far more dynamic and useful.

the most interesting feature of Google Maps. The user can drag the entire map by using the mouse. The map itself is composed of small tiled images, and if the user scrolls the map far enough to expose a new tile, it will be asynchronously downloaded. There is a noticeable lag at times, with a blank white area showing initially, which is filled in once the map tile is loaded; however, the user can continue to scroll, triggering fresh tile requests, while the download takes place. The map tiles are cached by the browser for the extent of a user's session, making it much quicker to return to a part of the map already visited.

Looking back to our discussions of usability, two important things are apparent. First, the action that triggers the download of new map data is not a specific click on a link saying "fetch more maps" but something that the user is doing anyway, namely, moving the map around. The user workflow is uninterrupted by the need to communicate with the server. Second, the requests themselves are asynchronous, meaning that the contextual links, zoom control, and other page features remain accessible while the map is gathering new data.

Internet-based mapping services are nothing new. If we looked at a typical pre-Ajax Internet mapping site, we would see a different set of interaction patterns. The map would typically be divided into tiles. A zoom control, and perhaps sideways navigation links at the map's edges, might be provided. Clicking on any of these would invoke a full-screen refresh, resulting in a similar page hosting different map tiles. The user workflow would be interrupted more, and after looking at Google Maps, the user would find the site slow and frustrating.

Turning to the server-side, both services are undoubtedly backed by some powerful mapping solutions. Both serve up map tiles as images. The conventional web server of the pre-Ajax site is continually refreshing boilerplate code when the user scrolls, whereas Google Maps, once up and running, serves only the required data, in this case image tiles that aren't already cached. (Yes, the browser will cache the images anyway, providing the URL is the same, but browser caching still results in server traffic when checking for up-to-date data and provides a less-reliable approach than programmatic caching in memory.) For a site with the prominent exposure of Google, the bandwidth savings must be considerable.

To online services such as Google, ease of use is a key feature in getting users to visit their service and to come back again. And the number of page impressions is a crucial part of the bottom line for the business. By introducing a better UI with the flexibility that Ajax offers, Google has clearly given traditional mapping services something to worry about. Certainly other factors, such as the quality of the back-end service, come into play, but other things being equal, Ajax can offer a strong business advantage.

We can expect the trend for this to rise as public exposure to richer interfaces becomes more prevalent. As a marketable technology, Ajax looks to have a bright future for the next few years. However, other rich client technologies are looking to move into this space, too. Although they are largely outside the scope of this book, it's important that we take a look at them before concluding our overview.

1.4   Alternatives to Ajax

Ajax meets a need in the marketplace for richer, more responsive web-based clients that don't need any local installation. It isn't the only player in that space, though, and in some cases, it isn't even the most appropriate choice. In the following section, we'll briefly describe the main alternatives.

1.4.1   Macromedia Flash-based solutions

Macromedia's Flash is a system for playing interactive movies using a compressed vector graphics format. Flash movies can be streamed, that is, played as they are downloaded, allowing users to see the first bits of the movie before the last bits have arrived. Flash movies are interactive and are programmed with ActionScript, a close cousin of JavaScript. Some support for input form widgets is also provided, and Flash can be used for anything from interactive games to complex business UIs. Flash has very good vector graphics support, something entirely absent from the basic Ajax technology stack.

Flash has been around for ages and is accessed by a plug-in. As a general rule, relying on a web browser plug-in is a bad idea, but Flash is *the* web browser plug-in, with the majority of browsers bundling it as a part of the installation. It is available across Windows, Mac OS X, and Linux, although the installation base on Linux is probably smaller than for the other two platforms.

For the purposes of creating rich clients with Flash, two very interesting technologies are Macromedia's Flex and the open source Laszlo suite, both of which provide simplified server-side frameworks for generating Flash-based business UIs. Both frameworks use Java/Java 2 Enterprise Edition (J2EE) on the server side. For lower-level control over creating Flash movies dynamically, several toolkits, such as PHP's libswf module, provide core functionality.

1.4.2   Java Web Start and related technologies

Java Web Start is a specification for bundling Java-based web applications on a web server in such a way that a desktop process can find, download, and run them. These applications can be added as hyperlinks, allowing seamless access from a Web Start–savvy web browser. Web Start is bundled with the more recent Java runtimes, and the installation process will automatically enable Web Start on Internet Explorer and Mozilla-based browsers.

Once downloaded, Web Start applications are stored in a managed "sandbox" in the filesystem and automatically updated if a new version is made available. This allows them to be run while disconnected from the network and reduces network traffic on reload, making the deployment of heavy applications weighing several megabytes a possibility. Applications are digitally signed, and the user may choose to grant them full access to the filesystem, network ports, and other resources.

Traditionally, Web Start UIs are written in the Java Swing widget toolkit, about which strong opinions are held on both sides. The Standard Widget Toolkit (SWT) widgets used to power IBM's Eclipse platform can also be deployed via Web Start, although this requires a bit more work.

Microsoft's .NET platform offers a similar feature called No Touch Deployment, promising a similar mix of easy deployment, rich UIs, and security.

The main downside to both technologies is the need to have a runtime preinstalled. Of course, any rich client needs a runtime, but Flash and Ajax (which uses the web browser itself as a runtime) use runtimes that are commonly deployed. Java and .NET runtimes are both very limited in their distribution at present and can't be relied on for a public web service.

1.5 Summary

We've discussed the differences between transient and sovereign applications and the requirements of each. Transient applications need to deliver the goods, but, when users are using them, they have already stepped out of their regular flow of work, and so a certain amount of clunkiness is acceptable. Sovereign applications, in contrast, are designed for long-term intensive use, and a good interface for a sovereign application must support the users invisibly, without breaking their concentration on the task at hand.

The client/server and related n-tier architectures are essential for collaborative or centrally coordinated applications, but they raise the specter of network latency, with its ability to break the spell of user productivity. Although a general-purpose solution to the conflict between the two exists in asynchronous remote event handling, the traditional request-response model of the classic web application is ill suited to benefit from it.

We've set a goal for ourselves, and for Ajax, in this chapter of delivering usable sovereign applications through a web browser, thereby satisfying the goals of user productivity, networking, and effortless, centralized maintenance of an application all at once. In order for this mission to succeed, we need to start thinking about our web pages and applications in a fundamentally different way. We've identified the key ideas that we need to learn and those that we need to unlearn:

- The browser hosts an application, not content.

- The server delivers data, not content.

- The user interacts continuously with the application, and most requests to the server are implicit rather than explicit.

- Our codebase is large, complex, and well structured. It is a first-class citizen in our architecture, and we must take good care of it.

The next chapter will unpack the key Ajax technologies and get our hands dirty with some code. The rest of the book will look at important design principles that can help us to realize these goals.

1.6 Resources

To check out some of our references in greater depth, here are URLs to several of the articles that we've referred to in this chapter:

- Jesse James Garrett christened Ajax on February 18, 2005, in this article: www.adaptivepath.com/publications/essays/archives/000385.php

- Alan Cooper's explanation of sovereign and transient applications can be found here: www.cooper.com/articles/art_your_programs_posture.htm

- Google Maps can be found here if you live in the United States: http://maps.google.com

  and here if you live in the United Kingdom: http://maps.google.co.uk

  and here if you live on the moon: http://moon.google.com

The images of the bicycle were taken from the Pedaling History website: www.pedalinghistory.com

First steps with Ajax

This chapter covers

- Introducing the technologies behind Ajax
- Using Cascading Style Sheets to define look and feel
- Using the Document Object Model to define the user interface structure
- Using XMLHttpRequest to asynchronously contact the server
- Putting the pieces together

In chapter 1 we focused on users and how Ajax can assist them in their daily activities. Most of us are developers, and so, having convinced ourselves that Ajax is a Good Thing, we need to know how to work with it. The good news is that, as with many brand-new, shiny technologies, most of this process will be reasonably familiar already, particularly if you've worked with the Internet.

In this chapter, we'll explain the Ajax technology. We'll discuss the four technological cornerstones of Ajax and how they relate to one another, using code examples to demonstrate how each technology works and how everything fits together.

You might like to think of this chapter as the "hello world" section of the book, in which we introduce the core technologies using some simple examples. We're more interested here in just getting things to work; we'll start to look at the bigger picture in chapter 3. If you're already familiar with some or all of the Ajax technologies, you may want to skim these sections. If you're new to Ajax and to web client programming, these introductions should be sufficient to orient you for the rest of the book.

2.1 The key elements of Ajax

Ajax isn't a single technology. Rather, it's a collection of four technologies that complement one another. Table 2.1 summarizes these technologies and the role that each has to play.

Table 2.1   The key elements of Ajax

JavaScript	JavaScript is a general-purpose scripting language designed to be embedded inside applications. The JavaScript interpreter in a web browser allows programmatic interaction with many of the browser's inbuilt capabilities. Ajax applications are written in JavaScript.
Cascading Style Sheets (CSS)	CSS offers a way of defining reusable visual styles for web page elements. It offers a simple and powerful way of defining and applying visual styling consistently. In an Ajax application, the styling of a user interface may be modified interactively through CSS.
Document Object Model (DOM)	The DOM presents the structure of web pages as a set of programmable objects that can be manipulated with JavaScript. Scripting the DOM allows an Ajax application to modify the user interface on the fly, effectively redrawing parts of the page.
XMLHttpRequest object	The (misnamed) XMLHttpRequest object allows web programmers to retrieve data from the web server as a background activity. The data format is typically XML, but it works well with any text-based data. While XMLHttpRequest is the most flexible general-purpose tool for this job, there are other ways of retrieving data from the server, too, and we'll cover them all in this chapter.

We saw in chapter 1 how an Ajax application delivers a complex, functioning application up front to users, with which they then interact. JavaScript is the glue that is used to hold this application together, defining the user workflow and business logic of the application. The user interface is manipulated and refreshed by using JavaScript to manipulate the Document Object Model (DOM), continually redrawing and reorganizing the data presented to the users and processing their mouse- and keyboard-based interactions. Cascading Style Sheets (CSS) provide a consistent look and feel to the application and a powerful shorthand for the programmatic DOM manipulation. The XMLHttpRequest object (or a range of similar mechanisms) is used to talk to the server asynchronously, committing user requests and fetching up-to-date data while the user works. Figure 2.1 shows how the technologies fit together in Ajax.

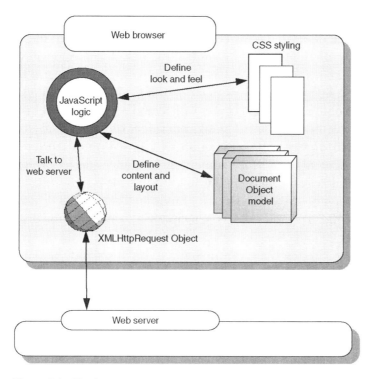

Figure 2.1 The four main components of Ajax: JavaScript defines business rules and program flow. The Document Object Model and Cascading Style Sheets allow the application to reorganize its appearance in response to data fetched in the background from the server by the XMLHttpRequest object or its close cousins.

Three of the four technologies—CSS, DOM, and JavaScript—have been collectively referred to as Dynamic HTML, or DHTML for short. DHTML was the Next Big Thing around 1997, but not surprisingly in this industry, it never quite lived up to its initial promise. DHTML offered the ability to create funky, interactive interfaces for web pages, yet it never overcame the issue of the full-page refresh. Without going back to talk to the server, there was only so much that we could do. Ajax makes considerable use of DHTML, but by adding the asynchronous request, it can extend the longevity of a web page considerably. By going back to the server while the interface is doing its stuff, without interruption, Ajax makes a great difference to the end result.

Rather conveniently, all of these technologies are already preinstalled in most modern web browsers, including Microsoft's Internet Explorer; the Mozilla/Gecko family of browsers, including Firefox, Mozilla Suite, Netscape Navigator, and Camino; the Opera browser; Apple's Safari; and its close cousin Konqueror, from the UNIX KDE desktop. Inconveniently, the implementations of these technologies are frustratingly different in some of the fine details and will vary from version to version, but this situation has been improving over the last five years, and we have ways of coping cleanly with cross-browser incompatibilities.

Every modern operating system comes with a modern browser preinstalled. So the vast majority of desktop and laptop computers on the planet are already primed to run Ajax applications, a situation that most Java or .NET developers can only dream about. (The browsers present in PDAs and Smartphones generally offer a greatly cut-down feature list and won't support the full range of Ajax technologies, but differences in screen size and input methods would probably be an issue even if they did. For now, Ajax is principally a technology for desktop and laptop machines.)

We'll begin by reviewing these technologies in isolation and then look at how they interoperate. If you're a seasoned web developer, you'll probably know a lot of this already, in which case you might like to skip ahead to chapter 3, where we begin to look at managing the technologies by using design patterns.

Let's start off our investigations by looking at JavaScript.

2.2 Orchestrating the user experience with JavaScript

The central player in the Ajax toolkit is undoubtedly JavaScript. An Ajax application downloads a complete client into memory, combining data and presentation and program logic, and JavaScript is the tool used to implement that logic.

JavaScript is a general-purpose programming language of mixed descent, with a superficial similarity to the C family of languages.

JavaScript can be briefly characterized as a loosely typed, interpreted, general-purpose scripting language. *Loosely typed* means that variables are not declared specifically as strings, integers, or objects, and the same variable may be assigned values of different types. For example, the following is valid code:

```
var x=3.1415926;
x='pi';
```

The variable x is defined first as a numeric value and reassigned a string value later.

Interpreted means that it is not compiled into executable code, but the source code is executed directly. When deploying a JavaScript application, you place the source code on the web server, and the source code is transmitted directly across the Internet to the web browser. It's even possible to evaluate snippets of code on the fly:

```
var x=eval('7*5');
```

Here we have defined our calculation as a piece of text, rather than two numbers and an arithmetic operator. Calling eval() on this text interprets the JavaScript it contains, and returns the value of the expression. In most cases, this simply slows the program execution down, but at times the extra flexibility that it brings can be useful.

General purpose means that the language is suitable for use with most algorithms and programming tasks. The core JavaScript language contains support for numbers, strings, dates and times, arrays, regular expressions for text processing, and mathematical functions such as trigonometry and random number generation. It is possible to define structured objects using JavaScript, bringing design principles and order to more complex code.

Within the web browser environment, parts of the browser's native functionality, including CSS, the DOM, and the XMLHttpRequest objects, are exposed to the JavaScript engine, allowing page authors to programmatically control the page to a greater or lesser degree. Although the JavaScript environment that we encounter in the browser is heavily populated with browser-specific objects, the underlying language is just that, a programming language.

This isn't the time or place for a detailed tutorial on JavaScript basics. In appendix B we take a closer look at the language and outline the fundamental differences between JavaScript and the C family of languages, including its namesake, Java. JavaScript examples are sprinkled liberally throughout this book, and several other books already exist that cover the language basics (see our Resources section at the end of this chapter).

Within the Ajax technology stack, JavaScript is the glue that binds all the other components together. Having a basic familiarity with JavaScript is a prerequisite for writing Ajax applications. Being fluent in JavaScript and understanding its strengths will allow you to take full advantage of Ajax.

We'll move on now to Cascading Style Sheets, which control the visual style of elements on a web page.

2.3 Defining look and feel using CSS

Cascading Style Sheets are a well-established part of web design, and they find frequent use in classic web applications as well as in Ajax. A stylesheet offers a centralized way of defining categories of visual styles, which can then be applied to individual elements on a page very concisely. In addition to the obvious styling elements such as color, borders, background images, transparency, and size, stylesheets can define the way that elements are laid out relative to one another and simple user interactivity, allowing quite powerful visual effects to be achieved through stylesheets alone.

In a classic web application, stylesheets provide a useful way of defining a style in a single place that can be reused across many web pages. With Ajax, we don't think in terms of a rapid succession of pages anymore, but stylesheets still provide a helpful repository of predefined looks that can be applied to elements dynamically with a minimum of code. We'll work through a few basic CSS examples in this section, but first, let's look at how CSS rules are defined.

CSS styles a document by defining rules, usually in a separate file that is referred to by the web page being styled. Style rules can also be defined inside a web page, but this is generally considered bad practice.

A style rule consists of two parts: the *selector* and the *style declaration*. The selector specifies which elements are going to be styled, and the style declaration declares which style properties are going to be applied. Let's say that we want to make all our level-1 headings in a document (that is, the <H1> tags) appear red. We can declare a CSS rule to do this:

```
h1 { color: red }
```

The selector here is very simple, applying to all <H1> tags in the document. The style declaration is also very simple, modifying a single style property. In practice, both the selector and the style declaration can be considerably more complex. Let's look at the variations in each, starting with the selector.

2.3.1 *CSS selectors*

In addition to defining a type of HTML tag to apply a style to, we can limit the rule to those within a specific context. There are several ways of specifying the context: by HTML tag type, by a declared class type, or by an element's unique ID.

Let's look at tag-type selectors first. For example, to apply the above rule only to `<H1>` tags that are contained within a `<DIV>` tag, we would modify our rule like this:

```
div h1 { color: red; }
```

These are also referred to as element-based selectors, because they decide whether or not a DOM element is styled based on its element type. We can also define classes for styling that have nothing to do with the HTML tag type. For example, if we define a style class called `callout`, which is to appear in a colored box, we could write

```
.callout { border: solid blue 1px; background-color: cyan }
```

To assign a style class to an element, we simply declare a class attribute in the HTML tag, such as

```
<div>I'll appear as a normal bit of text</div>
<div class='callout'>And I'll appear as a callout!</div>
```

Elements can be assigned more than one class. Suppose that we define an additional style class `loud` as

```
.loud { color: orange }
```

and apply both the styles in a document like so:

```
<div class='loud'>I'll be bright orange</div>
<div class='callout'>I'll appear as a callout</div>
<div class='callout loud'>
And I'll appear as an unappealing mixture of both!
</div>
```

The third `<div>` element will appear with orange text in a cyan box with a blue border. It is also possible to combine CSS styles to create a pleasing and harmonious design!

We can combine classes with element-based rules, to define a class that operates only on particular tag types. For example:

```
span.highlight { background-color: yellow }
```

will be applied only to <span> tags with a declared class attribute of highlight. Other <span> tags, or other types of tag with class='highlight', will be unaffected.

We can also use these in conjunction with the parent-child selectors to create very specific rules:

```
div.prose span.highlight { background-color: yellow }
```

This rule will be applied only to <span> tags of class highlight that are nested within <div> tags of class prose.

We can specify rules that apply only to an element with a given unique ID, as specified by the id attribute in the HTML. No more than one element in an HTML document should have a given ID assigned to it, so these selectors are typically used to select a single element on a page. To draw attention to a close button on a page, for example, we might define a style:

```
#close { color: red }
```

CSS also allows us to define styles based on pseudo-selectors. A web browser defines a limited number of pseudo-selectors. We'll present a few of the more useful ones here. For example:

```
*:first-letter {
  font-size: 500%;
  color: red;
  float: left;
}
```

will draw the first letter of any element in a large bold red font. We can tighten up this rule a little, like this:

```
p.illuminated:first-letter {
  font-size: 500%;
  color: red;
  float: left;
}
```

The red border effect will now apply only to <p> elements with a declared class of illuminated. Other useful pseudo-selectors include first-line, and hover, which modifies the appearance of hyperlinks when the mouse pointer passes over them. For example, to make a link appear in yellow when under the mouse pointer, we could write the following rule:

```
a:hover{ color:yellow; }
```

That covers the bases for CSS selectors. We've already introduced several style declarations informally in these examples. Let's have a closer look at them now.

2.3.2 *CSS style properties*

Every element in an HTML page can be styled in a number of ways. The most generic elements, such as the `<DIV>` tag, can have dozens of stylings applied to them. Let's look briefly at a few of these.

The text of an element can be styled in terms of the color, the font size, the heaviness of the font, and the typeface to use. Multiple options can be specified for fonts, to allow graceful degradation in situations where a desired font is not installed on a client machine. To style a paragraph in gray, terminal-style text, we could define a styling:

```
.robotic{
  font-size: 14pt;
  font-family: courier new, courier, monospace;
  font-weight: bold;
  color: gray;
}
```

Or, more concisely, we could amalgamate the font elements:

```
.robotic{
  font: bold 14pt courier new, courier, monospace;
  color: gray;
}
```

In either case, the multiple styling properties are written in a key-value pair notation, separated by semicolons.

CSS can define the layout and size (often referred to as the *box-model*) of an element, by specifying margins and padding elements, either for all four sides or for each side individually:

```
.padded{ padding: 4px; }
.eccentricPadded {
  padding-bottom: 8px;
  padding-top: 2px;
  padding-left: 2px;
  padding-right: 16px;
  margin: 1px;
}
```

The dimensions of an element can be specified by the `width` and `height` properties. The position of an element can be specified as either absolute or relative. Absolutely positioned elements can be positioned on the page by setting the `top` and `left` properties, whereas relatively positioned elements will flow with the rest of the page.

Background colors can be set to elements using the `background-color` property. In addition, a background image can be set, using the `background-image` property:

```
.titlebar{ background-image: url(images/topbar.png); }
```

Elements can be hidden from view by setting either `visibility:hidden` or `display:none`. In the former case, the item will still occupy space on the page, if relatively positioned, whereas in the latter case, it won't.

This covers the basic styling properties required to construct user interfaces for Ajax applications using CSS. In the following section, we'll look at an example of putting CSS into practice.

2.3.3 A simple CSS example

We've raced through the core concepts of Cascading Style Sheets. Let's try putting them into practice now. CSS can be used to create elegant graphic design, but in an Ajax application, we're often more concerned with creating user interfaces that mimic desktop widgets. As a simple example of this type of CSS use, figure 2.2 shows a folder widget styled using CSS.

CSS performs two roles in creating the widget that we see on the right in figure 2.2. Let's look at each of them in turn.

Using CSS for layout

The first job is the positioning of the elements. The outermost element, representing the window as a whole, is assigned an absolute position:

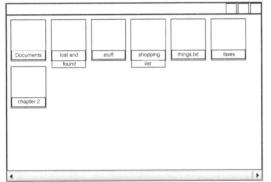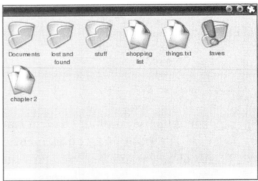

Figure 2.2   **Using CSS to style a user interface widget. Both screenshots were generated from identical HTML, with only the stylesheets altered. The stylesheet used on the left retains only the positioning elements, whereas the stylesheet used to render the right adds in the decorative elements, such as colors and images.**

```
div.window{
  position: absolute;
  overflow: auto;
  margin: 8px;
  padding: 0px;
  width: 420px;
  height: 280px;
}
```

Within the content area, the icons are styled using the `float` property so as to flow within the confines of their parent element, wrapping around to a new line where necessary:

```
div.item{
  position: relative;
  height: 64px;
  width: 56px;
  float: left;
  padding: 0px;
  margin: 8px;
}
```

The `itemName` element, which is nested inside the `item` element, has the text positioned below the icon by setting an upper margin as large as the icon graphic:

```
div.item div.itemName{
  margin-top: 48px;
  font: 10px verdana, arial, helvetica;
  text-align: center;
}
```

Using CSS for styling

The second job performed by CSS is the visual styling of the elements. The graphics used by the items in the folder are assigned by class name, for example:

```
div.folder{
  background:
    transparent url(images/folder.png)
    top left no-repeat;
}
div.file{
  background:
    transparent url(images/file.png)
    top left no-repeat;
}
div.special{
  background:
    transparent url(images/folder_important.png)
    top left no-repeat;
}
```

The background property of the icon styles is set to not repeat itself and be positioned at the top left of the element, with transparency enabled. (Figure 2.2 is rendered using Firefox. Transparency of .png images under Internet Explorer is buggy, with a number of imperfect proposed workarounds available. The forthcoming Internet Explorer 7 fixes these bugs, apparently. If you need cross-browser transparent images, we suggest the use of .gif images at present.)

Individual items declare two style classes: The generic item defines their layout in the container, and a second, more specific one defines the icon to be used. For example:

```
<div class='item folder'>
<div class='itemName'>stuff</div>
</div>
<div class='item file'>
<div class='itemName'>shopping list</div>
</div>
```

All the images in the styling are applied as background images using CSS. The titlebar is styled using an image as tall as the bar and only 1 pixel wide, repeating itself horizontally:

```
div.titlebar{
  background-color: #0066aa;
  background-image: url(images/titlebar_bg.png);
  background-repeat: repeat-x;
  ...
}
```

The full HTML for this widget is presented in listing 2.1.

Listing 2.1 window.html

```
<html>
<head>
<link rel='stylesheet' type='text/css'         Link to
  href='window.css' />                         stylesheet
</head>
<body>
<div class='window'>      <—  Top-level window element
  <div class='titlebar'>
    <span class='titleButton' id='close'></span>
    <span class='titleButton' id='max'></span>      Titlebar
    <span class='titleButton' id='min'></span>      buttons
  </div>
  <div class='contents'>
    <div class='item folder'>
      <div class='itemName'>Documents</div>
    </div>
    <div class='item folder'>
```

```
      <div class='itemName'>lost and found</div>
    </div>
    <div class='item folder'>                    An icon
      <div class='itemName'>stuff</div>          inside a
    </div>                                        window
    <div class='item file'>
      <div class='itemName'>shopping list</div>
    </div>
    <div class='item file'>
      <div class='itemName'>things.txt</div>
    </div>
    <div class='item special'>
      <div class='itemName'>faves</div>
    </div>
    <div class='item file'>
      <div class='itemName'>chapter 2</div>
    </div>
  </div>
</div>
</body>
</html>
```

The HTML markup defines the structure of the document, not the look. It also defines points in the document through which the look can be applied, such as class names, unique IDs, and even the tag types themselves. Reading the HTML, we can see how each element relates to the other in terms of containment but not the eventual visual style. Editing the stylesheet can change the look of this document considerably while retaining the structure, as figure 2.2 has demonstrated. The complete stylesheet for the widget is shown in listing 2.2.

Listing 2.2   window.css

```
div.window{
  position: absolute;
  overflow: auto;
  background-color: #eeefff;
  border: solid #0066aa 2px;
  margin: 8px;
  padding: 0px;
  width: 420px;          ➊ Geometry
  height: 280px;           of element
}
div.titlebar{
  background-color: #0066aa;
  background-image:                ➋ Background
  url(images/titlebar_bg.png);        texture
  background-repeat: repeat-x;
```

```
  color:white;
  border-bottom: solid black 1px;
  width: 100%;
  height: 16px;
  overflow:hidden;
}
span.titleButton{
  position: relative;
  height: 16px;
  width: 16px;
  padding: 0px;
  margin: 0px 1px; 0px 1px;
  float:right;                        ❸  Flow layout
}
span.titleButton#min{
  background: transparent
    url(images/min.png) top left no-repeat;
}
span.titleButton#max{
  background: transparent
    url(images/max.png) top left no-repeat;
}
span.titleButton#close{
  background: transparent
    url(images/close.png) top left no-repeat;
}
div.contents {
  background-color: #e0e4e8;
  overflow: auto;
  padding: 2px;
  height:240px;
}
div.item{
  position : relative;
  height : 64px;
  width: 56px;
  float: left;
  color : #004488;
  font-size: 18;
  padding: 0px;
  margin: 4px;
}
div.item div.itemName {
  margin-top: 48px;                   ❹  Text placement
  font: 10px verdana, arial, helvetica;
  text-align: center;
}
div.folder{
  background: transparent
    url(images/folder.png) top left no-repeat;
}
```

```
div.file{
  background: transparent
    url(images/file.png) top left no-repeat;
}
div.special{
  background: transparent
    url(images/folder_important.png)
    top left no-repeat;
}
```

We've already looked at a number of the tricks that we've employed in this stylesheet to tune the look and feel of individual elements. We've highlighted a few more here, to demonstrate the breadth of concerns to which CSS can be applied: on-screen placement ❶, texturing elements ❷, assisting in layout of elements ❸, and placing text relative to accompanying graphics ❹.

CSS is an important part of the web developer's basic toolkit. As we've demonstrated here, it can be applied just as easily to the types of interfaces that an Ajax application requires as to the more design-oriented approach of a static brochure-style site.

2.4 *Organizing the view using the DOM*

The Document Object Model (DOM) exposes a document (a web page) to the JavaScript engine. Using the DOM, the document structure, as seen in figure 2.3, can be manipulated programmatically. This is a particularly useful ability to have at our disposal when writing an Ajax application. In a classic web application, we are regularly refreshing the entire page with new streams of HTML from the server, and we can redefine the interface largely through serving up new HTML. In an Ajax application, the majority of changes to the user interface will be made using the DOM. HTML tags in a web page are organized in a tree structure. The root of the tree is the <HTML> tag, which represents the document. Within this, the <BODY> tag, which represents the document body, is the root of the visible document structure. Inside the body, we find table, paragraph, list, and other tag types, possibly with other tags inside them.

A DOM representation of a web page is also structured as a tree, composed of elements or nodes, which may contain child nodes within them, and so on recursively. The JavaScript engine exposes the root node of the current web page through the global variable *document*, which serves as the starting point for all our DOM manipulations. The DOM element is well defined by the W3C specification.

It has a single parent element, zero or more child elements, and any number of attributes, which are stored as an associative array (that is, by a textual key such as width or style rather than a numerical index). Figure 2.3 illustrates the abstract structure of the document shown in listing 2.2, as seen using the Mozilla DOM Inspector tool (see appendix A for more details).

The relationship between the elements in the DOM can be seen to mirror that of the HTML listing. The relationship is two-way. Modifying the DOM will alter the HTML markup and hence the presentation of the page.

This provides a top-level view of what the DOM looks like. In the following section, we'll see how the DOM is exposed to the JavaScript interpreter and how to work with it.

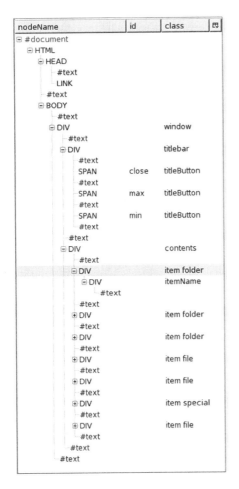

Figure 2.3
The DOM presents an HTML document as a tree structure, with each element representing a tag in the HTML markup.

2.4.1 *Working with the DOM using JavaScript*

In any application, we want to modify the user interface as users work, to provide feedback on their actions and progress. This could range from altering the label or color of a single element, through popping up a temporary dialog, to replacing large parts of the application screen with an entirely new set of widgets. By far the most usual is to construct a DOM tree by feeding the browser with declarative HTML (in other words, writing an HTML web page).

The document that we showed in listing 2.2 and figure 2.3 is rather large and complex. Let's start our DOM manipulating career with a small step. Suppose that we want to show a friendly greeting to the user. When the page first loads, we don't know his name, so we want to be able to modify the structure of the page to add his name in later, possibly to manipulate the DOM nodes programmatically. Listing 2.3 shows the initial HTML markup of this simple page.

Listing 2.3   Ajax "hello" page

```
<html>
<head>
<link rel='stylesheet' type='text/css'
  href='hello.css' />              ←—❶  Link to stylesheet
<script type='text/javascript'
  src='hello.js'></script>      ❷  Link to JavaScript
</head>
<body>
<p id='hello'>hello</p>
<div id='empty'></div>      ❸  Empty element
</body>
```

We have added references to two external resources: a Cascading Style Sheet ❶ and a file containing some JavaScript code ❷. We have also declared an empty `<div>` element with an ID ❸, into which we can programmatically add further elements.

Let's look at the resources that we've linked to. The stylesheet defines some simple stylings for differentiating between different categories of item in our list by modifying the font and color (listing 2.4).

Listing 2.4   hello.css

```
.declared{
  color: red;
  font-family: arial;
  font-weight: normal;
```

```
    font-size: 16px;
  }
  .programmed{
    color: blue;
    font-family: helvetica;
    font-weight: bold;
    font-size: 10px;
  }
```

We define two styles, which describe the origin of our DOM nodes. (The names of the styles are arbitrary. We called them that to keep the example easy to understand, but we could have just as easily called them `fred` and `jim`.) Neither of these style classes is used in the HTML, but we will apply them to elements programmatically. Listing 2.5 shows the JavaScript to accompany the web page in listing 2.4. When the document is loaded, we will programmatically style an existing node and create some more DOM elements programmatically.

Listing 2.5   hello.js

```
window.onload=function(){
  var hello=document.getElementById('hello');      ⟵ Find element by ID
  hello.className='declared';

  var empty=document.getElementById('empty');
  addNode(empty,"reader of");
  addNode(empty,"Ajax in Action!");

  var children=empty.childNodes;
  for (var i=0;i<children.length;i++){
    children[i].className='programmed';
  }

  empty.style.border='solid green 2px';        │ Style node
  empty.style.width="200px";                   │ directly
}
function addNode(el,text){
  var childEl=document.createElement("div");      ⟵ Create new element
  el.appendChild(childEl);
  var txtNode=document.createTextNode(text);      ⟵ Create text element
  childEl.appendChild(txtNode);
}
```

The JavaScript code is a bit more involved than the HTML or the stylesheet. The entry point for the code is the `window.onload()` function, which will be called programmatically once the entire page has been loaded. At this point, the DOM tree has been built, and we can begin to work with it. Listing 2.5 makes use of several DOM manipulation methods, to alter attributes of the DOM nodes, show and hide nodes, and even create completely new nodes on the fly. We won't cover every DOM manipulation method here—have a look at our resources section for that— but we'll walk through some of the more useful ones in the next few sections.

2.4.2 *Finding a DOM node*

The first thing that we need to do in order to work on a DOM with JavaScript is to find the elements that we want to change. As mentioned earlier, all that we are given to start with is a reference to the root node, in the global variable document. Every node in the DOM is a child, (or grandchild, great-grandchild, and so on) of document, but crawling down the tree, step by step, could be an arduous process in a big complicated document. Fortunately, there are some shortcuts. The most commonly used of these is to tag an element with a unique ID. In the onload() function in listing 2.5 we want to find two elements: the paragraph element, in order to style it, and the empty <div> tag, in order to add contents to it. Knowing, this, we attached unique ID attributes to each in the HTML, thus:

```
<p id='hello'>
```

and

```
<div id='empty'></div>
```

Any DOM node can have an ID assigned to it, and the ID can then be used to get a programmatic reference to that node in one function call, wherever it is in the document:

```
var hello=document.getElementById('hello');
```

Note that this is a method of a Document object. In a simple case like this (and even in many complicated cases), you can reference the current Document object as document. If you end up using IFrames, which we'll discuss shortly, then you have multiple Document objects to keep track of, and you'll need to be certain which one you're querying.

In some situations, we do want to walk the DOM tree step by step. Since the DOM nodes are arranged in a tree structure, every DOM node will have no more than one parent but any number of children. These can be accessed by the parentNode and childNodes properties. parentNode returns another DOM node object, whereas childNodes returns a JavaScript array of nodes that can be iterated over; thus:

```
var children=empty.childNodes;
for (var i=0;i<children.length;i++){
    ...
}
```

A third method worth mentioning allows us to take a shortcut through documents that we haven't tagged with unique IDs. DOM nodes can also be searched for based on their HTML tag type, using `getElementsByTagName()`. For example, `document.getElementsByTagName("UL")` will return an array of all `<UL>` tags in the document.

These methods are useful for working with documents over which we have relatively little control. As a general rule, it is safer to use `getElementById()` than `getElementsByTagName()`, as it makes fewer assumptions about the structure and ordering of the document, which may change independently of the code.

2.4.3 *Creating a DOM node*

In addition to reorganizing existing DOM nodes, there are cases where we want to create completely new nodes and add them to the document (say, if we're creating a message box on the fly). The JavaScript implementations of the DOM give us methods for doing that, too.

Let's look at our example code (listing 2.5) again. The DOM node with ID `'empty'` does indeed start off empty. When the page loads, we created some content for it dynamically. Our `addNode()` function uses the standard `document.create-Element()` and `document.createTextNode()` methods. `createElement()` can be used to create any HTML element, taking the tag type as an argument, such as

```
var childEl=document.createElement("div");
```

`createTextNode()` creates a DOM node representing a piece of text, commonly found nested inside heading, div, paragraph, and list item tags.

```
var txtNode=document.createTextNode("some text");
```

The DOM standard treats text nodes as separate from those representing HTML elements. They can't have styles applied to them directly and hence take up much less memory. The text represented by a text node may, however, be styled by the DOM element containing it.

Once the node, of whatever type, has been created, it must be attached to the document before it is visible in the browser window. The DOM node method `appendChild()` is used to accomplish this:

```
el.appendChild(childEl);
```

These three methods—`createElement()`, `createTextNode()`, and `appendChild()`—give us everything that we need to add new structure to a document. Having done so, however, we will generally want to style it in a suitable way, too. Let's look at how we can do this.

2.4.4 Adding styles to your document

So far, we've looked at using the DOM to manipulate the structure of a document—how one element is contained by another and so on. In effect, it allows us to reshape the structures declared in the static HTML. The DOM also provides methods for programmatically modifying the style of elements and reshaping the structures defined in the stylesheets.

Each element in a web page can have a variety of visual elements applied to it through DOM manipulation, such as position, height and width, colors, margins and borders. Modifying each attribute individually allows for very fine control, but it can be tedious. Fortunately, the web browser provides us with JavaScript bindings that allow us to exercise precision where needed through a low-level interface and to apply styling consistently and easily using CSS classes. Let's look at each of these in turn.

The className property

CSS offers a concise way of applying predefined, reusable styles to documents. When we are styling elements that we have created in code, we can also take advantage of CSS, by using a DOM node's `className` property. The following line, for example, applies the presentation rules defined by the `declared` class to a node:

```
hello.className='declared';
```

where `hello` is the reference to the DOM node. This provides an easy and compact way to assign many CSS rules at once to a node and to manage complex stylings through stylesheets.

The style property

In other situations, we may want to make a finer-grained change to a particular element's style, possibly supplementing styles already applied through CSS.

DOM nodes also contain an associative array called `style`, containing all the fine details of the node's style. As figure 2.4 illustrates, DOM node styles typically contain a large number of entries. Under the hood, assigning a `className` to the node will modify values in the `style` array.

The `style` array can be manipulated directly. After styling the items in the `empty` node, we draw a box around them; thus:

```
empty.style.border="solid green 2px";
empty.style.width="200px";
```

We could just as easily have declared a `box` class and applied it via the `className` property, but this approach can be quicker and simpler in certain circumstances, and it allows for the programmatic construction of strings. If we want to freely resize elements to pixel accuracy, for example, doing so by predefining styles for every width from 1 to 800 pixels would clearly be inefficient and cumbersome.

Using the above methods, then, we can create new DOM elements and style them. There's one more useful tool in our toolbox of content-manipulation techniques that takes a slightly different approach to programmatically writing a web page. We close this section with a look at the `innerHTML` property.

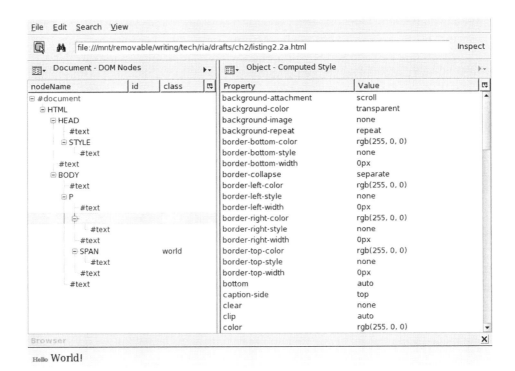

Figure 2.4 Inspecting the `style` attribute of a DOM node in the DOM Inspector. Most values will not be set explicitly by the user but will be assigned by the rendering engine itself. Note the scrollbar: we're seeing only roughly one-quarter of the full list of computed styles.

2.4.5 *A shortcut: Using the innerHTML property*

The methods described so far provide low-level control over the DOM API. However, `createElement()` and `appendChild()` provide a verbose API for building a document and are best suited for situations in which the document being created follows a regular structure that can be encoded as an algorithm. All popular web browsers' DOM elements also support a property named `innerHTML`, which allows arbitrary content to be assigned to an element in a very simple way. `innerHTML` is a string, representing a node's children as HTML markup. For example, we can rewrite our `addNode()` function to use `innerHTML` like this:

```
function addListItemUsingInnerHTML(el,text){
  el.innerHTML+="<div class='programmed'>"+text+"</div>";
}
```

The `<DIV>` element and the nested text node can be added in a single statement. Note also that it is appending to the property using the += operator, not assigning it directly. Deleting a node using `innerHTML` would require us to extract and parse the string. `innerHTML` is less verbose and suited to relatively simple applications such as this. If a node is going to be heavily modified by an application, the DOM nodes presented earlier provide a superior mechanism.

We've now covered JavaScript, CSS, and the DOM. Together, they went under the name Dynamic HTML when first released. As we mentioned in the introduction to this chapter, Ajax uses many of the Dynamic HTML techniques, but it is new and exciting because it throws an added ingredient into the mix. In the next section, we'll look at what sets Ajax apart from DHTML—the ability to talk to the server while the user works.

2.5 *Loading data asynchronously using XML technologies*

While working at an application—especially a sovereign one—users will be interacting continuously with the app, as part of the workflow. In chapter 1, we discussed the importance of keeping the application responsive. If everything locks up while a lengthy background task executes, the user is interrupted. We discussed the advantages of asynchronous method calls as a way of improving UI responsiveness when executing such lengthy tasks, and we noted that, because of network latency, all calls to the server should be considered as lengthy. We also noted that under the basic HTTP request-response model, this was a bit of a nonstarter. Classical web applications rely on full-page reloads with every call to the server leading to frequent interruptions for the user.

Although we have to accept that a document request is blocked until the server returns its response, we have a number of ways of making a server request look asynchronous to users so that they can continue working. The earliest attempts at providing this background communication used IFrames. More recently, the XMLHttpRequest object has provided a cleaner and more powerful solution. We'll look at both technologies here.

2.5.1 *IFrames*

When DHTML arrived with versions 4 of Netscape Navigator and Microsoft Internet Explorer, it introduced flexible, programmable layout to the web page. A natural extension of the old HTML Frameset was the *IFrame*. The *I* stands for *inline*, meaning that it is part of the layout of another document, rather than sitting side by side as in a frameset. An IFrame is represented as an element in the DOM tree, meaning that we can move it about, resize it, and even hide it altogether, while the page is visible. The key breakthrough came when people started to realize that an IFrame could be styled so as to be completely invisible. This allowed it to fetch data in the background, *while the visible user experience was undisturbed*. Suddenly, there was a mechanism to contact the server asynchronously, albeit rather a hacky one. Figure 2.5 illustrates the sequence of events behind this approach.

Like other DOM elements, an IFrame can be declared in the HTML for a page or it can be programmatically generated using `document.createElement()`. In a simple case, in which we want only a single nonvisible IFrame for loading data into, we can declare it as part of the document and get a programmatic handle on it using `document.getElementById()`, as in listing 2.6.

Listing 2.6 Using an IFrame

```
<html>
<head>
<script type='text/javascript'>
window.onload=function(){
  var iframe=document.getElementById('dataFeed');
  var src='datafeeds/mydata.xml';
  loadDataAsynchronously(iframe,src);
}
function loadDataAsynchronously(iframe,src){
  //...do something amazing!!
}
</script>
</head>
<body>
<!--
...some visible content here...
```

```
-->
<iframe
  id='dataFeed'
  style='height:0px;width:0px;'
>
</iframe>
</body>
</html>
```

The IFrame has been styled as being invisible by setting its width and height to zero pixels. We could use a styling of `display:none`, but certain browsers will optimize based on this and not bother to load the document! Note also that we need to wait for the document to load before looking for the IFrame, by calling `getElementById()` in the `window.onload` handler function. Another approach is to programmatically generate the IFrames on demand, as in listing 2.7. This has the added advantage of keeping all the code related to requesting the data in one place, rather than needing to keep unique DOM node IDs in sync between the script and the HTML.

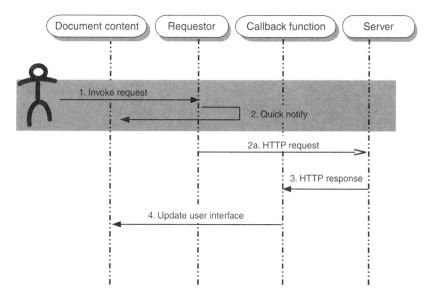

Figure 2.5 Sequence of events in an asynchronous communication in a web page. User action invokes a request from a hidden requester object (an IFrame or XMLHttpRequest object), which initiates a call to the server asynchronously. The method returns very quickly, blocking the user interface for only a short period of time, represented by the height of the shaded area. The response is parsed by a callback function, which then updates the user interface accordingly.

Listing 2.7 Creating an IFrame

```
function fetchData(){
  var iframe=document.createElement('iframe');
  iframe.className='hiddenDataFeed';
  document.body.appendChild(iframe);
  var src='datafeeds/mydata.xml';
  loadDataAsynchronously(iframe,src);
}
```

The use of `createElement()` and `appendChild()` to modify the DOM should be familiar from earlier examples. If we follow this approach rigidly, we will eventually create a large number of IFrames as the application continues to run. We need to either destroy the IFrames when we've finished with them or implement a pooling mechanism of some sort.

Design patterns, which we introduce in chapter 3, can help us to implement robust pools, queues, and other mechanisms that make a larger-scale application run smoothly, so we'll return to this topic in more depth later. In the meantime, let's turn our attention to the next set of technologies for making behind-the-scenes requests to the server.

2.5.2 *XmlDocument and XMLHttpRequest objects*

IFrames can be used to request data behind the scenes, as we just saw, but it is essentially a hack, repurposing something that was originally introduced to display visible content within a page. Later versions of popular web browsers introduced purpose-built objects for asynchronous data transfer, which, as we will see, offer some convenient advantages over IFrames.

The XmlDocument and XMLHttpRequest objects are nonstandard extensions to the web browser DOM that happen to be supported by the majority of browsers. They streamline the business of making asynchronous calls considerably, because they are explicitly designed for fetching data in the background. Both objects originated as Microsoft-specific ActiveX components that were available as Java-Script objects in the Internet Explorer browser. Other browsers have since implemented native objects with similar functionality and API calls. Both perform similar functions, but the XMLHttpRequest provides more fine-grained control over the request. We will use that throughout most of this book, but mention Xml-Document briefly here in case you come across it and wonder how it differs from XMLHttpRequest. Listing 2.8 shows a simple function body that creates an Xml-Document object.

Listing 2.8 getXmlDocument() function

```
function getXMLDocument(){
  var xDoc=null;
  if (document.implementation
    && document.implementation.createDocument){
    xDoc=document.implementation
      .createDocument("","",null);     <— Mozilla/Safari
  }else if (typeof ActiveXObject != "undefined"){
    var msXmlAx==null;
    try{
      msXmlAx=new ActiveXObject
        ("Msxml2.DOMDocument");     <— Newer Internet Explorer
    }catch (e){
      msXmlAx=new ActiveXObject
        ("Msxml.DOMDocument");     <— Older Internet Explorer

    }
    xDoc=msXmlAx;
  }
  if (xDoc==null || typeof xDoc.load=="undefined"){
    xDoc=null;
  }
  return xDoc;
}
```

The function will return an XmlDocument object with an identical API under most modern browsers. The ways of creating the document differ considerably, though.

The code checks whether the document object supports the implementation property needed to create a native XmlDocument object (which it will find in recent Mozilla and Safari browsers). If it fails to find one, it will fall back on ActiveX objects, testing to see if they are supported or unsupported (which is true only in Microsoft browsers) and, if so, trying to locate an appropriate object. The script shows a preference for the more recent MSXML version 2 libraries.

NOTE It is possible to ask the browser for vendor and version number information, and it is common practice to use this information to branch the code based on browser type. Such practice is, in our opinion, prone to error, as it cannot anticipate future versions or makes of browser and can exclude browsers that are capable of executing a script. In our getXml-Document() function, we don't try to guess the version of the browser but ask directly whether certain objects are available. This approach, known as *object detection*, stands a better chance of working in future versions of browsers, or in unusual browsers that we haven't explicitly tested, and is generally more robust.

Listing 2.9 follows a similar but slightly simpler route for the XMLHttp-
Request object.

Listing 2.9 `getXmlHttpRequest()` function

```
function getXMLHTTPRequest() {
  var xRequest=null;
  if (window.XMLHttpRequest) {
    xRequest=new XMLHttpRequest();    <— Mozilla/Safari
  }else if (typeof ActiveXObject != "undefined"){
    xRequest=new ActiveXObject
      ("Microsoft.XMLHTTP");    <— Internet Explorer
  }
  return xRequest;
}
```

Again, we use object detection to test for support of the native XMLHttpRequest
object and, failing that, for support for ActiveX. In a browser that supports neither, we will simply return `null` for the moment. We'll look at gracefully handling
failure conditions in more detail in chapter 6.

So, we can create an object that will send requests to the server for us. What do
we do now that we have it?

2.5.3 *Sending a request to the server*

Sending a request to the server from an XMLHttpRequest object is pretty
straightforward. All we need to do is pass it the URL of the server page that will
generate the data for us. Here's how it's done:

```
function sendRequest(url,params,HttpMethod){
  if (!HttpMethod){
    HttpMethod="POST";
  }
  var req=getXMLHTTPRequest();
  if (req){
    req.open(HttpMethod,url,true);
    req.setRequestHeader
        ("Content-Type",
          "application/x-www-form-urlencoded");
    req.send(params);
  }
}
```

XMLHttpRequest supports a broad range of HTTP calling semantics, including
optional querystring parameters for dynamically generated pages. (You may
know these as CGI parameters, Forms arguments, or ServletRequest parameters,

depending on your server development background.) Let's quickly review the basics of HTTP before seeing how our request object supports it.

HTTP—A quick primer

HTTP is such a ubiquitous feature of the Internet that we commonly ignore it. When writing classic web applications, the closest that we generally get to the HTTP protocol is to define a hyperlink and possibly set the `method` attribute on a form. Ajax, in contrast, opens up the low-level details of the protocol for us to play with, allowing us to do a few surprising things.

An HTTP transaction between a browser and a web server consists of a request by the browser, followed by a response from the server (with some exceptionally clever, mind-blowingly cool code written by us web developers happening in between, of course). Both request and response are essentially streams of text, which the client and server interpret as a series of headers followed by a body. Think of the headers as lines of an address written on an envelope and the body as the letter inside. The headers simply instruct the receiving party what to do with the letter contents.

An HTTP request is mostly composed of headers, with the body possibly containing some data or parameters. The response typically contains the HTML markup for the returning page. A useful utility for Mozilla browsers called Live-HTTPHeaders (see the Resources section at the end of this chapter and appendix A) lets us watch the headers from requests and responses as the browser works. Let's fetch the Google home page and see what happens under the hood.

The first request that we send contains the following headers:

```
GET / HTTP/1.1
Host: www.google.com
User-Agent: Mozilla/5.0
  (Windows; U; Windows NT 5.0; en-US; rv:1.7)
  Gecko/20040803 Firefox/0.9.3
Accept: text/xml,application/xml,
  application/xhtml+xml,text/html;q=0.9,
  text/plain;q=0.8,image/png,*/*;q=0.5
Accept-Language: en-us,en;q=0.5
Accept-Encoding: gzip,deflate
Accept-Charset: ISO-8859-1,utf-8;q=0.7,*;q=0.7
Keep-Alive: 300
Connection: keep-alive
Cookie: PREF=ID=cabd38877dc0b6a1:TM=1116601572
  :LM=1116601572:S=GD3SsQk3v0adtSBP
```

The first line tells us which HTTP method we are using. Most web developers are familiar with GET, which is used to fetch documents, and POST, used to submit

HTML forms. The World Wide Web Consortium (W3C) spec includes a few other common methods, including HEAD, which fetches the headers only for a file; PUT, for uploading documents to the server; and DELETE, for removing documents. Subsequent headers do a lot of negotiation, with the client telling the server what content types, character sets, and so on it can understand. Because I've visited Google before, it also sends a *cookie*, a short message telling Google who I am.

The response headers, shown here, also contain quite a lot of information:

```
HTTP/1.x 302 Found
Location: http://www.google.co.uk/cxfer?c=PREF%3D:
  TM%3D1116601572:S%3DzFxPsBpXhZzknVMF&prev=/
Set-Cookie: PREF=ID=cabd38877dc0b6a1:CR=1:TM=1116601572:
  LM=1116943140:S=fRfhD-u49xp9UE18;
  expires=Sun, 17-Jan-2038 19:14:07 GMT;
  path=/; domain=.google.com
Content-Type: text/html
Server: GWS/2.1
Transfer-Encoding: chunked
Content-Encoding: gzip
Date: Tue, 24 May 2005 17:59:00 GMT
Cache-Control: private, x-gzip-ok=""
```

The first line indicates the status of the response. A 302 response indicates a redirection to a different page. In addition, another cookie is passed back for this session. The content type of the response (aka MIME type) is also declared. A further request is made on the strength of the redirect instruction, resulting in a second response with the following headers:

```
HTTP/1.x 200 OK
Cache-Control: private
Content-Type: text/html
Content-Encoding: gzip
Server: GWS/2.1
Content-Length: 1196
Date: Tue, 24 May 2005 17:59:00 GMT
```

Status code 200 indicates success, and the Google home page will be attached to the body of this response for display. The content-type header tells the browser that it is html.

Our sendRequest() method is constructed so that the second and third parameters, which we probably won't need most of the time, are optional, defaulting to using POST to retrieve the resource with no parameters passed in the request body.

The code in this listing sets the request in motion and will return control to us immediately, while the network and the server take their own sweet time.

This is good for responsiveness, but how do we find out when the request has completed?

2.5.4 *Using callback functions to monitor the request*

The second part of the equation for handling asynchronous communications is setting up a reentry point in your code for picking up the results of the call once it has finished. This is generally implemented by assigning a callback function, that is, a piece of code that will be invoked when the results are ready, at some unspecified point in the future. The `window.onload` function that we saw in listing 2.6 is a callback function.

Callback functions fit the event-driven programming approach used in most modern UI toolkits—keyboard presses, mouse clicks, and so on will occur at unpredictable points in the future, too, and the programmer anticipates them by writing a function to handle them when they do occur. When coding UI events in JavaScript, we assign functions to the `onkeypress`, `onmouseover`, and similarly named properties of an object. When coding server request callbacks, we encounter similar properties called `onload` and `onreadystatechange`.

Both Internet Explorer and Mozilla support the `onreadystatechange` callback, so we'll use that. (Mozilla also supports `onload`, which is a bit more straightforward, but it doesn't give us any information that `onreadystatechange` doesn't.) A simple callback handler is demonstrated in listing 2.10.

Listing 2.10 Using a callback handler

```
var READY_STATE_UNINITIALIZED=0;
var READY_STATE_LOADING=1;
var READY_STATE_LOADED=2;
var READY_STATE_INTERACTIVE=3;
var READY_STATE_COMPLETE=4;
var req;
function sendRequest(url,params,HttpMethod){
  if (!HttpMethod){
    HttpMethod="GET";
  }
  req=getXMLHTTPRequest();
  if (req){
    req.onreadystatechange=onReadyStateChange;
    req.open(HttpMethod,url,true);
    req.setRequestHeader
        ("Content-Type", "application/x-www-form-urlencoded");
    req.send(params);
  }
}
```

```
function onReadyStateChange(){
  var ready=req.readyState;
  var data=null;
  if (ready==READY_STATE_COMPLETE){
    data=req.responseText;
  }else{
    data="loading...["+ready+"]";
  }
  //... do something with the data...
}
```

First, we alter our `sendRequest()` function to tell the request object what its callback handler is, before we send it off. Second, we define the handler function, which we have rather unimaginatively called `onReadyStateChange()`.

`readyState` can take a range of numerical values. We've assigned descriptively named variables to each here, to make our code easier to read. At the moment, the code is only interested in checking for the value 4, corresponding to completion of the request.

Note that we declare the request object as a global variable. Right now, this keeps things simple while we address the mechanics of the `XMLHttpRequest` object, but it could get us into trouble if we were trying to fire off several requests simultaneously. We'll show you how to get around this issue in section 3.1. Let's put the pieces together now, to see how to handle a request end to end.

2.5.5 *The full lifecycle*

We now have enough information to bring together the complete lifecycle of loading a document, as illustrated in listing 2.11. We instantiate the XMLHttp-Request object, tell it to load a document, and then monitor that load process asynchronously using callback handlers. In the simple example, we define a DOM node called `console`, to which we can output status information, in order to get a written record of the download process.

Listing 2.11 Full end-to-end example of document loading using XMLHttpRequest

```
<html>
<head>
<script type='text/javascript'>
var req=null;
var console=null;
var READY_STATE_UNINITIALIZED=0;
var READY_STATE_LOADING=1;
var READY_STATE_LOADED=2;
```

```
var READY_STATE_INTERACTIVE=3;
var READY_STATE_COMPLETE=4;
function sendRequest(url,params,HttpMethod){
  if (!HttpMethod){
    HttpMethod="GET";
  }
  req=initXMLHTTPRequest();
  if (req){
    req.onreadystatechange=onReadyState;
    req.open(HttpMethod,url,true);
    req.setRequestHeader
        ("Content-Type", "application/x-www-form-urlencoded");
    req.send(params);
  }
}
function initXMLHTTPRequest(){
  var xRequest=null;
  if (window.XMLHttpRequest){
    xRequest=new XMLHttpRequest();
  } else if (window.ActiveXObject){          Initialize
    xRequest=new ActiveXObject                request
      ("Microsoft.XMLHTTP");                  object
  }
  return xRequest;
}
function onReadyState(){      <—— Define callback handler
  var ready=req.readyState;
  var data=null;
  if (ready==READY_STATE_COMPLETE){    <—— Check readyState
    data=req.responseText;    <—— Read response data
  }else{
    data="loading...["+ready+"]";
  }
  toConsole(data);
}
function toConsole(data){
  if (console!=null){
    var newline=document.createElement("div");
    console.appendChild(newline);
    var txt=document.createTextNode(data);
    newline.appendChild(txt);
  }
}
window.onload=function(){
  console=document.getElementById('console');
  sendRequest("data.txt");
}
</script>
</head>
<body>
<div id='console'></div>
```

```
</body>
</html>
```

Let's look at the output of this program in Microsoft Internet Explorer and Mozilla Firefox, respectively. Note that the sequence of readyStates is different, but the end result is the same. The important point is that the fine details of the readyState shouldn't be relied on in a cross-browser program (or indeed, one that is expected to support multiple versions of the same browser). Here is the output in Microsoft Internet Explorer:

```
loading...[1]
loading...[1]
loading...[3]
Here is some text from the server!
```

Each line of output represents a separate invocation of our callback handler. It is called twice during the loading state, as each chunk of data is loaded up, and then again in the interactive state, at which point control would be returned to the UI under a synchronous request. The final callback is in the completed state, and the text from the response can be displayed.

Now let's look at the output in Mozilla Firefox version 1.0:

```
loading...[1]
loading...[1]
loading...[2]
loading...[3]
Here is some text from the server!
```

The sequence of callbacks is similar to Internet Explorer, with an additional callback in the loaded readyState, with value of 2.

In this example, we used the responseText property of the XMLHttpRequest object to retrieve the response as a text string. This is useful for simple data, but if we require a larger structured collection of data to be returned to us, then we can use the responseXML property. If the response has been allocated the correct MIME type of text/xml, then this will return a DOM document that we can interrogate using the DOM properties and functions such as getElementById() and childNodes that we encountered in section 2.4.1.

These, then, are the building blocks of Ajax. Each brings something useful to the party, but a lot of the power of Ajax comes from the way in which the parts combine into a whole. In the following section, we'll round out our introduction to the technologies with a look at this bigger picture.

2.6 *What sets Ajax apart*

While CSS, DOM, asynchronous requests, and JavaScript are all necessary components of Ajax, it is quite possible to use all of them *without* doing Ajax, at least in the sense that we are describing it in this book.

We already discussed the differences between the classic web application and its Ajax counterpart in chapter 1; let's recap briefly here. In a classic web application, the user workflow is defined by code on the server, and the user moves from one page to another, punctuated by the reloading of the entire page. During these reloads, the user cannot continue with his work. In an Ajax application, the workflow is at least partly defined by the client application, and contact is made with the server in the background while the user gets on with his work.

In between these extremes are many shades of gray. A web application may deliver a series of discrete pages following the classic approach, in which each page cleverly uses CSS, DOM, JavaScript, and asynchronous request objects to smooth out the user's interaction with the page, followed by an abrupt halt in productivity while the next page loads. A JavaScript application may present the user with page-like pop-up windows that behave like classic web pages at certain points in the flow. The web browser is a flexible and forgiving environment, and Ajax and non-Ajax functionality can be intermingled in the same application.

What sets Ajax apart is not the technologies that it employs but the interaction model that it enables through the use of those technologies. The web-based interaction model to which we are accustomed is not suited to sovereign applications, and new possibilities begin to emerge as we break away from that interaction model.

There are at least two levels at which Ajax can be used—and several positions between these as we let go of the classic page-based approach. The simplest strategy is to develop Ajax-based widgets that are largely self-contained and that can be added to a web page with a few imports and script statements. Stock tickers, interactive calendars, and chat windows might be typical of this sort of widget. Islands of application-like functionality are embedded into a document-like web page (figure 2.6). Most of Google's current forays into Ajax (see section 1.3) fit this model. The drop-down box of Google Suggest and the map widget in Google Maps are both interactive elements embedded into a page.

If we want to adopt Ajax more adventurously, we can turn this model inside out, developing a host application in which application-like and document-like fragments can reside (figure 2.7). This approach is more analogous to a desktop application, or even a window manager or desktop environment. Google's GMail

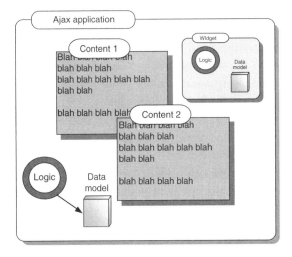

Figure 2.6
A simple Ajax application will still work like a web page, with islands of interactive functionality embedded in the page.

fits this model, with individual messages rendering as documents within an interactive, application-like superstructure.

In some ways, learning the technologies is the easy part. The interesting challenge in developing with Ajax is in learning how to use them together. We are accustomed to thinking of web applications as storyboards, and we shunt the user from one page to another following a predetermined script. With application-like functionality in our web application, we can provide the user with a more fine-grained handle on the business domain, which can enable a more free-form problem-solving approach to his work.

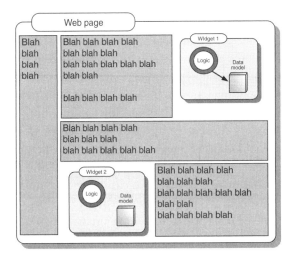

Figure 2.7
In a more complex Ajax application, the entire application is an interactive system, into which islands of document-like content may be loaded or programmatically declared.

In order to gain the benefits of this greater flexibility, we have to question a lot of our coding habits. Is an HTML form the only way for a user to input information? Should we declare all our user interfaces as HTML? Can we contact the server in response to user interactions such as key presses and mouse movements, as well as the conventional mouse click? In the fast-paced world of information technology, we place a large emphasis on learning new skills, but unlearning old habits can be at least as important.

2.7 Summary

In this chapter, we've introduced the four technical pillars of Ajax.

JavaScript is a powerful general-purpose programming language with a bad reputation for generating pop-up windows, back-button hacks, and image roll-overs. Appendix B contains a more detailed description of some of the features of the language, but from the examples here, you should be able to get a feel for how it can be used to genuinely enhance usability.

CSS and the DOM complement one another in providing a clear programmatic view of the user interface that we're working with, while keeping the structure separate from the visual styling. A clean document structure makes programmatic manipulation of a document much simpler, and maintaining a separation of responsibilities is important in developing larger Ajax applications, as we'll see in chapters 3 and 4.

We've shown how to work with the XMLHttpRequest object and with the older XmlDocument and IFrame. A lot of the current hype around Ajax praises XMLHttpRequest as the fashionable way to talk to the server, but the IFrame offers a different set of functionality that can be exactly what we need at times. Knowing about both enriches your toolkit. In this chapter, we introduced these techniques and provided some examples. In chapter 5, we will discuss client/server communications in more detail.

Finally, we looked at the way the technological pillars of Ajax can be combined to create something greater than the sum of its parts. While Ajax can be used in small doses to add compelling widgets to otherwise static web pages, it can also be applied more boldly to create a complete user interface within which islands of static content can be contained. Making this leap from the sidelines to center stage will require a lot of JavaScript code, however, and that code will be required to run without fail for longer periods, too. This will require us to approach our code differently and look at such issues as reliability, maintainability, and flexibility. In the next chapter, we look at ways of introducing order into a large-scale Ajax codebase.

2.8 *Resources*

For a deeper understanding of Cascading Style Sheets, we recommend the CSS Zen Garden (www.csszengarden.com/), a site that restyles itself in a myriad of ways using nothing but CSS.

Eric Meyer has also written extensively on CSS; visit his website at www.meyer-web.com/eric/css/. Blooberry (www.blooberry.com) is another excellent website for CSS information.

Early Ajax solutions using IFrames are described at http://developer.apple.com/internet/webcontent/iframe.html.

The LiveHttpHeaders extension for Mozilla can be found at http://livehttp-headers.mozdev.org/

Danny Goodman's books on JavaScript are an essential reference for DOM programming, and cover the browser environments in great detail: *Dynamic* HTML: *The Definitive Reference* (O'Reilly 2002) and *JavaScript Bible* (John Wiley 2004).

The W3Schools website contains some interactive tutorials on JavaScript, for those who like to learn by doing (www.w3schools.com/js/js_examples_3. asp).

Introducing order to Ajax

This chapter covers

- Developing and maintaining large Ajax client codebases
- Refactoring Ajax JavaScript code
- Exploring common design patterns used in Ajax applications
- Using Model-View-Controller on the server side of an Ajax app
- Overview of third-party Ajax libraries

In chapter 2, we covered all the basic technologies that make up an Ajax application. With what we've learned so far, it's possible to build that super-duper Ajax-powered web application that you've always dreamed of. It's also possible to get into terrible trouble and end up with a tangle of code, HTML markup, and styling that is impossible to maintain and that mysteriously stops working one day. Or worse, you end up with an application that continues to work so long as you don't breathe near it or make a sudden loud noise. To be in such a situation on a personal project can be disheartening. To be in such a situation with an employer's or paying customer's site—someone who wants a few tweaks here and there—can be positively frightening.

Fortunately, this problem has been endemic since the dawn of computing—and probably before that! People have developed ways to manage complexity and to keep increasingly large codebases in working order. In this chapter, we'll introduce the core tools for keeping on top of your code, allowing you to write and rewrite your Ajax application to your customer's heart's content, and still go home from work on time.

Ajax represents a break from the previous use of DHTML technologies not only in the way the technologies are put together but also in the scale at which they are used. We're dealing with much more JavaScript than a classic web application would, and the code will often be resident in the browser for a much longer time. Consequently, Ajax needs to manage complexity in a way that classic DHTML doesn't.

In this chapter, we'll give an overview of the tools and techniques that can help you keep your code clean. These techniques are most useful, in our experience, when developing large, complex Ajax applications. If you want to write only simple Ajax applications, then we suggest you skip ahead to the example-driven chapters, starting with chapter 9. If you already know refactoring and design patterns back to front, then you may wish to skim this chapter and move on to the application of these techniques to Ajax in chapters 4 through 6. Even so, the groundwork that we lay here is important in adapting these approaches to JavaScript, so we expect you'll return here at some point. We also take the opportunity at the end of this chapter to review the current state of third-party libraries for Ajax, so if you're shopping for frameworks to streamline your project, you may want to check out section 3.5.

3.1 Order out of chaos

The main tool that we will apply is *refactoring*, the process of rewriting code to introduce greater clarity rather than to add new functionality. Introducing greater clarity can be a satisfying end in itself, but it also has some compelling advantages that should appeal to the bottom-line, when-the-chips-are-down mentality.

It is typically easier to add new functionality to well-factored code, to modify its existing functionality, and to remove functionality from it. In short, it is understandable. In a poorly factored codebase, it is often the case that everything does what the current requirements specify, but the programming team isn't fully confident as to why it all works.

Changing requirements, often with short time frames, are a regular part of most professional coding work. Refactoring keeps your code clean and maintainable and allows you to face—and implement—changes in requirements without fear.

We already saw some elementary refactoring at work in our examples in chapter 2, when we moved the JavaScript, HTML, and stylesheets into separate files. However, the JavaScript is starting to get rather long at 120 lines or so and is mixing together low-level functionality (such as making requests to the server) with code that deals specifically with our list object. As we begin to tackle bigger projects, this single JavaScript file (and single stylesheet, for that matter) will suffer. The goal that we're pursuing—creating small, easily readable, easily changeable chunks of code that address one particular issue—is often called *separation of responsibilities*.

Refactoring often has a second motive, too, of identifying common solutions and ways of doing things and moving code toward that particular pattern. Again, this can be satisfying in its own right, but it has a very practical effect. Let's consider this issue next.

3.1.1 Patterns: creating a common vocabulary

Code conforming to any well-established pattern stands a good chance of working satisfactorily, simply because it's been done before. Many of the issues surrounding it have already been thought about and, we hope, addressed. If we're lucky, someone's even written a reusable framework exemplifying a particular way of doing things.

This way of doing things is sometimes known as a *design pattern*. The concept of patterns was coined in the 1970s to describe solutions to architectural and planning problems, but it has been borrowed by software development for the last ten years or so. Server-side Java has a strong culture of design patterns, and Microsoft has recently been pushing them strongly for the .NET Framework. The term often carries a rather forbidding academic aura and is frequently misused in an effort to sound impressive. At its root, though, a design pattern is simply a description of a repeatable way of solving a particular problem in software design. It's important to note that design patterns give names to abstract technical solutions, making them easier to talk about and easier to understand.

Design patterns can be important to refactoring because they allow us to succinctly describe our intended goal. To say that we "pull out these bits of code into objects that encapsulate the process of performing a user action, and can then undo everything if we want" is quite a mouthful—and rather a wordy goal to have in mind while rewriting the code. If we can say that we are introducing the Command pattern to our code, we have a goal that is both more precise and easier to talk about.

If you're a hardened Java server developer, or an architect of any hue, then you're probably wondering what's new in what we've said. If you've come from the trenches of the web design/new media world, you may be thinking that we're those weird sorts of control freaks who prefer drawing diagrams to writing real code. In either case, you may be wondering what this has to do with Ajax. Our short answer is "quite a lot." Let's explore what the working Ajax programmer stands to gain from refactoring.

3.1.2 *Refactoring and Ajax*

We've already noted that Ajax applications are likely to use more JavaScript code and that the code will tend to be longer lived.

In a classic web app, the complex code lives on the server, and design patterns are routinely applied to the PHP, Java, or .NET code that runs there. With Ajax, we can look at using the same techniques with the client code.

There is even an argument for suggesting that JavaScript needs this organization more than its rigidly structured counterparts Java and C#. Despite its C-like syntax, JavaScript is a closer cousin to languages such as Ruby, Python, and even Common Lisp than it is to Java or C#. It offers a tremendous amount of flexibility and scope for developing personal styles and idioms. In the hands of a skilled developer, this can be wonderful, but it also provides much less of a safety net for the average programmer. Enterprise languages such as Java and C# are designed to work well with teams of average programmers and rapid turnover of members. JavaScript is not.

The danger of creating tangled, unfathomable JavaScript code is relatively high, and as we scale up its use from simple web page tricks to Ajax applications, the reality of this can begin to bite. For this reason, I advocate the use of refactoring in Ajax more strongly than I do in Java or C#, the "safe" languages within whose communities design patterns have bloomed.

3.1.3 Keeping a sense of proportion

Before we move on, it's important to say that refactoring and design patterns are just tools and should be used only where they are actually going to be useful. If overused, they can induce a condition known as *paralysis by analysis*, in which implementation of an application is forestalled indefinitely by design after redesign, in order to increase the flexibility of the structure or accommodate possible future requirements that may never be realized.

Design patterns expert Erich Gamma summed this up nicely in a recent interview (see Resources at end of chapter) in which he described a call for help from a reader who had managed to implement only 21 of the 23 design patterns described in the seminal *Design Patterns* book into his application. Just as a developer wouldn't struggle to make use of integers, strings, and arrays in every piece of code that he writes, a design pattern is useful only in particular situations.

Gamma recommends refactoring as the best way to introduce patterns. Write the code first in the simplest way that works, and then introduce patterns to solve common problems as you encounter them. If you've already written a lot of code, or are charged with maintaining someone else's tangled mess, you may have been experiencing a sinking, left-out-of-the-party feeling until now. Fortunately, it's possible to apply design patterns retroactively to code of any quality. In the next section, we'll take some of the rough-and-ready code that we developed in chapter 2 and see what refactoring can do for it.

3.1.4 Refactoring in action

This refactoring thing might sound like a good idea, but the more practical-minded among you will want to see it working before you buy in. Let's take a few moments now to apply a bit of refactoring to the core Ajax functionality that we developed in the previous chapter, in listing 2.11. To recap the structure of that code, we had defined a `sendRequest()` function that fired off a request to the server. `sendRequest()` delegated to an `initHttpRequest()` function to find the appropriate XMLHttpRequest object and assigned a hard-coded callback function, `onReadyState()`, to process the response. The XMLHttpRequest object was defined as a global variable, allowing the callback function to pick up a reference to it. The callback handler then interrogated the state of the request object and produced some debug information.

The code in listing 2.11 does what we needed it to but is somewhat difficult to reuse. Typically when we make a request to the server, we want to parse the response and do something quite specific to our application with the results. To plug custom business logic into the current code, we need to modify sections of the `onReadyState()` function.

The presence of the global variable is also problematic. If we want to make several calls to the server simultaneously, then we must be able to assign different callback handlers to each. If we're fetching a list of resources to update and another list of resources to discard, it's important that we know which is which, after all!

In object-oriented (OO) programming, the standard solution to this sort of issue is to encapsulate the required functionality into an object. JavaScript supports OO coding styles well enough for us to do that. We'll call our object ContentLoader, because it loads content from the server. So what should our object look like? Ideally, we'd be able to create one, passing in a URL to which the request will be sent. We should also be able to pass a reference to a custom callback handler to be executed if the document loads successfully and another to be executed in case of errors. A call to the object might look like this:

```
var loader=new net.ContentLoader('mydata.xml',parseMyData);
```

where `parseMyData` is a callback function to be invoked when the document loads successfully. Listing 3.1 shows the code required to implement the Content-Loader object. There are a few new concepts here, which we'll discuss next.

Listing 3.1   ContentLoader object

```
var net=new Object();                              ❶  Namespacing object
net.READY_STATE_UNINITIALIZED=0;
net.READY_STATE_LOADING=1;
net.READY_STATE_LOADED=2;
net.READY_STATE_INTERACTIVE=3;
net.READY_STATE_COMPLETE=4;
net.ContentLoader=function(url,onload,onerror){    ❷  Constructor function
  this.url=url;
  this.req=null;
  this.onload=onload;
  this.onerror=(onerror) ? onerror : this.defaultError;
  this.loadXMLDoc(url);
}
net.ContentLoader.prototype={
```

```
loadXMLDoc:function(url){              ❸  Renamed initXMLHttpRequest function
 if (window.XMLHttpRequest){
   this.req=new XMLHttpRequest();                    ❹  Refactored
 } else if (window.ActiveXObject){                       loadXML
   this.req=new ActiveXObject("Microsoft.XMLHTTP");      function
 }
 if (this.req){
   try{
     var loader=this;
     this.req.onreadystatechange=function(){
       loader.onReadyState.call(loader);
     }
     this.req.open('GET',url,true);     ❺  Refactored
     this.req.send(null);                   sendRequest
   }catch (err){                            function
     this.onerror.call(this);
   }
 }
},
onReadyState:function(){       ❻  Refactored callback
 var req=this.req;
 var ready=req.readyState;
 if (ready==net.READY_STATE_COMPLETE){
   var httpStatus=req.status;
   if (httpStatus==200 || httpStatus==0){
     this.onload.call(this);
   }else{
     this.onerror.call(this);
   }
 }
},
defaultError:function(){
 alert("error fetching data!"
   +"\n\nreadyState:"+this.req.readyState
   +"\nstatus: "+this.req.status
   +"\nheaders: "+this.req.getAllResponseHeaders());
 }
}
```

The first thing to notice about the code is that we define a single global variable net ❶ and attach all our other references to that. This minimizes the risk of clashes in variable names and keeps all the code related to network requests in a single place.

We provide a single constructor function for our object ❷. It has three arguments, but only the first two are mandatory. In the case of the error handler, we test for null values and provide a sensible default if necessary. The ability to pass a varying number of arguments to a function might look odd to

OO programmers, as might the ability to pass functions as first-class references. These are common features of JavaScript. We discuss these language features in more detail in appendix B.

We have moved large parts of our initXMLHttpRequest() ❹ and send-Request() functions ❺ from listing 2.11 into the object's internals. We've also renamed the function to reflect its slightly greater scope here as well. It is now known as loadXMLDoc. ❸ We still use the same techniques to find an XMLHttp-Request object and to initiate a request, but the user of the object doesn't need to worry about it. The onReadyState callback function ❻ should also look largely familiar from listing 2.11. We have replaced the calls to the debug console with calls to the onload and onerror functions. The syntax might look a little odd, so let's examine it a bit closer. onload and onerror are Function objects, and Function.call() is a method of that object. The first argument to Function.call() becomes the context of the function, that is, it can be referenced within the called function by the keyword this.

Writing a callback handler to pass into our ContentLoader is quite simple, then. If we need to refer to any of the ContentLoader's properties, such as the XMLHttpRequest or the url, we can simply use this to do so. For example:

```
function myCallBack(){
  alert(
    this.url
    +" loaded! Here's the content:\n\n"
    +this.req.responseText
  );
}
```

Setting up the necessary "plumbing" requires some understanding of JavaScript's quirks, but once the object is written, the end user doesn't need to worry about it.

This situation is often a sign of good refactoring. We've tucked away the difficult bits of code inside the object while presenting an easy-to-use exterior. The end user is saved from a lot of unnecessary difficulty, and the expert responsible for maintaining the difficult code has isolated it into a single place. Fixes need only be applied once, in order to be rolled out across the codebase.

We've covered the basics of refactoring and shown how it can work to our benefit in practice. In the next section, we'll look at some more common problems in Ajax programming and see how we can use refactoring to address them. Along the way, we will discover some useful tricks that we can reuse in subsequent chapters and that you can apply to your own projects as well.

3.2 Some small refactoring case studies

The following sections address some issues in Ajax development and look at some common solutions to them. In each case, we'll show you how to refactor to ease the pain associated with that issue, and then we'll identify the elements of the solution that can be reused elsewhere.

In keeping with an honorable tradition in design patterns literature, we will present each issue in terms of a problem, the technical solution, and then a discussion of the larger issues involved.

3.2.1 Cross-browser inconsistencies: Façade and Adapter patterns

If you ask any web developers—be they coders, designers, graphics artists, or all-rounders—for their pet peeves in relation to their work, there's a good chance that getting their work to display correctly on different browsers will be on their list. The Web is full of standards for technology, and most browser vendors implement most of the standards more or less completely most of the time. Sometimes the standards are vague and open to different interpretations, sometimes the browser vendors extended the standards in useful but inconsistent ways, and sometimes the browsers just have good old-fashioned bugs in them.

JavaScript coders have resorted since the early days to checking in their code which browser they're using or to testing whether or not an object exists. Let's take a very simple example.

Working with DOM elements

As we discussed in chapter 2, a web page is exposed to JavaScript through the Document Object Model (DOM), a tree-like structure whose elements correspond to the tags of an HTML document. When manipulating a DOM tree programmatically, it is quite common to want to find out an element's position on the page. Unfortunately, browser vendors have provided various nonstandard methods for doing so over the years, making it difficult to write fail-safe cross-browser code to accomplish the task. Listing 3.2—a simplified version of a function from Mike Foster's x library (see section 3.5)—shows a comprehensive way of discovering the pixel position of the left edge of the DOM element *e* passed in as an argument.

Listing 3.2   `getLeft()` function

```
function getLeft(e){
  if(!(e=xGetElementById(e))){
    return 0;
  }
  var css=xDef(e.style);
  if (css && xStr(e.style.left)) {
    iX=parseInt(e.style.left);
    if(isNaN(iX)) iX=0;
  }else if(css && xDef(e.style.pixelLeft)) {
    iX=e.style.pixelLeft;
  }
  return iX;
}
```

Different browsers offer many ways of determining the position of the node via the style array that we encountered in chapter 2. The W3C CSS2 standard supports a property called `style.left`, defined as a string describing value and units, such as `100px`. Units other than pixels may be supported. `style.pixelLeft`, in contrast, is numeric and assumes all values to be measured in pixels. `pixelLeft` is supported only in Microsoft Internet Explorer. The `getLeft()` method discussed here first checks that CSS is supported and then tests both values, trying the W3C standard first. If no values are found, then a value of zero is returned by default. Note that we don't explicitly check for browser names or versions but use the more robust object-detection technique that we discussed in chapter 2.

Writing functions like these to accommodate cross-browser peculiarities is a tedious business, but once it is done, the developer can get on with developing the application without having to worry about these issues. And with well-tested libraries such as x, most of the hard work has already been done for us. Having a reliable adapter function for discovering the on-page position of a DOM element can speed up the development of an Ajax user interface considerably.

Making requests to the server

We've already come across another similar cross-browser incompatibility in chapter 2. Browser vendors have provided nonstandard mechanisms for obtaining the XMLHttpRequest object used to make asynchronous requests to the server. When we wanted to load an XML document from the server, we needed to figure out which of the possibilities to use.

Internet Explorer will only deliver the goods if we ask for an ActiveX component, whereas Mozilla and Safari will play nice if we ask for a native built-in object. Only the XML loading code itself knew about those differences. Once the

XMLHttpRequest object was returned into the rest of the code, it behaved identically in both cases. Calling code doesn't need to understand either the ActiveX or the native object subsystem; it only needs to understand the `net.ContentLoader()` constructor.

The Façade pattern

For both `getLeft()` and `new net.ContentLoader()`, the code that does the object detection is ugly and tedious. By defining a function to hide it from the rest of our code, we are making the rest of the code easier to read and isolating the object-detection code in a single place. This is a basic principle in refactoring—don't repeat yourself, often abbreviated to DRY. If we discover an edge case that our object-detection code doesn't handle properly, then fixing it once rolls that change out to all calls to discover the left coordinate of a DOM element, create an XML Request object, or whatever else we are trying to do.

In the language of design patterns, we are using a pattern known as *Façade*. Façade is a pattern used to provide a common access point to different implementations of a service or piece of functionality. The XMLHttpRequest object, for example, offers a useful service, and our application doesn't really care how it is delivered as long as it works (figure 3.1).

In many cases, we also want to simplify access to a subsystem. In the case of getting the left-edge coordinate of a DOM element, for example, the CSS spec provided us with a plethora of choices, allowing the value to be specified in pixels, points, ems, and other units. This freedom of expression may be more than we need. The `getLeft()` function in listing 3.2 will work as long as we are using pixels as the unit throughout our layout system. Simplifying the subsystem in this way is another feature of the Façade pattern.

The Adapter pattern

A closely related pattern is Adapter. In Adapter, we also work with two subsystems that perform the same function, such as the Microsoft and Mozilla approaches to getting an XMLHttpRequest object. Rather than constructing a new Façade for each to use, as we did earlier, we provide an extra layer over one of the subsystems that presents the same API as the other subsystem. This layer is known as the Adapter. The Sarissa XML library for Ajax, which we will discuss in section 3.5.1, uses the Adapter pattern to make Internet Explorer's ActiveX control look like the Mozilla built-in XMLHttpRequest. Both approaches are valid and can help to integrate legacy or third-party code (including the browsers themselves) into your Ajax project.

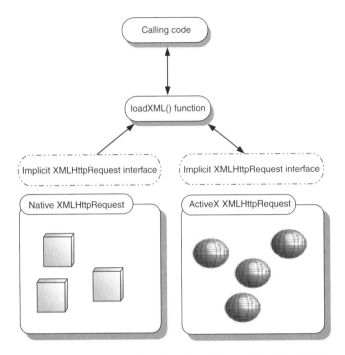

Figure 3.1 Schematic of the Façade pattern, as it relates to the XMLHttpRequest object across browsers. The `loadXML()` function requires an XMLHttpRequest object, but doesn't care about its actual implementation. Underlying implementations may offer considerably more complex HTTP Request semantics, but both are simplified here to provide the basic functionality required by the calling function.

Let's move on to the next case study, in which we consider issues with JavaScript's event-handling model.

3.2.2 *Managing event handlers: Observer pattern*

We can't write very much Ajax code without coming across event-based programming techniques. JavaScript user interfaces are heavily event-driven, and the introduction of asynchronous requests with Ajax adds a further set of callbacks and events for our application to deal with. In a relatively simple application, an event such as a mouse click or the arrival of data from the server can be handled by a single function. As an application grows in size and complexity, though, we may want to notify several distinct subsystems and even to expose a mechanism whereby interested parties can sign themselves up for such notification. Let's explore an example to see what the issues are.

Using multiple event handlers

It's common practice when scripting DOM nodes using JavaScript to define the script in the `window.onload` function, which is executed after the page (and therefore the DOM tree) is fully loaded. Let's say that we have a DOM element on our page that will display dynamically generated data fetched from the server at regular intervals once the page is loaded. The JavaScript that coordinates the data fetching and the display needs a reference to the DOM node, so it gets it by defining a `window.onload` event:

```
window.onload=function(){
   displayDiv=document.getElementById('display');
}
```

All well and good. Let's say that we now want to add a second visual display that provides alerts from a news feed, for example (see chapter 13 if you're interested in implementing this functionality). The code that controls the news feed display also needs to grab references to some DOM elements on startup. So it defines a `window.onload` event handler, too:

```
window.onload=function(){
   feedDiv=document.getElementById('feeds');
}
```

We test both sets of code on separate pages and find them both to work fine. When we put them together, the second `window.onload` function overwrites the first, and the data feed fails to display and starts to generate JavaScript errors. The problem lies in the fact that the window object allows only a single onload function to be attached to it.

Limitations of a composite event handler

Our second event handler overrides the first one. We can get around this by writing a single composite function:

```
window.onload=function(){
   displayDiv=document.getElementById('display');
   feedDiv=document.getElementById('feeds');
}
```

This works for our current example, but it tangles together code from the data display and the news feed viewer, which are otherwise unrelated to each other. If we were dealing with 10 or 20 systems rather than 2, and each needed to get references to several DOM elements, then a composite event handler like this would become hard to maintain. Swapping individual components in and out would become difficult and error prone, leading to exactly the sort of situation that we described in the introduction, where nobody wants to touch the code in case it should break. Let's try to refactor a little further, by defining a loader function for each subsystem:

```
window.onload=function(){
  getDisplayElements();
  getFeedElements();
}
function getDisplayElements(){
  displayDiv=document.getElementById('display');
}
function getFeedElements(){
  feedDiv=document.getElementById('feeds');
}
```

This introduces some clarity, reducing our composite `window.onload()` to a single line for each subsystem, but the composite function is still a weak point in the design and is likely to cause us trouble. In the following section, we'll examine a slightly more complex but more scalable solution to the problem.

The Observer pattern

It can be helpful sometimes to ask where the responsibility for an action lies. The composite function approach places responsibility for getting the references to DOM elements on the window object, which then has to know which subsystems are present in the current page. Ideally, each subsystem should be responsible for acquiring its own references. That way, if it is present on a page, it will get them, and if it isn't present, it won't.

To set the division of responsibility straight, we can allow systems to register for notification of the `onload` event happening by passing a function to call when the `window.onload` event is fired. Here's a simple implementation:

```
window.onloadListeners=new Array();
window.addOnLoadListener(listener){
  window.onloadListeners[window.onloadListeners.length]=listener;
}
```

When the window is fully loaded, then the window object need only iterate through its array of listeners and call each one in turn:

```
window.onload=function(){
  for(var i=0;i<window.onloadListeners.length;i++){
    var func=window.onlloadListeners[i];
    func.call();
  }
}
```

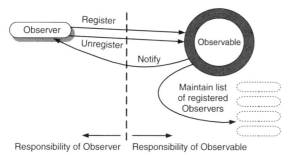

Figure 3.2
Division of responsibility in the Observer pattern. Objects wishing to be notified of an event, the Observers, can register and unregister themselves with the event source, Observable, which will notify all registered parties when an event occurs.

Provided that every subsystem uses this approach, we can offer a much cleaner way of setting up all the subsystems without tangling them up in one another. Of course, it takes only one rogue piece of code to directly override `window.onload` and the system will break. But we have to take charge of our codebase at some point to prevent this from happening.

It's worth pointing out here that the newer W3C event model also implements a multiple event handler system. We've chosen to build our own here on top of the old JavaScript event model because implementations of the W3C model aren't consistent across browsers. We discuss this in greater detail in chapter 4.

The design pattern into which our code here is refactored is called Observer. Observer defines an Observable object, in our case the built-in window object, and a set of Observers or Listeners that can register themselves with it (figure 3.2).

With the Observer pattern, responsibility is apportioned appropriately between the event source and the event handler. Handlers take responsibility for registering and unregistering themselves. The event source takes responsibility for maintaining a list of registered parties and firing notifications when the event occurs. The pattern has a long history of use in event-driven UI programming, and we'll return to Observer when we discuss JavaScript events in more detail in chapter 4. And, as we'll see, it can also be used in our own code objects independently of the browser's mouse and key event processing.

For now, let's move on to the next recurring issue that we can solve through refactoring.

3.2.3 *Reusing user action handlers: Command pattern*

It may be obvious to say that in most applications, the user is telling (through mouse clicks and keyboard presses) the app to do something, and the app then does it. In a simple program, we might present the user with only one way to perform an action, but in more complex interfaces, we will often want the user to be able to trigger the same action from several routes.

Implementing a button widget

Let's say that we have a DOM element styled to look like a button widget that performs a calculation when pressed and updates an HTML table with the result. We could define a mouse-click event-handler function for the button element that looks like this:

```
function buttonOnclickHandler(event){
  var data=new Array();
  data[0]=6;
  data[1]=data[0]/3;
  data[2]=data[0]*data[1]+7;
  var newRow=createTableRow(dataTable);
  for (var i=0;i<data.length;i++){
    createTableCell(newRow,data[i]);
  }
}
```

We're assuming here that the variable dataTable is a reference to an existing table and that the functions createTableRow() and createTableCell() take care of the details of DOM manipulation for us. The interesting thing here is the calculation phase, which could, in a real-world application, run to hundreds of lines of code. We assign this event handler to the button element like so:

```
buttonDiv.onclick=buttonOnclickHandler;
```

Supporting multiple event types

Let's say that we have now supercharged our application with Ajax. We are polling the server for updates, and we want to perform this calculation if a particular value is updated from the server, too, and update a different table with the data. We don't need to go into the details of setting up a repeated polling of the server here. Let's assume that we have a reference to an object called poller. Internally, it is using an XMLHttpRequest object and has set its onreadystatechange handler to call an onload function whenever it has finished loading an update from the server. We could abstract out the calculation and display phases into helper functions, like this:

```
function buttonOnclickHandler(event){
  var data=calculate();
  showData(dataTable,data);
}
function ajaxOnloadHandler(){
  var data=calculate();
```

```
    showData(otherDataTable,data);
  }
  function calculate(){
    var data=new Array();
    data[0]=6;
    data[1]=data[0]/3;
    data[2]=data[0]*data[1]+7;
    return data;
  }
  function showData(table,data){
    var newRow=createTableRow(table);
    for (var i=0;i<data.length;i++){
      createTableCell(newRow,data[i]);
    }
  }
  buttonDiv.onclick=buttonOnclickHandler;
  poller.onload=ajaxOnloadHandler;
```

A lot of the common functionality has been abstracted out into the `calculate()` and `showData()` functions, and we're only repeating ourselves a little in the `onclick` and `onload` handlers.

We've achieved a much better separation between the business logic and the UI updates. Once again, we've stumbled upon a useful repeatable solution. This time it is known as the Command pattern. The Command object defines some activity of arbitrary complexity that can be passed around in code easily and swapped between UI elements easily. In the classic Command pattern for object-oriented languages, user interactions are wrapped up as Command objects, which typically derive from a base class or interface. We've solved the same problem in a slightly different way here. Because JavaScript functions are first-class objects, we can treat them as Command objects directly and still provide the same level of abstraction.

Wrapping up everything that the user does as a Command might seem a little cumbersome, but it has a hidden payoff. When all our user actions are wrapped up in Command objects, we can easily associate other standard functionality with them. The most commonly discussed extension is to add an `undo()` method. When this is done, the foundations for a generic undo facility across an application are laid. In a more complex example, Commands could be recorded in a stack as they execute, and the user can use the undo button to work back up the stack, returning the application to previous states (figure 3.3).

Each new command is placed on the top of the stack, which may be undone item by item. The user creates a document by a series of write actions. Then she selects the entire document and accidentally hits the delete button. When she invokes the `undo` function, the topmost item is popped from the stack, and its

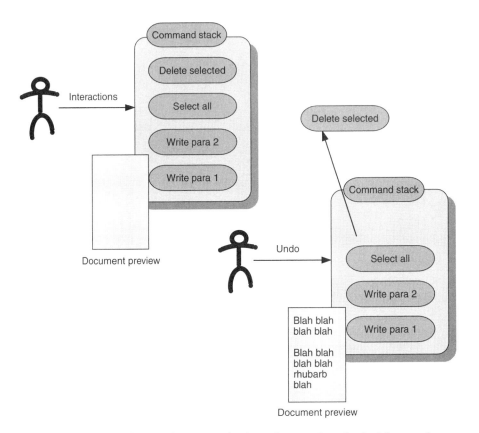

Figure 3.3 Using the Command pattern to implement a generic undo stack in a word processing application. All user interactions are represented as commands, which can be undone as well as executed.

undo() method is called, returning the deleted text. A further undo would deselect the text, and so on.

Of course, using Command to create an undo stack means some extra work for the developer, in ensuring that the combination of executing and undoing the command returns the system to its initial state. A working undo feature can be a strong differentiator between products, however, particularly for applications that enjoy heavy or prolonged use. As we discussed in chapter 1, that's exactly the territory that Ajax is moving into.

Command objects can also be useful when we need to pass information across boundaries between subsystems in an application. The network, of course, is just such a boundary, and we'll revisit the Command pattern in chapter 5, when we discuss client/server interactions.

3.2.4 Keeping only one reference to a resource: Singleton pattern

In some situations, it is important to ensure that there is only one point of contact with a particular resource. Again, this is best explained by working with a specific example, so let's look at one now.

A simple trading example

Let's say that our Ajax application manipulates stock market data, allowing us to trade on the real markets, perform what-if calculations, and run simulation games over a network against other users. We define three modes for our application, named after traffic lights. In real-time mode (green mode), we can buy and sell stocks on live markets, when they are open, and perform what-if calculations against stored datasets. When the markets are closed, we revert to analysis-only mode (red mode) and can still perform the what-if analyses, but we can't buy or sell. In simulation mode (amber mode), we can perform all the actions available to green mode, but we do so against a dummy dataset rather than interacting with real stock markets.

Our client code represents these permutations as a JavaScript object, as defined here:

```
var MODE_RED=1;
var MODE_AMBER=2;
var MODE_GREEN=2;
function TradingMode(){
  this.mode=MODE_RED;
}
```

We can query and set the mode represented in this object and will do so in our code in many places. We could provide getMode() and setMode() functions that would check conditions such as whether or not the real markets were open, but for now let's keep it simple.

Let's say that two of the options open to the user are to buy and sell stocks and to calculate potential gains and losses from a transaction before undertaking it. The buy and sell actions will point to different web services depending on the mode of operation—internal ones in amber mode, our broker's server in green mode—and will be switched off in red mode. Similarly, the analyses will be based on retrieving data feeds on current and recent prices—simulated in amber mode and live market data in green mode. To know which feeds to point to, both will refer to a TradingMode object as defined here (figure 3.4).

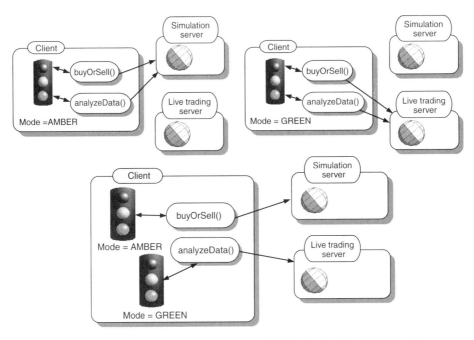

Figure 3.4 In our example Ajax trading application, both buy/sell and analysis functions determine whether to use real or simulated data based on a TradingMode object's status, talking to the simulation server if it is in amber mode and to the live trading server in green mode. If more than one TradingMode object is present in the system, the system can end up in an inconsistent state.

It is imperative that both activities point to the same TradingMode object. If our user is buying and selling in a simulated market but basing her decisions on analysis of live market data, she will probably lose the game. If she's buying and selling real stocks based on analysis of a simulation, she's apt to lose her job!

An object of which there is only one instance is sometimes described as a *singleton*. We'll look at how singletons are handled in an object-oriented language first and then work out a strategy for using them in JavaScript.

Singletons in Java

Singletons are typically implemented in Java-like languages by hiding the object constructor and providing a getter method, as illustrated in listing 3.3.

Listing 3.3 Singleton TradingMode object in Java

```
public class TradingMode{
  private static TradingMode instance=null;
  public int mode;
```

```
  private TradingMode(){
    mode=MODE_RED;
  }
  public static TradingMode getInstance(){
    if (instance==null){
      instance=new TradingMode();
    }
    return instance;
  }
  public void setMode(int mode){
    ...
  }
}
```

The Java-based solution makes use of the private and public access modifiers to enforce singleton behavior. The code

```
new TradingMode().setMode(MODE_AMBER);
```

won't compile because the constructor is not publicly accessible, whereas the following will:

```
TradingMode.getInstance().setMode(MODE_AMBER);
```

This code ensures that every call is routed to the same TradingMode object. We've used several language features here that aren't available in JavaScript, so let's see how we can get around this.

Singletons in JavaScript

In JavaScript, we don't have built-in support for access modifiers, but we can "hide" the constructor by not providing one. JavaScript is prototype-based, with constructors being ordinary Function objects (see appendix B if you don't understand what this means). We could write a TradingMode object in the ordinary way:

```
function TradingMode(){
  this.mode=MODE_RED;
}
TradingMode.prototype.setMode=function(){
}
```

and provide a global variable as a pseudo-Singleton:

```
TradingMode.instance=new TradingMode();
```

But this wouldn't prevent rogue code from calling the constructor. On the other hand, we can construct the entire object manually, without a prototype:

```
var TradingMode=new Object();
```

```
TradingMode.mode=MODE_RED;
TradingMode.setMode=function(){
  ...
}
```

We can also define it more concisely like this:

```
var TradingMode={
  mode:MODE_RED,
  setMode:function(){
    ...
  }
};
```

Both of these examples will generate an identical object. The first way of writing it is probably more familiar to Java or C# programmers. We've shown the latter approach as well, because it is often used in the Prototype library and in frameworks derived from it.

This solution works within the confines of a single scripting context. If the script is loaded into a separate IFrame, it will launch its own copy of the singleton. We can modify this by explicitly specifying that the singleton object be accessed from the topmost document (in JavaScript, top is always a reference to this document), as illustrated in listing 3.4.

Listing 3.4   Singleton TradingMode object in JavaScript

```
Function getTradingMode(){
  if (!top.TradingMode){
    top.TradingMode=new Object();
    top.TradingMode.mode=MODE_RED;
    top.TradingMode.setMode=function(){
      ...
    }
  }
  return top.TradingMode;
}
```

This allows the script to be safely included in multiple IFrames, while preserving the uniqueness of the Singleton object. (If you're planning on supporting a Singleton across multiple top-level windows, you'll need to investigate top.opener. Due to constraints of space, we leave that as an exercise for the reader.)

You're not likely to have a strong need for singletons when writing UI code, but they can be extremely useful when modeling business logic in JavaScript. In a traditional web app, business logic is typically modeled only on the server, but doing things the Ajax way changes that, and Singleton can be useful to know about.

This provides a first taste of what refactoring can do for us at a practical level. The cases that we've looked at so far have all been fairly simple, but even so, using refactoring to clarify the code has helped to remove several weak points that could otherwise come back to haunt us as the applications grow.

Along the way, we encountered a few design patterns. In the following section, we'll look at a large-scale server-side pattern and see how we can refactor some initially tangled code toward a cleaner, more flexible state.

3.3 *Model-View-Controller*

The small patterns that we've looked at so far can usefully be applied to specific coding tasks. Patterns have also been developed for the organization of entire applications, sometimes referred to as architectural patterns. In this section, we're going to look at an architectural pattern that can help us to organize our Ajax projects in several ways, making them easier to code and easier to maintain.

Model-View-Controller (MVC) is a way of describing a good separation between the part of a program that interacts with a user and the part that does the heavy lifting, number crunching, or other "business end" of the application.

MVC is typically applied at a large scale, covering entire layers of an application or even stretching between the layers. In this chapter, we introduce the pattern and show how to apply it to the web server when serving data to an Ajax application. In chapter 4, we'll look at the rather more involved case of applying it to the JavaScript client application.

The MVC pattern identifies three roles that a component in the system can fulfill. The Model is the representation of the application's problem domain, the thing that it is there to work with. A word processor would model a document; a mapping application would model points on a grid, contour lines, and so on.

The View is the part of the program that presents things to the user—input forms, pictures, text, or widgets. The View need not be graphical. In a voice-driven program, for example, the spoken prompts are the View.

The golden rule of MVC is that the View and the Model shouldn't talk to each other. Taken at face value, that might sound like a pretty dysfunctional program, but this is where the Controller comes in. When the user presses a button or fills in a form, the View tells the Controller. The Controller then manipulates the Model and decides whether the changes in the Model require an update of the View. If so, it tells the View how to change itself (see figure 3.5).

The advantage of this is that the Model and View remain loosely coupled, that is, neither has a deep understanding of the other. Obviously they need to

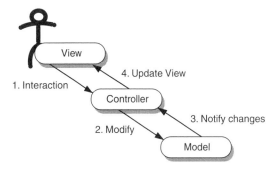

Figure 3.5
The main components of the Model-View-Controller pattern. The View and Model do not interact directly but always through the Controller. The Controller can be thought of as a thin boundary layer that allows the Model and View to communicate but enforces clear separation of the codebase, improving flexibility and maintainability of the code over time.

know enough to get the job done, but the View knows about the Model only in very general terms.

Let's consider a program for managing inventories. The Controller might provide the View with a function that returns a list of all product lines matching a given category ID, but the View knows nothing about how that list was derived. It may be that version 1 of this program stored the data used to generate the list in an array in memory or read it from a flat text file. With the second version of the program, there was a requirement to handle much larger datasets, and a relational database server was added to the architecture. The implications of this change on the Model would be significant, and a lot of code would need to be rewritten. Provided that the Controller could still deliver a list of product lines matching a category, the impact on the View code would be nil.

Similarly, the engineers working on the View should be free to improve the usability of the application without worrying about breaking hidden assumptions in the Model, so long as they stick to a basic agreement on the interfaces with which the Controller provides them. By dividing the system into subsystems, MVC provides an insurance policy against minor changes rippling right across a codebase and allows the team behind each subsystem to respond quickly without treading on one another's toes.

The MVC pattern is commonly applied to classic web application frameworks in a particular way, in order to serve up the succession of static pages that compose the interface. When an Ajax application is up and running and requesting data from the server, the mechanics of serving up the data are similar to those of a classic web app. Web server–style MVC can also benefit Ajax applications, and because it's well understood, we'll start here and move on to other more Ajax-specific ways of working with MVC later.

If you're new to web frameworks, this section should provide you with the information you need to understand how they can make an Ajax application more scalable and robust. If, on the other hand, you're familiar with web-tier tools such as template engines and Object-Relational Mapping (ORM) tools or with frameworks such as Struts, Spring, or Tapestry, you'll probably already know most of what we're going to say here. In this case, you might like to skim over this section and pick up the MVC trail in chapter 4, where we discuss its use in a very different way.

3.4 Web server MVC

Web applications are no stranger to MVC, even the classic page-based variety that we spend so much time bashing in this book! The very nature of a web application enforces some degree of separation between the View and the Model, because they are on different machines. Does a web application inherently follow the MVC pattern then? Or, put another way, is it possible to write a web application that tangles the View and the Model together?

Unfortunately, it is. It's very easy, and most web developers have probably done it at some point, the authors included.

Most proponents of MVC on the Web treat the generated HTML page, and the code that generates it, as the View, rather than what the user actually sees when that page renders. In the case of an Ajax application serving data to a JavaScript client, the View from this perspective is the XML document being returned to the client in the HTTP response. Separating the generated document from the business logic does require a little discipline, then.

3.4.1 The Ajax web server tier without patterns

To illustrate our discussion, let's develop an example web server tier for an Ajax application. We've already seen the fundamentals of the client-side Ajax code in chapter 2 and section 3.1.4, and we'll return to them in chapter 4. Right now, we'll concentrate on what goes on in the web server. We'll begin by coding it in the simplest way possible and gradually refactor toward the MVC pattern to see how it benefits our application in terms of its ability to respond to change. First, let's introduce the application.

We have a list of clothes in a clothing store, which are stored in a database, and we want to query this database and present the list of items to the user, showing an image, a title, a short description, and a price. Where the item is available in several colors or sizes, we want to provide a picker for that, too. Figure 3.6 shows the main components of this system, namely the database, a data structure representing a single product, and an XML document to be transmitted to our Ajax client, listing all the products that match a query.

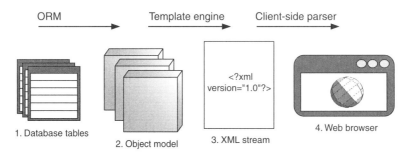

Figure 3.6 **Main components used to generate an XML feed of product data in our online shop example. In the process of generating the view, we extract a set of results from the database, use it to populate data structures representing individual garments, and then transmit that data to the client as an XML stream.**

Let's say that the user has just entered the store and is offered a choice between Menswear, Womenswear, and Children's clothing. Each product is assigned to one of these categories by the Category column of the database table named Garments. A simple piece of SQL to retrieve all relevant items for a search under Menswear might be

```
SELECT * FROM garments WHERE CATEGORY = 'Menswear';
```

We need to fetch the results of this query and then send them to the Ajax application as XML. Let's see how we can do that.

Generating XML data for the client

Listing 3.5 shows a quick-and-dirty solution to this particular requirement. This example uses PHP with a MySQL database, but the important thing to note is the general structure. An ASP or JSP page, or a Ruby script, could be constructed similarly.

Listing 3.5 Quick-and-dirty generation of an XML stream from a database query

```php
<?php
header("Content-type: application/xml");      <— Tell client we are returning XML
echo "<?xml version=\"1.0\" encoding=\"UTF-8\" ?>\n";
$db=mysql_connect("my_db_server","mysql_user");
mysql_select_db("mydb",$db);
$sql="SELECT id,title,description,price,colors,sizes"      Fetch the
  ."FROM garments WHERE category=\"{$cat}\"";              results from
$result=mysql_query($sql,$db);                             the database
echo "<garments>\n";
while ($myrow = mysql_fetch_row($result)) {      <— Iterate through resultset
    printf("<garment id=\"%s\" title=\"%s\">\n"
```

```
      ."<description>%s</description>\n<price>%s</price>\n",
      $myrow["id"],
      $myrow["title"],
      $myrow["description"],
      $myrow["price"]);
    if (!is_null($myrow["colors"])){
      echo "<colors>{$myrow['colors']}</colors>\n";
    }
    if (!is_null($myrow["sizes"])){
      echo "<sizes>{$myrow['sizes']}</sizes>\n";
    }
    echo "</garment>\n";
  }
  echo "</garments>\n";
  ?>
```

The PHP page in listing 3.5 will generate an XML page for us, looking something like listing 3.6, in the case where we have two matching products in our database. Indentation has been added for readability. We've chosen XML as the communication medium between client and server because it is commonly used for this purpose and because we saw in chapter 2 how to consume an XML document generated by the server using the XMLHttpRequest object. In chapter 5, we'll explore the various other options in more detail.

Listing 3.6   Sample XML output from listing 3.5

```
<garments>
  <garment id="SCK001" title="Golfers' Socks">
    <description>Garish diamond patterned socks. Real wool.
      Real itchy.</description>
    <price>$5.99</price>
    <colors>heather combo,hawaiian medley,wild turkey</colors>
  </garment>
  <garment id="HAT056" title="Deerstalker Cap">
    <description>Complete with big flappy bits.
    As worn by the great detective Sherlock Holmes.
    Pipe is model's own.</description>
    <price>$79.99</price>
    <sizes>S, M, L, XL, egghead</sizes>
  </garment>
</garments>
```

So, we have a web server application of sorts, assuming that there's a nice Ajax front end to consume our XML. Let's look to the future. Suppose that as our product range expands, we want to add subcategories (Smart, Casual, Outdoor, for example) and also a "search by season" function, maybe keyword searching, and a link to clearance items. All of these features could reasonably be served by a similar XML stream. Let's look at how we might reuse our current code for these purposes and what the barriers might be.

Problems with reusability

There are several barriers to reusing our script as it stands. First, we have hardwired the SQL query into the page. If we wanted to search again by category or keyword, we would need to modify the SQL generation. We could end up with an ugly set of `if` statements accumulating over time as we add more search options, and a growing list of optional search parameters.

There is an even worse alternative: simply accepting a free-form WHERE clause in the CGI parameters, that is,

```
$sql="SELECT id,title,description,price,colors,sizes"
    ."FROM garments
WHERE ".$sqlWhere;
```

which we can then call directly from the URL, for example:

```
garments.php?sqlWhere=CATEGORY="Menswear"
```

This solution confuses the Model and the View even further, exposing raw SQL in the presentation code. It also opens the door to malicious SQL injection attacks, and, although modern versions of PHP have some built-in defenses against these, it's foolish to rely on them.

Second, we've hardwired the XML data format into the page—it's been buried in there among the `printf` and `echo` statements somewhere. There are several reasons why we might want to change the data format. Maybe we want to show an original price alongside the sale price, to try to persuade some poor sap to buy all those itchy golfing socks that we ordered!

Third, the database result set itself is used to generate the XML. This may look like an efficient way to do things initially, but it has two potential problems. We're keeping a database connection open all the time that we are generating the XML. In this case, we're not doing anything very difficult during that `while()` loop, so the connection won't be too lengthy, but eventually it may prove to be a bottleneck. Also, it works only if we treat our database as a flat data structure.

3.4.2 Refactoring the domain model

We're handling our lists of colors and sizes in a fairly inefficient manner at present, by storing comma-separated lists in fields in the Garments table. If we normalize our data in keeping with a good relational model, we ought to have a

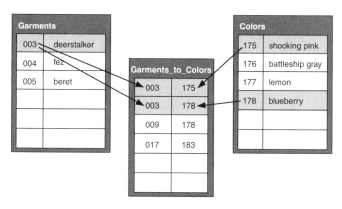

Figure 3.7   A many-to-many relationship in a database model. The table Colors lists all available colors for all garments, and the table Garments no longer lists any color information.

separate table of all available colors, and a bridging table linking garments to colors (what the database wonks call a many-to-many relationship). Figure 3.7 illustrates the use of a many-to-many relationship of this sort.

To determine the available colors for our deerstalker hat, we look up the Garments_to_Colors table on the foreign key `garment_id`. Relating the `color_id` column back to the primary key in the Colors table, we can see that the hat is available in shocking pink and blueberry but not battleship gray. By running the query in reverse, we could also use the Garments_to_Colors table to list all garments that match a given color.

We're making better use of our database now, but the SQL required to fetch all the information begins to get a little hairy. Rather than having to construct elaborate join queries by hand, it would be nice to be able to treat our garments as objects, containing an array of colors and sizes.

Object-relational Mapping tools

Fortunately, there are tools and libraries that can do that for us, known as Object-Relational Mapping (ORM) tools. An ORM automatically translates between database data and in-memory objects, taking the burden of writing raw SQL off the developer. PHP programmers might like to take a look at PEAR DB_DataObject, Easy PHP Data Objects (EZPDO), or Metastorage. Java developers are relatively spoiled for choice, with Hibernate (also ported to .NET) currently a popular choice. ORM tools are a big topic, one that we'll have to put aside for now.

Looking at our application in MVC terms, we can see that adopting an ORM has had a happy side effect, in that we have the beginnings of a genuine Model on our hands. We now can write our XML-generator routine to talk to the Garment object and leave the ORM to mess around with the database. We're no longer bound to a particular database's API (or its quirks). Listing 3.7 shows the change in our code after switching to an ORM.

In this case, we define the business objects (that is, the Model) for our store example in PHP, using the `Pear::DB_DataObject`, which requires our classes to extend a base `DB_DataObject` class. Different ORMs do it differently, but the point is that we're creating a set of objects that we can talk to like regular code, abstracting away the complexities of SQL statements.

Listing 3.7 Object model for our garment store

```php
require_once "DB/DataObject.php";
class GarmentColor extends DB_DataObject {
  var $id;
  var $garment_id;
  var $color_id;
}
class Color extends DB_DataObject {
  var $id;
  var $name;
}
class Garment extends  DB_DataObject {
  var $id;
  var $title;
  var $description;
  var $price;
  var $colors;
  var $category;
  function getColors(){
    if (!isset($this->colors)){
      $linkObject=new GarmentColor();
      $linkObject->garment_id = $this->id;
      $linkObject->find();
      $colors=array();
      while ($linkObject->fetch()){
        $colorObject=new Color();
        $colorObject->id=$linkObject->color_id;
        $colorObject->find();
        while ($colorObject->fetch()){
          $colors[] = clone($colorObject);
        }
      }
    }
    return $colors;
  }
}
```

As well as the central Garment object, we've defined a Color object and a method of the Garment for fetching all Colors that it is available in. Sizes could be implemented similarly but are omitted here for brevity. Because this library doesn't directly support many-to-many relationships, we need to define an object type for the link table and iterate through these in the getColors() method. Nonetheless, it represents a fairly complete and readable object model. Let's see how to make use of that model in our page.

Using the revised model

We've generated a data model from our cleaner database structure. Now we need to use it inside our PHP script. Listing 3.8 revises our main page to use the ORM-based objects.

Listing 3.8 Revised page using ORM to talk to the database

```php
<?php
header("Content-type: application/xml");
echo "<?xml version=\"1.0\" encoding=\"UTF-8\" ?>\n";
include "garment_business_objects.inc"
$garment=new Garment;
$garment->category = $_GET["cat"];
$number_of_rows = $garment->find();
echo "<garments>\n";
while ($garment->fetch()) {
    printf("<garment id=\"%s\" title=\"%s\">\n"
      ."<description>%s</description>\n<price>%s</price>\n",
      $garment->id,
      $garment->title,
      $garment->description,
      $garment->price);
    $colors=$garment->getColors();
    if (count($colors)>0){
      echo "<colors>\n";
      for($i=0;$i<count($colors);$i++){
        echo "<color>{$colors[$i]}</color>\n";
      }
      echo "</colors>\n";
    }
    echo "</garment>\n";
}
echo "</garments>\n";
?>
```

We include the object model definitions and then talk in terms of the object model. Rather than constructing some ad hoc SQL, we create an empty Garment object and partly populate it with our search criteria. Because the object model is included from a separate file, we can reuse it for other searches, too. The XML View is generated against the object model now as well. Our next refactoring step is to separate the format of the XML from the process of generating it.

3.4.3 *Separating content from presentation*

Our View code is still rather tangled up with the object, inasmuch as the XML format is tied up in the object-parsing code. If we're maintaining several pages, then we want to be able to change the XML format in only one place and have that apply everywhere. In the more complex case where we want to maintain more than one format, say one for short and detailed listings for display to customers and another for the stock-taking application, then we want to define each format only once and provide a centralized mapping for them.

Template-based systems

One common approach to this is a template language, that is, a system that accepts a text document containing some special markup notation that acts as a placeholder for real variables during execution. PHP, ASP, and JSP are themselves templating languages of sorts, written as web page content with embedded code, rather than the code with embedded content seen in a Java servlet or traditional CGI script. However, they expose the full power of the scripting language to the page, making it easy to tangle up business logic and presentation.

In contrast, purpose-built template languages, such as PHP Smarty and Apache Velocity (a Java-based system, ported to .NET as NVelocity), offer a more limited ability to code, usually limiting control flow to simple branching (for example, `if`) and looping (for example, `for`, `while`) constructs. Listing 3.9 shows a PHP Smarty template for generating our XML.

Listing 3.9 PHP Smarty template for our XML output

```
<?xml version="1.0" encoding="UTF-8" ?>
<garments>
{section name=garment loop=$garments}
  <garment id="{$garment.id}" title="{$garment.title}">
    <description>{$garment.description}</description>
    <price>{$garment.price}</price>
{if count($garment.getColors())>0}
    <colors>
{section name=color loop=$garment.getColors()}
      <color>$color->name</color>
{/section}
    </colors>
```

```
{/if}
  </garment>
{/section}
</garments>
```

The template expects to see an array variable `garments`, containing Garment objects, as input. Most of the template is emitted from the engine verbatim, but sections inside the curly braces are interpreted as instructions and are either substituted for variable names or treated as simple `branch` and `loop` statements. The structure of the output XML document is more clearly readable in the template than when tangled up with the code, as in the body of listing 3.7. Let's see how to use the template from our page.

Using the revised view

We've moved the definition of our XML format out of our main page into the Smarty template. As a result, now the main page needs only to set up the template engine and pass in the appropriate data. Listing 3.10 shows the changes needed to do this.

Listing 3.10   Using Smarty to generate the XML

```php
<?php
header("Content-type: application/xml");
include "garment_business_objects.inc";
include "smarty.class.php";
$garment=new DataObjects_Garment;
$garment->category = $_GET["cat"];
$number_of_rows = $garment->find();
$smarty=new Smarty;
$smarty->assign('garments',$garments);
$smarty->display('garments_xml.tpl');
?>
```

Smarty is very concise to use, following a three-stage process. First, we create a Smarty engine. Then, we populate it with variables. In this case, there is only one, but we can add as many as we like—if the user details were stored in session, we could pass them in, for example, to present a personalized greeting through the template. Finally, we call `display()`, passing in the name of the template file.

We've now achieved the happy state of separating out the View from our search results page. The XML format is defined once and can be invoked in a few lines of code. The search results page is tightly focused, containing only the information that is specific to itself, namely, populating the search parameters and defining an output format. Remember that we dreamed up a requirement earlier to be able to swap in alternative XML formats on the fly? That's easy with Smarty; we simply define an extra format. It even supports including templates within other templates if we want to be very structured about creating minor variations.

Looking back to the opening discussion about the Model-View-Controller pattern, we can see that we're now implementing it quite nicely. Figure 3.8 provides a visual summary of where we are.

The Model is our collection of domain objects, persisted to the database automatically using our ORM. The View is the template defining the XML format. The Controller is the "search by category" page, and any other pages that we care to define, that glue the Model and the View together.

This is the classic mapping of MVC onto the web application. We've worked through it here in the web server tier of an Ajax application that serves XML documents, but it's easy to see how it could also apply to a classic web application serving HTML pages.

Depending on the technologies you work with, you'll encounter variations on this pattern, but the principle is the same. J2EE enterprise beans abstract the Model and Controller to the point where they can reside on different servers. .NET "code-behind" classes delegate the Controller role to page-specific objects, whereas frameworks such as Struts define a "front controller" that intercepts and routes all requests to the application. Frameworks such as Apache Struts have worked this down to a fine art, refining the role of the Controller to route the user between pages, as well as applying at the single-page level. (In an Ajax application, we might do this in the JavaScript.) But in all cases, the mapping is

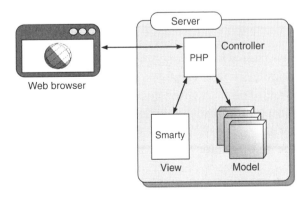

Figure 3.8
MVC as it is commonly applied in the web application. The web page/servlet acts as the Controller and first queries the Model to get the relevant data. It then passes this data to the template file (the View), which generates the content to be forwarded to the user. Note that this is a read-only situation. If we were modifying the Model, the flow of events would differ slightly, but the roles would remain the same.

basically the same, and this is how MVC is generally understood in the web application world.

Describing our web architecture using MVC is a useful approach, and it will continue to serve us well as we move from classic to Ajax-style applications. But it isn't the only use to which we can put MVC in Ajax. In chapter 4, we will examine a variation on the pattern that allows us to reap the advantages of structured design throughout our application. Before we do that, though, let's look at another way of introducing order to our Ajax applications.

As well as refactoring our own code, we can often rationalize a body of code by making use of third-party frameworks and libraries. With the growing interest in Ajax, a number of useful frameworks are emerging, and we conclude this chapter with a brief review of some of the more popular ones.

3.5 *Third-party libraries and frameworks*

A goal of most refactoring is reducing the amount of repetition in the codebase, by factoring details out to a common function or object. If we take this to its logical conclusion, we can wrap up common functionality into libraries, or frameworks, that can be reused across projects. This reduces the amount of custom coding needed for a project and increases productivity. Further, because the library code has already been tested in previous projects, the quality can be expected to be high.

We'll develop a few small JavaScript frameworks in this book that you can reuse in your own projects. There's the ObjectBrowser in chapters 4 and 5, the CommandQueue in chapter 5, the notifications frameworks in chapter 6, the Stop-Watch profiling tools in chapter 8, and the debugging console in appendix A. We'll also be refactoring the teaching examples in chapters 9 through 13 at the end of each chapter, to provide reusable components.

Of course, we aren't the only people playing this game, and plenty of JavaScript and Ajax frameworks are available on the Internet, too. The more established of these have the advantage of some very thorough testing by a large pool of developers.

In this section, we'll look at some of the third-party libraries and frameworks available to the Ajax community. There's a lot of activity in the Ajax framework space at the moment, so we can't cover all the contenders in detail, but we'll try to provide you with a taste of what sort of frameworks exist and how you can introduce order into your own projects by using them.

3.5.1 *Cross-browser libraries*

As we noted in section 3.2.1, cross-browser inconsistencies are never far away when writing Ajax applications. A number of libraries fulfill the very useful function of papering over cross-browser inconsistencies by providing a common façade against which the developer can code. Some focus on specific pieces of functionality, and others attempt to provide a more comprehensive programming environment. We list below the libraries of this type that we have found to be helpful when writing Ajax code.

x library

The x library is a mature, general-purpose library for writing DHTML applications. First released in 2001, it superseded the author's previous CBE (Cross-Browser Extensions) library, using a much simpler programming style. It provides cross-browser functions for manipulating and styling DOM elements, working with the browser event model, and includes out-of-the-box support libraries for animation and drag and drop. It supports Internet Explorer version 4 upward, as well as recent versions of Opera and the Mozilla browsers.

x uses a simple function-based coding style, taking advantage of JavaScript's variable argument lists and loose typing. For example, it wraps the common `document.getElementById()` method, which accepts only strings as input, with a function that accepts either strings or DOM elements, resolving the element ID if a string is passed in but returning a DOM element unmodified if that is passed in as argument. Hence, `xGetElementById()` can be called to ensure that an argument has been resolved from ID to DOM node, without having to test whether it's already been resolved. Being able to substitute a DOM element for its text ID is particularly useful when creating dynamically generated code, such as when passing a string to the `setTimeout()` method or to a callback handler.

A similarly concise style is used in the methods for manipulating DOM element styling, with the same function acting as both getter and setter. For example, the statement

```
xWidth(myElement)
```

will return the width of the DOM element `myElement`, where `myElement` is either a DOM element or the ID of a DOM element. By adding an extra argument, like so

```
xWidth(myElement,420)
```

we set the width of the element. Hence, to set the width of one element equal to another, we can write

```
xWidth(secondElement,xWidth(firstElement))
```

x does not contain any code for creating network requests, but it is nonetheless a useful library for constructing the user interfaces for Ajax applications, written in a clear, understandable style.

Sarissa

Sarissa is a more targeted library than x, and is concerned chiefly with XML manipulation in JavaScript. It supports Internet Explorer's MSXML ActiveX components (version 3 and up), Mozilla, Opera, Konqueror, and Safari for basic functionality, although some of the more advanced features such as XPath and XSLT are supported by a smaller range of browsers.

The most important piece of functionality for Ajax developers is cross-browser support for the XMLHttpRequest object. Rather than creating a Façade object of its own, Sarissa uses the Adapter pattern to create a JavaScript-based XMLHttpRequest object on browsers that don't offer a native object by that name (chiefly Internet Explorer). Internally, this object will make use of the ActiveX objects that we described in chapter 2, but as far as the developer is concerned, the following code will work on any browser once Sarissa has been imported:

```
var xhr = new XMLHttpRequest();
xhr.open("GET", "myData.xml");
xhr.onreadystatechange = function(){
  if(xhr.readyState == 4){
    alert(xhr.responseXML);
  }
}
xhr.send(null);
```

Compare this code with listing 2.11 and note that the API calls are identical to those of the native XMLHttpRequest object provided by Mozilla and Safari browsers.

As noted already, Sarissa also provides a number of generic support mechanisms for working with XML documents, such as the ability to serialize arbitrary JavaScript objects to XML. These mechanisms can be useful in processing the XML documents returned from an Ajax request to the server, if your project uses XML as the markup for response data. (We discuss this issue, and the alternatives, in chapter 5.)

Prototype

Prototype is a general-purpose helper library for JavaScript programming, with an emphasis on extending the JavaScript language itself to support a more object-oriented programming style. Prototype has a distinctive style of JavaScript coding, based on these added language features. Although the Prototype code itself can be difficult to read, being far removed from the Java/C# style, using Prototype, and libraries built on top of it, is straightforward. Prototype can be thought of a library for library developers. Ajax application writers are more likely to use libraries built on top of Prototype than to use Prototype itself. We'll look at some of these libraries in the following sections. In the meantime, a brief discussion of Prototype's core features will help introduce its style of coding and will be useful when we discuss Scriptaculous, Rico, and Ruby on Rails.

Prototype allows one object to "extend" another by copying all of the parent object's properties and methods to the child. This feature is best illustrated by an example. Let's say that we define a parent class `Vehicle`

```
function Vehicle(numWheels,maxSpeed){
   this.numWheels=numWheels;
   this.maxSpeed=maxSpeed;
}
```

for which we want to define a specific instance that represents a passenger train. In our child class we also want to represent the number of carriages and provide a mechanism for adding and removing them. In ordinary JavaScript, we could write

```
var passTrain=new Vehicle(24,100);
passTrain.carriageCount=12;
passTrain.addCarriage=function(){
   this.carriageCount++;
}
passTrain.removeCarriage=function(){
   this.carriageCount--;
}
```

This provides the required functionality for our passTrain object. Looking at the code from a design perspective, though, it does little to wrap up the extended functionality into a coherent unit. Prototype can help us here, by allowing us to define the extended behavior as an object and then extend the base object with it. First, we define the extended functionality as an object:

```
function CarriagePuller(carriageCount){
   this.carriageCount=carriageCount;
   this.addCarriage=function(){
     this.carriageCount++;
   }
   this.removeCarriage=function(){
     this.carriageCount--;
   }
}
```

Then we merge the two to provide a single object containing all of the required behavior:

```
var parent=new Vehicle(24,100);
var extension=new CarriagePuller(12);
var passTrain=Object.extend(parent,extension);
```

Note that we define the parent and extension objects separately at first and then mix them together. The parent-child relationship exists between these instances, not between the `Vehicle` and `CarriagePuller` classes. While it isn't exactly classic object orientation, it allows us to keep all the code related to a specific function, in this case pulling carriages, in one place, from which it can easily be reused. While doing so in a small example like this may seem unnecessary, in larger projects, encapsulating functionality in such a way is extremely helpful.

Prototype also provides Ajax support in the form of an Ajax object that can resolve a cross-browser XMLHttpRequest object. Ajax is extended by the `Ajax.Request` type, which can make requests to the server using XMLHttp-Request, like so:

```
var req=new Ajax.Request('myData.xml');
```

The constructor uses a style that we'll also see in many of the Prototype-based libraries. It takes an associative array as an optional argument, allowing a wide range of options to be configured as needed. Sensible default values are provided for each option, so we need only pass in those objects that we want to override. In the case of the `Ajax.Request` constructor, the options array allows post data, request parameters, HTTP methods, and callback handlers to be defined. A more customized invocation of `Ajax.Request` might look like this:

```
var req=new Ajax.Request(
  'myData.xml',
  {
    method: 'get',
    parameters: { name:'dave',likes:'chocolate,rhubarb' },
    onLoaded: function(){ alert('loaded!'); },
    onComplete: function(){
      alert('done!\n\n'+req.transport.responseText);
    }
  }
);
```

The options array here has passed in four parameters. The HTTP method is set to get, because Prototype will default to the HTTP post method. The parameters array will be passed down on the querystring, because we are using HTTP get. If we used POST, it would be passed in the request body. onLoaded and onComplete are callback event handlers that will be fired when the readyState of the underlying XMLHttpRequest object changes. The variable `req.transport` in the `onComplete` function is a reference to the underlying XMLHttpRequest object.

On top of `Ajax.Request`, Prototype further defines an `Ajax.Updater` type of object that fetches script fragments generated on the server and evaluates them. This follows what we describe as a "script-centric" pattern in chapter 5 and is beyond the scope of our discussion here.

This concludes our brief review of cross-browser libraries. Our choice of libraries has been somewhat arbitrary and incomplete. As we have noted, there is a lot of activity in this space at the moment, and we've had to limit ourselves to some of the more popular or well-established offerings. In the next section, we'll look at some of the widget frameworks built on top of these and other libraries.

3.5.2 Widgets and widget suites

The libraries that we've discussed so far have provided cross-browser support for some fairly low-level functionality, such as manipulating DOM elements and fetching resources from the server. With these tools at our disposal, constructing functional UIs and application logic is certainly simplified, but we still need to do a lot more work than our counterparts working with Swing, MFC, or Qt, for example.

Prebuilt widgets, and even complete widget sets for Ajax developers, are starting to emerge. In this section, we'll look at a few of these—again, more to give a flavor of what's out there than to provide a comprehensive overview.

Scriptaculous

The Scriptaculous libraries are UI components built on top of Prototype (see the previous section). In its current form, Scriptaculous provides two major pieces of functionality, although it is being actively developed, with several other features planned.

The Effects library defines a range of animated visual effects that can be applied to DOM elements, to make them change size, position, and transparency. Effects can be easily combined, and a number of predefined secondary effects are provided, such as `Puff()`, which makes an element grow larger and more transparent until it fades away completely. Another useful core effect, called `Parallel()`, is provided to enable simultaneous execution of multiple effects. Effects can be a useful way of quickly adding visual feedback to an Ajax user interface, as we'll see in chapter 6.

Invoking a predetermined effect is as simple as calling its constructor, passing in the target DOM element or its ID as an argument, for example:

```
new Effect.SlideDown(myDOMElement);
```

Underlying the effects is the concept of a transition object, which can be parameterized in terms of duration and event handlers to be invoked when the transition ends. Several base transition types, such as linear, sinusoidal, wobble, and pulse, are provided. Creating a custom effect is simply a matter of combining core effects and passing in suitable parameters. A detailed discussion of building custom effects is beyond the scope of this brief overview. We'll see Scriptaculous effects in use again in chapter 6, when we develop a notifications system.

The second feature that Scriptaculous provides is a drag-and-drop library, through the Sortable class. This class takes a parent DOM element as an argument and enables drag-and-drop functionality for all its children. Options passed in to the constructor can specify callback handlers for when the item is dragged and dropped, types of child elements to be made draggable, and a list of valid drop targets (that is, elements that will accept the dragged item if the user lets go of it while mousing over them). Effect objects may also be passed in as options, to be executed when the item is first dragged, while it is in transit, and when it is dropped.

Rico

Rico, like Scriptaculous, is based on the Prototype library, and it also provides some highly customizable effects and drag-and-drop functionality. In addition, it provides a concept of a Behavior object, a piece of code that can be applied to part of a DOM tree to add interactive functionality to it. A few example Behaviors are provided, such as an Accordion widget, which nests a set of DOM elements within a given space, expanding one at a time. (This style of widget is often referred to as *outlook bar*, having been popularized by its use in Microsoft Outlook.)

Let's build a simple Rico Accordion widget. Initially, we require a parent DOM element; each child of the parent will become a pane in the accordion. We define a DIV element for each panel, with two further DIVs inside that, representing the header and the body of each panel:

```
<div id='myAccordion'>
  <div>
    <div>Dictionary Definition</div>
    <div>
      <ul>
      <li><b>n.</b>A portable wind instrument with a small
      keyboard and free metal reeds that sound when air is
      forced past them by pleated bellows operated by the
      player.</li>
      <li><b>adj.</b>Having folds or bends like the bellows
```

```
        of an accordion: accordion pleats; accordion blinds.</li>
        </ul>
      </div>
    </div>
    <div>
      <div>A picture</div>
      <div>
      <img src='monkey-accordion.jpg'></img>
      </div>
    </div>
  </div>
```

The first panel provides a dictionary definition for the word *accordion* and the second panel a picture of a monkey playing an accordion (see figure 3.9). Rendered as it is, this will simply display these two elements one above the other. However, we have assigned an ID attribute to the top-level DIV element, allowing us to pass a reference to it to the Accordion object, which we construct like this:

```
var outer=$('myAccordion');
outer.style.width='320px';
new Rico.Accordion(
  outer,
  { panelHeight:400,
    expandedBg:'#909090',
    collapsedBg:'#404040',
  }
);
```

The first line looks rather curious. $ is actually a valid JavaScript variable name and simply refers to a function in the core Prototype library. $() resolves DOM nodes in a way similar to the x library's xGetElementById() function that we discussed in the previous section. We pass a reference to the resolved DOM element to the Accordion object constructor, along with an array of options, in the standard idiom for Prototype-derived libraries. In this case, the options simply provide some styling of the Accordion widget's visual elements, although callback handler functions to be triggered when panels are opened or closed can also be passed in here. Figure 3.9 shows the effect of styling the DOM elements using the Accordion object. Rico's Behaviors provide a simple way of creating reusable widgets from common markup and also separate the content from the interactivity. We'll explore the topic of applying good design principles to the JavaScript UI in chapter 4.

The final feature of the Rico framework to mention is that it provides very good support for Ajax-style requests to the server, through a global Rico Ajax-Engine object. The AjaxEngine provides more than just a cross-browser wrapper around the XMLHttpRequest object. It defines an XML response format that

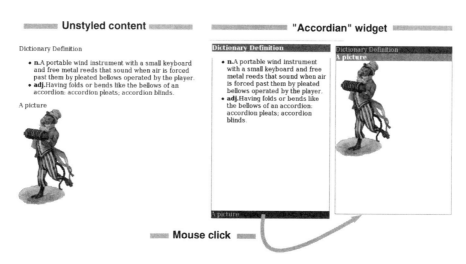

Figure 3.9 The Rico framework Behaviors allow plain DOM nodes to be styled as interactive widgets, simply by passing a reference to the top-level node to the Behavior object's constructor. In this case, the Accordion object has been applied to a set of DIV elements (left) to create an interactive menu widget (right), in which mouse clicks open and close the individual panels.

consists of a number of `<response>` elements. The engine will automatically decode these, and it has built-in support for two types of response: those that directly update DOM elements and those that update JavaScript objects. We'll look at a similar mechanism in greater detail in section 5.5.3, when we discuss client/server interactions in depth. For now, let's move on to the next type of framework: one that spans both client and server.

3.5.3 Application frameworks

The frameworks that we have looked at so far are executed exclusively in the browser and can be served up as static JavaScript files from any web server. The final category of frameworks that we will review here are those that reside on the server and generate at least some of the JavaScript code or HTML markup dynamically.

These are the most complex of the frameworks that we are discussing here, and we won't be able to discuss them in great detail but will give a brief overview of their features. We will return to the topic of server-side frameworks in chapter 5.

DWR, JSON-RPC, and SAJAX

We'll begin by looking at three small server-side frameworks together, because they share a common approach, although they are written for different server-side languages. SAJAX works with a variety of server-side languages, including PHP, Python, Perl, and Ruby. DWR (which stands for Direct Web Remoting) is a Java-based framework with a similar approach, exposing methods of objects rather than standalone functions. JSON-RPC (JavaScript Object Notation-based Remote Procedure Calls) is also similar in design. It offers support for server-side JavaScript, Python, Ruby, Perl, and Java.

All three allow objects defined on the server to expose their methods directly as Ajax requests. We will frequently have a server-side function that returns a useful result that has to be calculated on the server, say, because it looks up a value from a database. These frameworks provide a convenient way to access those functions or methods from the web browser and can be a good way of exposing the server-side domain model to the web browser code.

Let's look at an example using SAJAX, exposing functions defined on the server in PHP. We'll use a straightforward example function that simply returns a string of text, as follows:

```php
<?php
function sayHello(name){
  return("Hello! {$name} Ajax in Action!!!!");
?>
```

To export this function to the JavaScript tier, we simply import the SAJAX engine into our PHP and call the `sajax_export` function:

```php
<?php
require('Sajax.php');
sajax_init();
sajax_export("sayHello");
?>
```

When we write our dynamic web page, then, we use SAJAX to generate some Java-Script wrappers for the exported functions. The generated code creates a local JavaScript function with identical signatures to the server-side function:

```
<script type='text/javascript'>
<?
 sajax_show_javascript();
?>
...
alert(sayHello("Dave"));
...
</script>
```

When we call `sayHello("Dave")` in the browser, the generated JavaScript code will make an Ajax request to the server, execute the server-side function, and return the result in the HTTP response. The response will be parsed and the return value extracted to the JavaScript. The developer need not touch any of the Ajax technologies; everything is handled behind the scenes by the SAJAX libraries.

These three frameworks offer a fairly low-level mapping of server-side functions and objects to client-side Ajax calls. They automate what could otherwise be a tedious task, but they do present a danger of exposing too much server-side logic to the Internet. We discuss these issues in greater detail in chapter 5.

The remaining frameworks that we'll look at in this section take a more sophisticated approach, generating entire UI layers from models declared on the server. Although they use standard Ajax technologies internally, these frameworks essentially provide their own programming model. As a result, working with these frameworks is quite different from writing generic Ajax, and we will be able to provide only a broad overview here.

Backbase

The Backbase Presentation Server provides a rich widget set that binds at runtime to XML tags embedded in the HTML documents generated by the server. The principle here is similar to the Rico behavior components, except that Backbase uses a custom set of XHTML tags to mark up the UI components, rather than standard HTML tags.

Backbase provides server-side implementations for both Java and .NET. It is a commercial product but offers a free community edition.

Echo2

NextApp's Echo2 framework is a Java-based server engine that generates rich UI components from a model of the user interface that is declared on the server. Once launched in the browser, the widgets are fairly autonomous and will handle user interactions locally using JavaScript or otherwise send requests back to the server in batches using a request queue similar to the one employed by Rico.

Echo2 promotes itself as an Ajax-based solution that requires no knowledge of HTML, JavaScript, or CSS, unless you want to extend the set of components that are available. In most cases, the development of the client application is done using only Java. Echo2 is open source, licensed under a Mozilla-style license, allowing its use in commercial applications.

Ruby on Rails

Ruby on Rails is a web development framework written in the Ruby programming language. It bundles together solutions for mapping server-side objects to a database and presenting content using templates, very much in the style of the server-side MVC that we discussed in section 3.4. Ruby on Rails claims very fast development of simple to medium websites, since it uses code-generation techniques to generate a lot of common code. It also seeks to minimize the amount of configuration required to get a live application running.

In recent versions, Rails has provided strong Ajax support through the Prototype library. Prototype and Rails are a natural fit, since the JavaScript code for Prototype is generated from a Ruby program, and the programming styles are similar. As with Echo2, using Ajax with Rails does not require a strong knowledge of Ajax technologies such as JavaScript, but a developer who does understand JavaScript can extend the Ajax support in new ways.

This concludes our overview of third-party frameworks for Ajax. As we've already noted, this is currently a fast-moving area, and most of the frameworks that we have discussed are under active development.

Many of the libraries and frameworks have their own coding idioms and styles, too. In writing the code examples for this book, we have sought to provide a feel for the breadth of Ajax technologies and techniques and have avoided leaning too heavily on any particular framework. Nonetheless, you will encounter some of the products that we have discussed here, sprinkled lightly throughout the rest of the book.

3.6 Summary

In this chapter, we've introduced the concept of refactoring as a way of improving code quality and flexibility. Our first taste of refactoring was to roll up the XMLHttpRequest object—the very core of the Ajax stack—into a simple, reusable object.

We've looked at a number of design patterns that we can apply to solve commonly encountered problems when working with Ajax. Design patterns provide a semiformal way of capturing the knowledge of the programmers who have gone before us and can help us to refactor toward a concrete goal.

Façade and Adapter provide useful ways of smoothing over the differences between varying implementations. In Ajax, these patterns are especially useful in providing an insulating layer from cross-browser incompatibilities, a major and longstanding source of worry for JavaScript developers.

Observer is a flexible pattern for dealing with event-driven systems. We'll return to it in chapter 4 when looking at the UI layers of our application. Used together with Command, which offers a good way of encapsulating user interactions, it is possible to develop a robust framework for handling user input and providing an undo facility. Command also has its uses in organizing client/server interactions, as we will see in chapter 5.

Singleton offers a straightforward way of controlling access to specific resources. In Ajax, we may usefully use Singleton to control access to the network, as we will see in chapter 5.

Finally, we introduced the Model-View-Controller pattern, an architectural pattern that has a long history (in Internet time, at least!) of use in web applications. We discussed how the use of MVC can improve the flexibility of a server-side application through use of an abstracted data layer and a template system.

Our garment store example also demonstrated the way in which design patterns and refactoring go hand in hand. Creating a perfectly designed piece of code the first time round is difficult, but refactoring an ugly-but-functional bit of code such as listing 3.4 to gradually bring in the benefits of design patterns is possible, and the end results are every bit as good.

Finally, we looked at third-party libraries and frameworks as another way of introducing order to an Ajax project. A number of libraries and frameworks are springing up at present, from simple cross-browser wrappers to complete widget sets to end-to-end solutions encompassing both client and server. We reviewed several of the more popular frameworks briefly, and we will return to some of them in later chapters.

In the following two chapters, we'll apply our understanding of refactoring and design patterns to the Ajax client and then to the client/server communication system. This will help us to develop a vocabulary and a set of practices that will make it easier to develop robust and multifeatured web applications.

3.7 Resources

Martin Fowler (with coauthors Kent Beck, John Brant, William Opdyke, and Don Roberts) wrote the seminal guide to refactoring: *Refactoring: Improving the Design of Existing Code* (Addison-Wesley Professional, 1999).

Erich Gamma, Richard Helm, Ralph Johnson, and John Vlissides (also known as "The Gang of Four") wrote the influential *Design Patterns* (Addison-Wesley Professional, 1995).

Gamma later went on to become architect for the Eclipse IDE/platform (see appendix A), and discusses both Eclipse and design patterns in this recent interview: www.artima.com/lejava/articles/gammadp.html.

Michael Mahemoff has recently set up a website devoted to cataloging Ajax design patterns: www.ajaxpatterns.org.

Part 2

Core techniques

Now that you know what Ajax is all about, we'll cover the core techniques for designing an application. Our goals are to design code that is flexible, maintainable, and fun to work with. Chapter 4 looks at ways of getting the client code in shape, and keeping the CSS, HTML, and JavaScript out of each other's hair. Chapter 5 looks at ways of interacting with the server, and how to manage communication between the client and server tiers.

The page as
an application

This chapter covers

- Organizing complex user interface code
- Using the Model-View-Controller pattern with JavaScript
- Separating presentation from logic for maintainable code
- Creating a flexible event-handling mode
- Generating the user interface directly from your business objects

In chapters 1 and 2 we covered the basic principles of Ajax, from both a usability and a technology perspective. In chapter 3 we touched on the notion of creating *maintainable* code through refactoring and design patterns. In the examples that we've looked at so far, this may have seemed like overkill, but as we explore the subject of Ajax programming in more depth, they will prove themselves to be indispensable tools.

In this chapter and the next, we discuss the details of building a larger, scalable Ajax client, and the architectural principles needed to make it work. This chapter looks at the coding of the client itself, drawing heavily on the Model-View-Controller (MVC) pattern that we discussed in chapter 3. We'll also encounter the Observer and other smaller patterns along the way. Chapter 5 will look at the relationship between the client and the server.

4.1 A different kind of MVC

In chapter 3, we presented an example of refactoring a simple garment store application to conform to the MVC pattern. This is the context in which most web developers will have come across MVC before, with the Model being the domain model on the server, the View the generated content sent to the client, and the Controller a servlet or set of pages defining the workflow of the application.

However, MVC had its origins in desktop application development, and there are several other places in an Ajax application where it can serve us well too. Let's have a look at them now.

4.1.1 Repeating the pattern at different scales

The classic web MVC model describes the entire application in coarse-grained detail. The entire generated data stream is the View. The entire CGI or servlet layer is the Controller, and so on.

In desktop application development, MVC patterns are often applied at a much finer scale, too. Something as simple as a pushbutton widget can use MVC:

- The internal representation of states—pressed, unpressed, inactive, for example—is the Model. An Ajax widget would typically implement this as a JavaScript object.

- The painted-on-screen widget—composed of Document Object Model (DOM) nodes, in the case of an Ajax UI—with modifications for different states, highlights, and tooltips, is the View.

- The internal code for relating the two is the Controller. The event-handler code (that is, what happens in the larger application when the user presses the button) is also a Controller, but not the Controller for this View and Model. We'll get to that shortly.

A pushbutton in isolation will have very little behavior, state, or visible variation, so the payback for using MVC here is relatively small. If we look at a more complicated widget component, such as a tree or a table, however, the overall system is complicated enough to benefit from a clean MVC-based design more thoroughly.

Figure 4.1 illustrates MVC applied to a tree widget. The Model consists of tree nodes, each with a list of child nodes, an open/closed status, and a reference to some business object, representing files and directories in a file explorer, say. The View consists of the icons and lines painted onto the widget canvas. The Controller handles user events, such as opening and closing nodes and displaying pop-up menus, and also triggering graphical update calls for particular nodes, to allow the View to refresh itself incrementally.

That's one way of applying MVC outside of the more familiar web server scenario. But we're not finished yet. Let's turn our attention to the web browser next.

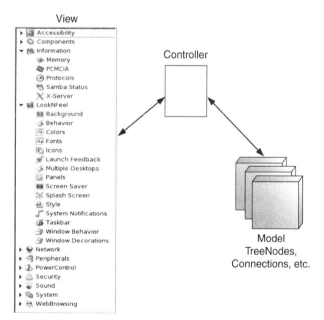

Figure 4.1
Model-View-Controller applied to the internal functioning of a tree widget. The view consists of a series of painted-on-screen elements composed of DOM elements. Behind the scenes, the tree structure is modeled as a series of JavaScript objects. Controller code mediates between the two.

4.1.2 Applying MVC in the browser

We've focused on the small details of our application. We can also zoom out our perspective, to consider the entire JavaScript application that is delivered to the browser on startup. This, too, can be structured to follow the MVC pattern, and it will benefit from clear separation of concerns if it is.

At this level, the Model consists of the business domain objects, the View is the programmatically manipulated page as a whole, and the Controller is a combination of all the event handlers in the code that link the UI to the domain objects. Figure 4.2 illustrates the MVC operating at this level. This is perhaps the most important use of MVC for an Ajax developer, because it is a natural fit to the Ajax rich client application. We'll examine the details of such use of the pattern, and what it buys us, in the remainder of the chapter.

If you think back to the conventional web MVC that we discussed in chapter 3 as well, you'll remember that we have at least three layers of MVC within a typical Ajax application, each performing different roles within the lifecycle of the application and each contributing to clean, well-organized code. Figure 4.3 illustrates

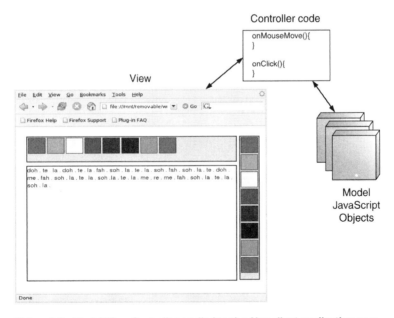

Figure 4.2   Model-View-Controller applied to the Ajax client application as a whole. The Controller at this level is the code that links the UI to the business objects in the JavaScript.

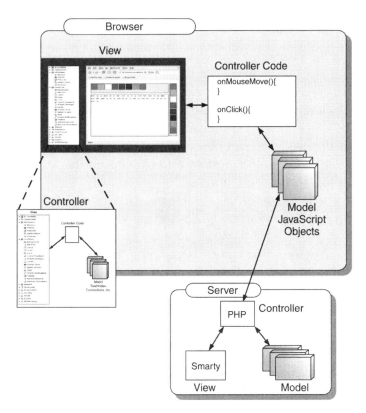

Figure 4.3 Nested MVC architecture, in which the pattern repeats itself at different scales. At the outermost level, we can see the pattern defining the workflow of the application as a whole, with the model residing on the web server. At a smaller scale, the pattern is replicated within the client application and, at a smaller scale than that, within individual widgets in the client application.

how these MVC patterns at different scales are nested within each other in the application architecture.

So, what does this mean to us when we're working on the code? In the following sections, we'll take a more practical look at using MVC to define the structure of our JavaScript application, how it will affect the way we write code, and what the benefits will be. Let's start with a look at the View.

4.2 *The View in an Ajax application*

From the position of the JavaScript application delivered to the browser when the application starts up, the View is the visible page, consisting of the DOM elements that are rendered by HTML markup or through programmatic manipulation. We've already shown how to manipulate the DOM programmatically in chapter 2.

According to MVC, our View has two main responsibilities. It has to provide a visible interface for the user to trigger events from, that is, to talk to the Controller. It also needs to update itself in response to changes in the Model, usually communicated through the Controller again.

If the application is being developed by a team, the View will probably be the area subject to the most contention. Designers and graphic artists will be involved, as will programmers, particularly as we explore the scope for interactivity in an Ajax interface. Asking designers to write code, or programmers to get involved in the aesthetics of an application, is often a bad idea. Even if you're providing both roles, it can be helpful to separate them, in order to focus on one at a time.

We showed in our overview of server MVC how code and presentation could become intertwined, and we separated them out using a template system. What are the options available to us here on the browser?

In chapter 3, we demonstrated how to structure our web pages so that the CSS, HTML, and JavaScript are defined in separate files. In terms of the page itself, this split follows MVC, with the stylesheet being the View and the HTML/DOM being the model (a Document Object Model). From our current perspective, though, the page rendering is a black box, and the HTML and CSS together should be treated as the View. Keeping them separate is still a good idea, and simply by moving the JavaScript out into a separate file we have started to keep the designers and the programmers off each other's backs. This is just a start, however, as you'll see.

4.2.1 *Keeping the logic out of the View*

Writing all our JavaScript in a separate file is a good start for enforcing separation of the View, but even with this in place, we can entangle the View with the logic roles (that is, Model and Controller) without having to try too hard. If we write JavaScript event handlers inline, such as

```
<div class='importButton'
onclick='importData("datafeed3.xml", mytextbox.value);'/>
```

then we are hard-coding business logic into the View. What is `datafeed3`? What does the value of `mytextbox` have to do with it? Why does `importData()` take two arguments, and what do they mean? The designer shouldn't need to know these things.

`importData()` is a business logic function. The View and the Model shouldn't talk to one another directly, according to the MVC canon, so one solution is to separate them out with an extra layer of indirection. If we rewrite our DIV tag as

```
<div class='importButton' onclick='importFeedData()'/>
```

and define an event handler like this

```
function importFeedData(event){
  importData("datafeed3.xml", mytextbox.value);
}
```

then the arguments are encapsulated within the `importFeedData()` function, rather than an anonymous event handler. This allows us to reuse that functionality elsewhere, keeping the concerns separate and the code DRY (at the risk of repeating myself, DRY means "don't repeat yourself").

The Controller is still embedded in the HTML, however, which might make it hard to find in a large application.

To keep the Controller and the View separate, we can attach the event programmatically. Rather than declare an event handler inline, we can specify a marker of some sort that will later be picked up by the code. We have several options for this marker. We can attach a unique ID to the element and specify event handlers on a per-element basis. The HTML would be rewritten as

```
<div class='importButton' id='dataFeedBtn'>
```

and the following code executed as part of the `window.onload` callback, for example:

```
var dfBtn=document.getElementById('dataFeedBtn');
dfBtn.onclick=importFeedData;
```

If we want to perform the same action on multiple event handlers, we need to apply a non-unique marker of some sort. One simple approach is to define an extra CSS class.

Adding events indirectly using CSS

Let's look at a simple example, in which we bind mouse events to keys on a virtual musical keyboard. In listing 4.1, we define a simple page containing an unstyled document structure.

Listing 4.1   musical.html

```
<!DOCTYPE html
PUBLIC "-//W3C//DTD XHTML 1.0 Strict//EN"
"http://www.w3.org/TR/xhtml1/DTD/xhtml1-strict.dtd">
<html>
<head>
<title>Keyboard</title>
<link rel='stylesheet' type='text/css' href='musical.css'/>
<script type='text/javascript' src='musical.js'></script>
<script type='text/javascript'>
window.onload=assignKeys;
</script>
</head>
<body>
<div id='keyboard' class='musicalKeys'>
  <div class='do musicalButton'></div>
  <div class='re musicalButton'></div>
  <div class='mi musicalButton'></div>
  <div class='fa musicalButton'></div>            ❶ Keys on our
  <div class='so musicalButton'></div>               "keyboard"
  <div class='la musicalButton'></div>
  <div class='ti musicalButton'></div>
  <div class='do musicalButton'></div>
</div>
<div id='console' class='console'>
</div>
</body>
</html>
```

We declare the page to conform to XHTML strict definition, just to show that it can be done. The keyboard element is assigned a unique ID, but the keys are not. Note that the keys designated ❶ are each defined as having two styles. musical-Button is common to all keys, and a separate style differentiates them by note. These styles are defined separately in the stylesheet (listing 4.2).

Listing 4.2   musical.css

```
.body{
  background-color: white;
}
.musicalKeys{
  background-color: #ffe0d0;
  border: solid maroon 2px;
  width: 536px;
  height: 68px;
  top: 24px;
  left: 24px;
```

```
    margin: 4px;
    position: absolute;
    overflow: auto;
  }
  .musicalButton{
    border: solid navy 1px;
    width: 60px;
    height: 60px;
    position: relative;
    margin: 2px;
    float: left;
  }
  .do{ background-color: red; }
  .re{ background-color: orange; }
  .mi{ background-color: yellow; }
  .fa{ background-color: green; }
  .so{ background-color: blue; }
  .la{ background-color: indigo; }
  .ti{ background-color: violet; }
  div.console{
    font-family: arial, helvetica;
    font-size: 16px;
    color: navy;
    background-color: white;
    border: solid navy 2px;
    width: 536px;
    height: 320px;
    top: 106px;
    left: 24px;
    margin: 4px;
    position: absolute;
    overflow: auto;
  }
```

The style `musicalButton` defines the common properties of each key. The note-specific styles simply define a color for each key. Note that whereas top-level document elements are positioned with explicit pixel precision, we use the float style attribute to lay the keys out in a horizontal line using the browser's built-in layout engine.

Binding the event-handler code

The JavaScript file (listing 4.3) binds the events to these keys programmatically.

Listing 4.3   musical.js

```
function assignKeys(){
    var keyboard=document.getElementById("keyboard");    <── Find parent DIV
```

```
var keys=keyboard.getElementsByTagName("div");        ◁— Enumerate children
if (keys){
  for(var i=0;i<keys.length;i++){
    var key=keys[i];
    var classes=(key.className).split(" ");
    if (classes && classes.length>=2
     && classes[1]=="musicalButton"){
      var note=classes[0];
      key.note=note;                    ◁— Add custom attribute
      key.onmouseover=playNote;
    }
  }
}
}
function playNote(event){
  var note=this.note;          ◁— Retrieve custom attribute
  var console=document.getElementById("console");
  if (note && console){
    console.innerHTML+=note+" . ";
  }
}
```

The `assignKeys()` function is called by `window.onload`. (We could have defined `window.onload` directly in this file, but that limits its portability). We find the keyboard element by its unique ID and then use `getElementsByTagName()` to iterate through all the DIV elements inside it. This requires some knowledge of the page structure, but it allows the designer the freedom to move the keyboard DIV around the page in any way that she wants.

The DOM elements representing the keys return a single string as `className` property. We use the inbuilt `String.split` function to convert it into an array, and check that the element is of class `musicalButton`. We then read the other part of the styling—which represents the note that this key plays—and attach it to the DOM node as an extra property, where it can be picked up again in the event handler.

Playing music through a web browser is rather tricky, so in this case, we simply write the note out to the "console" underneath the keyboard. `innerHTML` is adequate for this purpose. Figure 4.4 shows our musical keyboard in action. We've achieved good separation of roles here. Provided the designer drops the keyboard and console DIV tags somewhere on the page and includes the stylesheet and JavaScript, the application will work, and the risk of accidentally breaking the event logic is small. Effectively, the HTML page has become a template into which we inject variables and logic. This provides us with a good way of keeping

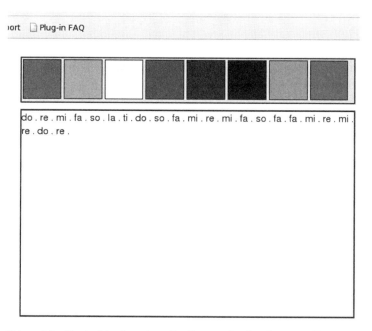

Figure 4.4 Musical keyboard application running in a browser. The colored areas along the top are mapped to music notes, which are printed out in the lower console area when the mouse moves over them.

logic out of the View. We've worked through this example manually, to demonstrate the details of how it's done. In production, you might like to make use of a couple of third-party libraries that address the same issue.

The Rico framework (www.openrico.org/) has a concept of Behavior objects that target specific sections of a DOM tree and add interactivity to them. We looked at the Rico Accordion behavior briefly in section 3.5.2.

A similar separation between HTML markup and interactivity can be achieved with Ben Nolan's Behaviour library (see the Resources section at end of chapter). This library allows event-handler code to be assigned to DOM elements based on CSS selector rules (see chapter 2). In our previous example, the `assignKeys()` function programmatically selects the document element with the id `keyboard`, and then gets all DIV elements directly contained by it, using DOM manipulation methods. We can express this using a CSS selector as

```
#keyboard div
```

Using CSS, we could style all our `keyboard` elements using this selector. Using the Behaviour.js library, we can also apply event handlers in the same way as follows:

```
var myrules={
  '#keyboard div' : function(key){
    var classes=(key.className).split(" ");
    if (classes && classes.length>=2
    && classes[1]=='musicalButton'){
      var note=classes[0];
      key.note=note;
      key.onmouseover=playNote;
    }
  }
};
Behaviour.register(myrules);
```

Most of the logic is the same as in our previous example, but the use of CSS selectors offers a concise alternative to programmatically locating DOM elements, particularly if we're adding several behaviors at once.

That keeps the logic out of the view for us, but it's also possible to tangle the View up in the logic, as we will see.

4.2.2 *Keeping the View out of the logic*

We've reached the point now where the designers can develop the look of the page without having to touch the code. However, as it stands, some of the functionality of the application is still embedded in the HTML, namely, the ordering of the keys. Each key is defined as a separate DIV tag, and the designers could unwittingly delete some of them.

If the ordering of the keys is a business domain function rather than a design issue—and we can argue that it is—then it makes sense to generate some of the DOM for the component programmatically, rather than declare it in the HTML. Further, we may want to have multiple components of the same type on a page. If we don't want the designer to modify the order of the keys on our keyboard, for example, we could simply stipulate that they assign a DIV tag with the class `keyboard` and have our initialization code find it and add the keys programmatically. Listing 4.4 shows the modified JavaScript required to do this.

Listing 4.4 musical_dyn_keys.js

```
var notes=new Array("do","re","mi","fa","so","la","ti","do");
function assignKeys(){
  var candidates=document.getElementsByTagName("div");
  if (candidates){
    for(var i=0;i<candidates.length;i++){
      var candidate=candidates[i];
      if (candidate.className.indexOf('musicalKeys')>=0){
        makeKeyboard(candidate);
```

```
        }
      }
    }
  }
  function makeKeyboard(el){
    for(var i=0;i<notes.length;i++){
      var key=document.createElement("div");
      key.className=notes[i]+" musicalButton";
      key.note=notes[i];
      key.onmouseover=playNote;
      el.appendChild(key);
    }
  }
  function playNote(event){
    var note=this.note;
    var console=document.getElementById('console');
    if (note && console){
      console.innerHTML+=note+" . ";
    }
  }
```

Previously, we had defined our key sequence in the HTML. Now it is defined as a global JavaScript array. The assignKeys() method examines all the top-level DIV tags in the document, to see if the className contains the value musical-Keys. If it does, then it tries to populate that DIV with a working keyboard, using the makeKeyboard() function. makeKeyboard() simply creates new DOM nodes and then manipulates them in the same way as listing 4.4 did for the declared DOM nodes that it encountered. The playNote() callback handler operates exactly as before.

Because we are populating empty DIVs with our keyboard controls, adding a second set of keys is simple, as listing 4.5 illustrates.

Listing 4.5 musical_dyn_keys.html

```
<!DOCTYPE html
PUBLIC "-//W3C//DTD XHTML 1.0 Strict//EN"
"http://www.w3.org/TR/xhtml1/DTD/xhtml1-strict.dtd">
<html>
<title>Two Keyboards</title>
<head>
<link rel='stylesheet' type='text/css'
  href='musical_dyn_keys.css'/>
<script type='text/javascript'
  src='musical_dyn_keys.js'>
</script>
<script type='text/javascript'>
```

```
window.onload=assignKeys;
</script>
</head>
<body>
<div id='keyboard-top' class='toplong musicalKeys'></div>
<div id='keyboard-side' class='sidebar musicalKeys'></div>
<div id='console' class='console'>
</div>
</body>
</html>
```

Adding a second keyboard is a single-line operation. Because we don't want them sitting one on top of the other, we move the placement styling out of the musical-Keys style class and into separate classes. The stylesheet modifications are shown in listing 4.6.

Listing 4.6   Changes to musical_dyn_keys.css

```
.musicalKeys{     <—  Common keyboard styling
  background-color: #ffe0d0;
  border: solid maroon 2px;
  position: absolute;
  overflow: auto;
  margin: 4px;
}
.toplong{     <—  Geometry of keyboard I
  width: 536px;
  height: 68px;
  top: 24px;
  left: 24px;
}
.sidebar{     <—  Geometry of keyboard 2
  width: 48px;
  height: 400px;
  top: 24px;
  left: 570px;
}
```

The musicalKeys class defines the visual style common to all keyboards. toplong and sidebar simply define the geometry of each keyboard.

By refactoring our keyboard example in this way, we have made it possible to reuse the code easily. However, the design of the keyboard is partly defined in the JavaScript, in the makeKeyboard() function in listing 4.4, and yet, as figure 4.5 shows, one keyboard has a vertical layout and the other a horizontal one. How did we achieve this?

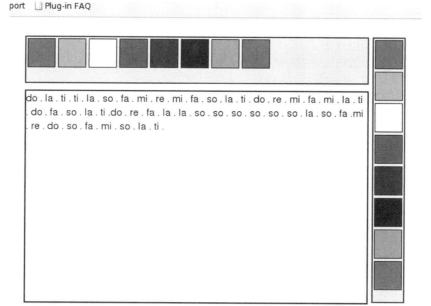

Figure 4.5 Our revised musical keyboard program allows the designer to specify multiple keyboards. Using CSS-based styling and the native render engine, we can accommodate both vertical and horizontal layouts without writing explicit layout code in our JavaScript.

makeKeyboard() could easily have computed the size of the DIV that it was targeting and placed each button programmatically. In that case, we would need to get quite fussy about deciding whether the DIV was vertical or horizontal and write our own layout code. To a Java GUI programmer familiar with the internals of LayoutManager objects, this may seem all too obvious a route to take. If we took it, our programmers would wrest control of the widget's look from the designers, and trouble would ensue!

As it is, makeKeyboard() modifies only the structure of the document. The keys are laid out by the browser's own layout engine, which is controlled by stylesheets—by the float style attribute in this case. It is important that the layout be controlled by the designer. Logic and View remain separate, and peace reigns.

The keyboard was a relatively simple widget. In a larger, more complex widget such as a tree table, it may be harder to see how the browser's own render engine can be coerced into doing the layout, and in some cases, programmatic styling is inevitable. However, it's always worth asking this question, in the interests of keeping View and Logic separate. The browser render engine is also a high-performing, fast, and well-tested piece of native code, and it is likely to beat any JavaScript algorithms that we cook up.

That about wraps it up for the View for the moment. In the next section, we'll explore the role of the Controller in MVC and how that relates to JavaScript event handlers in an Ajax application.

4.3 *The Controller in an Ajax application*

The role of the Controller in MVC is to serve as an intermediary between the Model and the View, decoupling them from one another. In a GUI application such as our Ajax client application, the Controller layer is composed of event handlers. As is often the case with web browsers, techniques have evolved over time, and modern browsers support two different event models. The classic model is relatively simple and is in the process of being superseded by the newer W3C specifications for event handling. At the time of writing, however, implementations of the new event-handling model vary between browsers and are somewhat problematic. Both event models are discussed here.

4.3.1 *Classic JavaScript event handlers*

The JavaScript implementation in web browsers allows us to define code that will be executed in response to a user event, typically either the mouse or keyboard. In the modern browsers that support Ajax, these event handlers can be assigned to most visual elements. We can use the event handlers to connect our visible user interface, that is, the View, to the business object Model.

The classic event model has been around since the early days of JavaScript, and is relatively simple and straightforward. DOM elements have a small number of predefined properties to which callback functions can be assigned. For example, to attach a function that will be called when the mouse is clicked on an element `myDomElement`, we could write

```
myDomElement.onclick=showAnimatedMonkey
```

`myDomElement` is any DOM element that we have a programmatic handle on. `showAnimatedMonkey` is a function, defined as

```
function showAnimatedMonkey(){
  //some skillfully executed code to display
  //an engaging cartoon character here
}
```

that is, as an ordinary JavaScript function. Note that when we assign the event handler, we pass the Function object, not a call to that object, so it doesn't have parentheses after the function name. This is a common mistake:

```
myDomElement.onclick=showAnimatedMonkey();
```

This looks more natural to programmers unaccustomed to treating functions as first-class objects, but it will not do what we think. The function will be called when we make the assignment, not when the DOM element is clicked. The `onclick` property will be set to whatever is returned by the function. Unless you're doing something extremely clever involving functions that return references to other functions, this is probably not desirable. Here's the right way to do it:

```
myDomElement.onclick=showAnimatedMonkey;
```

This passes a reference to our callback function to the DOM element, telling it that this is the function to invoke when the node is clicked on. DOM elements have many such properties to which event-handler functions can be attached. Common event-handler callbacks for GUI work are listed in table 4.1. Similar properties can be found elsewhere in web browser JavaScript, too. The `XML-HttpRequest.onreadystate` and `window.onload`, which we have encountered already, are also event handler functions that can be assigned by the programmer.

Table 4.1 Common GUI event handler properties in the DOM

Property	Description
onmouseover	Triggered when the mouse first passes into an element's region.
onmouseout	Triggered when the mouse passes out of an element's region.
onmousemove	Triggered whenever the mouse moves while within an element's region (i.e., frequently!).
onclick	Triggered when the mouse is clicked within an element's region.
onkeypress	Triggered when a key is pressed while this element has input focus. Global key handlers can be attached to the document's body.
onfocus	A visible element receives input focus.
onblur	A visible element loses input focus.

There is an unusual feature of the event handler functions worth mentioning here, as it trips people up most frequently when writing object-oriented Java-Script, a feature that we will lean on heavily in developing Ajax clients.

We've got a handle on a DOM element, and assigned a callback function to the `onclick` property. When the DOM element receives a mouse click, the callback is invoked. However, the function context (that is, the value that variable `this` resolves to—see appendix B for a fuller discussion of JavaScript Function objects) is assigned to the DOM node that received the event. Depending on where and how the function was originally declared, this can be very confusing.

Let's explore the problem with an example. We define a class to represent a button object, which has a reference to a DOM node, a callback handler, and a value that is displayed when the button is clicked. Any instance of the button will respond in the same way to a mouse click event, and so we define the callback handler as a method of the button class. That's a sufficient spec for starters, so let's look at the code. Here's the constructor for our button:

```
function Button(value,domEl){
  this.domEl=domEl;
  this.value=value;
  this.domEl.onclick=this.clickHandler;
}
```

We go on to define an event handler as part of the `Button` class:

```
Button.prototype.clickHandler=function(){
  alert(this.value);
}
```

It looks straightforward enough, but it doesn't do what we want it to. The alert box will generally return a message `undefined`, not the value property that we passed to the constructor. Let's see why. The function `clickHandler` gets invoked by the browser when the DOM element is clicked, and it sets the function context to the DOM element, not the Button JavaScript object. So, `this.value` refers to the `value` property of the DOM element, not the Button object. You'd never tell by looking at the declaration of the event-handler function, would you?

We can fix things up by passing a reference to the Button object to the DOM element, that is, by modifying our constructor like this:

```
function Button(value,domEl){
  this.domEl=domEl;
  this.value=value;
  this.domEl.buttonObj=this;
  this.domEl.onclick=this.clickHandler;
}
```

The DOM element still doesn't have a `value` property, but it has a reference to the Button object, which it can use to get the value. We finish up by altering the event handler like this:

```
Button.prototype.clickHandler=function(){
  var buttonObj=this.buttonObj;
  var value=(buttonObj && buttonObj.value) ?
    buttonObj.value : "unknown value";
  alert(value);
}
```

The DOM node refers to the Button, which refers to its `value` property, and our event handler does what we want it to. We could have attached the `value` directly to the DOM node, but attaching a reference to the entire backing object allows this pattern to work easily with arbitrarily complex objects. In passing, it's worth noting that we've implemented a mini-MVC pattern here, with the DOM element View fronting a backing object Model.

That's the classic event model, then. The main shortcoming of this event model is that it allows only one event-handler function per element. In the Observer pattern that we presented in chapter 3, we noted that an observable element could have any number of observers attached to it at a given time. When writing a simple script for a web page, this is unlikely to be a serious shortcoming, but as we move toward the more complex Ajax clients, we start to feel the constraint more. We will take a closer look at this in section 4.3.3, but first, let's look at the more recent event model.

4.3.2 *The W3C event model*

The more flexible event model proposed by the W3C is complex. An arbitrary number of listeners can be attached to a DOM element. Further, if an action takes place in a region of the document in which several elements overlap, the event handlers of each are given an opportunity to fire and to veto further calls in the event stack, known as "swallowing" the event. The specification proposes that the event stack be traversed twice in total, first propagating from outermost to innermost (from the document element down) and then bubbling up again from the inside to the outside. In practice, different browsers implement different subsets of this behavior.

In Mozilla-based browsers and Safari, event callbacks are attached using `addEventListener()` and removed by a corresponding `removeEventListener()`. Internet Explorer offers similar functions: `attachEvent()` and `detachEvent()`. Mike Foster's `xEvent` object (part of the x library—see the Resources section at the end of this chapter) makes a brave attempt at creating a Façade (see chapter 3) across these implementations in order to provide a rich cross-browser event model.

There is a further cross-browser annoyance here, as the callback handler functions defined by the user are called slightly differently. Under Mozilla browsers, the function is invoked with the DOM element receiving the event as a context object, as for the classic event model. Under Internet Explorer, the function context is always the Window object, making it impossible to work out which DOM element is currently calling the event handler! Even with a layer such as xEvent in place, developers need to account for these variations when writing their callback handlers.

The final issue to mention here is that neither implementation provides a satisfactory way of returning a list of all currently attached listeners.

At this point, I advise you not to use the newer event model. The main shortcoming of the classic model—lack of multiple listeners—can be addressed by the use of design patterns, as we will see next.

4.3.3 *Implementing a flexible event model in JavaScript*

Because of the incompatibilities of the newer W3C event model, the promise of a flexible event listener framework remains just out of reach. We described the Observer pattern in chapter 3, and that seems to fit the bill nicely, allowing us to add and remove observers from the event source in a flexible fashion. Clearly, the W3C felt the same way, as the revised event model implements Observer, but the browser vendors delivered inconsistent and just plain broken implementations. The classic event model falls far short of the Observer pattern, but perhaps we can enhance it a little with some code of our own.

Managing multiple event callbacks

Before going on to implement our own solution, let's come to grips with the problem through a simple example. Listing 4.7 shows a simple web page, in which a large DIV area responds to mouse move events in two ways.

Listing 4.7 mousemat.html

```
<html>
<head>
<link rel='stylesheet' type='text/css' href='mousemat.css' />
<script type='text/javascript'>
var cursor=null;
window.onload=function(){
  var mat=document.getElementById('mousemat');
  mat.onmousemove=mouseObserver;
  cursor=document.getElementById('cursor');
}
function mouseObserver(event){
  var e=event || window.event;
  writeStatus(e);
```

```
    drawThumbnail(e);
  }
  function writeStatus(e){
    window.status=e.clientX+","+e.clientY;
  }
  function drawThumbnail(e){
    cursor.style.left=((e.clientX/5)-2)+"px";
    cursor.style.top=((e.clientY/5)-2)+"px";
  }
  </script>
  </head>
  <body>
  <div class='mousemat' id='mousemat'></div>
  <div class='thumbnail' id='thumbnail'>
    <div class='cursor' id='cursor'/>
  </div>
  </body>
  </html>
```

First, it updates the browser status bar, in the writeStatus() function. Second, it updates a smaller thumbnail image of itself, by repositioning a dot in the thumbnail area, to copy the mouse pointer's movements, in the drawThumbnail() function. Figure 4.6 shows the page in action.

These two actions are independent of each other, and we would like to be able to swap these and other responses to the mouse movement in and out at will, even while the program is running.

The mouseObserver() function is our event listener. (The first line is performing some simple cross-browser magic, by the way. Unlike Mozilla, Opera, or Safari, Internet Explorer doesn't pass any arguments to the callback handler function, but stores the Event object in window.event.) In this example, we have hardwired the two activities in the event handler, calling writeStatus() and drawThumbnail() in turn. The program does exactly what we want it to do, and, because it is a small program, the code for mouseObserver() is reasonably clear. Ideally, though, we would like a cleaner way to wire the event listeners together, allowing the approach to scale to more complex or dynamic situations.

Implementing Observer in JavaScript

The proposed solution is to define a generic event router object, which attaches a standard function to the target element as an event callback and maintains a list of listener functions. This would allow us to rewrite our mousemat initialization code in this way:

```
window.onload=function(){
  var mat=document.getElementById('mousemat');
  ...
  var mouseRouter=new jsEvent.EventRouter(mat,"onmousemove");
  mouseRouter.addListener(writeStatus);
  mouseRouter.addListener(drawThumbnail);
}
```

We define an EventRouter object, passing in the DOM element and the type of event that we would like to register as arguments. We then add listener functions to the router object, which also supports a `removeListener()` method that we don't need here. It looks straightforward, but how do we implement it?

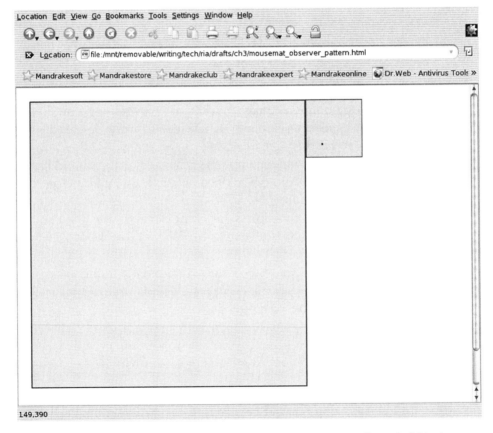

Figure 4.6 **The Mousemat program tracks mouse movement events on the main "virtual mousemat" area in two ways: by updating the browser status bar with the mouse coordinates and by moving the dot on the thumbnail view in sync with the mouse pointer.**

First, we write a constructor for the object, which in JavaScript is simply a function. (Appendix B contains a primer on the syntax of JavaScript objects. Take a look if any of the following code looks strange or confusing.)

```
jsEvent.EventRouter=function(el,eventType){
  this.lsnrs=new Array();
  this.el=el;
  el.eventRouter=this;
  el[eventType]=jsEvent.EventRouter.callback;
}
```

We define the array of listener functions, which is initially empty, take a reference to the DOM element, and give it a reference to this object, using the pattern we described in section 3.5.1. We then assign a static method of the `EventRouter` class, simply called `callback`, as the event handler. Remember that in JavaScript, the square bracket and dot notations are equivalent, which means

```
el.onmouseover
```

is the same as

```
el['onmouseover']
```

We use this to our advantage here, passing in the name of a property as an argument. This is similar to reflection in Java or the .NET languages.

Let's have a look at the callback then:

```
jsEvent.EventRouter.callback=function(event){
  var e=event || window.event;
  var router=this.eventRouter;
  router.notify(e)
}
```

Because this is a callback, the function context is the DOM node that fired the event, not the router object. We retrieve the `EventRouter` reference that we had attached to the DOM node, using the backing object pattern that we saw earlier. We then call the `notify()` method of the router, passing the event object in as an argument.

The full code for the Event Router object is shown in listing 4.8.

Listing 4.8   EventRouter.js

```
var jsEvent=new Array();
jsEvent.EventRouter=function(el,eventType){
  this.lsnrs=new Array();
  this.el=el;
  el.eventRouter=this;
```

```
    el[eventType]=jsEvent.EventRouter.callback;
}
jsEvent.EventRouter.prototype.addListener=function(lsnr){
  this.lsnrs.append(lsnr,true);
}
jsEvent.EventRouter.prototype.removeListener=function(lsnr){
  this.lsnrs.remove(lsnr);
}
jsEvent.EventRouter.prototype.notify=function(e){
  var lsnrs=this.lsnrs;
  for(var i=0;i<lsnrs.length;i++){
    var lsnr=lsnrs[i];
    lsnr.call(this,e);
  }
}
jsEvent.EventRouter.callback=function(event){
  var e=event || window.event;
  var router=this.eventRouter;
  router.notify(e)
}
```

Note that some of the methods of the array are not standard JavaScript but have been defined by our extended array definition, which is discussed in appendix B. Notably, addListener() and removeListener() are simple to implement using the append() and remove() methods. Listener functions are invoked using the Function.call() method, whose first argument is the function context, and subsequent arguments (in this case the event) are passed through to the callee.

The revised mousemat example is shown in listing 4.9.

Listing 4.9   Revised mousemat.html, using EventRouter

```
<html>
<head>
<link rel='stylesheet' type='text/css' href='mousemat.css' />
<script type='text/javascript' src='extras-array.js'></script>
<script type='text/javascript' src='eventRouter.js'></script>
<script type='text/javascript'>
var cursor=null;
window.onload=function(){
  var mat=document.getElementById('mousemat');
  cursor=document.getElementById('cursor');
  var mouseRouter=new jsEvent.EventRouter(mat,"onmousemove");
  mouseRouter.addListener(writeStatus);
  mouseRouter.addListener(drawThumbnail);
}
function writeStatus(e){
  window.status=e.clientX+","+e.clientY
```

```
}
function drawThumbnail(e){
  cursor.style.left=((e.clientX/5)-2)+"px";
  cursor.style.top=((e.clientY/5)-2)+"px";
}
</script>
</head>
<body>
<div class='mousemat' id='mousemat'></div>
<div class='thumbnail' id='thumbnail'>
  <div class='cursor' id='cursor'/>
</div>
</body>
</html>
```

The inline JavaScript is greatly simplified. All we need to do is create the `Event-Router`, pass in the listener functions, and provide implementations for the listeners. We leave it as an exercise for the reader to include checkboxes to add and remove each listener dynamically.

This rounds out our discussion of the Controller layer in an Ajax application and the role that design patterns—Observer in particular—can play in keeping it clean and easy to work with. In the following section, we'll look at the final part of the MVC pattern, the Model.

4.4 *Models in an Ajax application*

The Model is responsible for representing the business domain of our application, that is, the real-world subject that the application is all about, whether that is a garment store, a musical instrument, or a set of points in space. As we've noted already, the Document Object Model is *not* the model at the scale at which we're looking at the application now. Rather, the model is a collection of code that we have written in JavaScript. Like most design patterns, MVC is heavily based on object-oriented thinking.

JavaScript is not designed as an OO language, although it can be persuaded into something resembling object orientation without too much struggle. It does support the definition of something very similar to object classes through its prototype mechanism, and some developers have gone as far as implementing inheritance systems for JavaScript. We discuss these issues further in appendix B. When implementing MVC in JavaScript so far, we've adapted it to the JavaScript style of coding, for example, passing Function objects directly as event listeners. When it comes to defining the model, however, using JavaScript objects, and as much of an OO approach as we're comfortable with for the language, makes good sense. In the following section, we'll show how that is done.

4.4.1 *Using JavaScript to model the business domain*

When discussing the View, we are very much tied to the DOM. When we talk about the Controller, we are constrained by the browser event models. When writing the Model, however, we are dealing almost purely with JavaScript and have very little to do with browser-specific functionality. Those who have struggled with browser incompatibilities and bugs will recognize this as a comfortable situation in which to be.

Let's look at a simple example. In chapter 3 we discussed our garment store application, from the point of view of generating a data feed from the server. The data described a list of garment types, in terms of a unique ID, a name, and a description, along with price, color, and size information. Let's return to that example now and consider what happens when the data arrives at the client. Over the course of its lifetime, the application will receive many such streams of data and have a need to store data in memory. Think of this as a cache if you like—data stored on the client can be redisplayed very quickly, without needing to go back to the server at the time at which the user requests the data. This benefits the user's workflow, as discussed in chapter 1.

We can define a simple JavaScript object that corresponds to the garment object defined on the server. Listing 4.10 shows a typical example.

Listing 4.10 Garment.js

```
var garments=new Array();
function Garment(id,title,description,price){
  this.id=id;
  garments[id]=this;
  this.title=title;
  this.description=description;
  this.price=price;
  this.colors=new Object();
  this.sizes=new Object();
}
Garment.prototype.addColor(color){
  this.colors.append(color,true);
}
Garment.prototype.addSize(size){
  this.sizes.append(size,true);
}
```

We define a global array first of all, to hold all our garments. (Yes, global variables are evil. In production, we'd use a namespacing object, but we've omitted that for clarity here.) This is an associative array, keyed by the garment's unique ID, ensuring that we have only one reference to each garment type at a time. In the constructor function, we set all the simple properties, that is, those that aren't arrays. We define the arrays as empty and provide simple adder methods, which uses our enhanced array code (see appendix B) to prevent duplicates.

We don't provide getter or setter methods by default and don't support the full access control—private, protected, and public variables and methods—that a full OO language does. There are ways of providing this feature, which are discussed in appendix B, but my own preference is to keep the Model simple.

When parsing the XML stream, it would be nice to initially build an empty Garment object and then populate it field by field. The astute reader may be wondering why we haven't provided a simpler constructor. In fact, we have. JavaScript function arguments are mutable, and any missing values from a call to a function will simply initialize that value to null. So the call

```
var garment=new Garment(123);
```

will be treated as identical to

```
var garment=new Garment(123,null,null,null);
```

We need to pass in the ID, because we use that in the constructor to place the new object in the global list of garments.

4.4.2 *Interacting with the server*

We could parse the XML feed of the type shown in listing 4.10 in order to generate Garment objects in the client application. We've already seen this in action in chapter 2, and we'll see a number of variations in chapter 5, so we won't go into all the details here. The XML document contains a mixture of attributes and tag content. We read attribute data using the `attributes` property and `getNamedItem()` function and read the body text of tags using the `firstChild` and `data` properties, for example:

```
garment.description=descrTag.firstChild.data;
```

to parse an XML fragment such as

```
<description>Large tweedy hat looking
like an unappealing strawberry
</description>
```

Note that garments are automatically added to our array of all garments as they are created, simply by invoking the constructor. Removing a garment from the array is also relatively straightforward:

```
function unregisterGarment(id){
  garments[id]=null;
}
```

This removes the garment type from the global registry, but won't cascade to destroy any instances of Garment that we have already created. We can add a simple validation test to the Garment object, however:

```
Garment.prototype.isValid=function(){
  return garments[this.id]!=null;
}
```

We've now defined a clear path for propagating data all the way from the database to the client, with nice, easy-to-handle objects at each step. Let's recap the steps. First, we generate a server-side object model from the database. In section 3.4.2, we saw how to do this using an Object-Relational Mapping (ORM) tool, which gave us out-of-the-box two-way interactions between object model and database. We can read data into objects, modify it, and save the data.

Second, we used a template system to generate an XML stream from our object model, and third, we parsed this stream in order to create an object model on the JavaScript tier. We must do this parsing by hand for now. We may see ORM-like mapping libraries appearing in the near future.

In an administrative application, of course, we might want to edit our data too, that is, modify the JavaScript model, and then communicate these changes back to the server model. This forces us to confront the issue that we now have two copies of our domain model and that they may get out of sync with each other.

In a classic web application, all the intelligence is located on the server, so our model is located there, in whatever language we're using. In an Ajax application, we want to distribute the intelligence between the client and the server, so that the client code can make some decisions for itself before calling back to the server. If the client makes only very simple decisions, we can code these in an ad hoc way, but then we won't get much of the benefit of an intelligent client, and the system will tend to still be unresponsive in places. If we empower the client to make more important decisions for itself, then it needs to know something about our business domain, at which point it really needs to have a model of the domain.

We can't do away with the domain model on the server, because some resources are available only on the server, such as database connections for persistence, access to legacy systems, and so on. The client-side domain model has to work with the one on the server. So, what does that entail? In chapter 5 we will develop a fuller understanding of the client/server interactions and how to work cleanly with a domain model split across both tiers.

So far we've looked at Model, View, and Controller in isolation. The final topic for this chapter brings the Model and View together again.

4.5 *Generating the View from the Model*

By introducing MVC into the browser, we've given ourselves three distinct subsystems to worry about. Separating concerns may result in cleaner code, but it can also result in a lot of code, and a common critique of design patterns is that they can turn even the simplest task into quite an involved process (as Enterprise JavaBeans [EJB] developers know only too well!).

Many-layered application designs often end up repeating information across several layers. We know the importance of DRY code, and a common way of tackling this repetition is to define the necessary information once, and generate the various layers automatically from that definition. In this section, we'll do just that, and present a technique that simplifies the MVC implementation and brings together all three tiers in a simple way. Specifically, we'll target the View layer.

So far, we've looked at the View as a hand-coded representation of the underlying Model. This gives us considerable flexibility in determining what the user sees, but at times, we won't need this flexibility, and hand-coding the UI can become tedious and repetitive. An alternative approach is to automatically generate the user interface, or at least portions of it, from the underlying Model. There are precedents for doing this, such as the Smalltalk language environments and the Java/.NET Naked Objects framework (see the Resources section), and JavaScript is well suited to this sort of task. Let's have a look at what JavaScript reflection can do for us in this regard, and develop a generic "Object Browser" component, that can be used as a View for any JavaScript object that we throw at it.

4.5.1 *Reflecting on a JavaScript object*

Most of the time when we write code to manipulate an object, we already have a fairly good idea of what the object is and what it can do. Sometimes, however, we need to code blindly, as it were, and examine the object without any prior knowledge. Generating a user interface for our domain model objects is just such a case. Ideally, we would like to develop a reusable solution that can be equally applied to any domain—finance, e-commerce, scientific visualization,

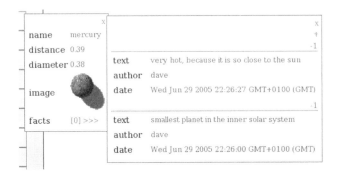

Figure 4.7
Here the ObjectViewer is used to display a hierarchical system of planets, each of which contains a number of informational properties, plus a list of facts stored as an array.

and so on. This section presents just such a JavaScript library, the ObjectViewer, that can be used in your own applications. To give you a taste of the Object-Viewer in action, figure 4.7 shows the ObjectViewer displaying several layers of a complex object graph.

The object being viewed, representing the planet Mercury, is quite sophisticated, with properties including an image URL, an array of facts, as well as simple strings and numbers. Our ObjectViewer can handle all of these intelligently without knowing anything specific about the type of object in advance.

The process of examining an object and querying its properties and capabilities is known as *reflection*. Readers with a familiarity to Java or .NET should already be familiar with this term. We discuss JavaScript's reflection capabilities in more detail in appendix B. To summarize briefly here, a JavaScript object can be iterated over as if it were an associative array. To print out all the properties of an object, we can simply write

```
var description="";
for (var i in MyObj){
  var property=MyObj[i];
  description+=i+" = "+property+"\n";
}
alert(description);
```

Presenting data as an alert is fairly primitive and doesn't integrate with the rest of a UI very well. Listing 4.11 presents the core code for the ObjectViewer object.

Listing 4.11   ObjectViewer object

```
objviewer.ObjectViewer=function(obj,div,isInline,addNew){
  styling.removeAllChildren(div);
  this.object=obj;
  this.mainDiv=div;
  this.mainDiv.viewer=this;
```

```
    this.isInline=isInline;
    this.addNew=addNew;
    var table=document.createElement("table");
    this.tbod=document.createElement("tbody");
    table.appendChild(this.tbod);
    this.fields=new Array();
    this.children=new Array();
    for (var i in this.object){
      this.fields[i]=new objviewer.PropertyViewer(
        this, i
      );
    }
  objviewer.PropertyViewer=function(objectViewer,name){
    this.objectViewer=objectViewer;
    this.name=name;
    this.value=objectViewer.object[this.name];
    this.rowTr=document.createElement("tr");
    this.rowTr.className='objViewRow';
    this.valTd=document.createElement("td");
    this.valTd.className='objViewValue';
    this.valTd.viewer=this;
    this.rowTr.appendChild(this.valTd);
    var valDiv=this.renderSimple();
    this.valTd.appendChild(valDiv);
    viewer.tbod.appendChild(this.rowTr);
  }
  objviewer.PropertyViewer.prototype.renderSimple=function(){
      var valDiv=document.createElement("div");
      var valTxt=document.createTextNode(this.value);
      valDiv.appendChild(valTxt);
      if (this.spec.editable){
        valDiv.className+=" editable";
        valDiv.viewer=this;
        valDiv.onclick=objviewer.PropertyViewer.editSimpleProperty;
      }
      return valDiv;
  }
```

Our library contains two objects: an ObjectViewer, which iterates over the members of an object and assembles an HTML table in which to display the data, and a PropertyViewer, which renders an individual property name and value as a table row.

This gets the basic job done, but it suffers from several problems. First, it will iterate over every property. If we have added helper functions to the Object prototype, we will see them. If we do it to a DOM node, we see all the built-in properties and appreciate how heavyweight a DOM element really is. In general, we want to be selective about which properties of our object we show to the user. We can specify which properties we want to display for a given object by attaching a special property, an Array, to the object before passing it to the object renderer. Listing 4.12 illustrates this.

Listing 4.12 Using the `objViewSpec` property

```
objviewer.ObjectViewer=function(obj,div,isInline,addNew){
  styling.removeAllChildren(div);
  this.object=obj;
  this.spec=objviewer.getSpec(obj);
  this.mainDiv=div;
  this.mainDiv.viewer=this;
  this.isInline=isInline;
  this.addNew=addNew;
  var table=document.createElement("table");
  this.tbod=document.createElement("tbody");
  table.appendChild(this.tbod);
  this.fields=new Array();
  this.children=new Array();
  for (var i=0;i<this.spec.length;i++){
    this.fields[i]=new objviewer.PropertyViewer(
      this,this.spec[i]
    );
  }
objviewer.getSpec=function (obj){
  return (obj.objViewSpec) ?
    obj.objViewSpec :
    objviewer.autoSpec(obj);
}
objviewer.autoSpec=function(obj){
  var members=new Array();
  for (var propName in obj){
    var spec={name:propName};
    members.append(spec);
  }
  return members;
}
objviewer.PropertyViewer=function(objectViewer,memberSpec){
  this.objectViewer=objectViewer;
  this.spec=memberSpec;
  this.name=this.spec.name;
  ...
}
```

We define a property `objViewSpec`, which the ObjectViewer constructor looks for in each object. If it can't find such a property, it then resorts to creating one by iterating over the object in the `autoSpec()` function. The `objViewSpec` property is a numerical array, with each element being a lookup table of properties. For now, we're only concerned with generating the `name` property. The PropertyViewer is passed the spec for this property in its constructor and can take hints from the spec as to how it should render itself.

If we provide a specification property to an object that we want to inspect in the ObjectViewer, then we can limit the properties being displayed to those that we think are relevant.

A second problem with our ObjectViewer is that it doesn't handle complex properties very well. When objects, arrays, and functions are appended to a string, the `toString()` method is called. In the case of an object, this generally returns something nondescriptive such as `[Object object]`. In the case of a Function object, the entire source code for the function is returned. We need to discriminate between the different types of properties, which we can do using the `instanceof` operator. With that in place, let's see how we can improve on our viewer.

4.5.2 *Dealing with arrays and objects*

One way of handling arrays and objects is to allow the user to drill down into them using separate ObjectViewer objects for each property. There are several ways of representing this. We have chosen here to represent child objects as pop-out windows, somewhat like a hierarchical menu.

To achieve this, we need to do two things. First, we need to add a `type` property to the object specification and define the types that we support:

```
objviewer.TYPE_SIMPLE="simple";
objviewer.TYPE_ARRAY="array";
objviewer.TYPE_FUNCTION="function";
objviewer.TYPE_IMAGE_URL="image url";
objviewer.TYPE_OBJECT="object";
```

We modify the function that generates specs for objects that don't come with their own to take account of the type, as shown in listing 4.13.

Listing 4.13 Modified `autoSpec()` function

```
objviewer.autoSpec=function(obj){
  var members=new Array();
  for (var propName in obj){
    var propValue=obj[name];
    var propType=objviewer.autoType(value);
    var spec={name:propName,type:propType};
```

```
      members.append(spec);
    }
    if (obj && obj.length>0){
      for(var i=0;i<obj.length;i++){
        var propName="array ["+i+"]";
        var propValue=obj[i];
        var propType=objviewer.ObjectViewer.autoType(value);
        var spec={name:propName,type:propType};
        members.append(spec);
      }
    }
    return members;
}
objviewer.autoType=function(value){
  var type=objviewer.TYPE_SIMPLE;
  if ((value instanceof Array)){
    type=objviewer.TYPE_ARRAY;
  }else if (value instanceof Function){
    type=objviewer.TYPE_FUNCTION;
  }else if (value instanceof Object){
    type=objviewer.TYPE_OBJECT;
  }
  return type;
}
```

Note that we also add support for numerically indexed arrays, whose elements wouldn't be discovered by the `for...in` style of loop.

The second thing that we need to do is to modify the PropertyViewer to take account of the different types and render them accordingly, as shown in listing 4.14.

Listing 4.14   Modified PropertyViewer constructor

```
objviewer.PropertyViewer=function
  (objectViewer,memberSpec,appendAtTop){
  this.objectViewer=objectViewer;
  this.spec=memberSpec;
  this.name=this.spec.name;
  this.type=this.spec.type;
  this.value=objectViewer.object[this.name];
  this.rowTr=document.createElement("tr");
  this.rowTr.className='objViewRow';
  var isComplexType=(this.type==objviewer.TYPE_ARRAY
                    ||this.type==objviewer.TYPE_OBJECT);
  if ( !(isComplexType && this.objectViewer.isInline
)
    ){
    this.nameTd=this.renderSideHeader();
```

```
    this.rowTr.appendChild(this.nameTd);
  }
  this.valTd=document.createElement("td");
  this.valTd.className='objViewValue';
  this.valTd.viewer=this;
  this.rowTr.appendChild(this.valTd);
  if (isComplexType){
    if (this.viewer.isInline){
      this.valTd.colSpan=2;
      var nameDiv=this.renderTopHeader();
      this.valTd.appendChild(nameDiv);
      var valDiv=this.renderInlineObject();
      this.valTd.appendChild(valDiv);
    }else{
      var valDiv=this.renderPopoutObject();
      this.valTd.appendChild(valDiv);
    }
  }else if (this.type==objviewer.TYPE_IMAGE_URL){
    var valImg=this.renderImage();
    this.valTd.appendChild(valImg);
  }else if (this.type==objviewer.TYPE_SIMPLE){
    var valTxt=this.renderSimple();
    this.valTd.appendChild(valTxt);
  }
  if (appendAtTop){
    styling.insertAtTop(viewer.tbod,this.rowTr);
  }else{
    viewer.tbod.appendChild(this.rowTr);
  }
}
```

To accommodate the various types of properties, we have defined a number of rendering methods, the implementation of which is too detailed to reproduce in full here. Source code for the entire ObjectViewer can be downloaded from the website that accompanies this book.

We now have a fairly complete way of viewing our domain model automatically. To make the domain model objects visible, all that we need to do is to assign objViewSpec properties to their prototypes. The Planet object backing the view shown in figure 4.7, for example, has the following statement in the constructor:

```
this.objViewSpec=[
  {name:"name",     type:"simple"},
  {name:"distance", type:"simple", editable:true},
  {name:"diameter", type:"simple", editable:true},
  {name:"image",    type:"image url"},
  {name:"facts",    type:"array",  addNew:this.newFact, inline:true }
];
```

The notation for this specification is the JavaScript object notation, known as JSON. Square braces indicate a numerical array, and curly braces an associative array or object (the two are really the same). We discuss JSON more fully in appendix B.

There are a few unexplained entries here. What do `addNew`, `inline`, and `editable` mean? Their purpose is to notify the View that these parts of the domain model can not only be inspected but also modified by the user, bringing in the Controller aspects of our system, too. We'll look at this in the next section.

4.5.3 *Adding a Controller*

It's nice to be able to look at a domain model, but many everyday applications require us to modify them too—download the tune, edit the document, add items to the shopping basket, and so on. Mediating between user interactions and the domain model is the responsibility of the Controller, and we'll now add that functionality to our ObjectViewer.

The first thing that we'd like to do is to be able to edit simple text values when we click on them, if our specification object flags them as being editable. Listing 4.15 shows the code used to render a simple text property.

Listing 4.15 `renderSimple()` function

```
objviewer.PropertyViewer.prototype.renderSimple=function(){
    var valDiv=document.createElement("div");
    var valTxt=document
      .createTextNode(this.value);      ◁— Show read-only value
    valDiv.appendChild(valTxt);
    if (this.spec.editable){      ❶ Add interactivity if editable
      valDiv.className+=" editable";
      valDiv.viewer=this;
      valDiv.onclick=objviewer.PropertyViewer.editSimpleProperty;
    }
    return valDiv;
}
objviewer.PropertyViewer.editSimpleProperty=function(e){      ❷ Begin editing
  var viewer=this.viewer;
  if (viewer){
    viewer.edit();
  }
}
objviewer.PropertyViewer.prototype.edit=function(){
  if (this.type=objviewer.TYPE_SIMPLE){
    var editor=document.createElement("input");
    editor.value=this.value;
    document.body.appendChild(editor);
```

```
        var td=this.valTd;
        xLeft(editor,xLeft(td));
        xTop(editor,xTop(td));
        xWidth(editor,xWidth(td));
        xHeight(editor,xHeight(td));
        td.replaceChild(editor,td.firstChild);    ❸  Replace with read/write view
        editor.onblur=objviewer.
          PropertyViewer.editBlur;       ❹  Add commit callback
        editor.viewer=this;
        editor.focus();
      }
    }
    objviewer.PropertyViewer
      .editBlur=function(e){    ❺  Finish editing
       var viewer=this.viewer;
       if (viewer){
         viewer.commitEdit(this.value);
       }
    }
    objviewer.PropertyViewer.prototype.commitEdit=function(value){
      if (this.type==objviewer.TYPE_SIMPLE){
        this.value=value;
        var valDiv=this.renderSimple();
        var td=this.valTd;
        td.replaceChild(valDiv,td.firstChild);
        this.objectViewer
          .notifyChange(this);    ❻  Notify observers
      }
    }
```

Editing a property involves several steps. First, we want to assign an `onclick` handler to the DOM element displaying the value, if the field is editable ❶. We also assign a specific CSS classname to editable fields, which will make them change color when the mouse hovers over them. We need the user to be able to realize that she can edit the field, after all.

`editSimpleProperty()` ❷ is a simple event handler that retrieves the reference to the PropertyViewer from the clicked DOM node and calls the `edit()` method. This way of connecting the View and Controller should be familiar from section 4.3.1. We check that the property type is correct and then replace the read-only label with an equivalent-sized HTML form text input, containing the value ❸. We also attach an `onblur` handler to this text area ❹, which replaces the editable area with a read-only label ❺ and updates the domain model.

We can manipulate the domain model in this way, but in general, we would often like to take some other action when the model is updated. The `notifyChange()`

method of the ObjectViewer ❻, invoked in the `commitEdit()` function, comes into play here. Listing 4.16 shows this function in full.

Listing 4.16 `ObjectViewer.notifyChange()`

```
objviewer.ObjectViewer.prototype
 .notifyChange=function(propViewer){
  if (this.onchangeRouter){
    this.onchangeRouter.notify(propViewer);
  }
  if (this.parentObjViewer){
    this.parentObjViewer.notifyChange(propViewer);
  }
}
objviewer.ObjectViewer.prototype
 .addChangeListener=function(lsnr){
  if (!this.onchangeRouter){
    this.onchangeRouter=new jsEvent.EventRouter(this,"onchange");
  }
  this.onchangeRouter.addListener(lsnr);
}
objviewer.ObjectViewer.prototype
 .removeChangeListener=function(lsnr){
  if (this.onchangeRouter){
    this.onchangeRouter.removeListener(lsnr);
  }
}
```

The problem we are facing—notifying arbitrary processes of a change in our domain model—is ideally solved by the Observer pattern and the EventRouter object that we defined in section 4.3.3. We could attach an EventRouter to the `onblur` event of the editable fields, but a complex model may contain many of these, and our code shouldn't have visibility of such fine details in the Object-Viewer implementation.

Instead, we define our own event type on the ObjectViewer itself, an `onchange` event, and attach an EventRouter to that. Because our ObjectViewers are arranged in a tree structure when drilling down on object and array properties, we pass `onchange` events to the parent, recursively. Thus, in general, we can attach listeners to the root ObjectViewer, the one that we create in our application code, and changes to model properties several layers down the object graph will propagate back up to us.

A simple example of an event handler would be to write a message to the browser status bar. The top-level object in a model of planets is the solar system, so we can write

```
var topview=new objviewer.ObjectViewer
  (planets.solarSystem,mainDiv);
topview.addChangeListener(testListener);
```

where `testListener` is an event-handler function that looks like this:

```
function testListener(propviewer){
  window.status=propviewer.name+" ["+propviewer.type+"] =
  "+propviewer.value;
}
```

Of course, in reality, we would want to do more exciting things when the domain model changes, such as contacting the server. In the next chapter, we'll look at ways of contacting the server and put our ObjectViewer to further use.

4.6 Summary

The Model-View-Controller pattern is an architectural pattern that has been applied to the server code of classic web applications. We showed how to reuse this pattern on the server in an Ajax application, in order to generate data feeds for the client. We also applied the pattern to the design of the client itself and developed a range of useful insights through doing so.

Looking at the View subsystem, we demonstrated how to effectively separate presentation from logic, with the very practical benefit of allowing designer and programmer roles to be kept separate. Maintaining clear lines of responsibilities in the codebase that reflect your team's organizational structure and skill sets can be a great productivity booster.

In the Controller code, we looked at the different event models available to Ajax and erred on the side of caution toward the older event model. Although it is limited to a single callback function for each event type, we saw how to implement the Observer pattern to develop a flexible, reconfigurable event-handler layer on top of the standard JavaScript event model.

Regarding the Model, we began to address the larger issues of distributed multiuser applications, which we will explore further in chapter 5.

Looking after a Model, a View, and a Controller can seem like a lot of work. In our discussion of the ObjectViewer example, we looked at ways of simplifying the interactions between these using automation, and we created a simple system capable of presenting an object model to the user and allowing interaction with it.

We'll continue to draw upon design patterns as we move on to explore client/server interactions in the next chapter.

4.7 Resources

The Behaviours library used in this chapter can be found at http://ripcord.co.nz/behaviour/. Mike Foster's x library can be found at www.cross-browser.com.

Autogeneration of the View from the Model is a technique inspired by the Naked Objects project (http://www.nakedobjects.org/). The book *Naked Objects* (John Wiley & Sons, 2002), by Richard Pawson and Robert Matthews, is somewhat out of date as far as the code goes, but provides an incisive critique of hand-coded MVC in the opening sections.

The images of the planets used in the ObjectViewer are provided by Jim's Cool Icons (http://snaught.com/JimsCoolIcons/), and are modeled using the POV-Ray modeler and textured with real images from NASA (according to the website)!

The role of the server

This chapter covers

- Using current web framework types with Ajax
- Exchanging data with the server as content, script, or data
- Communicating updates to the server
- Bundling multiple requests and replies into a single HTTP call

This chapter concludes the work that we started in chapter 4: making our applications robust and scalable. We've moved from the proof-of-concept stage to something that you can use in the real world. Chapter 4 examined ways of structuring the client code to achieve our goal; in this chapter, we look at the server and, more specifically, at the communication between the client and the server.

We'll begin by looking at the big picture and discuss what functions the server performs. We'll then move on to describe the types of architectures commonly employed in server-side frameworks. Many, many web frameworks are in use today, particularly in the Java world, and we won't try to cover them all, but rather we'll identify common approaches and ways of addressing web application development. Most frameworks were designed to generate classic web applications, so we're particularly interested to see how they adapt to Ajax and where the challenges lie.

Having considered the large-scale patterns, we'll look at the finer details of communicating between client and server. In chapter 2 we covered the basics of the XMLHttpRequest object and hidden IFrames. We'll return to these basics here as we examine the various patterns for updating the client from the server and discuss the alternatives to parsing XML documents using DOM methods. In the final section, we'll present a system for managing client/server traffic over the lifetime of the application, by providing a client-side queue for requests and server-side processes for managing them.

Let's start off, then, by looking at the role of the server in Ajax.

5.1 *Working with the server side*

In the lifecycle of an Ajax application, the server has two roles to fulfill, and these are fairly distinct. First, it has to deliver the application to the browser. So far, we've assumed that the initial delivery of content is fairly static, that is, we write the application itself as a series of .html, .css, and .js files that even a very basic web server would be able to deliver. Nothing is wrong with this approach—in fact, a lot can be said for it—but it isn't the only option available to us. We'll look at the alternatives later, when we discuss server-side frameworks in section 5.3.

The second role of the server is to talk to the client, fielding queries and supplying data on request. Because HTTP is the only transport mechanism available to us, we're limited to the client starting off any conversation. The server can only respond. In chapter 4, we discussed the need for an Ajax application to maintain a domain model on both the client (for fast responses) and the server (for access to resources such as the database). Keeping the models in sync with one another represents a major challenge, and one that the client can't solve on its own. We'll look at ways of writing data to the server in section 5.5 and present a solution to this problem based on one of the patterns that we encountered in chapter 3.

We can deliver the client application—and talk to the client—in several ways, as you will see in this chapter. Is one way better than the others? Do any particular combinations support each other? Can they be mixed and matched? How do the different solutions work with legacy server frameworks and architectures? To answer these questions, a vocabulary for describing our various options will be useful. And that's exactly what we're going to develop in this chapter. First, let's look at the way the server is set up in a web application, and how Ajax affects that.

5.2 *Coding the server side*

In a conventional web application, the server side tends to be a rather complex place, controlling and monitoring the user's workflow through the application and maintaining conversational state. The application is designed for a particular language, and set of conventions, that will determine what it can and can't do. Languages may in themselves be tied to specific architectures, operating systems, or hardware. Picking a programming environment is a big choice to make, so let's discuss the options available to us.

5.2.1 *Popular implementation languages*

Server-side programming is dominated by a handful of languages. Over the very brief course of Internet history, fashions in server-side languages have changed remarkably. The current kings of the hill are PHP, Java, and classic ASP, with ASP.NET and Ruby growing in popularity too. These names are undoubtedly familiar to most readers, so I won't try to explain what they are here. Ajax is primarily a client-side technology and can interoperate with any of these languages. Indeed, some ways of working with Ajax downplay the importance of the server-side language considerably, making it easy to port Ajax applications from one server platform to another.

Web frameworks are in many ways more important to Ajax than the implementation language. Web frameworks carry assumptions with them, about how the application is structured and where key responsibilities lie. Most frameworks have been designed for building classic web applications, and assumptions about the lifecycles of these—which are very different from those of an Ajax app—may be problematic in places. We'll look at server-side designs and frameworks in the following section, but first, let's review the basic principles of web-based architectures, in order to lay the groundwork for that discussion.

5.2.2 *N-tier architectures*

A core concept in distributed applications is that of the *tier*. A tier often represents a particular set of responsibilities for an application, but it also describes a subsystem that can be physically isolated on a particular machine or process. This distinguishes it from the roles in MVC, for example. Model, View, and Controller aren't tiers because they typically sit in the same process.

Early distributed systems consisted of a client tier and a server tier. The client tier was a desktop program using a network socket library to communicate to the server. The server tier was typically a database server.

Similarly, early web systems consisted of a browser talking to a web server, a monolithic system on the network sending files from the filesystem.

As web-based applications became more complex and began to require access to databases, the two-tier model of client/server was applied to the web server to create a three-tier model, with the web server mediating between the web browser client and the database. Later refinements on the model saw a further separation of the middle tier into presentation and business roles, either as distinct processes or as a more modular software design within a single process.

Modern web applications typically have two principal tiers. The business tier models the business domain, and talks directly to the database. The presentation tier takes data from the business tier and presents it to the user. The browser acts as a dumb client in this setup.

The introduction of Ajax can be considered to be the development of a further client tier, separating the presentation tier's traditional responsibilities of workflow and session management between the web server and the client (figure 5.1).

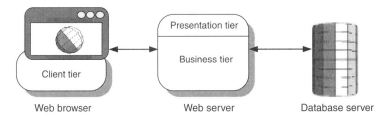

Figure 5.1   An Ajax application moves some of the responsibilities of the presentation tier from the server up to the browser, in a new entity that we call the client tier.

The role of the server-side presentation tier can be much reduced and workflow control partly or completely handed over to the new client tier, written in JavaScript and hosted on the browser.

This new tier in our application brings with it new possibilities, as we've already discussed. It also brings the potential for greater complexity and confusion. Clearly, we need a way to manage this.

5.2.3 *Maintaining client-side and server-side domain models*

In an Ajax application, we still need to model the business domain on the server, close to the database and other vital centralized resources. However, to give the client code sufficient responsiveness and intelligence, we typically will want to maintain at least a partial model in the browser. This presents the interesting problem of keeping the two models in sync with one another.

Adding an extra tier always adds complexity and communications overheads. Fortunately, the problem isn't entirely new, and similar issues are commonly encountered in J2EE web development, for example, in which there is a strict separation between the business tier and the presentation tier. The domain model sits on the business tier and is queried by the presentation tier, which then generates web content to send to the browser. The problem is solved in J2EE by the use of "transfer objects," which are simple Java objects designed to pass data between the tiers, presenting limited views of the domain model to the presentation tier.

Ajax provides us with new challenges, though. In J2EE, both tiers are written in a common language with a remote procedure mechanism provided, which is typically not the case with Ajax. We could use JavaScript on the server tier, through Mozilla's Rhino or Microsoft's JScript .NET, for example, but it is currently rather unorthodox to do so, and we'd still need to communicate between the two JavaScript engines.

The two basic requirements for communicating between the tiers are reading data from the server and writing data to the server. We'll look at the details of these in section 5.3 through 5.5. Before we conclude our overview of architectural issues, though, we will look at the main categories of server architecture currently in use. In particular, we'll be interested to see how they represent the domain model to the presentation tier and what restrictions this might place on an Ajax-based design.

A recent informal survey (see the Resources at the end of this chapter) listed over 60 presentation frameworks for Java alone (to be fair, Java probably suffers from this framework-itis more than any other server language). Most of these differ in the details, fortunately, and we can characterize the presentation tier (in whatever server language) as following one of several architectural patterns. Let's have a look at these now.

5.3 *The big picture: common server-side designs*

Server-side frameworks matter to all Ajax applications. If we choose to generate the client code from a sever-side model, it matters a great deal. If we hand-code the client code and serve it as static HTML and JavaScript pages, then the framework isn't involved in delivering the app, but the data that the application will consume still has to be dynamically generated. Also, as we noted in the previous section, the server-side framework typically contains a domain model of some sort, and the presentation tier framework stands between that model and our Ajax application. We need to be able to work with the framework in order for our application to function smoothly.

Web application servers can be unkindly characterized as developers' playgrounds. The problem of presenting a coherent workflow to a user through a series of web pages, while interfacing to back-end systems such as database servers, has never been adequately solved. The Web is littered with undernourished, ill-maintained frameworks and utilities, with new projects popping up on a monthly, if not weekly, basis.

Fortunately, we can recognize discrete families within this chaotic mixture. Reducing this framework soup to its essentials, there are possibly four main ways to get the job done. Let's examine each in turn and see how it can be adapted to the Ajax model.

5.3.1 *Naive web server coding without a framework*

The simplest kind of framework is no framework at all. Writing a web application without a framework defining the key workflow elements, or mediating access to the back-end systems, doesn't imply a complete lack of order. Many web sites are still developed this way, with each page generating its own views and performing its own back-end housekeeping, probably with the assistance of some shared library of helper functions or objects. Figure 5.2 illustrates this pattern of programming.

Modifying this approach for Ajax is relatively straightforward, if we assume that the client is hand-coded. Generating client code from the server is a big topic that's beyond the scope of this book. To deliver the client, we need to define a master page that will include any necessary JavaScript files, stylesheets, and other resources. For supplying data feeds, we simply need to replace the

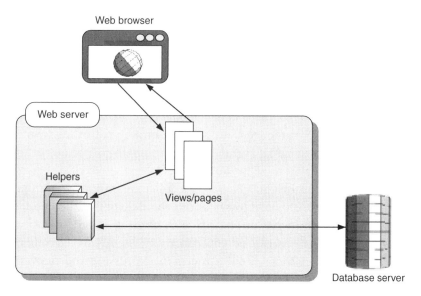

Figure 5.2   Web programming without a framework. Each page, servlet, or CGI script maintains its own logic and presentation details. Helper functions and/or objects may encapsulate common low-level functionality, such as database access.

generated HTML pages with XML or the other data stream of our choice (more on this topic later).

The key shortcoming of this approach in a classic web app is that the links between documents are scattered throughout the documents themselves. That is, the Controller role is not clearly defined in one place. If a developer needs to rework the user flow between screens, then hyperlinks must be modified in several places. This could be partly ameliorated by putting link-heavy content such as navigation bars inside include files or generating them programmatically using helper functions, but maintenance costs will still rise steeply as the app becomes more complicated.

In an Ajax application, this may be less of a problem, since hyperlinks and other cross-references will typically not be embedded in data feeds as densely as in a web page, but includes and forwarding instructions between pages will still pose a problem. Includes and forwards won't be required in a simple XML document, but larger applications may be sending complex structured documents assembled by several subprocesses, as we will see in section 5.5. The early generation of web frameworks used MVC as a cure for these ills, and many of these frameworks are still in use today, so let's look at them next.

5.3.2 *Working with Model2 workflow frameworks*

The Model2 design pattern is a variation of MVC, in which the Controller has a single point of entry and a single definition of the users' possible workflows. Applied to a web application, this means that a single Controller page or servlet is responsible for routing most requests, passing the request through to various back-end services and then out to a particular View. Apache Struts is probably the best-known Model2 framework, although a number of other Java and PHP frameworks follow this pattern. Figure 5.3 illustrates the structure of a Model2 web framework.

How can we apply this design to a server application talking to an Ajax client, then? Model2 has relatively little to say about the delivery of the client application, which will typically occur at startup as a single payload, identical for all authenticated users. The centralized controller may be involved in the authentication process itself, but there is little merit in expressing the delivery of the application itself through anything other than a single endpoint of the controller.

It provides a workable solution for delivery of data feeds, though. The Views returned by Model2 are essentially independent of the framework, and we may

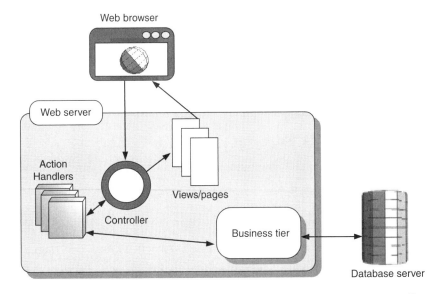

Figure 5.3   Model2 web framework. A single controller page or servlet accepts all requests and is configured with a complete graph of user workflows and interactions. The request will be handed to one of a number of ancillary classes or functions for more specialized processing and finally routed out to a View component (for example, a JSP or PHP page) before being sent to the browser.

easily swap HTML for XML or other data formats. Part of the Controller responsibility will be passed to the client tier, but some Controller functions may still be usefully expressed through server-side mappings.

Model2 for classic web apps provides a good way of expressing much of the Controller responsibility at a high level of abstraction, but it leaves the implementation of the View as a hand-coding task. Later developments in web frameworks attempted to provide a higher-level abstraction for the View, too. Let's examine them next.

5.3.3 Working with component-based frameworks

When writing an HTML page for a classic web application, the page author has a very limited set of predefined GUI components at hand, namely the HTML form elements. Their feature set has remained largely unchanged for nearly 10 years, and compared to modern GUI toolkits, they are very basic and uninspiring. If a page author wishes to introduce anything like a tree control or editable grid, a calendar control or an animated hierarchical menu, he needs to resort to low-level programming of basic document elements. Compared with the level of abstraction available to a developer building a desktop GUI using component toolkits such as MFC, GTK+, Cocoa, Swing, or Qt, this seems like a poor option.

Widgets for the web

Component-based frameworks aim to raise the level of abstraction for web UI programming, by providing a toolkit of server-side components whose API resembles that of a desktop GUI widget set. When desktop widgets render themselves, they typically paint onto a graphics context using low-level calls to generate geometric primitives, bitmaps, and the like. When web-based widgets render themselves, they automatically generate a stream of HTML and JavaScript that provides equivalent functionality in the browser, relieving the poor coder from a lot of low-level drudgery. Figure 5.4 illustrates the structure of a component-based web framework.

Many component-based frameworks describe user interaction using a desktop-style metaphor. That is, a Button component may have a click event handler, a text field component may have a `valueChange` handler, and so on. In most frameworks, event processing is largely delegated to the server, with a request being fired for each user interaction. Smarter frameworks manage to do this behind the scenes, but some will refresh the entire page with each user event. This leads to a decidedly clunky user experience, as an application designed as a

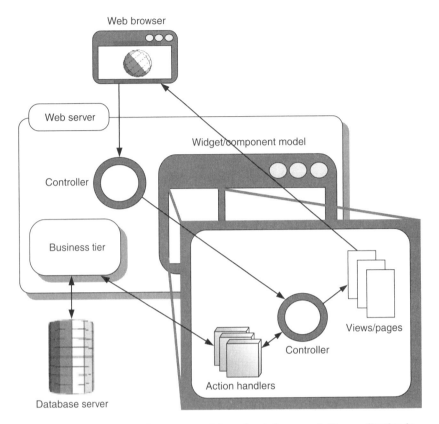

Figure 5.4 Architecture of a component-based web framework. The application is described as a collection of widgets that render themselves by emitting a stream of HTML and JavaScript into the browser. Each component contains its own small-scale Model, View, and Controller, in addition to the larger Controller that fields browser requests to individual components and the larger domain model.

widget set will typically have lots of fine-grained interactions compared to one designed as a set of pages, using Model2, say.

A significant design goal of these frameworks is to be able to render different types of user interface from a single widget model description. Some frameworks, such as Windows Forms for .NET and JavaServer Faces (JSF), are already able to do this.

Interoperating with Ajax

So how do Component-based frameworks fare with Ajax, then? On the surface, both are moving away from a document-like interface toward a widget-based one, so the overlap ought to be good. This type of framework may have strong possibilities as far as generating the client application goes, if pluggable renderers that understand Ajax can be developed. There is a considerable appeal to doing so, since it avoids the need to retrain developers in the intricacies of JavaScript, and it leaves an easy route for providing an alternative to older browsers through a plain-old HTML rendering system.

Such a solution will work well for applications that require only standard widget types. A certain degree of flexibility, however, will be lacking. Google Maps, for example (see chapter 1), is successful largely because it defines its own set of widgets, from the scrollable map to the zoom slider and the pop-up balloons and map pins. Trying to build this using a standard set of desktop widgets would be difficult and probably less satisfactory in the end.

That said, many applications do fit more easily within the conventional range of widget types and would be better served by these types of framework. This trade-off between flexibility and convenience is common to many code generation–based solutions and is well understood.

To fully serve an Ajax application, the framework must also be able to supply the necessary data feeds. Here, the situation may be somewhat more problematic, as the Controller is heavily tied to the server tiers and is tightly defined through the desktop metaphor. A responsive Ajax application requires more freedom in determining its own event handlers than the server event model seems to allow. Nonetheless, there is considerable momentum behind some of these frameworks, and solutions will undoubtedly emerge as Ajax rises in popularity. The CommandQueue approach that we will introduce in section 5.5.3 may be one way forward for JSF and its cousins, although it wasn't designed as such. For now, though, these frameworks tie the client a little too closely to their apron strings for my liking.

It will be interesting to see how these frameworks adapt to Ajax in the future. There is already significant interest in providing Ajax-enabled toolkits from within Sun and from several of the JSF vendors, and .NET Forms already support some Ajax-like functionality, with more being promised in the forthcoming Atlas toolkit (see the Resource section at the end of this chapter for URLs to all these).

This raises the question of what a web framework would look like if designed specifically for Ajax. No such beast exists today, but our final step on the tour of web frameworks may one day be recognized as an early ancestor.

5.3.4 *Working with service-oriented architectures*

The final kind of framework that we'll look at here is the service-oriented architecture (SOA). A *service* in an SOA is something that can be called from the network and that will return a structured document as a reply. The emphasis here is on data, not content, which is a good fit with Ajax. Web services are the most common type of service currently, and their use of XML as a lingua franca also works well with Ajax.

> **NOTE**   The term *Web Services*, with capital letters, generally refer to systems using SOAP as transport. The broader term *web services* (in lower case), encompasses any remote data exchange system that runs over HTTP, with no constraints on using SOAP or even XML. XML-RPC, JSON-RPC and any custom system that you develop using the XMLHttpRequest object are web services, but not Web Services. We are talking about the broader category of web services in this section.

When consuming a web service as its data feed, an Ajax client achieves a high degree of independence, similar to that of a desktop email client communicating to a mail server, for example. This is a different kind of reuse from that offered by the component-based toolkits. There, the client is defined once and can be exported to multiple interfaces. Here, the service is defined once and can be used by numerous unrelated clients. Clearly, a combination of SOA and Ajax could be powerful, and we may see separate frameworks evolving to generate, and to serve, Ajax applications.

Exposing server-side objects to Ajax

Many SOA and web service toolkits have appeared that make it possible to expose a plain-old server-side object written in Java, C#, or PHP directly as a web service, with a one-to-one mapping between the object's methods and the web service interface. Microsoft Visual Studio tools support this, as does Apache Axis for Java. A number of Ajax toolkits, such as DWR (for Java) and SAJAX (for PHP, .NET, Python, and several other languages) enhance these capabilities with JavaScript-specific client code.

These toolkits can be very useful. They can also be misused if not applied with caution. Let's look at a simple example using the Java DWR toolkit, in order to work out the right way to use these tools. We will define a server-side object to represent a person.

```
package com.manning.ajaxinaction;

public class Person{
  private String name=null;
  public Person(){
  }
  public String getName(){
    return name;
  }
  public void setName(String name){
    this.name=name;
  }
}
```

The object must conform to the basic JavaBeans specification. That is, it must provide a public no-argument constructor, and expose any fields that we want to read or write with getter and setter methods respectively. We then tell DWR to expose this object to the JavaScript tier, by editing the dwr.xml file:

```
<dwr>
  <init>
    <convert id="person" converter="bean"
      match="com.manning.ajaxinaction.Person"/>
  </init>
  <allow>
    <create creator="new" javascript="person">
      <param name="class" value="com.manning.ajaxinaction.Person"/>
    </create>
  </allow>
</dwr>
```

In the <init> section, we define a converter for our class of type bean, and in the <allow> section, we then define a creator that will expose instances of that object to JavaScript as a variable called person. Our Person object only has one public method, getName(), so we will be able to write in our Ajax client code

```
var name=person.getName();
```

and retrieve the value asynchronously from the server.

Our Person only has one method, so that's all we've exposed, right? Unfortunately, that's a false assumption. Our Java `Person` class is descended from `java.lang.Object` and inherits a few public methods from there, such as `hashCode()` and `toString()`, which we can also invoke from the server. This hidden feature is not peculiar to DWR. The `JSONRPCBridge.registerObject()` method will do the same, for example. To its credit, DWR does provide a mechanism for restricting access to specific methods within its XML config file. However, the default behavior is to expose everything. This problem is inherent in most reflection-based solutions. We ran across it in chapter 4 in our early versions of the ObjectViewer utility using JavaScript reflection. Let's see what we can do about it.

Limiting exposure

We've accidentally exposed our hashcodes to the Web, but have we really done any damage? In this case, probably not, because the superclass is `java.lang.Object`, which is unlikely to change. In a more complex domain model, though, we might be exposing implementation details of our own superclasses, which we might want to refactor later. By the time we get around to it, some bright spark is bound to have discovered our unwittingly exposed methods and used them in his client code, so that when we deploy the refactored object model, his client suddenly breaks. In other words, we've failed to separate our concerns adequately. If we're using a toolkit such as DWR or JSON-RPC, then we should take great care to decide which objects we are going to publish as our Ajax interface and preferably create a Façade object of some sort (figure 5.5).

Using a Façade in this situation offers several advantages. First, as already noted, it allows us to refactor our server-side model without fear. Second, it simplifies the publicly published interface that client code will use. In comparison to code written for internal consumption, interfaces published to other parties are expensive. Either we document them in detail up front or we don't document them—and become inundated with support calls from people writing to our published interfaces.

Another advantage of Façade is that it allows us to define the level of granularity of our services separately from the design of our domain model. A good domain model may contain lots of small, precise methods, because we require that precision and control within our server-side code. The requirements of a web service interface for an Ajax client are quite different, however, because of network latency. Many small method calls will kill the usability of the client, and, if deployed in sufficient number, may kill the server and even the network.

Think of it as the difference between a face-to-face conversation and a written correspondence (or an IM conversation and an email correspondence, for those too young and hip to remember what pen and paper are). When I talk directly to you, there are many small interchanges, possibly several just to establish that we are both "fine" today. When writing a letter, I may send a single exchange describing the state of my health, a recent vacation, what the family is doing, and a joke that I heard the other day, all in a single document.

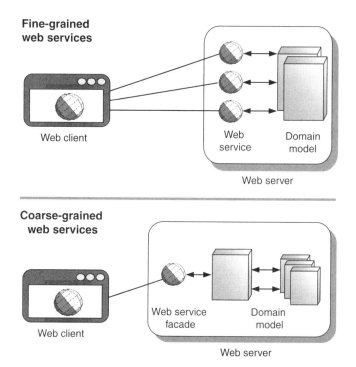

Figure 5.5 Comparison of a system in which all objects are fully exposed as Internet services to an Ajax client and one is using a Façade to expose only a few carefully chosen pieces of functionality. By reducing the number of publicly published methods, we can refactor our domain model without fear of breaking client code over which we have no control.

By bundling calls across the network into larger documents, service-oriented architectures are making better use of available network resources. Bandwidth is typically less of a problem than latency. They are also causing problems for themselves by standardizing on a bulky XML data format over a verbose transmission protocol (our familiar and well-loved HTTP), but that's a story for another day. If we look at the options available with Ajax, we can see that we are provided with good native support for HTTP and XML technologies in the browser, and so a document-centric approach to our distributed domain models makes sense.

A conventional document, such as this book, is composed of paragraphs, headings, tables, and figures. Likewise, a document in a call to a service may contain a variety of elements, such as queries, updates, and notifications. The Command pattern, discussed in chapter 3, can provide a good foundation for structuring our documents as a series of undoable actions to be passed between client and server. We'll look at an implementation of this later in the chapter.

This concludes our discussion of the server-side architectures of the day. None provides a perfect fit for Ajax yet, which is not surprising given that they were designed to serve a considerably different kind of web application. A lot of good work is underway to build Ajax into existing frameworks and the next year or so should prove interesting. Nonetheless, many web developers will be faced with the task of making Ajax work with these legacy systems, and this overview of the strengths and weaknesses for each ought to provide a starting point.

Let's assume for the moment that we have decided upon one architecture or another and begun the work of developing an Ajax application. We have already discussed the architecture of the client application itself in detail in chapter 4, and we provided examples of retrieving XML data from the server in chapter 2. XML is popular but not the only way of exchanging data between client and server. In the following section, we review the full spectrum of options for communicating between client and server.

5.4 *The details: exchanging data*

We've looked at the big architectural patterns that describe how our web application might behave and shown that there are many options. We've stressed the importance of communication between the client and the server's domain models, and we might naively assume that once we've settled on a framework, our design choices are made for us. In this and the following section, we'll see that this is far from true. If we focus on a single exchange of data, we have many options. We'll catalog the options here, with the aim of developing a pattern language for Ajax data exchange. With this in hand, we can make more informed decisions about what techniques to use in particular circumstances.

Exchanging pure data has no real analog in the classical web application, and so the pattern language is less well developed in this area. I'll attempt to fill that void by defining a few phrases of my own. As a first cut, I suggest that we break user interactions into four categories: *client-only, content-centric, script-centric*, and *data-centric*. Client-only interactions are simple, so we'll deal with them quickly in the next section, and then introduce an example that can see us through the other three.

5.4.1 *Client-only interactions*

A client-only interaction is one in which a user interaction is processed by a script that has already been loaded into the browser. No recourse to the web server (the old presentation tier) is necessary, which is good for responsiveness and for server load. Such an interaction is suitable for relatively trivial calculations, such as adding a sales tax or shipping charge to a customer's order. In general, for this approach to be effective, the client-side logic that processes the interaction needs to be small and unchanging during the lifetime of the customer interaction. In the case of shipping options, we are on safe ground because the number of options will be of the order of two to five, not several thousands (unlike, say, the full catalog of an online retailer), and the shipping costs are unlikely to change from one minute to the next (unlike, say, a stock ticker or first-come-first-served ticket-reservation system). This type of interaction has already been explored in chapter 4's discussion of the client-side Controller, so we'll say no more about it here.

The remaining three categories all involve a trip back to the server and differ primarily in what is fetched. The key differences are summarized in the following sections, along with the pros and cons of each.

5.4.2 *Introducing the planet browser example*

Before we dive in to the different data exchange mechanisms, let's introduce a simple example, to serve as a hook on which to hang our arguments. The application will present a range of facts about the planets of our solar system. Our main screen shows an idealized view of the solar system, with an icon for each planet. On the server, we have recorded various facts about these planets, which can be brought up in pop-up windows by clicking on the planet's icon (figure 5.6). We aren't using the ObjectViewer from chapter 4 here, but we will get back to it later in this chapter.

The part of the puzzle that interests us now is delivering the data shown in the pop-up from the server to the browser. We'll look at the format of data that the server sends us in each variation, but we won't go into the details of generating that data, as we've already covered the principles in our discussion of MVC in chapter 3. Listing 5.1 shows the skeleton of our client-side application, around which we can explore the various content-delivery mechanisms.

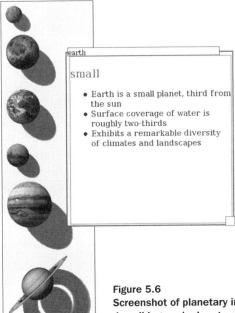

Figure 5.6
Screenshot of planetary info application, in which pop-up windows describing each planet can be brought up by clicking on the icons.

Listing 5.1 popups.html

```
<!DOCTYPE html PUBLIC
"-//W3C//DTD XHTML 1.0 Strict//EN"
"http://www.w3.org/TR/xhtml1/DTD/xhtml1-strict.dtd">
<html>
<head>
<title>Planet Browser</title>
<link rel=stylesheet type="text/css"
  href="main.css"/>
<link rel=stylesheet type="text/css"
  href="windows.css"/>
<link rel=stylesheet type="text/css"
  href="planets.css"/>

<script type="text/javascript"
  src="x/x_core.js"></script>          ◁
<script type="text/javascript"
  src="x/x_event.js"></script>         ◁
<script type="text/javascript"
  src="x/x_drag.js"></script>          ◁
<script type="text/javascript"
  src="windows.js"></script>          ◁
<script type="text/javascript"
  src="net.js"></script>              ◁
```

❶ Include JavaScript libraries

```
<script type="text/javascript">

window.onload=function(){
  var pbar=document.getElementById("planets");
  var children=pbar.getElementsByTagName("div");
  for(var i=0;i<children.length;i++){
    children[i].onclick=showInfo;        ➋  Assign event handler to icons
  }
}

</script>

</head>
<body>

<div class="planetbar" id="planets">     ➌  Add hard-coded icons of planets
<div class="planetbutton" id="mercury">
 <img src="img/ball-mercury.gif" alt="mercury"/>
</div>
<div class="planetbutton" id="venus">
 <img src="img/ball-venus.gif" alt="venus"/>
</div>
<div class="planetbutton" id="earth">
 <img src="img/ball-earth.gif" alt="earth"/>
</div>
<div class="planetbutton" id="mars">
 <img src="img/ball-mars.gif" alt="mars"/>
</div>
<div class="planetbutton" id="jupiter">
 <img src="img/ball-jupiter.gif" alt="jupiter"/>
</div>
<div class="planetbutton" id="saturn">
 <img src="img/ball-saturn.gif" alt="saturn"/>
</div>
<div class="planetbutton" id="uranus">
 <img src="img/ball-uranus.gif" alt="uranus"/>
</div>
<div class="planetbutton" id="neptune">
 <img src="img/ball-neptune.gif" alt="neptune"/>
</div>
<div class="planetbutton" id="pluto">
 <img src="img/ball-pluto.gif" alt="pluto"/>
</div>
</div>

</body>
</html>
```

We have included a few JavaScript libraries ❶ in our file. net.js handles the low-level HTTP request mechanics for us, using the XMLHttpRequest object that we described in chapter 2. windows.js defines a draggable window object that we can use as our pop-up window. The details of the implementation of the window needn't concern us here, beyond the signature of the constructor:

```
var MyWindow=new Window(bodyDiv,title,x,y,w,h);
```

where `bodyDiv` is a DOM element that will be added into the window body, `title` is a display string to show in the window titlebar, and `x,y,w,h` describes the initial window geometry. By specifying a DOM element as the argument, we give ourselves considerable flexibility as to how the content is supplied to the window. The downloadable source code accompanying the book contains the full listing for the Window object.

In the HTML, we simply define a `div` element for each planet ❸, to which we assign an `onclick` handler in the `window.onload` function ❷, using the standard DOM tree navigation methods. The `onclick` handler, `showInfo()`, isn't defined here, as we'll provide several implementations in this chapter. Let's start by looking at the various actions that we can take when we come to loading the content.

5.4.3 Thinking like a web page: content-centric interactions

The first steps that we take toward Ajax will resemble the classic web application that we are moving away from, as noted in chapter 1 when discussing horses and bicycles. Content-centric patterns of interaction still follow the classic web paradigm but may have a role to play in an Ajax application.

Overview

In a content-centric pattern of interaction, HTML content is still being generated by the server and sent to an IFrame embedded in the main web page. We discussed IFrames in chapter 2 and showed how to define them in the HTML markup of the page or generate them programmatically. In the latter case, we can still be looking at a fairly radically dynamic style of interface more akin to a window manager than a desktop. Figure 5.7 outlines the content-centric architecture.

Listing 5.2 shows an implementation of the event handler for our planetary info application, using a content-centric approach.

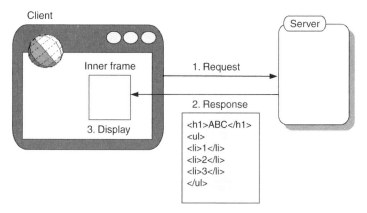

Figure 5.7 Content-centric architecture in an Ajax application. The client creates an IFrame and launches a request to the server for content. The content is generated from a Model, View, and Controller on the server presentation tier and returned to the IFrame. There is no requirement for a business domain model on the client tier.

Listing 5.2 ContentPopup.js

```
var offset=8;

function showInfo(event){
  var planet=this.id;
  var infoWin=new ContentPopup(
    "info_"+planet+".html",
    planet+"Popup",
    planet,offset,offset,320,320
  );
  offset+=32;
}

function ContentPopup(url,winEl,displayStr,x,y,w,h){

  var bod=document.createElement("div");
  document.body.appendChild(bod);

  this.iframe=document.createElement("iframe");
  this.iframe.className="winContents";
  this.iframe.src=url;
  bod.appendChild(this.iframe);

  this.win=new windows.Window(bod,displayStr,x,y,w,h);
}
```

showInfo() is the event-handler function for the DOM element representing the planet. Within the event handler, this refers to the DOM element, and we use that element's id to determine for which planet we display information.

We define a ContentPopup object that composes one of the generic Window objects, creates an IFrame to use as the main content in the window body, and loads the given URL into it. In this case, we have simply constructed the name of a static HTML file as the URL. In a more sophisticated system with dynamically generated data, we would probably add querystring parameters to the URL instead. The simple file that we load into the IFrame in this example, shown in listing 5.3, is generated by the server.

Listing 5.3 info_earth.html

```
<html>
<head>
<link rel=stylesheet type="text/css" href="../style.css"/>
</head>
<body class="info">
<div class="framedInfo" id="info">
<div class="title" id="infotitle">earth</div>
<div class="content" id="infocontent">
A small blue planet near the outer rim of the galaxy,
third planet out from a middle-sized sun.
</div>
</div>
</body>
</html>
```

Nothing remarkable there—we can just use plain HTML markup as we would for a classic web application.

In a content-centric pattern, the client-tier code needs only a limited understanding of the business logic of the application, being responsible for placing the IFrame and constructing the URL needed to invoke the content. Coupling between the client and presentation tiers is quite loose, with most responsibility still loaded onto the server. The benefit of this style of interaction is that there is plenty of HTML floating around on the Web, ready to use. Two scenarios in which it could be useful are incorporating content from external sites—possibly business partners or public services—and displaying legacy content from an application. HTML markup can be very effective, and there is little point in converting some types of content into application-style content. Help pages are a prime example. In many cases where a classic web application would use a pop-up window, an Ajax application might prefer a content-centric piece of code, particularly in light of the pop-up blocker features in many recent browsers.

This pattern is useful in a limited set of situations, then. Let's briefly review its limitations before moving on.

Problems and limitations

Because they resemble conventional web pages so much, content-centric interactions have many of the limitations of the old way of doing things. The content document is isolated within the IFrame from the page in which it is embedded. This partitions the screen real estate to some extent. In terms of layout, the IFrame imposes a single rectangular window for the child document, although it may be assigned a transparent background to help blend it into the parent document.

It may be tempting to use this mechanism to deliver highly dynamic subpages within the highly dynamic application, but the introduction of IFrames in this way can be problematic. Each IFrame maintains its own scripting context, and the amount of "plumbing" code required for scripts in the IFrame and parent to talk to one another can be considerable. For communication with scripts in other frames, the problem worsens. We'll return to this issue shortly when we look at script-centric patterns.

We also suffer many of the usability problems of traditional web applications. First, if the layout of the IFrame involves nontrivial boilerplate markup, we are still resending static content with each request for content. Second, although the main document won't suffer from "blinking" when data is refreshed, the IFrame might, if the same frame is reused for multiple fetches of content. This latter issue could be avoided with a bit of extra coding to present a loading message over the top of the frame, for example.

So, "content-centric" is the first new term for our vocabulary of Ajax server request techniques. Content-centric approaches are limited in usefulness, but it's good to have a name for them. There are many scenarios that can't be easily addressed by a content-centric approach, such as updating a small part of a widget's surface, for example, a single icon or a single row in a table. One way to perform such modifications is to send JavaScript code. Let's look at that option now.

Variations

The content-centric style that we've applied so far has used an IFrame to receive the server-generated content. An alternative approach that might be considered content-centric is to generate a fragment of HTML in response to an asynchronous request, and assign the response to the `innerHTML` of a DOM element in the current document. We use that approach in chapter 12 in our XSLT-driven phonebook, so we won't reproduce a full example here.

5.4.4 *Thinking like a plug-in: script-centric interactions*

When we send a JavaScript file from our web server to a browser, and it executes in that browser for us, we are actually doing something quite advanced. If we generate the JavaScript that we are sending from a program, we are setting up an even more complex system. Traditionally, client/server programs communicate data to one another. Communicating executable, mobile code across the network opens up a lot of flexibility. Enterprise-grade network languages such as Java and the .NET stack are only just catching on to the possibilities of mobile code, through technologies such as RMI, Jini, and the .NET Remoting Framework. We lightweight web developers have been doing it for years! As usual, Ajax lets us do a few new interesting things with this capability, so let's see what they are.

Overview

In a classic web application, a piece of JavaScript and its associated HTML are delivered in a single bundle, and the script is typically authored to work with that particular page. Using Ajax, we can load scripts and pages independently of one another, giving us the possibility of modifying a particular page in a number of different ways, depending on the script that we load. The code that constitutes our client-tier application can effectively be extended at runtime. This introduces both problems and opportunities, as we will see. Figure 5.8 illustrates the basic architecture of a script-centric application.

The first advantage of this approach over a content-centric solution is that the network activity is relegated to the background, eliminating visual blinking.

The exact nature of the script that we generate will depend on the hooks that we expose in the client tier itself. As with much code generation, success hinges on keeping the generated portion simple and making use of nongenerated library code where possible, either transmitted alongside the generated code or resident in the client application.

Either way, this pattern results in relatively tight coupling between the tiers. That is, the code generated by the server requires intimate knowledge of API calls on the client. Two problems emerge. First, changes to the server and client code can unintentionally break them. Good modular design principles can offset this to some extent, by providing a well-defined, well-documented API—implementing the Façade pattern. The second issue is that the stream of JavaScript is very

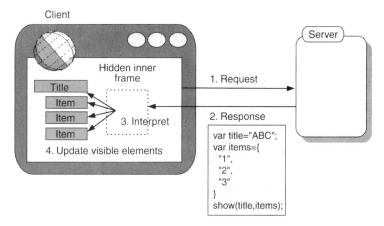

Figure 5.8 Script-centric architecture in an Ajax application. The client application makes a request to the server for a fragment of JavaScript, which it then interprets. The client app exposes several entry points for generated scripts to hook into, allowing manipulation of the client by the script.

specifically designed for this client, and it is unlikely to be as reusable in other contexts in comparison to, say, a stream of XML. Reusability isn't important in all cases, however.

Let's have a look at our planetary info example again. Listing 5.4 shows a simple API for displaying our information windows.

Listing 5.4 showPopup() function and supporting code

```
var offset=8;
function showPopup(name,description){
  var win=new ScriptIframePopup
    (name,description,offset,offset,320,320);
  offset+=32;
}

function ScriptIframePopup(name,description,x,y,w,h){

  var bod=document.createElement("div");
  document.body.appendChild(bod);

  this.contentDiv=document.createElement("div");
  this.contentDiv.className="winContents";
  this.contentDiv.innerHTML=description;
  bod.appendChild(this.contentDiv);

  this.win=new windows.Window(bod,name,x,y,w,h);
}
```

We define a function `showPopup` that takes a name and description as argument and constructs a window object for us. Listing 5.5 shows an example script that invokes this function.

Listing 5.5 script_earth.js

```
var name='earth';
var description="A small blue planet near the outer rim of the galaxy,"
  +"third planet out from a middle-sized sun.";

showPopup (name,description);
```

We simply define the arguments and make a call against the API. Behind the scenes, though, we need to load this script from the server and persuade the browser to execute it. There are two quite different routes that we can take. Let's examine each in turn.

Loading scripts into IFrames

If we load a JavaScript using an HTML document `<script>` tag, the script will automatically be executed by the interpreter when it loads. IFrames are the same as any other document in this respect. We can define a `showInfo()` method to create an IFrame for us, and load the script into it:

```
function showInfo(event){
  var planet=this.id;
  var scriptUrl="script_"+planet+".html";
  var dataframe=document.getElementById('dataframe');
  if (!dataframe){
    dataframe=document.createElement("iframe");
    dataframe.className='dataframe';
    dataframe.id='dataframe';
    dataframe.src=scriptUrl;
    document.body.appendChild(dataframe);
  }else{
    dataframe.src=scriptUrl;
  }
}
```

The DOM manipulation methods that we're using should be familiar by now. If we use an invisible IFrame to load our script, we need only concentrate on generating the script itself, since all other interactions are generated for us. So let's stitch our sample script into an HTML document, as shown in listing 5.6.

Listing 5.6 script_earth.html

```html
<html>
<head>
<script type='text/javascript' src='script_earth.js'>
</script>
</head>
<body>
</body>
</html>
```

When we try to load this code, it doesn't work, because the IFrame creates its own JavaScript context and can't directly see the API that we defined in the main document. When our script states

```
showPopup(name,description);
```

the browser looks for a function `showPopup()` defined inside the IFrame's context. In a simple two-context situation such as this, we can preface API calls with top, that is,

```
top.showPopup(name,description);
```

in order to refer to the top-level document. If we were nesting IFrames inside IFrames, or wanted to be able to run our application inside a frameset, things could get much more complicated.

The script that we load uses a functional approach. If we choose to instantiate an object in our IFrame script, we will encounter further complications. Let's say that we have a file PlanetInfo.js that defines a `PlanetInfo` type of object that we invoke in our script as

```
var pinfo=new PlanetInfo(name,description);
```

To use this type in our script, we could import PlanetInfo.js into the IFrame context, by adding an extra script tag:

```html
<script type='text/javascript' src='PlanetInfo.js'></script>
<script type='text/javascript'>
  var pinfo=new PlanetInfo(name,description);
</script>
```

The PlanetInfo object created within the IFrame would have identical behavior to one created in the top-level frame, but the two wouldn't have the same prototype. If the IFrame were later destroyed, but the top-level document kept a reference to an object created by that IFrame, subsequent calls to the object's methods would fail. Further, the `instanceof` operator would have counterintuitive behavior, as outlined in table 5.1.

Table 5.1 Behavior of `instanceof` operator across frames

Object Created In	`instanceof` Invoked In	Obj `instanceof` Object Evaluates To
Top-level document	Top-level document	true
Top-level document	IFrame	false
IFrame	Top-level document	false
IFrame	IFrame	true

Importing the same object definition into multiple scripting contexts is not as simple as it first looks. We can avoid it by providing a factory method as part of our top-level document's API, for example:

```
function createPlanetInfo(name,description){
  return new PlanetInfo(name,description);
}
```

which our script can then call without needing to refer to its own version of the PlanetInfo type, thus:

```
<script type='text/javascript'>
  var pinfo=createPlanetInfo(name,description);
</script>
```

The `showPopup()` function in listing 5.4 is essentially a factory for the Script-IframePopup object.

This approach works and does what we want it to. We need to send a small amount of HTML boilerplate with each page, but much less than with the content-centric solution. The biggest drawback of this approach appears to be the creation of a separate JavaScript context. There is a way to avoid that altogether, which we will look at now.

Loading scripts using XMLHttpRequest and eval()

JavaScript, like many scripting languages, has an `eval()` function, which allows any arbitrary text to be passed directly to the JavaScript interpreter. Using `eval()` is often discouraged, or noted as being slow, and this is indeed the case when it is called regularly on lots of small scripts. However, it has its uses, and we can exploit it here to evaluate scripts loaded from the server using the XMLHttp-Request object. `eval()` performs with reasonable efficiency when working on fewer, larger scripts.

Our planetary info example is rewritten to use `eval()` in the following code:

```
function showInfo(event){
  var planet=this.id;
  var scriptUrl="script_"+planet+".js";
  new net.ContentLoader(scriptUrl,evalScript);
}

function evalScript(){
  var script=this.req.responseText;
  eval(script);
}
```

The `showInfo()` method now uses the XMLHttpRequest object (wrapped in our `ContentLoader` class) to fetch the script from the server, without needing to wrap it in an HTML page. The second function, `evalScript()`, is passed to the `Content-Loader` as a callback, at which point we can read the `responseText` property from the XMLHttpRequest object. The entire script is evaluated in the current page context, rather than in a separate context within an IFrame.

We can add the term *script-centric* to our pattern language now and make a note that there are two implementations of it, using IFrames and `eval()`. Let's step back then, and see how script-based approaches compare with the content-based style.

Problems and limitations

When we load a script directly from the server, we are generally transmitting a simpler message, reducing bandwidth to some extent. We also decouple the logic from the presentation to a great degree, with the immediate practical consequence that visual changes aren't confined to a fixed rectangular portion of the screen as they are with the content-centric approach.

On the downside, however, we introduce a tight coupling between client and server code. The JavaScript emitted by the server is unlikely to be reusable in other contexts and will need to be specifically written for the Ajax client. Further, once published, the API provided by the client will be relatively difficult to change.

It's a step in the right direction, though. The Ajax application is starting to behave more like an application and less like a document. In the next style of client-server communication that we cover, we can release the tight coupling between client and server that was introduced here.

5.4.5 *Thinking like an application: data-centric interactions*

With the script-centric approach just described, we have started to behave more like a traditional thick client, with data requests to the server taking place in the background, decoupled from the user interface. The script content remained highly specific to the browser-based client, though.

Overview

In some situations, we may want to share the data feeds to our Ajax client with other front ends, such as Java or .NET smart clients or cell phone/PDA client software. In such cases, we would probably prefer a more neutral data format than a set of JavaScript instructions.

In a data-centric solution, the server serves up streams of pure data, which our own client code, rather than the JavaScript engine, parses. Figure 5.9 illustrates the features of a data-centric solution.

Most of the examples in this book follow a data-centric approach. The most obvious format for data is XML, but other formats are possible, too, as we'll see next.

Using XML data

XML is a near-ubiquitous data format in modern computing. The web browser environment in which our Ajax application sits, and the XMLHttpRequest object

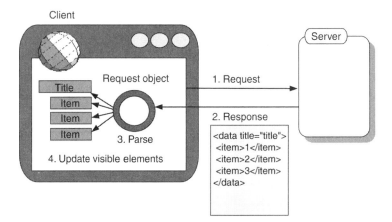

Figure 5.9 In a data-centric system, the server returns streams of raw data (XML in this case), which are parsed on the client tier and used to update the client tier model and/or user interface.

in particular, provides good native support for processing XML. If the XML-HttpRequest receives a response with an XML Content type such as `application/xml` or `text/xml`, it can present the response as a Document Object Model, as we have already seen. Listing 5.7 shows how our planetary data application adapts to using XML data feeds.

Listing 5.7   DataXMLPopup.js

```
var offset=8;
function showPopup(name,description){
  var win=new DataPopup(name,description,offset,offset,320,320);
  offset+=32;
}

function DataPopup(name,description,x,y,w,h){

  var bod=document.createElement("div");
  document.body.appendChild(bod);

  this.contentDiv=document.createElement("div");
  this.contentDiv.className="winContents";
  this.contentDiv.innerHTML=description;
  bod.appendChild(this.contentDiv);

  this.win=new windows.Window(bod,name,x,y,w,h);
}

function showInfo(event){
  var planet=this.id;
  var scriptUrl=planet+".xml";
  new net.ContentLoader(scriptUrl,parseXML);
}

function parseXML(){
  var name="";
  var descrip="";
  var xmlDoc=this.req.responseXML;
  var elDocRoot=xmlDoc.getElementsByTagName("planet")[0];
  if (elDocRoot){
    attrs=elDocRoot.attributes;
    name=attrs.getNamedItem("name").value;
    var ptype=attrs.getNamedItem("type").value;
    if (ptype){
      descrip+="<h2>"+ptype+"</h2>";
    }

    descrip+="<ul>";
    for(var i=0;i<elDocRoot.childNodes.length;i++){
      elChild=elDocRoot.childNodes[i];
```

```
    if (elChild.nodeName=="info"){
      descrip+="<li>"+elChild.firstChild.data+"</li>\n";
    }
  }
  descrip+="</ul>";
}else{
  alert("no document");
}
top.showPopup(name,descrip);
}
```

The `showInfo()` function simply opens up an XMLHttpRequest object, wrapped up in a ContentLoader object, providing the `parseXML()` function as a callback. The callback here is slightly more involved than the `evalScript()` method that we encountered in section 5.6.3, as we have to navigate the response DOM, pull out the data, and then manually invoke the `showPopup()` method. Listing 5.8 shows an example XML response generated by the server, which our XML data-centric app might consume.

Listing 5.8   earth.xml

```
<planet name="earth" type="small">
  <info id="a" author="dave" date="26/05/04">
    Earth is a small planet, third from the sun
  </info>
  <info id="b" author="dave" date="27/02/05">
    Surface coverage of water is roughly two-thirds
  </info>
  <info id="c" author="dave" date="03/05/05">
    Exhibits a remarkable diversity of climates and landscapes
  </info>
</planet>
```

A big advantage of XML is that it lends itself to structuring information. We have taken advantage of this here to provide a number of <info> tags, which we translate into an HTML unordered list in the `parseXML()` code.

We've achieved better separation of the server and client tiers by using XML. Provided that both sides understand the document format, client and server code can be changed independently of one another. However, getting the JavaScript interpreter to do all the work for us in the script-centric solutions of the previous section was nice. The following example, using JSON, gives us something of the best of both worlds. Let's look at it now.

Using JSON data

The XMLHttpRequest object is arguably misnamed, as it can receive any text-based information. A useful format for transmitting data to the Ajax client is the JavaScript Object Notation (JSON), a compact way of representing generic JavaScript object graphs. Listing 5.9 shows how we adapt our planetary info example to use JSON.

Listing 5.9 DataJSONPopup.js

```
function showInfo(event){
  var planet=this.id;
  var scriptUrl=planet+".json";
  new net.ContentLoader(scriptUrl,parseJSON);
}

function parseJSON(){
  var name="";
  var descrip="";
  var jsonTxt=net.req.responseText;
  var jsonObj=eval("("+jsonTxt+")");
  name=jsonObj.planet.name;
  var ptype=jsonObj.planet.type;
  if (ptype){
    descrip+="<h2>"+ptype+"</h2>";
  }

  var infos=jsonObj.planet.info;
  descrip+="<ul>";
  for(var i in infos){
    descrip+="<li>"+infos[i]+"</li>\n";
  }
  descrip+="</ul>";

  top.showPopup(name,descrip);
}
```

Once again, we fetch the data using a ContentLoader and assign a callback function, here `parseJSON()`. The entire response text is a valid JavaScript statement, so we can create an object graph in one line by simply calling `eval()`:

```
var jsonObj=eval("("+jsonTxt+")");
```

Note that we need to wrap the entire expression in parentheses before we evaluate it. We can then query the object properties directly by name, leading to somewhat more terse and readable code than the DOM manipulation methods that we used for the XML. The `showPopup()` method is omitted, as it is identical to that in listing 5.7.

So what does JSON actually look like? Listing 5.10 shows our data for planet Earth as a JSON string.

Listing 5.10   earth.json

```
{"planet": {
  "name": "earth",
  "type": "small",
  "info": [
    "Earth is a small planet, third from the sun",
    "Surface coverage of water is roughly two-thirds",
    "Exhibits a remarkable diversity of climates and landscapes"
  ]
}}
```

Curly braces denote associative arrays, and square braces numerical arrays. Either kind of brace can nest the other. Here, we define an object called `planet` that contains three properties. The `name` and `type` properties are simple strings, and the `info` property is an array.

JSON is less common than XML, although it can be consumed by any Java-Script engine, including the Java-based Mozilla Rhino and Microsoft's JScript .NET. The JSON-RPC libraries contain JSON parsers for a number of programming languages (see the Resources section at the end of this chapter), as well as a JavaScript "Stringifier" for converting JavaScript objects to JSON strings, for two-way communications using JSON as the medium. If a JavaScript interpreter is available at both the server and client end, JSON is definitely a viable option. The JSON-RPC project has also been developing libraries for parsing and generating JSON for a number of common server-side languages.

We can add *data-centric* to our vocabulary now and note the potential for a wide range of text-based data formats other than the ever-popular XML.

Using XSLT

Another alternative to manually manipulating the DOM tree to create HTML, as we have done in section 5.7.3, is to use XSLT transformations to automatically convert the XML into XHTML. This is a hybrid between the data-centric and content-centric approaches. From the server's perspective, it is data-centric, whereas from the client's, it looks more content-centric. This is quicker and easier but suffers the same limits as a content-centric approach, namely, the response is interpreted purely as visual markup typically affecting a single rectangular region of the visible UI. XSLT is discussed in more detail in chapter 11.

Problems and limitations

The main limitation of a data-centric approach is that it places the burden of parsing the data squarely on the client. Hence the client-tier code will tend to be more complicated, but, where this approach is adopted wholesale in a larger application, the costs can be offset by reusing parser code or abstracting some of the functionality into a library.

The three approaches that we have presented here arguably form a spectrum between the traditional web-app model and the desktop-style thick client. Fortunately, the three patterns are not mutually exclusive and may all be used in the same application.

Client/server communications run both ways, of course. We'll wrap up this chapter with a look at how the client can send data to the server.

5.5 Writing to the server

So far, we've concentrated on one side of the conversation, namely, the server telling the client what is going on. In most applications, the user will want to manipulate the domain model as well as look at it. In a multiuser environment, we also want to receive updates on changes that other users have made.

Let's consider the case of updating changes that we have made first. Technically, there are two main mechanisms for submitting data: HTML forms and the XMLHttpRequest object. Let's run through each briefly in turn.

5.5.1 Using HTML forms

In a classic web application, HTML form elements are the standard mechanism for user input of data. Form elements can be declared in the HTML markup for a page:

```
<form method="POST" action="myFormHandlerURL.php">
  <input type="text" name="username"/>
  <input type="password" name="password"/>
  <input type="submit" value="login"/>
</form>
```

This will render itself as a couple of blank text boxes. If I enter values of dave and letmein on the form, then an HTTP POST request is sent to myFormHandlerURL.php, with body text of username=dave&password=letmein. In most modern web programming systems, we don't directly see this encoded form data but have the name-value pairs decoded for us as an associative array or "magic" variables.

It's fairly common practice these days to add a little JavaScript to validate the form contents locally before submitting. We can modify our simple form to do this:

```
<form id="myForm" method="POST" action=""
      onsubmit="validateForm(); return false;">
  <input type="text" name="username"/>
  <input type="password" name="password"/>
  <input type="submit" value="login"/>
</form>
```

And we can define a validation routine in the JavaScript for the page:

```
function validateForm(){
  var form=document.getElementById('myForm');
  var user=form.elements[0].value;
  var pwd=form.elements[1].value;
  if (user && user.length>0 && pwd && pwd.length>0){
    form.action='myFormHandlerURL.php';
    form.submit();
  }else{
    alert("please fill in your credentials before logging in");
  }

}
```

The form is initially defined with no action attribute. The real URL is substituted only when the values in the form have been validated correctly. JavaScript can also be used to enhance forms by disabling the Submit button to prevent multiple submissions, encrypting passwords before sending them over the network, and so on. These techniques are well documented elsewhere, and we won't go into them in depth here. Chapters 9 and 10 contain more detailed working examples of Ajax-enhanced HTML forms.

We can also construct a form element programmatically and submit it behind the scenes. If we style it to not be displayed, we can do so without it ever being seen by the user, as illustrated in listing 5.11.

Listing 5.11   submitData() function

```
function addParam(form,key,value){
  var input=document.createElement("input");
  input.name=key;
  input.value=value;
  form.appendChild(input);
}
```

```
function submitData(url,data){
  var form=document.createElement("form");
  form.action=url;
  form.method="POST";
  for (var i in data){
    addParam(form,i,data[i]);
  }
  form.style.display="none";
  document.body.appendChild(form);
  form.submit();
}
```

submitData() creates the form element and iterates over the data, adding to the form using the addParam() function. We can invoke it like this:

```
submitData(
  "myFormHandlerURL.php",
  {username:"dave",password:"letmein"}
);
```

This technique is concise but has a significant drawback in that there is no easy way of capturing a server response. We could point the form at an invisible IFrame and then parse the result, but this is rather cumbersome at best. Fortunately, we can achieve the same effect by using the XMLHttpRequest object.

5.5.2 *Using the XMLHttpRequest object*

We've already seen the XMLHttpRequest object in action in chapter 2 and earlier in this chapter. The differences between reading and updating are minor from the client code's point of view. We simply need to specify the POST method and pass in our form parameters.

Listing 5.12 shows the main code for our ContentLoader object developed in section 3.1. We have refactored it to allow parameters to be passed to the request, and any HTTP method to be specified.

Listing 5.12   ContentLoader object

```
net.ContentLoader=function
  (url,onload,onerror,method,params,contentType){     ❶ Extra arguments

  this.onload=onload;
  this.onerror=(onerror) ? onerror : this.defaultError;
  this.loadXMLDoc(url,method,params,contentType);
}

net.ContentLoader.prototype.loadXMLDoc
```

```
=function(url,method,params,contentType){
if (!method){
  method="GET";
}
if (!contentType && method=="POST"){
  contentType="application/x-www-form-urlencoded";
}
if (window.XMLHttpRequest){
  this.req=new XMLHttpRequest();
} else if (window.ActiveXObject){
  this.req=new ActiveXObject("Microsoft.XMLHTTP");
}
if (this.req){
  try{
    this.req.onreadystatechange=net.ContentLoader.onReadyState;
    this.req.open(method,url,true);                    <—  HTTP method
    if (contentType){                       <—  Content type
      this.req.setRequestHeader("Content-Type", contentType);
    }
    this.req.send(params);      <—  Request parameters
  }catch (err){
    this.onerror.call(this);
  }
}
}
```

We pass in several new arguments to the constructor ❶. Only the URL (corresponding to the form action) and the onload handler are required, but the HTTP
method, request parameters, and content type may be specified, too. Note that if
we're submitting key-value pairs of data by POST, then the content type must be
set to application/x-www-form-urlencoded. We handle this automatically if no
content type is specified. The HTTP method is specified in the open() method of
XMLHttpRequest, and the params in the send() method. Thus, a call like this

```
var loader=net.ContentLoader(
  'myFormHandlerURL.php',
  showResponse,
  null,
  'POST',
  'username=dave&password=letmein'
);
```

will perform the same request as the forms-based submitData() method in
listing 5.11. Note that the parameters are passed as a string object using the
form-encoded style seen in URL querystrings, for example:

```
name=dave&job=book&work=Ajax_In+Action
```

This covers the basic mechanics of submitting data to the server, whether based on textual input from a form or other activity such as drag and drop or mouse movements. In the following section, we'll pick up our ObjectViewer example from chapter 4 and learn how to manage updates to the domain model in an orderly fashion.

5.5.3 *Managing user updates effectively*

In chapter 4, we introduced the ObjectViewer, a generic piece of code for browsing complex domain models, and provided a simple example for viewing planetary data. The objects representing the planets in the solar system each contained several parameters, and we marked a couple of simple textual properties—the diameter and distance from the sun—as editable. Changes made to any properties in the system were captured by a central event listener function, which we used to write some debug information to the browser status bar. (The ability to write to the status bar is being restricted in recent builds of Mozilla Firefox. In appendix A, we present a pure JavaScript logging console that could be used to provide status messages to the user in the absence of a native status bar.) This event listener mechanism also provides an ideal way of capturing updates in order to send them to the server.

Let's suppose that we have a script updateDomainModel.jsp running on our server that captures the following information:

- The unique ID of the planet being updated
- The name of the property being updated
- The value being assigned to the property

We can write an event handler to fire all changes to the server like so:

```
function updateServer(propviewer){
  var planetObj=propviewer.viewer.object;
  var planetId=planetObj.id;
  var propName=propviewer.name;
  var val=propviewer.value;
  net.ContentLoader(
    'updateDomainModel.jsp',
    someResponseHandler,
    null,
    'POST',
    'planetId='+encodeURI(planetId)
    +'&propertyName='+encodeURI(propName)
    +'&value='+encodeURI(val)
  );
}
```

And we can attach it to our ObjectViewer:

```
myObjectViewer.addChangeListener(updateServer);
```

This is easy to code but can result in a lot of very small bits of traffic to the server, which is inefficient and potentially confusing. If we want to control our traffic, we can capture these updates and queue them locally and then send them to the server in batches at our leisure. A simple update queue implemented in Java-Script is shown in listing 5.13.

Listing 5.13 CommandQueue object

```
net.CommandQueue=function(id,url,freq){            ❶  Create a queue object
  this.id=id;
  net.cmdQueues[id]=this;
  this.url=url;
  this.queued=new Array();
  this.sent=new Array();
  if (freq){
    this.repeat(freq);
  }
}

net.CommandQueue.prototype.addCommand=function(command){
  if (this.isCommand(command)){
    this.queue.append(command,true);
  }
}

net.CommandQueue.prototype.fireRequest=function(){       ❷  Send request to server
  if (this.queued.length==0){
    return;
  }
  var data="data=";
  for(var i=0;i<this.queued.length;i++){
    var cmd=this.queued[i];
    if (this.isCommand(cmd)){
      data+=cmd.toRequestString();
      this.sent[cmd.id]=cmd;
    }
  }
  this.queued=new Array();
  this.loader=new net.ContentLoader(
    this.url,
    net.CommandQueue.onload,net.CommandQueue.onerror,
    "POST",data
  );
}
```

```
net.CommandQueue.prototype.isCommand=function(obj){        ❸  Test object type
  return (
    obj.implementsProp("id")
    && obj.implementsFunc("toRequestString")
    && obj.implementsFunc("parseResponse")
  );
}

net.CommandQueue.onload=function(loader){        ❹  Parse server response
  var xmlDoc=net.req.responseXML;
  var elDocRoot=xmlDoc.getElementsByTagName("commands")[0];
  if (elDocRoot){
    for(i=0;i<elDocRoot.childNodes.length;i++){
      elChild=elDocRoot.childNodes[i];
      if (elChild.nodeName=="command"){
        var attrs=elChild.attributes;
        var id=attrs.getNamedItem("id").value;
        var command=net.commandQueue.sent[id];
        if (command){
          command.parseResponse(elChild);
        }
      }
    }
  }

}
net.CommandQueue.onerror=function(loader){
  alert("problem sending the data to the server");
}

net.CommandQueue.prototype.repeat=function(freq){        ❺  Poll the server
  this.unrepeat();
  if (freq>0){
    this.freq=freq;
    var cmd="net.cmdQueues["+this.id+"].fireRequest()";
    this.repeater=setInterval(cmd,freq*1000);
  }
}
net.CommandQueue.prototype.unrepeat=function(){        ❻  Switch polling off
  if (this.repeater){
    clearInterval(this.repeater);
  }
  this.repeater=null;
}
```

The CommandQueue object (so called because it queues Command objects—we'll get to that in a minute) is initialized ❶ with a unique ID, the URL of a server-side script, and, optionally, a flag indicating whether to poll repeatedly. If it doesn't, then we'll need to fire it manually every so often. Both modes of operation may be useful, so both are included here. When the queue fires a request to the server, it converts all commands in the queue to strings and sends them with the request ❷.

The queue maintains two arrays. `queued` is a numerically indexed array, to which new updates are appended. `sent` is an associative array, containing those updates that have been sent to the server but that are awaiting a reply. The objects in both queues are Command objects, obeying an interface enforced by the `isCommand()` function ❸. That is:

- It can provide a unique ID for itself.
- It can serialize itself for inclusion in the POST data sent to the server (see ❷).
- It can parse a response from the server (see ❹) in order to determine whether it was successful or not, and what further action, if any, it should take.

We use a function `implementsFunc()` to check that this contract is being obeyed. Being a method on the base class `Object`, you might think it is standard Java-Script, but we actually defined it ourselves in a helper library like this:

```
Object.prototype.implementsFunc=function(funcName){
  return this[funcName] && this[funcName] instanceof Function;
}
```

Appendix B explains the JavaScript prototype in greater detail. Now let's get back to our queue object. The `onload` method of the queue ❹ expects the server to return with an XML document consisting of `<command>` tags inside a central `<commands>` tag.

Finally, the `repeat()` ❺ and `unrepeat()` ❻ methods are used to manage the repeating timer object that will poll the server periodically with updates.

The Command object for updating the planet properties is presented in listing 5.14.

Listing 5.14   UpdatePropertyCommand object

```
planets.commands.UpdatePropertyCommand=function(owner,field,value){
  this.id=this.owner.id+"_"+field;
  this.obj=owner;
  this.field=field;
  this.value=value;
}

planets.commands.UpdatePropertyCommand.toRequestString=function(){
```

```
  return {
    type:"updateProperty",
    id:this.id,
    planetId:this.owner.id,
    field:this.field,
    value:this.value
  }.simpleXmlify("command");
}

planets.commands.UpdatePropertyCommand.parseResponse=function(docEl){
  var attrs=docEl.attributes;
  var status=attrs.getNamedItem("status").value;
  if (status!="ok"){
    var reason=attrs.getNamedItem("message").value;
    alert("failed to update "
     +this.field+" to "+this.value
     +"\n\n"+reason);
  }
}
```

The command simply provides a unique ID for the command and encapsulates the parameters needed on the server. The `toRequestString()` function writes itself as a piece of XML, using a custom function that we have attached to the Object prototype:

```
Object.prototype.simpleXmlify=function(tagname){
  var xml="<"+tagname;
  for (i in this){
    if (!this[i] instanceof Function){
      xml+=" "+i+"=\""+this[i]+"\"";
    }
  }
  xml+="/>";
  return xml;
}
```

This will create a simple XML tag like this (formatted by hand for clarity):

```
<command type='updateProperty'
  id='001_diameter'
  planetId='mercury'
  field='diameter'
  value='3'/>
```

Note that the unique ID consists only of the planet ID and the property name. We can't send multiple edits of the same value to the server. If we do edit a property several times before the queue fires, each later value will overwrite earlier ones.

The POST data sent to the server will contain one or more of these tags, depending on the polling frequency and how busy the user is. The server process needs to process each command and store the results in a similar response. Our CommandQueue's `onload` will match each tag in the response to the Command object in the sent queue and then invoke that Command's `parseResponse` method. In this case, we are simply looking for a status attribute, so the response might look like this:

```
<commands>
  <command id='001_diameter' status='ok'/>
  <command id='003_albedo' status='failed' message='value out of range'/>
  <command id='004_hairColor' status='failed' message='invalid property
  name'/>
</commands>
```

Mercury's diameter has been updated, but two other updates have failed, and a reason has been given in each case. Our user has been informed of the problems (in a rather basic fashion using the `alert()` function) and can take remedial action.

The server-side component that handles these requests needs to be able to break the request data into commands and assign each command to an appropriate handler object for processing. As each command is processed, the result will be written back to the HTTP response. A simple implementation of a Java servlet for handling this task is given in listing 5.15.

Listing 5.15   CommandServlet.java

```
public class CommandServlet extends HttpServlet {

  private Map commandTypes=null;

  public void init() throws ServletException {
    ServletConfig config=getServletConfig();
    commandTypes=new HashMap();        ❶ Configure handlers on startup
    boolean more=true;
    for(int counter=1;more;counter++){
      String typeName=config.getInitParameter("type"+counter);
      String typeImpl=config.getInitParameter("impl"+counter);
      if (typeName==null || typeImpl==null){
        more=false;
      }else{
        try{
          Class cls=Class.forName(typeImpl);
          commandTypes.put(typeName,cls);
        }catch (ClassNotFoundException clanfex){
          this.log(
```

```
                    "couldn't resolve handler class name "
                    +typeImpl);
          }
        }
      }
    }

    protected void doPost(
      HttpServletRequest req,
      HttpServletResponse resp
    ) throws IOException{
      resp.setContentType("text/xml");        ❷ Process a request
      Reader reader=req.getReader();
      Writer writer=resp.getWriter();
      try{
        SAXBuilder builder=new SAXBuilder(false);
        Document doc=builder.build(reader);     ❸ Process XML data
        Element root=doc.getRootElement();
        if ("commands".equals(root.getName())){
          for(Iterator iter=root.getChildren("command").iterator();
          iter.hasNext();){
            Element el=(Element)(iter.next());
            String type=el.getAttributeValue("type");
            XMLCommandProcessor command=getCommand(type,writer);
            if (command!=null){
              Element result=command.processXML(el);   ❹ Delegate to handler
              writer.write(result.toString());
            }
          }
        }else{
          sendError(writer,
            "incorrect document format - "
            +"expected top-level command tag");
        }
      }catch (JDOMException jdomex){
        sendError(writer,"unable to parse request document");
      }
    }

    private XMLCommandProcessor getCommand
      (String type,Writer writer)
      throws IOException{                    ❺ Match handler to command
      XMLCommandProcessor cmd=null;
      Class cls=(Class)(commandTypes.get(type));
      if (cls!=null){
        try{
          cmd=(XMLCommandProcessor)(cls.newInstance());
        }catch (ClassCastException castex){
          sendError(writer,
            "class "+cls.getName()
            +" is not a command");
```

```
        } catch (InstantiationException instex) {
          sendError(writer,
            "not able to create class "+cls.getName());
        } catch (IllegalAccessException illex) {
          sendError(writer,
            "not allowed to create class "+cls.getName());
        }
      }else{
        sendError(writer,"no command type registered for "+type);
      }
      return cmd;
    }`

  private void sendError
    (Writer writer,String message) throws IOException{
    writer.write("<error msg='"+message+"'/>");
    writer.flush();
    }
  }
```

The servlet maintains a map of XMLCommandProcessor objects that are configured here through the ServletConfig interface ❶. A more mature framework might provide its own XML config file. When processing an incoming POST request ❷, we use JDOM to parse the XML data ❸ and then iterate through the <command> tags matching type attributes to XMLCommandProcessors ❹. The map holds class definitions, from which we create live instances using reflection in the getCommand() method ❺.

The XMLCommandProcessor interface consists of a single method:

```
public interface XMLCommandProcessor {
    Element processXML(Element el);
}
```

The interface depends upon the JDOM libraries for a convenient object-based representation of XML, using Element objects as both argument and return type. A simple implementation of this interface for updating planetary data is given in listing 5.16.

Listing 5.16   PlanetUpdateCommandProcessor.java

```
public class PlanetUpdateCommandProcessor
  implements XMLCommandProcessor {

  public Element processXML(Element el) {
    Element result=new Element("command");       ❶ Create XML result node
    String id=el.getAttributeValue("id");
```

```
      result.setAttribute("id",id);
      String status=null;
      String reason=null;
      String planetId=el.getAttributeValue("planetId");
      String field=el.getAttributeValue("field");
      String value=el.getAttributeValue("value");
      Planet planet=findPlanet(planetId);      ❷  Access domain model
      if (planet==null){
        status="failed";
        reason="no planet found for id "+planetId;
      }else{
        Double numValue=new Double(value);
        Object[] args=new Object[]{ numValue };
        String method = "set"+field.substring(0,1).toUpperCase()
          +field.substring(1);
        Statement statement=new Statement(planet,method,args);
        try {
          statement.execute();      ❸  Update domain model
          status="ok";
        } catch (Exception e) {
          status="failed";
          reason="unable to set value "+value+" for field "+field;
        }
      }
      result.setAttribute("status",status);
      if (reason!=null){
        result.setAttribute("reason",reason);
      }
      return result;
    }

  private Planet findPlanet(String planetId) {
    // TODO use hibernate              ❹   Use ORM for domain model
    return null;
  }

}
```

As well as using JDOM to parse the incoming XML, we use it here to generate XML, building up a root node ❶ and its children programmatically in the `pro-cessXML()` method. We access the server-side domain model using the `find-Planet()` method ❷, once we have a unique ID to work with. `findPlanet()` isn't implemented here, for the sake of brevity—typically an ORM such as Hibernate would be used to talk to the database behind the scenes ❹. We use reflection to update the domain model ❸ and then return the JDOM object that we have constructed, where it will be serialized by the servlet.

This provides a sketch of the complete lifecycle of our queue-based architecture for combining many small domain model updates into a single HTTP transaction. It combines the ability to execute fine-grained synchronization between the client and server domain models with the need to manage server traffic effectively. As we noted in section 5.3, it may provide a solution for JSF and similar frameworks, in which the structure of the user interface and interaction model is held tightly by the server. In our case, though, it simply provides an efficient way of updating the domain models across the tiers.

This concludes our tour of client/server communication techniques for this chapter and our overview of key design issues for Ajax applications. Along the way, we've developed the start of a pattern language for Ajax server requests and a better understanding of the technical options available to us for implementing these.

5.6 *Summary*

We began this chapter by looking at the key roles of the application server in Ajax, of delivering the client code to the browser, and supplying the client with data once it is running. We looked at the common implementation languages on the server side and took a tour of the common types of server-side frameworks of the day. These are largely designed to serve classic web applications, and we considered how they can adapt to Ajax. The server-side framework space is crowded and fast moving, and rather than looking at particular products, we categorized in terms of generic architectures. This reduced the field to three main approaches: the Model2 frameworks, component-based frameworks, and service-oriented architectures. SOA seems to provide the most natural fit for Ajax, although the others can be adapted with varying degrees of success. We looked at how to enforce good separation of concerns in an SOA by introducing Façades.

Moving down to the fine-grained details, we contrasted three approaches to fetching data from the server, which we labeled as content-centric, script-centric, and data-centric. These form a continuum, with classic web applications tending heavily toward the content-centric style and Ajax toward a data-centric style. In discussing data-centric approaches, we discovered that there is life beyond XML, and we took a look at JSON as a means of transmitting data to the client.

Finally, we described ways of sending updates to the server, using HTML forms and the XMLHttpRequest object. We also considered bandwidth management using a client-side queue of Command objects. This sort of technique can give a significant performance boost by reducing both server load and network traffic, and it is in keeping with what we have observed about best practice in SOA, moving from an RPC-style approach toward a document-based communication strategy.

This chapter concludes our coverage of the core techniques of Ajax. We've now covered all the basics and touched on quite a few advanced topics along the way. In the following three chapters we return to the theme of usability and add some polish to the technical wizardry that we've accomplished here, in order to highlight key issues that can differentiate a clever hack from something that the lay user will actually want to use.

5.7 Resources

Several web frameworks were discussed in this chapter. Here are the URLs:

- Struts (http://struts.apache.org)
- Tapestry (http://jakarta.apache.org/tapestry/)
- JSF (http://java.sun.com/j2ee/javaserverfaces/faq.html)
- PHP-MVC (www.phpmvc.net)

There are over 60 web frameworks for Java alone listed by the Wicket developers: (http://wicket.sourceforge.net/Introduction.html).

JSF is a broad category covering many individual frameworks and products. Kito Mann, author of JavaServer Faces in Action (Manning, 2004), maintains the definitive portal site for all things JSF at www.jsfcentral.com/. Greg Murray and colleagues of Sun's Blueprints catalog discuss Ajax and JSF at https://bpcatalog.dev.java.net/nonav/ajax/jsf-ajax/frames.html. AjaxFaces is a commercial Ajax-enabled JSF implementation (www.ajaxfaces.com), and Apache's Open Source MyFaces is looking at Ajax, too (http://myfaces.apache.org/sandbox/inputSuggestAjax.html).

Microsoft's Atlas is still under development at the time of writing, but early releases are expected later this year (2005). Scott Guthrie is Project Manager of Atlas. His blog can be found at http://weblogs.asp.net/scottgu/archive/2005/06/28/416185.aspx.

You can find JSON-RPC libraries for a range of programming languages at www.json-rpc.org/impl.xhtml.

Part 3

Professional Ajax

Your Ajax application works end-to-end now and can read from the server and update data on the server. There's still some way to go though, if you want to deploy a professional-quality application to real users. We'll show you in this part how to make your application easier to use, safer to use, and fast enough to use.

The user experience

This chapter covers

- Key features of usable code
- Common notification features
- A reusable framework for notifications
- Highlighting updated data in situ

In chapter 1, we discussed usability, the keystone to any software application. No matter how well organized your codebase and how clever the technical merits of your application, if the usability stinks, you leave a bad association in the user's mind. This can be grossly unfair, but it's a fact of life. More people recognize Albert Einstein for his hangdog looks and wild hair than understand what he was trying to say about the nature of space-time. First impressions—and attention to detail—matters.

In chapters 2 to 5, we introduced a lot of cool technology and did some clever things with Ajax. The focus on organization throughout the latter part of this journey has enabled us to be flexible and highly adaptive about how we do these things. However, our examples have been rather rough around the edges, and rightly so while we focused on the cleverness at hand, but now we need to step back and assess what we have done in terms of creating something that people will actually want to use, possibly for several hours a day. The topics presented in this chapter will go a long way toward helping you get your Ajax application ready and presentable for the real world.

One of the biggest things that you can do to make your users feel comfortable with your application is to keep them informed about background events in a discrete and consistent fashion. They aren't the be-all and end-all of usability, but we will focus on them in this chapter in order to show how an in-depth, consistent treatment benefits the application as a whole. Most Ajax applications will want to notify the user at some point too, so we hope you'll find the finished components useful in your own projects as well.

We develop several solutions in this chapter for letting the users know what is going on, without getting in the way of their workflow. Before we go into these specifics, though, let's take a quick look at what we mean by quality and how to get there.

6.1 Getting it right: building a quality application

Usability is an especially hot topic for Ajax because web app users can be an extremely fickle bunch. The downside of being able to download and run your app with zero effort is that the users have invested no time and effort in it when they start to use the application and will be willing to throw it away and move on to the next of the 8 billion web pages that Google can point them to. To complicate matters further, with Ajax we are seeing the convergence of two different usability traditions, namely the desktop application and the web page. Getting the mixture right can be quite a challenge, and failing to get it right can consign your hard work to obscurity.

In chapter 1, we looked at usability from the users' point of view. What do they want in an application? And what are they willing to put up with? Let's turn the question around now and ask what qualities we need in our code to meet the goal of usability. With this as a starting point, we can figure out what we can do in practical terms to make our application work. The following sections detail a number of key features that add quality to your application.

6.1.1 *Responsiveness*

The most basic frustration that a computer user can suffer from is to have workflow interrupted while the computer struggles to catch up with him. Basic design mistakes, such as locking up the entire user interface while writing some lengthy configuration file to disk, can cause the user to lose track of what he is doing and force him to make the mental leap between the domain model in which he is engaged to the harsh reality of computer hardware.

When looking at responsiveness, it can be important to understand your target audience and its typical system setups. In the case of writing a configuration file, the speed may be acceptable on the developer's high-speed 7200-RPM SATA disk drive on the local workstation, but the customer writing the file to a congested network share or a USB thumb drive may have a different experience. In the specific case of web app development, a similar mistake is often made in only testing the application running over the loopback interface, that is, the web server running on the same development machine as the web browser. This doesn't give a useful evaluation of network latency issues, and all web apps ought to be either tested over a real LAN or WAN or simulated using a traffic-shaping tool.

Beyond network issues, the performance of the client code can make a huge difference to responsiveness. Performance is a big issue, so we'll defer a closer look at it to chapter 7.

6.1.2 *Robustness*

An application is *robust* if it can withstand the usual conditions encountered at a busy workstation. How does it cope with a temporary network outage? If a badly behaved program hogs the CPU for five minutes, will your application still work afterwards? At one recent project that I was involved in, we would test our application's robustness by pounding randomly on the keyboard for 10 seconds or so, and by "scribbling" the mouse across the page while clicking it. A crude sort of test—but effective—and quite good fun!

What can such a test reveal? For one thing, it can highlight inefficiencies in event-handler code. Keypresses, mouse moves, and the like need to return quickly, since they are apt to be called very frequently. Further, they can reveal unintentional dependencies between components. A particular condition may arise in a GUI, for example, where a modal dialog is blocking access to the main application, but an open menu item is blocking access to the modal dialog. If such a situation depends on precise timing in the opening of the dialog and the menu, it might take a single user two months of daily work to discover it. Once released to an audience of several thousand, however, it might start showing up within hours and be extremely hard to reproduce from field reports. Identifying the problem up front, and correcting it, increases the overall robustness of the application.

There is more to robustness than randomly thumping the keyboard. Just as valuable is the process of watching someone other than the developer trying to use the application. In the case of a complete newcomer, this can provide helpful information on the overall usability design, but it is also useful to let someone closely acquainted with the domain knowledge, even the product, test-drive a new bit of functionality. When the person who wrote the code runs the program, she can "see" the code behind it and may subconsciously avoid specific combinations of actions or particular actions in specific contexts. The end user won't have this insider knowledge, of course, and neither will the developer sitting next to you (unless you do pair programming). Getting someone else to informally run through your app workflow can help to build up robustness early on.

6.1.3 *Consistency*

As we already noted, the usability patterns of Ajax are still evolving from a mishmash of desktop application and web browser conventions. Some Ajax toolkits, such as Bindows, qooxdoo, and Backbase, even present widget sets deliberately styled to look like desktop application buttons, trees, and tables.

The right answer to this conundrum is still being worked out by webmasters, usability gurus, and everyday users of the Web as it continues to evolve. In the meantime, the best advice available is to keep things consistent. If one part of your application uses web-style single clicks to launch pop-up windows, and another part requires double-clicks on similar-looking icons, your user will quickly become confused. And if you must have a talking pig that guides your users around the site, make sure that it doesn't suddenly change its accent, costume, or hairstyle halfway through!

From the point of view of your codebase, consistency and reuse go hand in hand. If you cut and paste functionality from one location to another, and then respond to a change request in three copies of the button-rendering code but miss a fourth, the consistency of your interface will erode over time. If there is only one copy of the button-rendering code that everyone uses, then the consistency of your application is likely to remain high. This applies not only to visual UI behavior but also to less-visible parts of the interface, such as network timeouts and responses to bad data.

6.1.4 *Simplicity*

Finally, we need to stress the importance of simplicity. Ajax allows you to do a number of wild and creative things, the likes of which have never been seen in a web page before. Some of these things have never been seen because the necessary technology is only just arriving on the scene. In other cases, there are good reasons for not implementing a feature. Spring-loaded menus that bounce onto the screen and gradually dampen their oscillations may be great fun to code and great fun for a short-term user dropping by for five minutes to let off steam. If the user is going to use the application for several hours a day, though, she is less likely to appreciate the fun by the day's end.

It is always worth asking whether a new feature will actually improve the end experience. In many cases with Ajax, the answer will be yes, and the developer can concentrate on coding features that will be genuinely beneficial.

6.1.5 *Making it work*

It's probably the case that your code doesn't exhibit all the features we just mentioned. Mine certainly doesn't. These are merely ideals that we've presented. Making the effort to move toward these ideals can pay big dividends when it comes to maintaining your codebase in the future, and refactoring existing code can introduce these qualities as you go along. Choosing where to concentrate the effort is something of a black art, and the only way to get good at it is by practicing. If you're new to refactoring, start with something small and gradually work outward. Remember, refactoring is an incremental process, and you can add quality to your code without pulling it apart and leaving bits on the floor for weeks on end.

In the remainder of this chapter, we'll look at some specific features that you can build into Ajax applications. A large part of the chapter focuses on notification frameworks, which are ways of keeping the user informed while background processes such as calculations or network requests take place. By providing the user with a visual cue that the process is under way, we improve the responsiveness of the application. By running all such notifications through a common framework, we ensure that presentation is consistent and make it simple for the user to work with the notifications because everything works in the same way.

Let's start off by looking at the various ways in which we can notify the user of events taking place within the application.

6.2 *Keeping the user informed*

In an Ajax application, we may often need to run off across the network and fetch some resources from the server and then pick up the results in a callback function and do something with them. If we were handling server requests synchronously, we would have a relatively easy time working out how to handle this in user interface terms. The request would be initiated, the entire user interface would lock up and stop responding, and when the results come back from the server, the interface would update itself and then start responding to input. What's good for the developer here is lousy for the user, of course, so we make use of an asynchronous request mechanism. This makes the business of communicating server updates through the user interface that much more complicated.

6.2.1 *Handling responses to our own requests*

Let's pick up a concrete example to work with. The planetary information viewer that we developed in chapter 5 allowed the user to update a couple of editable properties for planets: the diameter and the distance from the sun (see section 5.5). These updates are submitted to the server, which then responds, saying whether it has accepted or rejected them. With the introduction of the command queue concept in section 5.5.3, we allowed each server response to carry acknowledgments to several updates from a given user. A sample XML response document follows, showing one successful and one unsuccessful command:

```
<commands>
  <command id='001_diameter' status='ok'/>
  <command id='003_albedo' status='failed'
   message='value out of range'/>
</commands>
```

From the user's perspective, she edits the property and then moves on to some other task, such as editing the list of facts associated with that planet or even staring out of the window. Her attention is no longer on the diameter of the planet Mercury. Meanwhile, in the background, the updated value has been wrapped in a JavaScript Command object, which has entered the queue of outgoing messages and will be sent to the server shortly thereafter. The Command object is then transferred to the "sent" queue and is retrieved when the response returns, possibly along with a number of other updates. The Command object is then responsible for processing the update and taking appropriate action.

Let's recap where we had left this code before we start refactoring. Here is our implementation of the Command object's `parseResponse()` method, as presented in chapter 5:

```
planets.commands.UpdatePropertyCommand
  .parseResponse=function(docEl){
  var attrs=docEl.attributes;
  var status=attrs.getNamedItem("status").value;
  if (status!="ok"){
    var reason=attrs.getNamedItem("message").value;
    alert("failed to update "+this.field
      +" to "+this.value+"\n\n"+reason);
  }
}
```

This is good proof-of-concept code, ripe for refactoring into something more polished. As it stands, if the update is successful, nothing happens at all. The local domain model was already updated before the data was sent to the server, so everything is assumed to be in sync with the server's domain model. If the update fails, then we generate an alert message. The alert message is simple for the developer but makes for poor usability, as we will see.

Let's return to our user, who is probably no longer thinking about the albedo of the planet Mercury. She is suddenly confronted with a message in an alert box saying, "Failed to update albedo to 180 value out of range," or something similar. Taken out of context, this doesn't mean very much. We could upgrade our error message to say "Failed to update albedo of Mercury...," but we would still be interrupting the user's workflow, which was the reason that we switched to asynchronous message processing in the first place.

We would, in this particular case, also be creating a more serious problem. Our editable fields implementation uses the `onblur` event to initiate the process of submitting data to the server. The `onblur()` method is triggered whenever the text input field loses focus, including when it is taken away by an alert box. Hence, if our user has moved on to editing another property and is midway through typing into the second textbox, our alert will result in the submission of partial data and either mess up the domain model on the server or generate an error—and a further alert box if our validation code catches it!

A more elegant solution than the alert box is needed. We'll develop one shortly, but first let's further complicate the picture by considering what other users are up to while we make our requests to the server.

6.2.2 *Handling updates from other users*

Our planetary viewer application allows more than one user to log in at once, so presumably other users may be editing data while we are. Each user would presumably like to be informed of changes made by other users more or less as they happen. Most Ajax applications will involve more than one browser sharing a domain model, so this is again a fairly common requirement.

We can modify our XML response, and the Command queue object, to cope with this situation in the following way. For each update to the server-side model, we generate a timestamp. We modify the server-side process that handles updates to also check the domain model for recent updates by other users, and attach them to the response document, which might now look like this:

```
<responses updateTime='1120512761877'>
  <command id='001_diameter' status='ok'/>
  <command id='003_albedo' status='failed' message='value out of range'/>
  <update planetId='002' fieldName='distance' value='0.76' user='jim'/>
</responses>
```

Alongside the `<command>` tags, which are identified by the ID of the Command object in the sent queue, there is an `<update>` tag, which in this case denotes that the distance from the sun of Venus has been set to a value of 0.76 by another user called Jim. We have also added an attribute to the top-level tag, the purpose of which we explain shortly.

Previously, our command queue sent requests to the server only if there were commands queued up. We would need to modify it now to poll the server even if the queue were empty, in order to receive updates. Implementing this touches upon the code in several places. Listing 6.1 shows the revised CommandQueue object, with the changes in bold.

Listing 6.1 CommandQueue object

```
net.cmdQueues=new Array();         ❶ Global lookup

net.CommandQueue=function(id,url,onUpdate,freq){   ❷ Extra parameters
  this.id=id;
  net.cmdQueues[id]=this;
  this.url=url;
  this.queued=new Array();
  this.sent=new Array();
```

```
    this.onUpdate=onUpdate;
    if (freq){                          ❸  Polling initializer
      this.repeat(freq);
    }
    this.lastUpdateTime=0;
}

net.CommandQueue.prototype.fireRequest=function(){
  if (!this.onUpdate && this.queued.length==0){
    return;
  }
  var data="lastUpdate="+this.lastUpdateTime+"&data=";   ⟵ Timestamp requests
  for(var i=0;i<this.queued.length;i++){
    var cmd=this.queued[i];
    if (this.isCommand(cmd)){
      data+=cmd.toRequestString();
      this.sent[cmd.id]=cmd;
    }
  }
  this.queued=new Array();
  this.loader=new net.ContentLoader(
    this.url,
    net.CommandQueue.onload,net.CommandQueue.onerror,
    "POST",data
  );
}

net.CommandQueue.onload=function(loader){
  var xmlDoc=net.req.responseXML;
  var elDocRoot=xmlDoc.getElementsByTagName("responses")[0];
  var lastUpdate=elDocRoot.attributes.getNamedItem("updateTime");
  if (parseInt(lastUpdate)>this.lastUpdateTime){
    this.lastUpdateTime=lastUpdate;      ❹  Updated timestamp
  }
  if (elDocRoot){
    for(i=0;i<elDocRoot.childNodes.length;i++){
      elChild=elDocRoot.childNodes[i];

      if (elChild.nodeName=="command"){
        var attrs=elChild.attributes;
        var id=attrs.getNamedItem("id").value;
        var command=net.commandQueue.sent[id];
        if (command){
          command.parseResponse(elChild);
        }
      }else if (elChild.nodeName=="update"){
        if (this.implementsFunc("onUpdate")){
          this.onUpdate.call(this,elChild);   ❺  Updated handler
        }
      }
```

```
      }
    }
  }
  net.CommandQueue.prototype.repeat=function(freq){        ❻  Server poller
    this.unrepeat();
    if (freq>0){
      this.freq=freq;
      var cmd="net.cmdQueues["+this.id+"].fireRequest()";
      this.repeater=setInterval(cmd,freq*1000);
    }
  }
  net.CommandQueue.prototype.unrepeat=function(){          ❼  Polling switch
    if (this.repeater){
      clearInterval(this.repeater);
    }
    this.repeater=null;
  }
```

We've added quite a bit of new functionality here. Let's step through it.

First, we've introduced a global lookup of command queue objects ❶. This is a necessary evil given the limitations of the setInterval() method, which we'll discuss shortly. The constructor takes a unique ID as an argument and registers itself with this lookup under this key.

The CommandQueue constructor now takes two other new arguments ❷. onUpdate is a Function object that is used to handle the <update> tags that we introduced into our response XML. freq is a numerical value indicating the number of seconds between polling the server for updates. If it is set, then the constructor initializes a call to the repeat() function ❻, which uses JavaScript's built-in setInterval() method to regularly execute a piece of code. setInterval() and its cousin setTimeout() accept only strings as arguments under Internet Explorer, so passing variable references directly into the code to be executed is not possible. We use the global lookup variable and the unique ID of this queue to develop a workaround to this problem in the repeat() method. We also keep a reference to the repeating interval, so that we can stop it using clearInterval() in our unrepeat() method ❼.

In the fireRequest() method, we previously exited directly if the queue of commands to send was empty. That test has been modified now so that if an onUpdate handler is set, we will proceed anyway and send an empty queue in order to fetch any <update> tags waiting for us. Alongside our own edited data, we send a timestamp telling the server the date that we last received updates ❸, so that it can work out to send us relevant updates. This is stored as a property of the command queue and set to 0 initially.

We pass these timestamps as UNIX-style dates, that is, the number of milliseconds elapsed since January 1, 1970. The choice of timestamp is based on portability. If we chose a date format that was easier to read, we would run into issues with localization, differences in default formats across platforms and languages, and so on. Getting localization right is an important topic for Ajax applications, since the application will be exposed to users worldwide if it is on the public Internet or the WAN of a large organization.

In the onload() function, we add the code required to update the last updated timestamp when a response comes in ❹ and to parse <update> tags ❺. The onUpdate handler function is called with the command queue as its context object and the <update> tag DOM element as the sole argument.

In the case of our domain model of the solar system, the update handler function is shown in listing 6.2.

Listing 6.2   updatePlanets() function

```
function updatePlanets(updateTag){
   var attribs=updateTag.attributes;
   var planetId=attribs.getNamedItem("planetId").value;
   var planet=solarSystem.planets[planetId];
   if (planet){
     var fld=attribs.getNamedItem("fieldName").value;
     var val=attribs.getNamedItem("value").value;
     if (planet.fld){
       planet[fld]=val;
     }else{
       alert('unknown planet attribute '+fld);
     }
   }else{
     alert('unknown planet id '+planetId);
   }
}
```

The attributes in the <update> tag give us all the information that we need to update the domain model on the JavaScript tier. Of course, the data coming from the server may not be correct, and we need to take some action if it isn't. In this case, we have fallen back on an alert() statement compounding the problems that were discussed in section 6.2.1.

We've added quite a bit more clever code to our command queue object in the process of handling updates from other users, including passing timestamps between the client and web tiers, and adding a pluggable update handler function. Eventually we come full circle to the issue of informing the user of changes and asynchronous updates as they take place. In the next section, we look at our options for presenting this information to the user in a more workable fashion, and we'll factor out that pesky `alert()` function.

6.3 *Designing a notification system for Ajax*

The `alert()` function that we've been relying on up to now is a primitive throwback to the earlier, much simpler days of JavaScript, when web pages were largely static and the amount of background activity was minimal. We can't control its appearance in any way through CSS, and for production-grade notification, we're much better off developing our own notification mechanisms using the techniques employed to build the rest of our Ajax user interface. This also provides a much greater degree of flexibility.

If we look across the full spectrum of computer systems, we see that notifications come in many shapes and sizes, varying considerably in their impact on the user. At the low end of the scale regarding obtrusiveness are changes to the mouse cursor (such as the Windows hourglass or the Mac "spinning beach ball") or the addition of secondary icons or emblems to an image denoting the status of the files or other items in a folder. These simple indicators offer relatively little information. A status bar can provide a bit more detail on background events, and finally the full-blown dialog can show a greater degree of detail than either. Figure 6.1 illustrates a range of notification conventions being used in the KDE desktop for UNIX.

The folder called lost+found is not accessible to the current user, so a secondary image of a padlock has been superimposed over that folder. The status bar at the bottom of the main window gives further information on the contents of the folder being viewed, without interrupting the user. Finally, the error window that is presented when the user tries to open the locked folder presents a stronger notification requiring immediate action by the user.

Compared to these notifications, the use of `alert()` is essentially ad hoc, as well as being simplistic and ugly. In our quest for robustness, consistency, and simplicity, it makes sense to develop a framework for presenting notifications to the user that we can reuse throughout our application. In the following sections we'll do just that.

Figure 6.1 Various conventions for providing status information in a user interface: modifying the icons to reflect particular characteristics (here access permissions), a status bar providing summary information, and a modal dialog. The interface shown here is the KDE desktop for UNIX workstations, but similar conventions are found in most popular graphical interfaces.

6.3.1 *Modeling notifications*

As a first step, let's define what a notification message looks like. It contains a text description for the user and optionally an icon to display alongside the message.

When we notify the user of background activity, some messages are going to be more urgent than others. Rather than working out each time whether or not to show a particular message, let's define some generic priority levels, which we can then assign to each message.

In general, we want to tell the user something, which they can acknowledge and dismiss. Some messages might be important enough to stay around indefinitely until the user does dismiss them, whereas others will be relevant only for a limited time. Where a message does remove itself without user intervention, it may be in response to a callback, if it is telling the user that some background process such as a network download is under way and the process finishes before the user dismisses the notification. In other cases, such as a news feed, we may simply wish to assign a given lifetime to a message, after which it will tidy itself away.

With these requirements in mind, listing 6.3 presents a Message object, which provides a generic behind-the-scenes representation of a notification that is to be presented to the user. Once we've established this model of notification messages, we can dress them up in various ways, as we will see later.

Listing 6.3 Message object

```
var msg=new Object();

msg.PRIORITY_LOW=     { id:1, lifetime:30, icon:"img/msg_lo.png" };
msg.PRIORITY_DEFAULT={ id:2, lifetime:60, icon:"img/msg_def.png" };
msg.PRIORITY_HIGH=    { id:3, lifetime:-1, icon:"img/msg_hi.png" };

msg.messages=new Array();

msg.Message=function(id,message,priority,lifetime,icon){
  this.id=id;
  msg.messages[id]=this;
  this.message=message;
  this.priority=(priority) ? priority : msg.PRIORITY_DEFAULT.id;
  this.lifetime=(lifetime) ? lifetime : this.defaultLifetime();
  this.icon=(icon) ? icon : this.defaultIcon();
  if (this.lifetime>0){
    this.fader=setTimeout(
      "msg.messages['"+this.id+"'].clear()",
      this.lifetime*1000
    );
  }
}
msg.Message.prototype.clear=function(){
  msg.messages[this.id]=null;
}

msg.Message.prototype.defaultLifetime=function(){
  if (this.priority<=msg.PRIORITY_LOW.id){
    return msg.PRIORITY_LOW.lifetime;
  }else if (this.priority==msg.PRIORITY_DEFAULT.id){
    return msg.PRIORITY_DEFAULT.lifetime;
  }else if (this.priority>=msg.PRIORITY_HIGH.id){
    return msg.PRIORITY_HIGH.lifetime;
  }
}

msg.Message.prototype.defaultIcon=function(){
  if (this.priority<=msg.PRIORITY_LOW.id){
    return msg.PRIORITY_LOW.icon;
  }else if (this.priority==msg.PRIORITY_DEFAULT.id){
    return msg.PRIORITY_DEFAULT.icon;
  }else if (this.priority>=msg.PRIORITY_HIGH.id){
    return msg.PRIORITY_HIGH.icon;
  }
}
```

We define a global namespace object msg for our notification system, and within that an associative array from which any message can be looked up by a unique ID. The ID generation scheme will depend on the application using the framework.

We define three constants defining the three priority levels—low, default, and high—to which a message can be assigned. Each priority defines a default icon and lifetime (in seconds), both of which may be overridden by optional arguments in the constructor function. A lifetime value of -1, assigned to high-priority messages, indicates that the message will not expire automatically but will need to be dismissed explicitly, either by the user or by a callback function.

6.3.2 *Defining user interface requirements*

In MVC terms, we have provided a Model for our notification system here. To make it useful, we need to define a View. There are many possible ways of visually representing notifications. For this example, we have chosen to provide a status bar of sorts, upon which notifications are represented as icons, as illustrated in figure 6.2.

Figure 6.2   Status bar user interface for our notification system. Individual messages are represented by their icons.

The red X icon is a standard icon provided for low-level notifications by our system. The third message object on the status bar has provided its own icon, a blue, shaded sphere, which overrides the default X. Each notification that is added to this status bar can be inspected as a tooltip device, as shown in figure 6.3.

Figure 6.3   Messages on the status bar can be inspected by rolling the mouse over the icon, causing a tooltip to appear.

This mechanism is designed to be unobtrusive. The status bar occupies relatively little screen space, but it is apparent to the user when a new notification has arrived by the presence of an additional icon. For more urgent messages, we may

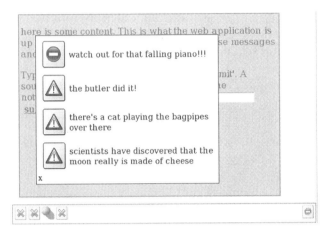

Figure 6.4   Higher-priority messages are shown in a pop-up dialog, in which messages are listed in order of priority.

wish for something more immediate. To this end, we will initially display only low-priority messages in the status bar; default and high-priority messages will first appear in a pop-up dialog, as illustrated in figure 6.4, before being dismissed.

The dialog can be modal or nonmodal. In the case of modal dialogs, we use a semitransparent layer to block off the rest of the user interface until the user dismisses the dialog. When dismissed, the dialog is represented by an icon on the right side of the status bar. In the following two sections, we'll look at implementations of these features.

6.4   *Implementing a notification framework*

We've defined two main parts to our user interface: the status bar and the pop-up dialog. Let's have a look at implementing this functionality now. The full notification system is quite complicated, so we'll break it down into stages. First, we'll enhance our Message object so that it knows how to render a user interface for itself, both for when it is sitting in the status bar as an icon and when it is showing its full details, either in a tooltip or within the pop-up dialog. Let's begin with the implementation of the status bar component.

6.4.1   *Rendering status bar icons*

The status bar needs to render itself on the screen and contain the icons representing active messages. We delegate rendering of the individual icons to the

Message objects themselves. The Message will effectively implement a small-scale MVC pattern, with the rendering ability delivering a View, whose interactive features fulfill the role of Controller. Designing it this way could be problematic if we wished to add arbitrary alternative rendering mechanisms to our notifications framework. We don't want to do that, however, because we want the notifications to be uniform across our application, for consistency's sake. Listing 6.4 shows a rendering method for the Message object.

Listing 6.4 Message framework with user interface

```
msg.Message.prototype.render=function(el){          ❶ Render message
  if (this.priority<=msg.PRIORITY_LOW.id){
    this.renderSmall(el);
  }else if (this.priority>=msg.PRIORITY_DEFAULT.id){
    this.renderFull(el);
  }
}

msg.Message.prototype.renderSmall=function(el){     ❷ Render as icon with tooltip
  this.icoTd=document.createElement("div");
  var ico=document.createElement("img");
  ico.src=this.icon;
  ico.className="msg_small_icon";
  this.icoTd.appendChild(ico);
  this.icoTd.messageObj=this;
  this.icoTd.onmouseover=msg.moverIconTooltip;
  this.icoTd.onmouseout=msg.moutIconTooltip;
  this.icoTd.onclick=msg.clickIconTooltip;

  el.appendChild(this.icoTd);
}

msg.moverIconTooltip=function(e){                    ❸ Handle mouse-over events
  var event=e || window.event;
  var message=this.messageObj;
  var popped=message.popped;
  if (!popped){
    message.showPopup(event,false);
  }
}
msg.moutIconTooltip=function(e){                     ❹ Handle mouse-out events
  var message=this.messageObj;
  var popped=message.popped;
  var pinned=message.pinned;
  if (popped && !pinned){
    message.hidePopup();
  }
}
```

```
msg.clickIconTooltip=function(e){                  ❺  Handle mouse-click events
  var event=e || window.event;
  var message=this.messageObj;
  var popped=message.popped;
  var pinned=message.pinned;
  var expired=message.expired;
  if (popped && pinned){
    message.hidePopup();
    if (expired){
      message.unrender();
    }
  }else{
    message.showPopup(event,true);
  }
}
msg.Message.prototype.showPopup=function(event,pinned){  ❻  Display tooltip
  this.pinned=pinned;
  if (!this.popup){
    this.popup=document.createElement("div");
    this.popup.className='popup';
    this.renderFull(this.popup);
    document.body.appendChild(this.popup);
  }
  this.popup.style.display='block';
  var popX=event.clientX;
  var popY=event.clientY-xHeight(this.popup)-12;
  xMoveTo(this.popup,popX,popY);
  if (msg.popper && msg.popper!=this){
    msg.popper.hidePopup();
  }
  this.popped=true;
  msg.popper=this;
}
msg.Message.prototype.hidePopup=function(){    ⟵  Hide tooltip
  if (this.popped){
    if (this.popup){
      this.popup.style.display='none';
    }
    this.popped=false;
  }
}
```

We've introduced the top-level rendering code for our Message object, and the specific details for the representation used in the status bar here. Let's address the top-level code first. We provide a render() method ❶, which takes a DOM element as an argument. This delegates to either a renderSmall() ❷ or render-Full() ❸ method, based on the priority of the message. Messages being shown in the status bar are always low priority, and will be displayed as an icon that presents a tooltip on mouseover (see figures 6.2 and 6.3).

renderSmall() renders the icon inside the DOM element and provides event handlers for displaying the pop-up tooltip.

Because this chapter is about adding professional polish to Ajax applications, the tooltip that we create for the icon has been implemented in a complete fashion, with three event handlers. It will appear when the mouse rolls over the icon ❹ and disappear when the mouse moves off the icon ❺. If the icon is clicked, however, the tooltip becomes "pinned" ❻ and will stay in place until either the icon is clicked again, the message expires, or another tooltip is selected (only one tooltip will be visible at any given time).

6.4.2 Rendering detailed notifications

Messages in the dialog are either default or high priority, and will display an icon and a message alongside (see figure 6.4). We also need this type of display for the status-bar icons' tooltips. When the tooltip is invoked in showPopup(), it calls the renderFull() method to present the full details of the message. The same method is reused to render messages in the dialog. This reuse saves us from duplicating unnecessary code and also ensures a high degree of visual consistency in the user interface. The renderFull() method is presented in listing 6.5.

Listing 6.5 renderFull() method

```
msg.Message.prototype.renderFull=function(el){
  var inTable=(el.tagName=="TBODY");
  var topEl=null;
  this.row=document.createElement("tr");
  if (!inTable){
    topEl=document.createElement("table");
    var bod=document.createElement("tbody");
    topEl.appendChild(bod);
    bod.appendChild(this.row);
  }else{
    topEl=this.row;
  }

  var icoTd=document.createElement("td");
  icoTd.valign='center';
  this.row.appendChild(icoTd);
  var ico=document.createElement("img");
  ico.src=this.icon;
  icoTd.className="msg_large_icon";
  icoTd.appendChild(ico);
```

```
var txtTd=document.createElement("td");
txtTd.valign='top';
txtTd.className="msg_text";
this.row.appendChild(txtTd);
txtTd.innerHTML=this.message;

el.appendChild(topEl);
}
```

The `renderFull()` method generates a table row for the message. It checks the DOM element that it is being appended to, and it will append itself directly if it is a `<tbody>` tag or generate the necessary `<table>` and `<tbody>` tags if not. This allows multiple messages to be presented in the same table in the main dialog and the tooltip `<div>` tag to be correctly populated.

Note that the message text is attached to the user interface using `innerHTML` rather than the W3C DOM methods that we usually use. This allows notifications to use HTML markup to present themselves in a richer fashion than if we were simply generating a text node.

6.4.3 *Putting the pieces together*

Having provided mechanisms for iconized and full-size display of messages, we've provided a comprehensive `render()` method for individual messages. The dialog and status bar themselves are generated by a top-level `render()` method, as shown in listing 6.6.

Listing 6.6 `msg.render()` function

```
msg.render=function(msgbar){
  if (!msgbar){
    msgbar='msgbar';
  }
  msg.msgbarDiv=xGetElementById(msgbar);        ❶ Ensure status
  if (!msg.msgbarDiv){                             bar exists
    msg.msgbarDiv=msg.createBar(msgbar);
  }
  styling.removeAllChildren(msg.msgbarDiv);
  var lows=new Array();
  var meds=new Array();
  var highs=new Array();
  for (var i in msg.messages){       ❷ Sort messages by priority
    var message=msg.messages[i];
    if (message){
      if (message.priority<=msg.PRIORITY_LOW.id){
        lows.append (message);
```

```
        }else if (message.priority==msg.PRIORITY_DEFAULT.id){
          meds.append(message);
        }else if (message.priority>=msg.PRIORITY_HIGH.id){
          highs.append(message);
        }
      }
    }
    for (var i=0;i<lows.length;i++){        ❸  Render low-priority messages
      lows[i].render(msg.msgbarDiv);
    }
    if (meds.length+highs.length>0){        ❹  Render higher-priority messages
      msg.dialog=xGetElementById(msgbar+"_dialog");
      if (!msg.dialog){
        msg.dialog=msg.createDialog(
          msgbar+"_dialog",
          msg.msgbarDiv,
          (highs.length>0) );         ❺  Ensure dialog exists

      }
      styling.removeAllChildren(msg.dialog.tbod);
      for (var i=0;i<highs.length;i++){
        highs[i].render(msg.dialog.tbod);
      }
      for (var i=0;i<meds.length;i++){
        meds[i].render(msg.dialog.tbod);
      }
      if (highs.length>0){
        msg.dialog.ico.src=msg.PRIORITY_HIGH.icon;
      }else{
        msg.dialog.ico.src=msg.PRIORITY_DEFAULT.icon;
      }
    }
  }
}

msg.createBar=function(id){        ❻  Create a status bar
  var msgbar=document.createElement("div");
  msgbar.className='msgbar';
  msgbar.id=id;
  var parentEl=document.body;
  parentEl.append(msgbar);
  return msgbar;
}

msg.createDialog=function(id,bar,isModal){        ❼  Create a pop-up dialog
  var dialog=document.createElement("div");
  dialog.className='dialog';
  dialog.id=id;
  var tbl=document.createElement("table");
  dialog.appendChild(tbl);
  dialog.tbod=document.createElement("tbody");
  tbl.appendChild(dialog.tbod);
```

```
var closeButton=document.createElement("div");
closeButton.dialog=dialog;
closeButton.onclick=msg.hideDialog;
var closeTxt=document.createTextNode("x");
closeButton.appendChild(closeTxt);
dialog.appendChild(closeButton);

if (isModal){        ❽  Add modal layer if need be
  dialog.modalLayer=document.createElement("div");
  dialog.modalLayer.className='modal';
  dialog.modalLayer.appendChild(dialog);
  document.body.appendChild(dialog.modalLayer);
}else{
  dialog.className+=' non-modal';
  document.body.appendChild(dialog);
}

dialog.ico=document.createElement("img");
dialog.ico.className="msg_dialog_icon";
dialog.ico.dialog=dialog;
dialog.ico.onclick=msg.showDialog;
bar.appendChild(dialog.ico);

return dialog;
}

msg.hideDialog=function(e){   ⟵  Hide the dialog
  var dialog=(this.dialog) ? this.dialog : msg.dialog;
  if (dialog){
    if (dialog.modalLayer){
      dialog.modalLayer.style.display='none';
    }else{
      dialog.style.display='none';
    }
  }
}

msg.showDialog=function(e){   ⟵  Show the dialog
  var dialog=(this.dialog) ? this.dialog : msg.dialog;
  if (dialog){
    if (dialog.modalLayer){
      dialog.modalLayer.style.display='block';
    }else{
      dialog.style.display='block';
    }
  }
}
```

render() can be called more than once. It will check for the presence of the common UI components ❶, ❺ and create them if necessary, using the createDialog() ❼ and createBar() ❻ functions. These assemble the UI components using standard DOM manipulation methods and event handlers, such as those used to show and hide the dialog.

To render all notifications, the system first sorts them by priority into three temporary arrays ❷. Low-priority messages are then rendered to the status bar ❸ and other messages to the dialog, higher-priority messages first ❹.

To implement a modal dialog, we simply nest the visible dialog within another DIV element that occupies the entire screen, blocking any mouse events from getting through to the main user interface ❽. This modal DIV has a background pattern of alternating white and transparent pixels to gray out the interface, giving a clear indication that the dialog is modal. We use this rather than CSS transparency settings because the latter will make any nested elements, such as the dialog itself, transparent, too. This is implemented in the CSS file for our notification framework, presented in listing 6.7.

Listing 6.7   msg.css

```
.msg_small_icon{
  height: 32px;
  width: 32px;
  position:relative;
  float:left;
}

.msg_dialog_icon{
  height: 32px;
  width: 32px;
  position:relative;
  float:right;
}

.msg_large_icon{
  height: 64px;
  width: 64px;
}

.msg_text{
  font-family: arial;
  font-weight: light;
  font-size: 14pt;
  color: blue;
}
```

```
.msgbar{
  position:relative;
  background-color: white;
  border: solid blue 1px;
  width: 100%;
  height: 38px;
  padding: 2px;
}

.dialog{
  position: absolute;
  background-color: white;
  border: solid blue 1px;
  width: 420px;
  top: 64px;
  left: 64px;
  padding: 4px;
}

.popup{
  position: absolute;
  background-color: white;
  border: solid blue 1px;
  padding: 4px;
}

.non-modal{
}

.modal{
  position: absolute;
  top: 0px;
  left: 0px;
  width: 100%;
  height: 100%;
  background-image:url(img/modal_overlay.gif);
}
```

It's worth noting the use of the CSS float attribute in the msg_small_icon and msg_dialog_icon classes, which are used to render the icons in the status bar. msg_small_icon, which renders the icons for low-priority messages that present the tooltips, uses a left float to align them to the left edge, and msg_dialog_icon uses a right float to align the icon that launches the dialog to the right edge. The framework allows the status bar to be rendered in any shape or size of DIV element. Floating elements will align themselves in a sensible fashion, wrapping into vertically aligned bars, if needed (figure 6.5).

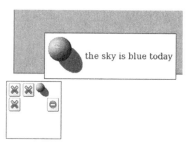

Figure 6.5
Using CSS float attributes allows a list of icons to fit into a variety of shapes of container. Here we have changed the status bar to a square, and the cross and blue sphere icons on the left wrap themselves into the new area automatically, while the launcher for the dialog floats to the right.

Finally, we need to modify our Message object now that we have a user interface for it. As individual messages are created, they have the ability to add themselves to the user interface and will remove themselves when the message expires. Listing 6.8 presents the changes needed to implement this functionality.

Listing 6.8   Modified Message object

```
var msg=new Object();

msg.PRIORITY_LOW=     { id:1, lifetime:30, icon:"img/msg_lo.png" };
msg.PRIORITY_DEFAULT={ id:2, lifetime:60, icon:"img/msg_def.png" };
msg.PRIORITY_HIGH=    { id:3, lifetime:-1, icon:"img/msg_hi.png" };

msg.messages=new Array();
msg.dialog=null;
msg.msgBarDiv=null;
msg.suppressRender=false;
msg.Message=function(id,message,priority,lifetime,icon){
  this.id=id;
  msg.messages[id]=this;
  this.message=message;
  this.priority=(priority) ? priority : msg.PRIORITY_DEFAULT.id;
  this.lifetime=(lifetime) ? lifetime : this.defaultLifetime();
  this.icon=(icon) ? icon : this.defaultIcon();
  if (this.lifetime>0){
    this.fader=setTimeout(
      "msg.messages['"+this.id+"'].clear()",
      this.lifetime*1000
    );
  }
  if (!msg.suppressRender){          ❶ Extra arguments
    this.attachToBar();
  }
}

msg.Message.prototype.attachToBar=function(){    ❷ Extra arguments
  if (!msg.msgbarDiv){
    msg.render();
```

```
  }else if (this.priority==msg.PRIORITY_LOW.id){
    this.render(msg.msgbarDiv);
  }else{
    if (!msg.dialog){
      msg.dialog=msg.createDialog(
        msg.msgbarDiv.id+"_dialog",
        msg.msgbarDiv,
        (this.priority==msg.PRIORITY_HIGH.id)
      );
    }
    this.render(msg.dialog.tbod);
    msg.showDialog();
  }
}

msg.Message.prototype.clear=function(){
  msg.messages[this.id]=null;
  if (this.row){                           ❸ Extra arguments
    this.row.style.display='none';
    this.row.messageObj=null;
    this.row=null;
  }
  if (this.icoTd){
    this.icoTd.style.display='none';
    this.icoTd.messageObj=null;
    this.icoTd=null;
  }
}
```

We want the framework to be easy for developers to work with, so when a message is created, we automatically attach it to the user interface ❶. Simply invoking the constructor will cause the new message to render itself. Depending on the message priority, it will attach itself to the status bar or dialog as appropriate ❷. For cases where we don't want the overhead of rendering for each message—such as when adding several messages at once—we provide a flag to suppress automatic rendering. In such cases, we can manually call msg.render() after creating a large number of messages.

Likewise, when removing a message in the clear() function, we automatically remove any user interface elements, so that the message goes away ❸.

We now have a useful framework for presenting notifications to the user. We can trigger it manually but also make use of it in our other reusable code components. In the following section, we demonstrate how to hook it up to our Content-Loader object to report on the progress of network downloads.

6.5 *Using the framework with network requests*

In chapter 5 we introduced the ContentLoader object as a common encapsulation for network traffic. We can make use of our notification framework to provide status reports on any data request that we make automatically. Let's scope out the requirements first.

When a request is made to the server, we would like to indicate that it is in progress, with a low-priority notification. To differentiate network requests from other low-level notifications, we would like to use a different icon. We have the image of the earth from our planetary viewer example in chapters 4 and 5, so let's use that.

When the network request completes, we would like the notification to be cleared and replaced by a low-level notification if everything went okay or by a medium-level notification if there was an error.

To implement this, we simply need to create Message objects at appropriate points in the lifecycle of the request, such as when the request is fired, when it completes or errors, and so on. The modified code for our ContentLoader object is given in listing 6.9.

Listing 6.9 ContentLoader with notifications

```
net.ContentLoader=function( ... ){ ... };
net.ContentLoader.msgId=1;
net.ContentLoader.prototype={
 loadXMLDoc:function(url,method,params,contentType){
  if (!method){
    method="GET";
  }
  if (!contentType && method=="POST"){
    contentType='application/x-www-form-urlencoded';
  }
  if (window.XMLHttpRequest){
    this.req=new XMLHttpRequest();
  } else if (window.ActiveXObject){
    this.req=new ActiveXObject("Microsoft.XMLHTTP");
  }
  if (this.req){
    try{
      var loader=this;
      this.req.onreadystatechange=function(){
        loader.onReadyState.call(loader);
      }
      this.req.open(method,url,true);
      if (contentType){
        this.req.setRequestHeader('Content-Type', contentType);
```

```
      }
      this.notification=new msg.Message(         ❶  Notify request has started
        "net00"+net.ContentLoader.msgId,
        "loading "+url,
        msg.PRIORITY_LOW.id,
        -1,
        "img/ball-earth.gif"
      );
      net.ContentLoader.msgId++;
      this.req.send(params);
    }catch (err){
      this.onerror.call(this);
    }
  }
},

onReadyState:function(){
 var req=this.req;
 var ready=req.readyState;
 if (ready==net.READY_STATE_COMPLETE){
    var httpStatus=req.status;
    if (httpStatus==200 || httpStatus==0){
      this.onload.call(this);
      this.notification.clear();        ❷  Clear initial notification
    }else{
      this.onerror.call(this);
    }
 }
},

defaultError:function(){                          ❸  Notify on error
  var msgTxt="error fetching data!"
    +"<ul><li>readyState:"+this.req.readyState
    +"<li>status: "+this.req.status
    +"<li>headers: "+this.req.getAllResponseHeaders()
    +"</ul>";
  if (this.notification){
    this.notification.clear();
  }
  this.notification=new msg.Message(
    "net_err00"+net.ContentLoader.msgId,
    msgTxt,msg.PRIORITY_DEFAULT.id
  );
  net.ContentLoader.msgId++;
  }
};
```

When we make a network request using `loadXMLDoc()`, we create a low-level notification ❶ and attach a reference to it to the ContentLoader object. Note that we set the lifetime to -1, so that the notification won't expire by itself.

In the `onReadyState()` method, we clear the notification if everything has gone well ❷. In the case of an error, we call the `defaultError()` method, which now generates a notification of its own ❸. The message for this notification uses HTML markup to create a richer report than plain text could.

Listing 6.10 demonstrates an example page using this modified Content-Loader.

Listing 6.10 Notifications sample page

```
<!DOCTYPE html PUBLIC "-//W3C//DTD XHTML 1.0 Strict//EN"
 "http://www.w3.org/TR/xhtml1/DTD/xhtml1-strict.dtd">
<html>
<head>
<title>Notifications test</title>
<link rel=stylesheet type="text/css" href="msg.css"/>

<script type="text/javascript" src="x/x_core.js"></script>
<script type="text/javascript" src="extras-array.js"></script>
<script type="text/javascript" src="styling.js"></script>
<script type="text/javascript" src="msg.js"></script>
<script type="text/javascript" src="net_notify.js"></script>
<script type="text/javascript">

window.onload=function(){
  msg.render('msgbar');
}
var msgId=1;

function submitUrl(){
  var url=document.getElementById('urlbar').value;
  var loader=new net.ContentLoader(url,notifyLoaded);    ❶ Make request
}                                                            to server

function notifyLoaded(){
  var doneMsg=new msg.Message(      ❷ Notify that resource is loaded
    "done00"+msgId,
    "loaded that resource you asked for: "+this.url,
    msg.PRIORITY_LOW.id
  );
  msgId++;
  msg.render('msgbar');
}

</script>
</head>
```

```
<body>
<div class='content'>
<p>here is some content. This is what the web
application is up to when not being bugged silly
by all these messages and notifications and stuff.
<p>Type in a URL in the box below (from the
same domain, see Chapter 7), and hit 'submit'.
A souped-up contentloader that understands the
notification system will be invoked.
<input id='urlbar' type='text'/> 
<a href='javascript:submitUrl()'>submit</a>
</div>
<div id='msgbar' class='msgbar'></div>
</body>
</html>
```

The page (as seen in figures 6.6 and 6.7) renders a simple HTML form into which
the user can type URLs. Clicking the submit link will attempt to load that URL ❶
and fire the `notifyLoaded()` callback function if successful. `notifyLoaded()`
doesn't actually do anything with the resource, other than report that it has
fetched it by creating another Message object ❷.

Note that the behavior on a successful request is not written into the framework but provided by a custom `onload` handler function. This allows the framework to be adapted to differing requirements. In the example in listing 6.9, we
have hard-coded the default behavior in case of error. In a real application, every
network failure may not be sufficiently important to warrant a big in-your-face
dialog. We leave it as an exercise for the reader to add a parameter to the
ContentLoader to denote the urgency of the notification required on failure (or
else provide an overridden `onError` handler with a gentler notification policy).

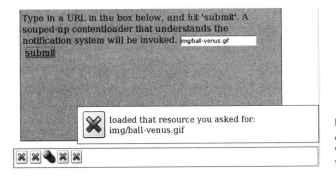

Figure 6.6
**A successfully loaded resource
will be displayed as a tooltip on
the status bar.**

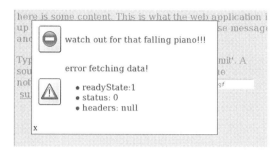

Figure 6.7
An unsuccessful network request will result in the notification dialog being shown. (There are two messages shown here, the second of which is a network error notification.)

We've taken this framework as far as we need to for now and demonstrated how it can play nicely with our existing code. In the following section, we'll look at an alternative graphical convention for notifications that can also serve us well.

6.6 *Indicating freshness of data*

The notifications framework that we developed in the previous section provides a series of new top-level components that display information about system activity. In some circumstances, we may want to display a more contextual form of notification, indicating a change to a piece of data in situ. In this section, we augment our ObjectViewer developed through chapters 4 and 5 to provide extra visual cues on recently changed data.

6.6.1 *Defining a simple highlighting style*

Let's start off with a simple way of highlighting the data by using a reverse video effect. The Object Viewer user interface is mostly quite pale, and uses blue/gray tones, so a deep red color will stand out nicely. The first thing that we need to do is to define an additional CSS class to represent newly changed data:

```
.new{
  background-color: #f0e0d0;
}
```

We have chosen a very simple styling here. In a more polished application, you may want to be a little more adventurous. Listing 6.11 shows the changes to the ObjectViewer code required to style recently edited properties as new and to remove the styling automatically after a given length of time.

Listing 6.11   ObjectViewer with styling of recent edits

```
objviewer.PropertyViewer.prototype.commitEdit=function(value){
  if (this.type=objviewer.TYPE_SIMPLE){
    this.value=value;
```

```
    var valDiv=this.renderSimple();
    var td=this.valTd;
    td.replaceChild(valDiv,td.firstChild);

    this.viewer.notifyChange(this);
    this.setStatus(objviewer.STATUS_NEW);          ❶ Set status as new
  }
}

objviewer.STATUS_NORMAL=1;
objviewer.STATUS_NEW=2;

objviewer.PropertyViewer.prototype.setStatus=function(status){
  this.status=status;
  if (this.fader){
    clearTimeout(this.fader);
  }
  if (status==objviewer.STATUS_NORMAL){
    this.valTd.className='objViewValue';
  }else if (status==objviewer.STATUS_NEW){
    this.valTd.className='objViewValue new';
    var rnd="fade_"+new Date().getTime();
    this.valTd.id=rnd;
    this.valTd.fadee=this;
    this.fader=setTimeout("objviewer.age('"+rnd+"')",5000);   ❷ Set timeout
  }
}

objviewer.age=function(id){
  var el=document.getElementById(id);
  var viewer=el.fadee;
  viewer.setStatus(objviewer.STATUS_NORMAL);      ❸ Reset status when
  el.id="";                                          timer expires
  el.fadee=null;
}
```

We define two statuses, normal and new. We could have set a boolean term isNew instead, but we chose this approach to allow for future expansion, say to style items whose updates are being submitted to the server. We call the setStatus() method when committing an edited value ❶. This sets the CSS class appropriately, and, in the case of the "new" status, it also sets up a timer that will reset the status to normal after five seconds ❷. (In real life, we'd probably want it to last longer, but five seconds is good for testing and demonstration purposes.) The object retains a reference to the timer, which it can cancel if another change of status takes place before it has expired.

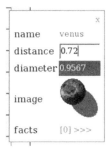

Figure 6.8
The modified ObjectViewer displaying a recently edited value for the `diameter` property, which is styled to have a colored background. The styling will disappear after a short period of time, when the edit is no longer new and noteworthy.

Because of the limitations of the JavaScript `setTimeout()` method, we assign a unique ID to the DOM node being styled, to allow us to find it again when the timer calls the `age()` function ❸. `age()` also tidies up the ID and other temporary references. Figure 6.8 shows the ObjectViewer with a recently edited value.

The user's eye will be drawn toward the recently edited value because of the change in color. Another way of drawing the user's attention is to use animation, and we'll see how simple that can be in the next section.

6.6.2 *Highlighting with the Scriptaculous Effects library*

We've created a simple styling effect by hand here, in part because it's easy to display in the static medium of a printed book with screen shots. For production, we recommend the Scriptaculous library's Effect objects as a simple way of adding sparkle to your inline notifications. We briefly introduced this library in section 3.5.2, where we noted that it provides one-line calls for styling DOM elements with a variety of animated effects and transitions.

We can easily rewrite our `setStatus()` method from listing 6.11 to make use of Scriptaculous Effects. Let's say that we want to make recently edited entries pulsate using the `Effects.Pulsate` object. This will make them fade in and out repeatedly, in a way that certainly catches the eye, but unfortunately can't be captured in a screen shot. Listing 6.12 shows the changes necessary to make this work.

Listing 6.12 Styling recent edits with Scriptaculous

```
objviewer.PropertyViewer.prototype.setStatus=function(status){
  this.status=status;
  if (this.effect){
    this.effect.cancel();
    this.effect=null;
  }
  if (status==objviewer.STATUS_NEW){
    this.effect=new Effect.Pulsate(
      this.valTd,
```

```
        {duration: 5.0}
      );
    }
  }
```

The Effect object takes care of some of the plumbing work for us, and we no longer need to manage our own timeouts. The `age()` function can be removed altogether. We simply invoke the constructor of the Pulsate effect, passing in a reference to the DOM element to operate on, and an associative array of any options whose defaults we wish to override. By default, the Pulsate effect runs for 3 seconds. We have modified it here to 5 seconds, in keeping with our previous example, by passing a duration parameter into the options array.

The same styling techniques could be applied to other events affecting the data, such as updates originating from the server. To prevent any clashes between effects, we check first for any effect that is already in progress, and cancel it. (As of version 1.1, all Scriptaculous effects respect a standard `cancel()` function.)

This kind of styling provides instant feedback to the user at the point at which his attention is already focused, unlike the status bar and dialog notifications, which are better suited to more general information. Taken together, these visual feedbacks can do a lot to improve the user experience.

6.7 *Summary*

In this chapter, we've looked at a number of topics that add a professional feel to an Ajax application. At the outset, we defined responsiveness, robustness, consistency, and simplicity as key factors in providing that sense of quality.

The majority of the chapter has been dedicated to looking at ways of providing the user with feedback while she works. Along the way, we developed several implementations of visual feedback mechanisms, including a status bar, a pop-up dialog, and inline highlighting of data. Going the extra distance to add these features can enrich the user experience considerably, and wrapping the functionality up as a reusable framework as we have done here removes a lot of burden from the developer. Having developed the frameworks, we showed how to easily integrate them with some of our previous code examples. We added status bar notifications to provide feedback on the progress of our server requests and inline highlighting of recently updated data in the ObjectBrowser that we use to view data about planets in the solar system.

That's enough glamour for now, though. The next two chapters look at topics that help the usability of an application from behind the scenes, namely security and performance.

6.8 Resources

The Scriptaculous Effects library can be found at http://wiki.script.aculo.us/scriptaculous/list?category=Effects.

Additional icons for the notifications examples were taken from the Nuvola icon set developed by David Vignoni (www.icon-king.com/).

Security and Ajax

This chapter covers

- The JavaScript security model
- Remote web services
- Protecting users' data on the Internet
- Protecting your Ajax data streams

Security is an increasingly important concern for Internet services. The Web is inherently nonsecure, and adding proper security measures to an Ajax application can be a strong differentiator for a product. Clearly, if a user's money is involved in any way, such as online shopping or providing a service that he has paid for, giving due consideration to security is essential.

Security is a big topic and deserves its own book. Many of the security issues that an Ajax application faces are the same as for a classical web application. For these reasons, we'll limit our discussion to security-related concerns that have particular implications for Ajax. First, we'll look at the security implications of shunting executable scripts around the network, and the steps that the browser vendors have taken to make this a safe experience. We'll also see the steps that may be taken to relax these safeguards, with the user's compliance. Second, we'll look at protecting a user's data when it is submitted to the server, allowing a user to work with our Ajax services confidently. Finally, we'll describe ways to secure the data services that our Ajax clients use to prevent them from being used illegitimately by external entities on the network. Let's kick off now with a look at the security implications of sending our client across the network.

7.1 JavaScript and browser security

When an Ajax application is launched, the web server sends a set of JavaScript instructions to a web browser running on a different machine, about which it knows very little. The browser proceeds to execute these instructions. In letting their web browser do this, the user of an Ajax application is placing a significant amount of trust in the application and its authors. The browser vendors and standards bodies recognized that this trust was not always appropriate, and have put safeguards in place to prevent it from being abused. In this section, we'll look at the safeguards and how to work with them. We'll then discuss situations where the constraints aren't appropriate and can thus be relaxed. The ability to talk directly to third-party web services is one such situation that should be of particular interest to Ajax developers.

Before diving any further into this topic, let us define what we mean by "mobile code." Everything on the hard disk of a computer is just a clump of binary data. We can distinguish, however, between data that is purely descriptive and data that represents machine instructions that can be executed. Descriptive data can do nothing until some executing process picks it up. In the early client/server applications, the client was installed on the user's machine just like any other desktop application, and all traffic over the network was purely descriptive data. The JavaScript code of an Ajax application, however, is executable code. As such, it offers the potential to do many more exciting things than "dead" data can. It can also be more dangerous. We describe code as *mobile* if it is stored on one machine and can transmit itself across the network to execute on another. The computer receiving the mobile code needs to consider whether it should trust the sender of the code, particularly over the public Internet. To what system resources should it grant access?

7.1.1 *Introducing the "server of origin" policy*

We noted that, when executing JavaScript in a web browser, a user is letting code written by somebody they don't know run on their own machine. Mobile code, capable of running automatically over a network in this fashion, is a potential security risk. In response to the potential dangers of mobile code, browser vendors execute JavaScript code in a *sandbox*, a sealed environment with little or no access to the computer's resources. An Ajax application can't read or write to the local filesystem. Nor can it establish network connections to any web domain other than the one from which it originated, in most cases. A programmatically generated IFrame *can* load pages from other domains and execute code, but the scripts from the two domains cannot interact with each other. This is sometimes referred to as the "server of origin" policy.

Let's take a (very) simple example. In our first script file, we define a variable:

```
x=3;
```

In the second script file, we make use of that variable:

```
alert(top.x+4);
```

The first script is included into our top-level document, which opens up an IFrame and loads a page that includes the second script into it (figure 7.1).

If both scripts are hosted on the same domain, then the alert fires successfully. If not, a JavaScript error is thrown instead, and the second script fails.

7.1.2 *Considerations for Ajax*

In the script-centric interaction that we discussed in chapter 5, JavaScript code is retrieved from the server and evaluated on the fly. In most cases, the client is consuming code from its own server, but let's consider the case where it is running code from a different domain, often referred to as "cross-scripting." Allowing the user to download scripts from arbitrary sites would open up the potential for a lot of mischief, effectively letting third parties re-author or deface websites by using

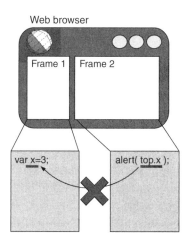

Figure 7.1
The JavaScript security model prevents scripts from different domains from interacting with one another.

DOM manipulation, for example. The limitations imposed by the JavaScript security model offer real protection from this kind of exploit. The model also prevents malicious sites from downloading your Ajax client code directly from your website and pointing it at a different server without your users knowing that they were talking to a different back-end.

In a data-centric interaction, the risk is slightly less, as the server is delivering data rather than live code. Nonetheless, if delivered from a third-party server the data might contain information crafted to do harm when parsed. For example, it might overwrite or delete vital information, or cause resources to be consumed on the server.

7.1.3 *Problems with subdomains*

Finally, note that web browsers have a fairly limited notion of what constitutes the same domain and can err frustratingly on the side of caution. The domain is identified solely by the first portion of the URL, with no attempt to determine whether the same IP address backs the two domains. Table 7.1 illustrates a few examples of how the browser security model "thinks."

Table 7.1   Examples of cross-browser security policy

URLs	Cross-Scripting Allowed?	Comments
http://www.mysite.com/script1.js	Yes	As expected!
http://www.mysite.com/script2.js		

continued on next page

Table 7.1   **Examples of cross-browser security policy** *(continued)*

URLs	Cross-Scripting Allowed?	Comments
http://www.mysite.com:8080/script1.js	No	The port numbers don't match (script 1 is served from port 8080).
http://www.mysite.com/script2.js		
http://www.mysite.com/script1.js	No	The protocols don't match (script 2 uses a secure HTTP protocol).
https://www.mysite.com/script2.js		
http://www.mysite.com/script1.js	No	ww.mysite.com resolves to IP address 192.168.0.1, but the browser doesn't try to work this out.
http://192.168.0.1/script2.js		
http://www.mysite.com/script1.js	No	Subdomains are treated as separate domains.
http://scripts.mysite.com/script2.js		
http://www.myisp.com/dave/script1.js	Yes	Although the scripts come from sites owned by different people, the domain is the same.
http://www.myisp.com/eric/script2.js		
http://www.myisp.com/dave/script1.js	No	www.mysite.com points to www.myisp.com/dave, but the browser won't check this.
http://www.mysite.com/script2.js		

In the case of subdomains, it is possible to truncate the part of the domain being matched by setting the `document.domain` property. Thus, for example, in a script served from http://www.myisp.com/dave, we can add a line to the script stating

```
document.domain='myisp.com';
```

which would allow interaction with a script served from the subdomain http://dave.myisp.com/, provided that it too sets the document.domain value. It isn't possible to set my document.domain to an arbitrary value such as www.google.com, however.

7.1.4 *Cross-browser security*

Our discussion wouldn't be complete without pointing out a glaring cross-browser inconsistency. Internet Explorer security operates on a series of "zones," with more or less restrictive security permissions. By default (for Internet Explorer 6, at least), files executing on the local filesystem are given permission to contact websites on the Internet without the user being prompted, with the

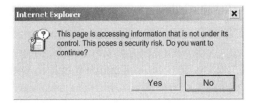

Figure 7.2
A security warning dialog is shown in Internet Explorer if the code tries to contact a web service not originating from its own server. If the user agrees to this interaction, subsequent interactions won't be interrupted.

local filesystem assumed to be a safe zone. The same code will trigger a security dialog if run from a local web server (figure 7.2).

It is possible to write sophisticated Ajax applications and test large parts of the functionality against dummy data served directly from the filesystem. Taking the web server out of the equation does simplify a development setup during intense coding sessions. However, we urge developers testing any code that is accessing Internet web services to test it on a local web server in addition to the filesystem. Under Mozilla, there is no concept of zones, and web applications served off the local filesystem are as restricted as any delivered from a web server. Under Internet Explorer, however, the code runs in different security zones under the two situations, making for a big difference in behavior.

This summarizes the key constraints within which our Ajax scripts must operate. The JavaScript security model has a few annoyances but generally works to our advantage. Without it, public confidence in rich Internet services such as those offered by Ajax would be so low that Ajax wouldn't be a viable technology for any but the most trivial of uses.

There are, however, legitimate reasons for invoking scripts from domains other than your own, such as when dealing with a publisher of web services. We'll see in the next section how to relax the security considerations for situations such as these.

7.2 *Communicating with remote services*

Building security into the web browser is a sensible move, but it can also be frustrating. Security systems have to distrust everyone in order to be effective, but there are situations where you will want to access a resource on a third-party server for legitimate reasons, having thought through the security implications for yourself. Now that we understand how the browsers apply their security policy, let's discuss ways of relaxing it. The first method that we'll look at requires additional server-side code, and the second one works on the client only.

7.2.1 *Proxying remote services*

Because of the "server of origin" policy, an Ajax application is limited to retrieving all its data from its own web domain. If we want our Ajax application to access information from a third-party site, one solution is to make a call to the remote server from our own server rather than from the client, and then forward it on to the client (figure 7.3).

Under this setup, the data appears to the browser to be coming from the local server, and so the server of origin policy is not violated. In addition, all data is subject to the scrutiny of the server, giving an opportunity to check for malicious data or code before forwarding it to the client.

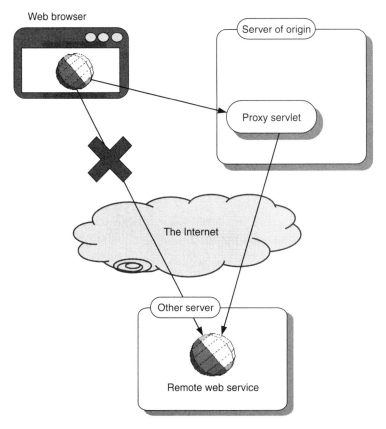

Figure 7.3   If an Ajax application needs to access resources from other domains, the server of origin can proxy the resources on the Ajax client's behalf.

On the downside, this approach does increase the load on the server. The second solution that we'll examine goes directly from the browser to the third-party server.

7.2.2 *Working with web services*

Many organizations these days provide web services that are intended to be used by external entities, including JavaScript clients. An Ajax client will want to contact a web service directly. The server of origin security policy is a problem here, but it can be overcome by programmatically requesting privileges to perform network activities. This request may be passed on to the user, or remembered by the browser and applied automatically, if the user has so instructed.

In this section, you'll learn how to call a third-party web service directly from an Ajax client application. Internet Explorer and Mozilla Firefox each handle these requests in their own ways, and we'll see how to keep them both happy.

Our example program will contact one of Google's web services using the Simple Object Access Protocol (SOAP). SOAP is an XML-based protocol built on top of HTTP. The basic principle of SOAP is that the request sends an XML document to the server, describing parameters to the service, and the server responds with an XML document describing the results. The XML sent by SOAP is rather bulky, itself consisting of headers and content wrapped up in an "envelope." Because of its use of XML, it is ideal for use with the XMLHttpRequest object.

Google offers a SOAP interface to its search engine, in which the user can transmit a search phrase in the request and get back an XML document that lists a page of results. The XML response is very similar to the data presented visually in a Google search results page, with each entry listing a title, snippet, summary, and URL. The document also lists the total estimated number of results for the phrase.

Our application is a guessing game for the Internet age. It is the estimated number of results that we are interested in. We're going to present the user with a simple form and a randomly generated large number (figure 7.4). The user must enter a phrase that they think will return a number of results within 1,000 of the number indicated when sent to Google.

Figure 7.4
Using the Google SOAP API in a simple Ajax application to entirely frivolous ends. The user can try to enter a phrase that will return an estimated number of results from Google within the specified range.

We are going to contact the Google SOAP service using the XMLHttpRequest object, wrapped up in the ContentLoader object that we developed in chapter 3. We last revised this object in chapter 6, when we added some notification capabilities to it. If we use that version of the ContentLoader to talk to Google, we will succeed in Internet Explorer but not in Mozilla. Let's quickly run through the behavior for each browser.

Internet Explorer and web services

As we already noted, Internet Explorer's security system is based on the concept of zones. If we are serving our guessing game application from a web server, even one running on the localhost port, then we are by default considered to be somewhat nonsecure. When we contact Google the first time using our ContentLoader, we receive a notification message like the one depicted in figure 7.2. If the user clicks Yes, our request, as well as any subsequent requests to that server, will go ahead. If the user clicks No, our request is canceled, and the ContentLoader's error handler is invoked. The user is not greatly inconvenienced, and a moderate level of security is attained.

Remember, if you're testing your Ajax client off the local filesystem, Internet Explorer will treat you as secure, and you won't see the dialog box.

Mozilla browsers, including Firefox, take a rather stricter approach to security, and are consequently more difficult to get right. Let's look at them next.

Mozilla's PrivilegeManager

The Mozilla browser security model is based on a concept of privileges. Various activities, such as talking to third-party web servers and reading and writing local files, are considered to be potentially unsafe. Application code seeking to undertake these activities must request the privilege of doing so. Privileges are handed out by the `netscape.security.PrivilegeManager` object. If we want our Ajax client to talk to Google, it'll have to talk nicely to the PrivilegeManager first. Unfortunately, Firefox can be configured so that the PrivilegeManager won't even listen to your code, and this setting is the default for content served from a web server rather than the local filesystem. Thus, the following technique is mainly suitable for use in intranets. If you are in such a situation, or just curious about how Firefox works, then read on.

To request a privilege, we can call the `enablePrivilege` method. The script will then be halted, and a dialog will be shown to the user (figure 7.5).

The dialog explains that the script is about to do something that might be unsafe. The user has the opportunity to grant or withhold the privilege. In either

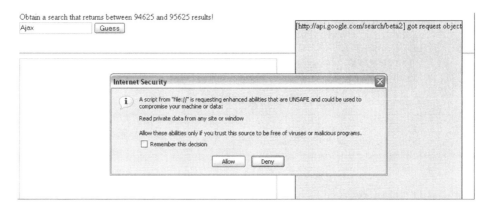

Figure 7.5 Requesting additional security privileges in the Firefox browser will result in a dialog being displayed, with a standardized warning message.

case, the script then resumes running. If the privilege has been granted, then all is well. If it hasn't, then trying to execute the action requiring the privilege will usually result in a scripting error.

We saw that Internet Explorer will automatically remember a user's first decision and stop bothering them after the first warning. Mozilla will only grant a privilege for the duration of the function in which it was requested, and unless the user clicks the "Remember my decision" checkbox, they will be interrupted by the dialog every time the privilege is required (which is twice per network request, as we will see). Security and usability seem to be at loggerheads here.

The other difference between Internet Explorer and Mozilla is that Mozilla will insist on being asked explicitly in the code before it will even show the user a dialog. Let's look at our ContentLoader object again (see chapters 3, 5, and 6), and see what we need to do to it to make the request to Google. The modified code contains requests to the PrivilegeManager object, as shown in listing 7.1. (We've also added the ability to write custom HTTP headers, which we'll need to create the SOAP message, as we'll see next.)

Listing 7.1 Security-aware ContentLoader object

```
net.ContentLoader=function(
  url,onload,onerror,method,params,contentType,headers,secure
){
  this.req=null;
  this.onload=onload;
  this.onerror=(onerror) ? onerror : this.defaultError;
  this.secure=secure;
  this.loadXMLDoc(url,method,params,contentType,headers);
}
```

```
net.ContentLoader.prototype={
  loadXMLDoc:function(url,method,params,contentType,headers){
    if (!method){
      method="GET";
    }
    if (!contentType && method=="POST"){
      contentType='application/x-www-form-urlencoded';
    }
    if (window.XMLHttpRequest){
      this.req=new XMLHttpRequest();
    } else if (window.ActiveXObject){
      this.req=new ActiveXObject("Microsoft.XMLHTTP");
    }
    if (this.req){
      try{
        try{
          if (this.secure && netscape
            && netscape.security.PrivilegeManager.enablePrivilege) {
            netscape.security.PrivilegeManager
              .enablePrivilege('UniversalBrowserRead');
          }
        }catch (err){}
        this.req.open(method,url,true);
        if (contentType){
          this.req.setRequestHeader('Content-Type', contentType);
        }
        if (headers){
          for (var h in headers){
            this.req.setRequestHeader(h,headers[h]);
          }
        }
        var loader=this;
        this.req.onreadystatechange=function(){
          loader.onReadyState.call(loader);
        }
        this.req.send(params);
      }catch (err){
        this.onerror.call(this);
      }
    }
  },

  onReadyState:function(){
    var req=this.req;
    var ready=req.readyState;
    if (ready==net.READY_STATE_COMPLETE){
      var httpStatus=req.status;
      if (httpStatus==200 || httpStatus==0){
        try{
          if (this.secure && netscape
            && netscape.security.PrivilegeManager.enablePrivilege) {
```

❶ Ask for privilege to make request

❷ Add custom HTTP headers

```
            netscape.security.PrivilegeManager        │ Ask for privilege to
                .enablePrivilege('UniversalBrowserRead');  │ parse response
            }
        }catch (err){}
        this.onload.call(this);
      }else{
        this.onerror.call(this);
      }
    }
  },
  defaultError:function(){
   alert("error fetching data!"
     +"\n\nreadyState:"+this.req.readyState
     +"\nstatus: "+this.req.status
     +"\nheaders: "+this.req.getAllResponseHeaders());
   }
 }
```

We have added two new arguments to our constructor. The first is an array of additional HTTP headers ❷, because we will need to pass these in during the construction of the SOAP request. The second is a boolean flag indicating whether the loader should request privileges at key points.

When we request privileges from the `netscape.PrivilegeManager` object, we are granted them only for the scope of the current function. Therefore, we request them at two points: when the request to the remote server is made ❶, and when we try to read the response that is returned ❷. We call the custom `onload` handler function within the scope of the `onReadyState` function, so the privilege will persist through any custom logic that we pass in there.

Internet Explorer doesn't understand the PrivilegeManager, and will throw an exception when it is referred to. For this reason, we simply wrap the references to it in `try...catch` blocks, allowing the exception to be caught and swallowed silently. When the previous code runs in Internet Explorer, it will fail silently within the `try...catch` block, pick itself up again, and keep going with no ill results. Under Mozilla, the PrivilegeManager will be communicated with and no exception will be thrown.

Let's make use of our modified ContentLoader, then, to send a request off to Google. Listing 7.2 shows the HTML required for our simple guessing game application.

Listing 7.2   googleSoap.html

```
<!DOCTYPE HTML PUBLIC "-//W3C//DTD HTML 4.0 Transitional//EN">
<html>
```

```
<head>
<title>Google Guessing</title>
  <script type="text/javascript" src='net_secure.js'></script>
  <script type="text/javascript" src='googleSoap.js'></script>
  <script type='text/javascript'>

    var googleKey=null;

    var guessRange = 1000;
    var intNum = Math.round(Math.random()
      * Math.pow(10,Math.round(Math.random()*8)));

    window.onload = function(){
      document.getElementById("spanNumber")
        .innerHTML = intNum + " and "
        + (intNum + guessRange);
    }

  </script>
</head>
<body>
  <form name="Form1" onsubmit="submitGuess();return false;">
  Obtain a search that returns between 
  <span id="spanNumber"></span>  results!<br/>
  <input type="text" name="yourGuess" value="Ajax">
    <input type="submit" name="b1" value="Guess"/><br/><br/>
    <span id="spanResults"></span>
  </form>
  <hr/>
  <textarea rows='24' cols='100' id='details'></textarea>
</body>
</html>
```

We set up the form elements in HTML, and calculate a suitably large random number here. We also declare a variable, googleKey. This is a license key allowing us to use the Google SOAP APIs. We haven't included a valid key here, because we aren't allowed to by the license terms. Keys are free, and offer a limited number of searches per day. They can be obtained from Google online through a simple process (see the URL in the Resources section at the end of this chapter).

Submitting the request

The bulk of the work is done by the submitGuess() function, which is invoked when the form is submitted. This is defined in the included JavaScript file, so let's have a look at that next. Listing 7.3 illustrates the first bit of JavaScript, which calls the Google API.

Listing 7.3 `submitGuess()` function

```
function submitGuess(){

  if (!googleKey){        ❶  Check license key
    alert("You will need to get a license key "
     +"from Google,\n and insert it into "
     +"the script tag in the html file\n "
     +"before this example will run.");
    return null;
  }
  var myGuess=document.Form1.yourGuess.value;

  var strSoap='<?xml version="1.0" encoding="UTF-8"?>'      ❷  Build SOAP message
    +'\n\n<SOAP-ENV:Envelope'
    +' xmlns:SOAP-ENV="http://schemas.xmlsoap.org/soap/envelope/"'
    +' xmlns:xsi="http://www.w3.org/1999/XMLSchema-instance"'
    +' xmlns:xsd="http://www.w3.org/1999/XMLSchema">'
    +'<SOAP-ENV:Body><ns1:doGoogleSearch'
    +' xmlns:ns1="urn:GoogleSearch"'
    +' SOAP-ENV:encodingStyle='
    +'"http://schemas.xmlsoap.org/soap/encoding/">'
    +'<key xsi:type="xsd:string">' + googleKey + '</key>'
    +'<q xsi:type="xsd:string">'+myGuess+'</q>'
    +'<start xsi:type="xsd:int">0</start>'
    +'<maxResults xsi:type="xsd:int">1</maxResults>'
    +'<filter xsi:type="xsd:boolean">true</filter>'
    +'<restrict xsi:type="xsd:string"></restrict>'
    +'<safeSearch xsi:type="xsd:boolean">false</safeSearch>'
    +'<lr xsi:type="xsd:string"></lr>'
    +'<ie xsi:type="xsd:string">latin1</ie>'
    +'<oe xsi:type="xsd:string">latin1</oe>'
    +'</ns1:doGoogleSearch>'
    +'</SOAP-ENV:Body>'
    +'</SOAP-ENV:Envelope>';

  var loader=new net.ContentLoader(          ❸  Create ContentLoader
    "http://api.google.com/search/beta2",    ❹  Provide URL to Google API
    parseGoogleResponse,
    googleErrorHandler,
    "POST",
    strSoap,
    "text/xml",
    {
      Man:"POST http://api.google.com/search/beta2 HTTP/1.1",
      MessageType:"CALL"
    },                                       Pass custom  ❺
    true                                     HTTP headers
  );
}
```

The first thing that we do in the `submitGuess()` function is check that we have a license key, and remind the user if we don't ❶. When you download the code for this example, the license key will be set to `null`, so you'll need to get your own key from Google if you want to play with it.

Our second task is to construct a monstrously huge SOAP message ❷, containing the phrase we're submitting and the license key value. SOAP is designed with automation in mind, and it is unusual to build the XML by hand as we have done here. Both Internet Explorer and Mozilla provide browser-specific objects for interacting with SOAP in a simpler fashion. Nonetheless, we thought it instructive to do it manually and look at the SOAP request and response data.

Having created the request XML text, we construct a ContentLoader object ❸, passing in the SOAP XML as the HTTP body content, along with the URL of the Google API ❹ and the custom HTTP headers ❺. We set the content-type to `text/xml`. Note that this represents the MIME type of the body of the request, not the MIME type we expect to receive in the response, although in this case the two are the same. The final parameter, set to a value of `true`, indicates that we should seek permission from the PrivilegeManager object.

Parsing the response

The ContentLoader will then make the request and, if the user grants permission, will receive an equally large chunk of XML in return. Here is a small sample of the response to a search on the term "Ajax":

```
<?xml version='1.0' encoding='utf-8'?>
<soap-env:envelope
  xmlns:soap-env="http://schemas.xmlsoap.org/soap/envelope/"
  xmlns:xsi="http://www.w3.org/1999/xmlschema-instance"
  xmlns:xsd="http://www.w3.org/1999/xmlschema">
<soap-env:body>
  <ns1:dogooglesearchresponse xmlns:ns1="urn:googlesearch"
    soap-env:encodingstyle="http://schemas.xmlsoap.org/soap/encoding/">
<return xsi:type="ns1:googlesearchresult">
<directorycategories
  xmlns:ns2="http://schemas.xmlsoap.org/soap/encoding/"
  xsi:type="ns2:array"
  ns2:arraytype="ns1:directorycategory[1]">

...

<estimateisexact xsi:type="xsd:boolean">false</estimateisexact>
<estimatedtotalresultscount
xsi:type="xsd:int">741000</estimatedtotalresultscount>

...
```

```
<hostname xsi:type="xsd:string"></hostname>
<relatedinformationpresent xsi:type="xsd:boolean">true</
   relatedinformationpresent>
<snippet xsi:type="xsd:string">de officiële site van afc &lt;b&gt;ajax&lt;/
   b&gt;.</snippet>
<summary xsi:type="xsd:string">official club site, including roster,
   history, wallpapers, and video clips.&lt;br&gt; [english/dutch]</summary>
<title xsi:type="xsd:string">
&lt;b&gt;ajax&lt;/b&gt;.nl - splashpagina
</title>

   . . .
```

The full SOAP response is too lengthy to include here, we've presented three snippets. The first part defines some of the transport headers, saying where the response comes from, and so on. Within the body, we find a couple of elements describing the estimated results count—the phrase returned 741,000 results, which is not considered to be an exact figure. Finally, we can see part of the first result returned, describing the link to the Dutch football team Ajax's home page. Listing 7.4 shows our callback handler, in which we parse the response.

Listing 7.4 `parseGoogleResponse()` function

```
function parseGoogleResponse(){
  var doc=this.req.responseText.toLowerCase();
  document.getElementById('details').value=doc;
  var startTag='<estimatedtotalresultscount xsi:type="xsd:int">';
  var endTag='</estimatedtotalresultscount>';
  var spot1=doc.indexOf(startTag);
  var spot2=doc.indexOf(endTag);
  var strTotal1=doc.substring(spot1+startTag.length,spot2);
  var total1=parseInt(strTotal1);
  var strOut="";
  if(total1>=intNum && total1<=intNum+guessRange){
    strOut+="You guessed right!";
  }else{
    strOut+="WRONG! Try again!";
  }
  strOut+="<br/>Your search for <strong>"
   +document.Form1.yourGuess.value
   +"</strong> returned " + strTotal1 + " results!";
  document.getElementById("spanResults").innerHTML = strOut;
}
```

For the moment, we aren't concerned with the structure of the SOAP message but only with the estimated number of results returned. The response is valid XML, and we could parse it using the XMLHttpRequest object's responseXML property. However, we take the path of least resistance here, and simply extract the estimated result count using string manipulation. We then use a few of our DOM manipulation techniques to present the verdict to the user (how good their guess was). For educational purposes, we also dump the entire XML response into a textarea element, for those who want to look at SOAP data in more detail.

Enabling the PrivilegeManager in Firefox

As we noted earlier, the PrivilegeManager can be configured not to respond to our programmatic pleas. To find out whether a Firefox browser is configured this way, type "about:config" into the address bar to reveal the preferences list. Use the filter textbox to find the entry signed.applets.codebase_principal_support. If the value is true, then our code above will work. If not, we won't be able to contact Google.

Earlier versions of Mozilla required that the configuration be edited by hand, followed by a complete browser restart. In Firefox, double-clicking the relevant row in the preferences list will toggle the preference value between true and false. Changes made in this way will take place immediately, without needing to restart the browser, or even refresh the page, if the preferences are opened in a separate tab.

Signing Mozilla client code

Because Internet Explorer bypasses the PrivilegeManager, the application functions smoothly enough in that browser. However, in Mozilla the user is confronted with the scary-looking dialog twice (assuming that the browser is configured to use the PrivilegeManager), making this sort of web service approach rather problematic for Mozilla users. They can prevent it from reappearing by selecting the "Remember my decision" checkbox (see figure 7.5), but we developers have no control over that (and quite rightly so!).

There is a solution, but it requires the application to be packaged in a way that is very specific to Mozilla. Web applications may be signed by digital certificates. To be signed, however, they must be delivered to Mozilla browsers in JAR files, that is, compressed zip archives with all scripts, HTML pages, images, and other resources in one place. JAR files are signed with digital certificates of the variety sold by companies such as Thawte and VeriSign. Resources inside signed JAR files are referred to using a special URL syntax, such as

```
jar:http://myserver/mySignedJar.jar|/path/to/someWebPage.html
```

When the user downloads a signed web application, they are asked once whether they want to allow it to grant any privileges that it asks for, and that is that.

Mozilla provides free downloadable tools for signing JAR files. For users who want to simply experiment with this technology, unauthenticated digital certificates can be generated by tools such as the keytool utility that ships with the Sun Java Development Kit (JDK). We, however, recommend using a certificate from a recognized authority for live deployments.

Signed JAR files are not portable. They will only work in Mozilla browsers. For that reason, we won't pursue them in any greater detail here. If you're interested in exploring this approach further, have a look at the URLs in the Resources section.

This concludes our discussion on interacting with remote services using Ajax. We've reached to the point where our application is running in the browser, exchanging data with its server and possibly with third-party servers as well. That data is unlikely to execute malicious code on your machine, but it may be a security risk of a different kind, particularly if the data is confidential. In the next section, we'll see how to safeguard your users' data from prying eyes.

7.3 Protecting confidential data

The web browser that your user is sitting in front of does not enjoy a direct connection to your server. When data is submitted to the server, it is routed across many intermediate nodes (routers and proxy servers, for instance) on the Internet before it finds your server. Ordinary HTTP data is transmitted in plain text, allowing any intermediate node to read the data in the packets. This exposes the data to compromise by anyone who has control of these intermediate nodes, as we will see.

7.3.1 The man in the middle

Let's suppose you've just written an Ajax application that sends financial details, such as bank account numbers and credit card details, across the Internet. A well-behaved router transmits the packet unchanged without looking at anything other than the routing information in the packet headers, but a malicious router (figure 7.6) may read the contents of the transmission (say, looking for credit card numbers in the content or valid email addresses to add to a spam list), modify routing information (for example, to redirect the user to a fake site that mimics the one she is visiting), or even modify the content of the data (to divert funds from an intended recipient to his own account, for instance).

Ajax uses HTTP both for transmitting the client code and for submitting data requests to the server. All of the communication methods we've looked at—

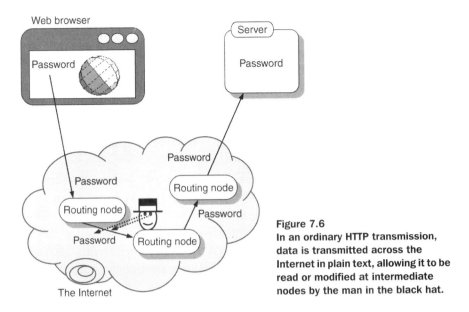

Figure 7.6
In an ordinary HTTP transmission, data is transmitted across the Internet in plain text, allowing it to be read or modified at intermediate nodes by the man in the black hat.

hidden IFrames, HTML forms, XMLHttpRequest objects—are identical in this respect. As with any web-based application, a malicious entity looking to interfere with your service has several points of leverage. Exploiting these weak points are known as "man-in-the-middle" attacks. Let's look at the measures we can take to protect ourselves from them.

7.3.2 *Using secure HTTP*

If you are concerned about protecting the traffic between your Ajax client and the server, the most obvious measure you can take is to encrypt the traffic using a secure connection. The Hypertext Transfer Protocol over Secure Socket Layer (HTTPS) provides a wrapper around plain-text HTTP, using public-private key pairs to encrypt data going in both directions. The man in the middle still sees the data packets, but because the content is encrypted, there is nothing much that he can do with them (figure 7.7).

HTTPS requires native code support on both the browser and the server. Modern browsers have good support for HTTPS built in, and most web-hosting firms now offer secure connections at a reasonable price. HTTPS is computationally expensive, and transfers binary data. JavaScript is not a natural choice here; just as we wouldn't try to reimplement the DOM, CSS, or HTTP using JavaScript, HTTPS is best viewed as a service that we use, rather than something we can override and replace for ourselves.

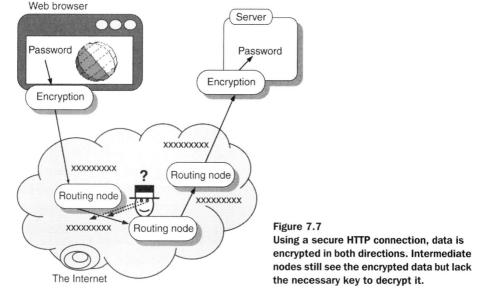

Figure 7.7
Using a secure HTTP connection, data is encrypted in both directions. Intermediate nodes still see the encrypted data but lack the necessary key to decrypt it.

Let us introduce a few caveats about HTTPS. First, the encryption and decryption do introduce a computational overhead. At the client end, this is not a significant problem, as a single client need only process one stream of traffic. On the server, however, the additional load can be significant on a large website. In a classic web application, it is common practice to transmit only key resources over HTTPS and send mundane content such as images and boilerplate markup over plain HTTP. In an Ajax application, you need to be aware of the impact that this may have on the JavaScript security model, which will recognize *http://* and *https://* as distinct protocols.

Second, using HTTPS secures only the transmission of data; it is not a complete security solution in itself. If you securely transmit your users' credit card details using 128-bit SSL encryption and then store the information in an unpatched database that has been infected with a backdoor exploit, the data will still be vulnerable.

Nonetheless, HTTPS is the recommended solution for transferring sensitive data across the network. However, we do recognize that it has its costs and might not be within easy reach of the small website owner. For those with more modest security requirements, we next present a plain HTTP mechanism for transmitting encrypted data.

7.3.3 Encrypting data over plain HTTP using JavaScript

Let's suppose that you run a small website that doesn't routinely transmit sensitive data requiring secure connections. You do ask users to log in, however, and are troubled by the passwords being sent as plain text for verification.

In such a scenario, JavaScript can come to your aid. First, let's describe the overview of the solution and then look at the implementation.

Public and private keys

Rather than transmitting the password itself, we can transmit an encrypted form of the password. An encryption algorithm will generate a random-looking, but predictable, output from an input string. MD5 is an example of such an algorithm. It has a few key features that make it useful for security. First, MD5-ing a piece of data will always generate the same result, every time. Second, two different resources are monumentally unlikely to generate the same MD5 digest. Taken together, these two features make an MD5 digest (that is, the output of the algorithm) of a resource a rather good fingerprint of that resource. The third feature is that the algorithm is not easy to reverse. The MD5 digest can therefore be freely passed about in the open, without the risk of a malicious entity being able to use it to decrypt the message.

For example, the MD5 algorithm will generate the digest string "8bd04bbe6ad2709075458c03b6ed6c5a" from the password string "Ajax in action" every time. We could encrypt it on the client and transmit the encrypted form to the server. The server would then fetch the password for the user from the database, encrypt it using the same algorithm, and compare the two strings. If they match, the server would log us in. At no time did our unencrypted password go across the Internet.

We can't transmit the straight MD5 digest across the Internet in order to log in, however. A malicious entity might not be able to figure out that it was generated from "Ajax in action", but they would soon learn that that particular digest grants them access to our site account.

This is where public and private keys come in. Rather than encrypting just our password, we will encrypt a concatenation of our password and a random sequence of characters supplied by the server. The server will supply us with a different random sequence every time we visit the login screen. This random sequence is transmitted across the Internet to the client.

On the client tier, when the user enters her password, we append the random string and encrypt the result. The server has remembered the random string for the duration of this login attempt. It can therefore retrieve the user id, pull the correct password for that user from its database, append the random term, encrypt it, and compare the results. If they match, it lets us in. If they don't (say we mistype our password), it presents the login form again, but with a different random string this time.

Let's say that the server transmits the string "abcd". The MD5 digest of "Ajax in actionabcd" is "e992dc25b473842023f06a61f03f3787." On the next request, it transmits the string "wxyz", for which we generate a completely different digest, "3f2da3b3ee2795806793c56bf00a8b94." A malicious entity can see each random string, and match them to the encrypted hashes, but has no way of deducing the password from these pairs of data. So, unless it gets lucky enough to be snooping a message whose random string it has seen before, it will be unable to hijack the login request.

The random string is the public key. It is visible to all, and disposable. Our password is the private key. It is long-lived, and is never made visible.

A JavaScript implementation

Implementing this solution requires an MD5 generator at both the client and the server. On the client, Paul Johnston has written a freely available generator library in JavaScript (see the Resources section). Using his code is just a matter of including the library and invoking a simple function:

```
<script type='text/javascript' src='md5.js'></script>
<script type='text/javascript'>
  var encrypted=str_md5('Ajax in action');
  //now do something with it...
</script>
```

On the server tier, MD5 algorithms are available for most popular languages. PHP has had a built-in md5() function since version 3. The java.security.Message-Digest class provides a base implementation for Java encryption algorithms and implementations of a number of common algorithms, including MD5. The .NET Framework provides a System.Security.Cryptography.MD5 class.

This technique has limited usefulness, since the server must already know the data being encrypted in order to facilitate a comparison. It is ideal as a means of providing secure login capabilities without recourse to HTTPS, although it can't substitute for HTTPS as an all-around secure transmission system.

Let's review where are now. The server of origin policy is safeguarding our users' computers from malicious code. Data exchanged between the client and the server is protected from man-in-the-middle attacks by HTTPS. In the final section, let's look at a third point of attack, the server itself. You'll learn how to secure your own web services from unwanted visitors.

7.4 Policing access to Ajax data streams

Let's begin by reviewing the standard Ajax architecture, in order to identify the vulnerability that we'll discuss in this section. The client, once it is running in the user's browser, makes requests to the server using HTTP. These requests are serviced by web server processes (servlets, dynamic pages, or whatever) that return streams of data to the client, which it parses. Figure 7.8 summarizes the situation.

The web services or pages are accessible by external entities, without any additional work on our part—that's just how the Internet works. It may be that we encourage outsiders to use our web services in this way, and we may even publish an API, as eBay, Amazon, and Google, among others, have done. Even in this case, though, we need to keep security in mind. There are two things we can do, which we discuss in the following two sections. First, we can design our web services interface, or API, in such a way that external entities cannot subvert the purpose of our web application—say, by ordering goods without paying for them. Second, we look at techniques to restrict access to the web services to particular parties.

7.4.1 Designing a secure web tier

When we design a web application, we typically have an end-to-end workflow in mind. In a shopping site, for example, the users will browse the store, adding items to their baskets, and then proceed to checkout. The checkout process itself will

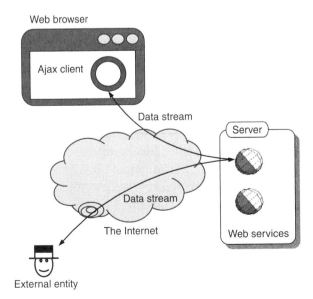

Figure 7.8
In an Ajax architecture, the server exposes web services to the Internet over a standard protocol, typically HTTP. The Ajax client fetches streams of data from the server. Because of the public nature of the web services, external entities may request the data directly, bypassing the client.

have a well-defined workflow, with choice of delivery address, shipping options, payment methods, and confirmation of order. As long as our application is calling the shots, we can trust that the workflow is being used correctly. If an external entity starts to call our web services directly, however, we may have a problem.

Screen scrapers and Ajax

A classic web application is vulnerable to "screen-scraping" programs that traverse these workflows automatically, crafting HTTP requests that resemble those generated by a user filling in a form. Screen-scrapers can deprive sites of advertising revenue and skew web statistics. More seriously, by automating what is intended to be an interaction between a human and the application, they can subvert the workflow of the application, calling server events out of order, or they can overload server processes by repetitive submission. From a security perspective, they are generally considered problematic.

The data in a classic web application's pages is often buried within a heap of boilerplate HTML and decorative content. In a well-factored Ajax application, the web pages sent to the client are much simpler, well-structured data. Separation of concerns between presentation and logic is good design, but it also makes the job of a screen-scraper easier, because the data returned from the server is designed to be parsed rather than rendered in a browser. Screen-scraping programs tend to be fragile and are prone to break when the look and feel of the site changes. Visual makeovers of an Ajax client are less likely to alter the signatures of the underlying web services that the client application uses to communicate to the server. To protect the integrity of our application, we need to give some thought to these issues when designing the structure of the high-level API used to communicate between client and server. By API, we don't mean HTTP or SOAP or XML, but the URLs of the dynamic pages and the parameters that they accept.

Example: online battleship game

To illustrate how the design of a web service API affects the security of the application, let's look at a simplistic example. We're developing an online version of the classic board game Battleship (see the Resources section), which will be played using an Ajax client that communicates to the server using web services. We want to ensure that the game is cheat-proof, even if a malicious player hacks the client, making it send data to the server out of turn.

The aim of the game is for each player to guess the position of the other's boats. The game consists of two phases. First, the players each position their pieces on the board. Once this is done, they take turns at guessing particular

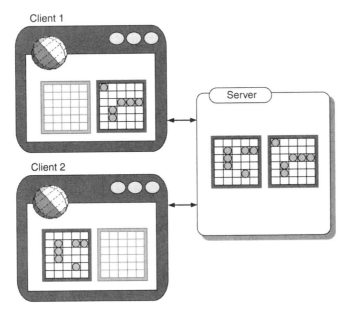

Figure 7.9 Data models in an Ajax-based game of Battleship. Once the pieces are positioned, the server will maintain a map of both players' pieces. The clients will initially model only their own pieces but build up a model of their opponent's as the game progresses.

squares on the board, to see if they can sink the other player's ships. The master copy of the board is stored on the server during a game, with each client also maintaining a model of its own half of the board and a blank copy of the other player's board, which gradually gets filled in as their ships are discovered (figure 7.9).

Let's look at the setup stage. First, the board is wiped clean. Then each piece is placed on the board, until all pieces are placed. There are two ways that we can design the service calls that the clients will make to the server during setup. The first is to use a fine-grained approach, with calls to clear the board and to add a given piece at a given position. During the setup phase, the server would be hit several times, once to clear the board and once to position each piece. Table 7.2 describes the fine-grained setup's API.

Table 7.2 Fine-grained web API for Battleship game setup phase

URL	Arguments	Return Data
clearBoard.do	userid	Acknowledgment
positionShip.do	userid shiplength coordinates (x,y) format orientation (N,S,E or W)	Acknowledgment or error

The second design is a coarse-grained approach, in which a single service call clears the board and positions all pieces. Under this approach, the server is hit only once during setup. Table 7.3 describes this alternative API.

Table 7.3 Coarse-grained web API for Battleship game setup phase

URL	Arguments	Return Data
setupBoard.do	userid coordinates array of (x,y,length, orientation) structs	Acknowledgment or error

We already contrasted these two styles of service architecture when we discussed SOA in chapter 5. The single network call is more efficient and provides better decoupling between tiers, but it also helps us to secure our game.

Under the fine-grained approach, the client takes on the responsibility of checking that the correct number and type of pieces are placed, and the server model takes on the responsibility of verifying the correctness of the system at the end of the setup. Under the coarse-grained approach, this checking is also written into the document format of the service call.

Once setup is completed, an additional service call is defined to represent a turn of the game, in which one player tries to guess the position of another's ship. By the nature of the game, this has to be a fine-grained service call representing a guess for a single square, as shown in table 7.4.

Table 7.4 Web API for Battleship game play phase (used for both fine- and coarse-grained setup styles)

URL	Arguments	Return Type
guessPosition.do	userid coordinates (x,y)	"hit," "miss," or "not your turn" plus update of other player's last guess

Under correct game play, both users may set up their pieces in any order and will then call the URL guessPosition.do in turn. The server will police the order of play, returning a "not your turn" response if a player tries to play out of turn.

Let's now put on our black hats and try to hack the game. We've written a client that is able to call the web service API in any order it likes. What can we do to tip the odds in our favor? We can't give ourselves extra turns because the server monitors that—it's part of the published API.

One possible cheat is to move a piece after the setup phase is finished. Under the fine-grained architecture, we can try calling positionShip.do while the game is in progress. If the server code has been well written, it will note that this is against the rules and return a negative acknowledgment. However, we have nothing to lose by trying, and it is up to the server-side developer to anticipate these misuses and code defensively around them.

On the other hand, if the server is using the coarse-grained API, it isn't possible to move individual pieces without also clearing the entire board. Fine-tuning the game in your favor isn't a possibility.

A coarse-grained API limits the flexibility of any malicious hacker, without compromising the usability for law-abiding users. Under a well-designed server model, use of a fine-grained API *shouldn't* present any exploits, but the number of entry points for potential exploits is much higher, and the burden of checking these entry points for security flaws rests firmly with the server tier developer.

In section 5.3.4, we suggested using a Façade to simplify the API exposed by a service-oriented architecture. We recommend doing so again here, from a security standpoint, because a simpler set of entry points from the Internet is easier to police.

Design can limit the exposure of our application to external entities, but we still need to offer some entry points for our legitimate Ajax client to use. In the following section, we examine ways of securing these entry points.

7.4.2 *Restricting access to web data*

In an ideal world, we would like to allow access to the dynamic data served from our app to the Ajax client (and possibly other authorized parties) and prevent anybody else from getting in. With some rich-client technologies, we would have the opportunity of using custom network protocols, but the Ajax application is limited to communicating over HTTP. Secure HTTP can keep the data in individual transactions away from prying eyes, as we discussed earlier, but it can't be used to determine who gets to call a particular URL.

Fortunately, HTTP is quite a rich protocol, and the XMLHttpRequest object gives us a good level of fine-grained control over it. When a request arrives on the server, we have access to a range of HTTP headers from which we can infer things about the origin of the request.

Filtering HTTP requests

For the sake of providing concrete examples, we'll use Java code here. Other server-side technologies offer similar ways to implement the techniques that we are describing, too. In the Java web application specification, we can define objects of type `javax.servlet.Filter`, which intercept specific requests before they are processed at their destination. Subclasses of `Filter` override the `doFil-ter()` method and may inspect the HTTP request before deciding whether to let it through or forward it on to a different destination. Listing 7.5 shows the code for a simple security filter that will inspect a request and then either let it through or forward it to an error page.

Listing 7.5 A generic Java security filter

```
public abstract class GenericSecurityFilter implements Filter {
  protected String rejectUrl=null;
  public void init(FilterConfig config)
  throws ServletException {
    rejectUrl=config.getInitParameter("rejectUrl");        ❶ Configure reject URL
  }

  public void doFilter(
    ServletRequest request, ServletResponse response,
    FilterChain chain)
    throws IOException, ServletException {
    if (isValidRequest(request)){                    ⬅❷ Check request validity
      chain.doFilter(request, response);
    }else if (rejectUrl!=null){                      ⬅❸ Forward to reject URL
      RequestDispatcher dispatcher
       =request.getRequestDispatcher(rejectUrl);
      dispatcher.forward(request, response);
    }
  }

  protected abstract boolean
   isValidRequest(ServletRequest request);

  public void destroy(){}
}
```

The filter is an abstract class, defining an abstract method `isValidRequest()` that inspects the incoming request object before passing a verdict. If the method fails ❷, it is forwarded to a different URL ❸, which is defined in the configuration file for the web application ❶, which we'll look at shortly.

    This filter provides us with considerable flexibility in defining a concrete subclass. We can adapt it to more than one security strategy.

Using the HTTP session

One common approach is to create a token in the user's HTTP session when she logs in and check for the existence of that object in session during subsequent requests before performing any other actions. Listing 7.6 demonstrates a simple filter of this type.

Listing 7.6   Session token-checking filter

```
public class SessionTokenSecurityFilter
extends GenericSecurityFilter {
  protected boolean isValidRequest(ServletRequest request) {
    boolean valid=false;
    HttpSession session=request.getSession();
    if (session!=null){
      UserToken token=(Token) session.getAttribute('userToken');
      if (token!=null){
        valid=true;
      }
    }
    return valid;
  }
}
```

This technique is commonly used in conventional web applications, typically forwarding to a login screen if validation fails. In an Ajax application, we are free to return a much simpler response in XML, JSON, or plain text, which the client could respond to by prompting the user to log in again. In chapter 11, we discuss a fuller implementation of such a login screen for our Ajax Portal application.

Using encrypted HTTP headers

Another common strategy for validating a request is to add an additional header to the HTTP request and check for its presence in the filter. Listing 7.7 shows a second example filter that looks for a specific header and checks the encrypted value against a known key held on the server.

Listing 7.7 HTTP header-checking filter

```
public class SecretHeaderSecurityFilter
extends GenericSecurityFilter {
  private String headerName=null;
  public void init(FilterConfig config) throws ServletException {
    super.init(config);
    headerName=config.getInitParameter("headerName");      ◁— Configure header
  }                                                              name

  protected boolean isValidRequest(ServletRequest request) {
    boolean valid=true;
    HttpServletRequest hrequest=(HttpServletRequest)request;
    if (headerName!=null){
      valid=false;
      String headerVal=hrequest.getHeader(headerName);     ❶  Get header value
      Encrypter crypt=EncryptUtils.retrieve(hrequest);
      if (crypt!=null){
        valid=crypt.compare(headerVal);     ❷  Compare header value
      }
    }
    return valid;
  }
}
```

When testing the request, this filter reads a specific header name ❶ and compares it with an encrypted value stored in the server session ❷. This value is transient and may be generated randomly for each particular session in order to make the system harder to crack. The `Encrypter` class uses the Apache Commons `Codec` classes and `javax.security.MessageDigest` classes to generate a hex-encoded MD5 value. The full class listing is available in the downloadable code that accompanies this book. The principle of deriving a hex-encoded MD5 in Java is shown here:

```
MessageDigest digest=MessageDigest.getInstance("MD5");
byte[] data=privKey.getBytes();
digest.update(data);
byte[] raw=digest.digest(pubKey.getBytes());
byte[] b64=Base64.encodeBase64(raw);
return new String(b64);
```

where `privKey` and `pubKey` are the private and public keys, respectively. To configure this filter to review all URLs under the path /Ajax/data, we can add the following filter definition to the web.xml configuration file for our web application:

```
<filter id='securityFilter_1'>
  <filter-name>HeaderChecker</filter-name>
  <filter-class>
   com.manning.ajaxinaction.web.SecretHeaderSecurityFilter
  </filter-class>
  <init-param id='securityFilter_1_param_1'>
    <param-name>rejectUrl</param-name>
    <param-value>/error/reject.do</param-value>
  </init-param>
  <init-param id='securityFilter_1_param_2'>
    <param-name>headerName</param-name>
    <param-value>secret-password</param-value>
  </init-param>
</filter>
```

This configures the filter to forward rejected requests to the URL /error/reject.do, after checking the value of HTTP header "secret-password." To complete the configuration, we define a filter mapping to match this filter to everything under a specific path:

```
<filter-mapping>
  <filter-name>HeaderChecker</filter-name>
  <url-pattern>/ajax/data/*</url-pattern>
</filter-mapping>
```

On the client side, the client can generate Base64 MD5 digests using Paul Johnston's libraries (which we discussed earlier in this chapter). To add the required HTTP header on our Ajax client, we use the setRequestHeader() method, as outlined here:

```
function loadXml(url){
  var req=null;
  if (window.XMLHttpRequest){
    req=new XMLHttpRequest();
  } else if (window.ActiveXObject){
    req=new ActiveXObject("Microsoft.XMLHTTP");
  }
  if (req){
     req.onreadystatechange=onReadyState;
     req.open('GET',url,true);
     req.setRequestHeader('secret-password',getEncryptedKey());
     req.send(params);
  }
}
```

where the encryption function is simply defined as the Base64 MD5 digest of a given string:

```
var key="password";
function getEncryptedKey(){
  return b64_md5(key);
}
```

This solution still requires us to initially communicate the variable `key` to the Ajax client. We might send the key for the session over HTTPS when the user logs into the application. In reality, the key would be something random, not a string as simple as "password" of course.

The strength of this particular solution is that the HTTP header information can't be modified from a standard hyperlink or HTML form. Requiring the hacker to use a programmatic HTTP client will stop the less determined ones, at least. Of course, as the use of XMLHttpRequest becomes more prevalent, the knowledge of how to craft HTTP headers within web page requests will spread. Programmatic HTTP clients such as Apache's HTTPClient and Perl LWP::User-Agent have been able to do this for a long time.

Ultimately, filters and similar mechanisms can't make it impossible for external agents to get into your site, but they can make it more difficult. Like any other developer, evil hackers have limited resources and time on their hands, and by securing your application in the various ways we have outlined above, you certainly discourage casual interference with your data services.

This concludes our discussion of security for Ajax applications. There are several aspects to securing an Ajax application that we haven't covered here, because they are largely the same as for a classic web application. A good authentication and authorization mechanism helps to control access to services based on roles and responsibilities. Standard HTTP headers can be used to verify the origin of callers, making it harder (but not impossible) to invoke the services outside the official channels. We recommend consulting the literature on web-based security for those of you with a deeper interest in securing your Ajax applications.

Finally, remember that security isn't an absolute state. Nothing is ever completely secure. The best that you can hope for is to be one step ahead of any intruders. Using HTTPS where relevant, minimizing exposure of your web-based API, and judiciously using HTTP request checking are all good steps in that direction.

7.5 Summary

In this chapter, we discussed security implications of using Ajax. We concentrated on security issues that were different for Ajax than for conventional web applications. First, we looked at the sandbox governing the use of JavaScript within the web browser and the rules that prevent code from different sources from interacting with each other. We saw how to relax the server of origin policy, with the user's consent, in order to access third-party Internet services such as the Google API.

Second, we looked at ways of protecting data as it passes between the client and the server. HTTPS is the recommended industry-strength solution here, but we also presented a simple Ajax-based way of transmitting passwords securely over plain-text HTTP. Finally, we saw how Ajax has a specific vulnerability owing to the way raw data is provided for consumption from the server. Having evaluated this as a serious threat in some cases, we looked at ways of designing the server architecture to minimize exposure to such risks. We also described ways of programming the server to make external access to data more difficult.

The issues that we've tackled in this chapter should help you to tighten up your Ajax applications for use in the real world. In the next chapter, we continue the theme of grim realities with a look at performance issues.

7.6 *Resources*

Keys for the Google web service APIs may be obtained at http://www.google.com/apis/.

The JavaScript MD5 libraries of Paul Johnston can be found at http://pajhome.org.uk/crypt/md5/md5src.html. For those wanting a quick taste of MD5, visit the online checksum generator at www.fileformat.info/tool/hash.htm?text=ajax+in+action.

The Apache Commons Codec library for Java, which we used to generate our Base64-MD5 on the server, can be downloaded at http://jakarta.apache.org/commons/codec/.

In section 7.1, we looked at signing JAR files to create secure applications for Mozilla browsers. The official word on that can be found at www.mozilla.org/projects/security/components/signed-scripts.html. You'll find some background information on the Battleship game at http://gamesmuseum.uwaterloo.ca/vexhibit/Whitehill/Battleship/.

Performance

This chapter covers

- Profiling Ajax applications
- Managing memory footprints
- Using design patterns for consistent performance
- Handling browser-specific performance issues

In the previous three chapters, we have built up our understanding of how Ajax applications can be made robust and reliable—able to withstand real-life usage patterns and changes in requirements. Design patterns help us to keep our code organized, and the principle of separation of concerns keeps the coupling in our code low enough to allow us to respond quickly to changes without breaking things.

Of course, to make our application really useful, it also has to be able to function at a reasonable speed and without bringing the rest of our user's computer to a grinding halt. So far, we've been operating in a high-tech Shangri-la in which our user's workstations have infinite resources and web browsers know how to make use of them effectively. In this chapter, we'll descend to the grubby side streets of the real world and look at the issue of performance. We'll be taking our idealistic refactoring and design patterns with us. Even down here, they can provide a vocabulary—and valuable insights—into performance issues that we might encounter.

8.1 What is performance?

The *performance* of a computer program hinges on two factors: how fast it can run and how much of the system resources (most crucially, memory and CPU load) it takes up. A program that is too slow is frustrating to work with for most tasks. In a modern multitasking operating system, a program that makes the rest of a user's activities grind to a halt is doubly frustrating. These are both relative issues. There is no fixed point at which execution speed or CPU usage becomes acceptable, and perception is important here, too. As programmers, we like to focus on the logic of our applications. Performance is a necessary evil that we need to keep an eye on. If we don't, our users will certainly remind us.

Like chess, computer languages offer self-contained worlds that operate by a well-specified set of rules. Within that set of rules, everything is properly defined and fully explicable. There is a certain allure to this comfortable clockwork world, and as programmers, we can be tempted to believe that the self-contained rules fully describe the system that we're working on to earn our daily bread. Modern trends in computer languages toward virtual machines reinforce this notion that we can write code to the spec and ignore the underlying metal.

This is completely understandable—and quite wrong. Modern operating systems and software are far too complicated to be understood in this mathematically pure way, and web browsers are no exception. To write code that can actually perform on a real machine, we need to be able to look beyond the shiny veneer of the W3C DOM spec or the ECMA-262 specification for JavaScript and come to grips with the grim realities and compromises built into the browsers that we know and love. If we don't acknowledge these lower layers of the software stack, things can start to go wrong.

If our application takes several seconds to respond to a button being clicked or several minutes to process a form, then we are in trouble, however elegant the design of the system. Similarly, if our application needs to grab 20MB of system memory every time we ask it what the time is and lets go of only 15MB, then our potential users will quickly discard it.

JavaScript is (rightly) not known for being a fast language, and it won't perform mathematical calculations with the rapidity of hand-tuned C. JavaScript objects are not light either, and DOM elements in particular take up a lot of memory. Web browser implementations too tend to be a little rough around the edges in many cases and prone to memory leaks of their own.

Performance of JavaScript code is especially important to Ajax developers because we are boldly going where no web programmer has gone before. The amount of JavaScript that a full-blown Ajax application needs is significantly more than a traditional web application would use. Further, our JavaScript objects may be longer lived than is usual in a classic web app, because we don't refresh the entire page often, if at all.

In the following two sections, we'll pursue the two pillars of performance, namely, execution speed and memory footprint. Finally, we'll round out this chapter with a case study that demonstrates the importance of naming and understanding the patterns that a developer uses when working with Ajax and with the DOM.

8.2　*JavaScript execution speed*

We live in a world that values speed, in which things have to get finished yesterday. (If you don't live in such a world, drop me a postcard, or better still, an immigration form.) Fast code is at a competitive advantage to slower code, provided that it does the job, of course. As developers of code, we should take an interest in how fast our code runs and how to improve it.

As a general rule, a program will execute at the speed of its slowest subsystem. We can time how fast our entire program runs, but having a number at the end of that won't tell us very much. It's much more useful if we can also time individual subsystems. The business of measuring the execution speed of code in detail is generally known as *profiling*. The process of creating good code, like creating good art, is never finished but just stops in interesting places. (Bad code, on the other hand, often just stops in interesting places.) We can always squeeze a little more speed out of our code by optimizing. The limiting factor is usually our time rather than our skill or ingenuity. With the help of a good profiler to identify the bottlenecks in our code, we can determine where to concentrate our efforts to get the best results. If, on the other hand, we try to optimize our code while writing it, the results can be mixed. Performance bottlenecks are rarely where one would expect them to be.

In this section, we will examine several ways of timing application code, and we'll build a simple profiling tool in JavaScript, as well as examine a real profiler in action. We'll then go on to look at a few simple programs and run them through the profiler to see how best to optimize them.

8.2.1 *Timing your application the hard way*

The simplest tool for measuring time that we have at our disposal is the system clock, which JavaScript exposes to us through the Date object. If we instantiate a Date object with no arguments, then it tells us the current time. If one Date is subtracted from another, it will give us the difference in milliseconds. Listing 8.1 summarizes our use of the Date object to time events.

Listing 8.1   Timing code with the Date object

```
function myTimeConsumingFunction(){
  var beginning=new Date();
  ...
  //do something interesting and time-consuming!
  ...
  var ending=new Date();
  var duration=ending-beginning;
  alert("this function took "+duration
    +"ms to do something interesting!");
}
```

We define a date at each end of the block of code that we want to measure, in this case our function, and then calculate the duration as the difference between the two. In this example, we used an alert() statement to notify us of the timing, but this will work only in the simplest of cases without interrupting the workflow that we are trying to measure. The usual approach to gathering this sort of data is to write it to a log file, but the JavaScript security model prevents us from accessing the local filesystem. The best approach available to an Ajax application is to store profiling data in memory as a series of objects, which we later render as DOM nodes to create a report.

Note that we want our profiling code to be as fast and simple as possible while the program is running, to avoid interfering with the system that we are trying to measure. Writing a variable to memory is much quicker than creating extra DOM nodes during the middle of the program flow.

Listing 8.2 defines a simple stopwatch library that we can use to profile our code. Profiling data is stored in memory while the test program runs and rendered as a report afterward.

Listing 8.2 stopwatch.js

```
var stopwatch=new Object();
stopwatch.watches=new Array();     ◁— Array of registered timers

stopwatch.getWatch=function(id,startNow){    ◁— Entry point for client code
  var watch=stopwatch.watches[id];
  if (!watch){
    watch=new stopwatch.StopWatch(id);
  }
  if (startNow){
    watch.start();
  }
  return watch;
}

stopwatch.StopWatch=function(id){    ◁— Stopwatch object constructor
  this.id=id;
  stopwatch.watches[id]=this;
  this.events=new Array();
  this.objViewSpec=[
    {name: "count", type: "simple"},
    {name: "total", type: "simple"},
    {name: "events", type: "array", inline:true}
  ];
}
stopwatch.StopWatch.prototype.start=function(){
  this.current=new TimedEvent();
}
stopwatch.StopWatch.prototype.stop=function(){
  if (this.current){
    this.current.stop();
    this.events.append(this.current);
    this.count++;
    this.total+=this.current.duration;
    this.current=null;
  }
}

stopwatch.TimedEvent=function(){    ◁— Timed event object constructor
  this.start=new Date();
```

```
    this.objViewSpec=[
      {name: "start", type: "simple"},
      {name: "duration", type: "simple"}
    ];
  }
  stopwatch.TimedEvent.prototype.stop=function(){
    var stop=new Date();
    this.duration=stop-this.start;
  }

  stopwatch.report=function(div){    ⟵  Profile report generator
    var realDiv=xGetElementById(div);
    var report=new objviewer.ObjectViewer(stopwatch.watches,realDiv);
  }
```

Our stopwatch system is composed of one or more categories, each of which can time one active event at a time and maintain a list of previous timed events. When client code calls stopwatch.start() with a given ID as argument, the system will create a new StopWatch object for that category or else reuse the existing one. The client code can then start() and stop() the watch several times. On each call to stop(), a TimedEvent object is generated, noting the start time and duration of that timed event. If a stopwatch is started multiple times without being stopped in between, all but the latest call to start() will be discarded.

This results in an object graph of StopWatch categories, each containing a history of timed events, as illustrated in figure 8.1.

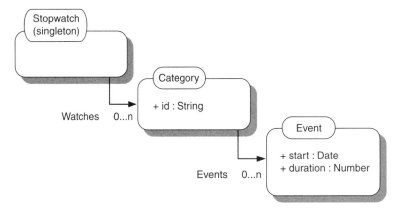

Figure 8.1   Object graph of stopwatch library classes. Each category is represented by an object that contains a history of events for that category. All categories are accessible from the stopwatch.watches singleton.

When data has been gathered, the entire object graph can be queried and visualized. The `render()` function here makes use of the ObjectViewer library that we encountered in chapter 5 to automatically render a report. We leave it as an exercise to the reader to output the data in CSV format for cutting and pasting into a file.

Listing 8.3 shows how to apply the stopwatch code to our example "time consuming" function.

Listing 8.3   Timing code with the stopwatch library

```
function myTimeConsumingFunction(){
  var watch=stopwatch.getWatch("my time consuming function",true);
  ...
  //do something interesting and time-consuming!
  ...
  watch.stop();
}
```

The stopwatch code can now be added relatively unobtrusively into our code. We can define as few or as many categories as we like, for different purposes. In this case, we named the category after the function name.

Before we move on, let's apply this to a working example. A suitable candidate is the mousemat example that we used in chapter 4 when discussing the Observer pattern and JavaScript events. The example has two processes watching mouse movements over the main mousemat DOM element. One writes the current coordinates to the browser status bar, and the other plots the mouse cursor position in a small thumbnail element. Both are providing us with useful information, but they involve some processing overhead, too. We might wonder which is taking up the most processor time.

Using our stopwatch library, we can easily add profiling capabilities to the example. Listing 8.4 shows us the modified page, with a new DIV element to hold the profiler report and a few stopwatch JavaScript methods sprinkled across the blocks of code that we are interested in.

Listing 8.4   mousemat.html with profiling

```
<html>

<head>
<link rel='stylesheet' type='text/css' href='mousemat.css' />
<link rel='stylesheet' type='text/css' href='objviewer.css' />
<script type='text/javascript' src='x/x_core.js'></script>
```

```
<script type='text/javascript' src='extras-array.js'></script>
<script type='text/javascript' src='styling.js'></script>
<script type='text/javascript' src='objviewer.js'></script>
<script type='text/javascript' src='stopwatch.js'></script>
<script type='text/javascript' src='eventRouter.js'></script>
<script type='text/javascript'>

var cursor=null;

window.onload=function(){
  var watch=stopwatch.getWatch("window onload",true);
  var mat=document.getElementById('mousemat');
  cursor=document.getElementById('cursor');

  var mouseRouter=new jsEvent.EventRouter(mat,"onmousemove");
  mouseRouter.addListener(writeStatus);
  mouseRouter.addListener(drawThumbnail);
  watch.stop();
}

function writeStatus(e){
  var watch=stopwatch.getWatch("write status",true);
  window.status=e.clientX+","+e.clientY;
  watch.stop();
}

function drawThumbnail(e){
  var watch=stopwatch.getWatch("draw thumbnail",true);
  cursor.style.left=((e.clientX/5)-2)+"px";
  cursor.style.top=((e.clientY/5)-2)+"px";
  watch.stop();
}
</script>
</head>

<body>
<div>
<a href='javascript:stopwatch.report("profiler")'>profile</a>
</div>

<div>
  <div class='mousemat' id='mousemat'></div>
  <div class='thumbnail' id='thumbnail'>
    <div class='cursor' id='cursor'></div>
  </div>
  <div class='profiler objViewBorder' id='profiler'></div>
</div>

</body>
</html>
```

We define three stopwatches: for the `window.onload` event and for each mouse listener process. We assign meaningful names to the stopwatches, as these will be used by the report that we generate. Let's load the modified application, then, and give it a quick spin.

When we mouse over the mousemat as before, our profiler is busy collecting data, which we can examine at any point by clicking the profile link in the top left. Figure 8.2 shows the application in the browser after a few hundred mouse moves, with the profiler report showing.

On both Firefox and Internet Explorer browsers we can see that in this case, the write status method takes less than one quarter the time of the draw thumbnail method.

Note that the `window.onload` event appears to have executed in 0 ms, owing to the limited granularity of the JavaScript Date object. With this profiling system, we're working entirely within the JavaScript interpreter, with all of the limitations that apply there. Mozilla browsers can take advantage of a native profiler built into the browser. Let's look at that next.

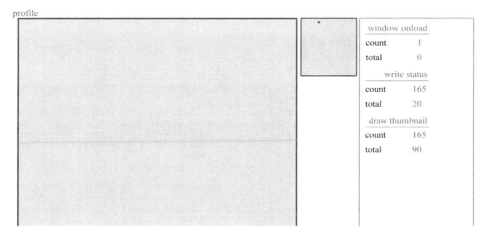

Figure 8.2   Mousemat example from chapter 4 with the JavaScript profiler running and generating a report on the active stopwatches. We have chosen to profile the `window.onload` event, the drawing of the thumbnail cursor in response to mouse movement, and the updating of the status bar with the mouse coordinates. `count` indicates the number of recordings made of each code block, and `total` the time spent in that block of code.

8.2.2 *Using the Venkman profiler*

The Mozilla family of browsers enjoys a rich set of plug-in extensions. One of the older, more established ones is the Venkman debugger, which can be used to step through JavaScript code line by line. We discuss Venkman's debugging features in appendix A. For now, though, let's look at one of its lesser-known capabilities, as a code profiler.

To profile code in Venkman, simply open the page that you're interested in, and then open the debugger from the browser's Tools menu. (This assumes that you have the Venkman extension installed. If you don't yet, see appendix A.) On the toolbar there is a clock button labeled Profile (figure 8.3). Clicking this button adds a green tick to the icon.

Venkman is now meticulously recording all that goes on in the JavaScript engine of your browser, so drag the mouse around the mousemat area for a few seconds, and then click the Profile button in the debugger again to stop profiling. From the debugger Window menu, select the Profile > Save Profile Data As option. Data can be saved in a number of formats, including CSV (for spreadsheets), an HTML report, or an XML file.

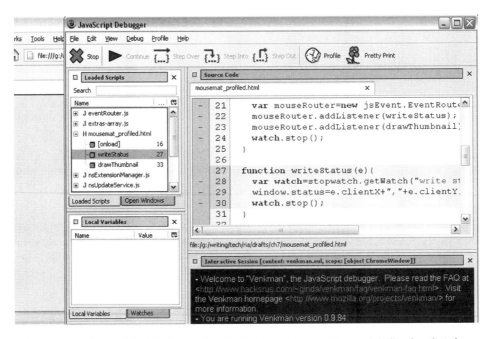

Figure 8.3   Venkman debugger for Mozilla with the Profile button checked, indicating that time spent executing all loaded scripts (as shown in the panel on the top left) is being recorded.

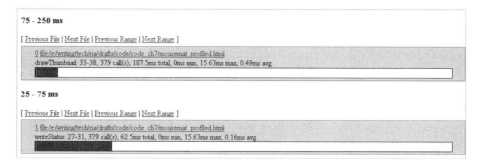

Figure 8.4 Fragment of the HTML profile report generated by Venkman showing the number of calls and total, minimum, maximum, and average time for each method that listens to the mouse movements over the mousemat DOM element in our example page.

Unfortunately, Venkman tends to generate rather too much data and lists various chrome:// URLs first. These are internal parts of the browser or plug-ins that are implemented in JavaScript, and we can ignore them. In addition to the main methods of the HTML page, all functions in all JavaScript libraries that we are using—including the stopwatch.js profiler that we developed in the previous section—have been recorded. Figure 8.4 shows the relevant section of the HTML report for the main HTML page.

Venkman generates results that broadly agree with the timings of our own stopwatch object—rewriting the status bar takes roughly one third as long as updating the thumbnail element.

Venkman is a useful profiling tool and it can generate a lot of data without us having to modify our code at all. If you need to profile code running across different browsers, then our stopwatch library can help you out. In the following section, we'll look at a few example pieces of code that demonstrate some refactorings that can be applied to code to help speed it up. We'll make use of our stopwatch library to measure the benefits.

8.2.3 *Optimizing execution speed for Ajax*

Optimization of code is a black art. Programming JavaScript for web browsers is often a hit-or-miss affair. It stands to reason, therefore, that optimizing Ajax code is a decidedly murky topic. A substantial body of folklore surrounds this topic, and much of what is said is good. With the profiling library that we developed in section 8.2.1, however, we can put our skeptic's hat on and put the folklore to the test. In this section, we'll look at three common strategies for improving execution speed and see how they bear out in practice.

Optimizing a for loop

The first example that we'll look at is a fairly common programming mistake. It isn't limited to JavaScript but is certainly easy to make when writing Ajax code. Our example calculation does a long, pointless calculation, simply to take up sufficient time for us to measure a real difference. The calculation that we have chosen here is the Fibonacci sequence, in which each successive number is the sum of the previous two numbers. If we start off the sequence with two 1s, for example, we get

```
1, 1, 2, 3, 5, 8, ...
```

Our JavaScript calculation of the Fibonacci sequence is as follows:

```
function fibonacci(count){
  var a=1;
  var b=1;
  for(var i=0;i<count;i++){
    var total=a+b;
    a=b;
    b=total;
  }
  return b;
}
```

Our only interest in the sequence is that it takes a little while to compute. Now, let's suppose that we want to calculate all the Fibonacci sequence values from 1 to n and add them together. Here's a bit of code to do that:

```
var total=0;
for (var i=0;i<fibonacci(count);i++){
  total+=i;
}
```

This is a pointless calculation to make, by the way, but in real-world programs you'll frequently come across a similar situation, in which you need to check a value that is hard to compute within each iteration of a loop. The code above is inefficient, because it computes `fibonacci(count)` with each iteration, despite the fact that the value will be the same every time. The syntax of the `for` loop makes it less than obvious, allowing this type of error to slip into code all too easily. We could rewrite the code to calculate `fibonacci()` only once:

```
var total=0;
var loopCounter=fibonacci(count);
for (var i=0;i<loopCounter;i++){
  total+=i;
}
```

So, we've optimized our code. But by how much? If this is part of a large complex body of code, we need to know whether our efforts have been worthwhile. To find out, we can include both versions of the code in a web page along with our profiling library and attach a stopwatch to each function. Listing 8.5 shows how this is done.

Listing 8.5 Profiling a `for` loop

```html
<html>

<head>
<link rel='stylesheet' type='text/css' href='mousemat.css' />
<link rel='stylesheet' type='text/css' href='objviewer.css' />
<script type='text/javascript' src='x/x_core.js'></script>
<script type='text/javascript' src='extras-array.js'></script>
<script type='text/javascript' src='styling.js'></script>
<script type='text/javascript' src='objviewer.js'></script>
<script type='text/javascript' src='stopwatch.js'></script>
<script type='text/javascript' src='eventRouter.js'></script>
<script type='text/javascript'>

function slowLoop(count){
  var watch=stopwatch.getWatch("slow loop",true);
  var total=0;
  for (var i=0;i<fibonacci(count);i++){      ⟵ Recompute loop counter every time
    total+=i;
  }
  watch.stop();
  alert(total);
}

function fastLoop(count){
  var watch=stopwatch.getWatch("fast loop",true);
  var total=0;
  var loopCounter=fibonacci(count);      ⟵ Compute loop counter once only
  for (var i=0;i<loopCounter;i++){
    total+=i;
  }
  watch.stop();
  alert(total);
}

function fibonacci(count){      ⟵ Compute Fibonacci sequence
  var a=1;
  var b=1;
  for(var i=0;i<count;i++){
    var total=a+b;
    a=b;
    b=total;
  }
```

```
    return b;
  }

function go(isFast){
  var count=parseInt(document.getElementById("count").value);
  if (count==NaN){
    alert("please enter a valid number");
  }else if (isFast){
    fastLoop(count);
  }else{
    slowLoop(count);
  }
}

</script>
</head>

<body>
<div>
<a href='javascript:stopwatch.report("profiler")'>profile</a> 
<input id='count' value='25'/> 
<a href='javascript:go(true)'>fast loop</a> 
<a href='javascript:go(false)'>slow loop</a>
</div>

<div>
  <div class='profiler objViewBorder' id='profiler'></div>
</div>

</body>
</html>
```

The functions slowLoop() and fastLoop() present our two versions of the algorithm and are wrapped by the go() function, which will invoke one or the other with a given counter value. The page provides hyperlinks to execute each version of the loop, passing in a counter value from an adjacent HTML forms textbox. We found a value of 25 to give a reasonable computation time on our testing machine. A third hyperlink will render the profiling report. Table 8.1 shows the results of a simple test.

Table 8.1 Profiling results for loop optimization

Algorithm	Execution Time (ms)
Original	3085
Optimized	450

From this, we can see that taking the lengthy calculation out of the `for` loop really does have an impact in this case. Of course, in your own code, it might not. If in doubt, profile it!

The next example looks at an Ajax-specific issue: the creation of DOM nodes.

Attaching DOM nodes to a document

To render something in a browser window using Ajax, we generally create DOM nodes and then append them to the document tree, either to `document.body` or to some other node hanging off it. As soon as it makes contact with the document, a DOM node will render. There is no way of suppressing this feature.

Re-rendering the document in the browser window requires various layout parameters to be recalculated and is potentially expensive. If we are assembling a complex user interface, it therefore makes sense to create all the nodes and add them to each other and then add the assembled structure to the document. This way, the page layout process occurs once. Let's look at a simple example of creating a container element in which we randomly place lots of little DOM nodes. In our description of this example, we referred to the container node first, so it seems natural to create that first. Here's a first cut at this code:

```
var container=document.createElement("div");
container.className='mousemat';
var outermost=document.getElementById('top');
outermost.appendChild(container);
for(var i=0;i<count;i++){
  var node=document.createElement('div');
  node.className='cursor';
  node.style.position='absolute';
  node.style.left=(4+parseInt(Math.random()*492))+"px";
  node.style.top=(4+parseInt(Math.random()*492))+"px";
  container.appendChild(node);
}
```

The element outermost is an existing DOM element, to which we attach our container, and the little nodes inside that. Because we append the container first and then fill it up, we are going to modify the entire document count+1 times! A quick bit of reworking can correct this for us:

```
var container=document.createElement("div");
container.className='mousemat';
var outermost=document.getElementById('top');
for(var i=0;i<count;i++){
  var node=document.createElement('div');
  node.className='cursor';
  node.style.position='absolute';
  node.style.left=(4+parseInt(Math.random()*492))+"px";
```

```
      node.style.top=(4+parseInt(Math.random()*492))+"px";
      container.appendChild(node);
    }
    outermost.appendChild(container);
```

In fact, we had to move only one line of code to reduce this to a single modification of the existing document. Listing 8.6 shows the full code for a test page that compares these two versions of the function using our stopwatch library.

Listing 8.6   Profiling DOM node creation

```
<html>

<head>
<link rel='stylesheet' type='text/css' href='mousemat.css' />
<link rel='stylesheet' type='text/css' href='objviewer.css' />
<script type='text/javascript' src='x/x_core.js'></script>
<script type='text/javascript' src='extras-array.js'></script>
<script type='text/javascript' src='styling.js'></script>
<script type='text/javascript' src='objviewer.js'></script>
<script type='text/javascript' src='stopwatch.js'></script>
<script type='text/javascript' src='eventRouter.js'></script>
<script type='text/javascript'>

var cursor=null;

function slowNodes(count){
  var watch=stopwatch.getWatch("slow nodes",true);
  var container=document.createElement("div");
  container.className='mousemat';
  var outermost=document.getElementById('top');
  outermost.appendChild(container);     ⟵ Append empty container at start
  for(var i=0;i<count;i++){
    var node=document.createElement('div');
    node.className='cursor';
    node.style.position='absolute';
    node.style.left=(4+parseInt(Math.random()*492))+"px";
    node.style.top=(4+parseInt(Math.random()*492))+"px";
    container.appendChild(node);
  }
  watch.stop();
}

function fastNodes(count){
  var watch=stopwatch.getWatch("fast nodes",true);
  var container=document.createElement("div");
  container.className='mousemat';
  var outermost=document.getElementById('top');
  for(var i=0;i<count;i++){
    var node=document.createElement('div');
```

```
      node.className='cursor';
      node.style.position='absolute';
      node.style.left=(4+parseInt(Math.random()*492))+"px";
      node.style.top=(4+parseInt(Math.random()*492))+"px";
      container.appendChild(node);
    }
    outermost.appendChild(container);    ⟵— Append full container at end
    watch.stop();
}

function go(isFast){
    var count=parseInt(document.getElementById("count").value);
    if (count==NaN){
      alert("please enter a valid number");
    }else if (isFast){
      fastNodes(count);
    }else{
      slowNodes(count);
    }
}

</script>
</head>

<body>
<div>
<a href='javascript:stopwatch.report("profiler")'>profile</a> 
<input id='count' value='640'/> 
<a href='javascript:go(true)'>fast loop</a> 
<a href='javascript:go(false)'>slow loop</a>
</div>

<div id='top'>
  <div class='mousemat' id='mousemat'></div>
  <div class='profiler objViewBorder' id='profiler'></div>
</div>

</body>
</html>
```

Again, we have a hyperlink to invoke both the fast and the slow function, using the value in an HTML form field as the argument. In this case, it specifies how many little DOM nodes to add to the container. We found 640 to be a reasonable value. The results of a simple test are presented in table 8.2.

Table 8.2 Profiling results for DOM node creation

Algorithm	Number of Page Layouts	Execution Time (ms)
Original	641	681
Optimized	1	461

Again, the optimization based on received wisdom does make a difference. With our profiler, we can see how much of a difference it is making. In this particular case, we took almost one third off the execution time. In a different layout, with different types of nodes, the numbers may differ. (Note that our example used only absolutely positioned nodes, which require less work by the layout engine.) The profiler is easy to insert into your code, in order to find out.

Our final example looks at a JavaScript language feature and undertakes a comparison between different subsystems to find the bottleneck.

Minimizing dot notation

In JavaScript, as with many languages, we can refer to variables deep in a complex hierarchy of objects by "joining the dots." For example:

```
myGrandFather.clock.hands.minute
```

refers to the minute hand of my grandfather's clock. Let's say we want to refer to all three hands on the clock. We could write

```
var hourHand=myGrandFather.clock.hands.hour;
var minuteHand=myGrandFather.clock.hands.minute;
var secondHand=myGrandFather.clock.hands.second;
```

Every time the interpreter encounters a dot character, it will look up the child variable against the parent. In total here, we have made nine such lookups, many of which are repeats. Let's rewrite the example:

```
var hands=myGrandFather.clock.hands;
var hourHand=hands.hour;
var minuteHand=hands.minute;
var secondHand=hands.second;
```

Now we have only five lookups being made, saving the interpreter from a bit of repetitive work. In a compiled language such as Java or C#, the compiler will often optimize these repetitions automatically for us. I don't know whether JavaScript interpreters can do this (and on which browsers), but I can use the stopwatch library to find out if I ought to be worrying about it.

The example program for this section computes the gravitational attraction between two bodies, called earth and moon. Each body is assigned a number of physical properties such as mass, position, velocity, and acceleration, from which the gravitational forces can be calculated. To give our dot notation a good testing, these properties are stored as a complex object graph, like so:

```
var earth={
  physics:{
    mass:10,
    pos:{ x:250,y:250 },
    vel:{ x:0, y:0 },
    acc:{ x:0, y:0 }
  }
};
```

The top-level object, physics, is arguably unnecessary, but it will serve to increase the number of dots to resolve.

The application runs in two stages. First, it computes a simulation for a given number of timesteps, calculating distances, gravitational forces, accelerations, and other such things that we haven't looked at since high school. It stores the position data at each timestep in an array, along with a running estimate of the minimum and maximum positions of either body.

In the second phase, we use this data to plot the trajectories of the two bodies using DOM nodes, taking the minimum and maximum data to scale the canvas appropriately. In a real application, it would probably be more common to plot the data as the simulation progresses, but I've separated the two here to allow the calculation phase and rendering phase to be profiled separately.

Once again, we define two versions of the code, an inefficient one and an optimized one. In the inefficient code, we've gone out of our way to use as many dots as possible. Here's a section (don't worry too much about what the equations mean!):

```
var grav=(earth.physics.mass*moon.physics.mass)
  /(dist*dist*gravF);
var xGrav=grav*(distX/dist);
var yGrav=grav*(distY/dist);

moon.physics.acc.x=-xGrav/(moon.physics.mass);
moon.physics.acc.y=-yGrav/(moon.physics.mass);
moon.physics.vel.x+=moon.physics.acc.x;
moon.physics.vel.y+=moon.physics.acc.y;
moon.physics.pos.x+=moon.physics.vel.x;
moon.physics.pos.y+=moon.physics.vel.y;
```

This is something of a caricature—we've deliberately used as many deep references down the object graphs as possible, making for verbose and slow code. There is certainly plenty of room for improvement! Here's the same code from the optimized version:

```
var mp=moon.physics;
var mpa=mp.acc;
var mpv=mp.vel;
var mpp=mp.pos;
var mpm=mp.mass;

...

    var grav=(epm*mpm)/(dist*dist*gravF);
    var xGrav=grav*(distX/dist);
    var yGrav=grav*(distY/dist);

    mpa.x=-xGrav/(mpm);
    mpa.y=-yGrav/(mpm);
    mpv.x+=mpa.x;
    mpv.y+=mpa.y;
    mpp.x+=mpv.x;
    mpp.y+=mpv.y;
```

We've simply resolved all the necessary references at the start of the calculation as local variables. This makes the code more readable and, more important, reduces the work that the interpreter needs to do. Listing 8.7 shows the code for the complete web page that allows the two algorithms to be profiled side by side.

Listing 8.7 Profiling variable resolution

```
<html>

<head>
<link rel='stylesheet' type='text/css' href='mousemat.css' />
<link rel='stylesheet' type='text/css' href='objviewer.css' />
<script type='text/javascript' src='x/x_core.js'></script>
<script type='text/javascript' src='extras-array.js'></script>
<script type='text/javascript' src='styling.js'></script>
<script type='text/javascript' src='objviewer.js'></script>
<script type='text/javascript' src='stopwatch.js'></script>
<script type='text/javascript' src='eventRouter.js'></script>
<script type='text/javascript'>

var moon={        <—  Initialize planetary bodies
  physics:{
    mass:1,
    pos:{ x:120,y:80 },
    vel:{ x:-24, y:420 },
```

```
    acc:{ x:0, y:0 }
  }
};
var earth={    <─── Initialize planetary bodies
  physics:{
    mass:10,
    pos:{ x:250,y:250 },
    vel:{ x:0, y:0 },
    acc:{ x:0, y:0 }
  }
};

var gravF=100000;

function showOrbit(count,isFast){
  var data=(isFast) ?              ❶ Select
    fastData(count) :                calculation
    slowData(count);                 type
  var watch=stopwatch.getWatch("render",true);
  var canvas=document.            ❷  Render orbit
    getElementById('canvas');
  var dx=data.max.x-data.min.x;
  var dy=data.max.y-data.min.y;
  var sx=(dx==0) ? 1 : 500/dx;
  var sy=(dy==0) ? 1 : 500/dy;
  var offx=data.min.x*sx;
  var offy=data.min.y*sy;
  for (var i=0;i<data.path.length;i+=10){
    var datum=data.path[i];
    var dpm=datum.moon;
    var dpe=datum.earth;

    var moonDiv=document.createElement("div");
    moonDiv.className='cursor';
    moonDiv.style.position='absolute';
    moonDiv.style.left=parseInt((dpm.x*sx)-offx)+"px";
    moonDiv.style.top=parseInt((dpm.x*sx)-offy)+"px";
    canvas.appendChild(moonDiv);

    var earthDiv=document.createElement("div");
    earthDiv.className='cursor';
    earthDiv.style.position='absolute';
    earthDiv.style.left=parseInt((dpe.x*sx)-offx)+"px";
    earthDiv.style.top=parseInt((dpe.x*sx)-offy)+"px";
    canvas.appendChild(earthDiv);
  }
  watch.stop();
}

function slowData(count){           ❸  Use dot notation a lot
  var watch=stopwatch.getWatch("slow orbit",true);
```

```
  var data={
    min:{x:0,y:0},
    max:{x:0,y:0},
    path:[]
  };
  ...

  }
  watch.stop();
  return data;
}

function fastData(count){          ❹  Use dot notation sparingly
  var watch=stopwatch.getWatch("fast orbit",true);
  var data={
    min:{x:0,y:0},
    max:{x:0,y:0},
    path:[]
  };
  ...

  }
  watch.stop();
  return data;
}

function go(isFast){
  var count=parseInt(document.getElementById("count").value);
  if (count==NaN){
    alert("please enter a valid number");
  }else{
    showOrbit(count,isFast);
  }
}

</script>
</head>

<body>
<div>
<a href='javascript:stopwatch.report("profiler")'>profile</a> 
<input id='count' value='640'/> 
<a href='javascript:go(true)'>fast loop</a> 
<a href='javascript:go(false)'>slow loop</a>
</div>

<div id='top'>
  <div class='mousemat' id='canvas'>
</div>
  <div class='profiler objViewBorder' id='profiler'></div>
</div>
```

```
</body>
</html>
```

The structure should be broadly familiar by now. The functions `slowData()` ❸ and `fastData()` ❹ contain the two versions of our calculation phase, which generates the data structures ❶. I've omitted the full algorithms from the listing here, as they take up a lot of space. The differences in style are described in the snippets we presented earlier and the full listings are available in the downloadable sample code that accompanies the book. Each calculation function has a stop-Watch object assigned to it, profiling the entire calculation step. These functions are called by the `showOrbit()` function, which takes the data and then creates a DOM representation of the calculated trajectories ❷. This has also been profiled by a third stopwatch.

The user interface elements are the same as for the previous two examples, with hyperlinks to run the fast and the slow calculations, passing in the text input box value as a parameter. In this case, it indicates the number of timesteps for which to run the simulation. A third hyperlink displays the profile data. Table 8.3 shows the results from a simple run of the default 640 iterations.

Table 8.3   Profiling results for variable resolution

Algorithm	Execution Time (ms)
Original calculation	94
Optimized calculation	57
Rendering (average)	702

Once again, we can see that the optimizations yield a significant increase, knocking more than one-third from the execution time. We can conclude that the folk wisdom regarding variable resolution and the use of too many dots is correct. It's reassuring to have checked it out for ourselves.

However, when we look at the entire pipeline of calculation and rendering, the optimization takes 760 ms, as opposed to the original's 796 ms—a savings closer to 5 percent than 40 percent. The rendering subsystem, not the calculation subsystem, is the bottleneck in the application, and we can conclude that, in this case, optimizing the calculation code is not going to yield great returns.

This demonstrates the broader value of profiling your code. It is one thing to know that a piece of code can be optimized in a particular way and another to know what the expected returns of such an operation would be. It might be tempting to conclude that DOM operations are roughly eight times more costly than pure JavaScript calculations, but that holds true only for this specific example. You may well find that to be the case in many situations, but a rule of thumb is best supplemented by a few measurements—and preferably on a range of different machines and browsers.

We won't spend more time now on profiling and execution speed. The examples that we have run through should give you a feel for the benefits that profiling can provide on your Ajax projects. Let's assume that your code is running at a satisfactory speed thanks to a bit of profiling. To ensure adequate performance, you still need to look at the amount of memory that your application is using. We'll explore memory footprints in the next section.

8.3 *JavaScript memory footprint*

The purpose of this section is to introduce the topic of memory management in Ajax programming. Some of the ideas are applicable to any programming language; others are peculiar to Ajax and even to specific web browsers.

A running application is allocated memory by the operating system. Ideally, it will request enough to do its job efficiently, and then hand back what it doesn't need. A poorly written application may either consume a lot of memory unnecessarily while running, or fail to return memory when it has finished. We refer to the amount of memory that a program is using as its *memory footprint*.

As we move from coding simple, transient web pages to Ajax rich clients, the quality of our memory management can have a big impact on the responsiveness and stability of our application. Using a patterns-based approach can help by producing regular, maintainable code in which potential memory leaks are easily spotted and avoided.

First, let's examine the concept of memory management in general.

8.3.1 *Avoiding memory leaks*

Any program can "leak" memory (that is, claim system memory and then fail to release it when finished), and the allocation and deallocation of memory are a major concern to developers using unmanaged languages such as C. JavaScript is a memory-managed language, in which a garbage-collection process automatically handles the allocation and deallocation of memory for the programmer. This takes care of many of the problems that can plague unmanaged code, but it is a fallacy to assume that memory-managed languages can't generate memory leaks.

Garbage-collection processes attempt to infer when an unused variable may be safely collected, typically by assessing whether the program is able to reach that variable through the network of references between variables. When a variable is deemed unreachable, it will be marked as ready for collection, and the associated memory will be released in the next sweep of the collector (which may be at any arbitrary point in the future). Creating a memory leak in a managed language is as simple as forgetting to dereference a variable once we have finished with it.

Let's consider a simple example, in which we define an object model that describes household pets and their owners. First let's look at the owner, described by the object Person:

```
function Person(name){
  this.name=name;
  this.pets=new Array();
}
```

A person may have one or more pets. When a person acquires a pet, he tells the pet that he now owns it:

```
Person.prototype.addPet=function(pet){
  this.pets[pet.name]=pet;
  if (pet.assignOwner){
    pet.assignOwner(this);
  }
}
```

Similarly, when a person removes a pet from his list of pets, he tells the pet that he no longer owns it:

```
this.removePet(petName)=function{
  var orphan=this.pets[petName];
  this.pets[petName]=null;
  if (orphan.unassignOwner){
    orphan.unassignOwner(this);
  }
}
```

The person knows at any given time who his pets are and can manage the list of pets using the supplied `addPet()` and `removePet()` methods. The owner informs the pet when it becomes owned or disowned, on the assumption that each pet adheres to a contract (in JavaScript, we can leave this contract as implicit and check for adherence to the contract at runtime).

Pets come in several shapes and sizes. Here we define two: a cat and a dog. They differ in the attitude that they take toward being owned, with a cat paying no attention to whom it is owned by, whereas a dog will attach itself to a given owner for life. (I apologize to the animal world for gross generalization at this point!)

So our definition of the pet cat might look like this:

```
function Cat(name){
  this.name=name;
}
Cat.prototype.assignOwner=function(person){
}
Cat.prototype.unassignOwner=function(person){
}
```

The cat isn't interested in being owned or disowned, so it provides empty implementations of the contractual methods.

We can define a dog, on the other hand, that slavishly remembers who its owner is, by continuing to hold a reference to its master after it has been disowned (some dogs are like that!):

```
function Dog(name){
  this.name=name;
}
Dog.prototype.assignOwner=function(person){
  this.owner=person;
}
Dog.prototype.unassignOwner=function(person){
  this.owner=person;
}
```

Both Cat and Dog objects are badly behaved implementations of Pet. They stick to the letter of the contract of being a pet, but they don't follow its spirit. In a Java or C# implementation, we would explicitly define a Pet interface, but that wouldn't stop implementations from breaching the spirit of the contract. In the real world of coding, object modelers spend a lot of time worrying about badly behaved implementations of their interfaces, trying to close off any loopholes that might be exploited.

Let's play with the object model a bit. In the script below, we create three objects:

1 jim, a Person
2 whiskers, a Cat
3 fido, a Dog

First, we instantiate a Person (step 1):

```
var jim=new Person("jim");
```

Next, we give that person a pet cat (step 2). Whiskers is instantiated inline in the call to `addPet()`, and so that particular reference to the cat persists only as long as the method call. However, jim also makes a reference to whiskers, who will be reachable for as long as jim is, that is, until we delete him at the end of the script:

```
jim.addPet(new Cat("whiskers"));
```

Let's give jim a pet dog, too (step 3). Fido is given a slight edge over whiskers in being declared as a global variable, too:

```
var fido=new Dog("fido");
jim.addPet(fido);
```

One day, Jim gets rid of his cat (step 4):

```
jim.removePet("whiskers");
```

Later, he gets rid of his dog, too (step 5). Maybe he's emigrating?

```
jim.removePet("fido");
```

We lose interest in jim and release our reference on him (step 6):

```
jim=null;
```

Finally, we release our reference on fido, too (step 7):

```
fido=null;
```

Between steps 6 and 7, we may believe that we have gotten rid of jim by declaring him to be null. In fact, he is still referenced by fido and so is still reachable by our code as `fido.owner`. The garbage collector can't touch him, leaving him lurking on the JavaScript engine's heap, taking up precious memory. Only in step 7, when fido is declared null, does Jim become unreachable, and our memory can be released.

In our simple script, this a small and temporary problem, but it serves to illustrate that seemingly arbitrary decisions affect the garbage-collection process. Fido may not be deleted directly after jim and, if he had the ability to remember more than one previous owner, might consign entire legions of Person objects to a shadow life on the heap before being destroyed. If we had chosen to declare fido inline and the cat as a global, we wouldn't have had any such problem. To assess the seriousness of fido's behavior, we need to ask ourselves the following questions:

1   How much memory might he consume in terms of references to otherwise deleted objects? We know that our simple fido can remember only one Person at a time, but even so, that Person might have a reference to 500 otherwise-unreachable pet cats, so the extra memory consumption might be arbitrarily large.

2   How long will the extra memory be held? In our simple script here, the answer is "not very long," but we might later add extra steps in between deleting jim and deleting fido. Further, JavaScript tends toward event-driven programming, and so, if the deletion of jim and of fido takes place in separate event handlers, we can't predict a hard answer, not even a probabilistic one without performing some sort of use-case analysis.

Neither question is quite as easy to answer as it might seem. The best that we can do is to keep these sorts of questions in mind as we write and modify our code and to conduct tests to see if we're right in our assumptions. We need to think about the usage patterns of our application while we code, not solely as an afterthought.

This covers the general principles of memory management. There are specific issues to be aware of in an Ajax application, so let's address them next.

8.3.2 Special considerations for Ajax

So far, we've covered some ground that is common to the memory management of most programming languages. Properly understanding concepts such as footprint and reachability are important when developing Ajax applications, but there are also issues that are specific to Ajax. With Ajax, we are operating in a managed environment, in a container that has exposed some of its native functionality and locked us out of others. This changes the picture somewhat.

In chapter 4, our Ajax application was divided into three notional subsystems: the Model, View, and Controller. The Model is usually composed of pure JavaScript objects that we have defined and instantiated ourselves. The View is composed largely of DOM nodes, which are native objects exposed to the JavaScript environment by the browser. The Controller glues the two together. It is in this layer that we need to pay special attention to memory management.

Breaking cyclic references

In section 4.3.1, we introduced a commonly used pattern for event handling, in which we attach domain model objects (that is, parts of the Model subsystem) to DOM nodes (that is, part of the View). Let's recap on the example that we presented. Here is a constructor for a domain model object representing a pushbutton:

```
function Button(value,domEl){
  this.domEl=domEl;
  this.value=value;
  this.domEl.buttonObj=this;
  this.domEl.onclick=this.clickHandler;
}
```

Note that a two-way reference between the DOM element `domEl` and the domain object itself is created. Below, the event-handler function referenced in the constructor:

```
Button.prototype.clickHandler=function(event){
  var buttonObj=this.buttonObj;
  var value=(buttonObj && buttonObj.value) ?
    buttonObj.value : "unknown value";
  alert(value);
}
```

Remember that the event-handler function will be called with the DOM node, not the Button object, as its context. We need a reference from the View to the Model in order to interact with the Model tier. In this case, we read its value property. In other cases where we have used this pattern in this book, we have invoked functions on the domain objects.

The domain model object of type Button will be reachable as long as any other reachable object has a reference to it. Similarly, the DOM element will remain reachable as long as any other reachable element refers to it. In the case of DOM elements, an element is always reachable if it is attached to the main document tree, even if no programmatic references are held to it. Thus, unless we explicitly break the link between the DOM element and the Button object, the Button can't be garbage-collected as long as the DOM element is still part of the document.

When scripted domain model objects interact with the Document Object Model, it is possible to create a local JavaScript object that remains reachable via the DOM rather than through any global variables we have defined. To ensure that objects aren't kept from garbage collection unnecessarily by we can write simple clean-up functions (a step back toward C++ object destructors in many ways, although we need to invoke them manually). For the Button object, we could write the following:

```
Button.prototype.cleanUp=function(){
  this.domEl.buttonObj=null;
  this.domEl=null;
}
```

The first line removes the reference that the DOM node has on this object. The second line removes this object's reference to the DOM node. It doesn't destroy the node but simply resets this local reference to the node to a null value. The DOM node was passed to our object as a constructor argument in this case, so it isn't our responsibility to dispose of it. In other cases, though, we do have that responsibility, so let's see how to handle it.

Disposing of DOM elements

When working with Ajax, and with large domain models in particular, it is common practice to construct new DOM nodes and interact with the document tree programmatically, rather than just via HTML declarations when the page first loads. Our ObjectViewer from chapters 4 and 5 and the notifications framework in chapter 6, for example, both contained several domain model objects capable of rendering themselves by creating additional DOM elements and attaching them to a part of the main document. With this great power comes great responsibility, and, for each node created programmatically, good housekeeping rules dictate that we are obliged to see to its disposal programmatically as well.

Neither the W3C DOM nor the popular browser implementations provide a way of destroying a DOM node outright once it has been created. The best we can do in destroying a created DOM node is to detach it from the document tree and hope that the garbage-collection mechanism in the browser will find it.

Let's look at a straightforward example. The following script demonstrates a simple pop-up message box that uses the DOM to find itself using `document.get-ElementById()` when being closed:

```
function Message(txt, timeout){
  var box=document.createElement("div");
  box.id="messagebox";
  box.classname="messagebox";
  var txtNode=document.createTextNode(txt);
  box.appendChild(txtNode);
  setTimeout("removeBox('messagebox')",timeout);
}

function removeBox(id){
  var box=document.getElementById(id);
  if (box){
    box.style.display='none';
  }
}
```

When we call `Message()`, a visible message box is created, and a JavaScript timer is set to call another function that removes the message after a given time.

The variables box and txtNode are both created locally and go out of scope as soon as the function `Message()` has exited, but the document nodes that are created will still be reachable, because they have been attached to the DOM tree.

The `removeBox()` function handles the job of making the created DOM node go away when we're done with it. We have several possible options for doing this, from a technical standpoint. In the example above, we removed the box simply by hiding it from view. It will still occupy memory when invisible, but if we are planning on redisplaying it soon, that won't be a problem.

Alternatively, we could alter our `remove()` method to dislocate the DOM nodes from the main document and hope that the garbage collector spots them before too long. Again, though, we don't actually destroy the variable, and the duration of its stay in memory is outside our control.

```
function removeBox(id){
  var box=document.getElementById(id);
  if (box && box.parentNode){
    box.parentNode.removeChild(box);
  }
}
```

We can discern two patterns for GUI element removal here, which we will refer to as *Remove By Hiding* and *Remove By Detachment*. The Message object here has no event handlers—it simply appears and disappears at its own speed. If we link the domain model and DOM nodes in both directions, as we did for our Button object, we would need to explicitly invoke the `cleanUp()` function if we were using a Remove By Detachment pattern.

Both approaches have their advantages and disadvantages. The main deciding factor for us is to ask whether we are going to reuse the DOM node at a later date. In the case of a general-purpose message box the answer is probably "yes," and we would opt for removal by hiding. In the case of a more specific use, such as a node in a complex tree widget, it is usually simpler to destroy the node when finished with it than to try to keep lots of references to dormant nodes.

If we choose to use Remove By Hiding, we can adopt a complementary approach of reusing DOM nodes. Here, we modify the message-creation function to first check for an existing node and create a new one only if necessary. We could rewrite our Message object constructor to accommodate this:

```
function Message(txt, timeout){
  var box=document.geElementById("messagebox");
  var txtNode=document.createTextNode(txt);
```

```
    if (box==null){
      box=document.createElement("div");
      box.id="messagebox";
      box.classname="messagebox";
      box.style.display='block';
      box.appendChild(txtNode);
    }else{
      var oldTxtNode=box.firstChild;
      box.replaceChild(txtNode,oldTxtNode);
    }
    setTimeout("removeBox('messagebox')",timeout);
  }
```

We can now contrast two patterns for GUI element creation, which we will refer to as *Create Always* (our original example) and *Create If Not Exists* (the modified version above). Because the ID that we check for is hard-coded, only one Message can be shown at a time (and that is probably appropriate here). Where we have attached a domain model object to a reusable DOM node, that domain object can be used to fetch the initial reference to the DOM node, allowing Create If Not Exists to coexist with multiple instances of an object.

> **NOTE**   When writing an Ajax application, then, it is important to be aware of memory-management issues regarding DOM elements, as well as conventional variables that we create ourselves. We also need to take account of the managed nature of DOM elements and treat their disposal differently. When mixing DOM nodes and ordinary variables, the use of clean-up code is advised, to break cyclic references.

In the following section, we'll look at further considerations that the Ajax programmer needs to take into account when working with Internet Explorer.

Further special considerations for Internet Explorer

Each web browser implements its own garbage collector, and some work differently than others. The exact mechanisms of the Internet Explorer browser garbage collection are not well understood, but, according to the consensus of the comp.lang.JavaScript newsgroup, it has specific difficulties with releasing variables where a circular reference exists between DOM elements and ordinary JavaScript objects. It has been suggested that manually severing such links would be a good idea.

To describe this by example, the following code defines a circular reference:

```
function MyObject(id){
  this.id=id;
  this.front=document.createElement("div");
```

```
        this.front.backingObj=this;
    }
```

`MyObject` is a user-defined type. Every instance will refer to a DOM node as this.front, and the DOM node will refer back to the JavaScript object as this.backingObj.

To remove this circular reference while finalizing the object, we might offer a method such as this:

```
MyObject.prototype.finalize=function(){
    this.front.backingObj=null;
    this.front=null;
}
```

By setting both references to null, we break the circular reference.

Alternatively, a DOM tree could be cleaned up in a generic fashion, by walking the DOM tree and eliminating references on the basis of name, type, or whatever. Richard Cornford has suggested such a function, specifically for dealing with event handler functions attached to DOM elements (see the Resources section at the end of this chapter).

My feeling is that generic approaches such as this should be used only as a last resort, as they may scale poorly to the large document trees typified by Ajax rich clients. A structured pattern-based approach to the codebase should enable the programmer to keep track of the specific cases where cleanup is required.

A second point worth noting for IE is that a top-level "undocumented" function called `CollectGarbage()` is available. Under IE v6, this function exists and can be called but seems to be an empty stub. We have never seen it make a difference to reported memory in the Task Manager.

Now that we understand the issues of memory management, let's explore the practicalities of measuring it and applying those measurements to a real-life application.

8.4 *Designing for performance*

We stated at the outset that performance consisted of both good execution speed and a controllable memory footprint. We also said that design patterns could help us to achieve these goals.

In this section, we'll see how to measure memory footprint in real applications, and we'll use a simple example to show how the use of design patterns can help us to understand the fluctuations in memory footprint that we may see in working code.

8.4.1 *Measuring memory footprint*

When we measured execution speed, we could do so either in JavaScript code using the Date object or with an external tool. JavaScript doesn't provide any built-in capabilities to read system memory usage, so we're dependent on external tools. Fortunately, we have several to choose from.

There are a variety of ways to see how much memory your browser is consuming during execution of your application. The simplest way to do so is to use a system utility appropriate to your operating system to see the underlying processes. On Windows systems, there is the Task Manager, and UNIX systems have the console-based top command. Let's look at each of these in turn.

Windows Task Manager

The Windows Task Manager (figure 8.5) is available on many versions of Windows (Windows 95 and 98 users are out of luck here). It provides a view of all processes running in the operating system and their resource use. It can usually be invoked

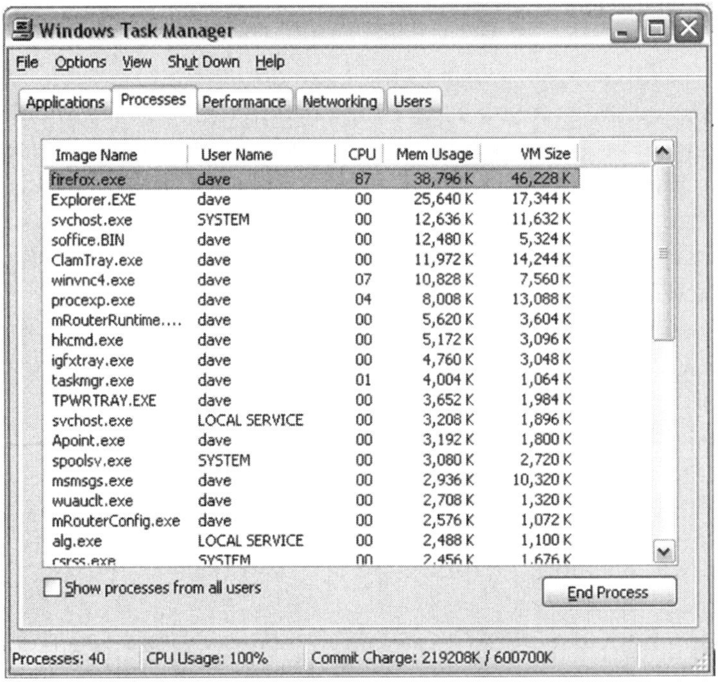

Figure 8.5   Windows Task Manager showing running processes and their memory usage. Processes are being sorted by memory usage, in descending order.

from the menu presented to the user when she presses the Ctrl+Alt+Delete key combination. The Task Manager interface has several tabs. We are interested in the tab labeled Processes.

The highlighted row shows that Firefox is currently using around 38MB of memory on our machine. In its default state, the Mem Usage column provides information on active memory usage by the application. On some versions of Windows, the user can add extra columns using the View > Select Columns menu (figure 8.6).

Showing the Virtual Memory Size of a process as well as Memory Usage can be useful. Memory Usage represents active memory assigned to an application, whereas Virtual Memory Size represents inactive memory that has been written to the swap partition or file. When a Windows application is minimized, the Mem Usage will typically drop considerably, but VM Size will stay more or less flat,

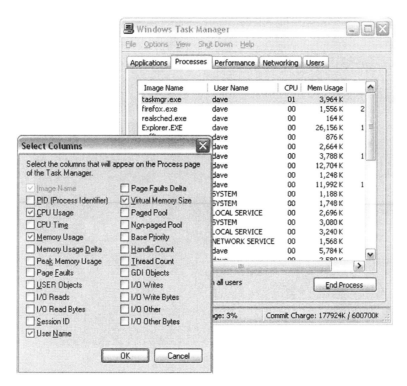

Figure 8.6 Selecting additional columns to view in the Task Manager's Processes tab. Virtual Memory Size shows the total amount of memory allocated to the process.

indicating that the application still has an option to consume real system resources in the future.

UNIX top

A console-based application for UNIX systems (including Mac OS X), `top` shows a very similar view of processes to the Windows Task Manager (figure 8.7).

As with Task Manager, each line represents an active process, with columns showing memory and CPU usage and other statistics. The `top` application is driven by keyboard commands, which are documented in the man or info pages and on the Internet. Space precludes a fuller tutorial on `top` here, or an exploration of the GUI equivalents such as the GNOME System Manager that may be present on some UNIX/Linux systems.

Power tools

Beyond these basic tools, various "power tools" are available for tracking memory usage, offering finer-grained views of the operating system's internal state. We can't do justice to the full range of these tools, but here are brief pointers to a couple of freeware tools that we have found useful.

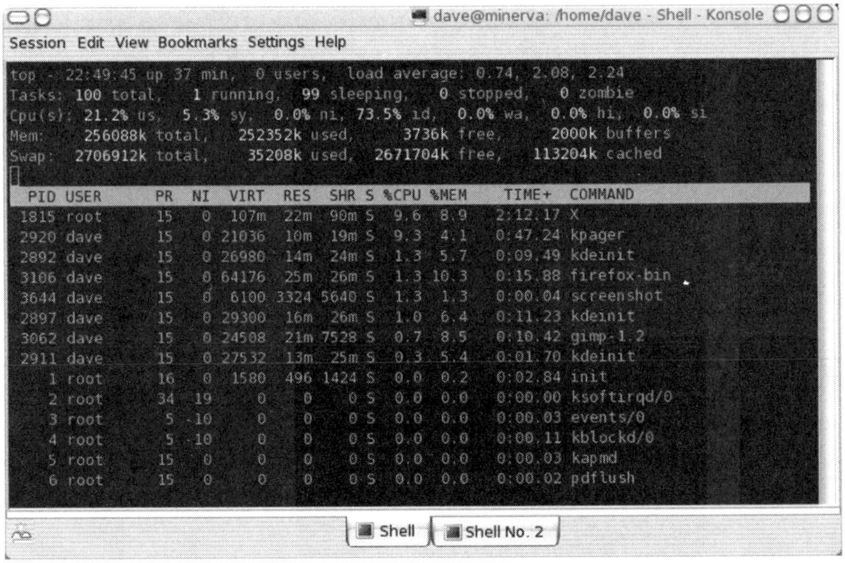

Figure 8.7   UNIX `top` command running inside a console, showing memory and CPU usage by process.

First, Sysinternal.com's Process Explorer tool (figure 8.8) is perhaps best described as a "task manager on steroids." It fulfills the same role as Task Manager but allows for detailed drilldown into the memory footprint and processor use of individual processes, allowing us to target Internet Explorer or Firefox specifically.

Second, J. G. Webber has developed Drip (see the Resources section), a simple but powerful memory management reporter for Internet Explorer that directly queries an embedded web browser about its known DOM nodes, including those that are no longer attached to the document tree (figure 8.9).

However, even with the basic tools, we can discover a lot about the state of a running Ajax application.

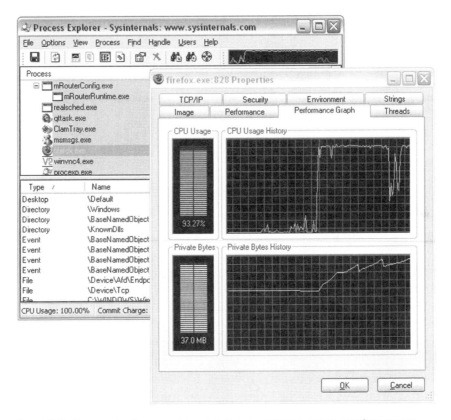

Figure 8.8   Process Explorer provides detailed reporting on memory and processor usage on a per-process basis, allowing for more accurate tracking of the browser's footprint on a Windows machine. This window is tracking an instance of Mozilla Firefox running the stress test described in section 8.4.2.

	Refs	Tag	Id	Class	
?\clickbox.html	1	DIV	box106	box1	
?\clickbox.html	1	DIV	box2	box1	
?\clickbox.html	1	DIV	box1	box1	
?\clickbox.html	1	DIV	box3	box1	
?\clickbox.html	1	DIV	box4	box1	
?\clickbox.html	1	DIV	box5	box1	
?\clickbox.html	1	DIV	box6	box1	
?\clickbox.html	1	DIV	box63	box1	
?\clickbox.html	1	DIV	box7	box1	
?\clickbox.html	1	DIV	box8	box1	
?\clickbox.html	1	DIV	box9	box1	
?\clickbox.html	1	DIV	box64	box1	
?\clickbox.html	1	DIV	box10	box1	
?\clickbox.html	1	DIV	box107	box1	
?\clickbox.html	1	DIV	box11	box1	
?\clickbox.html	1	DIV	box12	box1	
?\clickbox.html	1	DIV	box14	box1	
?\clickbox.html	1	DIV	box108	box1	
?\clickbox.html	1	DIV	box13	box1	
?\clickbox.html	1	DIV	box109	box1	
?\clickbox.html	1	DIV	box110	box1	

Figure 8.9   The Drip tool allows detailed queries on the internal state of Internet Explorer's DOM tree.

So far, we've looked at individual patterns and idioms for handling performance issues in small sections of code. When we write an Ajax application of even moderate size, the various patterns and idioms in each subsystem can interact with each other in surprising ways. The following section describes a case study that illustrates the importance of understanding how patterns combine with one another.

8.4.2   A simple example

In our discussion thus far, we have covered the theory of memory management and described a few patterns that might help us when programmatically creating interface elements. In a real-world Ajax application, we will employ several patterns, which will interact with one another. Individual patterns have impacts on performance, but so do the interactions between patterns. It is here that having access to a common vocabulary to describe what your code is doing becomes very valuable. The best way to illustrate this principle is by example, so in this section we introduce a simple one and present the performance impact of varying the combination of patterns that it uses.

In the simple test program, we can repeatedly create and destroy small Click-Box widgets, so called because they are little boxes that the user can click on with the mouse. The widgets themselves have a limited behavior, described by the following code:

```
function ClickBox(container){

  this.x=5+Math.floor(Math.random()*370);
  this.y=5+Math.floor(Math.random()*370);
  this.id="box"+container.boxes.length;
  this.state=0;
  this.render();
  container.add(this);
}

ClickBox.prototype.render=function(){
  this.body=null;
  if (this.body==null){
    this.body=document.createElement("div");
    this.body.id=this.id;
  }
  this.body.className='box1';
  this.body.style.left=this.x+"px";
  this.body.style.top=this.y+"px";
  this.body.onclick=function(){
    var clickbox=this.backingObj;
    clickbox.incrementState();
  }
}

ClickBox.prototype.incrementState=function(){
  if (this.state==0){
    this.body.className='box2';
  }else if (this.state==1){

    this.hide();
  }
  this.state++;
}

ClickBox.prototype.hide=function(){
  var bod=this.body;
  bod.className='box3';
}
```

When first rendered, the ClickBoxes are red in appearance. Click on them once, and they turn blue. A second click removes them from view. This behavior is implemented by creating two-way references between the domain model object and the DOM element that represents it onscreen, as discussed earlier.

Programmatically, each ClickBox consists of a unique ID, a position, a record of its internal state (that is, how many clicks it has received), and a body. The body is a DOM node of type DIV. The DOM node retains a reference to the backing object in a variable called backingObj.

A Container class is also defined that houses ClickBox objects and maintains an array of them, as well as a unique ID of its own:

```
function Container(id){
  this.id=id;
  this.body=document.getElementById(id);
  this.boxes=new Array();
}

Container.prototype.add=function(box){
  this.boxes[this.boxes.length]=box;
  this.body.appendChild(box.body);
}

Container.prototype.clear=function(){
  for(var i=0;i<this.boxes.length;i++){
    this.boxes[i].hide();
  }
  this.boxes=new Array();
  report("clear");
  newDOMs=0;
  reusedDOMs=0;
}
```

A screenshot of the application is shown in figure 8.10.

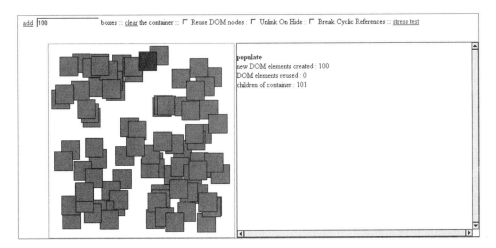

Figure 8.10 Our memory management demo application, after creation of the first 100 widgets. The user has just clicked one of the widgets with the mouse.

The debug panel on the right reports on the internal state of the system after various user events, such as adding or removing widgets from the container.

The code has been written to allow us to swap in different patterns for creation and destruction of DOM elements and cyclic references while the application is running. The user may choose between these at runtime by checking and unchecking HTML form elements on the page. When the links that add or remove boxes from the container are activated, the combination of patterns that is used to implement the user interface will match the state of the checkboxes. Let's examine each of these options and the corresponding code.

Reuse DOM Nodes checkbox

Checking this option will determine whether the ClickBox widget will try to find an existing DOM node when creating itself and create a new one only as a last resort. This allows the application to switch between the Create Always and Create If Not Exists patterns that we discussed in section 8.3.2. The modified rendering code follows:

```
ClickBox.prototype.render=function(){
  this.body=null;
  if (reuseDOM){
    this.body=document.getElementById(this.id);
  }
  if (this.body==null){
    this.body=document.createElement("div");
    this.body.id=this.id;
    newDOMs++;
  }else{
    reusedDOMs++;
  }
  this.body.backingObj=this;
  this.body.className='box1';
  this.body.style.left=this.x+"px";
  this.body.style.top=this.y+"px";
  this.body.onclick=function(){
    var clickbox=this.backingObj;
    clickbox.incrementState();
  }
}
```

Unlink On Hide checkbox

When a ClickBox is removed from the container (either by a second click or by calling `Container.clear()`), this switch will determine whether it uses the Remove By Hiding or Remove By Detachment pattern (see section 8.3.2):

```
ClickBox.prototype.hide=function(){
  var bod=this.body;
```

```
  bod.className='box3';
  if (unlinkOnHide){
    bod.parentNode.removeChild(bod);
  }
  ...
}
```

Break Cyclic References checkbox

When removing a ClickBox widget, this toggle determines whether the references between the DOM element and the backing object are reset to null or not, using the Break Cyclic References pattern in an attempt to appease the Internet Explorer garbage collector:

```
ClickBox.prototype.hide=function(){
  var bod=this.body;
  bod.className='box3';
  if (unlinkOnHide){
    bod.parentNode.removeChild(bod);
  }
  if (breakCyclics){
    bod.backingObj=null;
    this.body=null;
  }
}
```

Form controls allow the user to add ClickBoxes to the container and to clear the container. The application may be driven manually, but for the purposes of gathering results here, we have also written a stress-testing function that simulates several manual actions. This function runs an automatic sequence of actions, in which the following sequence is repeated 240 times:

1 Add 100 widgets to the container, using the `populate()` function.

2 Add another 100 widgets.

3 Clear the container.

The code for the stressTest function is provided here:

```
function stressTest(){
  for (var i=0;i<240;i++){
    populate (100);
    populate(100);
    container.clear();
  }
  alert("done");
}
```

Note that the functionality being tested here relates to the addition and removal of nodes from the container element, not to the behavior of individual Click-Boxes when clicked.

This test is deliberately simple. We encourage you to develop similar stress tests for your own applications, if only to allow you to see whether memory usage goes up or down when changes are made. Designing the test script will be an art in itself, requiring an understanding of typical usage patterns and possibly of more than one type of usage pattern.

Running the stress test takes over a minute, during which time the browser doesn't respond to user input. If the number of iterations is increased, the browser may crash. If too few iterations are employed, the change in memory footprint may not be noticeable. We found 240 iterations to be a suitable value for the machine on which we were testing; your mileage may vary considerably.

Recording the change in memory footprint was a relatively primitive business. We ran the tests on the Windows operating system, keeping the Task Manager open. We noted the memory consumption of iexplore.exe directly after loading the test page and then again after the alert box appeared, indicating that the test had completed. `top` or a similar tool could be used for testing on UNIX (see section 8.4.1). We closed down the browser completely after each run, to kill off any leaked memory, ensuring that each run started from the same baseline.

That's the methodology, then. In the following section, we'll see the results of performing these tests.

8.4.3 *Results: how to reduce memory footprint 150-fold*

Running the stress test we just described under various combinations of patterns yielded radically different values of memory consumption, as reported by the Windows Task Manager. These are summarized in table 8.4.

Table 8.4   Benchmark results for ClickBox example code

ID	Reuse DOM Nodes	Unlink On Hide	Break Cyclic Refs	Final Memory Use (IE)
A	N	N	N	166MB
B	N	N	Y	84.5MB
C	N	Y	N	428MB
D	Y	N	N	14.9MB
E	Y	N	Y	14.6MB

continued on next page

Table 8.4 Benchmark results for ClickBox example code *(continued)*

ID	Reuse DOM Nodes	Unlink On Hide	Break Cyclic Refs	Final Memory Use (IE)
F	Y	Y	N	574MB
G	Y	Y	Y	14.2MB

The results in table 8.4 were recorded for the stress test on a fairly unremarkable workstation (2.8GHz processor, 1GB of RAM) for Internet Explorer v6 on Windows 2000 Workstation under various permutations of patterns. Initial memory use was approximately 11.5MB in all cases. All memory uses reported are the Mem Usage column of the Processes tab of the Task Manager application (see section 8.4.1).

Since we're confronting real numbers for the first time, the first thing to note is that the application consumes quite a bit of memory. Ajax is often described as a thin client solution, but an Ajax app is capable of hogging a lot of memory if we make the right combination of coding mistakes!

The second important point about the results is that the choice of design patterns has a drastic effect on memory. Let's look at the results in detail. Three of our combinations consume less than 15MB of RAM after rendering and unrendering all the ClickBox widgets. The remaining combinations climb upward through 80MB, 160MB, to a staggering 430MB and 580MB at the top end. Given that the browser was consuming 11.5MB of memory, the size of additional memory consumed has varied from 3.5MB to 570MB—that's a difference of over 150 times, simply by modifying the combination of design patterns that we used. It's remarkable that the browser continued to function at all with this amount of memory leaking from it.

No particular pattern can be identified as the culprit. The interaction between design patterns is quite complex. Comparing runs A, D, and F, for example, switching on the Reuse DOM pattern resulted in a huge decrease in memory usage (over 90 percent), but switching on Unlink On Hide at the same time generated a threefold increase! In this particular case, the reason is understandable—because the DOM nodes have been unlinked, they can't be found by a call to `document.getElementById()` in order to be reused. Similarly, switching on Unlink On Hide by itself increased memory usage against the base case (comparing runs C to A). Before we discount Unlink On Hide as a memory hog, look at runs E and G—in the right context, it does make a small positive difference.

Interestingly, there is no single clear winner, with three quite different combinations all resulting in only a small increase in memory. All three of these reuse

DOM nodes, but so does the combination that results in the highest memory increase. We can't draw a simple conclusion from this exercise, but we can identify sets of patterns that work well together and other sets that don't. If we understand these patterns and have names for them, then it is much easier to apply them consistently throughout an application and achieve reliable performance. If we weren't using a fixed set of patterns but coding each subsystem's DOM lifecycle in an ad hoc fashion, each new piece of code would be a gamble that might introduce a large memory leak or might not.

This benchmarking exercise has provided an overview of the issues involved in developing a DHTML rich client that plays well with your web browser for extended periods of time, and it identified places where errors may occur, both in general and in some of the patterns discussed elsewhere in this book.

To really stay on top of memory issues, you must give them a place in your development methodology. Always ask yourself what the effect on memory usage will be as you introduce changes to your code, and always test for memory usage during implementation of the change.

Adopting a pattern-based approach to your codebase will help here, as similar memory issues will crop up repeatedly with the same patterns. We know, for example, that backing objects create cyclic references between DOM and non-DOM nodes, and that Remove By Detachment patterns interfere with Create If Not Exists patterns. If we use patterns consciously in our designs, we are less likely to run into these sorts of problems.

It can help to write and maintain automated test scripts and benchmark your changes against them. Writing the test scripts is probably the hardest part of this, as it involves knowledge of how users use your application. It may be that your app will have several types of user, in which case you would do well to develop several test scripts rather than a single average that fails to represent anyone. As with any kind of tests, they shouldn't be seen as set in stone once written but should be actively maintained as your project evolves.

8.5 Summary

Performance of any computer program is a combination of execution speed and resource footprint. With Ajax applications, we're working within a highly managed environment, far removed from the operating system and the hardware, but we still have the opportunity to affect performance greatly, based on the way we code.

We introduced the practice of profiling, both by using JavaScript libraries and using a native profiler tool such as the Venkman debugger. Profiling helps us to understand where the bottlenecks in our system are, and it also can be used to provide a baseline against which we can measure change. By comparing profiler results before and after a code change, we can assess its impact on the overall execution speed of our application.

We also looked at the issue of memory management and showed how to avoid introducing memory leaks into our code, either through generic bad practices or by running afoul of specific issues with the DOM or Internet Explorer. We saw how to measure memory consumption using the tools available to Windows and UNIX operating systems.

Finally, our benchmark example showed the real impact that attention to these details can have on our code. The role of design patterns was crucial in identifying where the great divergence in memory footprint lay and how to manage it.

Performance is an elusive goal—there is always room for a little more optimization—and we have to adopt a pragmatic approach to getting "good enough" performance from our Ajax apps. This chapter should have provided you with the tools needed to do just that.

8.6 Resources

We looked at a few useful development tools in this chapter.

- Drip, the Internet Explorer leak detector was created by Joel Webber. His blog, http://jgwebber.blogspot.com/2005/05/drip-ie-leak-detector.html, is no longer available, but Drip can currently be found at www.outofhanwell.com/ieleak/.

- Venkman Profiler: www.svendtofte.com/code/learning_venkman/advanced. php#profiling

- Process Explorer: www.sysinternals.com

The official line on Internet Explorer leakiness, and some workarounds, is presented here: http://msdn.microsoft.com/library/default.asp?url=/library/en-us/ IETechCol/dnwebgen/ie_leak_patterns.asp. Richard Cornford's suggested solution can be found on Google Groups by searching for "cornford javascript fix-CircleRefs()"—the full URL is too long to print out here.

Part 4

Ajax by example

The five complete Ajax projects in this section demonstrate the full process of building compelling interactive elements for your web applications. In each case, we've developed a straightforward example, step by step, so you can see how it works. We've then refactored the code so that the example can be dropped into your own projects easily. The examples cover the full spectrum of what Ajax can do, from enhancing form elements to developing complete portal solutions, communicating to both your own server-side processes and to standard Internet services. We've deliberately chosen a mixture of popular server-side programming languages in which to implement the server-side code, so you'll find a medley of PHP, Java, VB.Net and C# in this section. The downloadable code available from the website will contain multiple implementations of the sever-side back-end for each chapter. Have fun!

Dynamic double combo

This chapter covers
- The client-side JavaScript
- The server side in VB .NET
- Data exchange format
- Refactoring into a reusable component
- Dynamic select boxes

327

If you have ever shopped for a new shirt online, you may have run into the following problem. You pick the shirt size from one drop-down list, and from the next drop-down list you select the color. You then submit the form and get the message in giant red letters: "Sorry, that item is not in stock." Frustration sets in as you have to hit the back button or click a link to select a new color.

With Ajax we can eliminate that frustration. We can link the selection lists together, and when our user selects the size option from the first list, all of the available colors for that shirt can be populated to the second list directly from the database—without the user having to refresh the whole page. People have been linking two or more selection lists together to perform this action with either hard-coded JavaScript arrays or server-side postbacks, but now with Ajax we have a better way.

9.1 A double-combo script

In a double-combination linked list, the contents of one selection list are dependent on another selection list's selected option. When the user selects a value from the first list, all of the items in the second list update dynamically. This functionality is typically called a *double-combo script*.

There are two traditional solutions for implementing the dynamic filling of the second selection list: one is implemented on the client and the other on the server. Let's review how they work in order to understand the concepts behind these strategies and the concerns developers have with them.

9.1.1 Limitations of a client-side solution

The first option a developer traditionally had was to use a client-side-only solution. It uses a JavaScript method in which the values for the selection lists are hard-coded into JavaScript arrays on the web page. As soon as you pick a shirt size, the script seamlessly fills in the next selection list by selecting the values from the array. This solution is shown in figure 9.1.

One problem with this client-side method is that, because it does not communicate with the server, it lacks the ability to grab up-to-date data at the moment the user's first selection is made. Another problem is the initial page-loading time, which scales poorly as the number of possible options in the two lists grows. Imagine a store with a thousand items; values for each item would have to be placed in a JavaScript array. Since the code to represent this array would be part of the page's content, the user might face a long wait when first loading the page. There is no efficient way to transmit all of that information to the client up-front.

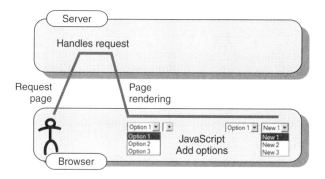

Figure 9.1
The client-side solution

On the other hand, the JavaScript method has one benefit: after the initial load time, it is fast. There is no major lag between selecting an option from the first selection list and the second list being populated. So this method is only usable if you have just a few double-combination options that will not impact the page-loading time significantly.

9.1.2 *Limitations of a server-side solution*

The next traditional solution is the submission of a form back to the server, which is known as a *page postback*. In this method, the onchange event handler in the first selection list triggers a postback to the server, via the submit() method of the form's JavaScript representation. This submits the form to the server, transmitting the user's choice from the first select element. The server, in turn, queries a database based on the value that the user selected, and dynamically fills in the new values for the second list, as it re-renders the page. You can see the process of the server-side method in figure 9.2.

A drawback to the server-side method is the number of round-trips to the server; each time the page is reloaded, there is a time delay, since the entire page

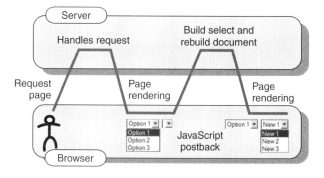

Figure 9.2
The server-side postback method

has to re-render. Figure 9.2 shows all of the extra processing required. Additional server-side code is also needed to reselect the user's choice on the first select element of the re-rendered page. Moreover, if the page was scrolled to a particular spot before the form was submitted, the user will have to scroll back to that location after the page reloads.

9.1.3 *Ajax-based solution*

We can avoid the problems of the JavaScript and server-side solutions by using Ajax to transfer data to the server and obtain the desired information for the second selection list. This allows the database to be queried and the form element to be filled in dynamically with only a slight pause. Compared with the JavaScript method, we are saving the extra page-loading time that was required to load all of the available options into the arrays. Compared with the server-side postback solution, we are eliminating the need to post the entire page back to the server; instead, we are passing only the information necessary. The page is not reloaded, so you do not have to worry about the scroll position of the page or what option was selected in the first drop-down field. The initial page loading time is also shortened since the JavaScript arrays do not have to be included in the page.

This example will involve two selection lists. The first selection list contains the sales regions for a company. The second selection list displays the related territories for the selected region, as shown in figure 9.3.

When the user selects a region from the first selection list, the client sends a request to the server containing only the necessary information to identify both the selected region, and the form control to populate with the list of territories. The server queries the database and returns an XML document containing the names of the territories in the selected region, and also the names of the form and the control that the client needs to update. Let's see how this works.

The first step in building the Ajax solution takes place on the client.

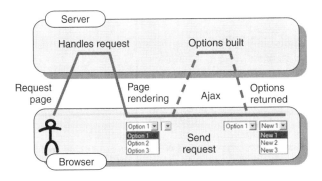

Figure 9.3
The Ajax solution

9.2 *The client-side architecture*

The client-side architecture is foreign territory to most developers who normally write server-side code. In this case, it is not that scary since we need to take only a few steps to get the options into our second selection list. If you have implemented the JavaScript or server-side solutions for a double combo before, then you have already have experience with part of the processes involved.

As you can see in figure 9.4, this application's client-side interaction does not require many steps. The first step is to build the initial form. The user then selects an item from the form's first `select`. This initiates the second step of the client-side architecture, which is to create an XMLHttpRequest object to interact with the server. This transmits the user's selection to the server, along with the names of the form and the control that will be updated when the server's response is received. The third part requires us to add the contents of the server's XML response to the second `select` element. JavaScript's XML DOM methods are used to parse the XML response.

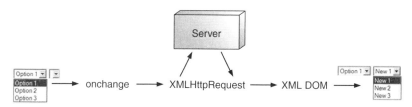

Figure 9.4   Client-side architecture, showing the Ajax interaction

Let's go over the first two steps, which happen before the Ajax request is sent to the server. We'll explain the third step (the DOM interaction with the server's XML response document) in more detail in section 9.4, since we need to talk about the server before we can implement the client-side architecture completely.

9.2.1 *Designing the form*

The form in this example involves two `select` elements. The first `select` element will initially contain values, while the second selection list will be empty. Figure 9.5 shows the form.

Figure 9.5
Available options in the first `select` element

The first form element can be filled in three separate ways initially, as shown in table 9.1.

Table 9.1 Three ways to populate a form element

Method	Advantages	Disadvantages
Hard-code the values into the `select` element.	No server-side processing.	Options cannot be dynamic.
Fill in the values by using a server-side script.	Options can be dynamic and pulled from the database.	Requires extra processing on the server.
Use Ajax to fill in the values; this method posts back to the server to retrieve the values.	Can be linked to other values on the page.	Requires extra processing on the server.

The first method is to hard-code the values into the `select` element. This method is good when you have a few options that are not going to change. The second method is to fill in the values by using a server-side script. This approach fills in the options as the page is rendered, which allows them to be pulled from a database or XML file. The third method is to use Ajax to fill in the values; this method posts back to the server to retrieve the values but does not re-render the entire page.

In this example, we are hard-coding the values into the selection list since there are only four options and they are not dynamic. The best solution for dynamically loading values into the first selection list is to use a server-side script that fills the list as the page is loaded. Ajax should not be used to populate the first selection list unless its contents depend on other values the user selects on the form.

The first selection list needs to have an `onchange` event handler added to its `select` element, as shown in listing 9.1. This event handler calls the JavaScript function `FillTerritory()`, which initiates the process of filling the second selection list by sending a request to the server.

Listing 9.1 The double-combo form

```
<form name="Form1">
  <select name="ddlRegion"
   onchange="FillTerritory(this,document.Form1.ddlTerritory)">
    <option value="-1">Pick A Region</option>
    <option value="1">Eastern</option>
    <option value="2">Western</option>
    <option value="3">Northern</option>
    <option value="4">Southern</option>
```

```
    </select>
    <select name="ddlTerritory"></select>
  </form>
```

The code in listing 9.1 creates a form that initiates the `FillTerritory()` process when an item is chosen in the first selection list. We pass two element object references to the `FillTerritory()` function. The first is the selection list object that the event handler is attached to, and the second is the selection list that is to be filled in. The next step for us is to develop the client-side code for `FillTerritory()`, which submits our request to the server.

9.2.2 *Designing the client/server interactions*

The `FillTerritory()` function's main purpose is to gather the information that is needed to send a request to the server. This information includes the selected option from the first list, the name of the form, and the name of the second selection list. With this information we can use the Ajax functions in our JavaScript library to send a request to the server. The first thing we need to do is add our Ajax functionality. The code needed to link to the external JavaScript file, `net.js`, which defines the ContentLoader object, is trivial. Just add this between the head tags of your HTML document:

```
    <script type="text/javascript" src="net.js"></script>
```

The ContentLoader object does all of the work of determining how to send a request to the server, hiding any browser-specific code behind the easy-to-use wrapper object that we introduced in chapter 3. It allows us to send and retrieve the data from the server without refreshing the page.

With the Ajax functionality added, we are able to build the function `Fill-Territory()`, shown in listing 9.2, which we also add between the head tags of our document.

Listing 9.2   The function `FillTerritory()` initializes the Ajax request.

```
    <script type="text/javascript">
    function FillTerritory(oElem,oTarget){
      var strValue = oElem.options[              ❶ Obtain value from
                  oElem.selectedIndex].value;       selection list
      var url = "DoubleComboXML.aspx";          ❷ Set the target URL
      var strParams = "q=" + strValue +         ❸ Build the
        "&f=" + oTarget.form.name +                parameter
        "&e=" + oTarget.name;                      string
```

```
    var loader1 = new                      ➍  Initiate the
    net.ContentLoader(url,FillDropDown,null,    content
                    "POST",strParams);          loader
}
```

The `FillTerritory()` function accepts two parameters, passed in this case from the `onchange` event handler on the first selection list. These are references to the first and second `select` elements. ➊ We access the value that the user selected in the first list. ➋ We set the URL of our target server-side script. ➌ We then build the parameters to be sent to the server by creating a string that has the same type of syntax as a querystring, using an ampersand to separate each name-value pair. For this example we are sending the value representing the selected region as `q`, the name of the form as `f`, and the name of the second `select` as `e`. The server-side code will use the selected region value to query the database, and it will send the names of the form and the `select` element back to the client in its XML response document. The client will use that information to determine which form and control to update. Once the parameter string is built, the only thing left is to initiate the Ajax process.

➍ To start the process, we call the `ContentLoader()` constructor, and pass in the target URL, the function to be called when the server's response is received, the error-handler function, the HTTP method to use, and the parameters to be sent. In this case, the `FillDropDown()` function will be called when the data is returned from the server, we will rely on ContentLoader's default error-handler function, and we are using a POST request.

At this point, the ContentLoader will wait for the server to return an XML document. The client-side code continues in section 9.4, but first, the server has some work to do.

9.3 *Implementing the server: VB .NET*

The server-side code needs to retrieve the territories belonging to the user's selected region from the database, and return them to the client in an XML document. The result set from the SQL query is used to create an XML document that is returned to the client side. Figure 9.6 shows the flow of the server-side process.

The server-side code is invoked by the request sent from the client-side ContentLoader object. The server-side code first retrieves the value of the request parameter `q`, representing the selected region. The value of `q` is used to create a

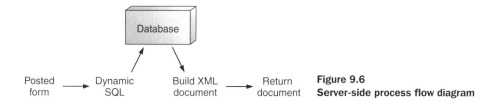

Figure 9.6
Server-side process flow diagram

dynamic SQL query statement, which is run against the database to find the text/ value pairs for the second drop-down list. The data that is returned by the database query is then formatted as XML and returned to the client. Before we write the code to do this, we need to define the basic XML document structure.

9.3.1 Defining the XML response format

We need to create a simple XML document to return the results of our database query to the client. It will contain the options to populate the second selection list. A pair of elements is needed to represent each option, one to contain the option text, and one to contain the option value.

The XML document in our example has a root element named `selectChoice`, containing a single element named `selectElement`, followed by one or more `entry` elements. `selectElement` contains the names of the HTML form and selection list that the results will populate on the client. Each `entry` element has two child elements, `optionText` and `optionValue`, which hold values representing each territory's description and ID. Listing 9.3 shows this structure.

Listing 9.3   Example of the XML response format

```xml
<?xml version="1.0" ?>
<selectChoice>
  <selectElement>
    <formName>Form1</formName>
    <formElem>ddlTerritory</formElem>
  </selectElement>
  <entry>
    <optionText>Select A Territory</optionText>
    <optionValue>-1</optionValue>
  </entry>
  <entry>
    <optionText>TerritoryDescription</optionText>
    <optionValue>TerritoryID</optionValue>
  </entry>
</selectChoice>
```

Notice in the example XML document in listing 9.3 that there is an entry containing the option text "Select A Territory". This is the first option shown in the selection list, prompting the user to choose a value. The server-side code includes this value at the start of every response document, before the dynamic options are obtained from the database.

Now that we have our response document defined, we can develop the code that dynamically creates the XML and returns it to the client.

9.3.2 *Writing the server-side code*

The VB .NET server-side code is straightforward. We perform a query on a database, which returns a record set. We then loop through the record set to create our XML document and send the XML back to the client. If we do not find any records, then we do not create any `entry` elements, also omitting the static "Select A Territory" option. As you can see in listing 9.4, the server-side code is not very complicated. It simply contains statements to retrieve the form values posted to the server, set the content type, perform a search, and output the XML document.

This example uses the Northwind sample database from Microsoft's SQL Server.

> **Listing 9.4   DoubleComboXML.aspx.vb: Server-side creation of the XML response**

```
Private Sub Page_Load( _
          ByVal sender As System.Object, _        Implement
          ByVal e As System.EventArgs) _          Page_Load
          Handles MyBase.Load                      method

    Response.ContentType = "text/xml"    ❶  Set the content type

    Dim strQuery As String
    strQuery = Request.Form("q")         ❷  Retrieve the
    Dim strForm As String                    posted data
    strForm = Request.Form("f")
    Dim strElem As String
    strElem = Request.Form("e")

    Dim strSql As String = "SELECT " & _
             "TerritoryDescription, " & _
             "TerritoryID" & _                  ❸  Create the SQL
             " FROM Territories" & _                statement
             " WHERE regionid = " & _
             strQuery & " ORDER BY " & _
             "TerritoryDescription"
```

```
    Dim dtOptions As DataTable
    dtOptions = FillDataTable(strSql)        ❹ Execute the SQL statement

    Dim strXML As StringBuilder
    strXML = New StringBuilder("<?xml " & _
                        "version=""1.0"" ?>")
    strXML.Append("<selectChoice>")
    strXML.Append("<selectElement>")         ❺ Begin XML
    strXML.Append("<formName>" & _             document
                strForm & _
                "</formName>")
    strXML.Append("<formElem>" & _
                strElem & _
                "</formElem>")
    strXML.Append("</selectElement>")

    If dtOptions.Rows.Count > 0 Then         ❻ Verify there are results

      strXML.Append("<entry>")
      strXML.Append("<optionText>" & _
                    "Select A Territory" & _  ❼ Add first
                    "</optionText>")            selection
      strXML.Append("<optionValue>-1" & _       element
                    "</optionValue>")
      strXML.Append("</entry>")

      Dim row As DataRow
      For Each row In dtOptions.Rows
        strXML.Append("<entry>")
        strXML.Append("<optionText>" & _
                row("TerritoryDescription") & _  ❽ Loop through
                "</optionText>")                   result set and
        strXML.Append("<optionValue>" & _          add XML
                    row("TerritoryID") & _         elements
                    "</optionValue>")
        strXML.Append("</entry>")
      Next

    End If

    strXML.Append("</selectChoice>")         ❾ Return the
    Response.Write(strXML.ToString)            XML document

End Sub

Public Function FillDataTable( _
                ByVal sqlQuery As String) _
                As DataTable
```

```
    Dim strConn As String = _
          "Initial Catalog = Northwind; " & _
          "Data Source=127.0.0.1; " & _
          "Integrated Security=true;"
    Dim cmd1 As _
    New SqlClient.SqlDataAdapter(sqlQuery, _
                                 strConn)

    Dim dataSet1 As New DataSet
    cmd1.Fill(dataSet1)
    cmd1.Dispose()
    Return dataSet1.Tables(0)
  End Function
```

Setting the page's content type ❶ to text/xml ensures that the XMLHttpRequest will parse the server response correctly on the client.

We obtain the value of the selected region, the HTML form name, and the element name from the request parameters ❷ received from the client. For added safety, we could add a check here to make sure that these values are not null. If the check does not find a value for each, the script could return an error response. We should also add checks for SQL injection before the application enters a production environment. This would ensure that the database is protected from malicious requests sent by attackers.

Having obtained the selected region's value, the next step is to generate a SQL string so we can retrieve the corresponding territories from the database ❸. The two columns we are interested in are TerritoryDescription and TerritoryID, from the database table Territories. We insert the region value into the SQL statement's WHERE clause. To ensure that the results appear in alphabetical order in our selection list, we also set the SQL ORDER BY clause to TerritoryDescription. Next, we must execute the SQL statement ❹. In this case, we call the function FillDataTable() to create a connection to the database server, perform the query, and return the results in a data table.

Now that we have obtained the result of the SQL query, we need to create the first part of the XML document ❺, which was discussed in listing 9.2. We begin the document and add the selectElement, containing the values of formName and formElem obtained from the request parameters.

A check is needed to verify if any results were returned by the SQL query ❻. If there are results, we add the preliminary "Select A Territory" option ❼ to the XML.

Next we loop through the results represented in the `DataTable` ❽, populating the value of the `TerritoryDescription` column into the `optionText` tag and the value of the `TerritoryID` column into the `optionValue` tag. By nesting each description/ID pair inside an `entry` tag, we provide an easier means to loop through the values on the client, with JavaScript's XML DOM methods. After we finish populating our results into the XML document, we need to close the root `selectChoice` element and write the response to the output page ❾. The XML response document is returned to the client, and the ContentLoader object is notified that the server-side process is complete. The ContentLoader calls the function `FillDrop-Down()` on the client, which will process the XML that we just created.

Let's recap what we've done on the server. We have taken the value from a selected item in a selection list and have run a query against a database without posting back the entire page to the server. We have then generated an XML document and returned it to the client. The next step in the process takes us back to the client side, where we must now convert the XML elements into options for our second selection list.

9.4 Presenting the results

We now have the results of our database query in an XML document, and we are going to navigate through its elements using JavaScript's DOM API. We can easily jump to a particular element in the document using a function called `getElementsByTagName()`. This function uses the element's name to look it up in the DOM, somewhat like the alphabetical tabs that stick out in an old-fashioned Rolodex. Since many elements in an XML document can have the same name, `getElementsByTagName()` actually returns an array of elements, in the order that they appear in the document.

9.4.1 Navigating the XML document

Now we will finish the client-side script that adds the options to the selection list. The names of the form and the selection element that we are going to populate are specified in the XML document along with all of the available options for the list. We need to traverse the document's elements in order to locate the options and insert them into our `select` element.

Once the ContentLoader receives the XML document from the server, it will call the `FillDropDown()` function that appears in listing 9.2. In `FillDropDown()`, we navigate the `entry` elements of the XML document, and create a new Option object for each. These Option objects represent the text and value pairs that will be added to the selection list. Listing 9.5 shows the `FillDropDown()` function in full.

Listing 9.5 Updating the page with data from the XML response

```
function FillDropDown(){
  var xmlDoc = this.req.responseXML.documentElement;    ❶ Get response XML
                                                            document
  var xSel = xmlDoc.
    getElementsByTagName('selectElement')[0];           ❷ Get name of
  var strFName = xSel.                                      form and
    childNodes[0].firstChild.nodeValue;                    select element
  var strEName = xSel.
    childNodes[1].firstChild.nodeValue;

  var objDDL = document.forms[strFName].                ❸ Obtain a
    elements[strEName];                                    reference the
  objDDL.options.length = 0;                               select element

  var xRows = xmlDoc.
    getElementsByTagName('entry');
  for(i=0;i<xRows.length;i++){
    var theText = xRows[i].
        childNodes[0].firstChild.nodeValue;
    var theValue = xRows[i].
        childNodes[1].firstChild.nodeValue;
    var option = new Option(theText,                    ❹ Loop through the
                            theValue);                     XML document
    try{                                                   adding options
      objDDL.add(option,null);
    }catch (e){
      objDDL.add(option,-1);
    }
  }
}
```

The `FillDropDown()` function is called by the ContentLoader once it has received and parsed the server's XML response. The ContentLoader object is accessible within `FillDropDown()` through the `this` reference, and we use it to obtain the response document, `responseXML`. Once we have a reference to the response's `documentElement` ❶, we can begin using JavaScript's DOM functions to navigate its nodes. The first information we want to obtain is the target `select` list to which we will add the new options. We look up the element named `selectElement` using `getElementsByTagName()`, taking the first item from the array it returns. We can then navigate to its child nodes ❷. The first child contains the form's name and the second child the `select` list's name.

Using these two values, we reference the target selection list itself ❸, and clear any existing options by setting the length of its options array to 0. Now we can add the new options to the list. We need to access the XML's document `entry` elements, so we call on `getElementsByTagName()` once again. This time we need to loop through the array of elements it returns, and obtain the text and value pairs from each ❹. The first child node of each `entry` is the option text that is to be displayed to the user, and the second child node is the value. Once these two values are obtained, we create a new Option object, passing the option text as the first constructor parameter and the option value as the second. The new option is then added to the target `select` element, and the process is repeated until all the new options have been added. The method signature for `select.add()` varies between browsers, so we use a `try...catch` statement to find one that works. This completes the coding for our double combo box. We can now load up our HTML page, select a region, and see the second drop-down populated directly from the database.

Figure 9.7 shows the double-combo list in action. In this example, the Eastern region is selected from the first list, and the corresponding territories are retrieved from the database and displayed in the second list. The Southern region is then selected from the first list, and its corresponding territories fill in the second list.

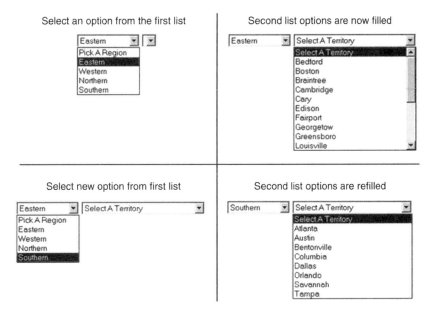

Figure 9.7   The double-combo list in action

As you can see in figure 9.7, we still have one job left: changing the selection list's appearance to make it more appealing. The second selection list's size expands as it is populated with options. We can fix this shift in size by applying a Cascading Style Sheet (CSS) rule to the element.

9.4.2 Applying Cascading Style Sheets

Cascading Style Sheets allow for changes in the visual properties of the selection element. We can change the font color, the font family, the width of the element, and so on. In figure 9.7 we saw that our second `select` element is initially only a few pixels wide since it contains no options. When the Eastern region is chosen from the first selection list, our second `select` element expands. This change of size is visually jarring and creates an unpleasant user experience.

The way to fix this issue is to set a width for the selection list:

```
<select name="ddlTerritory" style="width:200px"></select>
```

However, there may still be a problem if one of the displayed values is longer than the width we set. In Firefox, when the element is in focus the options under the drop-down list expand to display their entire text. However, in Microsoft Internet Explorer, the text is chopped off and is not visible to the user, as shown in figure 9.8.

To avoid the problem with Internet Explorer, we need to set the width of the selection list to the width of the longest option. Most of the time the only way to determine the number of pixels required to show the content is by trial and error.

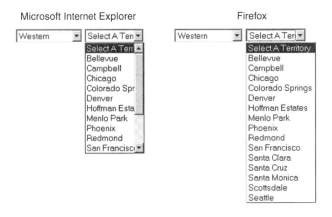

Figure 9.8   Cross-browser differences in how a `select` element is rendered

Some developers use browser-specific hacks in their CSS only to set the width wider for IE:

```
style="width:100px;_width:250px"
```

Internet Explorer recognizes the width with the underscore, while other browsers ignore it. Therefore, IE's selection box will be 250 pixels wide, while the other browsers' selection width will be 100 pixels wide. However, it's inadvisable to rely on browser bugs such as this one, as they may be fixed in a future version of the browser and break the way your page is displayed.

Let's look now at ways to add more advanced features to our double-combo script.

9.5 Advanced issues

In this chapter, we have built a simplified version of a double-combo script. We send a single parameter to the server, and we return a set of results for the single selected item. You may find that you need to change the way that this application works. You may want to add another element to the form so that you have a triple combo. You may even want to allow the user to select multiple items in the first list. If this is the case, then the following sections will give you ideas on how to implement them.

9.5.1 Allowing multiple-select queries

The code we have discussed so far is a simple example, allowing a user to select only one option from each selection list. In some cases, a user may be required to select more than one option from the first list. That means the second list in our combination will be populated with values corresponding to each selected option in the first list. With some simple changes to our client-side and server-side code, we can make this happen.

The first thing to do is to set up the first selection list to allow multiple items to be chosen. To do this, we need to add the `multiple` attribute to the `select` tag. To specify how many options to display, we can add the `size` attribute. If `size` is smaller than the number of options, the selection list will be scrollable to reveal those that are not visible.

```
<select name="ddlRegion" multiple size="4"
  onchange="FillTerritory(this,document.Form1.ddlTerritory)">
  <option value="1">Eastern</option>
  <option value="2">Western</option>
```

```
  <option value="3">Northern</option>
  <option value="4">Southern</option>
</select>
```

The next step is to change the `FillTerritory()` function. Instead of just referencing the selected index of the `select` element, we need to loop through all the options and find each of the selected values. We add the value of each selected option to the parameter string:

```
function FillTerritory(oElem,oTarget){
  var url = 'DoubleComboMultiple.aspx';
  var strParams = "f=" + oTarget.form.name +
     "&e=" + oTarget.name;
  for(var i=0;i<oElem.options.length;i++){
    if(oElem.options[i].selected){
      strParams += "&q=" + oElem.options[i].value;
    }
  }

  var loader1 = new
   net.ContentLoader(url,FillDropDown,null,"POST",strParams);
}
```

The last thing to do is change the code of the server-side script to handle the multiple values passed in the request. In .NET, the multiple values are represented in a single string, separated by commas. In order to get each item individually, we need to split the string into an array. We can then build our WHERE clause for the SQL statement by looping through the array.

```
Dim strQuery As String = Request.Form("q")
Dim strWhere As String = ""
Dim arrayStr() As String = strQuery.Split(",")
Dim i As Integer
For Each i In arrayStr
  If strWhere.Length > 0 Then
    strWhere = strWhere & " OR "
  End If
  strWhere = strWhere & " regionid = " & i
Next

Dim strSql As String = "SELECT " & _
            " TerritoryDescription, " & _
            " TerritoryID" & _
            " FROM Territories" & _
            " WHERE " & strWhere & _
            " ORDER BY TerritoryDescription"
```

With these changes, a user to can select multiple regions from the first selection list, and the territories corresponding with every selected region will appear in the second list.

9.5.2 *Moving from a double combo to a triple combo*

Moving to a double combo to a triple combo requires only a small number of changes, depending on how we want to handle the logic on the server. The first option is to move our logic into multiple server-side pages so that we can run a different query in each. That would mean adding another parameter to each selection list's `onchange` handler, representing the URL of the server-side script to call.

The other option can be as simple as adding an `if-else` or a `switch-case` statement to the server-side code. The `if-else` structure needs a way to determine which query to execute in order to return the appropriate values. The simplest check is to decide which SQL query to use based on the name of the `select` element to be populated. So, when we are performing a triple combo, we can check that the value of the `strElem` variable. This way, we do not need to make any changes to the `onchange` event handlers in the client-side code.

```
Dim strSql As String
If strElem = "ddlTerritory" Then
    strSql = "SELECT TerritoryDescription, " & _
             " TerritoryID" & _
             " FROM Territories" & _
             " WHERE " & strWhere & _
             " ORDER BY TerritoryDescription"
Else
    strSql = "SELECT Column1, Column2" & _
             " FROM TableName" & _
             " WHERE " & strWhere & _
             " ORDER BY Column2"
End If
```

With this solution, as long as the drop-down lists have unique names, you will be able to have multiple combination elements on the page without having to separate all of the logic into different server-side pages.

9.6 *Refactoring*

So what do you think is lacking at this point? I suspect I know what you're thinking—generality. This is an extremely cool, jazzed-up technique for implementing double combos, but it needs a little polish to be a generalized component.

We'll get there, so hang tight. But first, let's address something even more fundamental: encapsulation of some of the Ajax plumbing itself. The net.ContentLoader introduced briefly in chapter 3, and more thoroughly in chapter 5, is a good start. Let's build on this object to make our handling of AJAX even more seamless. Ideally we should be able to think of this entity as an Ajax "helper" object that does all the heavy lifting associated with Ajax processing. This will allow our component to focus on double combo–specific behaviors and reduce the amount of code required by the rest of our components as well. Our improved net.ContentLoader object should ideally encapsulate the state and behavior required to perform the following tasks:

- Creation of the XMLHttpRequest object in a cross-browser fashion, and as an independent behavior from sending requests. This will allow callers to use the creation method independently from the rest of the object. This is useful if the caller is using another idiom, framework, or mechanism for request/response activities.

- Provide a more convenient API for dealing with request parameters. Ideally the caller should just be able to pass state from the application and let the net.ContentLoader "helper" worry about creating querystrings.

- Routing the response back to a component that knows how to handle it and performing appropriate error handling.

So let's start our refactoring of net.ContentLoader, and then we'll move on to repackaging our double combo as a component.

9.6.1 *New and improved net.ContentLoader*

Let's start by thinking about how the constructor should be changed. Consider the following constructor:

```
net.ContentLoader = function( component, url, method, requestParams ) {
    this.component     = component;
    this.url           = url;                    net.ContentLoader
    this.requestParams = requestParams;          state
    this.method        = method;
}
```

The constructor shown here is called with four arguments. The first, `component`, designates the object that is using the services of this helper. The helper object will assume that `component` has an `ajaxUpdate()` method to handle responses and a `handleError()` method to handle error conditions. More about that later. Second, as before, `url` designates the URL that is invoked by this helper to asynchronously get data from the server. The `method` parameter designates the HTTP request method. Valid values are `GET` and `POST`. Finally, the `requestParameters` argument is an array of strings of the form `key=value`, which designate the request parameters to pass to the request. This allows the caller to specify a set of request parameters that do not change between requests. These will be appended to any additional request parameters passed into the `sendRequest` method discussed below. So our helper can now be constructed by a client as follows:

```
var str = "Eastern";
var aComp = new SomeCoolComponent(...);
var ajaxHelper = new net.ContentLoader( aComp,
                    "getRefreshData.aspx", "POST",
                    [ "query=" + str, "ignore_case=true" ] );
```

Now let's consider the rest of the API. One thing I should mention at this point is the stylistic nature of the code sample. The methods of this object are scoped to the prototype object attached to the constructor function. This is a common technique when writing object-oriented JavaScript, as it applies the method definitions to all instances of the object. However, there are several ways of syntactically specifying this. One of my favorites (a pattern I picked up from the prototype.js library packaged within Ruby On Rails) is to create the prototype object literally, as shown here:

```
net.ContentLoader.prototype = {

    method1: function(a, b, c) {      First method attached
    },                                to prototype

    method2: function() {      <── Second method
    },

    method3: function(a) {
    }

};
```

The thing we like about this syntactically is that it is expressed minimally. The way to read this is that the outermost open and close curly braces represent an object literal, and the content is a comma-delimited list of property-value pairs within the object. In this case our properties are methods. The property-value pairs are specified as the name of the property, followed by a colon, followed by the value of the property. In this case the values (or definitions if you prefer) are function literals. Piece of cake, huh? Just bear in mind that the methods shown from here on out are assumed to be contained within the prototype object literal as shown here. Also, note that the last property doesn't need—indeed can't have—a comma after it. Now let's go back to the task at hand: refactoring the API.

The API should address the requirements that we mentioned above, so let's take each one in turn. The first thing we need is an independent behavior to handle the creation of the XMLHttpRequest object in a cross-browser fashion. That sounds like a method. Fortunately, we've implemented this one a few times already. All we need to do is create it as a method of our helper, as shown in listing 9.6, and we'll never have to write it again.

Listing 9.6 The `getTransport` method

```
getTransport: function() {
   var transport;
   if ( window.XMLHttpRequest )              Native
      transport = new XMLHttpRequest();      object
   else if ( window.ActiveXObject ) {
      try {
         transport = new ActiveXObject('Msxml2.XMLHTTP');    IE ActiveX
      }                                                      object
      catch(err) {
         transport = new ActiveXObject('Microsoft.XMLHTTP');
      }
   }
   return transport;
},
```

There's not much explanation required here, since we've covered this ground many times, but now we have a cleanly packaged method to provide a cross-browser Ajax data transport object for handling our asynchronous communications.

The second requirement we mentioned was to provide a more convenient API for dealing with request parameters. In order for it to be used across a wide variety of applications, it is almost certain that the request being sent will need runtime values as parameters. We've already stored some initial state that represents request parameters that are constant across requests, but we'll also need runtime values. Let's decide on supporting a usage such as the following code:

```
var a,b,c;         ◁— Assume initialized with runtime values
var ajaxHelper = new net.ContentLoader(...);
ajaxHelper.sendRequest( "param1=" + a, "param2=" + b,
                        "param3=" + c );
```

So given this usage requirement, `sendRequest` is defined as shown in listing 9.7.

Listing 9.7   The sendRequest method

```
sendRequest: function() {

    var requestParams = [];                                   ❶ Store
    for ( var i = 0 ; i < arguments.length ;  i++ ) {           arguments
        requestParams.push(arguments[i]);                       in an array
    }

    var request = this.getTransport();                        ❷ Create the
    request.open( this.method, this.url, true );                 request
    request.setRequestHeader( 'Content-Type',
                        'application/x-www-form-urlencoded');

    var oThis = this;                               Specify the  ❸
    request.onreadystatechange = function() {          callback
                        oThis.handleAjaxResponse(request) };
    request.send( this.queryString(requestParams) ); ❹  Send the request
},
```

This method splits the process of sending a request into four steps. Let's look at each step of the process in detail:

❶ This step takes advantage of the fact that JavaScript creates a pseudo-array named `arguments` that is scoped to the function. As the name suggests, `arguments` holds the arguments that were passed to the function. In this case the arguments are expected to be strings of the form `key=value`. We just copy them into a first-class array for now. Also, note that all variables created in this method are preceded by the keyword `var`. Although JavaScript is perfectly happy if we leave the `var` keyword off, it's very important that we don't. Why? Because, if we omit the `var` keyword, the variable is created at a global scope—visible to all the code in your JavaScript universe! This could cause unexpected interactions with other code (for example, someone names a variable with the same name in a third-party script you have included). In short, it's a debugging nightmare waiting to happen. Do yourself a favor and get accustomed to the discipline of using locally scoped variables whenever possible.

❷ Here our method uses the `getTransport` method we defined in listing 9.6 to create an instance of an XMLHttpRequest object. Then the request is opened and its `Content-Type` header is initialized as in previous examples. The object reference is held in a local variable named `request`.

❸ This step takes care of the response-handling task. I'll bet you're wondering why the variable `oThis` was created. You'll note that the following line—an anonymous function that responds to the `onreadystatechange` of our request object—references `oThis`. The name for what's going on here is a *closure*. By virtue of the inner function referencing the local variable, an implicit execution context or scope is created to allow the reference to be maintained after the enclosing function exits. (See appendix B for more on closures.) This lets us implement handling of the Ajax response by calling a first-class method on our `ajaxHelper` object.

❹ Finally, we send the Ajax request. Note that the array we created in step 1 is passed to a method named `queryString` that converts it to a single string. That string becomes the body of the Ajax request. The `queryString` method isn't really part of the public contract we discussed earlier, but it's a helper method that keeps the code clean and readable. Let's take a look at it in listing 9.8.

Listing 9.8 The `queryString` method

```
queryString: function(args) {

  var requestParams = [];
  for ( var i = 0 ; i < this.requestParams.length ; i++ ) {    Constant
    requestParams.push(this.requestParams[i]);                  parameters
  }
  for ( var j = 0 ; j < args.length ; j++ ) {    Runtime
    requestParams.push(args[j]);                  parameters
  }

  var queryString = "";
  if ( requestParams && requestParams.length > 0 ) {
    for ( var i = 0 ; i < requestParams.length ; i++ ) {
      queryString += requestParams[i] + '&';
    }
    queryString = queryString.substring(0, queryString.length-1);
  }
  return queryString;
},
```

This method takes the request parameters that our net.ContentLoader was constructed with, along with the additional runtime parameters that were passed into the `sendRequest` method, and places them into a single array. It then iterates over the array and converts it into a querystring. An example of what this achieves is shown here:

```
var helper = new net.ContentLoader( someObj, someUrl,
                         "POST", ["a=one", "b=two"] );
var str = ajaxHelper.queryString( ["c=three", "d=four"] );

str => "a=one&b=two&c=three&d=four"
```

The last thing we need to do to have a fully functional helper object is to collaborate with a component to handle the response that comes back from Ajax. If you've been paying attention, you probably already know what this method will be named. Our `sendRequest` method already specified how it will handle the response from the `onreadystatechange` property of the request:

```
request.onreadystatechange = function(){
  oThis.handleAjaxResponse(request)
}
```

That's right, kids; all we need to do is implement a method named `handleAjax-Response`. Listing 9.9 contains the implementation.

Listing 9.9 The Ajax response handler methods

```
handleAjaxResponse: function(request) {
   if ( request.readyState == net.READY_STATE_COMPLETE ) {
      if ( this.isSuccess(request) )
         this.component.ajaxUpdate(request);      ◁— Message component
      else                                           with response
         this.component.handleError(request);     ◁— Message component
   }                                                  with error
},

isSuccess: function(request){
   return request.status == 0
      || (request.status >= 200 && request.status < 300);
}
```

All the method does is check for the appropriate `readyState` of 4 (indicating completion) and notifies the `this.component` that the response is available. But we're not quite finished yet. The other requirement we said we would address is to handle errors appropriately. But what is appropriate? The point is, we don't know what's appropriate. How to handle the error is a decision that should be deferred to another entity. Therefore we assume that our client, `this.component`, has a `handleError` method that takes appropriate action when the Ajax response comes back in a way we didn't expect. The component may in turn delegate the decision to yet another entity, but that's beyond the scope of what we care about as a helper object. We've provided the mechanism; we'll let another entity provide the semantics. As mentioned earlier, we're assuming that `this.component` has an `ajaxUpdate` and a `handleError` method. This is an implicit contract that we've created, since JavaScript isn't a strongly typed language that can enforce such constraints.

Congratulations! You've morphed net.ContentLoader into a flexible helper to do all the Ajax heavy lifting for your Ajax-enabled DHTML components. And if you have a DHTML component that's not yet Ajax-enabled, now it'll be easier! Speaking of which, we have a double-combo component to write.

9.6.2 *Creating a double-combo component*

We've laid some groundwork with our net.ContentLoader to make our task here much easier, so let's get started. Let's assume that our assignment as a rock-star status developer is to create a double-combo script that can be reused in many contexts across an application, or many applications for that matter. We need to consider several features in order to meet this requirement:

- Let's assume that we may not be able or want to directly change the HTML markup for the select boxes. This could be the case if we are not responsible for producing the markup. Perhaps the `select` is generated by a JSP or other server-language-specific tag. Or perhaps a designer is writing the HTML, and we want to keep it as pristine as possible to avoid major reworks caused by a round or two of page redesigns.

- We want a combo script that is able to use different URLs and request parameters to return the `option` data. We also want the design to accommodate further customization.

- We want to be able to apply this double-combo behavior potentially across multiple sets of `select` tags on the same page, also potentially setting up triple or quadruple combos, as discussed earlier.

Starting from the perspective of our first task, keeping the HTML markup as pristine as possible, let's assume the markup shown in listing 9.10 is representative of the HTML on which we will be operating.

Listing 9.10   Double-combo HTML markup listing

```
<html>
<body>

<form name="Form1">
   <select  id="region" name="region" >
      <options...>
   </select>
   <select id="territory" name="territory" />
</form>
```

```
  </body>
</html>
```

What we need is a `DoubleCombo` component that we can attach to our document to perform all of the double-combo magic. So let's work backwards and consider what we would want our markup to look like; then we'll figure out how to implement it. Let's change the markup to look something like listing 9.11.

Listing 9.11 Double-combo HTML modified markup listing

```
<html>
<head>
  ...
  <script>
    function injectComponentBehaviors() {
      var doubleComboOptions = {};
      new DoubleCombo( 'region',                          DoubleCombo
                       'territory',                       component
                       'DoubleComboXML.aspx',
                       doubleComboOptions );
    }
  </script>
</head>

<body onload="injectComponentBehaviors()">

<form name="Form1">
  <select  id="region" name="region" >
    <option value="-1">Pick A Region</option>
    <option value="1">Eastern</option>
    <option value="2">Western</option>
    <option value="3">Northern</option>
    <option value="4">Southern</option>
  </select>
  <select id="territory" name="territory" />
</form>

</body>
</html>
```

The markup has now changed in the following ways:

- A function has been created that injects all desired component behaviors into our document.

- An `onload` handler has been added to the body element that calls this function.

Note that nothing within the body section of the page has been modified. As stated earlier, this is a good thing. We've already satisfied our first requirement. But, looking at our `injectComponentBehaviors()` function, it's apparent that we have some more work to do. Namely, we need to create a JavaScript object named DoubleCombo that, when constructed, provides all the behaviors we need to support double-combo functionality.

DoubleCombo component logic

Let's start by looking more closely at the semantics of our component creation. Our `injectComponentBehaviors()` function creates a DoubleCombo object by calling its constructor. The constructor is defined in listing 9.12.

Listing 9.12 DoubleCombo constructor

```
function DoubleCombo( masterId, slaveId, url, options ) {
    this.master     = document.getElementById(masterId);         Initialize
    this.slave      = document.getElementById(slaveId);          state
    this.options    = options;
    this.ajaxHelper = new net.ContentLoader( this, url, "POST",
                            options.requestParameters || [] );

    this.initializeBehavior();      ⟵ Initialize behavior
}
```

This should be a familiar construct at this point; our constructor function initializes the state of our DoubleCombo. A description of the arguments that should be passed to the constructor is shown in table 9.2.

Table 9.2 Description of arguments

Argument	Description
`masterId`	The ID of the element in the markup corresponding to the master `select` element. The selection made in this element determines the values displayed by a second `select` element.
`slaveId`	The ID of the element in the markup corresponding to the slave `select` element. This is the element whose values will be changed when the user makes a choice from the master `select`.
`options`	A generic object that provides other data required by the double combo.

Consider the nature of the state maintained by the DoubleCombo object—particularly the URL and options. These two pieces of state satisfy the second functional requirement mentioned earlier. That is, our component can accommodate any URL for data retrieval and is customizable via the options parameter. Currently the only thing we assume we'll find within the options object is a requestParameters property. But, because the options parameter is just a general object, we could set any property on it needed to facilitate further customizations down the road. The most obvious kinds of properties we could place in our options object are such things as CSS class stylings and the like. However, the style and function of the double combo are fairly independent concepts, so we'll leave the styling to the page designer.

To many of you, we're sure, the more interesting part of the constructor comes in the last two lines. Let's look at each in turn:

```
this.ajaxHelper = new net.ContentLoader( this, url, "POST",
                        options.requestParameters || [] );
```

Obviously, we know that our component requires Ajax capabilities. As fortune and a little planning would have it, we already have an object to perform the lion's share of our Ajax-related work—that is, the net.ContentLoader we cleverly refactored earlier. The DoubleCombo simply passes itself (via this) as the component parameter to the ContentLoader helper. The url parameter is also passed through to the helper as the target URL of Ajax requests, and the HTTP request method is specified with the string "POST". Finally, the requestParameters property of the options object, or an empty array if none was defined, is passed as the "constant" parameter array to send with every Ajax request. Also recall that because we passed this as a component argument, the DoubleCombo object is obligated to implement the implied contract with the net.ContentLoader object we discussed earlier. That is, we must implement an ajaxUpdate() and a handleError() method. We'll get to that in a bit, but first let's look at the last line of our constructor:

```
this.initializeBehavior();
```

Finally our constructor is doing something that looks like behavior. Yes, the moment we've all been waiting for: the behavior implementation. Everything we'll do from here on out is directly related to providing double-combo functionality. So without further ado, let's take a look at this method along with all the other DoubleCombo methods that will be required. Thanks to all of the infrastructure we've put in place, our task is far from daunting at this point. Keep in mind that all the methods that appear throughout the rest of the example are assumed to be embedded within a prototype literal object, exactly as we did for the net.ContentLoader implementation.

```
DoubleCombo.prototype = {
    // all of the methods….
};
```

So, let's peek under the hood. First, the `initializeBehavior()` method is shown here:

```
initializeBehavior: function() {
    var oThis = this;
    this.master.onchange = function() { oThis.masterComboChanged(); };
},
```

Short and sweet. This method puts an `onchange` event handler on the master `select` element (formerly done in the HTML markup itself). When triggered, the event handler invokes another method on our object, `masterComboChanged()`:

```
masterComboChanged: function() {
    var query = this.master.options[
                this.master.selectedIndex].value;
    this.ajaxHelper.sendRequest( 'q=' + query );
},
```

Wow, also short and sweet. All this method has to do is create a request parameter and send our Ajax request. Since the Ajax-specific work has been factored out into another object, this is a single line of code. Recall that `sendRequest()` will create and send an XMLHttpRequest, then route the response back to our `ajaxUpdate()` method. So let's write that:

```
ajaxUpdate:  function(request) {
    var slaveOptions =  this.createOptions(
                        request.responseXML.documentElement);
    this.slave.length = 0;    ⟵ Clear any existing options
    for ( var i = 0 ; i < slaveOptions.length ; i++ )
      try{
        this.slave.add(slaveOptions[i],null);       Populate
      }catch (e){                                    new options
        this.slave.add(slaveOptions[i],-1);
      }
},
```

This method takes the response XML from the `request` object and passes it to a method named `createOptions()`, which creates our slave `select`'s `option` elements. The method then simply clears and repopulates the slave `select` element. The `createOptions()` method, although not part of any public contract, is a helper method that makes the code cleaner and more readable. Its implementation, along with another helper method, `getElementContent()`, is shown in listing 9.13.

Listing 9.13   Combo population methods

```
createOptions: function(ajaxResponse) {
    var newOptions = [];
    var entries = ajaxResponse.getElementsByTagName('entry');
    for ( var i = 0 ; i < entries.length ; i++ ) {
        var text  = this.getElementContent(entries[i],
                    'optionText');
        var value = this.getElementContent(entries[i],
                    'optionValue');
        newOptions.push( new Option( text, value ) );
    }
    return newOptions;
},

getElementContent: function(element,tagName) {
    var childElement = element.getElementsByTagName(tagName)[0];
    return (childElement.text != undefined) ? childElement.text :
                                              childElement.textContent;
},
```

These methods perform the hard work of actually fetching values from the XML response document, and creating options objects from them. To recap, the XML structure of the response is as follows:

```
<?xml version="1.0" ?>
<selectChoice>
  ...
  <entry>
    <optionText>Select A Territory</optionText>
    <optionValue>-1</optionValue>
  </entry>
  <entry>
    <optionText>TerritoryDescription</optionText>
    <optionValue>TerritoryID</optionValue>
  </entry>
</selectChoice>
```

The createOptions() method iterates over each entry element in the XML and gets the text out of the optionText and optionValue elements via the get-ElementContent() helper method. The only thing particularly noteworthy about the getElementContent() method is that it uses the IE-specific text attribute of the XML element if it exists; otherwise it uses the W3C-standardized text-Content attribute.

Error handling

We're all finished. Almost. We've implemented all the behaviors needed to make this component fully operational. But, dang, we said we'd handle error conditions, too. You will recall that we have to implement a `handleError()` method in order to play nicely with the net.ContentLoader. So let's implement that, and then we'll really be finished. So what's the appropriate recovery action if an error occurs? At this point we still can't really say. The application using our Double-Combo component ultimately should decide. Sounds like a job for our options object—remember the one we passed to the constructor? Let's think about that contract for a second. What if we constructed our double-combo component with code that looks something like this?

```
function myApplicationErrorHandler(request) {
    // Application function that knows how
    // to handle an error condition
}

var comboOptions = { requestParameters: [
                "param1=one", "param2=two" ],
                errorHandler: myApplicationErrorHandler };

var doubleCombo = new DoubleCombo( 'region',
                                'territory',
                                'DoubleComboXML.aspx',
                                comboOptions );
```

In this scenario, we've let the application define a function called `myApplication-ErrorHandler()`. The implementation of this method is finally where we can put application-specific logic to handle the error condition. This could be an alert. Or it could be a much less intrusive "oops" message a la GMail. The point is we've deferred this decision to the application that's using our component. Again, we've provided the mechanism and allowed someone else to provide the semantics. So now we have to write the DoubleCombo object's `handleError()` method:

```
handleError: function(request) {
    if ( this.options.errorHandler )
        this.options.errorHandler(request);
}
```

Component bliss

Congratulations are in order! We're finally all done. We have a general component that we can construct with the IDs of any two `select` elements and some configuration information, and we have instant double-combo capability. And it's just so … *door slams open!*

Enter pointy-haired manager, 2:45 P.M. Friday. "Johnson," he says. "We have to support subterritories! ... And we need it by Monday morning!" Dramatic pause. "Ouch!" you finally retort. Then you regain your composure and say, "I'll make it happen, sir. Even if I have to work all weekend." He hands you the new page design:

```
<form>
  <select id="region"       name="region"><select>
  <select id="territory"    name="territory"></select>
  <select id="subTerritory" name="subTerritory"></select>
</form>
```

Pointy-hair retreats. You open the HTML page in Emacs, because that's the way you roll. You go directly to the head section. The cursor blinks. You begin to type:

```
<script>
   function injectComponentBehaviors() {
      var opts1 = { requestParameters: "master=region" };
      var opts2 = { requestParameters: "master=territory" };

      new DoubleCombo( 'region',
                       'territory',
                       'DoubleComboXML.aspx', opts1 );
      new DoubleCombo( 'territory',
                       'subTerritory',
                       'DoubleComboXML.aspx', opts2 );
</script>
```

You press a key that runs a macro to nicely format your code. You save. You exclaim over your shoulder, "I'll be working from home," as you pass by Pointy's office at 2:57. You plop down on the sofa and think to yourself, "Boy, I am a rock star!" Okay, already. Enough of the fantasy. Let's tie a bow around this thing and call it a day.

9.7 Summary

The double combination `select` element is an efficient method to create dynamic form elements for the user. We can use JavaScript event handlers to detect changes in one `select` element and trigger a process to update the values in the second element. By using Ajax, we are able to avoid the long page-loading time that you would see using a JavaScript-only solution. Using Ajax, we can make a database query without the entire page being posted back to the server and disrupting the user's interaction with the form. Ajax makes it easy for your web application to act more like a client application.

With this code, you should be able to develop more sophisticated forms without having to worry about the normal problems of posting pages back to the server. With the ability to extend this script to act on multiple combinations of selection lists, your users can drill down more precisely through several layers of options to obtain the information or products they are looking for.

Finally, we did some refactoring of the code to build ourselves an industrial-strength component to facilitate reuse and customization down the road. From our perspective, we've encapsulated this functionality in a reusable component and won't ever need to write it again. From our users' perspective, they won't be getting that screen that says the product is not available when buying items from our online store. Everybody's happy.

10

Type-ahead suggest

This chapter covers

- Type-ahead suggest
- Caching search results on the client
- Rico library
- Prototype library
- JavaScript `apply()` function
- Parameterizing components

Type-ahead suggest is one of the main applications of Ajax that has helped put Ajax into the mainstream world of programming. Google Suggest amazed people as they discovered a list of choosable suggestions appearing while they were typing (and even now, several months later, it still gives a buzz). It is as if a little helper is sitting next to you and telling you what you are looking for. Some people first thought they were storing values on the page, and others thought they were using a hidden IFrame to get the data. Google was actually using the XMLHttpRequest object to obtain the values for each keystroke.

In this chapter, you'll learn how to send Ajax requests while the user is typing. We also examine the flaws of the available type-ahead suggest implementations and find ways to avoid these pitfalls in our application. At first we take a low-level approach that is easy to understand. After we get our application functioning, we reexamine it at a higher level, and use an object-oriented approach to gain more flexibility and usability. Before we build the application, though, let's take a quick look at some of the typical type-ahead suggest features, and how we will design our application to use the best of those features.

10.1 *Examining type-ahead applications*

Since Ajax has become popular, the type-ahead suggest has been one of the most sought-after pieces of code. Many people have created different versions of the type-ahead suggest that handle the interaction with the server in many ways. A lot of the solutions out there have flaws, while others go way overboard. We first evaluate some of the functionality in many type-ahead suggest applications and then take a quick look at Google Suggest. After that, we'll design our application.

10.1.1 *Common type-ahead suggest features*

Numerous type-ahead applications are available, from basic to advanced. Each of them does the same basic thing; some have fancy interfaces with fading transition effects. If you do a search for "type-ahead suggest Ajax," you will find plenty of examples.

If you look at a few of them, you should see that they all perform the same type of actions:

1 You type a character.
2 The type-ahead makes a request to the server.
3 It returns data to the client.
4 The client takes that data and displays the results in the table, div, textbox, or some other format.

However, there are things that some of the scripts do not handle well. Developers need to take into consideration bandwidth, server capacity, and the client's configuration. If you forget about these factors, Ajax may hurt your user's experience instead of improving it.

The problems listed in table 10.1 are very common with Ajax applications.

Table 10.1   Problems with type-ahead suggest

Problem	Result
Posting back on every keystroke	Large bandwidth consumption. Imagine the server-side bandwidth required for 1,000 users typing 10-characters words.
Not caching data	Requests are hitting the database each time even though they are returning a subset of data they already have.
The 56K modem	Yes, there are still people who dial in, and these users may see a lag in response time.
Returning too many results	Not limiting the results can send too much data to the client, slowing down response time.
Too fancy an interface	Fancy interfaces can be bad if they take a long time to render.
Fast typists	Some people can type fast. Certain type-ahead scripts have problems if the user is not a hunt-and-peck typist.

Many developers tend to forget about bandwidth. Even one user who is filling in a simple word can post back a number of times. Combine this with a fast typist, and you can have more hits in a second than you normally would for the user's entire session in a non-Ajax application.

Keeping the user interface responsive is also very important. The more time a control takes to render, the longer the user has to wait before seeing it, and the less effective the type-ahead suggest is. Delays can also be introduced by hitting the server too hard. If requests are made too frequently, or if they return too much data, the responsiveness of the user interface will suffer.

A good strategy for improving responsiveness is to cache the data *on the client*. (We can also cache data on the server, but that's another issue, more familiar to developers of classic web apps.) A type-ahead suggest system will typically return fewer results as extra characters are typed, and these will often be a subset of earlier results. A simple implementation will discard previous requests and fetch all data from the server every time. A more intelligent solution might retain the results of the initial request and whittle away unwanted entries as the user types, refreshing the user interface without going back to the server for every keystroke. This improves the application by increasing responsiveness and reducing the bandwidth. We'll just be going through the result set that we have, making it quicker to pull the necessary information and eliminating the extra postbacks to the server.

That's enough of the theory for now. In the next section, we'll take a look at a production-ready implementation of the type-ahead suggest.

10.1.2 Google Suggest

Some people consider Google Suggest to be the cream of the crop of the type-ahead suggest applications. Google Suggest is fast and user-friendly and does its job efficiently. In figure 10.1, Google Suggest is giving suggestions for the letter e.

In figure 10.1, the result set for the letter e is limited to 10 results. Knowing the vast collection of data Google has, it could be billions of results. Google uses an algorithm to determine what should be displayed. Developers have dissected Google's JavaScript code to figure out how it is accomplishing the task. Remember, JavaScript code cannot be completely hidden from view, although obfuscation can help.

One of the impressive things about Google Suggest is that it accounts for fast typists by using timers to limit multiple postbacks in a short span of time. This had to be one of Google's biggest concerns since they have such a large user base. Lots of postbacks to their servers could lead to problems, and limiting the number of postbacks saves resources.

Web Images Groups News Froogle Local **more »**	
ebay	Advanced Search
	Preferences
ebay	206,000,000 results Language Tools
expedia	11,200,000 results
easyjet	1,020,000 results
espn	11,200,000 results
As you type, Goo e bay	24,200,000 results sults. Learn more
ebay.com	1 result
e cards	18,300,000 results
exchange rates	22,800,000 results
ebay uk	15,700,000 results
eminem	11,900,000 results

Figure 10.1   Google Suggest showing the available suggestions for the letter e

Google has inspired us (and many others). In the next section, we'll incorporate the best of the features we've reviewed as we design our own type-ahead Ajax application.

10.1.3 *The Ajax in Action type-ahead*

The type-ahead for this application will try to limit the impact on the server as much as possible. Smaller sites cannot handle the traffic that Google, Amazon, and Yahoo! can, since they do not have fancy load-balancing and multiple servers to handle the requests. Therefore, the more bandwidth that can be saved, the cheaper it is for the smaller websites in the long run.

To do this, we use the server only when we need new data. In this application, we use a script-centric interaction between the server and the client. The server formats the results as JavaScript statements that can be executed on the client. The data returned by the server contains only the text to display to the user and any identification field we want to relate with this data. This identification field can be compared to the value or an option tag. Most scripts do not allow us to send an ID; this one allows that. Then the browser handles the returned data, as JavaScript. With the data in the form of JavaScript variables, DHTML takes its turn in the process. You can see a diagram of this process in figure 10.2.

The Ajax portion of the script, as shown in figure 10.2, allows us to grab the data from the server. The server returns a text document containing a JavaScript statement to the client. The client processes the data contained in the JavaScript statement and checks to see if there are any results. If there are, the options are displayed for the user to choose.

The concept sounds easy until you realize that a large amount of JavaScript is involved. But with a number of small steps, the process of building a type-ahead script that minimizes the impact on the server is rather simple. The easiest part of this project is the server-side code, so that's a good place to start.

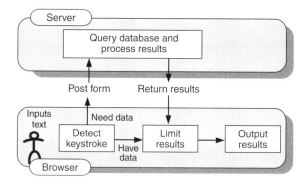

Figure 10.2
The system architecture for the type-ahead suggest

10.2 *The server-side framework: C#*

The type-ahead suggest that we are about to tackle involves three parts: the server, the database, and the client. The database could actually be an XML file, but the same basic concept can be applied.

10.2.1 *The server and the database*

The server and the database code can be handled at the same time since we are just going to connect to a database of information. In this example, we will use Microsoft's Northwind database and obtain the data from the Products table, but you can make this work for any database you want.

The idea behind the XMLHttpRequest object is to be able to send a request from the client to the server and receive back a formatted data structure. In this case, we create a text document dynamically with the data that we obtained from a database query. The text document will hold JavaScript code to create an array containing the data. You can see the steps for building the JavaScript array in listing 10.1.

Listing 10.1   typeAheadData.aspx.cs

```
private void Page_Load(object sender,        ❶ Initialize code
System.EventArgs e)                             on page load
{
    Response.ContentType = "text/html";      ❷ Set content type
    string strQuery =
      Request.Form.Get("q").ToString();      ❸ Request form element
    string strAny  = "";
    if (Request.Form.Get("where").ToLower()
      == "true")            ❹ Declare a
    {                          string
        strAny = "%";
    }
    string strSql = "Select top 15 " +
            "ProductName, " +
            "ProductId FROM Products " +     ❺ Build SQL
            "WHERE ProductName like '" +        statement
            strAny + strQuery + "%"
            "' ORDER BY ProductName";
DataTable dtQuestions  = FillDataTable(
                      strSql);               ❻ Initialize database query
System.Text.StringBuilder strJSArr =
    new System.Text.StringBuilder(
    "arrOptions = new Array(");              ❼ Build JavaScript array
```

```
        int iCount = 0;
        foreach (DataRow row in
            dtQuestions.Rows)
        {
            if (iCount > 0)
            {
                strJSArr.Append(",");
            }
            strJSArr.Append("[");
            strJSArr.Append("\"" +
                row["ProductName"].ToString()
                + "\",");
            strJSArr.Append("\"" +
                row["Productid"].ToString()
                + "\"");
            strJSArr.Append("]");
            iCount++;
        }
        strJSArr.Append(");");
        Response.Write(strJSArr.ToString());
    }

    public static DataTable
        FillDataTable(string sqlQuery)
    {
    string strConn = "Initial Catalog = "+
        "Northwind;Data Source=127.0.0.1; "
        "Integrated Security=true;";
        SqlConnection conn = new
            SqlConnection(strConn);
        SqlDataAdapter cmd1 = new
            SqlDataAdapter();
        cmd1.SelectCommand = new
            SqlCommand(sqlQuery,conn);
        DataSet dataSet1 = new DataSet();
        cmd1.Fill(dataSet1);
        cmd1.Dispose();
        conn.Close();
        return dataSet1.Tables[0];
    }
```

8 Loop through results

9 Write string to page

10 Execute query

The code in listing 10.1 lets us receive the values from the client and process the data into a string forming a JavaScript array. This newly created array is returned to the client where it will be processed. We need to initialize this on the page load **1** of the document. The first step when we return the string is to make sure that the content type of the page is set to text/html **2**.

The client-side code will post the values to this page via the XMLHttpRequest object. Therefore, we need to request the form element q for the text we are supposed to query ❸. Unlike most type-ahead suggests, we'll allow users to find results in the middle of a word, so we declare a string ❹ to handle this situation. The client script passes the boolean string within the form element named where. If it is true, we add a % to the start of our search term to enable searching from anywhere in the string.

We can now build the SQL statement ❺ to obtain the values from the database based on user input. To minimize the impact on the user, we limit the search by only allowing 15 records to be returned. We can then initialize ❻ our procedure to query the database ❿ and return a data table with the available search results.

Once the results have been returned from the database, we can start building the JavaScript array ❼. We then loop through our record set ❽, building the two-dimensional array containing the product name and ID. When the looping is complete, we write our string to the page ❾ so that our JavaScript statement can use it.

If you are using a server-side language that has a code-behind page and an HTML page, you need to remove all the extra tags from the HTML page. With our C# page, the only tag that should be on the ASPX page is the following:

```
<%@ Page Language="c#" AutoEventWireup="false"
Codebehind="TypeAheadXML.aspx.cs" Inherits="Chapter10CS.TypeAheadXML"%>
```

If we did not remove the extra HTML tags that are normally on the ASPX page by default, we would not have a valid text (with JavaScript) file, meaning that our JavaScript DOM methods would not be able to use the data. To ensure that the data being transferred back to our client is correct, we need to run a quick test.

10.2.2 *Testing the server-side code*

It is important to test the server-side code when you are working with Ajax since JavaScript is known for its problems, the causes of which are hard to find. Improvements have been made with Mozilla's JavaScript console, but it is always a good idea to make sure that the server is performing properly to eliminate the chances of error.

We have two options for testing the server-side code. Since we will be using the HTTP POST method with our XMLHttpRequest object, either we have to create a simple form with two textboxes and submit it to the server-side page, or we can comment out the lines that check for the form submission and hard-code values in its place. As you can see in the partial code listing in listing 10.2, the form request statements are commented out and replaced with hard-coded values.

Listing 10.2 Partial listing for commenting out the request lines for testing

```
//string strQuery = Request.Form.Get("q").ToString();
string strQuery = "a";

string strAny = "";
//if (Request.Form.Get("where").ToLower() == "true")
//{
    strAny = "%";
//}
```

This code is looking for all the words that contain the letter *a*. Therefore, when this code is executed, the JavaScript array declaration appears as shown in figure 10.3.

arrOptions = new Array(["Alice Mutton","17"],["Aniseed Syrup","3"],["Boston Crab Meat","40"],["Camembert Pierrot","60"],["Carnarvon Tigers","18"],["Chai","1"], ["Chang","2"],["Chartreuse verte","39"],["Chef Anton's Cajun Seasoning","4"],["Chef Anton's Gumbo Mix","5"],["Chocolade","48"],["Côte de Blaye","38"],["Escargots de Bourgogne","58"],["Gnocchi di nonna Alice","56"],["Gorgonzola Telino","31"]);

Figure 10.3   JavaScript statement output of the server-side page for a test run

As you can see, the string in figure 10.3 is correct. Therefore, we can remove the comments and hard-coded values and continue building the type-ahead suggest. You may be wondering where all the caching of the data returned from the server is. The client-side code will handle this. The only time the server will be called is for the very first keystroke or when the results are greater than or equal to 15. There is no reason to keep requesting the same data if we are only going to get a subset of the returned results. Now that we've finished the server-side code, let's develop the client-side framework.

10.3 The client-side framework

The client-side framework involves Ajax's XMLHttpRequest object and a good amount of DHTML. The first thing we tackle is building the textboxes.

10.3.1 The HTML

The HTML we'll use is very simple since we're dealing with only three form elements: two textboxes and a hidden field. The first textbox is the type-ahead suggest form element. The hidden field accepts the value of the selected item that the user picks from our type-ahead suggest. The other textbox does nothing other than keep our form from posting back to the server when the Enter key is pressed. The default action of the Enter key in a form with one text field is to submit the form. Adding another textbox to the page is the easiest way to get around the default action of the form. If you're adding the type-ahead suggest on a page that contains multiple form elements, then you don't need to add it. The basic HTML layout is shown in listing 10.3.

Listing 10.3 The basic HTML layout for the type-ahead suggest

```
<form name="Form1" AUTOCOMPLETE="off" ID="Form1">
  AutoComplete Text Box: <input type="text" name="txtUserInput" />
  <input type="hidden" name="txtUserValue" ID="hidden1" />
  <input type="text" name="txtIgnore" style="display:none" />
</form>
```

In listing 10.3, we added a form with autocomplete turned off. We need to do this to prevent the browser from putting values into the fields when the page is first loaded. It is a great feature when you need it, but in this case it disrupts the flow for our type-ahead suggest. Note that this is an Internet Explorer–specific fix, to prevent the built-in autocomplete drop-downs from interfering with our DHTML drop-down. Other browsers will ignore this attribute.

We added a textbox with the name txtUserInput, a hidden element with the name txtUserValue, and our dummy textbox with the name txtIgnore. The txtIgnore textbox, used to prevent automatic submission of the form, also has a CSS style applied to it to hide it from view, so the user cannot see it. There are other ways around this with coding, but this is the easiest and quickest solution. Now that we have added our text fields to the form, we can start coding the JavaScript.

10.3.2 *The JavaScript*

The JavaScript for the type-ahead suggest performs three main tasks:

- Monitoring the user's actions on the keyboard and mouse
- Sending and receiving data from the server
- Producing HTML content with which the user can interact

Before we start coding, it's a good idea to see exactly what we're going to be coding in action.

Figure 10.4
The output for the type-ahead suggest
for this application

When the user types a letter, a hidden span is made visible with the information that relates to the typed letter. In figure 10.4, the highlighted letter in all of the available options is the letter *a*, which appears in the textbox also. The first option in the list is highlighted. By pressing the Up and Down Arrow keys, we can move this selection. Pressing the Enter key allows us to select the option. We can also select the option by clicking on one of the words from the list with the mouse.

Because of the complexity of this script, the explanation may seem rather jumpy, since it involves the use of many functions to perform the type-ahead suggest. One function monitors the keystrokes, another one loads the text and Java-Script code, a third one builds the list, a fourth one underlines the typed letters, and so on. You can download the code from Manning's website so you can follow along and look at the code in your favorite editor.

Adding the external Ajax JavaScript file

To add Ajax functionality to this application, we must include the external Java-Script file, net.js (introduced in chapter 3), in the head tag. It contains the ContentLoader object, which allows us to initiate the Ajax request without having to do all the `if-else` checking:

```
<script type="text/javascript" src="net.js"></script>
```

To add the external file, we add the JavaScript tag and include the `src` attribute that specifies the external file. We link to the file just as we would link to an image or CSS file. This file does all the work of determining how to send the information to the server, hiding any browser-specific code behind the easy-to-use wrapper object. This now allows us to send and retrieve the data from the server without refreshing the page. With this file attached to our project, we can start to develop the type-ahead suggest.

The output span

Figure 10.4 shows a gray box that contains all the available options. The box is an HTML span element that is dynamically positioned to line up directly under the textbox. Instead of having to add the span to the page every time we want to use this script, we can add the span to the page from the script.

In listing 10.4, we create a new span element with DOM on the page load event. We are inserting a span to the HTML page with an ID of `spanOutput` and a CSS class name of `spanTextDropdown`. The span is then added by appending the new child element to the body element. The CSS class reference that we added allows us to assign the rules so that we can position the span dynamically. Since we are going to be dynamically positioning the span on the screen depending on where the textbox is located, we set the CSS class of the span to absolute positioning.

Listing 10.4   The JavaScript code to output the positioned span

```
window.onload = function(){
  var elemSpan = document.createElement("span");
  elemSpan.id = "spanOutput";
  elemSpan.className = "spanTextDropdown";
  document.body.appendChild(elemSpan);
}
```

We are using the page `onload` event handler to allow us to dynamically add a span element to the page. This prevents us from having to manually add it to the page every time we want to use this script. The DOM method `createElement` is used to create the span. We then need to assign our new span an ID and a `className` attribute. Once we add those new attributes, we can append the element to the page. At this point, let's create our CSS class (listing 10.5) so that we can dynamically position the element on the page.

Listing 10.5   CSS class for drop-down span

```
span.spanTextDropdown{ position: absolute;
                       top: 0px;
                       left: 0px;
                       width: 150px;
                       z-index: 101;
```

```
      background-color: #C0C0C0;
      border: 1px solid #000000;
      padding-left: 2px;
      overflow: visible;
      display: none;
}
```

The position of the span is initially set to arbitrary positions on the screen by adding the `top` and `left` parameters. We set a default width for our span and set the `z-index` to be the uppermost layer on the page. The CSS rule also lets us style the background and border of our span so it stands out on the page. The `display` property is set to `none` so that it is hidden from the user's view when the page is initially loaded. As the user starts to input data in the type-ahead text field, the `display` property is changed so that we can see the results.

Assigning the type-ahead functionality to a textbox

Because we may want to use the type-ahead functionality on multiple fields, we should develop a way to have different properties assigned to the various elements. The properties are used to determine how the script reacts. We set properties to match text with case sensitivity, match anywhere in the text, use timeouts, and perform other features we will discuss shortly. One way to do this is to build an object that contains all the needed parameters that are unique to the individual textbox. Therefore, when we have the textbox in focus, we can reference the object that is attached to the element to obtain the correct settings. In listing 10.6, a new object is created so we are able to organize the list of parameters that we assign to the textbox.

Listing 10.6 Building a custom object

```
function SetProperties(xElem,xHidden,xserverCode,
  xignoreCase,xmatchAnywhere,xmatchTextBoxWidth,
  xshowNoMatchMessage,xnoMatchingDataMessage,xuseTimeout,
  xtheVisibleTime){
    var props={
      elem: xElem,
      hidden: xHidden,
      serverCode: xserverCode,
      regExFlags: ( (xignoreCase) ? "i" : "" ),
      regExAny: ( (xmatchAnywhere) ? "^" : "" ),
      matchAnywhere: xmatchAnywhere,
      matchTextBoxWidth: xmatchTextBoxWidth,
      theVisibleTime: xtheVisibleTime,
      showNoMatchMessage: xshowNoMatchMessage,
```

```
      noMatchingDataMessage: xnoMatchingDataMessage,
      useTimeout: xuseTimeout
   };
   AddHandler(xElem);
   return props;
}
```

The first step in creating our objects for the type-ahead suggest is to create a new function called setProperties(), which can assign properties to the object. In this example, we are going to be passing in several parameters to this function. The list of parameters includes the textbox that the type-ahead is assigned to, the hidden element used to hold the value, the URL to the server-side page, a boolean to ignore case in the search, a boolean to match the text anywhere in the string, a boolean to match the textbox width, a boolean to show no matching message, the message to display, a boolean to determine if the options should hide after a given period of time, and the time span it should remain open.

This is a large list of parameters to pass into the function. We must take these parameters and assign them to our object. To do this, we use the JavaScript Object Notation (JSON), which we describe in more detail in appendix B. The keyword is defined before the colon, and the value afterward. Our treatment of two parameters, ignoreCase and matchAnywhere, is slightly more complex. Instead of storing the boolean value, we store the regular expression equivalent in the property. In this case, we use i to ignore case and ^ to match the beginning of a string in regular expressions. It is easier for us to set the regular expression parameters here instead of using if statements each time the functions are called.

The last step in our function is assigning the event handlers to the textbox. For this example, we'll call a function that adds the event handlers automatically. We develop the code for the function in a moment, but first let's call the function SetProperties() to create our object. The code in listing 10.7 is executed on the page onload event handler, enabling us to set the properties to the textbox.

Listing 10.7 Initializing the script

```
window.onload = function(){
  var elemSpan = document.createElement("span");
  elemSpan.id = "spanOutput";
  elemSpan.className = "spanTextDropdown";
  document.body.appendChild(elemSpan);

  document.Form1.txtUserInput.obj =
    SetProperties(document.Form1.txtUserInput,
```

```
document.Form1.txtUserValue,'typeAheadData.aspx',
true,true,true,true,"No matching Data",false,null);
}
```

The event handlers must be assigned when the page is loading. Therefore, we need to assign them to the `window.onload` event handler that we created earlier to add the new span element. In this example, we are using just one textbox for the type-ahead. We must reference the form element to which we want to add the type-ahead suggest and add a new property to it called `obj`. We will assign our custom object to this property so we can reference it throughout the script to obtain our values instead of using global variables.

We set the reference equal to the function `SetProperties()`. We then assign all the parameters that we created in listing 10.6. The important things to point out are that we are referencing the two form elements we created in listing 10.3 and we are calling the server-side page typeAheadData.aspx, which we created in listing 10.1. Now that the `onload` handler is initializing the process, we can add the event handlers, which our function `SetProperties()` is calling.

The event handlers

In order for us to determine the user's actions within the textbox for the type-ahead suggest, we need to add event handlers to the form. The two main things to consider are the user's typing on the keyboard and whether the user has left the text field. In listing 10.8, we use event handlers to detect the user's actions.

Listing 10.8   Attaching the event handlers

```
var isOpera=(navigator.userAgent.toLowerCase().indexOf("opera")!= -1);
    function AddHandler(objText){
      objText.onkeyup = GiveOptions;
      objText.onblur = function(){
        if(this.obj.useTimeout)StartTimeout();
      }
      if(isOpera)objText.onkeypress = GiveOptions;
}
```

Listing 10.8 begins with a browser-detection statement. The browser detection is going to be used in a few places in this example since Opera behaves differently with keypress detection. This is the easiest way to determine if the browser used is Opera, but it is not always the most reliable way since Opera can act like other browsers.

Our function `AddHandler()` is given a reference to the textbox. This reference allows us to add the `onkeyup` and `onblur` event handlers to the element. The `onkeyup` event handler fires a function called `GiveOptions()` when the key is released on the keyboard. Therefore, when the user types a five-letter word, the function `GiveOptions` is fired five times as the keys are released.

The `onblur` event handler that we attach to our textbox calls the function `StartTimeout()` when the user removes the focus from the textbox. Actions that can remove the focus from the textbox include clicking on another part of the screen or pressing the Tab key. We will be developing the `StartTimeout()` function in listing 10.19.

The reason we did the browser detection for Opera is that it does not fire the `onkeyup` event handler in the same manner as the other browsers do. When `onkeyup` is fired, Opera does not show the value in the textbox that includes that current keystroke. Adding the `onkeypress` event handler to Opera corrects this problem. You can see that we check for the browser using our boolean variable `isOpera`, and we then assign our `onkeypress` event handler to our textbox. With this event handler, Opera performs in the same way as other browsers. Since we now are able to detect the user's typing, we can determine what actions need to take place in the function `GiveOptions()`.

Handling the user's keypress

The `GiveOptions()` function that we are about to create is called when keypress events are fired. This function has two main jobs: determining the action to take depending on the keystroke, and determining whether we need to use Ajax to obtain the data from the server or use the data we already have. Therefore, the `GiveOptions()` function is performing the same role as the data caching that we discussed in section 10.1.1. By using client-side code to handle the additional keystrokes, we are decreasing the bandwidth consumption of the type-ahead suggest. To implement our cache of options, let's set some global variables on the client. The code in listing 10.9 contains a list of global variables that we need to start with.

Listing 10.9   Global variables used throughout the project

```
var arrOptions = new Array();
var strLastValue = "";
var bMadeRequest;
var theTextBox;
var objLastActive;
```

```
var currentValueSelected = -1;
var bNoResults = false;
var isTiming = false;
```

The first global variable is `arrOptions`. This variable references an array that holds all the available options from the server query. The next variable is `str-LastValue`, which holds the last string that was contained in the textbox. The variable `bMadeRequest` is a boolean flag that lets us know that a request has already been sent to the server so we do not keep sending additional requests. The flag is meant for very fast typists, so we do not have to worry about using timeouts as Google does.

The variable `theTextBox` will hold a reference to the textbox that the user has in focus, whereas `objLastActive` will hold the reference to the last active textbox. This is used to determine whether the data set needs to be refreshed if the user switches textboxes. While there is only one visible textbox on our example, if this solution is implemented on a window with multiple textboxes, we need to know which one has the focus. The next variable, `currentValueSelected`, will act like the `selectedIndex` of a select list. If the value is -1, nothing is selected. The final global variable that we need right now is a boolean `bNoResults`. This will tell us that there are no results, so we should not bother trying to find any. The variable `isTiming` allows us to determine whether a timer is running on the page. The timer runs to hide the options from the user's view if there is a period of inactivity.

Even though you might not completely understand what these global variables' roles are at this time, you'll understand better when we start using them. With all our global variables referenced, we can build the `GiveOptions()` function, which is called from the keystrokes in the textbox. The `GiveOptions()` function in listing 10.10 lets us determine the action the user has performed in the textbox.

Listing 10.10 The JavaScript code that detects the user's keypresses

```
function GiveOptions(e){
  var intKey = -1;
  if(window.event){
    intKey = event.keyCode;
    theTextBox = event.srcElement;
  }
  else{
    intKey = e.which;
    theTextBox = e.target;
  }
```

❶ **Detect the keypress**

```
if(theTextBox.obj.useTimeout){
  if(isTiming)EraseTimeout();
  StartTimeout();
}
```

❷ Reset the timer

```
if(theTextBox.value.length == 0
  && !isOpera){
  arrOptions = new Array();
  HideTheBox();
  strLastValue = "";
  return false;
}
```

❸ Determine if text exists

```
if(objLastActive == theTextBox){
  if(intKey == 13){
    GrabHighlighted();
    theTextBox.blur();
    return false;
  }
  else if(intKey == 38){
    MoveHighlight(-1);
    return false;
  }
  else if(intKey == 40){
    MoveHighlight(1);
    return false;
  }
}
```

❹ Determine function keys

```
if(objLastActive != theTextBox ||
  theTextBox.value
  .indexOf(strLastValue) != 0 ||
  ((arrOptions.length==0 ||
  arrOptions.length==15 )
  && !bNoResults) ||
  (theTextBox.value.length
    <= strLastValue.length)){

  objLastActive = theTextBox;
  bMadeRequest = true
  TypeAhead(theTextBox.value)
}
else if(!bMadeRequest){
  BuildList(theTextBox.value);
}
strLastValue = theTextBox.value;
}
```

❺ Handle keypress action

❻ Save user input

If the user is typing a word, either this function will start a new search, checking the server for matching data, or it will work with the cached result set. If we do not need to get new data from the server, then we can call a BuildList() function, which will limit the result set. We explain more about that in the section "Building the results span," later in this chapter.

The GiveOptions() function is declared with the parameter e, which allows us to detect the source of the event. The first thing we need to declare is a local variable intKey. This variable holds the code of the key that the user pressed ❶. To determine which key was pressed, we must determine what method the user's browser needs to function. If the window.event property is supported, then we know the browser is IE. We use event.keyCode to obtain the key code value, and we also use event.srcElement to get the object of the user's textbox. For the other browsers, we use e.which to obtain the key code value and e.target to obtain the textbox object reference.

We then need to check whether the textbox is using a timer to hide the textbox ❷. To do so, we reference the textbox's obj property (which we created earlier) and the boolean useTimeout. If the timer is running, we cancel it and then restart it by calling the functions EraseTimeout() and StartTimeout(), which we will code in the section "Using JavaScript timers."

We then check to see if anything is in the textbox ❸. If nothing is there, we call a HideTheBox() function (which is developed in the section "Setting the selected value"), set the strLastValue to null, and return false to exit the function. If the textbox contains text, then we can continue. Before we can detect the Enter key and arrow keys, we need to verify that the current active textbox is the same textbox as the last textbox that was active.

The first key to detect is the Enter key, which has a key code of 13 ❹. The Enter key will allow us to grab the value of the selected drop-down item and place it into the visible textbox. Therefore, we call a GrabHighlighted() function (which we will also code in the section "Setting the selected value"). We then remove the focus from the textbox and exit the function.

The next two keys we want to capture are the Up and Down Arrow keys, which have the values 38 and 40, respectively. The arrow keys move the highlighted option up and down the list. In figure 10.4, the dark gray bar is the selected item. By using the Down Arrow key, you can select the next item in the list. This functionality will be discussed in the section "Highlighting the options." The important thing to note is that the Down Arrow key sends a value of 1 to the function MoveHighlight(), while the Up Arrow key sends -1.

If no special key was pressed, then we check to see if we should hit the server to obtain the values or use the list that we already obtained from the server ❺. Here again we are using the caching mechanism of this script to limit the postbacks and reduce the load on the server. We can perform a couple of checks to see if we have to get new results. The first check is to determine whether or not the last active textbox is the textbox that currently has the focus. The next check is to make sure that the text the user typed into the textbox is the same as last time with only an addition at the end. If there are no results or our result set has 15 elements or less, then we need to check the server for data. The last check is to make sure that the current value's length is greater than the last value. If any of these checks pass, then we need to obtain new data from the server. We set the `objLastActive` with the current textbox. We then set a boolean saying that a request has been sent so we do not perform multiple requests, and we call our function `TypeAhead()` to grab the values.

Then we set the current string in the textbox to the last-known string ❻. We'll use that value again to see if we need to request data from the server on the next keystroke. This brings us to accessing the server to obtain the data.

10.3.3 *Accessing the server*

The XMLHttpRequest object allows us to transfer the text from the textbox to the server and to receive the results from the server. In this case, we are posting the data to the server since the server-side page we created in listing 10.1 is referencing the elements submitted in a form. We must specify in our ContentLoader the location of the page on the server, the function to call when it is completed, and the form parameters to be submitted to the form, as shown in listing 10.11.

> **Listing 10.11 Ajax functionality to send data back to the server**

```
function TypeAhead(xStrText){
  var strParams = "q=" + xStrText +
    "&where=" + theTextBox.obj.matchAnywhere;
  var loader1 = new net.ContentLoader(
    theTextBox.obj.serverCode,
    BuildChoices,null,"POST",strParams);
}
```

When we called the function `TypeAhead()` from the function `GiveOptions()`, we passed the current string value from the textbox to perform the search. We need to build the parameter string, `strParams`, that contains our textbox string value and also the `matchAnywhere` boolean value. Both of these were used in listing 10.1 to develop the results. Then we start to load the document by calling the Content-Loader. We are sending the URL of the server-side page and the JavaScript function to call when the results are returned as the first two parameters in the ContentLoader. The third parameter is `null` since we want to ignore any error messages. Ignoring the errors allows the type-ahead to act like a normal text field. The last two properties inform the ContentLoader to post the data to the server and send the form parameters contained in the string `strParams`.

When the results are returned from the server, the function `BuildChoices()` is called to allow us to finish the processing of the data on the client. When we developed the server-side code, we returned the results as a two-dimensional JavaScript array. This array contained the option's text-value pairs for the choices. However, in the response, it is just a string of characters. We need to take this returned string and make it accessible as a JavaScript array. Listing 10.12 contains the functionality that executes the information returned from our ContentLoader using the `eval()` method.

Listing 10.12 Transforming the `responseText` property to a JavaScript array

```
function BuildChoices(){
  var strText = this.req.responseText;
  eval(strText);
  BuildList(strLastValue);
  bMadeRequest = false;
}
```

The `responseText` property of the returned request object lets us obtain the text from the Ajax request. To allow this returned string to be used by our JavaScript code, we need to use the `eval()` method. The `eval()` method evaluates the string contained within its parentheses. In this case, it recognizes that the string is a variable declaration to make a new array. It processes the array so that we can access it. If we were just to write the string to the page, it would not be accessible to the JavaScript statement. Developers frown on using the `eval()` method since it is known to be slow. However, in this case we are eliminating the need to loop through an XML document on the client to obtain the values. Now we can call the function `BuildList()` to format and display the returned results. We also want to set our boolean `bMadeRequest` to `false` to inform the rest of the script that the request to the server is complete.

Building the results span

The use of JavaScript to manipulate the current document is normally considered to be DHTML. In this example, we are taking a two-dimensional array and turning it into lines of text on the screen. Looking back at figure 10.4, we see a list of words that have a portion of their text underlined. The underlined text is the text that matches what the user entered. We are going to display those words in the span element.

The BuildList() function that we create in listing 10.13 utilizes a series of three functions. The functions include finding the matched words, setting the position of the span, and formatting the results with the underline.

Listing 10.13 Formatting the results into a displayable format

```
function BuildList(theText){
  SetElementPosition(theTextBox);     <— Set element position
  var theMatches = MakeMatches(theText);   <— Format matches
  theMatches = theMatches.join().replace(/\,/gi,"");
  if(theMatches.length > 0){
    document.getElementById("spanOutput")
      .innerHTML = theMatches;
    document.getElementById(
      "OptionsList_0").className =       Show
      "spanHighElement";                 results
    currentValueSelected = 0;
    bNoResults = false;
  }
  else{
    currentValueSelected = -1;
    bNoResults = true;
    if(theTextBox.obj.showNoMatchMessage)
      document.getElementById(
        "spanOutput").innerHTML =
        "<span class='noMatchData'>" +    Show no
        theTextBox.obj                    matches
        .noMatchingDataMessage +
        "</span>";
    else HideTheBox();
  }
}
```

The function BuildList() in listing 10.13 takes the string the user entered and formats the results. The first thing we need to do is dynamically position the span element directly under the textbox from which the type-ahead is being implemented. To do this, we call the function SetElementPosition() (which we develop in the section "Dynamically setting an element's position"). After we position the span element, we can start to manipulate the array to find the matches by using the `MakeMatches()` function (see the section "Using regular expressions"). This function returns an array that contains only the information that matches the user's input. We are using JavaScript to limit the results on the client rather than requiring the processing to be done on the server like most of the type-ahead applications available online.

The `MakeMatches()` function formats the results and returns them as an array. We then turn this array into a string by using the `join` method. If the length of the string is greater than 0, then we can display the results in a span by setting its `innerHTML` property. Then we select the first element in the list and set its `class-Name` so it is highlighted.

If the returned array contains no data, then we display our "no matches" message if the textbox allows it. We make sure that we set the `currentSelectedValue` to `-1` so we know there are no matches. If no message is to be displayed, then we just hide the box.

We've finished the `BuildList()` function, so now we have to create all the functions that it calls. The first one we'll tackle is `SetElementPosition()`.

Dynamically setting an element's position

The input textbox is positioned on the page by the browser's layout engine. When we construct the DHTML drop-down suggest, we want to place it exactly in line with the textbox. One of our most difficult tasks is finding the position of a non-positioned element, in this case the textbox, so that we can compute the drop-down's coordinates. A nonpositioned element is one that is relatively set on the page without specifying the absolute left and top positions. If we reference the left and top positions for our textbox, we'll get an undefined string returned. Therefore, we need to use some JavaScript to determine the position of our element so that our box of choices lines up directly underneath it. In listing 10.14, we are dynamically positioning the span element to line up under our textbox.

Listing 10.14 Dynamically finding the position of a nonpositioned element

```
function SetElementPosition(theTextBoxInt){

  var selectedPosX = 0;
  var selectedPosY = 0;
  var theElement = theTextBoxInt;
  if (!theElement) return;
  var theElemHeight = theElement.offsetHeight;
  var theElemWidth = theElement.offsetWidth;
```

```
while(theElement != null){
  selectedPosX += theElement.offsetLeft;
  selectedPosY += theElement.offsetTop;
  theElement = theElement.offsetParent;
}
xPosElement = document.getElementById("spanOutput");
xPosElement.style.left = selectedPosX;
if(theTextBoxInt.obj.matchTextBoxWidth)
  xPosElement.style.width = theElemWidth;
xPosElement.style.top = selectedPosY + theElemHeight
xPosElement.style.display = "block";
if(theTextBoxInt.obj.useTimeout){
  xPosElement.onmouseout = StartTimeout;
  xPosElement.onmouseover = EraseTimeout;
}
else{
  xPosElement.onmouseout = null;
  xPosElement.onmouseover = null;
}
}
```

In listing 10.14, we declare our function SetElementPosition(), which accepts one parameter: the textbox object reference. Two local variables, selectedPosX and selectedPosY, are set to 0. These two integers are used to calculate the position of the element. The textbox reference is set into another local variable. The textbox's width and height are obtained by referencing the offsetHeight and offsetWidth properties.

A while loop is used to loop through the document tree. The document tree allows us to obtain the X and Y positions of the element relative to its parent. By looping through each positioned parent, we can find the exact position of the element by adding the offset position to the two local variables that we created.

Once we obtain the position of the textbox, we can retrieve the span's object reference, which is used to set the left and top positions of the drop-down suggest element. We then look at the textbox's obj object that we created to see if its width property is supposed to match the width of the textbox. If the boolean is true, then we set the width of the span. If the boolean is false, the width comes from the value specified in the stylesheet. The last step is to change the visibility of the span so it is not hidden from the user's view any more. We do this by setting the display property to block.

Now that our span is adequately positioned and visible to the user, we can develop the code that fills in the selectable option's content.

Using regular expressions

Since we are going to be searching for string segments, regular expressions are one of the best ways to find matches with added flexibility. The `MakeMatches()` function that we create next allows us to find the words in the options list that match the user's text in the textbox. This means we can avoid a trip to the server after every keystroke, since the function narrows the choices for us. The code in listing 10.15 lets us save bandwidth by limiting our result set.

Listing 10.15 Using regular expressions to limit results

```
var countForId = 0;
function MakeMatches(xCompareStr){

  countForId = 0;
  var matchArray = new Array();
  var regExp = new RegExp(theTextBox.obj.regExAny +
    xCompareStr,theTextBox.obj.regExFlags);
  for(i=0;i<arrOptions.length;i++){
    var theMatch = arrOptions[i][0].match(regExp);
    if(theMatch){
      matchArray[matchArray.length]=
        CreateUnderline(arrOptions[i][0],
                        xCompareStr,i);
    }
  }
  return matchArray;
}
```

We create the function `MakeMatches()`, which accepts one parameter: the string the user entered. We then reset the variable `countForId` to 0 and create a local array variable `matchArray`. (Note that `countForId` is a global variable. That keeps the example simple for now. We'll do away with it in the refactoring section later!) The key to this function is creating a regular expression that finds the options that match the user's input. Since we have already determined the parameters for the regular expression when we created the code in listing 10.6, we just need to reference our textbox's object. We add the property `reqExAny`, which allows us to match at the beginning of or anywhere in the string. The `regExFlags` property lets us determine whether to ignore the case when performing the matches.

With the regular expression completed, we loop through the array `arrOptions` to verify that the options in the array match our regular expression. If they match, then we add the text to our array `matchArray` after we call the function `CreateUnderline()`. `CreateUnderline()` formats the code to be displayed.

After we loop through all the elements in our array, we return the matched options to the main function `BuildList()`, where the matches are displayed to the user. `MakeMatches()` provides the caching mechanism that we talked about earlier. Instead of returning to the server to limit the search for every keystroke, regular expressions allow us to limit the available options to the user. The `CreateUnderline()` function is the last step in formatting the results.

Manipulating strings

The final step for formatting the strings so that the user can view and interact with them is to manipulate the string so that it is contained within a span tag, has an underline under the matching text, and has the `onclick` event handler attached to it so we can select it with the mouse. This section uses regular expressions again to build the formatted string, as you can see in listing 10.16.

Listing 10.16   Performing string manipulation with JavaScript

```
var undeStart = "<span class='spanMatchText'>";
var undeEnd = "</span>";

var selectSpanStart = "<span style='width:100%;display:block;'
  class='spanNormalElement' onmouseover='SetHighColor(this)' ";
var selectSpanEnd ="</span>";

function CreateUnderline(xStr,xTextMatch,xVal){
  selectSpanMid = "onclick='SetText(" + xVal + ")'" +
    "id='OptionsList_" +
    countForId + "' theArrayNumber='"+ xVal +"'>";
  var regExp = new RegExp(theTextBox.obj.regExAny +
    xTextMatch,theTextBox.obj.regExFlags);
  var aStart = xStr.search(regExp);
  var matchedText = xStr.substring(aStart,
                        aStart + xTextMatch.length);
  countForId++;
  return selectSpanStart + selectSpanMid +
        xStr.replace(regExp,undeStart +
        matchedText + undeEnd) + selectSpanEnd;
}
```

In listing 10.16, we define two variables to hold strings that are used to insert a CSS class around the portion of text that matches the string. This allows us to style the text easily. The first variable, `undeStart`, holds our start span tag, while the second variable, `undeEnd`, holds the closing span tag.

The next two variables form the container for the entire string. This container lets us manipulate the background color and determine whether the cell is clicked on. You can see that in the variable selectSpanStart, we added a mouse-over to highlight the cell. The selectSpanEnd variable is just the closing tag for the span.

Our function CreateUnderline() is called by the MakeMatches() function that we just coded. MakeMatches() passes in three parameters: the string the user entered, the option's text, and the option's value. With the passed-in data, we can develop the onclick handler and add an ID for the span. The onclick handler allows us to select the option, and the ID allows us to use DOM to select the option from the list.

We use a regular expression again to match the text typed by the user. This is so that we can insert the underline spans we created in the string. The search method is used to determine where the match is located in the string. After we find the location of the string, we can obtain the substring so that we can keep the original formatting. Our counter countForId is incremented, and we return our formatted string by joining together all the span elements that we created. The returned text is now formatted, but we still need to finish the CSS classes we added to the span elements.

The span elements were assigned CSS class names, so we do not have to manually go into the JavaScript code to change certain properties of the text. This allows us to fit the autocomplete textbox into any color scheme by simply changing these few CSS rules:

```
span.spanMatchText{ text-decoration: underline;
                    font-weight: bold; }
span.spanNormalElement{ background: #C0C0C0; }
span.spanHighElement{ background: #000040;
                      color: white;
                      cursor: pointer; }
span.noMatchData{ font-weight: bold;
                  color: #0000FF; }
```

Remember that in figure 10.4 the matching text was bold and underlined. You can see those two properties listed in the CSS rule span.spanMatchText. The span default style is represented with span.spanNormalElement, which contains a gray background color. The selected item is applied the CSS rule span.spanHigh-Element. By looking back at that figure you can see that the background color is dark gray and the text color is white. The cursor is also changed to a pointer, so the user knows she can select that option with the mouse. We can add more properties to any of the elements, such as fonts, sizes, borders, and so on. Now that we have built the stylesheet rules, we have finished working with outputting the results. All that is left is handling the Enter and arrow keys and creating our timer (which hides the options in case of inactivity).

Highlighting the options

Earlier in the chapter, we captured the keypresses of the Up and Down Arrow keys so that the user could move the selectedIndex up or down without having to use her mouse. The arrow keys send us either 1 (to move down the selection) or -1 (to move up the selection). When we move a selection, we apply CSS classes to the span elements. We are also adjusting the global variable currentValueSelected so that it holds our current index. The MoveHighlight() function in listing 10.17 gives us a richer user interface since it interacts with both the mouse and the keyboard.

Listing 10.17 Changing the CSS class names of elements with JavaScript

```
function MoveHighlight(xDir){
  if(currentValueSelected >= 0){
    newValue = parseInt(currentValueSelected) + parseInt(xDir);
    if(newValue > -1 && newValue < countForId){
      currentValueSelected = newValue;
      SetHighColor (null);
    }
  }
}

function SetHighColor(theTextBox){
  if(theTextBox){
   currentValueSelected =
   theTextBox.id.slice(theTextBox.id.indexOf("_")+1,
   theTextBox.id.length);
  }
  for(i = 0; i < countForId; i++){
    document.getElementById('OptionsList_' + i).className =
      'spanNormalElement';
  }
  document.getElementById('OptionsList_' +
    currentValueSelected).className = 'spanHighElement';
}
```

The MoveHighlight() function enables the user to use the Up and Down Arrow keys to make a selection. The function accepts one parameter, xDir, symbolizing the direction in which the highlight should be moved. The first check verifies that we have options to select. If there are options, we can obtain the new value. We verify that the new value is within the range of the selection. If it is, we set currentValueSelected and proceed to the next function, SetHighColor(), to highlight the new selection.

SetHighColor() is called from two different events: the arrow keys and the onmouseover event handler. This function is called to remove the highlight from the last selected option and add it to the new option that has been chosen. The onmouseover event in listing 10.16 passes in the object of the span; therefore, we need to obtain the index number of the span by ripping apart the ID. The arrow keys pass this value, so we are not required to perform this action since the move-Highlight() function already set currentValueSelected.

We loop through all of the span tags and set their CSS class to spanNormal-Element. This resets their appearance to their nonselected state. After the looping is completed, we add the CSS class to the selected option. With the two functions that we just created, we have given the user the ability to select an option with either the mouse or the keyboard. All that is left is to take this selected value and add it to the textbox.

Setting the selected value

The purpose of the type-ahead suggest is to allow the users to select available options to limit the amount of effort required to fill in a form field. In order to do this, we need to take the index of the item that the user selected and set the text to the textbox and the value to the hidden text field. These three functions in listing 10.18 allow our span element to act like an HTML select element.

> **Listing 10.18 Handling the arrow keys and mouse click events**

```
function SetText(xVal){
  theTextBox.value = arrOptions[xVal][0];  //set text value
  theTextBox.obj.hidden.value = arrOptions[xVal][1];
  document.getElementById("spanOutput").style.display = "none";
  currentValueSelected = -1;  //remove the selected index
}

function GrabHighlighted(){
  if(currentValueSelected >= 0){
    xVal = document.getElementById("OptionsList_" +
      currentValueSelected).getAttribute("theArrayNumber");
    SetText(xVal);
    HideTheBox();
  }
}
```

```
function HideTheBox(){
  document.getElementById("spanOutput").style.display = "none";
  currentValueSelected = -1;
  EraseTimeout();
}
```

The function that allows us to obtain the text and value of the selected item is `GrabHighlighted()`. First we need to see if the user has selected a value. If a value is selected, then we obtain the index number of the `arrOptions` array in which the text resides. To do this, we grab the value from the attribute, `theArrayNumber`, that we set earlier. Then, we call the function `SetText()` to set the selected option's text and value into their respective form elements.

`SetText()` uses the index value passed in as a parameter to index the array `arrOptions`. The visible text the user sees is set by indexing the first index of the array. The hidden form element receives the second index value stored in our array. After we retrieve the values, we remove the option list from the screen by calling our function `HideTheBox()`.

`HideTheBox()` allows us to remove the span, `spanOutput`, from the view. To do this, we reference the span and set its `style.display` property to `none`. We remove the selected index by setting the variable `currentValueSelected` to -1. Any timers that we may have set are removed by calling `EraseTimeout()`, which we develop next.

Using JavaScript timers

This is the final JavaScript section before the type-ahead project is complete, so your brain may be hurting from all of this client-side code. The JavaScript's `setTimeout()` method executes a statement after an elapsed time has passed. The elapsed time is specified in milliseconds, which we added to the object we created back in listing 10.6. The reason for using a timer is to hide the selection span if there is an inactive timeout period. If we set the parameter in our object `useTimeout` to `true`, then this function will be called. The timer in listing 10.19 gives us one more feature for a rich user interface.

Listing 10.19   Attaching and removing timing events

```
function EraseTimeout(){
  clearTimeout(isTiming);
  isTiming = false;
}
function StartTimeout(){
```

```
isTiming = setTimeout("HideTheBox()",
            theTextBox.obj.theVisibleTime);
}
```

The function `StartTimeout()` sets the timer when the function is executed. We initialize the timer by setting the variable `isTiming` to the `setTimeout` method. The `setTimeout` method should call the function `HideTheBox()` after the set time span, indicated by `theVisibleTime`.

The only other thing we have to do is to remove the timeout. To cancel it, we create the `EraseTimeout()` function that uses JavaScript's built-in `clearTimeout()` function for preventing `HideTheBox()` from firing. We set our boolean `isTiming` to `false`.

Upon finishing that last line of code, we can now run the type-ahead suggest project! Save the project, open it, and start typing in a word. Figure 10.5 shows the progression of the type-ahead suggest. The first letter, *s*, returned more than 15 options. The second letter, *h*, reduced the list to five options. The third letter, *o*, reduced the list to one, which we selected by pressing the Enter key. By adding this project to any form, you can increase the efficiency of your users so they do not have to type in entire words.

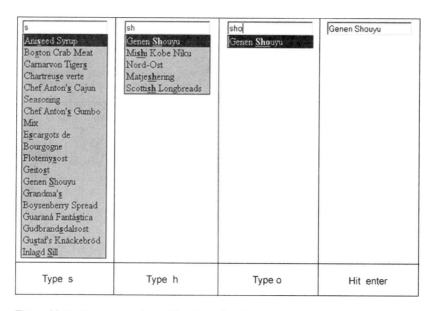

Figure 10.5   The progression of the type-ahead project

10.4 Adding functionality: multiple elements with different queries

With the way that we designed the script, we can have multiple type-ahead select elements on the page. We just need to add declarations with new calls to Set-Properties() for each element. The downside to this method is that in order to have different values fill in the drop-down, we would have to reference different server-side pages. In most cases we will be fine with this, but the only difference between these methods is most likely the SQL statement.

We can come up with an elaborate solution to this problem by adding an additional parameter to our custom object and sending it to the server. Another option is to work with what we have now so that we can make a minimum number of changes to our code. In this case, the simple solution involves changing one line in our code and adding an if statement on the server-side code.

The goal is to be able to somehow differentiate between the elements on the server to determine which element has caused the postback. A simple way to tell the difference is to use the name that is on the element. In this case, we'll reference the name of our textbox. In listing 10.20, we alter the parameter string to allow for this new functionality.

Listing 10.20 Altering the `TypeAhead()` function to allow for different queries

```
function TypeAhead(xStrText){
  var strParams = "q=" + xStrText + "&where=" +
    theTextBox.obj.matchAnywhere + "&name=" + theTextBox.name;
  var loader1 = new net.ContentLoader(theTextBox.obj.serverCode,
    BuildChoices,null,"POST",strParams);
}
```

By making the slight change to the variable strParams in the function Type-Ahead(), we are passing the name of the textbox in the form parameters being passed to the server. That means we can reference this value on the server and use either an if-else or a case statement to run a different query. Now we do not need multiple pages for multiple elements.

10.5 Refactoring

Now that we've developed a fairly robust set of features for providing type-ahead suggest capabilities, it's time to think about how to package all of this functionality in a more palatable way for the consuming web developer. What we've developed to this point provides the functionality needed for the suggest behavior, but it has some drawbacks in terms of the work required for a developer to plug it into a web page—or 20 to 30 web pages, for that matter.

So let's imagine for a moment that we are the grand architect of an Ajax-based web framework and we've been assigned the task of writing a suggest component for the rest of the company to use. As the requirements-gathering meeting disperses, we're handed a sheet giving us our loose set of functional requirements. Unsure of what we're getting into, we glance down at the list (table 10.2).

Table 10.2 Our functional requirements

Number	Requirement Description	Priority
1	The component must work with existing HTML markup without requiring any changes to the markup. Simple changes to the head section to inject the component's behavior are acceptable.	1
2	The component must support being instantiated multiple times on the same page with no additional effort.	1
3	Each component instance should be independently configurable, in terms of both the behavioral aspects (e.g., case matching, match anywhere) and the CSS styling.	1
4	The component should not introduce any global variables. The company uses third-party JavaScript libraries, and the global namespace is already cluttered. Any global names, with the exception of the component itself, are strictly prohibited.	1
5	The component should provide reasonable defaults for all of the configuration options.	1
6	The component must work in IE and Firefox.	1
7	The component should use an open source framework to reduce the amount of coding effort required and improve the quality and robustness of the solution.	1
8	Oh, and if you can, get it done by the end of the week.	1

As we survey the list, several thoughts run through our head. Okay, first of all, the powers that be don't seem understand the concept of a priority. But we're fairly used to that, so we look to the heart of the matter—the requirements. And despite all our hard work, we've satisfied less than half of them. Our script is already done, so that satisfies number 7 in the sense that we don't need to reduce the effort because the script is already implemented. Obviously requirement 8 is satisfied for the same reason. Our script supports multiple browsers, so number 6 is covered as well. As for the rest, we've got some work to do. We have only a week, so we'd better get started.

10.5.1 Day 1: developing the TextSuggest component game plan

The first thing to decide is how to boost productivity to accommodate the short time schedule. One of the best ways to do this is by leveraging the work of others. If someone else can do some of the work, that's less for us to do. So for this component, we're going to leverage the open source efforts of Rico (http://open-rico.org) and by extension Prototype.js (http://prototype.conio.net/). Rico provides some Ajax infrastructure, effects, and utility methods that will boost our development speed. Prototype provides some infrastructure for nice syntactic idioms that will make our code look cleaner and also take less time to develop. Let's take a look at the implications of using Prototype and Rico.

Prototype

Prototype provides developers with a few extensions to the core JavaScript object as well as a few functions that make for a nice coding style. Here are the ones we'll use in this example:

The Class object

The Class object introduced in the Prototype library has a single method called `create()`, which has the responsibility of creating instances that can have any number of methods. The `create()` method returns a function that calls another method in the same object named `initialize()`. It sounds complicated from the inside, but in practical use, it is straightforward. What this effectively does is create a syntactical way for specifying types in JavaScript. The idiom is as follows:

```
var TextSuggest = Class.create();

TextSuggest.prototype = {

    initialize: function( p1, p2, p3 ) {    <— Called during construction
    },
    ...
};
```

This segment of code creates what we can think of as a "class" (even though the language itself doesn't support such a concept) and defines a constructor function named `initialize()`. The client of the component can create an instance via this line of code:

```
var textSuggest = new TextSuggest(p1, p2, p3);
```

The `extend()` *method*

The Prototype library extends the JavaScript base object and adds a method to it named `extend()`, thus making this method available to all objects. The `extend()` method takes as its parameters two objects, the base object and the one that will extend it. The properties of the extending object are iterated over and placed into the base object. This allows for a per-instance object extension mechanism. We'll exploit this later when we implement the default values of the configurability parameters of the TextSuggest component.

The `bind/bindAsEventListener()` *method*

The Prototype library also adds two methods to the Function object called `bind()` and `bindAsEventListener()`. These methods provide a syntactically elegant way to create function closures. You will recall other examples where we created closures, such as

```
oThis = this;
this.onclick = function() { oThis.callSomeMethod() };
```

With the `bind()` method of Prototype, this can be expressed more simply as

```
this.onclick = this.callSomeMethod.bind(this);
```

The `bindAsEventHandler()` API passes the Event object to the method and normalizes the differences between IE and the W3C standard event model to boot!

The $ method—syntactic sugar

A little-known fact about JavaScript is that you can name methods with certain special characters, such as the dollar sign ($). The Prototype library did just that to encapsulate one of the most common tasks in DHTML programming, namely, getting an element out of the document based on its ID. So, in our code we will be able to write constructs such as

```
$('textField').value = aNewValue;
```

rather than

```
var textField = document.getElementById('textField')
textField.value = aNewValue;
```

Rico

We got Prototype for free by virtue of using Rico. Let's talk about what we'll be using from Rico. Rico has a rich set of behaviors, drag-and-drop capability, and cinematic effects, but since we are writing a component that uses a single text field, we won't need most of these. What we will be able to use, however, is a nice

Ajax handler and some of the utility methods provided by Rico. We will discuss the utility methods of Rico as the example progresses, but first let's take a moment to discuss the Rico Ajax infrastructure.

The Rico Ajax capabilities are published via a singleton object available to the document named `ajaxEngine`. The `ajaxEngine` API provides support for registering logical names for requests as well as for registering objects that know how to process Ajax responses. For example, consider the following:

```
ajaxEngine.registerRequest( 'getInvoiceData',
                            'someLongGnarlyUrl.do' );
ajaxEngine.registerAjaxObject( 'xyz', someObject );
```

The first line registers a logical name for a potentially ugly Ajax URL. This logical name can then be used when sending requests rather than having to keep track of the aforementioned ugly URL. An example is shown here:

```
ajaxEngine.sendRequest('getInvoiceData', request parameters... );
```

The `registerRequest()` method isolates the usage of URLs to a single location, usually in the `onload` of the body element. If the URL needs to be changed, it can be changed at the point of registration without affecting the rest of the code.

Then `registerAjaxObject()` illustrates the registration of an Ajax handling object. The previous example implies that the object reference `someObject` should be referred to in responses by the logical name `xyz` and be set to handle Ajax responses via an `ajaxUpdate()` method.

Given that these functionalities of the `ajaxEngine` object are used, the only thing left to consider is the XML response expected by the Ajax engine. This is somewhat different from the dynamically generated JavaScript returned by the previous version of this example, but Rico expects to see XML. The response should have a top-level element around all of the `<response>` elements named `<ajax-response>`. Within that element, the server can return as many `<response>` elements as required by the application. This is a nice feature, as it allows the server to return responses handled by different objects that update potentially unrelated portions of a web page—for example, to update a status area, a data area, and a summary area. The XML response for the previous example is shown here:

```
<ajax-response>

    <response type="object" id="xyz">
       ... the rest of the XML response as normal ...
    </response>
```

```
<response...> more response elements if needed..
</response>

</ajax-response>
```

This XML indicates to the `ajaxEngine` that an object registered under the identifier `xyz` should handle this response. The engine finds the object registered under the name `xyz` and passes the content of the appropriate `<response>` element to its `ajaxUpdate()` method.

Well, it was a short day overall. We spent some time researching open source frameworks to boost our productivity, and we came up with a game plan for incorporating them into our component. We've not yet written any code, but we have decided on a jump-start. We also have a good handle on a platform that will boost our performance, satisfying number 7 on our requirements list. Tomorrow we code.

10.5.2 *Day 2: TextSuggest creation—clean and configurable*

Now that there's a good technology platform to build on, let's start writing the component. It's often good to work backward from the desired result in order to think about the contract of our component up front. Let's recap our first requirement:

Requirement 1—The component must work with existing HTML markup without requiring any changes to the markup. Simple changes to the head section to inject the component's behavior are acceptable.

This requirement forces us to leave pretty much everything inside the `<body>` alone. In light of that, let's assume we're going to inject our script into the HTML via code that looks similar to the HTML in listing 10.21.

Listing 10.21 TextSuggest HTML markup

```
<html>
<head>
    <script>
      var suggestOptions = { /*details to come*/ };
      function injectSuggestBehavior() {    ◁— Create component in <head>
        suggest = new TextSuggest( 'field1',
                                   'typeAheadData.aspx',
                                   suggestOptions );
        } );
    </script>
</head>
```

```
<body onload="injectSuggestBehavior()">
   <form name="Form1">
      AutoComplete Text Box:
      <input type="text" id="field1" name="txtUserInput">
   </form>
</body>

</html>
```

The implication of this HTML is that we're going to construct our object with the ID of the text field we will be attaching to, the URL for the Ajax data source, and a set of configuration objects yet to be specified. (Note that the text field needs an ID attribute for this to work properly.) Everything inside the <body> element is left untouched. With that established, let's start with a look at the constructor. We'll put a name for our TextSuggest component into the global namespace via the constructor function that, as you recall, is generated by the Prototype library's Class.create() method, as shown in listing 10.22.

Listing 10.22   TextSuggest constructor

```
TextSuggest = Class.create();

TextSuggest.prototype = {

   initialize: function(anId, url, options) {
      this.id        = anId;                    ❶ Reference the
      this.textInput = $(this.id);                 input element

      var browser    = navigator.userAgent.toLowerCase();
      this.isIE      =
        browser.indexOf("msie") != -1;          ❷ Detect the
      this.isOpera =                               browser type
        browser.indexOf("opera")!= -1;

      this.suggestions = [];
      this.setOptions(options);        ❸ Set the defaults
      this.initAjax(url);
      this.injectSuggestBehavior();
   },
   ...
};
```

Now let's deconstruct the constructor. As already mentioned, we pass into our constructor the ID of the text input to which we'll be attaching the suggest behavior. A reference is held to both the ID and the DOM element for the input field ❶. Next we do a little browser sniffing and store the state for the few things in the rest of the component that need to know specifics about the browser run-time environment ❷. In this case, special case code is needed only for IE and Opera, so we sniff only for them.

We'll discuss the complex part of setting up Ajax and injecting behavior later ❸. Let's concentrate for the rest of the day on component configurability. As you recall, earlier we created a `SetProperties()` function to hold all of the config-urable aspects of our suggest script:

```
function SetProperties
            (xElem, xHidden, xserverCode,
             xignoreCase, xmatchAnywhere,
             xmatchTextBoxWidth, xshowNoMatchMessage,
             xnoMatchingDataMessage, xuseTimeout,
             xtheVisibleTime){
    ...
}
```

This meets the requirement of providing configurability but not of providing a convenient API or appropriate defaults. For this, we introduce an options object that is passed into the constructor. The options object has a property for each configuration parameter of the suggest component. Let's now fill in the options with some configuration parameters:

```
var suggestOptions = {
   matchAnywhere  : true,
   ignoreCase     : true
};

function injectSuggestBehavior() {
   suggest = new TextSuggest( 'field1',
                              'typeAheadXML.aspx',
                              suggestOptions );
   } );
```

This simple idiom comes with a big-time payload:

- It keeps the signature of the constructor clean. The client pages using our component can construct it with only three parameters.

- Configuration parameters can be added over time without changing the contract of the constructor.

- We can write a smart `setOptions()` that provides appropriate default val-ues for any unspecified properties, allowing the caller to specify only the properties that she wants to override.

The last bullet is exactly what the ❸ setOptions() method shown earlier in the constructor does. Let's look at how it works:

```
setOptions: function(options) {
    this.options = {
        suggestDivClassName: 'suggestDiv',
        suggestionClassName: 'suggestion',
        matchClassName    : 'match',
        matchTextWidth    : true,
        selectionColor    : '#b1c09c',
        matchAnywhere     : false,
        ignoreCase        : false,
        count             : 10
    }.extend(options || {});
},
```

Each property in the options object that has an appropriate default value is specified here. Then, the extend() method of the Prototype library is called to override any properties specified in the options object passed in at construction time. The result is a merged options object that has the defaults and overrides specified in a single object! In the example we used here, the matchAnywhere and ignoreCase boolean properties were both overridden to values of true. The values of the configuration properties are explained in table 10.3.

Table 10.3 Values of configuration properties

Value	Explanation
suggestDivClassName	Specifies the CSS class name of the div element that will be generated to hold the suggestions.
suggestionClassName	Specifies the CSS class name of the span element that is generated for each suggestion.
matchClassName	Specifies the CSS class name of the span holding the portion of the suggestion that matches what the user has typed in.
matchTextWidth	A boolean value indicating whether or not the div generated for the suggestions should size itself to match the width of the text field it is attached to.
selectionColor	Specifies a hex value (or any valid value used as a CSS color specification) for the background color of the selected suggestion.
matchAnywhere	A boolean value that specifies whether the match should be looked for only at the beginning of a string or anywhere.

continued on next page

Table 10.3 Values of configuration properties *(continued)*

Value	Explanation
ignoreCase	A boolean value indicating whether or not the matching should be case sensitive.
count	The maximum number of suggestions to render.

Note that there are several options that specify which CSS class names should be generated internally when building the HTML structure for the pop-up list of suggestions. Recall the configurability requirements from table 10.2:

Requirement 3—Each component instance should be independently configurable, in terms of both the behavioral aspects (for example, case matching, match anywhere) and the CSS styling.

Requirement 5—The component should provide reasonable defaults for all of the configuration options.

Our code will use this configuration mechanism to provide per-instance configurability in terms of behavior (for example, case matching) as well as styling (for example, the CSS class names).

So, here at the end of day 2, we've made a good start on our component. With our constructor out of the way, and with a clean way to make our component highly configurable, it's time to move on to making it Ajax aware.

10.5.3 *Day 3: Ajax enabled*

Let's put some Ajax into action, shall we? A TextSuggest component without Ajax is like a burger without the beef. With no disrespect to vegetarians, it's time for the beef. You already saw a hint of some Ajax setup when we were looking at the constructor. As you might recall, we placed a method call within the constructor called initAjax(). The initAjax() method does the setup required for the Rico Ajax support discussed earlier. Here's the implementation:

```
initAjax: function(url) {
   ajaxEngine.registerRequest( this.id + '_request', url );
   ajaxEngine.registerAjaxObject( this.id + '_updater', this );
},
```

Recall that the registerRequest() method provides the Rico Ajax engine a logical name for the URLs to invoke for a given request via the sendRequest() method. Given that we have to support the requirement of having multiple suggest components on the same page using different URLs (but using the same `ajax-Engine` singleton), we need to generate a unique logical name for each. So, we generate the name for the request based on the ID of the component, which we assume to be unique. The same goes for the handler registration. We register `this` as the object that will handle responses routed to the ID we're generating.

An example would probably help at this point. Suppose we attach the suggest behavior to a field with `id='field1'`, and then we effectively register ourselves as `'field1_updater'`. The XML we expect to come back to this component should have a response element that looks like this:

```
<ajax-response>
    <response type='object' id='field1_updater'>.
        ...same xml content as before.
    </response>
</ajax-response>
```

Internally, we will be sending requests via the following:

```
ajaxEngine.sendRequest( 'field1_request',
                        'param1=val1', 'param2=val2', ... );
```

With that in mind, there are two things we have to do from the client to make our component Ajax enabled: send the request and handle the response. Let's look at each in turn.

Text suggest—sending the Ajax request

Obviously there's a little bit of work involved in getting to the point where we can send a request. The text input will have to generate an `onchange` event that we will listen to and conditionally send a request for the suggestions. We've not put any of that code in place yet, but that's okay. We can still think in terms of our method responsibilities and the contracts we'd like to enforce independently of that being done. So, let's assume that some piece of code yet to be written will decide that it needs to send a request to get some suggestions. Let's call it `sendRequestFor-Suggestions()` and implement it as follows:

```
sendRequestForSuggestions: function() {

  if ( this.handlingRequest ) {
    this.pendingRequest = true;
    return;
  }

  this.handlingRequest = true;
  this.callRicoAjaxEngine();
},
```

All this code does is to conditionally call `this.callRicoAjaxEngine()` if a request is not still being processed. This simple mechanism turns an internal boolean property, `this.handlingRequest`, to `true` as soon as an Ajax request is made and back to `false` (shown later) once the request has been handled. This is a very simple mechanism to use to throttle the sending of events based on the speed of the server. The boolean property `this.pendingRequest` is set to `true` if the method is called while a request is currently being processed. This state will let the handler know that it may have to send another request once the one being processed is finished. Now let's peek under the hood and look at the `callRicoAjaxEngine()` method shown in listing 10.23.

Listing 10.23   Using the Rico `ajaxEngine`

```
callRicoAjaxEngine: function() {
  var callParms = [];
  callParms.push( this.id + '_request');
  callParms.push( 'id='             + this.id);
  callParms.push( 'count='          + this.options.count);
  callParms.push( 'query='          + this.lastRequestString);
  callParms.push( 'match_anywhere=' + this.options.matchAnywhere);
  callParms.push( 'ignore_case='    + this.options.ignoreCase);

  var additionalParms = this.options.requestParameters || [];
  for( var i=0 ; i < additionalParms.length ; i++ )
     callParms.push(additionalParms[i]);

  ajaxEngine.sendRequest.apply( ajaxEngine,
                          callParms );     ⟵ Send the Ajax request
},
```

Build the parameter array

To understand what this method does, we first need to talk about a JavaScript mechanism we are making use of on the very last line of the method:

```
ajaxEngine.sendRequest.apply( ajaxEngine, callParms );
```

This uses a method called `apply()`, which is available to all function objects (see appendix B for more details). Let's illustrate the usage with a simpler example:

```
Greeter.prototype.greetPeople = function(str1, str2) {
   alert('hello ' + str1 + 'and ' + str2)
};
```

Suppose we have an instance of `Greeter` called `friendlyPerson`, and we want to call the `greetPeople()` method on that object. But we don't have the parameters in a form that is easy to pass. We actually have an array of `people`. This is where the `apply` method comes in handy. We can write the code as

```
var people = [ "Joe", "Sally" ];
friendlyPerson.greetPeople.apply( friendlyPerson, people );
```

The `apply()` method converts the array passed in as the second argument to first-class method parameters and invokes the method on the object passed in as the first parameter. The previous code is equivalent to

```
friendlyPerson.greetPeople( people[0], people[1] );
```

Now back to the task at hand. We have to call `ajaxEngine`'s `sendRequest()` method, which takes as its first parameter the logical name of the request, and a variable number of string parameters of the form `key=value` representing the request parameters. Therein lies the rub. We have request parameters from different sources, and we don't know how many we have. Let's look at the code again:

```
var callParms = [];                                      ❶
callParms.push( this.id + '_request');
...
callParms.push( 'ignore_case='    + this.options.ignoreCase);

var additionalParms =
   this.options.requestParameters || [];                 ❷
for( var i=0 ; i < additionalParms.length ; i++ )
   callParms.push(additionalParms[i]);
```

The array of parameters to send to the `sendRequest()` method via `apply` is populated from a combination of the internal state of the object, things like the ID and the `lastRequestString`, as well as specific properties of the Options object (for example, `count`, `matchAnywhere`, `ignoreCase`) ❶.

However, we also have to provide a mechanism for the user of our component to pass in external request parameters as well ❷. For this, we look for the existence of a `requestParameters` property on the options object. If it is non-`null`, it's assumed to be an array of strings of the form `key=value`. The array is iterated over and added to the `callParms` already populated with the component-specific parameters. Finally, the request is sent via

```
ajaxEngine.sendRequest.apply( ajaxEngine, callParms );
```

Whew! Request sending all done. Now let's hope the server is up and running and we get a response. And let's talk about how we will handle it when it does.

Text suggest—handling the Ajax response

We went to a lot of trouble to provide a robust request-sending capability, so we'd better make sure we properly handle the response or all our hard work will be in vain. Recall that Rico's `ajaxEngine` routes the request back to the handler object's `ajaxUpdate()` method, passing the content of the `<response>` element. So, by implication, we must write an `ajaxUpdate()` method, and that method will be the entry point into our response handling. The `ajaxUpdate()` method is shown in listing 10.24 along with its parsing helper methods, `createSuggestions()` and `getElementContent()`.

Listing 10.24   Ajax response handling

```
ajaxUpdate: function( ajaxResponse ) {

   this.createSuggestions( ajaxResponse );          ⟵— Create suggestions

   if ( this.suggestions.length == 0 ) {
      this.hideSuggestions();
      $( this.id + "_hidden").value = "";
   }
   else {
      this.updateSuggestionsDiv();         Create and
      this.showSuggestions();              show UI
      this.updateSelection(0);
   }

   this.handlingRequest = false;           ⟵— Finish handling response

   if ( this.pendingRequest ) {
      this.pendingRequest    = false;
      this.lastRequestString = this.textInput.value;
      this.sendRequestForSuggestions();     ⟵— Send another request
   }
},
createSuggestions: function(ajaxResponse) {
   this.suggestions = [];
   var entries = ajaxResponse.getElementsByTagName('entry');
   for ( var i = 0 ; i < entries.length ; i++ ) {
      var strText  = this.getElementContent(
                     entries[i].getElementsByTagName('text')[0]);
      var strValue = this.getElementContent(
                     entries[i].getElementsByTagName('value')[0]);
      this.suggestions.push({ text: strText, value: strValue });
   }
},
getElementContent: function(element) {
   return element.firstChild.data;
}
```

Because we want to focus solely on the Ajax mechanisms being put in place, we'll just cover much of the content here at a high level and talk about our response handling in terms of the algorithm. The first thing we do is to parse the response via the `createSuggestions()` method into an in-memory representation of the suggestions held in the `suggestions` property. The `suggestions` property is an array of objects, each with a text and a value property corresponding to the `<text>` and `<value>` elements of each `<entry>` in the XML response.

The remainder of the `ajaxUpdate()` method's algorithm is fairly straightforward and should be easy to follow. If no suggestions were found, the pop-up is hidden and the internal value held by the component via a hidden field is cleared. If suggestions were found, the drop-down UI element is created, populated with the suggestions, and displayed, and the selection is updated to be the first one in the list. At this point, the response is considered to be handled, so the `this.handlingRequest` property discussed earlier is set back to `false`. Finally, the `ajaxUpdate()` method checks if there are any pending requests. If so, it sets the `pendingRequest` flag back to `false`, takes the current value in the input field for the `lastRequestString`, and initiates another request cycle via `sendRequest-ForSuggestions()`.

This concludes the full request/response cycle for the Ajax support and wraps up day 3. We've accomplished quite a bit today, plugging in an open source framework that fully "Ajax-enables" our component-meeting requirement, number 7, as well as making sure that it's done in a way that's configurable and supports multiple instances on the same page, satisfying requirements 2 and 3. We'll get into the details of what it means to create, position, show, and hide the UI for the pop-up on day 5. In the meantime, we'll hook up the component events and take care of the keyboard and mouse handling.

10.5.4 Day 4: handling events

Now that the suggest component is fully Ajax enabled, it's time to hook it into the events produced by the native input field's responses to the keyboard. If you are an astute reader, you will have guessed that the code that initiates this process was back in the constructor hiding in a call to the `injectSuggestBehavior()` method. This is the code that initiates all modifications to the DOM of the existing markup, including the event handling, extra inputs, and the container for the suggestions. It's all done programmatically so we don't have to touch any of the HTML code on the page, per requirement number 1. The behavior injection is shown in listing 10.25.

Listing 10.25 The behavior injection

```
injectSuggestBehavior: function() {

   if ( this.isIE ) {
      this.textInput.autocomplete = "off";     <—  Remove IE interference
   }
   var keyEventHandler =
      new TextSuggestKeyHandler(this);    <—  Create controller
   new Insertion.After( this.textInput,
                        '<input type="text" id="' +  this.id +
                        '_preventtsubmit'+
                        '" style="display:none"/>' );
   new Insertion.After( this.textInput,
                        '<input type="hidden" name="'+
                        this.id+'_hidden'+
                        '" id="'+this.id+'_hidden'+'"/>' );

   this.createSuggestionsDiv();    <—  Create UI
},
```

This method first checks to see if the browser is IE and, if so, sets the proprietary autocomplete property value to off. This keeps the autocompletion pop-up from interfering with our own pop-up. Next an object called TextSuggestKeyHandler is created to be the controller object for brokering the events to the right methods. Yes, the event mechanics are enough of a chore on their own that we split this behavior out into a separate object that we will discuss in a moment. The method next inserts a couple of input elements into the markup. You will recall that in the previous round of our script code, we added a hidden input field for storing the value of the component and an invisible text field to prevent the Enter key from causing the form to be submitted. Because our first requirement forbids us from monkeying with the HTML, we programmatically perform these chores with the two Insertion.After() calls. Insertion.After() is brought to us courtesy of the Prototype library. Finally, createSuggestionsDiv() is called to create the containing div element, which holds the UI for the suggestions.

The TextSuggestKeyHandler

We've decided to put the broker of the events into a dedicated controller class. There's nothing new or revolutionary about it, but it's definitely a helpful way to separate class responsibilities. In reality, the design could be further separated by creating explicit classes for the model and view roles to provide a full MVC pattern. This exercise is left to the user, but we will break down the architecture of the RSS reader in chapter 13 with a set of classes that satisfies a traditional MVC pattern.

The controller is constructed in the same way as our main class—using `Class.create()` and an `initialize()` method. The constructor is shown in listing 10.26.

Listing 10.26   The TextSuggestKeyHandler constructor

```
TextSuggestKeyHandler = Class.create();

TextSuggestKeyHandler.prototype = {

   initialize: function( textSuggest ) {
      this.textSuggest = textSuggest;    ◁— Reference to TextSuggest
      this.input       = this.textSuggest.textInput;
      this.addKeyHandling();
   },
   // rest of API
},
```

Upon construction, the controller holds a reference to the suggest component along with the native HTML form input field. It then adds the handlers onto the input field via `this.addKeyHandling()`. The `addKeyHandling()` method is shown in listing 10.27.

Listing 10.27   The keyboard handler

```
addKeyHandling: function() {
   this.input.onkeyup =
      this.keyupHandler.bindAsEventListener(this);
   this.input.onkeydown =
      this.keydownHandler.bindAsEventListener(this);
   this.input.onblur =
      this.onblurHandler.bindAsEventListener(this);
   if ( this.isOpera )
      this.input.onkeypress =
         this.keyupHandler.bindAsEventListener(this);
},
```

All the relevant events that we need to listen to along with the Opera-specific hack mentioned in the first round of our script development are set up in this method. You will recall that the `bindAsEventListener()` method is a closure mechanism provided courtesy of the Prototype library. This mechanism allows our handlers to call first-class methods on the controller and normalizes the IE and W3C event models. Very nice, indeed. keyupHandler(), keydownHandler(), onblurHandler(), and their helper methods are mostly a repackaging of what's already been covered with a few changes. We'll show the full range of methods next and point out differences from the original script along the way. We'll start by discussing keydownHandler() and its manipulation of the selection. The keydownHandler() method is shown in listing 10.28.

Listing 10.28 keydownHandler() method

```
keydownHandler: function(e) {
   var upArrow   = 38;
   var downArrow = 40;

   if ( e.keyCode == upArrow ) {
      this.textSuggest.moveSelectionUp();
      setTimeout( this.moveCaretToEnd.bind(this), 1 );
   }
   else if ( e.keyCode == downArrow ) {
      this.textSuggest.moveSelectionDown();
   }
},
```

The most significant difference from the original script in terms of functionality is in the handling of the arrow keys. The arrow keys in our TextSuggest component handle the movement of the selection based on the onkeydown event rather than the onkeyup event. This is done solely as a usability improvement. It's somewhat disconcerting to see the selection remain where it is when you press one of the arrow keys, only to see it move once you release the key. keydownHandler() therefore handles the movement of the selection. Note that the selection manipulation methods are methods of the TextSuggest component. The controller, because it saved a reference to the component at construction time, can call these methods through the saved object reference this.textSuggest. The selection manipulation methods of TextSuggest are shown in listing 10.29 for the sake of completeness.

Listing 10.29 TextSuggest selection manipulation methods

```
moveSelectionUp: function() {
   if ( this.selectedIndex > 0 ) {
      this.updateSelection(this.selectedIndex - 1);
   }
},
```

```
moveSelectionDown: function() {
   if ( this.selectedIndex < (this.suggestions.length - 1)  ) {
      this.updateSelection(this.selectedIndex + 1);
   }
},
updateSelection: function(n) {
   var span = $(this.id +"_"+this.selectedIndex);
   if (span){
      span.style.backgroundColor = "";      <—— Clear previous selection
   }
   this.selectedIndex = n;
   var span = $(this.id+"_"+this.selectedIndex);
   if (span){
      span.style.backgroundColor =
         this.options.selectionColor;
   }
},
```

The `updateSelection()` method does all the real work of actually changing the visual state of the selection. It updates the span created in the selection list—we'll write that code on day 5—and sets its `style.backgroundColor` to the value specified as the `options.selectionColor` of our component's Configuration object.

Before we leave the topic of key-down handling, there's one more bit of bookkeeping to take care of. Because we handle the arrow keys on the key-down rather than the key-up, we have to change the Up Arrow from its default behavior of moving the caret backward within the text field. We do this with the `moveCaretToEnd()` method called on a one-millisecond delay via `setTimeout`. The `moveCaretToEnd()` method is implemented as shown in listing 10.30.

Listing 10.30 TextSuggest `moveCaretToEnd()` method

```
moveCaretToEnd: function() {
   var pos = this.input.value.length;
   if (this.input.setSelectionRange) {
      this.input.setSelectionRange(pos,pos);
   }
   else if(this.input.createTextRange){
      var m = this.input.createTextRange();
      m.moveStart('character',pos);
      m.collapse();
      m.select();
   }
},
```

Now, let's move onto the key-up handling. The key-up implementation is a bit simpler than the key-down. All it has to do is broker its event to one of a couple of places based on the value in the input field and the key that was pressed. Let's take a look at the details in listing 10.31.

```
keyupHandler: function(e) {
   if ( this.input.length == 0 && !this.isOpera )
      this.textSuggest.hideSuggestions();

  if ( !this.handledSpecialKeys(e) )
     this.textSuggest.handleTextInput();
},
handledSpecialKeys: function(e) {
   var enterKey  = 13;
   var upArrow    = 38;
   var downArrow = 40;

   if ( e.keyCode == upArrow || e.keyCode == downArrow ) {
      return true;
   }
   else if ( e.keyCode == enterKey ) {
      this.textSuggest.setInputFromSelection();
      return true;
   }

   return false;
},
```

The key-up handler first checks to see if the input field contains any text. If not, it tells the TextSuggest component to hide its pop-up list of suggestions. Next it checks to see if the key pressed was one of the special keys: Up Arrow, Down Arrow, or the Enter key. If either the Up or Down Arrow key was pressed, the method just returns without performing any action, since the arrow keys have already been handled during the key-down processing. However, if the Enter key was pressed, the method tells the TextSuggest component to set its input value based on the currently selected item in the suggestion list. Finally, if the input field has a value and the key pressed was *not* one of the special keys, the key-up handler tells the TextSuggest component to consider that there is some input to be processed via the `textSuggest.handleTextInput()` method. This is the method of the TextSuggest component that finally calls the Ajax infrastructure we diligently put in place yesterday. The code for `handleTextInput()` is implemented in listing 10.32.

Listing 10.32   Text input handler

```
handleTextInput: function() {
  var previousRequest =
     this.lastRequestString;    <— Previous request value
  this.lastRequestString =
     this.textInput.value;    <— Current request value
  if ( this.lastRequestString == "" )
     this.hideSuggestions();
  else if ( this.lastRequestString != previousRequest ) {
     this.sendRequestForSuggestions();    <— Ajax request for data
  }
},
```

The handleTextInput() method first sets a local variable called previousRequest to the prior value of this.lastRequestString. It then sets the lastRequestString property to the current value of the input field so that it can compare the two to make sure that it's not trying to send a request for the same information that has already been requested. If the request is an empty string, the pop-up list is hidden. If the request is a valid request for new information, the handleTextInput() method calls the sendRequestForSuggestions() method that we wrote yesterday to call the Ajax-based data source to get some suggestions from the server. If the request is the same as the last one, the request is ignored and no action is taken. Finally, the pieces are starting to come together. The construction, the configuration, the Ajax handling, the event handling—it's almost as if we know what we're doing. And just in the nick of time; it's already day 4!

We have one more method of our controller class to cover—the onblur handler. The onblur handler is a very simple method that sets the value of the text field from the current selection and hides the suggestion. The implementation is as follows:

```
onblurHandler: function(e) {
  if ( this.textSuggest.suggestionsDiv.style.display == '' )
     this.textSuggest.setInputFromSelection();
  this.textSuggest.hideSuggestions();
}
```

The onblurHandler and handledSpecialKeys both reference a method of the Text-Suggest component that we've not seen yet—setInputFromSelection(). This method does essentially the same thing that our SetText() function did earlier—namely, to take the currently selected suggestion; set both the input field and the hidden field with its text and value, respectively; and hide the list of suggestions. The implementation is shown here:

```
setInputFromSelection: function() {
  var hiddenInput = $( this.id + "_hidden" );
  var suggestion  = this.suggestions[ this.selectedIndex ];

  this.textInput.value = suggestion.text;    <⎯  Update visible value
  hiddenInput.value    = suggestion.value;   <⎯  Update hidden value
  this.hideSuggestions();
}
```

We may have put in a little overtime to accomplish all that's been done today. We created a `controller` class to handle all of our event management. We used the Prototype library's `bindAsEventListener()` method to automatically create closures for us and normalize the IE and W3C event models. We implemented our key-up/down handlers to encapsulate the complexities of processing the selection as well as normal text input. We ensured that we initiate only requests for new information. We managed the showing and hiding of the suggestions UI as appropriate. We updated the DOM programmatically to manage the hidden input value and the invisible text field that prevents form submission when the Enter key is pressed. And we handled the updating of the hidden and visible values of the TextSuggest component. On day 5, we wrap a bow around our refactored component by implementing all the methods required to create the pop-up, position it, show it, hide it, and manage its mouse events. The once dim light at the end of the tunnel is now clearly in view.

10.5.5 Day 5: the suggestions pop-up UI

Now that we're fully plugged in, so to speak, it's time to tie up all the loose ends. To this point, we've created infrastructure for configurability and defaults, Ajax request and response handling, and the events that tie everything together. All that's left to cover is the graphical part. What we're referring to here, obviously, is the pop-up list of suggestions and all that implies. The tasks left to handle with respect to the UI are as follows:

- Creation of the suggestion pop-up UI. This entails the creation of the div for the suggestions as well as the span for each suggestion.
- The positioning of the pop-up.
- The population of the pop-up with suggestions.
- The showing and hiding of the suggestions.

Creating the suggestion pop-up

Let's go back and examine the implementation of the `injectSuggestBehavior()` method. Recall that this code was more or less the entry point to all the DOM manipulation done by the TextSuggest component:

```
injectSuggestBehavior: function() {
    // HTML Dom Behavior Injection...
    this.createSuggestionsDiv();
},
```

The last line of the `injectSuggestBehavior()` method calls the `createSuggestionsDiv()` method, which creates the outermost containing div of the suggestion pop-up. Since this is the container of all GUI artifacts, it's the logical place to start looking at UI code. The details of the implementation are shown in listing 10.33.

Listing 10.33   Creating the suggestion pop-up UI

```
createSuggestionsDiv: function() {
    this.suggestionsDiv =
        document.createElement("div");        ❶ Create the div
    this.suggestionsDiv.className =
        this.options.suggestDivClassName;     ❷ Style the div

    var divStyle =
        this.suggestionsDiv.style;            ❸ Add
    divStyle.position = 'absolute';              behavioral
    divStyle.zIndex   = 101;                     style
    divStyle.display  = "none";

    this.textInput.parentNode.appendChild
                (this.suggestionsDiv);        ❹ Insert into document
},
```

The creation method of the container has four basic responsibilities. First, it has to create the DIV via the document's `createElement()` API ❶.

Second, it has to style the DIV according to the client configuration ❷. Recall that one of our requirements was to make the CSS styling of each component instance individually configurable. We achieve that in this case by setting the div's `className` attribute according to the `suggestDivClassName` property of the options object. You will recall that we set the default value of this property to `suggestDiv` within the `setOptions` method. So if the user doesn't explicitly specify a value for a property, this is what she will get. This is a convenient feature because it allows the client of our component to have a default stylesheet that uses our default class names to style all TextSuggest component instances used across the application. Other stylesheets could also be provided (for example, product- or customer-specific stylesheets) that override the definitions of these standard style names. And finally, an individual page can override the value of the suggestDiv-ClassName parameter to provide a page-level or instance-level styling to the component. Sounds pretty flexible to us.

There are certain aspects of the style of the pop-up that are nonnegotiable, annotated as "Behavioral style," so we style them explicitly through the style attribute of the element ❸. Note that anything styled programmatically via the style attribute overrides anything specified via a CSS className, typically by a stylesheet. These nonnegotiable aspects are 1) position='absolute' because the component must manage the positioning of the div internally, 2) zIndex=101, which we use to make sure the pop-up is on top of everything on the page, and 3) display="none" because the pop-up has to be hidden from the user's view until the user's keystrokes trigger it. Note that the value of 101 for the zIndex is somewhat arbitrary.

Finally, the method inserts the div into the document as a sibling of the text field ❹. The parent in this case really doesn't matter, since the div will be positioned absolutely.

Positioning the pop-up

Now that our pop-up has been created, at some point it will have to be shown. But before it can be shown, it has to be positioned. When we show the pop-up, we want it to appear just below the text field and to be aligned with the left side of the text field. Let's write the positionSuggestionsDiv method in listing 10.34.

Listing 10.34 Positioning the pop-up UI

```
positionSuggestionsDiv: function() {
   var textPos = RicoUtil.toDocumentPosition(this.textInput);
   var divStyle = this.suggestionsDiv.style;
   divStyle.top  = (textPos.y + this.textInput.offsetHeight)
                   + "px";
   divStyle.left = textPos.x + "px";

   if ( this.options.matchTextWidth )
      divStyle.width = (this.textInput.offsetWidth -
                        this.padding()) + "px";
},
```

You will recall that in the previous version of this script, we wrote a method to calculate the absolute position of the text field. In this refactored version, we are relying on a utility method provided by Rico—toDocumentPosition(). All we have to do is to use this method to get our reference point and perform the appropriate calculations to get our pop-up below and align on the left with the text field. We then check for the existence of the configuration option matchTextWidth, and if it is true, we also size the width of the div element to match the width of the text input. Note that we adjust the width by the padding value. We do this because, as you recall, we've allowed the div element to be externally styled through a CSS class. We don't know if the user will have put margins and borders on the component, which would throw off the visual alignment to the width of the text field. Let's write a padding() method (listing 10.35) to compute the left and right padding values and margins to subtract from the overall width.

Listing 10.35 Calculation of left and right padding

```
padding: function() {
  try{
    var styleFunc = RicoUtil.getElementsComputedStyle;
    var lPad    = styleFunc( this.suggestionsDiv,
                             "paddingLeft",
                             "padding-left" );
    var rPad    = styleFunc( this.suggestionsDiv,
                             "paddingRight",
                             "padding-right" );
    var lBorder = styleFunc( this.suggestionsDiv,
                             "borderLeftWidth",
                             "border-left-width" );
    var rBorder = styleFunc( this.suggestionsDiv,
                             "borderRightWidth",
                             "border-right-width" );
    lPad    = isNaN(lPad)    ? 0 : lPad;
    rPad    = isNaN(rPad)    ? 0 : rPad;
    lBorder = isNaN(lBorder) ? 0 : lBorder;
    rBorder = isNaN(rBorder) ? 0 : rBorder;
    return parseInt(lPad) + parseInt(rPad) +
           parseInt(lBorder) + parseInt(rBorder);
  }catch (e){ return 0; }
},
```

Getting the calculated style of an element—the actual value of an attribute regardless of how it was set—is tricky business. To achieve this, IE provides a proprietary currentStyle attribute for each element. Mozilla-based browsers use a getComputedStyle() method of the defaultView property of the document to calculate this. Each one of these mechanisms expects a different specification for the attribute being queried, as well. The IE `currentStyle` expects style attributes specified via the JavaScript-like binding (for example, `borderRightWidth`), whereas the Mozilla `getComputedStyle()` expects attributes specified with the stylesheet-like syntax (for example, `border-right-width`). Luckily, Rico provides a method that takes care of all of this for us—`RicoUtil.getElementsComputedStyle()`. We just pass it the element, the IE name for the attribute, and the Mozilla name for the attribute, and the method returns a value. Our method here gets the values of the left and right borders and margins, sums them up, and returns them.

The `Rico.getElementsComputedStyle()` is known to have issues with some versions of Safari, and so we provide a default return value within a `try...catch` block.

Creating the pop-up contents

Now that we have the code to create and position the pop-up, we need to write a method to populate it with actual suggestions before it can be useful. Recall that our `ajaxUpdate()` method parses the XML from the response into an array of suggestion objects. And, if at least one suggestion exists, it calls a method named `this.updateSugggestionsDiv()`. This method is the transformer of the in-memory collection of suggestions to actual SPAN elements within the pop-up div. Let's look at how that's done now:

```
updateSuggestionsDiv: function() {
  this.suggestionsDiv.innerHTML = "";    <— Remove prior content
  var suggestLines = this.createSuggestionSpans();
  for (var i = 0; i < suggestLines.length; i++)          Create new
  this.suggestionsDiv.appendChild(suggestLines[i]);      content
},
```

This method is deceptively simple, but there's still lots of work to do, so hang with us. This method simply sets the value of the `innerHTML` property of the `suggestionsDiv` created earlier to an empty string in order to wipe out any prior content. Then it calls `createSuggestionSpans()` to create a span for each suggestion in the suggestions array. Finally, it iterates over the created spans and appends them to the div. This is where the real work starts. Let's continue by looking at `createSuggestionSpans()` in listing 10.36 to see what's involved in creating them.

Listing 10.36 Creation of suggestion list items

```
createSuggestionSpans: function() {
  var regExpFlags = "";
  if ( this.options.ignoreCase )
    regExpFlags = 'i';
  var startRegExp = "^";
```

```
        if ( this.options.matchAnywhere )
           startRegExp = '';

        var regExp  = new RegExp( startRegExp +
                                       this.lastRequestString,
                                  regExpFlags );

        var suggestionSpans = [];
        for ( var i = 0 ; i < this.suggestions.length ; i++ )
           suggestionSpans.push(
               this.createSuggestionSpan( i, regExp ) );

        return suggestionSpans;
     },
```

This method first looks at our options object to find the value of the `ignoreCase` and `matchAnywhere` properties. This has to be done so that a regular expression can be created with the appropriate parameters that will facilitate the retrieval of the portion of the string in the response that actually matches what the user has typed in. The method then iterates over the `suggestions` property, which you will recall is an array of objects that have a `.text` and a `.value` property. For each suggestion in the array, the `createSuggestionSpan()` method is called with the index of the suggestion and the regular expression created earlier. All the real work is done in `createSuggestionSpan()`, shown in listing 10.37.

Listing 10.37 Creation of a list item span

```
createSuggestionSpan: function( n, regExp ) {
   var suggestion = this.suggestions[n];

   var suggestionSpan = document.createElement("span");
   suggestionSpan.className = this.options.suggestionClassName;
   suggestionSpan.style.width   = '100%';
   suggestionSpan.style.display = 'block';
   suggestionSpan.id            = this.id + "_" + n;
   suggestionSpan.onmouseover   =
              this.mouseoverHandler.bindAsEventListener(this);
   suggestionSpan.onclick       =
              this.itemClickHandler.bindAsEventListener(this);

   var textValues = this.splitTextValues( suggestion.text,
                                 this.lastRequestString.length,
                                 regExp );

   var textMatchSpan = document.createElement("span");
   textMatchSpan.id          = this.id + "_match_" + n;
   textMatchSpan.className    = this.options.matchClassName;
```

```
        textMatchSpan.onmouseover    =
                this.mouseoverHandler.bindAsEventListener(this);
        textMatchSpan.onclick        =
                this.itemClickHandler.bindAsEventListener(this);

        textMatchSpan.appendChild(
           document.createTextNode(textValues.mid) );

        suggestionSpan.appendChild(
           document.createTextNode(textValues.start) );
        suggestionSpan.appendChild(textMatchSpan);
        suggestionSpan.appendChild(
           document.createTextNode(textValues.end) );

        return suggestionSpan;
    },
```

This task is starting to look daunting, but don't bail out just yet. This method probably looks more complicated than it is, although it does quite a bit of work. Perhaps it would be best to back up at this point and look at this method in terms of what it is attempting to produce: namely, some HTML for a suggestion. Let's imagine HTML markup for a suggestion that looks something like this:

```
<span>before <span>matching text</span>, and after</span>
```

This is a gross simplification of what's actually generated, but it illustrates the structure. Suppose that the user has typed "matching text," and one of the values in the database is "before matching text, and after." What's generated for a suggestion is basically what we just showed but with some extra attributes added to the spans for identification, styling, and event handling. All the hard work of splitting up the before and after portions of the text is done by the following line of code:

```
    var textValues = this.splitTextValues( suggestion.text,
                                this.lastRequestString.length,
                                regExp );
```

The textValues value returned is an object that has three properties: .start, .mid, and .end. So in the example just shown, textValues is an object that looks like the following:

```
    textValues = { start: 'before ',
                   mid:   'matching text',
                   end:   ', and after'   };
```

Finally, the splitTextValues() method implementation is shown here:

```
splitTextValues: function( text, len, regExp ) {
   var startPos   = text.search(regExp);
   var matchText  = text.substring( startPos, startPos + len );
   var startText  = startPos == 0 ?
                       "" : text.substring(0, startPos);
   var endText    = text.substring( startPos + len );
   return { start: startText, mid: matchText, end: endText };
},
```

Now that we've covered the basic structure of a suggestion span, let's talk about the relevant attributes that get generated on the spans. Both the outer span and the inner span are created with CSS class names based on the value of the suggestionClassName and matchClassName properties of the Options object, respectively. Just as the suggestionsDiv has an entirely customizable look and feel via CSS classes, so does all of the internal HTML structure of each suggestion.

The other noteworthy attributes generated within the spans are ID attributes so that the spans can be retrieved later by the aforementioned event handlers. An onmouseover event handler has to be placed on the spans so that the component can update the selection to the suggestion that the mouse is currently over. Also, an onclick event handler must be placed on each suggestion so that when a suggestion line is clicked on, its value can be placed within the text field. The two event handlers are implemented as shown in listing 10.38.

Listing 10.38   List item mouse event handlers

```
mouseoverHandler: function(e) {
   var src = e.srcElement ? e.srcElement : e.target;
   var index = parseInt(src.id.substring(src.id.lastIndexOf('_')+1));
   this.updateSelection(index);
},

itemClickHandler: function(e) {
   this.mouseoverHandler(e);
   this.hideSuggestions();
   this.textInput.focus();
},
```

mouseoverHandler() simply finds the target of the event and parses out the ID that we generated on it to get an index representing which suggestion it is. It can then use the updateSelection() method we wrote on day 4 to update the selection to the suggestion over which the mouse is currently hovering.

Similarly, itemClickHandler() has to update the selection, so it just calls mouseoverHandler() to do the selection update work. It then has to do the additional behavior of hiding the suggestions pop-up via a call to the `hideSuggestions()` method and giving the focus back to the text field so the user can continue typing.

We've finally completed the pop-up creation task. Now let's concentrate on the infinitely simpler task of hiding and showing it.

Showing and hiding the pop-up

Now that we've developed code to handle all of the complex details of creating a pop-up list of suggestions, we need to write the code that shows and hides it. Fortunately, this is an extremely straightforward process, as any seasoned developer of DHTML like yourself knows. The showing and hiding of an element are typically done by manipulating the `display` property of an element's style. This component will be no different. So without further ado, listing 10.39 contains the code that shows the pop up and the code that hides the pop-up.

Listing 10.39 Showing and hiding the suggestions pop-up

```
showSuggestions: function() {
  var divStyle = this.suggestionsDiv.style;
  if ( divStyle.display == '' )
     return;
  this.positionSuggestionsDiv();    <-- Position the pop-up
  divStyle.display = '';            <-- Show the pop-up
},

hideSuggestions: function() {
  this.suggestionsDiv.style.display =
      'none';    <-- Hide the pop-up
},
```

The show and hide, as shown here, simply manipulate the `style.display` property of `suggestionsDiv` in order to show it (via an empty string value) and hide it (via `none`). The `showSuggestions()` method does the additional work of positioning the pop-up before showing it. That's it! We mean that's really it. Our component is done. Let's take a few seconds to debrief.

10.5.6 *Refactor debriefing*

This was certainly a fairly complex component with a lot of moving parts. Grand architects or not, we've developed a reusable component to be proud of. Our TextSuggest component handles a wide range of configuration parameters, it's extensible, it's server-agnostic, it's unobtrusive, it's cross-browser, it has a simple API for creation, it slices, it dices… Well, maybe it's not all that, but seriously, it's pretty cool, and it covers all the bases that we listed in table 10.2. The component source code is available in its entirety at http://www.manning.com/crane. Rico can be found at http://openrico.org/ and Prototype at http://prototype.conio.net/.

10.6 *Summary*

The type-ahead suggest lets your users save time by offering the options that they may need as they are typing. When they type a few keystrokes on the keyboard, the data that they want is available for selection. This chapter has looked at the downfalls of the currently available implementations and has initiated an application that lets us eliminate any unnecessary postbacks to the server by doing most of the processing on the client. We have worked with DHTML to create a dynamic user interface that allows interaction with the keyboard and the mouse. This example shows how Ajax can be used effectively to add a seamless interaction with the server without disrupting the user's interactions with the web page. This script also degrades well with browsers that do not support Ajax, since the type-ahead textbox acts like a plain textbox into which users can enter data rather than just having a quick solution at their fingertips. Finally, we pushed the envelope of object-oriented JavaScript component development by refactoring the script into an easily created, configured, and used TextSuggest component.

11

The enhanced
Ajax web portal

This chapter covers

- Constructing an Ajax portal
- Implementing a login framework
- Creating dynamic windows
- Remembering window state
- Adapting library code

More and more companies have been adopting a portal-based intranet. Portals give users an easy gateway for obtaining large quantities of information on one page. This eliminates the need for the user to go to multiple locations to get the information they need. Online portals such as Yahoo! allow us to obtain news, weather, sports scores, mail, games, and so much more on just one page. Another portal is Amazon's A9.com search portal, which lets us do searches on multiple areas without going to separate pages. We can search for web pages, books, images, and much more on one page. A9.com utilizes Ajax to display the information on the screen. This allows for a great user experience since the user does not have to sit and wait for page re-rendering when new search results are displayed.

In this chapter, we are incorporating Ajax into a portal to improve the user's experience: specifically, how he logs into the system and how the system remembers his details. The portal project will allow the user to customize the layout of the portal with a minimum amount of effort. The user will not even realize that his actions are sending information back to the server to remember the exact location of the objects on the page. This means that his personal settings are the same every time he logs into the system. We first take a low-level approach to building the portal. We implement a basic portal framework in a less-structured manner to shed light on the concept behind the portal. We then look at the portal in a more advanced light using an object-oriented approach. Before we implement the portal, let's examine some current portals and see how adding Ajax can improve the user's experience.

11.1 The evolving portal

Over time, portals have evolved from simple sites that let us check our mail and do a search to elaborate setups that allow us to obtain a large amount of information in little time and with little effort. By comparison, in the past we had to check one site for news, another for weather, another for comics, another for a search, and so on. Either we had tons of bookmarks for the sites that we checked daily, or we just memorized our routine of what addresses to type into the browser.

11.1.1 The classic portal

We are all accustomed to classic portals—we've been using them for years—and a lot of company intranets are using them to improve company performance by having everything in one place. The classic portal is one that allows a user to log into the system and have the content personalized to her tastes. For example, a company portal can have one setup for a salesperson and another setup for a computer programmer. Both of these employees may need to have a window to the company calendar, but they both may not need to see the sales figures or the bug report for the applications. By limiting what they can see, we increase company security and improve the employees' performance since they do not have to search for information all over the company intranet.

Another example of a classic portal is Yahoo!. When we log into Yahoo!, we can check mail, change the weather to fit our current location, change the look, and so much more. As you can see in figure 11.1, Yahoo!'s portal is customized to the needs of the user.

Yahoo! accomplishes this by sending us to maintenance screens to alter the information. One example of the maintenance page allows us to select the city that we live in so that the weather forecast is for our area. In figure 11.1, you can

Figure 11.1   Yahoo!'s portal shows customized information.

see that the weather is customized to Laurel, Maryland. While it is great that we can customize the information we want to see, we can enhance the user experience even more by incorporating Ajax into the portal in the same way that Amazon did with the A9.com portal.

11.1.2   *The rich user interface portal*

With an Ajax portal, the rich user interface is more dynamic than a classic portal while positively impacting the user's experience. We can add new content and change the way the content is displayed in a seamless manner. A great example of this seamless interaction is in Amazon's A9.com search portal. Let's look at how that works. In figure 11.2, a search has been performed for Eric Pascarello with only the Web checkbox selected.

Now let's narrow the search results. We know that we are looking for a book that Pascarello has written, so we click the Books checkbox. The Book Results pane is inserted into the right-hand side of the page. The search results for Eric Pascarello's books are displayed without posting the entire page back to the server to obtain them, as shown in figure 11.3.

Another example of using Ajax to enhance the portal experience is in the configuration of the portal. Ajax allows the user interface to become part of the

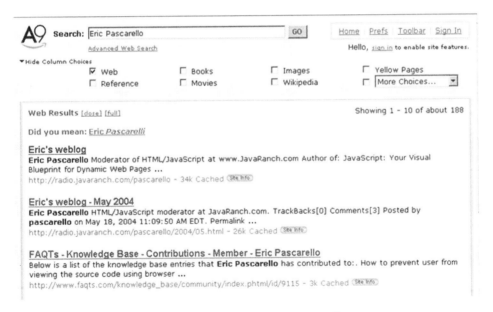

Figure 11.2   A9.com's portal with the web results for Eric Pascarello

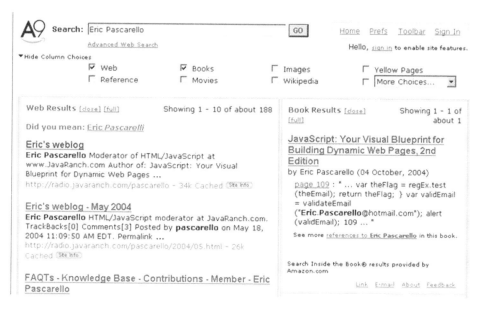

Figure 11.3 A9.com's portal showing the search results with the Book Results column

configuration-management tools by having the user click on objects in the window instead of going to another web page to configure the setup. The user can dynamically resize and position the elements on the screen, thus customizing his portal to fit his needs exactly.

Now that we've seen some of the advantages of an Ajax portal, let's look at the architecture of the portal we will be building.

11.2 *The Ajax portal architecture using Java*

To provide a highly customizable Ajax portal for multiple users, we need client-side code, server-side code, and a database. The client side handles the users' interactions with the windows, such as dragging, dropping, and sending data back to the server with Ajax. The server, in return, handles our users' sessions, data transfer back to the client, and interaction with the database. The database holds our users' logins and passwords in one table, and a second table holds the portal window metadata, such as the position, size, and content.

This project has a lot of steps since it contains dynamic results. To get this project started, let's look at how the project flows (figure 11.4).

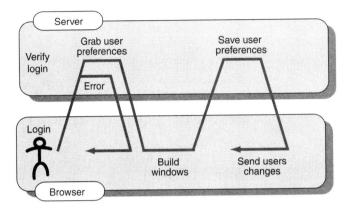

Figure 11.4 Ajax portal flow. Users log in to the portal and manage their windows. Changes are saved automatically in the background while they work.

The basic idea of the rich user interface portal that uses Ajax to interact with the server sounds difficult, but you will be amazed at how simple it is to implement the project. The portal architecture illustrated in figure 11.4 contains two major portions: the initial login and the dynamic interaction with the windows. Thus, we can break our processes into two different sections and adapt the Ajax functionality to meet those needs. The first operation validates a user's credentials against a database, and the second operation interacts with DHTML elements and returns values to our client.

In this chapter, we use a DHTML library to handle a lot of the client-side code. The DHTML library allows us to develop customizable windows that use IFrames to display content. The DHTML windows created by this library can be positioned anywhere on the page since the library supports dragging functionality. Another feature the library supports is resizing of the windows, so we can make the window any size we want. The DHTML library frees us from dwelling on the cross-browser problems that we might encounter with these actions. Instead we can focus on adding the Ajax technology into this library to make a dynamic script even more powerful by integrating it with the server.

The implementation that we'll present here uses Java on the server side, simply to provide a little variety from the previous two chapters, which used .NET languages. We've kept the implementation fairly simple. Because Ajax can work equally well against any server-side technology, we won't concentrate on the server-side details. The full source code for the server tier is available as part of the download for this book. Let's start off by introducing the Ajax login.

11.3 The Ajax login

The first action we need to take care of is the login procedure to access our portal. To do this, we create the database table, the server-side code to handle the request, and the client-side code that obtains the login information from the user and processes the request. The first step is to design our user table in the database.

11.3.1 The user table

The first table we will look at in the database is the `users` table. It contains three columns. We are using only the bare minimum of information for this project, but we can add more depending on our needs. The three columns in our user table are `id`, `username`, and `password`, and they are created with the basic SQL statement in listing 11.1. Figure 11.5 shows the table in design view mode with the SQL Squirrel database client program (http://squirrel-sql.sourceforge.net).

Listing 11.1 The users table schema

```
create table users(
  id int primary key unique not null,
  username varchar(50) not null,
  password varchar(50) not null
);
```

Now that we have created the table, we need to add some users. In this case, we hard-code in the usernames and passwords. As you can see in figure 11.6, two users have been added to the table with the ID numbers of 1 and 2. Those ID numbers will be important later on in this chapter.

Next, we need to set up the user accounts for the users in the table. As it stands, the portal doesn't present an administrative user interface for adding new users, and this would have to be done manually using the database tool of your

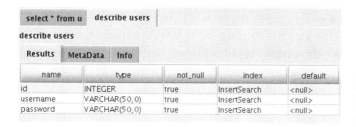

Figure 11.5
The `users` table properties in SQL Squirrel, the graphical database explorer

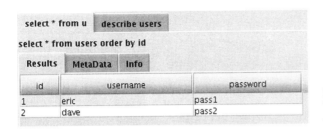

Figure 11.6
The contents of the
users table

choice. Developing an Ajax-based user administration front-end is possible, but we don't have the space to explore it here.

The last step is to make sure that we assign the permissions to the table. The user accounts that will be accessing the table must have the read and write permission set. Without setting the permissions, we would have trouble using our SQL query since we would get errors.

Now that we have our users table, let's write the code for the login process, starting with the server.

11.3.2 *The server-side login code: Java*

The server-side code for the Ajax portal is simple in nature, but it will have numerous steps by the time we get finished because of all the functionality that the portal contains. Right now, we are concerned with coding the login portion of the Ajax portal.

Let's review the process. When the user logs into the portal, the client-side code sends a request to the server, passing the user's credentials with the request. The server-side process that intercepts this request will determine whether the credentials that were sent to the server are correct. If they are correct, we start to process the building of the portal windows. If the user's credentials are incorrect, we pass an error message back to the client page.

Because we are developing in Java, we'll use a servlet filter to secure all our interactions with the server. To those unfamiliar with the term, a *filter* is simply a bit of logic that can be assigned to one or more resources, which is given the opportunity to modify a request before it reaches its destination servlet. We discussed using filters for security in chapter 7. If you're using a system that doesn't support filters, you can simply create a helper object or function that checks to see whether the user is logged in and invoke it manually at the top of each page that you want to protect. Listing 11.2 shows our login filter.

Listing 11.2   LoginFilter.java : server-side login code

```java
public class LoginFilter implements Filter {

  public void init(FilterConfig config)
  throws ServletException { }

  public void doFilter(
    ServletRequest request,
    ServletResponse response,
    FilterChain filterChain)
  throws IOException, ServletException {
    boolean accept=false;
      HttpSession session=(
      (HttpServletRequest)request).getSession();
      User user=(User)
        (session.getAttribute("user"));        ❶ Check session for User object
      if (user==null){
      accept=login(request);        ❷ Authenticate request
      }else{
      accept=true;        ❸ Let them in
      }
        if (accept){
          filterChain.doFilter
            (request,response);        ❹ Proceed
        }else{
          Writer writer=response.getWriter();
          writer.write
            (JSUtil.getLoginError());        ❺ Return error code
          writer.flush();
          writer.close();
        }
  }

  private boolean login(ServletRequest request){
      String user=request
        .getParameter("username");        ❻ Get credentials
      String password=request                 from request
        .getParameter("password");
    User userObj=findUser(user,password);
    if (userObj!=null){
        HttpSession session=
          ((HttpServletRequest)request).getSession(true);
      session.setAttribute("user",userObj);        ❼ Store in session for future use
    }
    return (userObj!=null);
  }

  private User findUser(String user, String password) {
    User userObj=null;
        Connection conn=DBUtil.getConnection();
```

```
      try{
        String sql="SELECT id FROM users WHERE username='"
            +user+"' AND password='"+password+"'";    ❽  Build SQL statement
        Statement stmt=conn.createStatement();
        ResultSet rs=stmt.executeQuery(sql);
        if (rs.next()){
              int id=rs.getInt("id");
              userObj=new User(id,user);    ❾  Create User object
        }
      }catch (SQLException sqlex){

      }
      return userObj;
  }

  public void destroy() { }


}
```

In this case, we will apply a filter that checks to see whether a User object is already held in session ❶. If it is, then we accept it ❸; otherwise, we authenticate it against the username and password supplied in the request ❷. If the request is accepted, it is passed on to the servlet ❹; otherwise, it will return an instruction to display an error message ❺. We have wrapped all generated JavaScript up into an object called JSUtil. The method that generates the error message is shown here:

```
    public static String getLoginError() {
      StringBuffer jsBuf=new StringBuffer()
      .append("document.getElementById('spanProcessing')\n")
      .append("  .innerHTML = ")
      .append("'The Username and Password are invalid';\n");
    return jsBuf.toString();
  }
```

The login() method in listing 11.2 provides the details on authentication. We extract the username and password from the request ❻ and then invoke find-User(), which contacts the database for a matching row ❽. (We've abstracted away the details of the database behind a DBUtil object here.) If a row matching the user is found, the function returns a User object ❾, which is then stored in session ❼ for the next time we pass through this filter. On subsequent passes through this filter, we won't need to provide the username and password in the querystring, because the User object will already be in session.

Another nice feature of this approach is that it makes it easy to log the user out. All we need to do is remove the User object from session.

The User object itself is a simple representation of the database structure, as shown in listing 11.3.

Listing 11.3 User.java

```java
public class User {
  private int id=-1;
  private String userName=null;

  public User(int id, String userName) {
    super();
    this.id = id;
    this.userName = userName;
  }
  public int getId() { return id;}
  public String getUserName() { return userName;}
}
```

We do not store the password field in this object. We won't need to refer to it again during the lifecycle of our portal, and having it sitting in session would be something of a security risk, too! So, that's our login framework from the server side. Nothing very unusual there. Let's move on now to see how our client-side code interacts with it.

11.3.3 The client-side login framework

The client-side login framework consists of two parts. The first is the visual part, which the user is able to view and interact with. We will dynamically create this with HTML; you'll see how easy it is to create a layout with divs, spans, and CSS.

The second part is our Ajax or our JavaScript code, which sends the request to the server and also processes the data. In this case, we are going to introduce JavaScript's `eval()` method. The `eval()` method evaluates the string passed to it as JavaScript code. If the string contains a variable name, it creates the variable. If the `eval` input contains a function call, it will execute that function. The `eval()` method is powerful, but its performance can be slow depending on the complexity of the operation.

The HTML layout

As in previous chapters, we are not using a table to do our layout. Table layouts lengthen the page-rendering time, and since we are using Ajax, we would like everything to be faster and more responsive. We need to place a textbox, a password field, and a submit button on a form that we can submit to the server. We also need a span so that we can display the error message from the server if the username or password is invalid. By putting the entire form inside divs and spans, we format the HTML to produce the portal's header. Listing 11.4 shows the basic HTML framework of our login header.

Listing 11.4   HTML login layout

```
<form name="Form1">        ❶  Define form
  <div id="header">          ❷  Add header
    <span id="login">          ❸  Insert login span
      Name:
        <input type="text" name="username">     ❹  Add username textbox
        <br>Password:
       <input type="password" name="password">    ❺  Add password element
        <br/>
        <span id="spanProcessing"></span>     ❻  Insert processing span
        <input type="button" name="btnSub" value="login"
        onclick="LoginRequest()">     ❼  Add submit button
    </span>
    <span id="sloganText">Ajax Portal</span>      ❽  Append slogan
  </div>
  <div id="defaultContent">           ❾  Add default
    <p>Some text goes here!</p>              content
  </div>
  <div id="divSettings" class="hidden"></div>
</form>
```

First, we add our form ❶ to our HTML document. The form provides a semantically meaningful container for the textboxes. It also provides a degradation path for a non-Ajax-based authentication via normal form submission. We create a header div ❷, which surrounds all our content. A span ❸ is then added to house our username textbox ❹ or password field ❺, our processing span ❻, and our submit button ❼.

The button we use to submit the data back to the server needs an onclick event handler. The onclick event handler initializes the Ajax by calling a Java-Script function, LoginRequest(). LoginRequest() is explained in the section "The JavaScript login code."

The only things left for the header are to add the slogan ❽ for the portal and to add a place for the default content ❾ to be shown when the page is loaded. Any message can be displayed inside the div defaultContent. In this example, we just put in a string of text, but we can add links, images, text, or whatever we think

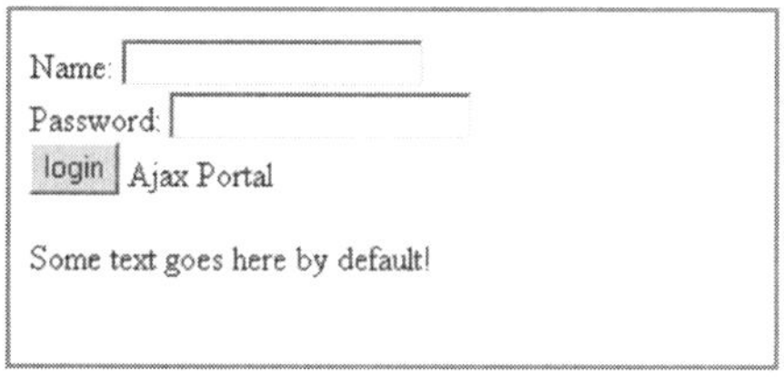

Name: [_____]
Password: [_____]
[login] Ajax Portal

Some text goes here by default!

Figure 11.7
The HTML login form with no CSS applied

is appropriate. Then we save the HTML; you can see how unsightly it looks without any CSS applied to the elements (figure 11.7).

To fix this drab-looking layout, we need to apply CSS to our elements. Since we have given the elements their own IDs, it makes the process simple. We reference the element's ID by placing a pound sign in front of it. We can add the stylesheet as an external file or inline via the `<style>` tag. In this case, we are using an inline `<style>` tag that we add to the head tag of the document. The CSS rules are added to alter the colors, fonts, sizes, location, margins, and so on, as shown in listing 11.5.

Listing 11.5 Login form CSS rules

```
<style type="text/css">
  html, body{ margin: 0px; padding:0px;          ❶ HTML and
          height:100%; }                            body elements
  #header{ background-color: #C0C0C0;
          height: 100px;                          ❷ Style the header
          border-bottom: 1px solid black;            element
          font-weight: bold; }
  #login{ text-align: right; float: right;        ❸ Position
          margin-top:15px;                           login span
          margin-right:15px; }
  #sloganText{ font-size: 25px;                   ❹ Format
          margin-left: 15px;                         slogan text
          line-height: 100px; }
</style>
```

We start out by removing any margins or padding from the body ❶ of the document. We specify the `height` as `100%` so that it is easier to define document heights in percentages if we need to in the future. It is important to note that we need to specify these properties both for the HTML and the body tags, since different browsers look at either one tag or the other for this information.

For the header ❷, we can apply a background color to the div. We can also set the height and add a bottom border to separate the header from the content in a more dynamic manner. We can also adjust any of the font properties as we think necessary.

We take the login information ❸ and move it to the right side of the screen. We use the `float` property and set the value to `right`. To make the text boxes uniform, we use the `text-align` property so that the content within the span is also aligned on the right margin. This gives our textboxes a more uniform look. Without it, the textboxes would not line up correctly since the string name is shorter than the password. We can also add some margins to adjust the position of the login information so that its right edge is not directly on the border of our header div.

The last thing to style in our header is the slogan ❹. By setting the `line-height` to the height of the div, we are allowing the slogan to be centered vertically in the header. We also set the font properties to make the text noticeable. Just as we did for the login span, we add a margin so the *A* in *Ajax* is not directly sitting on the edge of the header. After applying the CSS to our header, we can save the document and view how the CSS has changed the look and feel of the header, as shown in figure 11.8.

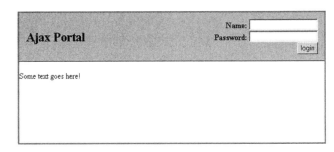

Figure 11.8
Ajax portal's login page with the CSS stylesheet attached

Here you can see that our textboxes are aligned on the right side and that our slogan is on the left side. We have taken the basic HTML structure and created an attractive login header that did not require a table. Now that the header is styled, we can add some functionality to this form. We need to add our JavaScript functionality so that we can make a request back to the server without submitting the entire page.

The JavaScript login code

The JavaScript login code will use the power of Ajax to allow us to send only the username and password to the server without having to submit the entire page. In order to do this, we need to reference our external JavaScript file, net.js, which contains the ContentLoader object, so we can use Ajax to send and retrieve the request:

```
<script type="text/javascript" src="net.js"></script>
```

The ContentLoader file does all of the work of determining how to send the information to the server, hiding any browser-specific code behind the easy-to-use wrapper object that we introduced in chapter 3. Now that the net.js file is referenced, we are able to perform the request. The request is initiated by the button click from our login form. The login form needs to perform three actions. The first is to inform the user that his request is being processed, the next is to gather the information, and the third is to send the request to the server (listing 11.6).

Listing 11.6 The XMLHttpRequest login request

```
function LoginRequest(){
  document.getElementById("spanProcessing").innerHTML =
    " Verifying Credentials";
  var url = 'portalLogin.servlet';
  var strName = document.Form1.username.value;
  var strPass = document.Form1.password.value;
  var strParams = "user="+strName
    + "&pass=" + strPass
  var loader1 = new net.ContentLoader(
    url,CreateScript,null,"POST",strParams
  );
}
```

Before we send the information to the server, we display a message to the user saying that his action of clicking the button is allowing him to log into the system. This keeps the user from clicking the button repeatedly, thinking that nothing happened.

We obtain the username and password field values and place them into a string that we will submit to the server. We submit the values to the server with our ContentLoader object, which accepts our parameters for the URL, the function to call for success, the function to call for an error, the POST form action, and the string containing the parameters to post. Let's look at the function we call when the server returns success: CreateScript(). It will process the data returned from the server-side page:

```
function CreateScript(){
  strText = this.req.responseText;
  eval(strText);
}
```

When we built the server-side code, we returned text strings that contained Java-Script statements in the `responseText` of our returned object. In order to effectively use the JavaScript statements, we must process them with the `eval()` method, which determines exactly what the strings contain and executes it. In this case, the string is either going to contain the error message generated by the `LoginFilter` failing, or the code to build the windows, if the filter lets us through to the `SelectServlet` (see listing 11.8).

What does the string consist of? In this application, we are not going to be sending back an XML document, as we have done in many of our examples. Instead, we will be sending back structured JavaScript statements with which we will be able to use the `eval()` method. Using the terms that we developed in chapter 5, we would say that our solution here is script-centric rather than data-centric. Again, we've chosen this approach simply for variety's sake. A portal solution could equally well be coded using XML or JSON as the communication medium.

We can now save the portal and run it to see if our login procedure is working correctly. As you can see in figure 11.9, the wrong username and password were entered into the fields.

The text beside the login button in figure 11.9 shows an error message to the user, informing her that the credentials that were provided are incorrect.

If, on the other hand, the login is successful, then the request will be forwarded to the main portal page. In this case, the next step is to build our windows. This will require a large amount of DHTML to develop our rich user interface, but the hard work is already done for us because we are using a prewritten JavaScript DHTML library.

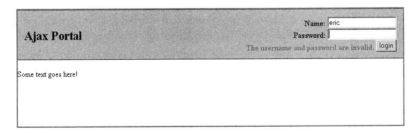

Figure 11.9   An error message is displayed because of invalid credentials.

11.4 *Implementing DHTML windows*

Our Ajax portal has a rich user interface that allows the user to dynamically position the windows. The user can also set the size of the window to the desired width and height. When the user changes these settings, we can use Ajax to interact with the server to store them as values in our database without the user even knowing anything is happening.

To enable this, we need to develop a database table to store the window properties such as `height`, `width`, and `position`. The server-side code needs to receive these new window properties and update the values in the database.

Writing browser-compliant DHTML can be complicated, so we are using a DHTML library script to perform the drag, drop, and resizing of the window. A library is nothing more than an external JavaScript file that contains all of the code for a given functionality. You can obtain the JavaScript library, JSWindow.js, for this project with the rest of the book's downloads. We will need to make only a few modifications to the library to enable Ajax.

11.4.1 *The portal windows database*

We need a database table that can hold the properties of several DHTML windows for each user. Each user can have multiple rows in this table, one for every window she has in her portal. The table is used to retrieve the last-known position and size of the window when the user first logs in. When the user makes changes, the values are then updated so that she can access them at future times and still see the same layout. The following SQL will create the `portal_windows` table:

```
create table portal_windows(
  id int primary key not null,
  user_id int not null,
  xPos int not null,
  yPos int not null,
  width int not null,
  height int not null,
  url varchar(255) not null,
  title varchar(255) not null
);
```

Each user can have multiple windows, all with different configurations. The column named `user_id` relates to our `users` database. Each of the windows must have an `id` as the primary key, so we can use this to save and update properties. Make sure you add the auto increment for the window's `id` column. This `id` column is used by the Ajax code and the DHTML window library to obtain and update the user's window properties.

describe portal | select * from p

describe portal_windows

Results | MetaData | Info

name	type	not_...	index	default
id	INTEGER	true	InsertSearch	<null>
user_id	INTEGER	true	InsertSearch	<null>
xPos	INTEGER	true	InsertSearch	<null>
yPos	INTEGER	true	InsertSearch	<null>
width	INTEGER	true	InsertSearch	<null>
height	INTEGER	true	InsertSearch	<null>
url	VARCHAR(255,0)	true	InsertSearch	<null>
title	VARCHAR(255,0)	true	InsertSearch	<null>

Figure 11.10 `portal_windows` database table structure

We need two columns to hold the x and y coordinates of our DHTML window. These give us the location of the window on the screen from the upper-left corner of the browser. The column names for coordinates are `xPos` and `yPos`. Two other properties we need to capture are the `width` and `height` properties of the DHTML window. These are all stored as integers in the table.

The last two columns in our database determine the URL of the content within the window and the title of the content that the user assigns as a quick reference. All of the database properties for `portal_windows` are shown in figure 11.10.

Now we need to enter some default values so we can perform some testing. We can add as many windows as we want for any of the users in the database table `users`. You can see in figure 11.10 that we have added three DHTML windows for user 1.

In figure 11.11, the three DHTML window parameters give us the information needed to create three windows on the screen with different dimensions and positions. The three windows in this table display three different websites: JavaRanch, Google, and Eric's Ajax Blog. Now that the database table has been built, we have to get this information to the user when he logs into the portal. You'll see how straightforward this is in the next section.

describe portal | select * from p

select * from portal_windows order by id,user_id

Results | MetaData | Info

id	user_id	xPos	yPos	width	height	url	title
1	1	612	115	615	260	http://www.javaranch.com	JavaRanch
2	1	10	115	583	260	http://www.google.com	Google
3	1	10	387	1220	300	http://radio.javaranch.com/pascarello	Ajax Blog!

Figure 11.11 Data entered for the user with the `id` of `1`

11.4.2 *The portal window's server-side code*

Let's assume that our login request has made it through the security filter. The next step is to retrieve the list of portal windows for our authenticated user and send back the JavaScript telling the browser what to display. We define a Portal-Window object that represents a row of data in the database, as shown in listing 11.7.

Listing 11.7   PortalWindow.java

```java
public class PortalWindow {
  private int id=-1;
  private User user=null;
  private int xPos=0;
  private int yPos=0;
  private int width=0;
  private int height=0;
  private String url=null;
  private String title=null;

  public PortalWindow(
      int id, User user, int xPos, int yPos,
      int width,int height,
      String url, String title
  ) {
      this.id = id;
      this.user = user;
      this.xPos = xPos;
      this.yPos = yPos;
      this.width = width;
      this.height = height;
      this.url = url;
      this.title = title;
  }
  public int getHeight() {return height;}
  public void setHeight(int height) {this.height = height;}
  public int getId() {return id;}
  public void setId(int id) {this.id = id;}
  public String getTitle() {return title;}
  public void setTitle(String title) {this.title = title;}
  public String getUrl() {return url;}
  public void setUrl(String url) {this.url = url;}
  public User getUser() {return user;}
  public void setUser(User user) {this.user = user;}
  public int getWidth() {return width;}
  public void setWidth(int width) {this.width = width;}
  public int getXPos() {return xPos;}
  public void setXPos(int pos) {xPos = pos;}
```

```
public int getYPos() {return yPos;}
public void setYPos(int pos) {yPos = pos;}
}
```

Again, this object is pretty much a straightforward mapping of the database structure. In production, we'd probably use an ORM system such as Hibernate or iBATIS to help us out, but we want to keep things fairly simple and platform-agnostic for now. Note that we provide setter methods as well as getters for this object, because we'll want to update these objects dynamically in response to user events.

The URL that we requested on login, portalLogin.servlet, is mapped to a servlet that retrieves all the portal windows for that user and sends back JavaScript instructions. Listing 11.8 shows the main servlet.

Listing 11.8 SelectServlet.java (mapped to 'portalLogin.servlet')

```
public class SelectServlet extends HttpServlet {
  protected void doPost(
    HttpServletRequest request,
       HttpServletResponse response
  ) throws ServletException, IOException {
    HttpSession session=request.getSession();
    User user=(User)
      (session.getAttribute("user"));        ❶ Check session
    StringBuffer jsBuf=new StringBuffer();
        if (user==null){
          jsBuf.append(JSUtil.logout());
        }else{
          List windows=DBUtil               ❷ Define object
            .getPortalWindows(user);     ◁─┘
          jsBuf.append(JSUtil.initUI());    ◁─❸ Utilize the JSUtil object
          for (Iterator iter=windows.iterator();iter.hasNext();){
            PortalWindow window=(PortalWindow)(iter.next());
            session.setAttribute("window_"+window.getId(),window);
            jsBuf.append
              (JSUtil.initWindow(window));    ❹ Declare portal window
          }
        }
    Writer writer=response.getWriter();
    writer.write(jsBuf.toString());        ❺ Write to output stream
    writer.flush();
  }
}
```

Again, we use the DBUtil object to abstract out the database interactions and the JSUtil to generate JavaScript code. DBUtil provides a `getPortalWindows()`

method ❷ that takes a User object as an argument. We have one of those sitting in the session, so we pull it out now ❶. The actual JavaScript is written by the JSUtil object again, providing some user interface initialization code ❸, declaring each of the portal windows that we've extracted from the database ❹ and then writing them directly to the servlet output stream ❺.

Let's briefly review the helper objects that we've used along the way, DBUtil and JSUtil. We used DBUtil to get a list of the portal windows. As we noted, we'd probably automate this in production using Hibernate or something similar; but listing 11.9 provides a method from DBUtil that is a simple home-rolled implementation of accessing the portal_windows table in the database, for teaching purposes. We're using straightforward SQL directly here, so it should be easy to adapt to the server language of your choice.

Listing 11.9 `getPortalWindows()` **method**

```
public static List getPortalWindows(User user){
  List list=new ArrayList();
  Connection conn=getConnection();
  try{
    String sql="SELECT * FROM portal_windows "
      +"WHERE user_id="+user.getId();     ❶ Construct SQL statement
      Statement stmt=conn.createStatement();
      ResultSet rs=stmt.executeQuery(sql);
      PortalWindow win=null;
      while (rs.next()){      ❷ Iterate through results
      int id=rs.getInt("id");
        int x=rs.getInt("xPos");
        int y=rs.getInt("yPos");
        int w=rs.getInt("width");
        int h=rs.getInt("height");
        String url=rs.getString("url");
        String title=rs.getString("title");

        win=new PortalWindow(      ❸ Add Object

          id,user,x,y,w,h,url,title
        );
        list.add(win);
      }
    rs.close();
    stmt.close();
  }catch (SQLException sqlex){
  }
  return list;
}
```

We simply construct the SQL statement ❶, iterate through the result set that it generates ❷, and add a PortalWindow object to our list in each case ❸.

Second, we use the JSUtil helper object to generate some initialization code and declare our window objects in JavaScript. The methods are basically exercises in string concatenation, and we won't show the full class here. The following code gives a flavor of how it works:

```
public static String initWindow(PortalWindow window) {
  StringBuffer jsBuf=new StringBuffer()
   .append("CreateWindow(new NewWin('")
   .append(window.getId())
   .append("','")
   .append(window.getXPos())
   .append(",")
   .append(window.getYPos())
   .append(",")
   .append(window.getWidth())
   .append(",")
   .append(window.getHeight())
   .append(",'")
   .append(window.getUrl())
   .append("','")
   .append(window.getTitle())
   .append("'));\n");
  return jsBuf.toString();
}
```

The `initWindow()` method generates the JavaScript code for initializing a single portal window. The JavaScript code from a successful request might look like this, with `initWindow()` being called for each window in turn (the code has been formatted here for improved readability):

```
document.getElementById('login')
  .innerHTML='Welcome back!'
document.getElementById('defaultContent')
  .style.display='none';

CreateWindow(
  new NewWin(
    '1',612,115,615,260,
    'http://www.javaranch.com','JavaRanch'
  )
);
CreateWindow(
  new NewWin(
    '2',10,115,583,260,
    'http://www.google.com','Google'
  )
);
```

```
CreateWindow(
  new NewWin(
    '3',10,387,1220,300,
    'http://radio.javaranch.com/pascarello','Ajax Blog!'
  )
);
```

Since we are now logged in, we can remove the login textboxes and submit button by placing a welcome message in their place. After we put up the welcome message, we need to hide the content that's on the screen by default. To do this, we set the `defaultContent` DOM element's `display` property to `none` so it is removed from the user's view.

The JavaScript statement that instantiates the window involves two parts for each window. The first part is a function call to `CreateWindow()`, which is part of the JavaScript library that we added. Inside the function call, we will call a new object constructor. The constructor creates a window class, to make it easier to reference the window properties. The JavaScript function that produces the `window` class needs to receive the `id`, `width`, `height`, `xPos`, `yPos`, `url`, and `title` of the window. When the servlet returns this string to the client, our JavaScript `eval()` method will execute it.

For the most part, we're following good code-generation conventions in generating simple, repetitive code that calls out to our JavaScript library functions. Our initialization code could be wrapped up into a single client-tier call, but we leave that as an exercise for the reader.

The JavaScript library that we use creates JavaScript floating windows. Let's now see how to make those window-building functions available on the client tier.

11.4.3 *Adding the JS external library*

As mentioned earlier, we are using a DHTML library that you can download from Manning's website. The file, called JSWindow.js, contains all of the JavaScript DOM methods to produce the window elements. The library also applies event handlers to the window objects so that we can use drag-and-drop functionality. It is convenient to use code libraries that are already developed since it cuts down on development time and the code is normally cross-browser compliant.

The first thing we need to do is rename the file so we can make changes to it. Rename the JavaScript file to AjaxWindow.js, and save it to the directory in which you are working.

To use the functions contained in AjaxWindow.js, we need to reference the external JavaScript file with a `script` tag. We use the `src` attribute of the JavaScript element tag. The `script` element that links to our .js file should be included within the head tags of our HTML page:

```
<script type="text/javascript" src="AjaxWindow.js"></script>
```

We also need to get the DHTML windows stylesheet, so we can style the window. To do this, download the file AjaxWindow.css from Manning's website and link to it using the `link` tag and the `href` attribute:

```
<link rel="stylesheet" type="text/css"
  href="AjaxWindows.css"></link>
```

Now that we have the JavaScript and the CSS files attached to the HTML page, we can test to make sure that we have linked to them correctly. We are also verifying that our server-side code is calling our JavaScript library correctly. If the code is linked correctly and we have obtained the data from the server properly, we should see three windows created from the information contained in the database, as shown in figure 11.12, after logging in with a username and password from our database. Remember that the library function we created is building the windows and adding all of the functionality to them. In a sense it is magic, since we just call it and it works.

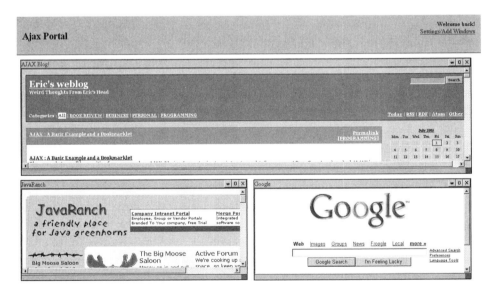

Figure 11.12   The Ajax portal with three windows open on the screen

With the portal windows open, we can test the functionalities built into the DHTML library without the Ajax functionality we are going to add next. Here are some of the things we can do:

- Maximize and minimize the windows by clicking on the button labeled with an *O*.

- Hide the window by clicking the button labeled with an *X*.

- Open the DHTML window into its own pop-up window by clicking on the *w*.

- Drag the window by holding down the left mouse button on the title bar and moving the mouse around. Releasing the mouse button stops the drag operation.

- Resize the window by clicking on the green box on the lower-right corner and dragging it around the screen.

You can see that the windows in figure 11.13 are in different positions than in figure 11.12.

Now that we have the ability to position and resize the windows with the library, we need to make our changes to the external .js file. The changes will allow us to call a function that utilizes Ajax to send the new property values to our database.

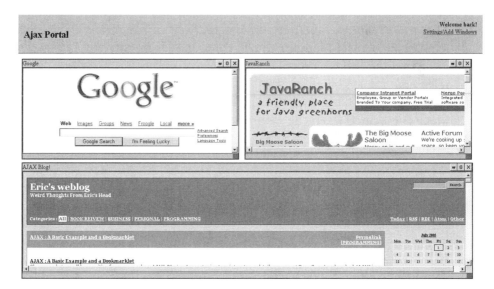

Figure 11.13   Ajax portal showing windows with different positions

11.5 *Adding Ajax autosave functionality*

Using Ajax allows us to implement an autosave feature that can be fired by any event without the user knowing that it is happening. Normally, the user would have to click a button to force a postback to the server. In this case, we will be firing the autosave with the onmouseup event, which ends the process of dragging and resizing events. If we were to fire a normal form submission on the onmouseup event, the user would lose all of the functionality of the page, disrupting her workflow. With Ajax, the flow is seamless.

11.5.1 *Adapting the library*

As we mentioned earlier, the code from JavaScript DHTML libraries is normally cross-browser compliant, which frees us from spending time getting cross-browser code to work correctly. If you look at the code in the external JavaScript file, Ajax-Window.js, you'll see a lot of functionality (which we will not discuss here because of its length). There are functions that monitor the mouse movements, and one function that builds the windows. There are functions that set the position of the windows, and another function that sets the size. Out of all of these functions, we need to adapt only one to have our window save back to the database with Ajax.

Adapting the DHTML library for Ajax

The DHTML library functions for dragging and resizing windows use many event handlers and DOM methods to overcome the inconsistencies between browsers. The dragging and resizing of the windows is completed when the mouse button is released ("up"). Therefore, we should look for a function that is called with the onmouseup event handler in the AjaxWindow.js file. It contains the following code, which is executed when the mouse button is released:

```
document.onmouseup = function(){
  bDrag = false;
  bResize = false;
  intLastX = -1;
  document.body.style.cursor = "default";
  elemWin="";
  bHasMoved = false;
}
```

In this code, a lot of booleans are being set to false to indicate that their actions have been canceled. The cursor is being set back to the default. The line that we need to change is the one where the elemWin reference is being canceled. At this point, we want to take the reference and pass it to another function to initialize our XMLHttpRequest object, in order to transfer the information to the server.

Although sometimes when we adapt libraries, it might take a lot of trial and error to adapt them to our needs, in this case, the functionality is pretty straightforward. Just add the following line, shown in bold, to your document's `onmouseup` event handler:

```
document.onmouseup = function(){
  bDrag = false;
  bResize = false;
  intLastX = -1;
  document.body.style.cursor = "default";
  if(elemWin && bHasMoved)SaveWindowProperties(elemWin);
  bHasMoved = false;
}
```

The bold line in the previous code snippet checks to make sure that the object has been moved or resized and that the element still exists. If the user did not perform either of these actions, then there would be no reason to send the request to the server. If one of these actions was performed, we pass the element reference to the function `SaveWindowProperties()`, which initiates the request to the server.

Obtaining the active element properties

After the user has moved or resized an element, we must update the server with the new parameters. The DHTML window library uses CSS to position the elements and to set their width and height. This means that all we have to do is obtain the database ID, the coordinates, and the size of the window. We can obtain the coordinates and size by looking at the CSS parameters assigned to the window that had focus. We then can take these new parameters and send them to the server to be saved in the database with Ajax (listing 11.10).

Listing 11.10 `SaveWindowProperties()` function

```
function SaveWindowProperties(){
  winProps = "ref=" +
    elemWin.id;           ❶  Obtain window ID
  winProps += "&x=" +
    parseInt(elemWin.style.left);     ❷  Find
  winProps += "&y=" +                     window
    parseInt(elemWin.style.top);        position
  winProps += "&w=" +
    parseInt(elemWin.style.width);    ❸  Grab
  winProps += "&h=" +                     window size
    parseInt(elemWin.style.height);
  Settings("saveSettings",winProps);  ❹  Call Settings function
  elemWin = "";        ❺  Remove element reference
}
```

As you can see in listing 11.11, we obtain the ID of the window ❶ by referencing the window object. The ID that we obtained was assigned to the window when the library built it. When it assigns an ID, it appends `win` in front of the number from the database `id` column; we can see that by looking at the JavaScript code that is building the windows.

The `x` and `y` positions of the window are obtained ❷ by referencing the `left` and `top` properties in the stylesheet. We also use the stylesheet properties to obtain the size ❸ of the window by referencing its `width` and `height` properties.

After obtaining the information, we can call another function, `Settings()` ❹, which we will be creating shortly, to send our request to the server. Once we call the function, we should remove the element object from our global variable `elemWin` ❺. To do this, we assign an empty string to the variable `elemWin`. Now with the `SaveWindowProperties()` function complete, we can initiate our silent Ajax request to the server with the JavaScript function `Settings()`.

11.5.2 Autosaving the information to the database

Ajax lets us send information to the server without the user even knowing it is happening. We can see this in action with two projects in this book. We can easily submit requests to the server as a result of both monitoring keystrokes, as we do in the type-ahead suggest (chapter 10), and monitoring mouse movements, as we do in this chapter. This invisible submission is great for developers since we can update the user's settings without him having to lift a finger. In most cases, reducing steps increases the user's satisfaction. For this application, the action of the user releasing the mouse button is all we need to initiate the XMLHttpRequest object. Now it's time to initiate the process to send the request to the server.

The client: sending the silent request

The XMLHttpRequest process in this case will not require anything sophisticated. The user's interaction with the form sends all of the form properties to our function. We first need to initialize the XMLHttpRequest object:

```
function Settings(xAction,xParams){
  var url = xAction + ".servlet";
  var strParams = xParams;
  var loader1 = new net.ContentLoader(url,
              BuildSettings,
              ErrorBuildSettings,
              "POST",
              strParams);
}
```

For the function `Settings()`, we are passing the action string that contains all of our window's properties. We attach the parameters that we're going to post back to the server. If we get a successful round-trip to the server, the loader will call the function `BuildSettings()`. If we get an error during the round-trip, we will call the function `ErrorBuildSettings()`:

```
function BuildSettings(){
  strText = this.req.responseText;
  document.getElementById("divSettings").innerHTML = strText;
}
function ErrorBuildSettings(){
  alert('There was an error trying to connect to the server.');
  document.getElementById("divSettings").style.display = "none";
}
```

The function `BuildSettings()` shown here is quite basic; all we are doing is finishing up our XMLHttpRequest received from the server. We can set a message on the portal status bar to show that we have updated the information on the server. We can add an error message to the status bar if we encounter a problem updating the information on the server. We also generate an alert, which tells the user of the error, but will also disrupt their workflow. We presented production-ready notification mechanisms in chapter 6, and leave it as an exercise for the reader to integrate those systems into the portal. Now let's see what happens on the server.

The server: gathering information from the client

All we have left to do is to extract the values from our form submission. The values were sent by our XMLHttpRequest object, which was triggered by the `onmouseup` event handlers. We need to create our SQL query with this information and update the record in the database to save the new information. We define an UpdateServlet for this purpose, which is shown in listing 11.11.

Listing 11.11   UpdateServlet.java (mapped to 'saveSettings.servlet')

```
public class UpdateServlet extends HttpServlet {
  protected void doPost(
    HttpServletRequest request,
    HttpServletResponse response
  )throws ServletException, IOException{
    String windowId=
      request.getParameter("ref");        ❶ Get unique ID from request
    HttpSession session=request.getSession();
    PortalWindow window=(PortalWindow)
     (session.getAttribute
       ("window_"+windowId));        ❷ Get Window object from session
    window.setXPos(getIntParam(request,"x"));
```

```
      window.setYPos(getIntParam(request,"y"));
      window.setWidth(getIntParam(request,"w"));
      window.setHeight(getIntParam(request,"h"));
      DBUtil.savePortalWindow(window);    ❸ Save changes
      Writer writer=response.getWriter();
      writer.write("Save Complete");    ⟵─ Return simple text reply
      writer.flush();
    }
    private int getIntParam(HttpServletRequest request, String param) {
      String str=request.getParameter(param);
      int result=Integer.parseInt(str);
      return result;
    }
  }
```

Given the window ID as a request parameter ❶, we can extract the PortalWindow from session ❷ and update its geometry based on further request parameters. We then call another method on our DBUtil object to save the portal window settings in the database ❸. Again, the implementation that we've provided here in listing 11.12 has been written to be simple and easy to translate to other languages.

Listing 11.12   `savePortalWindows()` method

```
public static void savePortalWindow(PortalWindow window){
  Connection conn=getConnection();
  int x=window.getXPos();
  int y=window.getYPos();
  int w=window.getWidth();
  int h=window.getHeight();
  int id=window.getId();
  String sql="UPDATE portal_windows SET xPos="+x
    +",yPos="+y
    +",width="+w
    +",height="+h
    +" WHERE id="+id;
  try{
    Statement stmt=conn.createStatement();
    stmt.execute(sql);
    stmt.close();
  }catch (SQLException sqlex){
  }
}
```

The code in listing 11.12 is very straightforward. We read the relevant details from the PortalWindow object and construct a SQL update statement accordingly. Rather than returning any JavaScript this time, we issue a simple text acknowledgment.

To test the new functionality, log into the portal as our test user. Drag the windows around the screen, and resize them so they are in different positions from their defaults. Close the browser to force an end to the session. When we reopen the browser and log back into the portal as that user, we see the windows in the same position. Move the windows to a new position and look at the database table. We are automatically saving the user's preferences without him even knowing it.

We've now provided all the basic functionality for a working portal system, including a few things that a classic web application just couldn't do. There are several other requirements that we could classify as "nice to have," such as being able to add, remove, and rename windows. Because of limited space, we are not going to discuss them here. The full code for the portal application is available to download and includes the ability to add, delete, rename, and adjust the window's properties without leaving the single portal page. If you have any questions about the code in this section or need a more thorough understanding, you can always reach us on Manning.com's Author Online at www.manning.com.

Our code so far has been somewhat rough and ready so that we could demonstrate how the individual pieces work. Let's hand it over to our refactoring team now, to see how to tighten things up and make the system easier to reuse.

11.6 *Refactoring*

The concept of an Ajax-based portal client that interacts with a server-side portal "manager" is, as you've seen, a compelling notion. In our refactoring of this chapter's client-side code, let's consider our component as an entity that serves as the arbitrator of portal commands sent to the portal manager on the server. Throughout this refactoring discussion, let's make it our goal to isolate the pieces of code that might change over time and facilitate those changes as easily as possible. Since the portal is a much coarser-grained component and something that will more or less take over the real estate of our page, we won't be so stringent with the requirement of not interrupting the HTML as we have in the previous two refactoring examples.

But, before discussing the client-side semantic, let's first stop and contemplate the contract with the server. Our previous server-side implementation was written in Java, so we had a servlet filter perform the authentication functionality: one servlet to return the window configurations, and another servlet to save window configurations. Similarly, for adding new windows and deleting the current ones, we would provide further standalone servlets. In a Java web application, the servlets can be mapped to URLs in a very flexible fashion, defined in the web.xml file of the web archive (.war) file. For example, our SelectServlet, which returned the script defining the initial windows, was mapped to the URL portalLogin.servlet.

One of the strengths of Ajax is the loose coupling between the client and the server. Our portal example uses Java as a back-end, but we don't want to tie it to Java-specific features such as servlet filters and flexible URL rewriting. An alternative back-end architecture might use a request dispatch pattern, in which a single servlet, PHP page, or ASP.NET resource accepts all incoming requests and then reads a GET or POST parameter that specifies what type of action is being undertaken. For example, the URL for logging in to the portal might be portal?action=login&userid=user&password=password or, more likely, the equivalent using POST parameters. In Java, we might implement a request dispatcher approach by assigning a specific URL prefix, say .portal, to the dispatcher servlet, allowing us to write URLs such as login.portal.

In our refactored component, we will generalize our assumptions about the back-end to allow either a request dispatcher architecture or the multiple address option that we used for our Java implementation. We don't, however, need to introduce complete flexibility, so we'll predefine a number of commands that the portal back-end will be expected to understand, covering login, showing the user's portal windows, and adding and deleting windows from the portal. With these changes to the server in mind, let's return our attention to the client-side implementation.

Let's begin our discussion of the portal refactoring by redefining the usage contract from the perspective of the page's HTML; then we'll delve into the implementation. Recall that the hook from our HTML page into the portal script was via the login, specifically through the login button:

```
<input type="button" name="btnSub" value="login"
       onclick="LoginRequest('login')">
```

We'll change the onclick handler to be a call to a function that will use our portal component. Let's assume that the portal component will be instantiated via a script that executes once the page loads. A representative example of what this should look like is shown in listing 11.13.

Listing 11.13   Portal creation and login

```
function createPortal() {
  myPortal = new Portal(
    'portalManager',      ❶   Base URL for portal
```

```
        {
          messageSpanId: 'spanProcessing',
          urlSuffix: '.portal'
        }
      );

      myPortal.loadPage(Portal.LOAD_SETTINGS_ACTION);
      document.getElementById('username').focus();
    }
    function login() {
    myPortal.login( document.getElementById('username').value,
                    document.getElementById('password').value );
    }
```

❷ Optional parameters

❸ Call to load windows

In this usage semantic, `createPortal()`, which should get called once the page loads, creates an instance of the portal component. The first argument is the base URL for the portal's server-side application ❶, and the second provides optional parameters used to customize it for a particular context ❷. In this case, we tell it the ID of the DOM element into which status messages should be written and the name of the request parameter that will denote which action to execute. Once created, an API on the portal named `loadPage` is called. This loads the page's portal windows if there is already a user login present in the server session ❸. If nobody is logged in, this server will return an empty script, leaving only the login form on the screen.

The `login()` function is just a utility function in the page that calls the `login()` method of our portal component, passing the username and password values as arguments. Given this contract, the login button's `onclick` handler now calls the page's `login()` method, as shown here:

```
<input type="button" name="btnSub" value="login" onclick="login()">
```

11.6.1 *Defining the constructor*

Now that you have a basic understanding of how the component will be used from the perspective of the page, let's implement the logic, starting with the constructor:

```
function Portal( baseUrl, options ) {
    this.baseUrl    = baseUrl;
    this.options    = options;
    this.initDocumentMouseHandler();
```

The constructor takes the URL of the Ajax portal management on the server as its first argument and an options object for configuration as the second. In our

earlier development of the script, recall that we had a servlet filter and two servlets perform the back-end processing. Throughout the rest of this example, we'll
assume a single servlet or resource, `portalManager`, which intercepts all requests
to the portal back-end, as configured in listing 11.13. If we wanted to configure
the portal against a back-end that didn't use a single request dispatcher, we could
simply pass different arguments to the constructor, for example:

```
myPortal = new Portal(
  'data',
  { messageSpanId: 'spanProcessing', urlSuffix: '.php' }
);
```

This will pass a base URL of "data" and, because no `actionParam` is defined in the
options array, append the command to the URL path, with the suffix .php, resulting in a URL such as data/login.php. We've given ourselves all the flexibility we'll
need here. We'll see how the options are turned into URLs in section 11.6.3. For
now, let's move on to the next task. The final line of the constructor introduces
the issue of adapting the AjaxWindows.js library.

11.6.2 *Adapting the AjaxWindows.js library*

Recall that the implementation of this portal used an external library called Ajax-
Windows.js for creating the individual portal windows and managing their size
and position on the screen. One of the things we had to do was to adapt the
library to send Ajax requests to the portal manager for saving the settings on the
`mouseup` event. This was the hook we needed; all move and resize operations are
theoretically terminated by a `mouseup` event. The way we performed the adaptation in round one was to make a copy of the AjaxWindows.js library code and
change the piece of code that puts a `mouseup` handler on the document. If we
think of the AjaxWindow.js library as a third-party library, the drawback to this
approach is evident. We've *branched* a third-party library codebase, that is, modified the source code and behavior of the library in such a way that it's no longer
compatible with the version maintained by its original author. If the library
changes, we have to merge in our changes with every new version we upgrade to.
We haven't done a good job of isolating this change point and making it as painless as possible. Let's consider a less-radical approach of adaptation and see if we
can rectify the situation. Recall the last line of our constructor:

```
this.initDocumentMouseHandler();
```

Our `initDocumentMouseHandler()` method is an on-the-fly adaptation of the Ajax-
Windows.js library. It just overrides the `document.onmouseup` as before, but within

our own codebase instead. Now our own method will perform the logic required to perform the adaptation within the portal's `handleMouseUp()` method. This is shown in listing 11.14.

Listing 11.14   Adaptation of the AjaxWindows.js mouse hander

```
initDocumentMouseHandler: function() {
   var oThis = this;
   document.onmouseup = function() { oThis.handleMouseUp(); };
},

handleMouseUp: function() {
   bDrag    = false;
   bResize  = false;
   intLastX = -1;
   document.body.style.cursor = "default";

   if ( elemWin && bHasMoved )
      this.saveWindowProperties(elemWin.id);

   bHasMoved = false;
},
```

This solution is much better, but we could take it one step further. If the AjaxWindows.js library defined the `mouseup` handler within a named function rather than anonymous, we could save the handler under a different name and invoke it from our own handler. This would have the benefit of not duplicating the logic already defined in the AjaxWindows.js library. This approach is illustrated in the following code:

```
function ajaxWindowsMouseUpHandler() {
   // logic here...
}
document.onmouseup = ajaxWindowsMouseUpHandler;
```

`ajaxWindowsMouseUpHandler()` is a callback defined by the AjaxWindows.js external library. Using it would allow us to save the definition of the method and use it later, as shown here:

```
initDocumentMouseHandler: function() {
   this.ajaxWindowsMouseUpHandler =
      ajaxWindowsMouseUpHandler;        ❶ Store our own reference
   var oThis = this;
   document.onmouseup = function() { oThis.handleMouseUp(); };
},
```

```
handleMouseUp: function() {
    this.ajaxWindowsMouseUpHandler();        ❷  Call library function
    if ( elemWin && bHasMoved )
        this.saveWindowProperties(elemWin.id);   ❸  Add our functionality
},
```

Now our `handleMouseUp()` method doesn't have to duplicate the AjaxWindows.js library functionality. We just invoke the functionality ❷ through our saved reference ❶ and then add our own functionality ❸. And if the `mouseup` handler of AjaxWindows changes in the future, we pick up the changes without requiring any code modifications. This is a much more palatable change-management situation. Of course, it does assume that the implied contract with the library doesn't change—the contract being two global variables named `elemWin` and `bHasMoved`. Given that the library currently defines the `mouseup` handler as an anonymous function, we could still save a reference to the existing `mouseup` functionality with a line of code such as

```
this.ajaxWindowsMouseUpHandler = this.document.onmouseup;
```

This would achieve the same thing, but it's a slightly more brittle proposition, since the contract in this situation is much looser. This solution relies on the fact that we've included our script libraries in the appropriate order and that the AjaxWindows.js library has already executed the code that placed the `mouseup` handler on the document. It also assumes no other library has placed a different `mouseup` handler on the document or has performed some other wrapping technique just as we've done.

That's probably about as much as we can hope to do with the library adaptation. Let's move on to the portal API. The `handleMouseUp()` method reveals one of the three portal commands that the portal component has to accommodate. When the mouse button is released, the `saveWindowProperties()` method is called to save the size and position of the current window. The following discussion will detail that along with the other portal command APIs.

11.6.3 *Specifying the portal commands*

As already discussed, our portal component is primarily a sender of commands. The commands that are sent are Ajax requests to a server-side portal management system. We've already discussed the notion of commands and the formal Command pattern in Ajax, in chapters 3 and 5. Here is another opportunity to put that knowledge to use.

The commands that we've supported up to this point in our portal are logging in, loading settings, and saving settings. We're going to throw in the ability to add and delete windows, which we alluded to although we didn't show the full implementation. We can think of each of these in terms of a method of our portal. But before we start looking at code, let's do a bit of prep work to help with the task of isolating change points. What we're referring to is the names of the commands themselves. Let's define symbols for each command name so that the rest of our components can use them. Consider the following set of symbols:

```
Portal.LOGIN_ACTION          = "login";
Portal.LOAD_SETTINGS_ACTION  = "PageLoad";
Portal.SAVE_SETTINGS_ACTION  = "UpdateDragWindow";
Portal.ADD_WINDOW_ACTION     = "AddWindow";
Portal.DELETE_WINDOW_ACTION  = "DeleteWindow";
```

Even though the language doesn't really support constants, let's assume that based on the uppercase naming convention, these values are intended to be constant values. We could lazily sprinkle these string literals throughout our code, but that's a fairly sloppy approach. Using constants in this way keeps our "magic" strings in a single location. If the server contract changes, we can adapt. For example, imagine the ways in which the server contract could change, as shown in table 11.1.

Table 11.1   Public contract changes

Server Contract Change	Action Required
A command is renamed (e.g., `PageLoad` gets renamed to its verb-noun form `LoadPage`).	Change the right side of the assignment of the `LOAD_SETTINGS_ACTION` constant to the new value. The rest of the code remains unaffected.
The server no longer supports a command.	Remove the constant, and do a global search for all references. Take appropriate action at each reference point.
The server supports a new command.	Add a constant for the command, and use its name within the code.

Now that we can reference commands by these symbols, let's look at a generic mechanism for issuing the commands to the portal management server. We need a helper method that generically sends Ajax-based portal commands to the server. Consider this usage contract:

```
myPortal.issuePortalCommand( Portal.SAVE_SETTINGS_ACTION,
                             "setting1=" + setting1Value,
                             "setting2=" + setting2Value, ... );
```

In this scenario, we're contemplating a method named `issuePortalCommand()` that takes the name of a command as its first argument (for example, one of our constants) and a variable number of arguments corresponding to the parameters the command expects/requires. The parameters are, quite intentionally, of the exact form as that required by the net.ContentLoader's `sendRequest()` method. The `issuePortalCommand()` method we've defined could be implemented as follows:

```
issuePortalCommand: function( commandName ) {
  var actionParam = this.options['actionParam'];      ❶ Get action parameter

  var urlSuffix = this.options['urlSuffix'];           ❷ Get URL suffix

  if (!urlSuffix) urlSuffix="";
  var url = this.baseUrl;
  var callParms = [];
  if (actionParam){
    callParms.push(
      actionParam + "=" + commandName              ❸ Apply action parameter
    );
  }else{
    url += "/" + commandName                       ❹ Apply URL
      + urlSuffix;                                     suffix
  }
  for ( var i = 1 ; i < arguments.length ; i++ )
    callParms.push( arguments[i] );
  var ajaxHelper = new
    net.ContentLoader( this, url, "POST", [] );    ❺ Create ContentLoader
  ajaxHelper.sendRequest
    .apply( ajaxHelper, callParms );               ❻ Send request
},
```

This method builds a URL based on the configuration options that we discussed in section 11.6.1. If we have supplied a value for actionParam ❶, then it will be added to the parameters that are POSTed to the server ❸. If not, we will append the command to the URL path ❹, adding the URL suffix if we have supplied one in our options ❷. The first function argument is the command name. All remaining arguments are treated as request parameters. The URL that we have constructed is then passed to the ContentLoader ❺, and the request is sent with the request parameters in tow ❻, as illustrated in the example usage shown previously. With this method in place, each of our portal command APIs will have a nicely minimal implementation. Another "for free" feature of having a generic method like this is that we can support new commands that become available on the server without having to change any client code. For now, let's look at the commands we do know about.

Login

Recall that our login button's `onclick` handler initiates a call to the `login()` method of our page, which in turn calls this method. The `login` command, at least from the perspective of the server, is a command that the server must handle by checking the credentials and then (if they are valid) responding with the same response that our `load-page` command would perform. With that in mind, let's look at the implementation shown in listing 11.15.

Listing 11.15 The portal login method

```
login: function(userName, password) {

    this.userName = userName;
    this.password = password;

    if ( this.options.messageSpanId )
        document.getElementById(
            this.options.messageSpanId).innerHTML =
            "Verifying Credentials";
    this.issuePortalCommand( Portal.LOGIN_ACTION,
                             "user=" + this.userName,
                             "pass=" + this.password );
},
```

The method puts a "Verifying Credentials" message into the span designated by our configurable option `this.options.messageSpanId`. It then issues a `login` command to the portal back end, passing the credentials that were passed into the method as request parameters. The `issuePortalCommand()` method we've just put in place does all the hard work.

Load settings

Recall that the `createPortal()` function of our page calls this method to load the initial configuration of our portal windows. The method to load the settings for the page is even simpler than the login method just discussed. It's just a thin wrapper around our `issuePortalCommand()`. It passes the user as the lone parameter that the server uses to load the relevant window settings, since the settings are on a per-user basis:

```
loadPage: function(action) {
    this.issuePortalCommand( Portal.LOAD_SETTINGS_ACTION,
                             "user=" + this.userName,
                             "pass=" + this.password );
},
```

Save settings

The save settings method is equally simplistic. Recall that this method is called by our AjaxWindows.js library adaptation on the `mouseup` event in order to store all move and size operations:

```
saveWindowProperties: function(id) {
    this.issuePortalCommand( Portal.SAVE_SETTINGS_ACTION,
                    "ref=" + id,
                    "x="    + parseInt(elemWin.style.left),
                    "y="    + parseInt(elemWin.style.top),
                    "w="    + parseInt(elemWin.style.width),
                    "h="    + parseInt(elemWin.style.height) );
    elemWin = null;
},
```

Adding/deleting windows

Although we didn't fully develop the concept out of adding and deleting windows, at least from the perspective of providing a nice UI to initiate these actions, we can certainly define the command API methods that would support these operations, as shown here:

```
addWindow: function(title, url, x, y, w, h) {
    this.issuePortalCommand( Portal.ADD_WINDOW_ACTION,
                    "title=" + title,
                    "url="   + url,
                    "x="     + x,
                    "y="     + y,
                    "w="     + w,
                    "h="     + h );

},

deleteWindow: function(id) {
    var doDelete =
        confirm("Are you sure you want to delete this window?");
    if(doDelete)
        this.issuePortalCommand( Portal.DELETE_WINDOW_ACTION,
                        "ref=" + id );
},
```

This concludes our discussion of the APIs required to support the portal commands. Now let's look at our portal Ajax handling.

11.6.4 Performing the Ajax processing

As already noted, in this example we're using an Ajax technique for handling responses in a script-centric way. The technique relies on the fact that the expected response is valid JavaScript code. The thing that's very desirable about this kind of approach is that the client doesn't have to do any data-marshaling or parsing to grok (geek-speak for *understand*) the response. The response is simply evaluated via the JavaScript `eval()` method, and the client is absolved from all further responsibility. The negative side of this approach is that it puts the responsibility on the server to be able to understand the client-side object model and generate a syntactically correct language-specific (JavaScript) response. The second downside of this approach is partially addressed by the popular variety of this technique of using JSON to define our responses. There are some server-side libraries that aid in the generation of JSON responses (see chapter 3), although these are moving more toward what we described in chapter 5 as a data-centric approach.

For now, we're going to stick to a script-centric system, so let's look at our implementation and see what we can do to help it along. Let's start with our `ajax-Update()` function and its helper `runScript()`:

```
ajaxUpdate: function(request) {
    this.runScript(request.responseText);
},

runScript: function(scriptText) {
    eval(scriptText);
},
```

As already discussed, the response handling is simple to a fault. All we do is call the `runScript()` method with the `responseText`, and the `runScript()` simply `eval()`s the response text. So why, you might ask, don't we just get rid of the `run-Script()` method altogether and just call `eval()` from within the `ajaxUpdate()` method? Well, that's certainly a valid and useful approach. It might be nice, however, to have a method that encapsulates the concept of running a script. For example, what if we added a preprocessing step or a postprocessing step to our `runScript()` implementation? Again, we've isolated a change point. Our `ajax-Update()` method is happily oblivious of the change, and we pick up the new behavior. One interesting application of this technique would be a preprocessor that does token replacement of values that reside on the client before executing.

Finishing out our Ajax discussion with the ever-important handling of errors, let's show our `handleError()` method. Recall that just as the `ajaxUpdate()` method is an implied contract required for collaboration with the net.Content-Loader, so is the `handleError()`. The `handleError()` method is shown here:

```
handleError: function(request) {
  if ( this.options.messageSpanId )
    document.getElementById
      (this.options.messageSpanId).innerHTML =
      "Oops! Server error.  Please try again later.";
},
```

This method checks for the existence of the `messageSpanId` configuration property and, if it exists, uses it as the element to place an "Oops!" message onto the UI. The actual text of the message that's presented is something that could also be parameterized with the options object. This is an exercise left to the reader.

With that, our portal component refactoring session has come to a close. We've created a deceptively simple mechanism for providing Ajax portal management. Now let's take a few moments to review the focus of our refactoring and recap what we've accomplished.

11.6.5 *Refactoring debrief*

In a couple of ways, the development of this component is quite different than the other component examples in this book. First, the portal component is a more coarse-grained component for providing an Ajax-based portal capability. A third-party developer is unlikely to want to drop a portal system into the corner of his page! Second, it uses a technique for handling Ajax responses as JavaScript code. Our refactoring of this component focused on ways to isolate change points. This was illustrated in several ways:

- We provided a clean way to adapt the AjaxWindows.js library.
- We isolated string literals as pseudo-constants.
- We wrote a generic method for issuing commands.
- We isolated via a method the concept of running an Ajax response script.

11.7 *Summary*

The portal can be one of the most powerful tools a company has. The company can set up business logic to allow users to see only the information that pertains to them. Portals also allows users to customize the look and feel of the window to fit their needs in order to increase their performance since the page is laid out exactly as they want it to be.

By using Ajax in the portal, we can keep all of the functionality in one area without having to send the server to multiple pages. There is no more worrying about what the back button is going to do when the user logs out. There will be no page history, since we never left the page. We talked about the drawbacks of navigating away from the page, but we were able to solve the problem by using Ajax to perform a request to the server.

We also sent requests back to the server without the user knowing that data was being saved. By triggering Ajax with event handlers, we are able to save data quickly without disrupting the user's interaction. A portal that uses Ajax introduces a new level of performance in a rich user interface.

In the final section of this chapter, we looked at refactoring the portal code. In previous sections, we have focused on creating a reusable component that can be dropped in to an existing page. In this case, that isn't appropriate, as the portal is the shell within which other components will reside. Our emphasis in these refactorings has been on increasing the maintainability of the code by isolating String constants, creating some generic methods, and separating the third-party library from our project code in a cleaner way.

In this chapter, we've generated simple XML responses from the server and decoded them manually using JavaScript. In the next chapter, we'll look at an alternative approach: using XSLT stylesheets on the client to transform abstract XML directly into HTML markup.

Live search using XSLT

This chapter covers

- Dynamic search techniques
- Using XSLT to translate XML to HTML
- Bookmarking dynamic information
- Building a live search component

With Ajax, it's easy to perform server-side actions while controlling what is happening on the client. If a process takes an extended period of time, we can show animated GIFs that display messages that let the user know what's happening. The user can perform other actions while the server-side process is taking place and will be less likely to think that the browser has frozen.

In this chapter, we use this Ajax technique to create a live search. It utilizes Extensible Stylesheet Language Transformations (XSLT) to transform an XML document into an HTML layout. The XSLT translation is easier to maintain than the code to manually parse the XML and produce HTML using JavaScript statements. It uses a tree-oriented transformation on a dynamically generated XML document, which replaces the server-side code and the JavaScript on which the previous projects relied. We are eliminating the hassles of manually making sure that all the HTML elements are formed properly.

As with previous examples, we first develop the code in a straightforward way and then refactor it into a reusable component. By the end of this chapter, you should understand the principles of using XSLT with Ajax and have a ready-rolled search component that you can drop into your own projects.

12.1 Understanding the search techniques

When we perform searches, we are accustomed to seeing the page freeze while the search is conducted on the server. (At least, this is the case on websites that do not have 1,200 clustered servers that perform a search over 8 billion pages in less than a second. The budget constraints of your project may vary.) To eliminate the pause, some developers implement pop-up windows and frames. The additional window is used to perform the processing so the user's experience can be enhanced, but this also creates problems. With Ajax, we can eliminate the common delays of the classic form and frame submissions.

12.1.1 Looking at the classic search

In a classic search process, when we include a search form on our website, one or more form elements are posted back to the server. Google's main search page is an example. Google's search page (www.google.com) contains a single textbox and two search buttons. Depending on what search action we select, the form either directs us to a list of records, which we can navigate, or takes us to a single result in that list. This design is well suited for a page that doesn't have any other functionality, but if it is part of a larger project, the design may cause problems, such as losing the state of the page, clearing form fields, and so on. Figure 12.1 is

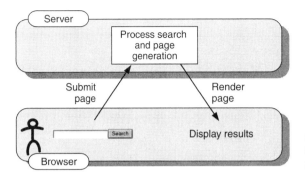

Figure 12.1
Classic search model showing the processing over a period of time

a diagram of the classic search model, where the entire page is posted back to the server for processing and a complete, new results page is returned.

One source of delay is that database queries can take an extended period of time. The browser is not accessible to the user until the results are displayed, causing the page to seem as if it has become frozen or inaccessible. Developers attempt to alleviate this inaccessibility period by adding functionality to the page to notify the user that the process is happening. It's important to note that this inaccessibility problem is not limited to search operations. It can appear when updating or deleting records in a database, running a complicated server-side transaction, and so on.

One way developers try to cope with this is to display an animated GIF, such as a status bar, while the server is processing the submission. A common question on forums such as JavaRanch (www.JavaRanch.com) is how this can be done. The problem with an animated GIF is that it does not always run. The GIF tends to remain on the first frame with Microsoft Internet Explorer and does not loop through the GIF animation cycle. Developers have reported that some users think that their browser has frozen since they do not see the animation, and they click the refresh button or close their browser.

The classic search form also suffers from the same problems as some of the previous examples in which the page has to be re-rendered. The scroll position of the page may be lost because the new page is loaded at the top of the page instead of where the action took place. The form fields may not stay filled in, which requires the user to enter the data again. Developers attempt to solve these problems by using frames and pop-up windows, but they end up creating more problems. Let's take a look at the underlying reasons.

12.1.2 *The flaws of the frame and pop-up methods*

Developers have traditionally used frames, IFrames, and pop-up windows to avoid the problems with pages appearing to be frozen, losing scroll position, and so on. The frames and the pop-up window allow the processing to be continued in another part of the web page, so the user can manipulate the part of the form where the action originated. Not only can the user manipulate the form, but other JavaScript functions can be executed as well.

The frame and pop-up windows have other added benefits. The frame solution allows the returned record set to be scrolled while the search form elements remain in the view of the user. The pop-up window permits the result to be displayed in a separate window, taking the processing away from the main window. With some parent/child window communication, we can pass data from the child window back to the parent window to return results. The pop-up window is great for adding searches in large forms when the user needs specific information that can be hard to memorize. The window can also be set to close after the processing is complete. That is useful when we want to perform updates without returning any data.

Figure 12.2 shows how a search in a frame is implemented. The bottom frame is responsible for submitting the search request to the server, allowing the results to be processed. As a result of having the bottom frame initiate the search, the frame at the top of the window is still accessible to the user, unlike the classic search shown in figure 12.1.

Although these solutions solve the problems that we talked about earlier, they also introduce new problems. Frames have been (and still are) one of developers' worst nightmares. The main problem is navigation, since we do not know how the frame will react with the browser. We wonder how the back button will affect the frame. Will the frame take us to the right page, will it destroy our

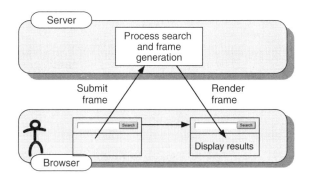

Figure 12.2
Process flow of a search
executed in the frame model

frameset, or will it just not seem to work? These are the questions that are typically in our minds when testing. And what if the pages are opened in a browser that does not support framesets? To avoid this latter problem, we would have to include frame-detection scripts on the page, adding more weight to our application and introducing more code to manage, and thus increasing the complexity of our codebase.

Pop-up windows, on the other hand, are subject to pop-up blockers as users increasingly turn them on. Pop-up windows should have no problem if they are explicitly initiated by the user's button click, but pop-up windows can be spawned by the browser automatically, such as an onload or onunload pop-up. These onload pop-up windows are often prevented from opening since they tend to be abused as advertisements. Some users block all pop-up windows—which means users will never get their results since no window will open.

Other problems can occur with pop-up windows, such as when the child window appears underneath its parent; the pop-up window cannot be seen since it is covered by the parent window. This is known as a *pop-under*. Another problem can happen when an action takes place in the parent window. If the user clicks a link or refreshes the page, the action can sever the child-parent relationship, resulting in loss of communication between the windows. When the page refreshes, the pop-up window object is destroyed; there is no way to carry the object from page to page in a reasonable manner.

As you can see, although the frame and pop-up methods solve the problems inherent in traditional form submission, their solutions may lead to bigger problems. One way to fix these problems is to use Ajax. Ajax handles server communication independently of the browser page, which allows our animations to play and maintains the page state; we do not have to worry about outside factors such as pop-up blockers and users closing the window because they think it is frozen.

12.1.3 Examining a live search with Ajax and XSLT

We can improve the functionality of certain search features on a website by turning the search into a *live search*, which is how some developers are naming the functionality of Ajax searches. This search is performed without posting the entire page to the server (as in the traditional search), which means that the current state of the page can be maintained. In addition, we can run JavaScript and GIF animations without any major problems, since the results are displayed within the browser with `innerHTML` or other DOM methods.

Let's say we have a search that triggers a long database transaction that appears to lock the page. With Ajax, the animation can start when the database transaction starts. When we begin to output the results, we can simply set the CSS `display` property of the animated image to `none`, which will make the animation disappear. A variation on this is to place the animation image in the output location where the results are to be displayed. When the transaction is complete, we replace the GIF with the results, so the wait image is removed. Either way, the user can still use the form while the XMLHttpRequest object is processing the data of the server.

Let's look at a popular example of allowing the user to work with an application while processing is being done on the server: Google Maps. We send out a request to the server for, say, restaurants on Main Street, and we are still able to manipulate the map while the server processes our request. We do not have to wait as we would with a normal form submission. The server-side process then returns the results to the page, where they are displayed to the user. In the same way, our live search allows the user to interact with the page while the server is processing the data. Figure 12.3 shows Ajax's process flow.

The Ajax approach to handling searches and long transitions allows us to eliminate the problems that we have faced with the other options used in the past. This live search feature is not only useful when used with a search engine like Google or Yahoo, but it can also be helpful for smaller lookups. For instance, we can use a live search to perform a lookup to a database table to retrieve information for some of the form fields, such as an address, based on what the user has entered so far—all while the user is filling in other fields. Any long transaction with the server can be turned into a live process, with the server providing incremental updates to the client, which are displayed in an unobtrusive way (see chapter 6). With Ajax, we can improve data transfer and get the results to the client in a richer environment.

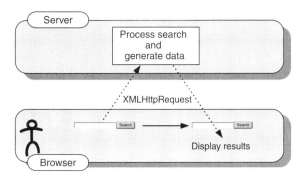

Figure 12.3
Process flow of the Ajax model. The server-side process generates data, which the client-side code inserts into the page directly. Less bandwidth is used, and the user interface is smoother.

12.1.4 *Sending the results back to the client*

When the server returns the result of a live search, we can send the information back to the client in one of several ways. We can format the results as XML, plain text, or HTML tags. In previous examples, we created an XML document on the server. The JavaScript code on the client side then called XML DOM methods to build the results table on the client side by looping through the XML nodes. This process used two loops. The first loop was on the server when we built the XML document, and the second was the loop to build the HTML table on the client.

We can avoid the client-side XML DOM loop by building the HTML table on the server before we send it back, rather than building the XML file. With this technique, we concatenate HTML tags into a large string, similar to what we did to create the XML document. However, instead of building it with XML tags, we use table elements. The HTML string is returned to the client, and we can apply it directly to an element's `innerHTML` property. In this case, we would use the XMLHttpRequest object's `responseText` property since we would have no need to navigate through the nodes.

The problem with these techniques is that—whether it happens on the server or the client—there is a requirement to loop through the data and build the table dynamically. If we need to make changes to the table format in the future, it may be a tedious task, depending on the complexity of the table. Adding or subtracting a column may cause a problem, since we must alter the code inside the loop. We also need to take into account the extra quotes that are contained inside our string; we must make sure that we are escaping the quotes when building the string. Also, if we embed JavaScript into this HTML tag, it adds even more quotes and apostrophes to worry about—we have to verify that all of the tags are closed and that they are properly formatted. The only way we can do that effectively is by examining the text after we build the string.

One option that lets us avoid these problems is to use XSLT. With Ajax, it is possible to combine an XSLT file with an XML document and display the results, thus avoiding DOM methods. If a developer knows XSLT and is not great at coding JavaScript, this may be an excellent solution.

One thing to note about an Ajax search is that it does not require a postback to the server, and consequently the URL of the page does not change to match the search results. Therefore bookmarking the URL will not give us the results we want. In a classic search, such as Google, we can easily copy a URL from a page found by the search and paste it into an e-mail; when the recipient clicks the link, they see the results. However, with an Ajax search, we need to add a little extra code to make this happen. We will look at this solution in section 12.5.4.

12.2 *The client-side code*

Formatting XML data using XSLT is a popular technique since XML has a structured layout that can be easily manipulated. In previous projects such as the type-ahead suggest in chapter 10, we used JavaScript, XML, and DOM manipulation to create the HTML that we were to display. In this example, we use XSLT to produce the same effect.

XSLT enables us to format our data by building the HTML layout in another file and combining it with the XML document. The XSLT file takes all of the guesswork out of navigating through the XML nodes and building our tables, menus, and HTML layouts. With Ajax, we can retrieve a static or dynamic XML file and a static or dynamic XLST file from the server, and combine them on the client to build our HTML document. XSLT could also be undertaken on the server side, but we'll look at client-side transformations here.

12.2.1 *Setting up the client*

For this project, we perform a phonebook search on a user's name. We use one textbox and one submit button to do this. Our simple search form is shown in listing 12.1.

Listing 12.1 Client-side form

```
<form name="Form1"  ID="Form1"
  onsubmit="GrabNumber();return false;">      ❶  Add onsubmit handler

  Name: <input name="user" type="text"/>      ❷  Insert textbox
  <input type="submit" name="btnSearch"
    value="Search" />      ❸  Add submit button
  <br/><br/>
  <div id="results"></div>      ❹  Add div for results
</form>
```

To initialize the live search, we need to add an event handler to the `form` tag. The `onsubmit` event handler ❶ intercepts clicks on both the Enter key on the textbox and the submit button. This event handler calls the function `GrabNumber()`, which initiates the XMLHttpRequest without submitting the form back to the page. (In a production environment, we would check to see whether the user has JavaScript disabled. In that case, the form would have to be submitted back to the server, and we could use a classic search form to support that user. However, we are not adding that functionality to this project.)

The form that we have created is basic, containing only one event handler to initialize the XMLHttpRequest. The textbox ❷ and the submit button ❸ are added to the form to collect the user's search criteria. If we wanted to get fancy, we could also add an `onblur` handler to the textbox that calls the function `Grab-Number()`, and when the user removes focus from the textbox, it would perform the search. In this example, we stick with the `onsubmit` handler to perform the search.

We next add our `div` element ❹ to the document as the output location for the search results. We can position the `div` wherever we want the results to appear on the page. The ID is added to the `div` so that we can reference it to add the results and an animated GIF. We are not required to use a `div` element to output the results. We could easily output the results into a cell in a table or even a span; in fact, we can use any HTML element whose `innerHTML` property can be manipulated. We are using a `div` because it is a block element, which contains a line break before and after the element. The `div` also takes up 100 percent of the available width of the browser, making it easier for larger results tables to be displayed to the user.

It is important to note that the `onsubmit` handler must return `false` when the event handler is executing. This informs the browser that the form should not be submitted back to the server, which would trigger a full-page refresh and interrupt our JavaScript programming of the form. We'll see the return value in listing 12.2 in the next section.

12.2.2 Initiating the process

In this example, we use two files on the server: an XML document and an XSL document. The XML document is created dynamically by PHP when the client requests it. The PHP code takes the user input posted from the page, runs a query against the database, and then formats the results into an XML document. The static XSL document transforms our dynamic XML file into an HTML document. Because it is static, it does not have to be created by the server at the time of the client request, but can be set up ahead of time.

Just as with the other projects in this book, we are using a function to initialize our XMLHttpRequest object. We gather this information and call the function in listing 12.2.

Listing 12.2   Initiation function

```
function GrabNumber(){    ⟵— Create the function
  var urlXML='PhoneXML.php?q='
    + document.Form1.user.value;    ❶ Build XML URL

  var urlXSL='Phone.xsl';    ❷ Build XSL URL

  var newImg=document.createElement('img');    ❸ Create image element

  newImg.setAttribute('src',
    'images/loading.gif');    ❹ Set the source

  document.getElementById("results")
.appendChild(newImg);    ❺ Append image to page

  LoadXMLXSLTDoc(urlXML,urlXSL,"results");    ❻ Start loading
}
```

This function assembles the information needed for the call to the server, sets the "in progress" image, and calls the server, which will dynamically build the response data based on the querystring value we send. The first parameter of the LoadXMLXSLTDoc() function is the URL of the PHP page that generates the XML document, combined with the querystring, which is built by referencing the value of HTML form field ❶. The second parameter is the name of the XSLT file ❷ that is used in the transformation of the XML data. The third parameter that we need for the function LoadXMLXSLTDoc() is the ID of the div where the search results are to appear. The ID is just the string name of the output element and is not the object's reference; in this case, the string is "results".

The next step is to add the loading image to the web page, using DOM methods. The image element ❸ is created and the source attribute ❹ of the image is set. We append the newly created element ❺ to the results div. This places the image file on the page when our function is called from the onsubmit handler of the form. It is important to show the user visual feedback, such as a message or an image, to indicate that the request processing is happening. This eliminates the chance of the user repeatedly clicking the submit button, thinking that nothing has happened, since Ajax is a "silent" process.

The last step is to call the function LoadXMLXSLTDoc() ❻, which initiates the process of sending the information to the server. The LoadXMLXSLTDoc() function that we will build in section 12.4 will handle calling our ContentLoader(), which requests the documents from the server. By specifying the output location as a parameter instead of hard-coding the value into our `LoadXMLXSLTDoc()` function, we can reuse this function multiple times on the same page without having to add multiple functions or `if` statements to separate the functionality. Therefore, we redirect the output of different searches to different parts of the page. But before we do this, let's look at how we build the XML and XSLT documents on the server.

12.3 *The server-side code: PHP*

In this section, we create the dynamic XML document for this project using the popular open source scripting language PHP (remember, Ajax is able to work with any server-side language or platform). The XML document is dynamically generated from the result set of a database query at the time of the client's request. We also show how to create the static XSLT document, which resides on the server and is retrieved each time the dynamic file is requested. Both of these documents are sent back to the client separately when the ContentLoader requests each of them in two separate requests, as shown in listing 12.7. The XSLT transforms our dynamic XML document on the client and creates an HTML table that is displayed to the user.

12.3.1 *Building the XML document*

Since we are using XSLT, we need a structured XML document that is just a simple listing of information, so the XSLT file can perform a basic transformation. For this project, we develop a dynamic XML file when the PHP file is requested from the client.

Designing the XML structure

Before we can start to build the XML file, we need to create a template for that file. The template should reflect the structure of the data returned by the search. For our address book example, we'll return the company name, the name of a contact person, the country, and a phone number. Listing 12.3 shows our basic XML template containing the four fields.

Listing 12.3 Basic XML file

```
<?xml version="1.0" ?>
  <phonebook>
    <entry>
      <company>Company Name</company>
      <contact>Contact Name</contact>
      <country>Country Name</country>
      <phone>Phone Number</phone>
```

```
  </entry>
</phonebook>
```

The first element is `phonebook`. The next one is the `entry` element, which contains the subelements that hold all the details that relate to each contact found in the query. If we have five results, there will be five `entry` elements in our XML document. The company name is displayed in the `company` element. We are also adding the contact name, the country name, and the phone number. We are not limited to just these fields; we can add and subtract fields depending on the information we want to display.

Instead of displaying an alert message to the user if results are not found, we can create an entry displaying that information to the user. This makes it easy for us to return the result to the user without having to add any extra client-side code. The code in listing 12.4 is almost the same as that in listing 12.3, but this time we are inserting text into the XML elements that we want to display to the user to show that no results were returned.

Listing 12.4 XML file with no results

```
<?xml version="1.0" ?>
  <phonebook>
    <entry>
      <company>No Results</company>          ❶ Display "No Results"
                                                 for company name
      <contact>N/A</contact>         ❷ Display "N/A"
      <country>N/A</country>            for remaining
      <phone>N/A</phone>               fields
    </entry>
  </phonebook>
```

With this code, we display a single row to the user showing that there is no information. In the `company` tag ❶, we display a message to the user informing her that there were no results. In the other tags ❷, we are telling the user that there is no information. If we do not want to display "N/A", we can add a nonbreaking space, ` `, instead, which allows the table cells to show up. If we were to not add any information, the cells would not appear in the table.

As you can see, the XML format has a very simple structure. If this XML file were static, it would be rather easy for any user to add a new customer to the file. Because we are creating it dynamically, we will have to create a loop, which builds our XML document from our result set.

Building the dynamic XML document

As always, we build our XML document on the server. Following our policy of using different server languages for our illustrations, we've implemented the server code for this chapter in PHP. Ajax can work with any server-side language, and the fine details of the server code aren't important to our story here. Listing 12.5 shows the server-side code. The code obtains the querystring parameter and generates a result set of a database query. We then loop through the result set and create an entry in the XML file for each phone entry returned from the query, following our basic template (listing 12.4).

Listing 12.5   phoneXML.php: Server-side XML generation

```php
<?php
header("Content-type: text/xml");        ❶  Declare mime type
echo("<?xml version='1.0' ?>\n");

$db = mysql_connect("localhost","ajax","action");     ❷  Connect to
mysql_select_db("ajax",$db);                               database
$result = mysql_query("SELECT * FROM Contacts WHERE ContactName like '%".
$_GET['q']."%'",$db);      ❸  Populate query
?>
<phonebook>
<?
if ($myrow = mysql_fetch_array($result)) {      ❹  Test results
  do {      ❺  Iterate through results
?>
<entry id='<?=$myrow['id']?>001'>
  <company><?=$myrow['companyName']?></company>
  <contact><?=$myrow['contactName']?></contact>
  <country><?=$myrow['country']?></country>
  <phone><?=$myrow['phone']?></phone>
</entry>
<?
  }while ($myrow = mysql_fetch_array($result));
}else{
?>
<entry id='001'>      ❻  Show empty dataset
  <company>No Results</company>
  <contact>N/A</contact>
  <country>N/A</country>
  <phone>N/A</phone>
</entry>
<?
}
?>
</phonebook>
```

In order for this dynamic XML document generation to work, we must set the document's type to `text/xml` ❶; if we skip this step, the XSLT transformation may not take place, especially with Mozilla and Firefox.

The data that we are searching for is stored in a database table. We need to select the relevant entries. In this case, we are using PHP's built-in MySQL functions to talk to the database directly, in order to keep things as simple as possible. We connect to the database ajax running on the local database server as the user ajax with password *action* ❷. We then construct our SQL query string using the `request` parameter passed in from the client code to populate the WHERE clause ❸.

For a more robust server-side implementation, we recommend an Object-Relational Mapping system such as Pear `DB_DataObject` (see chapter 3) rather than talking directly to the database as we have done here. However, the current implementation is simple and can be easily configured by readers wanting to test the example for themselves. Having returned the result set, we check whether it is empty ❹, and then either iterate over it ❺ to create the phone entries, or print out the "No Results" message ❻.

12.3.2 *Building the XSLT document*

We can use XSLT to transform our XML file into a nice HTML table with only a few lines of code. The XSLT document allows for pattern matching if necessary to display the data in any format we want. The pattern matching uses a template to display the data. We loop through the source tree nodes with the XSLT to display the data. The XSLT takes the structured XML file and converts it into a viewable format that is easy to update and change. Our XSLT document will be defined statically.

Explaining the XSLT structure

An XSLT transformation contains the rules for transforming a source tree into a result tree. The whole XSLT process consists of pattern matching. When a pattern is matched against the source tree elements, the template then creates our result tree.

The result tree structure does not have to be related to the source tree structure. Since they can be different, we can take our XML file and convert it into any format we want. We are not required to stick with a tabular dataset.

This XSLT transformation is called a stylesheet since it styles the result tree. The stylesheet contains template rules, which have two parts. The first part is the pattern, which is matched against the nodes of the source tree. When a match is found, the XSLT processor uses the second part, the template, which contains the tags to build the source tree.

Building the XSLT document

Building the XSLT transformation for this project is rather simple. Since we are developing a table, we won't need any special pattern matching; instead, we will loop through the source tree element nodes. The template that we'll develop outputs an HTML table with four columns. Listing 12.6 shows the XSLT file for this project.

Listing 12.6   XSLT file

```
<?xml version="1.0" encoding="ISO-8859-1"?>          ❶  Set XML version and encoding
<xsl:stylesheet version="1.0"
xmlns:xsl=
   "http://www.w3.org/1999/XSL/Transform">           ❷  Specify XSLT namespace

<xsl:template match="/">        ❸  Set template rule

    <table id="table1">    ❹  Add table element
      <tr>
        <th align="left">Company</th>
        <th align="left">Contact</th>          ❺  Create
        <th align="left">Country</th>              heading
        <th align="left">Phone</th>                row
      </tr>
      <xsl:for-each
        select="phonebook/entry">    ❻  Loop through phonebook entries
      <tr>
        <td><xsl:value-of
         select="company"/></td>
        <td><xsl:value-of          ❼  Output the
         select="contact"/></td>       entry data
        <td><xsl:value-of
         select="country"/></td>
        <td><xsl:value-of
         select="phone"/></td>
      </tr>
      </xsl:for-each>
    </table>
  </xsl:template>
</xsl:stylesheet>
```

When we create an XSLT transformation, we need to state the version and encoding ❶ of the XML. The XSLT namespace ❷ needs to be specified. The namespace gives the document the rules and specifications that it is expected to follow. The elements in the XML namespace are recognized in the source document and not in the results document. The prefix `xsl` is used to define all our elements in the XSLT namespace. We can then set the template rule to the match pattern of / ❸, which references the whole document.

We can start building the table template that displays our results. We add the `table` tag ❹, giving the table an ID. The table header row ❺ is next inserted, which contains the column names to be displayed to the user so she can understand what information is contained in the table.

By looping through the source node set, we obtain the remaining rows of the table. For this, we use the `for-each` loop ❻ to iterate over the records to obtain the nodes that are located in `phonebook/entry`.

The column values have to be selected as we are looping through the document tree. To select the values from the nodes, we use `value-of` ❼, which extracts the value of an XML element and adds it to the output stream of the transformation. To specify the XML element whose text we want to retrieve, we use the `select` attribute with the element's name. Now that we have built the XSLT file and created the code to dynamically generate the XML document, we can finish building the JavaScript code to see how the XSLT transformation structures our XML file into a viewable table when we combine them.

The next step takes us back to the client, which retrieves the files that we just created with the HTTP response.

12.4 Combining the XSLT and XML documents

Back on the client, we need to combine the XSLT and XML documents from the server. When using an XSLT transformation, we'll find that the browsers differ on how they combine the two documents. Therefore, we first check to see what method the browser supports in order to load and combine our two documents.

Again we're using the ContentLoader object, introduced in chapter 3. It is contained in the external JavaScript file, net.js. This file does all of the work of determining how to send the information to the server, hiding any browser-specific code behind the easy-to-use wrapper object.

```
<script type="text/javascript" src="net.js"></script>
```

Now we can begin the process of obtaining the server-side files and combining them on the client. In listing 12.7, the `LoadXMLXSLTDoc()` function is being called from the function `GrabNumber()` in listing 12.2. The function `GrabNumber()` passes in the values for the URL that generates the XML data, the XSL file, and the output reference ID. With these three values, we are able to load the two documents and combine them when both have been completely loaded. After they have been loaded, we have to do some cross-browser coding in order to combine the XML and XSL files. You can see all of this happening in listing 12.7.

Listing 12.7 LoadXMLXSLTDoc

```
var xmlDoc;              ❶ Declare global
var xslDoc;                 variables
var objOutput;
function LoadXMLXSLTDoc(urlXML,urlXSL,elementId){
  xmlDoc=null;           ❷ Set variables
  xslDoc=null;              to null
  objOutput = document.getElementById(          ❸ Reference
                          elementId);              output element
  new net.ContentLoader(urlXML,onXMLLoad);      ❹ Load XML and
  new net.ContentLoader(urlXSL,onXSLLoad);         XSL files
}

function onXMLLoad(){          ❺ Handle XML
  xmlDoc=this.req.responseXML;    document
  doXSLT();
}

function onXSLLoad(){          ❻ Handle XSL
  xslDoc=this.req.responseXML;    document
  doXSLT();
}

function doXSLT(){
  if (xmlDoc==null || xslDoc==null){ return; }   ❼ Check for loaded documents
  if (window.ActiveXObject){
    objOutput.innerHTML=xmlDoc.transformNode(xslDoc);
  }
  else{
    var xsltProcessor = new XSLTProcessor();      ❽ Transform
    xsltProcessor.importStylesheet(xslDoc);          XML
    var fragment  =xsltProcessor.                    document
                transformToFragment(
                        xmlDoc,document);
    objOutput.innerHTML = "";
    objOutput.appendChild(fragment);
  }

}
```

To simplify the client-side script, we need to declare three global variables ❶ to hold three different objects. The first two variables, xmlDoc and xslDoc, are going to hold the XML and XSLT files returned from the server. The third variable, objOutput, holds the object reference to our DOM element where the results are to be inserted. With these variables defined, we can now build the function Load-XMLXSLTDoc(), which we invoked from the function GrabNumber().

Since we are loading two documents, we need a way to determine when they are both loaded. We do this by looking to see if the variables xmlDoc and xslDoc contain their respective documents. Before we start, we must set the variables to null ❷. This removes any data that may exist in the variables if this function is run more than once on the page. The output location for the results is set ❸ by using the passed element ID from the function call. Now we call the Content-Loader ❹ twice, once for the XML document and once for the XSL document. In each call, the ContentLoader will get the URL and then call another function to load the documents. onXMLLoad() ❺ loads the returned XML results into our global variable xmlDoc and then calls the function doXSLT() for future processing. onXSLLoad() ❻ loads the XSL document into the global variable xslDoc and also calls the doXSLT() function.

Processing cannot continue until both documents have been loaded, and there is no way of knowing which will be loaded first, so the doXSLT() function first checks for that. It is called twice, once after the XML document is loaded and once after the XSL document is loaded. The first time it is called, one of our global variables is still set to null and we exit the function ❼. The next time it is called, the function will not exit since neither of the variables will be null. With both documents now loaded, we are able to perform the XSLT transformation ❽.

Once the two documents are loaded, we need to transform the XML document with the XSLT. As you can see by looking at the code in the listing, there are two different ways to do this, depending on the browser. Internet Explorer uses transformNode(), whereas Mozilla uses the XSLTProcessor object. Let's examine these two different implementations of performing the transformation in greater detail.

12.4.1 *Working with Microsoft Internet Explorer*

Internet Explorer makes it easy to transform the XML document with the XSLT with only a few lines of code. We use the transformNode() method, which takes the XML and XSLT documents and combines them in one step:

```
if (window.ActiveXObject){
    objOutput.innerHTML=xmlDoc.transformNode(xslDoc);
}
```

We first check to see if the browser supports the `transformNode()` method. We've done this here by testing for ActiveX object support. If it supports it, we call the `transformNode()` method on the global variable containing our XML data, passing it the global variable containing our XSLT data. The result of this transformation is added to the `innerHTML` of our result element, which then contains the newly formatted search results.

Now that we are able to format the results for Internet Explorer, let's get this functioning for Mozilla-compatible browsers.

12.4.2 *Working with Mozilla*

With Mozilla, we need to use the XSLTProcessor object, which lets us combine the XML and XSLT documents. Note that even though Opera and Safari both support the XMLHttpRequest object, they still do not support the XSLTProcessor object, and they cannot run this project without support from the server (we will address this issue in section 12.5.2). In the listing 12.8, we transform the XML document using the XSLT and display the formatted result set.

Listing 12.8   Invoking XSLT for Mozilla

```
else{
    var xsltProcessor = new XSLTProcessor();
    xsltProcessor.importStylesheet(xslDoc);
    var fragment=xsltProcessor.transformToFragment(xmlDoc,document);
    objOutput.innerHTML = "";
    objOutput.appendChild(fragment);
}
```

The first step is to initialize the XSLTProcessor object, which enables us to join the XML and XSLT files together. The `importStylesheet` method of the XSLTProcessor object allows us to import the XSLT file so that we can join it to the XML file in the upcoming steps. When the XSLT file is loaded into the processor, we are left with transforming the XML document. The XSLTProcessor is used again with a new method called `transformToFragment()`. The `transformToFragment()` method takes the XML file and combines it with the XSLT, and then returns the formatted result tree.

We replace the content that exists in our `result` element by setting the `innerHTML` with a blank string. This removes our loading animation from the

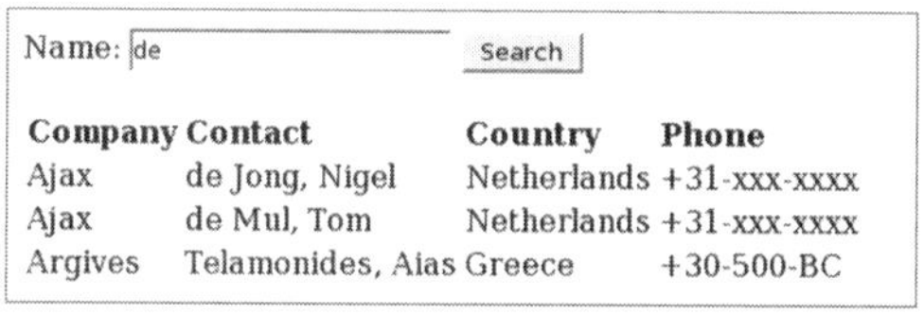

Figure 12.4
The search results are displayed from the Ajax live search.

page. Finally, we take the result we obtained from the `transformToFragment()` method and append it to the element. The newly formatted search results are now displayed to the user.

This code introduced some new concepts to us, including the XSLTProcessor object, which allows us to combine arbitrary XML and XSLT files. The Mozilla and Firefox browsers require us to use more DOM methods to combine the two documents. Internet Explorer, on the other hand, required only a single line of code to transform the XML document. The overall end result is exactly the same: they both show our results formatted according to the XSLT file.

Now that the client-side code is finished, we can save our documents and run a test of our live search. Enter some text into the textbox, and click the search button. The results should appear in the table format shown in figure 12.4.

As you can see, we have finished building our XSLT document and were able to run a successful search. The table displayed in figure 12.4 is rather dull since it has no formatting. That means the only thing that we have left to do is style our results table to make it more visually appealing. To do that, we need to use Cascading Style Sheets (CSS).

12.5 Completing the search

Now that we have combined our XML and XSLT documents to get our results, we need to enhance the style of the search results by applying CSS to our elements. Styling the elements will make it easier for the users to read the results. The first step in improving the user experience is to apply our CSS rules to the HTML elements.

12.5.1 Applying a Cascading Style Sheet

We introduced Cascading Style Sheets in chapter 2. A Cascading Style Sheet will make the results look professional with a minimum amount of effort on our part, separating the presentation of the results from the document structure and from the transformation logic. Along the way, if the manager or client hates the colors, we can make the changes quickly and easily. If we're on a large project with separate design and coding teams, CSS helps to keep them from treading on each other's toes. We can either include the stylesheet as an external file on our search page or embed the code into the search page. Using an external CSS file is preferable since it is cached by the browser and decreases the page-loading time in the future. The stylesheet rules are shown in listing 12.9.

Listing 12.9 Cascading Style Sheet

```
table{
  border: 1px solid black;          ❶ Style the
  border-collapse: collapse;            table
  width: 50%;
}
th, td{
  border: 1px solid black;          ❷ Style the
  padding: 3px;                         table cells
  width: 25%;
}
th{                                 ❸ Style the
  background-color: #A0A0A0;            header cells
}
```

The first CSS rule we are applying is to the `table` tag ❶. In this case, we want to make the border a solid-black line one pixel wide. We set the table's `border-collapse` property to `collapse`. The collapse CSS model basically allows the properties of the table to be uniform. The borders become even thicknesses, with adjacent cells sharing borders rather than accumulating to double or triple thicknesses. The final step for the `table` tag is to set the table `width` property. In this case, we are setting the width of the table to 50% of the `div` that it is contained in since we are not returning a large number of columns. Each of our columns will contain only a small amount of data, so the table does not need wide spacing.

After styling the `table` element, our next step is to format the table's body and header cells ❷. Just as we did for the table, we are setting the border to be a solid-black one-pixel line. We insert padding into the cells so that the text is not sitting directly on the cell borders. We also set the `width` property of the cells to 25% of the width of the table so that all four columns are uniform in size.

The final step to apply CSS to our table is to change the properties of the header cell so it stands out from the body cell. We reference the header cell ❸ and change the `background-color` of the cell to a shade of gray. We can change other properties here, such as `font-weight`, `color`, and so on. After we finish

Figure 12.5
The search results are displayed from the Ajax live search with CSS applied to the elements.

applying the stylesheet properties, we save our document and run the same search again. Our new formatted table is shown in figure 12.5.

As you can see, the table has a structured format that was easily created by applying CSS properties to our table elements. If we wanted to add more functionality to our stylesheet, we could add class references to the XSLT file to make it even more flexible. CSS lets us customize the table any way we want, but we may want to improve the search in other areas as well.

12.5.2 *Improving the search*

One of the benefits of Ajax is that it's easy to pass information back to the server. This project was a simple exercise for creating a search utilizing Ajax and XSLT to display a formatted results table with a minimum amount of effort. We can make the live search as sophisticated as we want. Let's look at some ways to improve it.

Including new features

The search form we created uses a single textbox and a single submit button to perform the search. We can easily adapt this search to use multiple parameters, such as additional search parameters with the contact name or country. All we have to do is send the additional parameters back to the server and have the server-side code check for them. That means the users can have additional ways to look for information, making the form more useful.

We could add other Ajax features to this script, such as the double combination script, as we did in chapter 9. This would help reduce the possibilities from which the user can choose. We can implement techniques from chapter 10 with the type-ahead suggest, too.

Supporting Opera and Safari

If you recall, we have a problem with Opera and Safari not supporting either the `transformNode()` method or the XSLTProcessor object. We have two options for supporting Opera and Safari. The first one is to use Ajax to send the files to a server-side page for processing. The server-side code can combine the XML and

XSLT documents. We would then fetch the result of the transformation using a single ContentLoader object, rather than fetching the XML data and the XSLT stylesheet independently. This is not the best solution since we have to use two round-trips to perform the transformation.

Our second option is to submit the entire page back to the server without the use of Ajax. The server in this case would handle the submission and combine the XML and XSLT documents on the server as we would do traditionally. This approach is better because it lets all users use the search. If a person is using an early version of a browser that does not support the XMLHttpRequest object, then that user can use the form. If we used the Ajax-only technique, the people without the ability to use Ajax would not be able to retrieve the two files for processing. Our second approach gives them the ability to use the form since Ajax is not required. In order to add this functionality, we need to make two changes to the LoadXMLXSLTDoc() function, as shown in listing 12.10. We must alter the first if statement to include a check for the XSLT processor. Then we must add an else statement to force the submit back to the server.

Listing 12.10 Altering LoadXMLXSLTDoc to support Opera and Safari

```
function LoadXMLXSLTDoc(urlXML,urlXSL,elementID){
  var reqXML;
  var reqXSL;
if (window.XMLHttpRequest && window.XSLTProcessor){
  //...do Mozilla client XSLT
}else if (window.ActiveXObject){
  //...do Internet Explorer client XSLT
}else{
    document.Form1.onsubmit = function(){return true;}
    document.Form1.submit();
  }
}
```

In listing 12.10, we remove the onsubmit event handler inside the else branch of the conditional check so that we submit the form to the server. Without removing the onsubmit handler, the form would not submit back to the server.

The server-side page then has to do all of the processing and put the element on the form. In return, we get a fast response for those users who can combine XSLT with JavaScript, and we do not alienate the users who do not support Ajax or the XSLTProcessor. Remember that Ajax is giving us the benefit of not having to re-render the entire page, which can lose the current state of the page. We do not have to worry about the scroll position, form values, and so on. Since we were able to solve this problem with Opera and Safari, that is one less argument we have to face when determining whether it is a wise solution to use an XSLT transformation.

12.5.3 *Deciding to use XSLT*

One of the discussions that we may have with our development team or boss is why we're using XSLT in the first place. The argument starts out with "You have to generate the XML file dynamically on the server, so why don't you just generate the results table instead?"

The major point that our fellow developers are trying to make is that we are using more processing in order to display the results to the user. That is true in the sense that the web page has to perform extra work when the browser renders the results table. Instead of loading one file, the Ajax code has to load two files, which then have to be combined.

We can dynamically build the table on the server with no major problems. The results table is displayed by using the `responseText` property of the XMLHttp-Request object and applying the returned value to our HTML element. There is nothing wrong with this method since it means one less step to deal with.

The one problem that we face when building the HTML table with the server-side code is the effort required to update the table if changes need to be made. As we discussed earlier in this chapter, we as developers may face many problems when building the table. We have to worry about quotes, tag syntax, attributes, event handlers, and so much more. If the users want us to change the order of the columns of the results table, we have to alter a bunch of code to perform this task.

By using XSLT, we are taking the building of the table away from our server-side code. The server can build a simplified version of the results table in XML format. XML format is very easy to look at and makes it easy to find mistakes. Also, the XSLT looks like an HTML page. We do not have to sit and count quotation marks or search through strings to see if a tag is there. With XSLT we can look directly at it and know that it is correct.

Another feature is that we can easily take a table layout that a web designer has designed and place it into an XSLT file. If we ever need to make a change such as swapping columns, it is as easy as cutting and pasting the data. No more scratching our heads wondering if the tags are still going to be right when we paste them. By using XSLT, we are removing the processing of the HTML from our dynamic code. This allows us to change the results table without any major problems.

And finally, using JavaScript lets us do some things very easily that we couldn't do if we did the transformation on the server:

- We can retrieve different XSL documents based on a theme, screen dimensions, language, and so on.

- We can retrieve an XML document and an XSL document without help from the server.

- We can examine an XML log file on our local machine without having control over the XML document structure.

When performing your daily tasks, you'll find that Ajax gives you so many possibilities.

We still have one issue with the live search that we need to address: allowing the user to bookmark the results page.

12.5.4 *Overcoming the Ajax bookmark pitfall*

There is one downside to using Ajax to perform searches: Bookmarking the page in the traditional manner is not an option. (This same problem occurs with frames and pop-up windows.) Bookmarks allow us to come back to the search results in the future without having to type in the request information, and they can be easily sent to friends and colleagues by email or messaging. Since an Ajax search does not require a postback to the server, we are not changing the URL of the page during the search, and therefore bookmarking the URL will simply mark the starting point for our application, not the results that we want to preserve.

An easy solution for this is to add a behavior that lets us remember the search. We can build a dynamic string that will be used to create a dynamic bookmark. This dynamic string will contain a direct link to the page it's on and will include a querystring parameter with the search value. Therefore, when we write this string to the page to form the link, the user can either bookmark it (by right-clicking on the link) or copy the link, and her search will be automatically saved. We add this functionality of reading the querystring value when the page is loaded after we build the link.

The link can be built when our `GrabNumber()` function is executed. We add another span to our document so that we have a location to put this link on the page. In this case, the span has an ID of `spanSave`, as you can see in listing 12.11 by looking at the statement where `getElementById` is invoked. We can position the span wherever we want on the page so it is convenient for the user.

Listing 12.11   Altering the `GrabNumber` function to integrate a bookmarking link

```
function GrabNumber(){
  var strLink = "<a href='" +
```

```
            location.href.split("?")[0] + "?q=" +
            document.Form1.user.value + "'>Save Search</a>";
    document.getElementById("spanSave").innerHTML = strLink;
```

The code in listing 12.11 generates a dynamic link to our current search page and adds the querystring parameter q with the value of the textbox. The querystring parameter is what allows us to remember the search. This new link is then added to the span on the page so the user can select the link and send it to others or bookmark it by clicking on the link and setting it to their favorites for future use. In listing 12.12, we obtain the querystring value from the URL when the page loads and then perform the search automatically so the results are shown.

Listing 12.12   Obtaining the querystring value and performing the search

```
window.onload = function(){
  var strQS = window.location.search;
  var intQS = strQS.indexOf("q=");
  if(intQS != -1){
    document.Form1.user.value = strQS.substring(intQS+2);
    GrabNumber();
  }
}
```

We add a handler for the onload event to our window object that will execute a function when the page is loaded. We check to see if our querystring value is in the URL; if it is, we obtain the value. The querystring value is placed inside the textbox, and then the GrabNumber() function is executed automatically to build the results table. Adding this code lets us bookmark the search pages and have the search results appear when we come to the page, instead of having to type in the value each time. This makes our Ajax project even more user-friendly.

12.6 *Refactoring*

It's time to take our XSLT live search to the next level by—you know the drill—componentizing! We need to take this nifty script and refactor it until we have an object-oriented reusable component. So let's start with the client-side XSLT processing. This example is different than all the others in the sense that it handles all the DOM manipulation aspects of response handling with XSLT. So let's start there. We should be able to refactor our XSLT processing in such a way that we can use it with other components—not just the live search. Once we do that, we'll focus on refactoring the live search in such a way that it can be quickly added to any page as an easy-to-use pluggable component.

12.6.1 *An XSLTHelper*

We've gone through a lot of trouble to learn the ins and outs of XSLT processing on the client side. For example, we've noticed that there are completely different APIs for doing XSLT processing on the client based on whether we're targeting an IE browser or a Mozilla-based browser. And each API has its own set of quirks and peculiarities. So, it would be a shame for us not to encapsulate that hard-earned knowledge so that our colleagues who come behind us don't have to go through the same pains to do some seemingly simple XSLT transformations. Therefore, let's do just that by creating an XSLTHelper object to encapsulate all of our XSLT concerns.

All XSLT processing typically requires two sources of information: the XML document to transform and the XSL document to provide the transformation rules. With that in mind, let's write a constructor for our helper that will give us a way to store that state:

```
function XSLTHelper( xmlURL, xslURL  ) {
    this.xmlURL = xmlURL;
    this.xslURL = xslURL;
}
```

The constructor is probably one of the simplest you've seen in this book yet. It stores the URLs for the documents we just noted: the XML data document and the XSLT transformation document. But before we get too giddy about the simplicity of it all, we need to think about an API to support graceful degradation. You'll note that our script conditionally performs only XSLT processing if the browser supports it. So if we're writing a helper, it would be nice for the helper to provide an API to tell the client whether or not it can perform XSLT operations. However, instantiating some object with XSLT in its name just to find out whether XSLT is supported doesn't seem right. The solution to this conundrum is an API function that's *not* scoped to the prototype object but rather to the constructor function itself. We can think of this function much like a static method in the Java world. The intent is that a client should be able to write code that looks something like this:

```
XSLTHelper.isXSLTSupported();
```

rather than having to instantiate an object like this:

```
var helper = new XSLTHelper( 'phoneBook.xml',
                             'transformation.xsl' );
var canDoThis = helper.isXSLTSupported();
```

So let's accommodate our inquisitive users with a pseudo-static method, which is expressed as follows:

```
XSLTHelper.isXSLTSupported = function() {
    return (window.XMLHttpRequest && window.XSLTProcessor ) ||
           XSLTHelper.isIEXmlSupported();
}

XSLTHelper.isIEXmlSupported = function() {
    if ( ! window.ActiveXObject )
       return false;
    try { new ActiveXObject("Microsoft.XMLDOM");
          return true; }
    catch(err) { return false; }
}
```

There's nothing new here. The logic is identical to the logic defined earlier; we've just encapsulated that knowledge about how to detect XSLT support. I'm sure someone will thank us for this. So now we can get on to the business of fleshing out the rest of the XSLTHelper API.

Let's keep things simple. How about saying that we'll have a single method for clients of our class to call to perform XSLT processing? Our helper will have ancillary methods to separate the responsibilities of all the internal logic, but we'll provide a single API for our clients to use. The semantics will be as follows:

```
var helper = new XSLTHelper ( 'phoneBook.xml',
                              'transformation.xsl' );
helper.loadView( 'someContainerId' );
```

In this example usage, the phoneBook.xml document should be transformed into HTML by the transformation.xsl document, and the resulting HTML should be placed within the element whose ID is someContainerId. Let's further specify that the parameter to loadView() can be either a string representing the ID of an element or the element itself. We'll internally figure out what we're dealing with and react accordingly. And, by the way, if the client doesn't care to reuse the helper instance, we can express all this with a single line of code:

```
new XSLTHelper('phoneBook.xml',
               'transformation.xsl').loadView('someContainerId');
```

Now that we've defined our API and its semantics, let's implement it as shown in listing 12.13.

Listing 12.13 The `loadView` method

```
loadView: function ( container ) {

    if ( ! XSLTHelper.isXSLTSupported() )          ❶ Check for XSLT
        return;                                         support

    this.xmlDocument    = null;                    ❷ Reinitialize
    this.xslStyleSheet  = null;                      helper state
    this.container      = $(container);

    new Ajax.Request( this.xmlURL,        ❸ Request documents
                    {onComplete: this.setXMLDocument.bind(this)} );
    new Ajax.Request( this.xslURL,
                    {method:"GET",
                     onComplete:
        this.setXSLDocument.bind(this)} );

},
```

The first thing the `loadView()` method does is makes sure it's operating within a browser runtime that supports XSLT ❶. The client should have already done this, as in our earlier example, but just in case the user of our code is sloppy, we take a better-safe-than-sorry approach and check again. Second, the method sets the state variables holding the XML and XSL documents to `null` and sets the reference to the container to be updated ❷. Lastly, we send the Ajax requests to retrieve the XML and XSL documents ❸. When the server responds to the request for the XML document, the `setXMLDocument()` method is called. Likewise, when the server responds to the request for the XSL document, the `setXSLDocument()` method is called. These functions are shown in listing 12.14.

Listing 12.14 Setting the XML and XSL documents

```
setXMLDocument: function(request) {
    this.xmlDocument = request.responseXML;
    this.updateViewIfDocumentsLoaded();
},

setXSLDocument: function(request) {
    this.xslStyleSheet = request.responseXML;
    this.updateViewIfDocumentsLoaded();
},
```

These methods set the state variables of the XSLTHelper corresponding to the XML document and XSL document, respectively. They then call the updateView-IfDocumentsLoaded() method, which checks to see if both documents have been initialized, and if this is the case, updates the view. The updateViewIfDocuments-Loaded() method is implemented as shown here:

```
updateViewIfDocumentsLoaded: function() {
    if ( this.xmlDocument == null || this.xslStyleSheet == null )
        return;
    this.updateView();
},
```

Once both responses have come back from the server, we are ready to update the UI. We know that both responses have come back when both the this.xmlDocument and the this.xslStyleSheet state variables are non-null. The updateView() method is shown in listing 12.15.

Listing 12.15 Updating the view

```
updateView: function () {
    if ( ! XSLTHelper.isXSLTSupported() )
        return;

    if ( window.XMLHttpRequest && window.XSLTProcessor )
        this.updateViewMozilla();
    else if ( window.ActiveXObject )
        this.updateViewIE();
},
```

As we've noted already, we require different implementations for each browser type being supported, so we've separated out the details. Let's look at each implementation, beginning with the Mozilla implementation, shown in listing 12.16.

Listing 12.16 Updating the view in Mozilla

```
updateViewMozilla: function() {
    var xsltProcessor = new XSLTProcessor();    ←— Initialize transformer
    xsltProcessor.importStylesheet(this.xslStyleSheet);
    var fragment = xsltProcessor.
      TransformToFragment(        ❶ Perform XSLT
        this.xmlDocument,            transform
        document);

    this.container.innerHTML = "";               ❷ Update
    this.container.appendChild(fragment);           the UI
},
```

The specific update implementations, whether IE or Mozilla, perform two basic steps: ❶ performing the XSLT transformation, and ❷ updating the UI with the result. Recall that the result of the Mozilla transformation process is a document fragment that is added to an element via `appendChild()`, whereas the IE transformation results in a string that is added via the `innerHTML` property. So with that in mind, the `updateViewIE()` implementation is shown here:

```
updateViewIE: function() {
    this.container.innerHTML =
        this.xmlDocument.transformNode(this.xslStyleSheet);
},
```

The same two steps are performed in the IE implementation, which is a good deal more compact because the steps of applying the transformation and updating the UI are all done in a single line of code. As to which one is more efficient, we'll let you decide.

Our XSLTHelper is now complete, and we have a clean, simple, one-method API for performing XSLT transformations. Our helper should prove to be very useful and more than worth the relatively small amount of effort we have put into it. Now let's refocus our efforts on the live search and contemplate a simple component design.

12.6.2 *A live search component*

Now that we have some sweet XSLT help in our back pocket, let's implement our live search script as a component that uses it. The component should satisfy the component requirements that we've discussed in detail in our other refactoring examples. These include such things as providing a clean API, being configurable while providing appropriate default values, being unobtrusive to the surrounding HTML, and being able to have multiple instantiations on a page. Let's develop a clean object-oriented solution with the guiding principle that each responsibility should be encapsulated in a dedicated method. One responsibility, one method. With that in mind, let's get started in the usual place—considering construction.

From the perspective of component state, the live search component has to keep track of more "stuff" than most other components we've written. It needs to know about an XML document source, an XSL document source, a field that initiates the search, and the URL of the page that it should use to support bookmarking. So, that means our constructor is going to be a little heavier in this example than in previous ones. However, it should still be quite manageable. Let's take a stab at a live search constructor now:

```
function LiveSearch( pageURL, lookupField, xmlURL,
xsltURL, options ) {
   this.pageURL      = pageURL;
   this.lookupField  = lookupField;
   this.xmlURL       = xmlURL;
   this.xsltURL      = xsltURL;
   this.setOptions(options);    ❶  Configure the component

   var oThis = this;
   lookupField.form.onsubmit = function(){
     oThis.doSearch(); return false; };
   this.initialize();    ◁— Go to previous search
}
```

The first four arguments of our constructor are the things we just indicated we'd have to keep up with: the URL of the page, the search field, and the two document URLs. The last parameter is our familiar `options` parameter for providing component configurability. The `options` argument is passed to the `setOptions()` method, which, as you recall, provides some default values for all configurable data ❶. Let's look briefly at the defaults before moving on:

```
setOptions: function(options) {
   this.options = options;
   if ( !this.options.loadingImage )
      this.options.loadingImage = 'images/loading.gif';
   if ( !this.options.bookmarkContainerId )
      this.options.bookmarkContainerId = 'bookmark';
   if ( !this.options.resultsContainerId )
      this.options.resultsContainerId  = 'results';
   if ( !this.options.bookmarkText )
      this.options.bookmarkText = 'Bookmark Search';
},
```

The `setOptions()` method is not as succinct as its counterpart in the TextSuggest component (see chapter 10), which used the Prototype library's `extend()` method to make the expression of this nice and compact. This method performs the same chores, however, and provides default values for the loading image, the ID of the element to contain the bookmark, the ID of the element to contain the result data, and, finally, the text of the generated bookmark. Recapping the mechanism, any values to these properties that live in the options object passed in by the user will override the defaults that are specified here. The resulting options object is a merged set of defaults and their overrides in a single object. These options are then used at the appropriate points throughout the rest of the example to configure the component.

With component configurability and defaults squared away, let's turn our attention back to the constructor for a moment and recall these two unassuming lines of code:

```
var oThis = this;
lookupField.form.onsubmit = function(){
  oThis.doSearch(); return false; };
```

You will recall that our script in its original form modified the HTML by putting an `onsubmit` handler on the search form:

```
<form name="Form1" onsubmit="GrabNumber();return false;">
```

Because we are striving to make our components as unobtrusive as possible, at least in terms of the amount of HTML that needs to be modified to use them, the same functionality has been provided by these two aforementioned lines of our constructor. The difference from a naming point of view is that we've renamed `GrabNumber()` to a more generic name, `doSearch()`, and `doSearch()` is a method of our component rather than a global function. Speaking of which, let's now take a look at the `doSearch()` method implementation:

```
doSearch: function() {
    if ( XSLTHelper.isXSLTSupported() )
       this.doAjaxSearch();
    else
       this.submitTheForm();
},
```

Our smarty-pants component knows that it should be checking for XSLT support before trying to actually *do* XSLT processing, so the search method uses the XSLTHelper API we wrote earlier to determine whether to use XSLT processing or to just do a standard form submission. Pretty smart indeed. Our client can just call the `doSearch()` method and not have to worry about whether it's doing XSLT. We've taken care of all the worrying for it. Let's take each of the two forms of searching and look at them in detail. Because the form submission is simpler, we'll look at it first:

```
submitTheForm: function() {
   var searchForm = this.lookupField.form;
   searchForm.onsubmit = function() { return true; };
   searchForm.submit();
},
```

This method simply finds the reference to the appropriate form through the lookup field and changes its `onsubmit` to a function that returns `true`. This allows the search request to be submitted back to the server in an explicit way. Then the method just calls the `submit()` method of the native HTML form, which causes a traditional form submission. In this scenario, the component assumes that there is an appropriate action attribute of the form and that the result of the action returns an appropriate page with search results.

Now let's look at the Ajax implementation of searching:

```
doAjaxSearch: function() {

    this.showLoadingImage();          ❶  Show loading image

    var searchUrl = this.appendToUrl( this.xmlURL,
                        'q',
                        this.lookupField.value);  ❷  Formulate URL

    new XSLTHelper(searchUrl,    ❸  Perform XSLT processing

                    this.xsltURL).loadView(
                    this.options.resultsContainerId);
    this.updateBookmark ();    ❹  Update bookmark
},
```

The `doAjaxSearch()` method performs the same steps that the first iteration of our script did, but it puts each step into a method to perform each responsibility. At this point, you might object and say that this method has four responsibilities. Well, actually it just has one: searching. However, the responsibility of searching has four parts, each a responsibility on its own. So let's look at each in turn:

❶ *Show the loading image*—The search is started by calling the method to show the "busy loading" image. The image used is determined by the options object:

```
showLoadingImage: function() {
    var newImg = document.createElement('img');
    newImg.setAttribute('src', this.options.loadingImage );
    document.getElementById(
    this.options.resultsContainerId).appendChild(newImg);
},
```

❷ *Formulate the search URL*—The search URL is built using the `xmlURL` attribute that was passed in at construction time with a `q=` parameter appended to it with the value currently contained in the lookup field. The appending is performed by a method that checks the URL for the existence of a previous querystring to make sure the correct parameter separators are used:

```
appendToUrl: function(url, name, value) {

    var separator = '?';
    if (url.indexOf(separator) > 0; )
        separator = '&';

    return url + separator + name + '=' + value;
},
```

❸ *Do the XSLT processing and update the UI*—Because we had the presence of mind to factor out the task of client-side XSLT processing, this seemingly heavy-duty responsibility is achieved within a single line of code:

```
new XSLTHelper(searchUrl,
    this.xsltURL).loadView(this.options.resultsContainerId);
```

❹ *Update the bookmark*—Once the user has initiated a search, the bookmark should be updated as well. This responsibility is performed via the `update-Bookmark()` method:

```
updateBookmark: function() {
  var container = document.getElementById(
    this.options.bookmarkContainerId);
  var bookmarkURL = this.appendToUrl(
    this.pageURL, 'q', this.lookupField.value );
  if ( container )
    container.innerHTML = '<a href="' +
      bookmarkURL + '" >' +
      this.options.bookmarkText + '</a>';
}
```

This method gets the `container` element and the text for the bookmark from the options object. The URL for the generated bookmark is the value passed into the constructor as the `pageURL` argument. The q= parameter with the value of the current search are appended to that URL. The `innerHTML` property of the container is updated with all of these values to produce the appropriate URL.

If a bookmark is stored and used to hit our page, the user is returned to our page with a q=someValue parameter. But what initiates the search to produce the result? Recall that the final line of the constructor called `this.initialize();`. We've not peeked at what that actually does yet, so we should do so now. As you've probably guessed, the `initialize()` method is there to support our bookmarking feature. The implementation is as follows:

```
initialize: function() {
  var currentQuery  = document.location.search;
  var qIndex = currentQuery.indexOf('q=');
  if ( qIndex != -1 ) {
    this.lookupField.value =
      currentQuery.substring( qIndex + 2 );
    this.doSearch();
  }
},
```

The `initialize()` method takes the current location of the document and looks for a parameter named `q` in the querystring. If one exists, it parses the value of the parameter and places it into the lookup field. Then, it simply initiates a search via the `doSearch()` method. Mystery solved.

12.6.3 *Refactoring debriefing*

Let's take a moment to consider what we've accomplished so far. We've written a helper class called `XSLTHelper`, which encapsulates the hard-earned knowledge of providing XSLT support on the browser client. We've taken advantage of that helper in our live search component. We've written a simple yet generic configurable live search component that can take just a few pieces of information and transform the user's web page into a responsive searching animal. We've written our component in a clean OO style that exemplifies simple design and separation of responsibilities. Overall, not bad for a day's work.

12.7 *Summary*

In this chapter, we took a basic search page and added Ajax functionality to it. The search allows the process to flow so that we can control the window while the server-side process is taking place. This means that we are able to place an animation in the browser. Having control of the browser allows us to perform other operations so we can make sure that the users of the application know that their search is taking place.

We then implemented XSLT processing to transform our XML document into formatted HTML code, which we applied to our `div` element's `innerHTML` property. This let us avoid using JavaScript to dynamically loop through the XML nodes and build a large string to apply to the document. Instead, we could rely on XSLT to produce the document from the XML.

Just because we used the processing animation and the XSLT with the live search does not mean we cannot apply these concepts to other projects. We can easily add this capability to a normal transaction with the server. I always hear people say that they have a process that takes several minutes to complete. Is there a way to show a message? We can easily use the `innerHTML` property that we used in this project to add an image or message telling the user that the processing of the search is under way. With almost every Ajax application, we should show that an action is taking place so the user does not repeatedly click the submit or the refresh buttons.

We can use XSLT to style RSS feeds or to change any of the other projects that we have done by using XSLT instead of performing the XML DOM looping on the client.

In the four examples that we've developed so far, we've implemented our own server-side processes specifically to serve our Ajax clients. In the final chapter, we'll look at an Ajax client that communicates directly to an Internet standard web service: an RSS news syndication feed.

Building stand-alone
applications with Ajax

13

This chapter covers

- Handling RSS feeds
- Ajax for accessing websites directly
- Ajax without a server
- Fade-in, fade-out

In the last four chapters, we've developed a range of neat Ajax applications and shown the client-side and server-side code for each. In this chapter, we don't need to present you with any server-side code, because we're not going to write any. This may come as a surprise to most people, but we can run Ajax applications directly against any web server-based stream of data, including those that are generated by third-party applications. We can develop a rich user interface for a web page that acts like a client application.

Many websites offer XML feeds in the formats of Really Simple Syndication (RSS), Resource Descriptor Framework (RDF), or Atom, which are the three most common syndication feeds that we see. The information contained in these syndication feeds can be daily news articles, comics, weblogs (*blogs*), jokes, weather, and so on. With Ajax we have the ability to get the syndication information without having to visit these websites or buy a client application that will read the XML syndication feeds on our computers.

In this chapter, we develop our own client application, an XML reader that obtains feeds from various websites. It can be run in the browser on any computer that has an active Internet connection.

13.1 Reading information from the outside world

An XML syndication feed consists of articles that are freely available for the public to read and display on other websites. A blog is good example of a syndicated XML feed for our purposes because it is so widely available. These XML feeds are different from plain old articles on a website since they can be shared and displayed in multiple formats. It is like finding a newspaper or magazine that fits perfectly on your table as you eat your morning breakfast. You can eat and read at the same time without having to shift everything around and spilling your coffee. The syndicated feeds can be formatted in any style that fits your needs, allowing you to obtain just the information you want.

We can view the contents of an XML syndication feed in several ways. For instance, for a single blog, we could go to the website where the XML feed is located. To view several feeds at once, we could go to sites such as JavaCrawl.com, which allow us to view multiple XML feeds without going to multiple sites. We can also view the RSS feed in its raw unedited form by directly opening up the path of the XML file directly in our web browser, or we can use downloadable software to organize and format the feeds we want to see.

A new option is to use Ajax to view the syndication feeds. Without Ajax, we were stuck with downloading a client application or having to visit a website to grab this information, but with Ajax we do not have to download anything or visit a website. Instead we are able to develop a JavaScript-based RSS reader that can be run directly on our desktop with just a browser. In this chapter, we build an application that obtains multiple RSS feeds from multiple sources and allows us to view them in an orderly fashion. We also integrate transition effects to add to the flashiness of the user interface. But before we develop this application with Ajax, we need to understand the format of an XML feed and where we can find XML feeds.

13.1.1 Discovering XML feeds

One of the most popular places to find an XML feed is on a blog. Many people today publish blogs, for all kinds of reasons. They can contain information such as a personal diary, personal musings, news articles, jokes, or technology discussions. Let's look at one example of a blog by Eric Pascerello, in figure 13.1.

Eric's blog is accessible, which means that it can be linked to by anyone. While many people simply read it on the JavaRanch site, it can also be accessed as a syndication feed. We can read this feed by accessing it directly in its native XML form, or we can go to other websites (such as JavaLobby) that obtain the syndication feed and display it in their format.

Figure 13.1   Eric Pascarello's blog, which has an accessible RSS feed

In figure 13.1, we see in the upper-right corner of the screen that there are links to RSS, RDF, and Atom. As we mentioned earlier, these are the most common XML syndication feeds that we can find.

Each of the syndication feeds has a different XML specification. That means if we were to look at the different XML files, we would see different naming schemes for the elements. Each feed has a specification clarifying what information must be defined in the feed. Since we are dealing with different formats, the easiest way to address it is to pick a single format and design the reader around it.

One of the most popular syndication feeds is Really Simple Syndication, better known as the RSS feed.

13.1.2 *Examining the RSS structure*

Before we create our Ajax XML reader, let's examine the structure of the RSS file. Knowing the structure allows us to navigate the XML DOM more efficiently to obtain the information that we want to display. The RSS document has two parts: the channel and the items. The channel gives us the information about where the RSS feed is from, and the items are the articles that we can read.

The channel elements

The channel can be considered to be the header information of the RSS feed. The channel elements tell the user where the RSS feed is coming from, what the title of the document is, when it was last updated, and so on. Only a few items are required by the RSS specification, as shown in table 13.1.

Table 13.1 Channel required elements

Element	Description	Example
description	Phrase describing the channel.	Weird thoughts from Eric's Head
link	The URL to the HTML website referring to the channel.	http://radio.javaranch.com/pascarello
title	The name of the channel and how people refer to the service. The name should be related to the name of the website.	Eric's blog on JavaRanch.com

The three required elements in table 13.1 give us the basic information about the RSS feed. The RSS feed's required elements tell us where the RSS channel is from, what the title of the channel is, and what the channel is about. If we want to obtain other information about the RSS feed, we need to check for optional elements.

The RSS feed can contain any number of the optional channel elements. The RSS feed developer can select none, one, or all 16. The optional elements (table 13.2) give us more options to learn about the feed.

Table 13.2 Optional channel elements

Element	Description	Example
category	Specifies which categories the channel belongs to.	Programming
cloud	Allows processes to register with a cloud so they can be notified of updates to the channel, implementing a lightweight publish-subscribe protocol.	
copyright	The copyright notice for the content in the channel.	Eric Pascarello
docs	A URL that points to the documentation for an RSS feed.	http://backend.userland.com/rss
generator	A string that indicates what program was used to generate the protocol.	Pebble
image	Specifies an image that can be displayed along with the feed.	http://pebble.soundforge.net/common/images/powered-by-pebble.gif
language	The language the channel is written in.	En
lastBuildDate	The last time the content was changed.	
managing editor	Email address for person who is responsible for the editorial content.	pascarello@javaranch.com
pubDate	The publication date for the content.	
rating	The PICS rating for the channel. See http://www.w3.org/PICS/.	
skipDays	Informs aggregators what days they can skip checking for updates.	
skipHours	Informs aggregators what hours they can skip checking for updates.	
textInput	Specifies a text input box that can be displayed.	

continued on next page

Table 13.2 Optional channel elements *(continued)*

Element	Description	Example
ttl	Indicates the Time to Live (TTL), or number of minutes the channel can be cached before it is updated.	
webmaster	Email address for the person who is responsible for technical issues.	webmaster@javaranch.com

Some of the element options include email addresses in case we have problems with the feed's content or layout. There is also information that explains when the syndication feed is updated.

The channel's required and optional elements describe the content of the RSS feed so that we can determine the characteristics of the feed. Just like the channel, the item elements have optional elements as well.

The item elements

The RSS feed can contain multiple item elements, similar to the way a newspaper consists of multiple articles. Each item element is required to have at least one of the following two elements: the title or the description. Only one is needed, according to the RSS specifications, but both are allowed in an item element.

There are also eight other optional elements that can be added to the item. Returning to the newspaper analogy, an article normally contains the story, the author, the source, and a title. In the same way, each item element in an RSS feed can have separate titles, authors, sources, and so on. All of the optional elements that are available for the item element are shown in table 13.3.

Table 13.3 Item elements

Element	Description	Example
author	The item author's email address	Pascarello@javaranch.com
category	Includes the item in one or more categories	Programming
comments	The URL of the page for comments that relates to this item	http://radio.javaranch.com/pascarello/2005/05/25/ 1117043999998.html#comments

continued on next page

Table 13.3   Item elements *(continued)*

Element	Description	Example
description	The item summary	Ajax allows developers to improve the UI by making a web application act like a client application.
enclosure	Describes the media object that is attached to the item	`<enclosure url="http://radio.javaranch.com/ pascarello/media/TheAjaxInActionSong.mp3" length="5908124" type="audio/mpeg"/>`
guid	A string that is a unique identifier	http://radio.javaranch.com/pascarello/2005/05/25/ 1117043999998.html
link	The URL of the item	http://radio.javaranch.com/pascarello/
pubDate	The date the item was published	Wed, 25 May 2005 17:59:59 GMT
source	The RSS channel the item came from	`<source url="http://radio.javaranch.com/ pascarello/blog.xml">Eric's Blog</source>`
title	The title of the element	Ajax Improves UI Development

The heart and soul of the RSS feed are the title and the description. The title gives us a small insight into what the article is, whereas the description element can be one of two things: a synopsis about the article or the entire article itself. There is no set standard on how the description element is used. To determine how to handle it, we have to look at the individual feeds before we start to write the RSS feed reader. If it's a synopsis, we can compare it to a blurb on the front of a magazine where it says, "see page 10 for more information." That is where the link element comes into use. The link is the URL to the entire article on the author's site.

Most RSS feeds try to utilize as many of the optional elements as possible in order to provide developers, like us, the tools to make our RSS reader as robust as possible. With better data at our hands, we can better display the RSS feed content. For more information about the RSS specification, visit http://backend.userland.com/rss.

Now that we understand the basic elements of the RSS document, we can create our Ajax-based RSS reader.

13.2 *Creating the rich user interface*

In this chapter, we create an RSS feed viewer that obtains the XML feeds from websites without using a server-side language or a client application RSS reader.

Ajax allows us to view the information with a web page that is stored on our desktop. This example demonstrates that Ajax does not have to run with a web server that has a server-side language such as .NET or JSP. As long as we have an active Internet connection, we are able to access RSS feeds from any site we desire. (If you are running a Mozilla browser, see section 13.6.1. You must overcome Mozilla's security restrictions, which we discussed in chapter 7, before you try to execute the code in this project.)

13.2.1 *The process*

If you find yourself scanning multiple websites for content every day, you will be able to avoid that by running this reader. The viewer will be able to show multiple feeds on one page.

The unique feature of this application is that we are not using any server-side code; we are only obtaining RSS XML documents that are created by the other websites. The complete application resides on a web page saved on our desktop environment or delivered as part of our website.

The first thing is to understand the steps for what we are going to develop. We are developing an RSS reader that is going to set up a slideshow that uses two layers. Each layer will contain one feed, which will be displayed for a set period of time, after which the next feed fades in. In figure 13.2, we can see the control flow of the application.

The process has a lot of steps. The first step is to load our multiple feeds. We will use a master array to hold the information we need from each feed source. We do not require all the optional item elements that we listed in table 13.2.

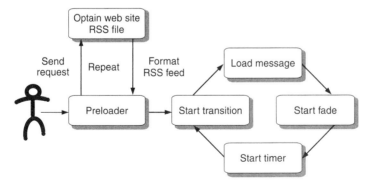

Figure 13.2   RSS reader project's process flow diagram

After we load all the files, we need to create our transition effect of fading in and out. In this case, we'll use CSS classes to do this. We'll use a timer to switch between messages and loop through all the messages.

Other features that we want to incorporate into this application are back, forward, and pause buttons. We can also add the ability to insert additional feeds from a selection list. The first step is to create our client-side form and layers.

13.2.2 *The table-less HTML framework*

The biggest part of this project is presentation. We'll use a series of div and span elements to make a table-like layout that contains a header, a body, and a footer. We can see how this looks in figure 13.3.

We could have used tables to create the layout, but tables were the pre-CSS page layout tool (see chapter 2 for an introduction to CSS). Today, tables should not be used for layout since they require more time to render and they are not as easy to change as a CSS layout. Listing 13.1 shows the markup on which our XML viewer's layout is based.

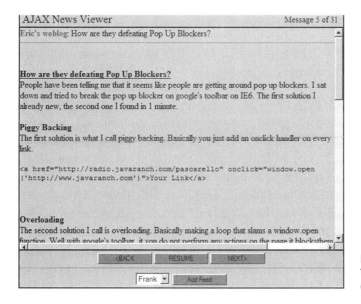

Figure 13.3
The RSS syndication reader developed in this project

Listing 13.1 Basic HTML for the RSS reader

```
<form name="Form1">
  <div id="divNewsHolder">        ❶ Container div

    <div id="divNewsTitle">       ❷ Header div

      <span id="spanCount">Loading</span>   ❸ Feed count holder

       Ajax News Viewer      ❹ Title
    </div>
    <div id="divAd">       ❺ News feed container
      <div id="divNews1">          ❻ First news
        Loading Content...              feed layers
      </div>
      <div id="divNews2">          ❼ Layout
        Loading Content...              footer
      </div>
    </div>
    <div id="divControls">      ❽
      <input type="button" name="btnPrev"
        id="btnPrev" value="<BACK" />
      <input type="button" name="btnPause"          ❾ Action
        id="btnPause" value="PAUSE" />                 buttons
      <input type="button" name="btnNext"
        id="btnNext" value="NEXT>" />
      <hr/>
      <select name="ddlRSS">
      </select>                         ❿ Additional feed
      <input type="button" name="btnAdd"     element
        value="Add Feed" />
    </div>
  </div>
</form>
```

The first div that we added is divNewsHolder ❶, our container, which we use to set the overall size of our display window. The next div that we add is divNewsTitle ❷, which is the header in our layout. Inside this div, we add a span ❸ that contains a placeholder for our feed count. The other line of text ❹ is the title of our feed viewer. We can make that line say anything we want.

The div divAd ❺ is our next row. This row is the placeholder for our RSS feed information that we will retrieve later. We insert two more div elements inside of the div divAd. The two new divs, divNews1 ❻ and divNews2 ❼, are used to hold the RSS feed information. The CSS properties of these elements will be altered by the JavaScript to create a fading transition.

The footer row is made up of a div divControls ❽. The footer row contains our navigation and our feed management functions. The next, back, and pause

Figure 13.4
HTML elements are shown
without any CSS

❾ buttons are added to the div. The select form element and a button ❿ are added that allow a user to select additional XML feeds. This now finishes up the basic framework for the viewer, as seen in figure 13.4.

Figure 13.4 is not visually appealing since we have not formatted our HTML elements. The viewer lacks any structure, but that changes when we add CSS rules to the elements. By looking at figure 13.3, we see that our two divs, divNews1 and divNews2, need to be sitting on top of each other in order for our fading effect to work properly.

13.2.3 *Compliant CSS formatting*

Without CSS, our web pages would all look like those in figure 13.4: very boring and unpleasant on the eyes. We'll apply some CSS to make this example more pleasing. The style allows us to easily edit the properties in the future without having to edit the HTML. The first thing we can apply style to is our holder div and our header row.

Applying style to the holder and header divs

The divNewsHolder div mentioned earlier can be considered our container for the viewer. It allows us to position the reader on the page and also set the width of the reader. Since we are using divs for our other rows, they take up 100 percent of the width that is available to them. By setting the width in the holder, we can dictate the width of the other elements, making future updates easier. Listing 13.2 shows how we achieve this using CSS.

Listing 13.2 CSS for the holder and header divs

```
#divNewsHolder{        ❶  The holder div
  width: 600px;
  border: 2px solid black;
  padding: 0px;
}
#divNewsTitle{         ❷  The title div
  font-size: 20px;
  height: 26px;
```

```
    background-color: #BACCD9;
    line-height: 26px;      ❸   Height of line
  }
  #spanCount{       ❹   The count span
    float: right;      ❺   Float-based layout
    font-size: 15px;
    padding-right: 10px;
  }
```

We apply style to our form elements by referencing its ID along with the pound (#) sign ❶. This specifies that the style should be applied to only our div with the id divNewsHolder. For our divNewsHolder, we can assign width and border rules to it and set the padding to 0.

Now that we have set our holder div, we can style our first row. We want to set the height, background color, and font size of div divNewsTitle ❷. The line-height property ❸ is set to the height of the div. This ensures that our single line of text that is 20 pixels high is centered vertically in the div. Without the line height, the text would be located at the top border of the div.

The last step for formatting our header row is to move the spanCount ❹ to the right portion of the header instead of it being in front of our title. To do this, we use the float property ❺ and set it to right. This right-aligns our text, whatever the width of the containing element, and does not affect our title. The font size can be set to a smaller pixel height so it is not as prominent as our title. The padding-right property moves the text from the right edge so it is not sitting directly on the border. We are now finished with our holder and our header row; see figure 13.5.

In figure 13.5, we can see that the header row is very different compared to the other rows that have not been styled. The word *Loading* appears on the right side of the div, and our text is centered in the div. The holder div border surrounds the rest of the elements; now we need to work on the content divs.

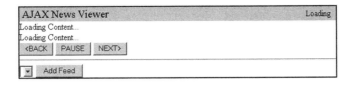

Figure 13.5
CSS is applied to the holder and header divs.

Styling the content divs

The next step is to style the middle section or the body of our RSS reader (listing 13.3). The body section will contain our formatted RSS feed information. We position the divs, `divNews1` and `divNews2`, on top of each other for our transition effect to work. The transition effect is to change the opacity of the layer so the layer contained below shows through. By increasing the opacity level of the layer, we are able to create a fading effect.

Listing 13.3   CSS for the content divs

```
#divAd{          ❶  Format divAd
  width: 100%;      ❷  Set width
  height: 400px;       ❸  Set height
  overflow: hidden;       ❹  Hide scrollbars
  border-top: 2px solid black;        ❺  Format
  border-bottom: 2px solid black;          borders
}
#divNews1, #divNews2{        ❻  Style both news divs
  width: 100%;          ❼  Set width and
  height: 400px;           height
  background: #D9CCBA;
  position: relative;        ❽  Use relative positioning
  overflow: auto;          ❾  Show scrollbars if necessary
  left: 0px;        ❿  Move divs to the edge
}
#divNews1{top: 0px;}       ⓫  Position first div
#divNews2{top: -400px;}        ⓬  Position second div
```

The first step is to style our div `divAd` ❶ that is the container for our feed spans. The width ❷ is set to 100 percent, and the height ❸ is set to `400px`. We do not want scrollbars to appear for the row; therefore, the `overflow` ❹ property to set to `hidden`. This means if any content is larger than 400 pixels, it is hidden from the view. The other divs inside this holder allow for scrolling so we do not lose the content. We then set our top and bottom borders ❺ styles by setting a solid 2-pixel black line. A side border is not needed since our holder div contains a border thickness. If we applied the borders all the way around our row, it would be 4 pixels wide instead of 2 on the sides and only 2 pixels tall on the top and bottom of the row, which makes it look awkward.

We have to format our two content holder divs, `divNews1` and `divNews2` ❻. We can style the properties that are the same between them by separating both of their IDs with a comma. The width and height values ❼ are set to take up the space of our holder div. By setting our divs' position ❽ to `relative`, it allows us to position the divs in relation to our parent div `divAd`, unlike the `absolute` position, which is in relation to the top-left corner of the browser window. We set the divs' `overflow` property ❾ to `auto`, allowing scrollbars to appear if necessary. The last step is to set the left ❿ position of the divs to 0 pixels, allowing the div to be flush so there are no gaps around the edges.

We want the two content divs to sit exactly on top of each other. Because we are using relative layout, separate position properties are required to be applied to our two feed divs. The div `divNews1`'s vertical position ⓫ is set to 0 pixels. This forces it to sit flush to the top border of the parent div. The `divNews2` position ⓬ is set to `-400px`. The reason for the negative number is that the second div is positioned lower down the page than the first div, as shown in figures 13.4 and 13.5. Since we set the height of the container div to 400 pixels, we need to move `divNews2` up 400 pixels so it is flush on the top of the parent div, just like `divNews1`. In figure 13.6, we can see how our two divs are now on top of each other, unlike in figure 13.5.

Since the two divs are on top of each other, we are only able to see the content from one of them. In this case, the opacity level is set at 100 percent; therefore, the content underneath is not visible. The level of 100 percent is going to be the last step in our fade transition, but before we can get to that we have to finish styling our reader.

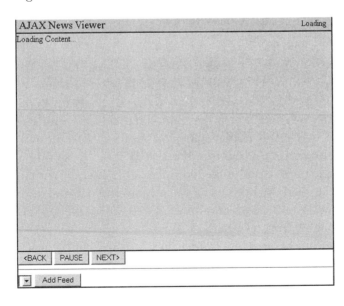

Figure 13.6
CSS applied to the content divs

Configuring the footer

The last section we want to add CSS to is our footer. In this section, we have to set the background color and standardize the form elements so that the section is more structured. To accomplish this, we set the colors, the font sizes, and the size of the buttons (listing 13.4).

Listing 13.4   CSS for the footer div

```
#divControls{         ❶ Style footer div
   background-color: #BACCD9;   ❷ Set background color
   text-align: center;     ❸ Center the text
   padding-top: 4px;
   padding-bottom: 4px;
                          ❹ Add padding
}
#divControls input{   ❺ Style form elements
   width: 100px;
   background-color: #8C8C8C;  ❻ Set size and
   color: #000000;                colors
   font-size: 10px;
}
```

We apply the CSS to our footer div `divControls` ❶ so it matches the header row. The background color ❷ is added to the div to match the header's background color. We align the text ❸ so the content is centered in the div horizontally. Top and bottom padding ❹ is added to the div, which means the content doesn't have to sit on the border. We don't have to add a border to our div since the middle row has the top border defined and the holder div has the other three borders covered.

The last step in the CSS for formatting our footer is applying styles to our form elements so they fit in with the style of the reader. The button elements ❺ that are located inside the `divControl` div are referenced with the div's name and then a space followed by the tag name. That means only the elements within that div tag get these properties assigned to them. Any of the other elements with the same tag name on the page will not.

Since the text in each of our buttons is a different length, we apply the `width` property ❻ to the buttons so they will all be the same width, causing the buttons to look more uniform. We change the background color so it is not the default color of the user's operating system. The text color and the size of the font for the element's text can be assigned also. Figure 13.7 shows us how our footer is now styled to match the feel of the RSS reader.

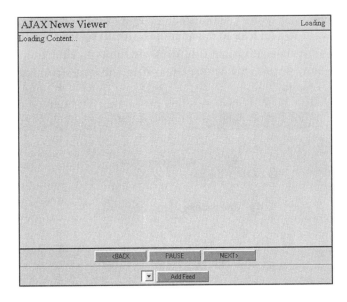

Figure 13.7
CSS applied to the footer

In figure 13.7, we see all of the properties that we applied to the divs. We applied widths, colors, font sizes, borders, padding, and much more. We can customize the CSS properties of these elements so they fit the needs and styles of any website theme or personal taste. The next thing we need to do is get content into our RSS reader!

13.3 Loading the RSS feeds

In this example, we will load files from multiple feeds. We will use our Content-Loader object to do the work, as we have throughout this book. In the first version, we use a series of global variables to quickly develop an RSS feed viewer.

13.3.1 Global scope

Global variables allow for easy adjustments to our script so we do not have to change the functionality inside the `for` loops and timers. We will be able to adjust the contents of the global variables to make changes throughout the script and communicate between the different functions. We want to use global variables rather than local variables in this script so they can be shared and we don't have to pass them from function to function. Later on in this chapter, when we refactor our script, you will see a solution that doesn't use global variables; but for now, they keep our example simple.

One downfall to JavaScript is that there is no variable type for constants, so we are simulating the effect with global variables. However, global variables can be overwritten, so we must be careful when using them. The variables in listing 13.5 will not be overwritten at any time during the application.

Listing 13.5   Global constant variables

```
var flipLength = 5000;
var timeColor = 100;
var strErrors = "<hr/>Error List: <br/>"
var arrayRSSFeeds = new Array(
   "http://radio.javaranch.com/news/rss.xml",
   "http://radio.javaranch.com/pascarello/rss.xml",
   "http://radio.javaranch.com/bear/rss.xml",
   "http://radio.javaranch.com/lasse/rss.xml");
```

In listing 13.5, we assign the global variables that affect how our viewer performs. The first global variable, `flipLength`, determines how many milliseconds our current message is displayed before it is replaced with the next message. In this case, the value `5000` represents the total number of milliseconds between messages. Another timer variable is `timeColor`. This time span is the number of milliseconds between the coloring or fading steps in our script. The larger the number, the longer the transition takes to complete.

The next global variable that we use is `strErrors`. This line is the heading for any errors we encounter during the loading process. We can change the message or add style parameters to it. The last global variable that is going to affect the outcome of the script is the array, `arrayRSSFeeds`. In this array, we add the URLs of the RSS feeds that we want to access. In this case, we access four separate RSS feeds from JavaRanch.com's radio blogs.

The next set of global variables that we declare, in listing 13.6, are used to communicate between our separate functions. These global variables hold the state of the RSS feeder. Their values change depending on the action that is being performed.

Listing 13.6   Global variables that maintain the state

```
var currentMessage = 0;
var layerFront = 2;
var timerSwitch;
var bPaused = false;
var arrayMessage = new Array();
var intLoadFile = 0;
var bLoadedOnce = false;
```

The first global variable that we instantiate in listing 13.6 is `currentMessage`. The variable `currentMessage` keeps track of the message that is being viewed. It can be considered a counter that is reset when it reaches the maximum number of records. The next global variable is `layerFront`, which holds the state of our layers. When we designed our RSS reader layout, we had two layers on top of each other. This variable is keeping track of the state of those layers.

The variable `timerSwitch` holds the timer object that determines when the next frame is going to be loaded. If the user pauses the feeder, we cancel this timer and change the state of our next variable, `bPaused`. The boolean value that `bPaused` holds allows us to determine the state of the timer: `true` if it is paused and `false` if it is running.

The global variable `arrayMessage` holds the formatted messages that we retrieved from the RSS items. The array is multidimensional and holds all the information we want to show. As stated earlier, the item elements in the RSS feed hold more information than we may need; therefore, we only grab the few items that interest us and store them in `arrayMessage`.

The last variable, `intLoadFile`, leads us into our next section of code. The variable is a counter, which holds the current file count that is being loaded from our array, `arrayRSSFeeds`, during the preloading process.

Now that all the global variables have been declared, we can see a global picture of where this project is heading. We preload the RSS feeds from an array of URLs. We use a counter to track the status of the preload process. During the preloading, we are only selecting the desired information from each XML file. After the preload process has finished, the messages are displayed with a fading transition to create a slideshow, which we can pause and manipulate. With the global variables that we declared, we are able to control the functionality of the script. This has led us to the starting point of the RSS preloader function.

13.3.2 *Ajax preloading functionality*

One of the problems developers face with Ajax is how to preload multiple files without sending too many requests to the external websites and having them step all over each other. One solution is to use queuing, and that is what our Ajax ContentLoader does.

Making the repeated requests

The ContentLoader allows the queuing mechanism to fire the requests in an orderly fashion. In listing 13.7, we take our array (which was populated when the page was loaded in listing 13.5) that contains the URLs to our feeds and prepare them for our ContentLoader.

Listing 13.7 Preload JavaScript function

```
window.onload = function(){
  var loader= new Array()
  for(i=0;i<arrayRSSFeeds.length;i++){
    loader[loader.length] = new
        net.ContentLoader(arrayRSSFeeds[i],
        BuildXMLResults,BuildError);
  }
}
```

The code in listing 13.7 is fired with the `onload` event handler. As the page is loaded, we prepare an array variable, `loader`, to hold all the requests to the server. We loop through our array `arrayRSSFeeds` to obtain all of the URLs from which we want to obtain information. For each iteration, we increment our `loader` array to hold the new ContentLoader request. We pass in the URL of the feed, the function `BuildXMLResults()` that formats the content, and the function `BuildError()` that will be called if there is an error obtaining the feed. Now that we have begun the loading process, we need to format the returned XML feeds.

Adapting the function

When the request is made, it is going to call either `BuildXMLResults()` (if it was successful) or `BuildError()` (if it encountered any problems). `BuildXMLResults()` takes the XML feed and formats it into a usable format. `BuildError()` logs the error to the error list. Both functions update the status so we can see the progress of the loading. Listing 13.8 shows the implementation of this logic.

Listing 13.8 Formatting the XML results into a JavaScript array

```
function BuildXMLResults(){
  var xmlDoc = this.req.responseXML.documentElement;
  var RSSTitle =
   xmlDoc.getElementsByTagName('title')[0].firstChild.nodeValue;
  var xRows = xmlDoc.getElementsByTagName('item');
  for(iC=0;iC<xRows.length;iC++){
    intMessage = arrayMessage.length;
    arrayMessage[intMessage] = new Array(
    RSSTitle,
    xRows[iC].getElementsByTagName('title')[0]
.firstChild.nodeValue,
    xRows[iC].getElementsByTagName('link')[0]
```

```
.firstChild.nodeValue,
    xRows[iC].getElementsByTagName('description')[0]
.firstChild.nodeValue);
  }
  UpdateStatus();
}
```

The function `BuildXMLResults()` in listing 13.8 retrieves the XML document by referencing our request object's `responseXML` property. With the XML document stored in our local variable `xmlDoc`, we are able to obtain the RSS title information for the feed. To do this, we reference the title element tag and reference the first child node's value.

We obtain the item elements and prepare to loop through the resulting array stored in `xRows`. By looping through the array, we are able to create a multidimensional array, storing it in the next position of our global array, `arrayMessage`. The global array holds the title of the RSS feed and the title, link, and description of the article. We build this multidimensional array for every item element stored in `xRows`. After we've finished traversing the document, we call the function `Update-Status()` (listing 13.9) to display the current state of the process to the user.

Listing 13.9   Function informing user of preloading functionality

```
function UpdateStatus(){
  intLoadFile++;
  if(intLoadFile < arrayRSSFeeds.length){
  document.getElementById("divNews2").innerHTML =
    "Loaded File " + intLoadFile + " of "
    + arrayRSSFeeds.length + strErrors;
  }else if(intLoadFile >= arrayRSSFeeds.length && !bLoadedOnce){
    document.getElementById("divNews2").innerHTML =
      "Loading Completed" + strErrors;
    if(arrayMessage.length == 0){
      alert("No RSS information was collected.");
      return false;
    }
    bLoadedOnce = true;
    var timerX = setTimeout("ChangeView()",1500);
  }
}
```

The function `UpdateStatus()` performs two services, as shown in listing 13.9. The first service displays the status of the preloader to the user. The second service determines if the slideshow has to be started. We first increment our global variable `intLoadFile` to update the file count. If `intLoadFile` is less than the total files we are to load, we display our loading status by setting the `innerHTML` of our top layer `divNews2` with our output string.

If the file count is greater than or equal to the number of files in our array (and also the slideshow has not been started), then we can start the transitions. Before we can start the slideshow, we need to verify that we actually have data to show. We verify the data by checking the length of our formatted message array, `arrayMessage`. If there are no messages, we notify the user and exit the function by returning `false`.

If there is data to display, we set `bLoadedOnce` to `true` and call the function `ChangeView()` after a slight pause in time. The slight pause allows the user to read any error messages that we may have encountered. As mentioned previously, if the loader encountered a problem with loading the XML document, it calls our function `BuildError()` (see listing 13.10).

Listing 13.10   Function to handle the errors generated from the XMLHttpRequest

```
function BuildError(){
  strErrors += "Error:" + "" + "<br/>";
  UpdateStatus();
}
```

`BuildError()` allows us to display an error to the user. This tells the user that not all of the files were loaded. We just append the error to our global variable `strErrors` and call our `UpdateStatus()` function that we just developed to inform the user of the application's current loading state. We can verify that our preloader works by saving the document and running the web page in our browser (figure 13.8).

When we test the viewer, we should see the status update on the screen. In figure 13.8, the preloader is loading file 2 of 4 and there have been no error messages. When all of the files have loaded, we should see that the files have been loaded successfully and there are no errors in the list. However, there is a JavaScript error indicated in our status bar since we still have not created our function `ChangeView()`. We'll do that in the next section, but first we will create the cross-browser fading transition effect.

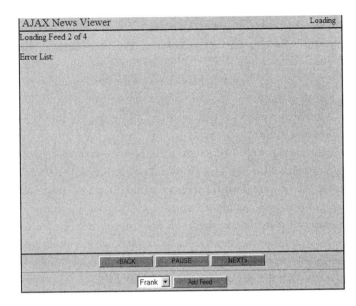

Figure 13.8
The preloader is loading file 2 of 4 as indicated by the status message with no errors.

13.4 Adding a rich transition effect

The code that we have written so far has loaded the files into an array. We now have to take the data stored in an array and build a slideshow. The slideshow is based on DHTML. By changing the content within divs by using `innerHTML`, we can display the different articles that our preloader has loaded. Changing CSS classes of the elements and altering the `z-Index` of layers allows us to create fading transition effects with the divs. By placing all of the steps together, we are going to create a dynamic fading slideshow.

13.4.1 Cross-browser opacity rules

When we are creating the fading effect, we need to change the opacity of the top layer. Changing the opacity of the layer lets the content underneath show through. With an opacity level of 0 percent, we are allowing all of the content to show through. An opacity level of 100 percent blocks anything on the layer underneath from showing through.

Now, as always, we have issues with Internet Explorer and Mozilla-based browsers. Both browsers view opacity differently, so in our stylesheet rules we must account for the differences. Mozilla uses opacity, whereas Internet Explorer uses a filter specifying the alpha opacity, as listing 13.11 shows.

Listing 13.11 CSS Opacity filter classes

```
.opac0{opacity: .0;filter: alpha(opacity=0);}
.opac1{opacity: .2;filter: alpha(opacity=20);}
.opac2{opacity: .4;filter: alpha(opacity=40);}
.opac3{opacity: .6;filter: alpha(opacity=60);}
.opac4{opacity: .8;filter: alpha(opacity=80);}
```

Listing 13.11 shows that we created a series of style rules that have different opacity levels. Using CSS rules instead of using JavaScript to manipulate the values is a matter of preference. By using CSS rules, we can change other properties; maybe we want the colors to change as the fading occurs, or maybe we want to increase the text size. Using CSS classes allows us to do that without adding any extra JavaScript code, and it also encapsulates the cross-browser differences in a single place.

Now that we have created our classes, we can start the process of loading the RSS feed information into our divs.

13.4.2 *Implementing the fading transition*

In section 13.3.2, we received an error message when testing the code since we had not created the function ChangeView(). ChangeView() initiates the process of the fading in and out of the content divs. For the fading process to work correctly, we alter the CSS classes and position the divs on different z-Index levels. Listing 13.12 shows how this is implemented.

Listing 13.12 ChangeView() function

```
function ChangeView(){          ❶ Declare ChangeView()
  strDisplay = "<span class='RSSFeed'>" +
    arrayMessage[currentMessage][0] + "</span>: "      ❷ Display RSS title
  strDisplay += "<span class='itemTitle'>" +
    arrayMessage[currentMessage][1] + "</span><hr>";   ❸ Show element title
  strDisplay += arrayMessage[currentMessage][3]
    + "<hr>";                                           ❹ Insert item description
  strDisplay += "<a href='" +
    arrayMessage[currentMessage][2] +
    "' title='View Page'>View Page</a>";               ❺ Output feed's URL
  document.getElementById("spanCount").innerHTML =
    "Message " + (currentMessage+1) +
    " of " + arrayMessage.length;                       ❻ Change feed status
  var objDiv1 = document.getElementById("divNews1");
  var objDiv2 = document.getElementById("divNews2");
  if(layerFront == 1){                                  ❼ Prepare transition
    objDiv2.className = "opac0";
```

```
      objDiv1.style.zIndex = 1;
      objDiv2.style.zIndex = 2;
      objDiv2.innerHTML = strDisplay;
      layerFront = 2;
   }
   else{
      objDiv1.className = "opac0";
      objDiv2.style.zIndex = 1;
      objDiv1.style.zIndex = 2;
      objDiv1.innerHTML = strDisplay;
      layerFront = 1;
   }
   SetClass(0);
}
```

7 Prepare transition

8 Start transition

The ChangeView() **1** function has two major roles. The first is to build the HTML to display our data obtained from the RSS feeds. The second role is to prepare our divs for the fading in. Building the HTML is simple since we are using a basic layout. The hardest part is making sure that we keep track of quotes and apostrophes so we do not encounter any errors.

The first line of text we want to display is the RSS channel's title **2**, which we stored in the first index of the array, arrayMessage. We need to surround the title with a span and assign a CSS class name of RSSFeed. The next step is to display the item element's title **3** by referencing the second index of the array. By surrounding the title with a span and assigning a CSS class of itemTitle to the span, we are able to apply a separate style to our titles. To allow for a separation between the title and the message body, a horizontal rule is inserted.

The item description **4** was stored in the fourth index of the arrayMessage. We divide the description from our next section, which holds the last item element we collected. The last item is the link **5**; we assign the value of the URL element to the link's HREF attribute. The text that is visible to the user is "View Page," which the user is able to click. The link sends the user to the RSS feed's website.

We want to update the current message display counter that we built into our RSS header. To do this, we alter the innerHTML **6** of our span spanCount by using the arrayMessage length and our current message counter. We need to prepare the divs **7** for the transition effect. We initialize the div by setting the zIndex so it is on top of the current one and set the class to our first CSS rule for opacity.

After we load the current message into our div, we start the process of fading the div into view. To do this, we need to create a function that loads the CSS classes in order; therefore, we call the function SetClass() **8**.

13.4.3 *Integrating JavaScript timers*

The process of loading our div into view creates a smooth transition effect between messages instead of an abrupt change. Altering the opacity level of the layer with the CSS classes we created earlier creates the effect. The opacity level allows the layers underneath the div to show through, as if we were looking through a window that was tinted. We increase the opacity level in order to block out all the content that is below the div.

As mentioned in section 13.4.1, we are using five CSS classes to handle the fading in and out. The reason for using the classes is that in the future we can add colors to the fading or anything else that we would like to display in the transition effect. In this case, we loop through the classes. This is illustrated in listing 13.13.

Listing 13.13 JavaScript function to set CSS class and to execute the transition effect

```
function SetClass(xClass){        ❶  Declare SetClass()
  if(xClass<5){        ❷  Verify transition step
    document.getElementById("divNews" +         ❸  Set next className
layerFront).className = "opac" + xClass;
    timerAmt = setTimeout("SetClass(" +          ❹  Initiate fade timer
    (xClass+1) + ")",timeColor);
  }
  else{
    document.getElementById("divNews"            ❺  Remove CSS class
    + layerFront).className = "";
    currentMessage++;        ❻  Increment count
    if(currentMessage>=arrayMessage.length)      ❼  Verify next message
      currentMessage = 0;
    if(!bPaused)                                  ❽  Start viewer
      timerSwitch = setTimeout(                      timer
        "ChangeView()",flipLength);
  }
}
```

Listing 13.13 shows the function SetClass()❶, which has a parameter, xClass, passed to it. This parameter allows us to track the current state of our transition effect without using another global variable. We call this function for every step of our transition to update the status until the fading transition is complete.

Since we are dealing with five CSS classes, we need to verify that the current step of our transition ❷ has a value under five. If that's the case, we know that there are still more CSS classes that need to be applied to our transition. If we are below five, we apply the next CSS class to the element. We reference the attribute className ❸ and apply the next class to the element.

After we set the new class, we need to create a timer to call the next step. The setTimeout ❹ method has two parameters. The first is the function or JavaScript statement to execute, and the second is the amount of time in milliseconds before it is executed. In this case, we are going to call our SetClass() function with the incremented state of our class. The timeout is set to our global variable, flip-Length, which we declared in section 13.3.1.

The else portion of our script handles the situation when we have looped through our five CSS classes and applied them to the div. First, we remove the CSS Class ❺ from our div. The default opacity is 100 percent and allows the div to cover the other one completely with nothing showing through from the bottom layer.

We increment the currentMessage ❻ variable, allowing the next message to be loaded. We check to see if that message number ❼ is greater than the number of messages contained in our array arrayMessage. If it is greater, we set the current message back to the start. The timer is restarted to load the next message ❽ after our set period of time. The setTimeout method calls our function, ChangeView(), and our global variable, flipLength, determines the length of time. In order for this to execute, we make sure that our global variable, bPaused, is not true. We will be coding the pause feature of this script in section 13.5.2.

The transition effect of the slideshow is now complete. We can test what we have created so far and see if it works. If everything is working correctly, we should see the page-loading counter slowly increasing as the files are being loaded into the script, and the first message should begin to fade in.

As you can see in figure 13.9, there are two different messages in the viewer since the one is slightly transparent. The current message (6) is displayed in the header, and we are able to see that in total 31 messages were loaded. Now, all we have left to do is add the pause, back, forward, and add functionality to our viewer.

13.5 Additional functionality

The code that we already developed can be used on its own, without the other features, but they can make the script more flexible for users and for us. The first feature that we want to add allows us to import other RSS feeds that are not included in the preload function. Perhaps we want to check a site once in a while for new content, or maybe we want to grab a weather RSS feed. This feature allows us to obtain the syndication feed when we need it. The other features that we can include will let us skip through messages and pause them if we want more time to read them.

13.5.1 *Inserting additional feeds*

Adding additional messages to our feed is easier than you may think. Take a look at figure 13.9 again. The selection list contains the names and URLs of additional feeds we want to check occasionally; we just select a name and click the Add Feed button. We have already built most of the functionality in section 13.3; all we need to do now is execute our ContentLoader, in listing 13.14, which will add the feed selected in the `select` element.

Listing 13.14   JavaScript function to load additional RSS feeds

```
function LoadNews(){
  var sel = document.Form1.ddlRSS;
  if(sel.options[sel.selectedIndex].className!="added"){
    var url = sel.options[sel.selectedIndex].value;
    sel.options[sel.selectedIndex].className="added";
    var loader1 = new net.ContentLoader(url,
                         BuildXMLResults);
  }
}
```

We create a function called `LoadNews()` that we initiate from our button named `btnAdd`. Since we are obtaining the additional RSS feeds' URLs from a `select` element, we need to reference our `select` element, `ddlRSS`, so we can access its values.

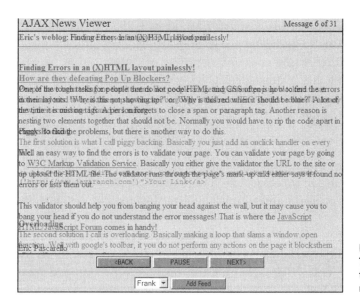

Figure 13.9
The fading transition is taking place between message 5 and 6.

When we want to add an RSS feed from the `select` element, we need to have some way to tell if it already has been added. One way to do this is to add a CSS class to the option element. Therefore, we need to add a check to verify that we have not added this RSS feed already. If the feed is new, we grab the value of the selected option and change the `className` to `added`.

We execute the ContentLoader with the URL of the feed and also the function `BuildXMLResults()`. We can use the default error message of the ContentLoader if it encounters an error. Now that we have the ability to load a document from the selection list, we need to add RSS feeds to the selection list and also add the event handler to the button, shown in listing 13.15.

Listing 13.15 HTML selection list

```
<select name="ddlRSS">
  <option
    value="http://radio.javaranch.com/frank/rss.xml">
    Frank</option>
  <option
    value="http://radio.javaranch.com/gthought/rss.xml">
    Gregg</option>
</select>
<input type="button" name="btnAdd"
  value="Add Feed" onclick="LoadNews()" />
```

In the selection list, we add URLs to RSS feeds that are not contained in our pre-loader RSS feed array. In this case, two additional RSS syndication feeds were added from JavaRanch's radio blog. We add the `onclick` event handler to our button `btnAdd` so the function `LoadNews()` can be executed.

The last step to loading the individual feeds is to create a CSS class to add to our stylesheet. This gives an added benefit to the users by giving a visual aid that the feed has been loaded.

```
.added{background-color: silver;}
```

In the CSS class, we can add any CSS rule so we are able to distinguish the added feeds from the others. In this case, we change the background color of the option to silver so that the option stands out in the list. After we add the class, we can test our application.

As figure 13.10 shows, we have added the RSS feed of Frank since it is highlighted in silver. The feed labeled Gregg is not added since it still has the default white background color. The number of messages in our RSS reader also

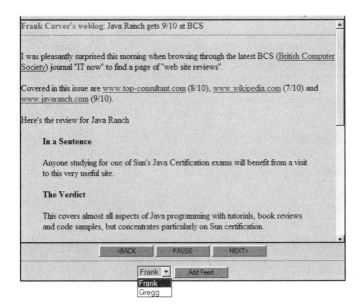

Figure 13.10
The Frank feed has been
added to the Ajax reader.

increased from 31 to 54 after we added the feed. The only features remaining to add are our back, forward, and pause buttons.

13.5.2 *Integrating the skipping and pausing functionality*

One of the most useful features that we can add is the ability to skip through messages. If we find a message that is not interesting to us, we can click a button to see the next one instead of having to wait for the timeout to execute. The pause feature allows us to have more time to read a message that is interesting or long. Since we have used global variables for our timers, pause, and the currentMessage counter, we are able to affect the current state of the RSS reader very easily. Listing 13.16 shows the code that lets the user flip through the feed.

Listing 13.16   JavaScript function to pause and skip the RSS reader feeds

```
function MoveFeed (xOption){      ❶  Create function MoveFeed()
  if(xOption == 0){       ❷  Check for pause/resume action
    if(!bPaused){
      bPaused = true;
      if(timerSwitch)                           ❸  Pause the reader
        clearTimeout(timerSwitch);
      document.getElementById("btnPause").value =
        "RESUME";
    }
```

```
    else{
      bPaused = false;
      setTimeout("ChangeView()",300);
      document.getElementById("btnPause").value =
        "PAUSE";
    }
  }
  else{
  if(timerSwitch)
    clearTimeout(timerSwitch);
  if(xOption == -1)currentMessage += -2;
  if(currentMessage < 0)
  currentMessage = arrayMessage.length
    + currentMessage;
  ChangeView();
  }
}
```

❹ **Resume the reader**

❺ **Change current message**

By creating a function, MoveFeed() ❶ and allowing it to accept a single parameter, we can handle all three situations; pause, skip forward, and skip backward. We can use an integer to differentiate between the different actions. To pause the reader, we pass in a 0. To skip forward, we use 1, and to skip backward we use -1.

The first functionality we check for is the pause. We verify ❷ that the passed-in parameter is a 0. The pause button has two behaviors. The first is to enter the pause mode, which stops the transitions from executing. The second is resume, which allows for the slideshow to restart the transitions.

If the feed is not paused ❸, then we need to set our bPaused variable to true and check to see if our timer timerSwitch is running. If the timer is running, we need to cancel it by using the clearTimeout method. We change the button's text to display the string "RESUME". If the button is clicked to resume the feed, we do the opposite of pausing the feed ❹. We set the bPaused variable to false; we call our function ChangeView() with a slight pause in time, and we change the text of our button value back to "PAUSE".

The pause behavior is now complete.

We have to create our skipping and backtracking functionality ❺. Since we are changing messages, we should remove the timer to avoid problems with skipping multiple messages. After we remove the timeout, we need to see if the action was -1. If we are moving backward, we need to subtract 2 from the currentMessage variable. This is because the variable, currentMessage, is actually holding the value of the next message since it already has been incremented. By subtracting 1 from the variable, we stay on the same message. Since we are already have the next message variable stored in `currentMessage`, we do not have to do anything for the forward button.

We have to be sure that our number is not less than 0. If it is, we need to set our variable to the last message in our array. After we have changed the `current-Message`, we can call our `ChangeView()` function to load our message. All we have to do is add the event handlers to the buttons (listing 13.17) so we can execute the function, `MoveFeed()`.

Listing 13.17 `onclick` event handlers for button actions

```
value=" <BACK " onclick="MoveFeed(-1)">
value=" PAUSE " onclick="MoveFeed(0)">
value="NEXT>" onclick="MoveFeed(1)">
```

To initialize the function, we add `onclick` handlers to our buttons. The `onclick` handlers call our function `MoveFeed()`, which passes the integers of `-1` to skip backwards, `0` to pause the reader, and `1` to skip forward a message. By saving the document and opening our browser to this page, we can test the last of the functionality.

Now that we have the ability to skip messages, we can advance to the messages in the middle of the RSS feed list. Figure 13.11 shows that the reader is paused since the button `btnAdd`'s text says RESUME. With the additional features that we

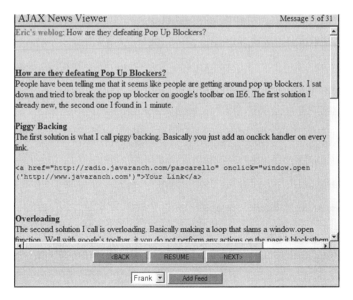

Figure 13.11
This window shows the RSS feeder being paused since the center button is now labeled RESUME.

have created, the RSS viewer allows us to read the feeds from our desktops without visiting the individual websites that host the feeds.

13.6 Avoiding the project's restrictions

With the Ajax-based RSS syndication feed reader that we have developed, we are able to view RSS feeds from an HTML file stored on the desktop with no server-side code required. We can use this application to grab the RSS feeds we read without having to go to the websites. We may want to offer this page as a download for the users on our websites. We can set it up to read our site's RSS feeds. Because we can run this script on our website too, we can use it for other things as well. One use can be a banner ad rotator, a company news banner, or anything else we can think of. But there are some limitations to what this script can do, and we may have trouble running this application with Mozilla on our desktop.

13.6.1 Overcoming Mozilla's security restriction

Unlike Microsoft Internet Explorer, Firefox and Mozilla cannot execute the application from our desktop due to security restrictions. The security restrictions keep Ajax from communicating from our desktop to other websites since they want to protect us from having code send information without our knowledge.

To verify that this is the problem with the Ajax script, we need to look for an error message. In Mozilla, we need to open up the JavaScript Console. The JavaScript console is located under Tools > Web Development > JavaScript Console (figure 13.12).

When we click on the JavaScript Console menu option, another window opens (figure 13.13).

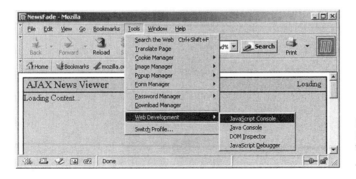

Figure 13.12
In Mozilla, choose Tools >
Web Development >
JavaScript Console.

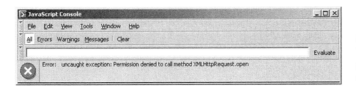

Figure 13.13
The permission denied error message caused by the XMLHttpRequest object

In figure 13.13, we see a permission denied error caused by the XMLHttpRequest object. There are two ways to correct this. The first is to go into the configuration file of Mozilla and set the permission setting to allow the XMLHttpRequest object to perform its desired task. To do this, we type *about:config* into the address bar of the browser and adjust the setting, but that is not a safe procedure to perform.

The reason it is not safe is that we are enabling it for anything that runs on our computer. That means any script that wants to talk to the outside world would be able to do so. How can we avoid this and allow only our Ajax application to talk to the outside? The solution is to set the security with JavaScript. We showed how to do this in chapter 7, provided the browser is configured to listen to programmatic requests to the Privilege Manager, but let's recap briefly here. Listing 13.18 shows the generic code for enabling the additional privileges required to read external resources.

Listing 13.18 Security Privilege Manager code

```
if(window.netscape &&
  window.netscape.security.PrivilegeManager.enablePrivilege)
  netscape.security.PrivilegeManager.enablePrivilege(
    'UniversalBrowserRead');
```

In listing 13.18, we check if we can access the Privilege Manager. If we can, we enable the `UniversalBrowserRead` privilege. We need to add this code in two separate places inside our ContentLoader object that handles the Ajax functionality.

The first place we need to add it is directly after the `loadXMLDoc` declaration, as shown in listing 13.19.

Listing 13.19 Code placement for `loadXMLDoc`

```
net.ContentLoader.prototype.loadXMLDoc = function(
url,method,params,contentType){
  if(window.netscape &&
  window.netscape.security.PrivilegeManager.enablePrivilege)
  netscape.security.PrivilegeManager.enablePrivilege(
    'UniversalBrowserRead');
```

We also need to add it to our `onReadyState` function (listing 13.20).

Listing 13.20   Code placement for `onReadyState`

```
net.ContentLoader.onReadyState=function(){
  if(window.netscape &&
    window.netscape.security
    .PrivilegeManager.enablePrivilege)
  netscape.security.PrivilegeManager
    .enablePrivilege('
UniversalBrowserRead');
```

Both of these functions interact with the data from the outside world. That is why we are required to add this functionality in both locations. When the script is executed, we will get a message prompt informing us of the request to change the security settings (figure 13.14).

If we simply click the Allow button at the prompt, the security prompt will still open every single time the function is accessed. To avoid this, click the "Remember this decision" checkbox. That way, the browser makes a note of your decision and allows the XMLHttpRequest to execute every time it is accessed without issuing the prompt.

With the security settings of the browser changed, we are able to make this application work off the desktop with Mozilla, Firefox, and Netscape. We can

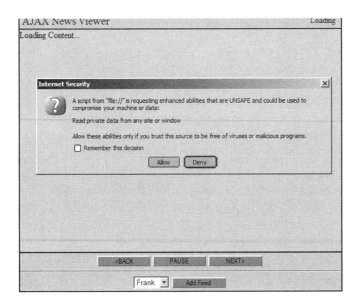

Figure 13.14
The security prompt notifies the user about the request for access rights.

access XML feeds from any site without having to open multiple tabs or windows by using this reader. We also have the ability to alter this application to obtain other information from the Web, such as weather and comics.

13.6.2 *Changing the application scope*

This application is not limited to being an XML syndication reader from sites. We can easily adapt it as a banner ad rotator, company news updater, an event calendar, and so much more.

For instance, we can store our banner ads within an XML document. That way, anyone can update the XML file with new ads without having to touch any of the HTML files or the server-side code. We can preload the banner ads and have them displayed in the reader. Instead of just having one ad on the screen, we can have them rotate through as the user is reading the site.

We can set up the XML document to hold the company news so we can display our current articles to the employees or customers. We just need to fill in the basic items of the XML feed. We can also make it display the updates to the site or any other information we want. As you can see, we are not limited to just the plain XML feeds.

13.7 Refactoring

Now that we have a fully developed script for reading RSS feeds, let's take the time once again to improve upon our efforts. As mentioned earlier, there are lots of possibilities for extending our script in terms of perusing different types of content. In this section, we concentrate on reorganizing the script along Model-View-Controller (MVC) boundaries. As we explained in chapters 3 and 4, the MVC pattern is a very common design pattern for separating the responsibilities of software. We'll start our discussion with defining the Model types, then we'll create a View for the Model, and finally we'll round out the discussion with the Controller that ties everything together.

13.7.1 *RSS reader Model*

The RSS reader we've developed in this example will definitely benefit from having some first-class Model types to deal with. This will make the software conceptually cleaner and easier to read and maintain. With Ajax-based applications putting a heavier emphasis on the client DHTML than more traditional web applications, it becomes increasingly important to write clean, maintainable software. The Model classes we develop should also be generally applicable to other applications that deal with RSS feeds. As a syntactic simplification, we'll use the Prototype library to define types just as we did in chapter 10.

Let's start by defining a Model class for an RSS feed. An RSS feed is for our purposes an XML document that adheres to a predefined structure and has a URL that specifies how it can be accessed. The primary attributes of the structure are the `title`, `link`, and `description`, with many other optional attributes, as discussed earlier. The feed also has several items, which can be thought of as the articles of its content. Let's start by capturing what we know so far, as represented in listing 13.21.

Listing 13.21   The `RSSFeed` Model class

```
RSSFeed = Class.create();
RSSFeed.prototype = {

   initialize: function( title, link, description ) {
      this.title       = title;
      this.link        = link;
      this.description = description;
      this.items       = [];
   },

   addItem: function(anItem) {
      this.items.push(anItem);
   }
};
```

This code defines the `RSSFeed` type via the Prototype library `Class.create()`. You will recall that using this idiom, the `initialize` method is invoked by the generated constructor. So with this definition of our RSS feed Model class, a feed could be constructed via the following line of code:

```
var rssFeed = new RSSFeed( 'JavaRanch News',
                           'http://radio.javaranch.com/news/',
                           'Stories from around the ranch' );
```

This is pretty much all that's required for the definition of an RSSFeed Model object. Notice that the RSSFeed has an `addItem` API that enables the addition of items to the internal item's array. Each item should be a Model object as well—one that encapsulates the attributes of each item in the feed. Given what we know about the RSS items, let's define our item Model class as shown in listing 13.22.

Listing 13.22 The `RSSItem` Model class

```
RSSItem = Class.create();
RSSItem.prototype = {
    initialize: function( rssFeed, title, link, description ) {
        this.rssFeed     = rssFeed;
        this.title       = title;
        this.link        = link;
        this.description = description;
    }
};
```

Nothing much to get excited about here. The item encapsulates the `title`, `link`, and `description` attributes but also holds a reference to the RSSFeed object that it belongs to. Given these two Model classes, now we can envision that an item and one of its feeds could be constructed as shown here:

```
var rssFeed = new RSSFeed( 'JavaRanch News',

    'http://radio.javaranch.com/news/',
    'Stories from around the ranch' );
var feed1 = new RSSItem( rssFeed,
    'Win a copy of JBoss',
    'http://radio.javaranch.com/news/05/07/20/9.html',
    'Text of Article' );
rssFeed.addItem(feed1);
```

So far, so good. The Model is a very straightforward encapsulation of the attributes of an RSS feed and its items. The two Model classes that encapsulate these two concepts are `RSSFeed` and `RSSItem`, respectively. Now let's consider the construction of the Model itself. We know that these objects will get instantiated as a result of the XML data being loaded into the client by an Ajax request. So let's define an API that our Ajax handler can call for converting the XML response into an instance of our `RSSFeed` Model class. Let's start by defining the contract of our Model creator as follows:

```
var rssFeed = RSSFeed.parseXML( rssXML );
```

This contract implies that we'll pass the XML response returned from our Ajax handler to the parse method of our `RSSFeed` type, and it will return to us an instance of an `RSSFeed`. Given that assumption, let's implement the `parseXML()` method as shown in listing 13.23.

Listing 13.23   The RSS XML parsing

```
RSSFeed.parseXML = function(xmlDoc) {

   var rssFeed = new RSSFeed(
     RSSFeed.getFirstValue(xmlDoc, 'title'),
     RSSFeed.getFirstValue(xmlDoc, 'link' ),
     RSSFeed.getFirstValue(xmlDoc, 'description'));

   var feedItems = xmlDoc.getElementsByTagName('item');
   for ( var i = 0 ; i < feedItems.length ; i++ ) {
     rssFeed.addItem(new RSSItem(rssFeed,
       RSSFeed.getFirstValue(feedItems[i], 'title'),
       RSSFeed.getFirstValue(feedItems[i], 'link' ),
       RSSFeed.getFirstValue(feedItems[i], 'description'))
   }
   return rssFeed;
}
```

This method does the textbook response XML parsing that we've done many
times already. It takes the values of the title, link, and description elements and
uses them to create the RSSFeed. It then iterates over all of the item elements and
does the same, creating an RSSItem instance for each. Within each iteration, the
addItem() method is used to add the item to its parent RSS feed. Note that a
helper method is used here to get the node value from the first child of an element with a given tag name. The helper method, getFirstValue, is shown in listing 13.24.

Listing 13.24   Parsing helper method

```
RSSFeed.getFirstValue = function(element, tagName) {
   var children = element.getElementsByTagName(tagName);
   if ( children == null || children.length == 0 )
     return "";
   if ( children[0].firstChild &&
       children[0].firstChild.nodeValue )
     return children[0].firstChild.nodeValue;
    return "";
}
```

This is everything we need from a Model perspective. Obviously, we could add
attributes for all the optional parts of an RSS feed and populate them if they are
present in the feed. We didn't do that in this case because the RSS reader doesn't
use or need any of the optional attributes. But it's definitely an opportunity to

provide extended metadata for future features. We could also define accessor methods for the attributes to provide a more formal contract for accessing them. For example, we could write a `getTitle()`/`setTitle()` method pair for accessing the `title` attribute. Since JavaScript doesn't support visibility semantics like other object-oriented languages (for example, the `private`/`protected` keywords in Java), we didn't bother. Now let's take a gander at our View.

13.7.2 *RSS reader view*

With our Model classes securely in place, we can now consider a View class. We could develop a View class for the RSSFeed, and another for the RSSItem, but because our RSSReader doesn't really view a feed independently of an item, we'll define a single View class called RSSItemView, which encapsulates the View for an RSSItem in the context of its parent RSSFeed. Since the View in this case is obviously HTML, our View class is really just responsible for the generation of HTML. Let's start by looking at the constructor in listing 13.25.

Listing 13.25 The `RSSItemView` View class

```
RSSItemView = Class.create();

RSSItemView.prototype = {

    initialize: function(rssItem, feedIndex, itemIndex, numFeeds) {
        this.rssItem = rssItem;
        this.feedIndex = feedIndex + 1;
        this.itemIndex = itemIndex + 1;
        this.numFeeds  = numFeeds;
    },
}
```

Let's take a moment to consider the parameters. The first parameter is an instance of an `RSSItem`. This tells the View what Model instance it's providing a view for. Note that it's not generally copasetic for the Model classes to have any knowledge of the View, but the View by necessity typically has intimate knowledge of the Model. The other parameters provide some supplemental context for the View. The `feedIndex` tells the View which feed number it's in. The `itemIndex` tells the View where this item resides within its parent RSSFeed's array of items. The `numFeeds` tells the View how many feeds there are. All of these index-based parameters are for the View to indicate its place in the world, so to speak. The View might want to display a context area that indicates, for example, "this is feed number 1 of 7 and article number 3 of 5." These attributes could be embedded within the Model, but they're not really attributes that the Model should typically care about, so this context that the View needs is passed into the View constructor by the client.

As mentioned previously, the responsibility of the View is to generate HTML. So our View class will need a single method that does precisely that. Let's see what that might look like in listing 13.26.

Listing 13.26   The HTML generation method

```
toHTML: function() {
   var out = ""
   out += '<span class="rssFeedTitlePrompt">RSS Feed '
   out += '(' + this.feedIndex + ' of ' + this.numFeeds + ') : ';
   out += '</span>';
   out += '<span class="rssFeedTitle">';
   out += '<a href="' + this.rssItem.rssFeed.link + '">' +
                    this.rssItem.rssFeed.title + '</a>';
   out += '</span>';
   out += '<br/>';
   out += '<span class="rssFeedItemTitlePrompt">Article ';
   out += '(' + this.itemIndex + ' of ' +
                    this.rssItem.rssFeed.items.length + ') : ';
   out += '</span>';
   out += '<span class="rssFeedItemTitle">';
   out += '<a href="' + this.rssItem.link + '">' +
                    this.rssItem.title  + '</a>';
   out += '</span>';

   out += '<div class="rssItemContent">';
   out += this.rssItem.description;
   out += '</div>';

   return out;
},
```

The `toHTML` method produces the contextual elements of the display followed by the text of the article. The first portion of the code displays the RSS *Feed (x of y) : RSS Feed Title*. The `link` attribute of the `rssFeed` parent is used to generate the HREF of the anchor produced, and the `title` is used to generate the text of the anchor. A CSS class name is generated for each span, one for the prompt, and another for the anchor, allowing each to be styled independently. This is illustrated in figure 13.15.

RSS Feed (2 of 4) :
Eric's weblog

```
var out = ""
out += '<span class="rssFeedTitlePrompt">Rss Feed '
out += '(' + this.feedIndex + ' of ' + this.nubFeeds + ') : ';
out += '</span>';
out += '<span class="rssFeedTitle">';
out += '<a href="' + this.rssItem.rssFeed.link + '">'
                    + this.rssItem.rssFeed.title + '</a>';
out += '</span>';
out += '<br/>';
```

Figure 13.15   RSS Feed (x of y) : RSS Feed Title

The next portion of code generates the *Article (x of y) : RSS Item Title*. The `link` attribute of the RSS item is used to generate the HREF of the anchor produced, and the `title` of the item is used to generate the text of the anchor. This code also provides CSS class names for both the prompt and the title, as illustrated in figure 13.16.

Article (1 of 3) :
Sending XML to the Server

```
out += '<span class="rssFeedItemTitlePrompt">Article ';
out += '(' + this.itemIndex + ' of '
            + this.rssItem.rssFeed.items.length + ') : ';
out += '</span>';
out += '<span class="rssFeedItemTitle">';
                    + this.rssItem.title + '</a>';
out += '</span>';
```

Figure 13.16   Article (x of y) : RSS Item Title

The last few lines of the `toHTML` method generate a div element to hold the content of the RSSItem's article (the `description` attribute). The code for this is as follows:

```
out += '<div class="rssItemContent">';
out += this.rssItem.description;
out += '</div>';
```

The CSS class name `rssItemContent` is generated for the article content. It should have a little bit of margin and padding in order for the content to visually reside within the display without touching any borders. It should also have a fixed height and `overflow` set to `auto` so that the content scrolls when needed—independently of the contextual information shown previously. A representative CSS definition for this class is shown here:

```
.rssItemContent {
   border-top : 1px solid black;
   width      : 590px;
   height     : 350px;
```

```
    overflow   : auto;
    padding    : 5px;
    margin-top : 2px;
}
```

Given the code and style shown in this code, the content area produced should look something like the sample shown in figure 13.17.

Putting it all together, the view generated by our RSSItemView class is shown in figure 13.18.

Before we leave the topic of our View, let's add one more little method to the View to make its usage more convenient:

```
toString: function() {
    return this.toHTML();
}
```

The reason we give the View a toString method is that it allows us to use the View instance and the HTML string that it generates interchangeably. For example, we can assign the View to the innerHTML attribute of an element, and the string representation, which is the HTML that it generates, will be used. For instance, the following code would assign the generated HTML of a view to the innerHTML of a div with the ID contentDiv:

```
var rssItemView = new RSSItemView( anRSSFeed, 0, 0, 5 );
$('contentDiv'). innerHTML = rssItemView;
```

A Basic Ajax Content Management Framework

One of the projects that I just took control of tracks documents that the Webmaster is placing manually into a folder and pastes a separate URL into a database so it can be linked to multiple records, other tables, and other crap. That part is not important, but I thought I would tell you where I thought of this. As I was coding the checking to see if a file exists I was like man, Ajax could be the missing link to those web content management tools out there. You have a site builder like on Brinkster or any of the other host and Ajax can improve its effectiveness. I was always annoyed by how slow they were to react when navigating since it always had to do the full-page refresh to get the documents and such. If you had to go 10 files deep in the tree, I needed a beer and a bag of pretzels waiting for it to happen.

So I just made a quick vb.net project that is not fancy. It is a basic framework for you to be able to navigate through a directory on a web server and look at the files and folders. The code is a basic starting point for anyone that wants to create a way for a user to look for files on the server. I see a lot of people saying that they want a file input to be able to search the server. With this code, you can create it. If I had more time, I would create a look like file browser, but I am busy with the book! If anyone out there does it, make sure to post a link in the comments.

Now, you really need to address security here since you are allowing people to access the folder structure on the server. I did a very $^{(infite+1)}$ small check that I am sure could be bypassed. If

Figure 13.17   Article (x of y) : RSS Item Title

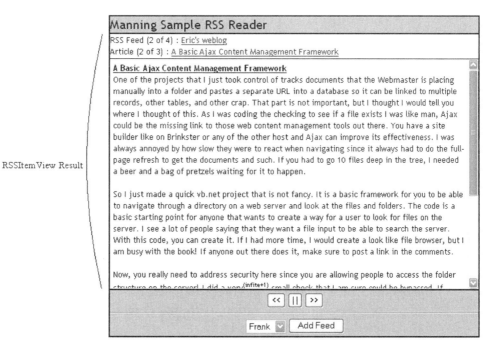

RSSItemView Result

Figure 13.18   RSSItemView result

(Remember, $()$ is a function provided by Prototype for retrieving DOM elements by their ID.) Now that we have a good set of abstractions for our Model classes and our View, let's tackle the RSS reader Controller that ties all the pieces together.

13.7.3   *RSS reader Controller*

The RSSReader class will perform functions related to manipulation of the Model and View classes to coordinate all of the activities associated with the reader. Recall that the RSS reader provides a slideshow-type interface to the feeds where each article is presented for a certain period of time, and then a transition effect is created to move from one article to the next. Buttons are provided to move backward and forward within the articles, as well as pause and resume the slide-show. Finally, a select list and an add button are provided to add supplemental feeds to the initial set of RSS feeds in the list. The RSS reader has to perform five categories of behaviors to implement these features, as outlined here:

- Constructing objects and initial setup
- Creating slideshow functionality
- Creating the transition effects
- Loading the RSS feeds via Ajax
- Updating the UI

To reduce the complexity and amount of code required to do all of this, we'll use the Prototype library for syntactical brevity, the Rico library to provide the functionality for our transition effects, and the net.ContentLoader for the Ajax support. Let's tackle the initial construction and setup first.

Construction and setup

The de facto starting point for our component development has been constructors. Let's stick with that practice here and start by defining our constructor. The constructor in this case is a simple method to set the initial defaults for some of the component state and, as in other examples, to set our configuration options and perform behavior initialization. With that in mind, our RSSReader constructor is defined as shown in listing 13.27.

Listing 13.27 The RSSReader constructor

```
RSSReader = Class.create();
RSSReader.prototype = {
    initialize: function( readerId, options ) {
        this.id               = readerId;
        this.transitionTimer  = null;        ❶  Set default
        this.paused           = false;           values
        this.visibleLayer     = 0;
        this.setOptions(options);  ❷  Set configuration options

        this.start();   ❸  Initialize behavior
    },
    ...
};
```

The constructor takes two arguments: an ID and an options object. The ID is used as a unique identifier for the reader and is used as a prefix for the IDs of the buttons that it will need to identify from the DOM. This will be shown shortly in the `applyButtonBehaviors` method. The first thing the constructor does ❶ is to set the default values for its state. Next, the options object, as with most of the components we've written, is used ❷ to specify configuration options to the component. This is done via the setOptions method. Finally, everything that needs to happen to bring the component to life happens in the start method ❸. Let's ponder configuration first, and then we'll move on to behavior.

Our boilerplate configuration idiom, setOptions, shown in listing 13.28, provides the configuration. Let's establish the setOptions implementation now and talk about our configuration options.

Listing 13.28 The setOptions method

```
setOptions: function(options) {
   this.options = {
       slideTransitionDelay: 7000,
       fadeDuration       : 300,
       errorHTML          : '<hr/>Error retrieving content.<br/>'
   }.extend(options);
},
```

The properties we've decided to make configurable in our RSS reader are indicated within the setOptions method shown here. The slideTransitionDelay property specifies the number of milliseconds an article's "slide" is visible before transitioning to the next one. The fadeDuration property specifies the amount of time in milliseconds it takes to fade out and subsequently fade in the next slide. Finally, if an error occurs while loading an RSS feed, the errorHTML property specifies the HTML to display as an error message. The defaults for these values, if not explicitly overridden by the user, are shown in this code. It's worth noting here that the component will expect an rssFeeds property of the options object to be passed in as the initial set of feeds to peruse. Because we can't really assume a reasonable default for this value, it's not defaulted within the setOptions method. The intent is that a reader will be created with an options object similar to the example shown here:

```
var options = {
  rssFeeds: [ "http://radio.javaranch.com/news/rss.xml",
             "http://radio.javaranch.com/pascarello/rss.xml",
             "http://radio.javaranch.com/bear/rss.xml",
             "http://radio.javaranch.com/lasse/rss.xml" ] };

var rssReader = new RSSReader('rssReader', options );
```

With creation and configuration quickly coded, it's time to peek behind the curtain at the magical start method that kicks everything off. We'll look at it briefly and cover its implications in the relevant sections that follow. Let's start by illustrating the implementation shown in listing 13.29.

Listing 13.29   The start method

```
start: function() {
    this.applyButtonBehaviors();
    new Effect.FadeTo( this.getLayer(1), 0.0, 1, 1, {} );
    this.loadRSSFeed(0,true);
    this.startSlideShow(false);
},
```

The `applyButtonBehaviors` method sets up the `onclick` handlers for the previous, pause, next, and Add Feed buttons. This is the next method we'll discuss. The fade effect on the second line fades out the visible div element so that when the first slide is loaded it can be faded in. Note that in this implementation, we're using an effect provided by Rico rather than writing our own, which reduces the amount of code we have to write, debug, and maintain. The `loadRSSFeed` method initiates the Ajax request to load in the first feed, and the `startSlideShow` method starts a timer with the value of the `slideTransitionDelay` to initiate the slideshow. The `loadRSSFeed` method will be explored in more detail in the "Loading RSS feeds with Ajax" section (page 556), and the `startSlideShow` method will be dissected in the "Slideshow functionality" (page 549) section. As promised, we'll close our discussion of construction and setup by looking at the `applyButton-Behaviors` method in listing 13.29.

The `applyButtonBehaviors` method, as mentioned previously, hooks the buttons up to methods that implement their behaviors. The implementation is shown in listing 13.30.

Listing 13.30   The applyButtonBehaviors method

```
applyButtonBehaviors: function() {
    $(this.id + '_prevBtn').onclick  = this.previous.bind(this);
    $(this.id + '_nextBtn').onclick  = this.next.bind(this);
    $(this.id + '_pauseBtn').onclick = this.pause.bind(this);
    $(this.id + '_addBtn').onclick   = this.addFeed.bind(this);
},
```

Let's start with some refresher notes about the syntax and idioms being used here. We're using a couple of syntactical elements of the Prototype library. First, the $ method, as you will recall, can be thought of as a call to `document.getElementById`. Second, the `bind` method implicitly creates a closure for us so that the `onclick` handler for each button can call first-class methods of our component. Now to the details of the implementation.

The implementation reveals an implicit contract between the component and the HTML markup for the reader. The component is constructed with an ID that it stores in its `this.id` attribute. The ID is then used as a prefix to find various elements within the markup. In this case, the IDs of the buttons are assumed to be the ID passed into the constructor, followed by _prevBtn, _nextBtn, _pauseBtn, and addBtn. To illustrate this, in the example construction just mentioned that uses rssReader for the ID, the component expects the buttons to be specified as follows:

```
<input type="button" id="rssReader_prevBtn"  value=" << "  />
<input type="button" id="rssReader_pauseBtn" value=" | | " />
<input type="button" id="rssReader_nextBtn"  value=" >> "  />
<input type="button" id="rssReader_addBtn"   value="Add Feed" />
```

Now that our RSSReader controller is starting to take shape, let's take a look at the implementation details of providing the slideshow behavior.

Slideshow functionality

Now would probably be a good time to talk about a change in semantic from our previous version of the script. In our first version of the RSS reader, we loaded all of the RSS feeds into memory at start time and then just transitioned through our in-memory representation. This had the advantage of simplicity but the decided disadvantage of not being very scalable. If we have dozens or even hundreds of RSS feeds that we read on a regular basis, each with dozens of articles, preloading them all would bring our browser to its knees. So in this refactoring, we'll take the opportunity to improve the scalability and performance of our RSS reader by changing our semantic to load only a single RSS feed into memory at a time. All of the RSSItems of a single feed will be in memory, but only a single RSSFeed will be in memory at a time. Three attributes of the Controller keep track of where the slideshow is in its list of displayable content. These are outlined in table 13.4.

Table 13.4 Attributes of the Controller

Attribute	Purpose
this.currentFeed	The RSSFeed instance currently loaded into memory.
this.feedIndex	The index of the currently visible feed. This is an index into the `this.options.rssFeeds` array.
this.itemIndex	The index of the currently visible item. This is an index into the currently visible RSSFeed object's internal items array.

With that overview of semantic change, let's ponder navigation. There are a number of methods that we must contemplate in order to navigate through each of the articles (item elements) of each one of the RSS feeds. Let's consider previous/next method pairs. A mechanism for moving forward and backward is needed not only to provide the implementation for the explicit button events but also for the passive perusal via the automated slideshow.

Let's start by looking at the boolean method pair that tells the reader whether it can move forward or backward. These two methods, hasPrevious and hasNext, are shown in listing 13.31.

Listing 13.31 The hasPrevious/hasNext method pair

```
hasPrevious: function() {
    return !(this.feedIndex == 0 && this.itemIndex == 0);
},

hasNext: function() {
    return !(this.feedIndex == this.options.rssFeeds.length - 1 &&
            this.itemIndex == this.currentFeed.items.length - 1);
},
```

These methods will be used in the previous and next processing to determine whether a previous or next slide is available. As implemented here, a previous slide is available unless we are on the first item of the first feed, and a next slide is available unless we are on the last item of the last feed.

Now let's examine what it means to move backward and forward. Let's start with the previous() method, shown in listing 13.32.

Listing 13.32 The previous() method

```
previous: function() {
    if ( !this.hasPrevious() ) return;

    var requiresLoad = this.itemIndex == 0;
    this.fadeOut( this.visibleLayer, Prototype.emptyFunction );
    this.visibleLayer = (this.visibleLayer + 1 ) % 2;
    if ( requiresLoad )
        this.loadRSSFeed( this.feedIndex - 1, false );
    else
        setTimeout( this.previousPartTwo.bind(this),
                    parseInt(this.options.fadeDuration/4) );
},
```

```
previousPartTwo: function() {
   this.itemIndex--; this.updateView();
},
```

The first thing the `previous()` method does is to put a guard condition at the beginning of the method. If there isn't a previous content item, then `previous()` just returns without performing any action. If the `requiresLoad` value is `true`, then the RSS content for the item being navigated to isn't loaded yet. When moving backward as we are here, a load is required if we're currently on the first item of a feed. The previous RSS feed will have to be loaded in order to be displayed. The fade-out method, which we'll examine in the "Transition effects" section on page 554, fades out the visible layer. What the method does next depends on whether or not it needs to load some content before it can display it. If we have to load content, then we initiate the load of that content via the `loadRSSFeed()` method. The first parameter is the index of the feed to be loaded, and the second parameter is a boolean value indicating a forward direction (`false` in this case). But if the content is already loaded, we call `previousPartTwo()` after a delay of one fourth of the overall `fadeDuration`. The "part two" of the method simply updates the `itemIndex` property and then calls `updateView()`, which fades in the appropriate slide.

Confused? Well, what's going on is that if the content that needs to be displayed isn't loaded, then the load is initiated immediately, which causes an update of the UI as soon as the response comes back. The time it takes for the response to come back provides a natural delay for the fade-in! On the other hand, if the content is already loaded (that is, we're looking at a different article in the same RSS feed that's loaded), then we intentionally delay by a quarter of the fade duration before we fade-in the next slide. Pretty slick, huh?

The `next()` method, shown in listing 13.33, is an inverse of the algorithm described previously.

Listing 13.33 The next() method

```
next: function() {
   if ( !this.hasNext() ) return;
   var requiresLoad =
      this.itemIndex == (this.currentFeed.items.length - 1);
   this.fadeOut( this.visibleLayer, Prototype.emptyFunction );
   this.visibleLayer = (this.visibleLayer + 1 ) % 2;
   if ( requiresLoad )
      this.loadRSSFeed( this.feedIndex + 1, true );
```

```
     else
        setTimeout( this.nextPartTwo.bind(this),
                      parseInt(this.options.fadeDuration/4) );
    },
    nextPartTwo: function() {
       this.itemIndex++; this.updateView();
    },
```

Look familiar? The `next()` method reverses the logic in terms of indexing but otherwise is identical to the algorithm shown previously. Note that the `previous()`/`next()` method pairs toggle the visible layer with each transition from one slide to the next with the expression

```
this.visibleLayer = (this.visibleLayer + 1) % 2;
```

This just tells the code that ultimately updates the UI as a result of the content load or the explicit call to `updateView()` into which layer to put the result. Recall that the content area of the reader has HTML markup that looks something like the following:

```
<!-- Content area -->
<div class="content" id="rssReader_content">
   <div class="layer1">Layer 0</div>
   <div class="layer2">Layer 1</div>
</div>
```

The `visibleLayer` is just an integer property that keeps track of into which div to put content. An index of `0` tells the UI update to put the content into `Layer 0`. A value of `1` indicates to put the content into `Layer 1`.

Now that we have the methods in place to provide forward and backward functionality, we can use these to create our slideshow methods. Let's dissect those now. The `startSlideShow` method, which you will recall was invoked from our `start()` method, and its companion `nextSlide()` are shown in listing 13.34.

Listing 13.34   The slideshow navigation methods

```
startSlideShow: function(resume) {
   var delay = resume ? 1 : this.options.slideTransitionDelay;
   this.transitionTimer = setTimeout(
                              this.nextSlide.bind(this),
                              delay );
},

nextSlide: function() {
   if ( this.hasNext() )
      this.next();
```

```
   else
      this.loadRSSFeed(0, true);

   this.transitionTimer = setTimeout(
                        this.nextSlide.bind(this),
                        this.options.slideTransitionDelay );
},
```

Our `startSlideShow` method just calls `nextSlide` on a delay. The delay is either the `slideTransitionDelay` or a single millisecond (effectively immediate), based on whether or not we're resuming the slideshow after having paused it. The `nextSlide` method is equally uncomplicated. It just calls our `next()` method as long as there is another slide available. If we're at the last slide, `loadRSS-Feed(0,true)` is called to wrap back to the beginning. It then just sets a timer to repeat the process. Piece of cake!

We mentioned that we can pause the slideshow via the pause button, but we haven't implemented that method yet. Let's do that now. This is shown in listing 13.35.

Listing 13.35 The pause method

```
pause: function() {
   if ( this.paused )
      this.startSlideShow(true);
   else
      clearTimeout( this.transitionTimer );
   this.paused = !this.paused;
},
```

The `pause` method toggles the paused state of the slideshow. This is tracked by the boolean attribute `this.paused`. If the slideshow is already paused, the `pause` method calls `startSlideShow`, passing `true` as the `resume` property; otherwise it clears the `transitionTimer` attribute, which suspends all slide transitions until the pause button is clicked again.

The final piece related to our slideshow functionality is to allow the slideshow to be augmented with additional RSS feeds via a select box and add button. We saw in the `applyButtonBehaviors()` function that the add button calls the `addFeed` method. Let's implement that to round out our slideshow functionality (see listing 13.36).

Listing 13.36 The addFeed method

```
addFeed: function() {
    var selectBox = $(this.id + '_newFeeds');
    var feedToAdd = selectBox.options[
                        selectBox.selectedIndex ].value;
    this.options.rssFeeds.push(feedToAdd);
},
```

This method also relies on an implicit contract with the HTML markup in terms of a naming convention for the select box of additional RSS feeds. The ID of the select box should be the ID of the reader with the suffix _newsFeeds. The method simply takes the selected RSS feed in the select box and appends it to the end of the this.options.rssFeeds array. Nothing more required! Don't you love it when adding functionality can happen in just a few lines of code?

This rounds out all of the slideshow-related methods. Let's now briefly look at the methods supporting our transition effects.

Transition effects

There are a few methods that we've already referenced that support our fade transitions between slides. Let's take a moment to decipher transitions. First, we defined a fadeIn() and fadeOut() method pair, as shown in listing 13.37.

Listing 13.37 The fadeIn()/fadeOut() method pair

```
fadeIn: function( layer, onComplete )  {
    this.fadeTo( 0.9999, layer, onComplete );
},

fadeOut: function( layer, onComplete ) {
    this.fadeTo( 0.0001, layer, onComplete );
},
```

These two methods both delegate to the fadeTo() method (shown next). They pass to the fadeTo() method an opacity value between 0 and 1—0 indicating the layer is invisible, 1 indicating the layer is completely visible. A value that is mathematically very close to 1 without actually being 1 seemed to cause less flicker in some browsers, which is why we used 0.9999 instead of 1. The layer number (0 or 1) is passed to indicate which layer to fade, and finally a function is passed in that provides a completion callback hook once the fade has completed. The fadeTo() method is implemented as shown in listing 13.38.

Listing 13.38 The `fadeTo()` method

```
fadeTo: function( n, layer, onComplete ) {
    new Effect.FadeTo( this.getLayer(layer),
                       n,
                       this.options.fadeDuration,
                       12,
                       {complete: onComplete} );
},
```

In a bout of utter laziness, or perhaps as a methodical well-thought-out strategy, we decided not to reinvent a fade effect. Instead, we use the Effect.FadeTo provided by the Rico library to perform the fancy fading magic for us. The Effect.FadeTo parameters are illustrated in table 3.5.

Table 13.5 The `Effect.FadeTo` parameters

Parameter	Description
`this.getLayer(layer)`	The DOM element to fade
`n`	An opacity value between 0 and 1
`this.options.fadeDuration`	How long it should take the fade to occur
`12`	The number of steps in the fade
`{complete: onComplete}`	The completion callback to call once done

We use the helper method `getLayer()` to get the div element corresponding to the content layer to be faded. The `getLayer()` method is shown in listing 13.39.

Listing 13.39 The `getLayer()` method

```
getLayer: function(n) {
    var contentArea = $(this.id+'_content');
    var children = contentArea.childNodes;
    var j = 0;
    for ( var i = 0 ; i < children.length ; i++ ) {
        if ( children[i].tagName &&
             children[i].tagName.toLowerCase() == 'div' ) {
            if ( j == n ) return children[i];
            j++;
        }
    }
    return null;
},
```

This method simply finds the content area, assuming its ID to be the ID of the reader with the value _content appended to the end. Once it finds the content element, it navigates to the children and finds the nth div child and returns it.

This finishes our treatment of transitions. Let's now examine the topic of loading our RSS feeds via the magic of Ajax.

Loading RSS feeds with Ajax

We've given a fair amount of attention to the topics of creating a component and providing a rich slideshow semantic and fancy DHTML techniques for transitioning between slides. But without Ajax at the core, the fanfare would be for naught. The point is that it's the synergy between Ajax, with its scalability and fine-grained data retrieval, and sophisticated DHTML, with its rich affordances and effects, that provides a superior user experience. Okay, enough of the soapbox. Let's look at some Ajax, starting with the method in listing 13.40 that loads an RSS feed into memory.

Listing 13.40   The `loadRSSFeed` method

```
loadRSSFeed: function(feedIndex, forward) {
   this.feedIndex = feedIndex;
   this.itemIndex = forward ? 0 : "last";
   new net.ContentLoader(this,
                    this.options.rssFeeds[feedIndex],
                    "GET", [] ).sendRequest();
},
```

This method uses our ever-familiar net.ContentLoader to make an Ajax request, passing the URL of an RSS feed as specified in the `this.options.rssFeeds` array. The `forward` parameter is a boolean specifying whether or not we're loading in new content as a result of moving forward. Given this knowledge, the `itemIndex` property is updated accordingly. Note that `itemIndex` is given the value of `last` rather than an integer if we're moving backward. That's because we want `itemIndex` to indicate the index of the last item in the previous RSS feed. The only problem is that we don't know how many items are in the feed, because it isn't loaded yet.

You'll recall that the `ajaxUpdate` and `handleError` methods are required as an implicit contract with the net.ContentLoader. We will look next at the `ajaxUpdate` method, shown in listing 13.41, to see how the implementation resolves our indexing dilemma.

Listing 13.41 The ajaxUpdate method

```
ajaxUpdate: function(request) {

if ( window.netscape &&
  window.netscape.security.PrivilegeManager.enablePrivilege)
    netscape.security.PrivilegeManager.enablePrivilege(
      'UniversalBrowserRead');

  this.currentFeed =
    RSSFeed.parseXML(request.responseXML.documentElement);
  if ( this.itemIndex == "last" )
    this.itemIndex = this.currentFeed.items.length - 1;
  this.updateView();
},
```

The `ajaxUpdate` method starts with a check to see if it's running in an environment that provides a `PrivilegeManager`. If so, it asks to grant the `Universal-BrowserRead` privilege. As noted earlier, this is done so that our reader can run locally within a Mozilla-based browser.

The `this.currentFeed` is an instance of our RSSFeed model object that we defined in the Model section. It corresponds to the single RSSFeed loaded into memory, as populated from the Ajax response. If `this.itemIndex` has a value of `last`—as set by the `loadRSSFeed` method when moving backward—the `itemIndex` property is updated to contain the actual number of items in the newly loaded RSSFeed. Finally, the UI is updated via a call to `updateView()`.

Let's not forget to do our due diligence and define a `handleError` method both to satisfy our contract with the net.ContentLoader and because we really should do something to handle errors. If an RSS feed fails to load, we'll just provide a "punt" message, as shown in our `handleError` implementation. More sophisticated implementations are certainly possible—and desirable.

```
handleError: function(request) {
  this.getLayer(this.visibleLayer).innerHTML =
    this.options.errorHTML;
},
```

Now that our RSSReader is fully Ajax-ified, the only remaining piece of our puzzle it to write a couple of methods that handle updating the UI.

UI manipulation

Recall that early on we took the time to create Model and View classes to support our refactoring effort. Now that we've come to the portion of the Controller that has responsibility for updating the UI, we should expect our work to be mostly done. If that's your expectation, then you're right on target. To illustrate this, our `updateView()` method that has been referenced numerous times throughout our refactoring session is shown in listing 13.42.

Listing 13.42   The `updateView()` method

```
updateView: function() {

  var rssItemView = new RSSItemView(
     this.currentFeed.items[this.itemIndex],
     this.feedIndex,
     this.itemIndex,
     this.options.rssFeeds.length );

  this.getLayer(this.visibleLayer).innerHTML = rssItemView;
  this.fadeIn( this.visibleLayer,
    this.bringVisibleLayerToTop.bind(this) );
},
```

As you can see, the `updateView()` method delegates all of the hard work to our View class by instantiating an instance of it, setting it as the value of the visible layer's `innerHTML` property, and finally fading the layer into visibility. Three lines of code. Not too shabby. Notice that once the layer is faded into view, we call a completion callback named `bringVisibleLayerToTop`. What this does is update the layer's `zIndex` style property to ensure that it's above the other layer being faded out. The `bringVisibleLayerToTop()` function is implemented as follows:

```
bringVisibleLayerToTop: function() {
   this.getLayer(this.visibleLayer).style.zIndex = 10;
   this.getLayer((this.visibleLayer+1)%2).style.zIndex = 5;
}
```

That's all we have to do from a UI-manipulation perspective. The separation of concerns across our Model, View, and Controller classes has facilitated a clean, maintainable architecture.

13.7.4   *Refactoring debrief*

Our refactoring session concentrated on repackaging our script in such a way as to provide an MVC implementation of our RSS reader. We created an RSSFeed Model class to encapsulate the concept of an RSS feed, as well as an RSSItem class. We created a View class to encapsulate the concept of providing a View for an RSSItem in context of its parent RSSFeed, the RSSItemView. Finally, we tied the

Model and View classes together with an `RSSReader` Controller class that provided all of the event-management glue and sophisticated interaction of a slideshow with transition effects.

13.8 *Summary*

In this chapter, Ajax allowed us to obtain information straight from our desktop without requiring a commercial client application, saving us money and allowing us to customize the solution to our needs. We were able to load multiple XML files and only obtain the information that is relevant to our needs. We developed an HTML framework and applied CSS to allow easy customization of the reader. By using DHTML, we were able to develop a rich user interface that allows users to skip messages, pause messages, and add additional feeds as needed. All of this was possible by taking advantage of Ajax functionality to obtain the syndication feeds from websites. By changing a few statements, we can easily adapt the reader to read any XML feed. We can even develop our own custom XML formats to display news, ads, and anything else that may be of importance for our websites. Finally, we repackaged the script along the lines of a Model-View-Controller architecture in order to facilitate the readability and maintainability of our code.

The Ajax
craftsperson's toolkit

Ajax is a very easy technology to work with. The toolset required to get the job done is minimal, and it is possible to develop complex Ajax applications using nothing more than a web browser, a text editor, and access to a web server—either on your development machine or through your ISP or hosting provider. Nonetheless, tools are important to programmers, and toolsets are becoming increasingly sophisticated.

As yet, there are no dedicated Ajax IDEs, although these will probably appear in time. Several development tools do, however, offer support for some parts of the Ajax development process. In this appendix, we present an overview of the types of tools available and how they can help you to work smarter and faster.

A.1 Working smarter with the right toolset

The right development tools can be invaluable in speeding up repetitive or difficult processes, and they can have an enormous impact on a developer's productivity. The wrong tools can be distracting, gimmicky, and constraining, forcing a project into a particular process or way of doing things that doesn't really fit. Different tools suit different people and will suit them better or worse on different kinds of projects. It's arguably a key part of a developer's job to devote time and effort to finding the right toolset. Abraham Lincoln put it nicely:

> *Give me six hours to chop down a tree and I will spend the first four sharpening the axe.*

If sufficient attention is invested in doing so, the returns can be considerable. Finding the balance between perfecting your tools and actually using them is important, too, particularly in a fragmented situation such as the current Ajax tools offerings, as you'll see in the following section.

A.1.1 Acquiring tools that fit

Many tools can be acquired relatively easily, in the form of free downloads, open source projects, or commercial products. There are no mature tools dedicated to Ajax yet, but several are available that are designed for developing web applications, and many of these support JavaScript, HTML, and CSS.

Ajax uses the same technologies as classical web applications but in quite different ways, as we outlined in chapter 1. Instead of being built out of lots of little pages presented in sequence, an Ajax application will tend to have only a few pages—and often only one—that undergo a variety of programmatic transitions as the user works with them and that talk to the server asynchronously in the background. Further, because of the much greater volume of JavaScript being generated, the Ajax programmer is more likely to be developing with JavaScript frameworks (see appendix C for a round-up of frameworks, and chapter 3 for a discussion of a few of the more popular ones).

These differences raise two concerns, then. First, the tool may make assumptions about page-based workflows that are at odds with the Ajax approach. Second, support for JavaScript may be based on the use of a particular set of functions or coding practices that don't play well with third-party frameworks that the user is employing.

The differences, then, are mainly in the high-level structure of an application rather than in the details. The concerns raised here are more likely to apply to complex tools, such as IDEs, than to simpler tools, such as JavaScript-aware text editors.

It's important to bear these considerations in mind when evaluating tools for an Ajax project. We'll raise them again later when we look at the different classes of tools on the market.

Finally, it's worth noting that many tools these days provide extensible feature sets, in the form of plug-ins. Complex tools such as general-purpose IDEs and web browsers are used by different types of users in different ways. Plug-ins allow users to customize a base application with the specific features that they need, avoiding bloat in the base feature set, and empower them to extend the functionality of an app in ways that the original development team hadn't anticipated. Two notable cases of plug-in–based applications are the Eclipse IDE, which, although it is mainly a Java developer's tool, supports a range of Ajax functionality through plug-ins, and the Firefox browser, which has an active plug-in (a.k.a. extensions) community and several useful extensions targeted at web developers.

Eclipse and Firefox both have very active plug-in communities, and the chances are that a plug-in already exists that does more or less what you want. There is also a strong tradition in computing, and in web development, of building your own tools, to which the plug-in approach also caters. Let's have a look at that tradition now.

A.1.2 *Building your own tools*

As an alternative to buying or downloading a ready-made tool, you can always write your own tool. This may sound daunting and unrealistic, given that the discussion has focused so far on IDEs and large-scale tools. We certainly wouldn't suggest that you begin an Ajax project by writing its own IDE!

There's a strong tradition in UNIX culture of developing small tools that do a single job. These kinds of tools are easily developed in a short time and are simple enough to be maintained easily, too. The stopwatch classes that we developed for profiling JavaScript code in chapter 7 are an example of this kind of tool, as is the output console that we'll demonstrate in section A.3.4.

Tools written in JavaScript and other Ajax technologies have the advantage of being portable across any browser. However, the capabilities available within the browser are severely limited, owing to the JavaScript security model that we discussed in chapter 6. Sometimes it makes more sense to write a tool as a stand-alone program, whether in .NET, Java, or any other programming language. The HTTP debuggers that we describe in section A.3.3 are a case in point here.

A middle way between writing tools within the browser and writing a standalone tool is to develop a plug-in. Many of the larger web development tools support the development of plug-ins these days, and some have made it quite easy to develop plug-ins, too. Two notable examples are the Firefox web browser and the Eclipse IDE, as discussed in the previous section. Eclipse even offers a set of plug-ins, bundled with the core download, that make it easy to write plug-ins. Nonetheless, plug-in development is somewhat more advanced than developing in-browser tools and probably only justifiable within the time budget of a larger project.

A variety of tools can be useful in Ajax development. These are rather scattered at present, and actively maintaining them is an ongoing task. Let's say a few words about that before moving on to look at some specific tools.

A.1.3 Maintaining your toolkit

As noted, Ajax tools are currently rather fragmented, a rather different situation for the Java or .NET programmer used to sitting in front of the comfortable bulk of Eclipse, NetBeans, or Visual Studio.

Developers owe it to themselves to keep their toolkit up to date. Without the central focus of a de facto standard IDE, this task is somewhat more problematic and will generally rely on word of mouth, mailing lists, portal sites, blogs, and the other distributed communications media of the Internet.

The most fundamental tool for any developer is the editor into which he types his code. Let's take a look at them next.

A.2 Editors and IDEs

Code-editing tools vary a great deal in complexity, from the simple Notepad to complex IDEs that model the code objects in a variety of ways as you type. Java-Script, HTML, and CSS aren't as well supported as enterprise-class languages such as C#, Visual Basic, and Java, but there's still quite a wide range of functionality from which to choose. Let's run through the types of features that we might look for before we consider the products available today.

A.2.1 What to look for in a code editor

Code editors can do many things, arguably too many. A lot of it comes down to individual tastes. Some developers prefer a simple tool that processes text; others like the visual aids and cues of a full-blown IDE.

When it comes to supporting Ajax code, in the form of HTML, CSS, and Java-Script, there are a number of ways in which the editor can help us. Many of these may seem like overkill for the web content of a classic web app, but as the code-base of an Ajax application is typically much larger and more structured, support for that structuring becomes more critical. Here's a quick rundown of useful features to look for.

Multiple file support

This is a very basic requirement but worth noting anyway. Ajax projects will typically entail a large number of files, and an editor that cannot manage multiple files or buffers (such as Windows Notepad) will quickly become annoying. Nearly all coding editors support multiple files through tabbed panels, a selector panel, or something similar.

Syntax highlighting

This is a fairly basic feature nowadays and one that most programmer's editors will support. Syntax highlighting simply colors, italicizes, or otherwise marks language keywords, symbols, quoted strings, and code comments, making it easier to read a sequence of code.

Most editors support syntax coloring for a range of languages, often with pluggable syntax definition files. The key issue for Ajax programming is that a variety of languages are typically used. There are HTML, CSS, XML, and Java-Script on the client side, all of which can benefit from syntax highlighting, and some or all of Java, C#, VB, and the more complex ASP, PHP, and JSP, in which blocks of HTML and code alternate with one another. Not all syntax-aware editors support the full range of languages in use in an Ajax project.

Higher-level code support

Coloring in the code provides useful visual cues, but some editors go beyond this to model the code at a higher level of function, methods, and object declarations. This higher-level understanding of a codebase opens up a broader range of tools such as outliners that summarize a file's contents, navigational aids such as maps of object hierarchies, and the ability to search for uses of a specific property or invocations of a method or function. Tools of this type become invaluable as a codebase matures.

Project-level support tools

Taking another step up from modeling individual object definitions, some IDEs will also manage a codebase as an integrated project, recognizing linkages between the various components and resources that lead to a deployed product. In an IDE for a compiled language, a key benefit of this is the ability to build the entire project into executable form, but this isn't a concern for Ajax, in which all client-side resources are deployed in their human-readable form. Nonetheless, this capability may be useful when working with server-side code.

Further, project-level support may provide the ability to deploy a project to a web server, even to manage the web server itself, either by controlling an external server through RPC calls or by embedding a simple server into the IDE. A tool that supports the codebase at the project level can release the developer from maintaining a build-and-deploy system.

Version control integration

Version control is a necessity in larger projects and good practice in a project of any size. Version-control systems themselves generally work on text and binary files without understanding their higher-level semantics, so there is little to say about them that is specific to Ajax, but integrating version control into your toolset can be a great help.

Mixed-language development: client and server integration

As we noted earlier, many Ajax projects will require a server-side component in addition to the many web browser technologies being employed. Server-side Java-Script is possible but not fashionable, and the Ajax developer will usually make use of different languages on the server side and the client side. It is possible to use completely different tools for server and client coding, but some tasks will involve rapidly switching between the tiers, and an editor that can support the full range of languages can be a distinct advantage.

Those, then, are our main criteria for choosing a code editor, whether it be a plain text editor or an IDE. In the next section, we'll have a look at some of the available tools at the time this book was written.

Two-way visual designers

Many web-design tools provide visual WYSIWYG designers for web pages. These can be useful for prototyping, although they are often poorly adapted to Ajax's more dynamic approach to rearranging the user interface through DOM manipulation. Most visual editors will also allow the programmer to switch to a text-based view of the HTML. When you're using this kind of tool with Ajax, it is important that the visual editor preserve elements that it does not understand, such as comments and custom tag types and attributes, particularly as the latter may be used by the JavaScript code that rearranges the DOM tree.

A.2.2 Current offerings

A variety of text editors and IDEs offer some support for Ajax technologies. We'll start by looking at the programmer's editors and move on from there to the more complex IDEs.

Text editors

Depending on your operating system, a wide range of open source, freeware, and shareware text editors is available these days, such as shareware tools TextPad, Notepad2, EditPlus, the UNIX veterans Vim and Emacs, and the extensible cross-platform jEdit, whose plug-in system enables some IDE-like functionality. Figure A.1 shows a few common text editors in JavaScript mode.

TextPad provides a staggeringly diverse base of user-contributed syntax definition files, including several for CSS, JavaScript, XML, and HTML, and for most popular server-side languages. There is minimal support for running user-defined commands such as compilers against the current file. TextPad runs on Microsoft Windows only. NotePad2 and EditPlus fill similar niches.

jEdit is Java based and can run on any platform that supports Java. It supports syntax highlighting for over 100 languages, including all the main Ajax ones. Several more advanced features are available through a plug-in system, which is well integrated. Plug-ins can be automatically browsed, downloaded, and installed from within jEdit itself. Useful plug-ins include support for syntax checkers, debuggers, compilers, and version-control interfaces, and specific support for CSS and XSLT.

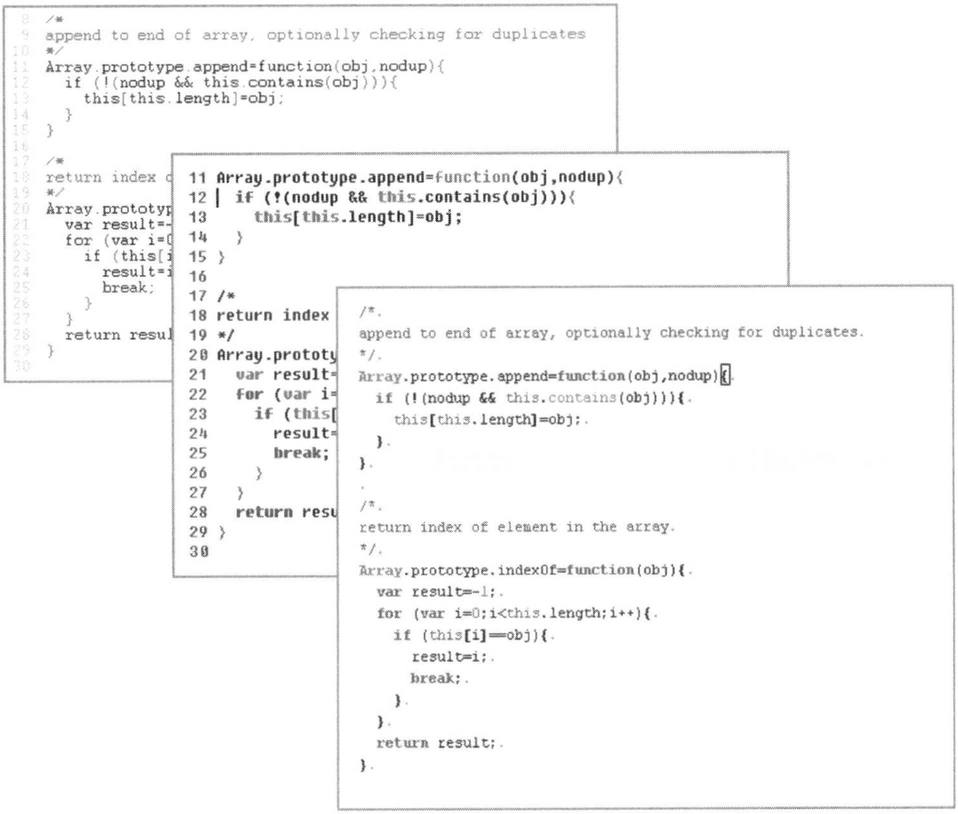

Figure A.1 Syntax highlighting support for JavaScript in (left to right) the TextPad, Gvim, and jEdit programmer's editors

Vim and Emacs are powerful extensible text editors with a long tradition in UNIX operating systems, although both have been ported to Windows, too. Both have well-developed modes for JavaScript coding.

Integrated development environments

Enterprise programming languages such as .NET and Java have a long history of integrated development environments. The market for these is mature, and in recent years, a number of mature, feature-rich open source and freeware IDEs have appeared. IDEs designed for server-side coding languages are often extensible enough to allow for client-side development using Ajax.

Microsoft technologies are still dominated by Microsoft's own Visual Studio. Visual Studio includes support for web development through the Visual InterDev component, which supports JavaScript and CSS. Free, cut-down versions have recently become available under the name Visual Studio Express, including one targeted at web developers.

The most prominent Java IDE at present is the IBM-sponsored Eclipse. Eclipse is mostly a Java development tool and ships with a complex set of plug-ins specifically written for Java developers. A thriving plug-in community exists, including some relatively simple JavaScript plug-ins providing syntax highlighting and outline views of methods and classes (figure A.2).

With the recent Eclipse version 3.1, a broader range of web developer plug-ins is being developed by the Web Tools Platform project, which in addition to supporting server-side J2EE technologies, has editors for JavaScript, XML, HTML, and CSS. Eclipse also offers strong project-level codebase-management features and full integration with CVS version control out of the box. Third-party integration with Subversion, Visual SourceSafe, and other version-control systems is available.

Some enterprise Java development tools such as the Sun Java Studio Creator and SAP NetWeaver offer high-level design facilities for web applications. In our experience, these are based heavily on the classic web application metaphor, with an application being modeled as a series of discrete pages, and may translate poorly to the Ajax approach. Studio Creator uses Java ServerFaces (JSF) behind the scenes, however. We discussed JSF and Ajax in chapter 5, and although the two technologies have some challenges to overcome before being fully interoperable, it may be possible that JSF-based tools will support Ajax better in the near future.

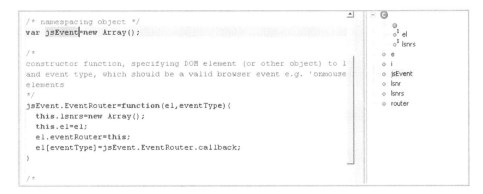

Figure A.2   The JavaScript editor plug-in for Eclipse provides rudimentary outlining support for JavaScript objects but doesn't handle the full object-based syntax.

As well as having a foot in the enterprise-development camp, Ajax has roots in the web-design community, for whom an entirely different type of toolset has developed. Macromedia Dreamweaver and Microsoft FrontPage are two notable web-design tools of this type, and both offer support for the basic client-side technologies used by Ajax. Dreamweaver provides good support for basic JavaScript and CSS editing (figure A.3) and a two-way HTML editor with visual and text modes, but for WYSIWYG orchestration of complex JavaScript user interfaces, it supports only its own code library. Integrating third-party libraries such as x, Prototype, and Rico into a Dreamweaver or FrontPage project would require a lot of hand-crafting the scripts, making use of the text editor functionality of the tools and relatively little else.

The final tool worth a mention here is ActiveState's Komodo, which is a cross-language scripting IDE, supporting Perl, Python, PHP, Tcl, JavaScript, and XSLT. Komodo has very good support for JavaScript codebase navigation and a sophis-

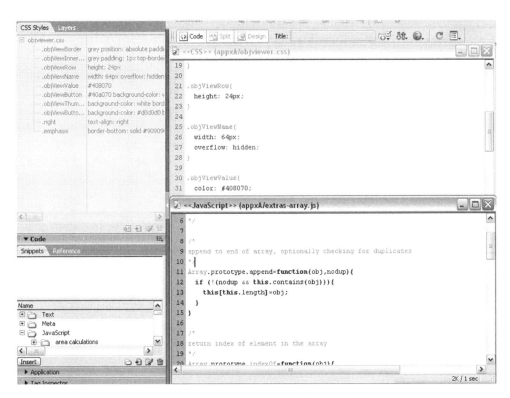

Figure A.3 Dreamweaver's editor supports JavaScript and CSS. The CSS file being edited in the upper-right pane is also shown in outline form in the upper left.

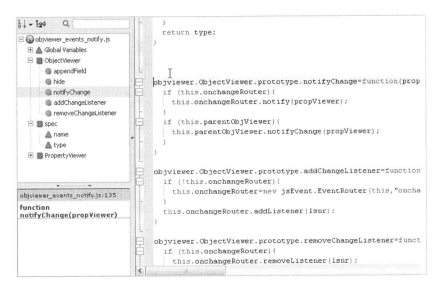

Figure A.4 **The Komodo IDE provides high-quality outlining features for JavaScript objects and can understand a number of coding idioms. Here the code outliner has recognized that various functions belong to the ObjectViewer prototype.**

ticated outliner that recognizes JavaScript classes as well as functions and methods (figure A.4). As a general-purpose scripting IDE, it deals only with JavaScript the generic language, not the browser-based implementations. As such, it is most useful when developing domain models for Ajax. Komodo is a commercial tool with free trials available. As an interesting aside, the Komodo UI is built using the XML-based XUL toolkit used to create the Firefox web browser.

In the next section, we'll consider another key tool in the developer's arsenal: the source code debugger.

A.3 Debuggers

The behavior of simple computer programs can often be figured out by looking at the code, but larger, more complex programs are often too large to hold in your mind all at once. Debugger tools provide a way of controlling the flow of execution of a piece of running code, allowing it to be stopped and started manually and the state of the program inspected while it is running.

A.3.1 *Why we use a debugger*

Debuggers provide a very practical way of finding out what a program does. In any programming effort, a debugger can be useful in testing whether you have understood a piece of code correctly. In Ajax, this is particularly valuable.

When the term *debugger* is used, most developers tend to think of source code debuggers, and server-side and JavaScript debuggers are indeed handy to have at your disposal when writing Ajax. However, it is also helpful to be able to debug network traffic when writing Ajax, as HTTP can be surprisingly complicated, too. In the following sections, we'll consider both source code and HTTP debugging tools. Let's look at the state of JavaScript debuggers first.

A.3.2 *JavaScript debuggers*

Being able to debug JavaScript code is especially useful because of the fluidity of the language. A C# or Java programmer generally knows which properties and methods are available on a given object by examining its class definition and knows the types and number of a method's arguments from its declared signature. It isn't always possible with JavaScript, though, to work out from the code how many arguments a function will be invoked with, or even what the variable `this` will resolve to inside a function. This latter issue is particularly problematic for callback handlers, for which the invocation of the function may be done by an unknown object or by the browser itself.

At its simplest, a source code debugger allows the user to set breakpoints that halt program execution and hand it over to the user when that line of code is executed. The user may then step through the code a line at a time, inspecting the values of any variables that are in scope, or resume normal execution until the next breakpoint is encountered. In JavaScript, breakpoints may be set by the debugger tool itself or by the coder, by adding a `debugger` statement to the code. For example, when the browser executes the following code

```
var x=3;
var y=x*7;
debugger;
var z=x+y;
```

control will be handed over to any debugger that is registered with the browser on the third line of code (figure A.5), at which point the values of variables x and y can be inspected. z has not been declared yet and so can be inspected only after the user has stepped the debugger forward over the fourth line.

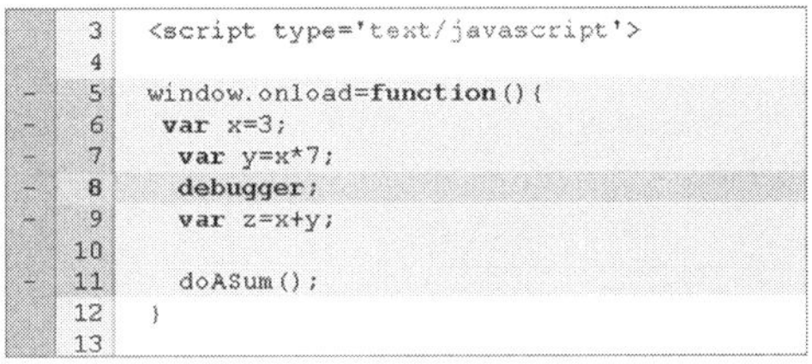

```
 3   <script type='text/javascript'>
 4
 5   window.onload=function(){
 6     var x=3;
 7     var y=x*7;
 8     debugger;
 9     var z=x+y;
10
11     doASum();
12   }
13
```

Figure A.5
Using the JavaScript `debugger` **statement**
triggers a breakpoint programmatically.

This defines the basic functionality of a source-debugging tool. A more sophisticated debugger may support further features, as discussed next.

Call stack navigation

When a function is executed in JavaScript, a new execution context is created, with its own set of local variables. When a debugger stops inside a function, it can see the local variables inside that function but not those in the function that called it. Consider the following example:

```
function doASum(){
  var a=3;
  var b=4;
  var c=multiply(a-2,b+6);
  return (a+b)/c;
}

function multiply(var1,var2){
  var n1=parseFloat(var1);
  var n2=parseFloat(var2);
  debugger;
  return n1*n2;
}
```

At the point at which the debugger is invoked, we can see variables n1, n2, var1, and var2. While examining a problem with our program, we may decide that the issue lies with the arguments being passed into our function. We need to know what values **a** and **b** held in the enclosing doASum() method. We could set an extra breakpoint in doASum() and run the program again, but it might take us some time to return to this state in a complex program. If the debugger supports call stack navigation, then we can simply move up the call stack to the doASum() function and inspect its state as though we had set a breakpoint on the third line, where multiply() is invoked (figure A.6). In a complex program, the call stack may be very deep, and the debugger is capable of moving up and down among all layers.

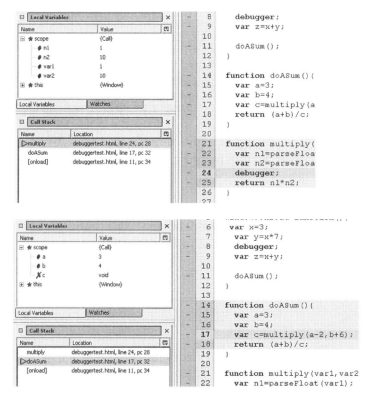

Figure A.6 The Mozilla Venkman debugger allows inspection of local variables in functions higher up the call stack than the current point of execution.

Watching expressions

Some debugger tools are capable of evaluating expressions on the fly and allow the user to predefine code expressions that will be reevaluated as the debugger moves across the code. These expressions can make use of any variables currently in scope, allowing the developer to interact with the program while it is running.

Conditional breakpoints

Setting a breakpoint at a particular point in the code can give a developer fine-grained control over when to invoke the debugger, but in some cases, this control is not enough. When executing a loop, for example, any breakpoint inside the body of the loop will be executed each time the loop is executed. Let's take the following example:

```
for (var i=0;i<100;i++){
  var divisor=i-57;
  var val=42/divisor;
  plotOnGraph(i,val);
}
```

Running this code causes an exception to be thrown midway through the loop. In this case, a quick inspection of the code tells us that this will happen when i is 57, and we attempt to divide by zero. However, let's pretend for now that it isn't so obvious, as will often be the case with real-world code. We suspect that the divisor being set to zero is the problem but don't know when such a condition will occur.

We could set a debugger breakpoint inside the loop:

```
for (var i=0;i<100;i++){
  var divisor=i-57;
  debugger;
  var val=42/divisor;
  plotOnGraph(i,val);
}
```

but we would need to click the resume button on our debugger numerous times to step through the loop to the point where we encounter the error condition. If we're being clever, we can test for the error condition in our code:

```
for (var i=0;i<100;i++){
  var divisor=i-57;
  if (divisor==0){ debugger; }
  var val=42/divisor;
  plotOnGraph(i,val);
}
```

This will take us straight to the fifty-seventh iteration of the loop, the one at which our error condition occurs. We could describe this as a conditional breakpoint—that is, it will break the flow of execution only if a certain condition is met.

We can set up conditions in this way only by modifying the code. However, if we are assigning breakpoints through the debugger IDE, we can set a condition on the breakpoint independently of the actual code (figure A.7). Some debuggers do support this facility, allowing the user to attach expressions to a breakpoint, and break the flow only if the expression evaluates to true.

Changing the values of variables

If we encounter an error condition, our program execution halts. In a debugging session, we may realize what the solution is but want to coerce the program into continuing anyway, in order to test some later piece of code under the current set of conditions.

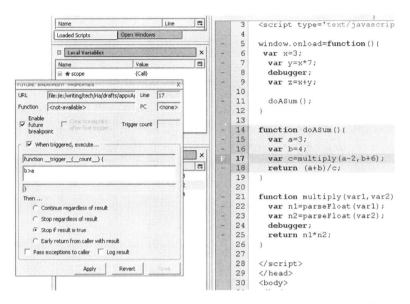

Figure A.7   Setting up a conditional breakpoint in the Mozilla Venkman debugger

Some debuggers will allow us to do this by providing write as well as read access to local variables (figure A.8). In the case of our loop example shown previously, if we know that a divisor value of 0 is going to be problematic but want to explore some code following the loop, we could temporarily reassign a value of 1 to the divisor, letting the flow of execution continue.

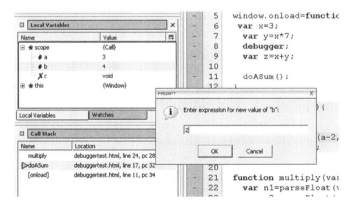

Figure A.8   Changing the value of a variable in a running program using the Mozilla Venkman debugger

A number of debuggers for JavaScript are available. Free debugging tools include the Venkman plug-in for Mozilla Firefox and the Microsoft Script Debugger (see the Resources section at the end of this appendix for information on both of these) for Internet Explorer. Venkman supports all of the advanced features described previously, as well as having an inbuilt profiling tool, which we describe in chapter 7. The Microsoft Script Debugger supports call stack navigation and an "immediate window" for executing JavaScript on the fly, including querying and reassigning local variable values.

Visual Studio and Komodo IDEs also support JavaScript debuggers with an advanced set of capabilities.

Server-side debugging

In addition to being able to debug JavaScript on the client, it is often useful to debug the server-side code, too. Java and .NET IDEs generally ship with high-quality debuggers. Eclipse's Java tools and Visual Studio both offer debugging out of the box, as do most other IDEs. For debugging Java-based web applications, the JBoss application server and Eclipse plug-ins provide a simple system for deploying and debugging web applications. Web development versions of Visual Studio ship with a built-in ASP.NET-enabled web server for development purposes. Visual Studio is the only development environment to my knowledge to support debugging of client-side and server-side code within the same user interface.

It can be also very useful to debug network traffic. Again, a range of free and commercial tools is available for this purpose. Let's look at them now.

A.3.3 HTTP debuggers

Between the Ajax client and the web server, all communications take place over HTTP. This in itself can be a complex business and may be a source of errors. At times, it is reassuring to be able to inspect the HTTP traffic, to look at the headers, querystrings, content of the request and response, and sequence of interchanges.

LiveHTTPHeader

Mozilla Firefox supports an extension called LiveHTTPHeaders, which is capable of logging HTTP traffic from the browser (figure A.9). Request and response headers are recorded and displayed, and they can be exported as text files to provide a permanent record of an Ajax session. Querystrings from GET and POST methods are also recorded, but the response content is not.

The Ajax craftsperson's toolkit

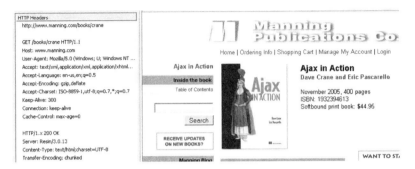

Figure A.9   The Mozilla LiveHTTPHeaders extension can log HTTP traffic and present details of request and response headers.

LiveHTTPHeaders supports only reading headers. Other Firefox extensions are available for modifying headers in transit, such as the Modify Headers extension.

Fiddler

Microsoft Research recently released a .NET-based application called Fiddler that fulfills a similar role to LiveHTTPHeaders but also allows for scripted rewriting of headers on the fly, using JavaScript. This provides a similar capability to the ability to change variable values in some debuggers during a session, and it can be used to quickly work around bugs in an application while it is running.

Unlike LiveHTTPHeaders, which is integrated into the browser, Fiddler is an independent process that acts as a proxy between the client and server. As such, it can be used with any combination of browser and web server.

Charles

Charles is a shareware tool written in Java. Like Fiddler, it acts as a proxy between browser and server. It can log request and response data, including the content, and export sessions as spreadsheet files. It also provides a highly configurable built-in bandwidth-shaping tool, which allows easy simulation of very slow connections over a fast LAN or even when the client and server are both deployed to the same machine.

There are a number of other useful tools in this category, which we don't have space to cover fully here. If Charles and Fiddler don't do what you want, a quick online search for "Ethereal" or "Apache TCPMon" might help you out.

This concludes our review of off-the-shelf debugging tools. By combining a server-side code debugger, a JavaScript debugger on the client, and an HTTP debugger in between, it is possible to intercept your application at any point in its lifecycle and be able to see what it is really getting up to.

Debuggers are, by their nature, intrusive. Although they are very powerful in many ways, there are times when a background logging system is preferable. Plenty of mature server-side logging frameworks are available, such as Apache log4j for Java, but, once again, the JavaScript toolset is lagging. In the final part of this section, we'll look at a simple logging tool written in JavaScript that can be integrated into your browser code to provide a record of background activity.

A.3.4 *Building your own cross-browser output console*

A debugger gives a developer a very detailed view of running code, but it interrupts the ordinary flow of events. When tracking a user's interactions for usability testing or monitoring the execution of code in a tight loop, it is sometimes more useful to log activity without interrupting the flow.

Web browser JavaScript doesn't provide a built-in logging facility. (The Mozilla JavaScript console may look like one at first glance, but it can only be written to by the browser and by extensions.) In this section, we'll develop our own simple logging system and demonstrate its use in one of our example applications. Let's sketch out our requirements first. We can't write to a local file because of the JavaScript security model, so we'll opt to write to an on-screen console element instead. We want to be able to append messages to our console. Ideally, we'd like to be able to use HTML markup in our logging, as well as plain text. We'd also like to clear the console of existing messages.

To keep things simple, we'll pass a DOM element in as an argument to the object constructor. The placement of the console can then be determined on a page-by-page basis. The constructor simply sets up a two-way reference between the DOM element and the console object itself:

```
Console=function(el){
  this.el=document.getElementById(el);
  this.el.className='console';
  this.el.consoleModel=this;
  this.clear();
}
```

To append to the console, we simply pass in an argument, which may be a textual string or a DOM element, and optionally pass in a CSS class name as well:

```
Console.prototype.append=function(obj,style){
  var domEl=styling.toDOMElement(obj);
  if (style) {
    domEl.className=style;
```

```
    }
    this.el.appendChild(domEl);
  }
```

The toDOMElement() method calls a generic styling function, which ensures that the message is wrapped up as a DOM element. If the argument is already a DOM element, it is returned unchanged. If it is a string, it is wrapped in a DIV element:

```
styling.toDOMElement=function(obj){
  var result=null;
  if (obj instanceof Element){
    result=obj;
  }else{
    var txtNode=document.createTextNode(String(obj));
      var wrapper=document.createElement('div');
      wrapper.appendChild(txtNode);
      result=wrapper;
  }
  return result;
}
```

To clear the console, we simply remove all child elements from it, one by one:

```
Console.prototype.clear=function(){
  while(this.el.firstChild){
    this.el.removeChild(this.el.firstChild);
  }
}
```

That provides a simple implementation of an in-browser logging console. Let's have a look at how we use it now. We'll take the ObjectViewer example from chapters 4 and 5. First, we define a DOM element in our page to contain the logging console

```
<div id='console'></div>
```

and a CSS class to position it on screen for us:

```
div.console {
  position:absolute;
  top:32px;
  left:600px;
  width:300px;
  height:500px;
  overflow:auto;
  border: 1px solid black;
  background-color: #eef0ff;
}
```

We are using absolute positioning here, but we could use any Ajax user interface technique to do the job for us. Next, we need to create the logging object. We'll define it as a global variable in this example for convenience.

```
var logger=null;
window.onload=function(){
  logger=new Console("console");
  logger.append("starting planets app");
  ...
}
```

We initialize the logger in the `window.onload` event, so that the DOM element that it requires is guaranteed to be created. Now let's suppose that we want to log a message whenever a planet object is created in our domain model. We simply need to invoke `logger.append()`:

```
planets.Planet=function
  (id,system,name,distance,diameter,image){
  this.id=id;
  ...
  logger.append("created planet object '"+this.name+"'");
}
```

Similarly, we can add logging statements to the ObjectViewer code when we edit values and launch pop-up subwindows, to the ContentLoader object when we load network resources, and so on, in order to track the behavior of our codebase while it is running. We can style important messages, for example, network failures:

```
net.ContentLoader.prototype.defaultError=function(){
  logger.append("network error! "+this.url, "urgent");
}
```

Figure A.10 illustrates the logger console in operation as part of the modified planet viewer application.

This demonstration shows how straightforward it is to add simple logging capabilities to an Ajax application. The system is considerably simpler than server-side logging frameworks such as Apache's log4j. We leave it as an exercise for the reader to add multiple categories of logging that can be turned on and off independently.

Now let's move on to our next type of tool: the DOM inspector.

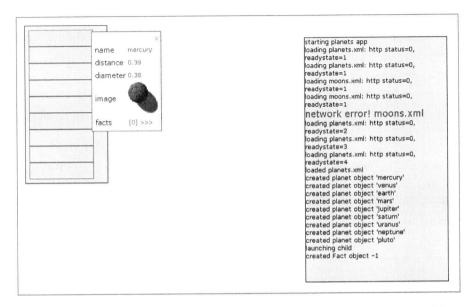

Figure A.10 The logging console in operation, monitoring object creation, network activity, user edits, and so on. We have added a second network request to a nonexistent server resource, moons.xml, to demonstrate the display of the styled logging message.

A.4 *DOM inspectors*

In an Ajax application, it is common to modify the user interface by modifying the DOM programmatically. Using a JavaScript debugger, we can walk through our DOM manipulation code one step at a time and ensure that it is doing what we want it to do.

The DOM, however, is still one step removed from the view presented to the user. We may be confident that our code is altering the DOM in the way that we think it is, but this won't necessarily translate into the user interface that we expect. A DOM inspector is a tool that allows the developer to inspect the relationships between the DOM tree that our code works with and the visible interface that the end user sees.

DOM inspectors need to be tightly integrated with the browser and always support only one make of browser. The most popular DOM inspector is the one that ships with Mozilla Firefox, so we'll look at that first, and then we'll look at the alternatives for Internet Explorer.

A.4.1 *Using the Mozilla DOM Inspector*

The DOM Inspector tool is bundled with Firefox but needs to be selected as a custom option during installation. If the DOM Inspector is installed, it will appear in the browser's menu system under the Tools menu as the option DOM Inspector. When initially opened, the DOM Inspector consists of two panes side by side (figure A.11). The left-hand pane presents a tree-table widget, typically showing only a document and an HTML node initially. The nodes may be opened to reveal a head and body to the document, and within the body, an assortment of nodes representing the HTML markup of a page, plus any elements that have been constructed programmatically. Where nodes have been assigned ID or CSS class attributes, these will be displayed in additional columns of the tree-table widgets.

This tree widget is synchronized to the page being displayed in the main browser window. Selecting a tree node with the mouse will make the related element in the page layout flash a red border. The relationship is two-way, too. By invoking the Search > Select Element by Click menu option on the DOM Inspector, the user can click on the web browser window and highlight the tree element corresponding to the element clicked upon. (There's also a toolbar button for this functionality.)

The right-hand pane lists information about the current node in one of several possible formats, including DOM node, CSS style rules, and as a JavaScript object (figure A.12). In the latter mode, the object may be programmatically scripted by right-clicking on the right-hand pane and selecting the Evaluate JavaScript button. The currently selected DOM element can be referred to as `target`, so, for example, typing in

```
target.style.border='4px solid blue'
```

will outline that element with a thick blue border.

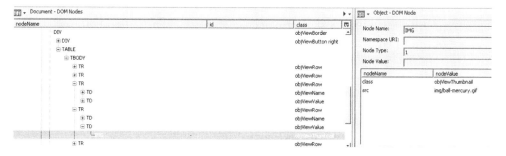

Figure A.11 The Mozilla DOM Inspector presents a structural view of the DOM behind a web page, including nodes declared in the HTML and those generated programmatically.

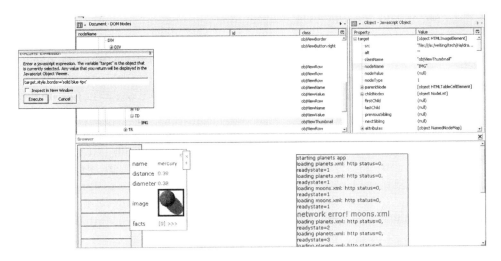

Figure A.12 The Mozilla DOM Inspector allows direct scripting access to elements in the DOM. The variable name `target` refers to the currently selected DOM node, in this case the image of the planet, whose border we have just altered.

The DOM Inspector also has a third pane, below the other two, into which the visible content of a document can be rendered (figure A.13). If the user types a page address into the URL bar and clicks on the Inspect button, this pane will appear, allowing the abstract DOM and the visible document to be examined side by side.

A.4.2 DOM inspectors for Internet Explorer

As with all the Mozilla-based toolkits, a major drawback is that the inspectors can't be used to inspect problems that occur only in Internet Explorer. Several DOM inspectors with similar functionality are available for Internet Explorer. Many are commercial or shareware, but some workable free versions also exist, such as the IEDocMon utility (see the Resources section for URLs).

Like the Mozilla DOM Inspector, IEDocMon provides a simple two-pane view of the DOM, with a tree on the left and node details on the right (figure A.13).

That concludes our discussions of specific types of development tools. One very active source of Ajax tools is the community that has sprung up around the Firefox browser's extensions capabilities. In the following section, we'll briefly outline how to find and install Firefox extensions.

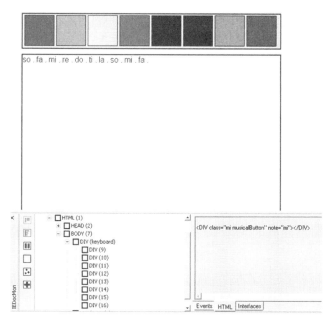

Figure A.13   The IEDocMon toolbar for Internet Explorer provides functionality similar to the Firefox DOM Inspector, allowing for rapid resolution of rendering issues with programmatically generated user interfaces.

A.4.3 *The Safari DOM Inspector for Mac OS X*

The Mac OS X browser Safari has a built-in DOM inspector too. This is available from the debug menu. The debug menu is not enabled by default. To enable it, open the Terminal application and type in the following:

```
defaults write com.apple.Safari IncludeDebugMenu 1
```

Depending on your privileges, you may need to `sudo` this command. Once it has executed, restart Safari and the debug menu should appear.

A.5 *Installing Firefox extensions*

We've already looked at two very useful Firefox extensions, the Venkman debugger and the LiveHTTPHeaders network debugger. There are many extensions available for Firefox, and several are designed for use by web developers. In this

Figure A.14 **The Firefox browser lists all installed extensions in a pop-up dialog. More extensions can be installed from the Web.**

section, we'll walk briefly through the process of installing a Firefox plug-in, using the Modify Headers extension as an example.

Firefox extensions are installed from the web browser itself. Initially, you need to locate the download page for the extension; in this case it's found at https://addons.mozilla.org/extensions. The Mozilla add-ons site can also be launched from the browser by clicking the Tools > Extensions menu and then selecting the Get More Extensions link in the pop-up dialog. Figure A.14 shows Firefox pointing at the Mozilla Update site page for the Modify Headers extension.

In this case, the hyperlink we need is the large Install Now button. We click on it, and a dialog appears, warning us of the dangers of installing unsigned extensions (figure A.15).

Unlike ordinary JavaScript code, extensions have full access to the local filesystem. Signing extensions offers a guarantee from the author that the extension hasn't been tampered with, but in practice, not all extensions are signed. After installation, the extension is registered in the pop-up Extensions dialog (figure A.16).

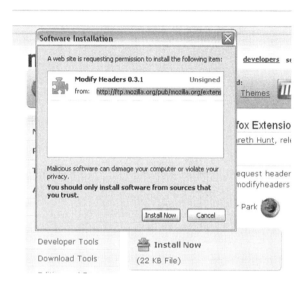

Figure A.15
Firefox extensions can be installed from the Web, using a special downloadable archive format.

All that remains is to close down all open Firefox windows (including DOM inspectors, debuggers, and so on), and restart Firefox. The extension is then ready to run, appearing as an option in the Tools menu (figure A.17).

Firefox supports a large number of extensions, many of which are aimed at web developers. Not all extensions are hosted on the addons.mozilla.org site, but this is certainly the first port of call for such things. The installation procedure is generally similar for all extensions, including the Venkman debugger that we discussed earlier.

This concludes our review of development tools for Ajax. We hope that it has provided you with some useful advice in getting your project off the ground.

Figure A.16
Newly installed extensions are visible in the Extensions dialog immediately but won't become active until the browser is restarted.

Figure A.17
After you restart the browser, the extension is ready to use.

A.6 Resources

This chapter was all about tools. Here are links to those that we featured:

- Textpad: www.textpad.com

- jEdit: www.jedit.org

- Eclipse: www.eclipse.org

- Eclipse JavaScript plug-ins: http://jseditor.sourceforge.net/

- Visual Studio Express: http://lab.msdn.microsoft.com/express/

- Dreamweaver: www.macromedia.com/software/dreamweaver/

- Komodo: www.activestate.com/Products/Komodo/

- Venkman Debugger: www.mozilla.org/projects/venkman/

- Microsoft Script debugger: www.microsoft.com/downloads/details.aspx?FamilyID=2f465be0-94fd-4569-b3c4-dffdf19ccd99&displaylang=en

- Charles: www.xk72.com/charles/

- Fiddler: www.fiddlertool.com

- LiveHttpHeaders: http://livehttpheaders.mozdev.org/

- Modify Headers extension: https://addons.mozilla.org/extensions/more-info.php?id=967&vid=4243

- IEDocMon DOM inspector for IE: www.cheztabor.com/IEDocMon/index.htm

JavaScript for object-oriented programmers

There are many routes into becoming a JavaScript programmer, ranging from graphic design to a serious programmer coming up from the business tiers.

This appendix won't aim to teach you how to program in JavaScript—there are already many good books and articles to help you do that. What I intend to record here are a few core concepts that will help Java and C# programmers make the leap to JavaScript programming in a relatively painless way. (The same is true to a lesser extent of C++ programmers, but C++ inherits a lot of strange flexibility from C, so that JavaScript should prove less of a shock to the system.) If you are a serious enterprise programmer with a grounding in OO design principles, then your first approaches to JavaScript may be overly influenced by your experience with languages such as Java and C#, and you may find yourself fighting against the language rather than working with it. I certainly did, and I've based this on my own experience as a programmer and in mentoring others along the same route.

JavaScript can do a lot of clever things that Java and C# can't. Some of these can help you to write better code, and some can only help you to shoot yourself in the foot more accurately! It's worth knowing about both, either to make use of the techniques or to avoid doing them unwittingly. If you are coming to Ajax from a structured OO language such as Java or C++, then I hope that reading this appendix will help you as much as I think it would have helped me a few years back!

B.1 JavaScript is not Java

What's in a name? In the case of Java and JavaScript, a lot of marketing and relatively little substance. JavaScript was renamed from "livescript" at the last minute by Netscape's marketing department, and now the name has stuck. Contrary to popular perception, JavaScript is not a descendent of the C family of languages. It owes a lot more to functional languages such as Scheme and Self, and it has quite a lot in common with Python, too. Unfortunately, it's been named after Java and syntactically styled to look like Java. In places, it will behave like Java, but in many places, it just plain won't.

Table B.1 summarizes the key differences.

Table B.1 Key features of JavaScript and their implications

Feature	Implications
Variables are loosely typed.	Variables are just declared as variables, not as integers, strings, or objects of a specific class. In JavaScript, it is legal to assign values of different types to the same variable.

continued on next page

Table B.1 Key features of JavaScript and their implications *(continued)*

Feature	Implications
Code is dynamically interpreted.	At runtime, code is stored as text and interpreted into machine instructions as the program runs, in contrast to precompiled languages such as Java, C, and C#. Users of your website can generally see the source code of your Ajax application. Furthermore, it allows for the possibility of code being generated dynamically by other code without resorting to special bytecode generators.
JavaScript functions are first-class objects.	A Java object's methods are tied to the object that owns them and can be invoked only via that object. JavaScript functions can be attached to objects so that they behave like methods, but they can also be invoked in other contexts and/or reattached to other objects at runtime.
JavaScript objects are prototype-based.	A Java, C++, or C# object has a defined type, with superclasses and virtual superclasses or interfaces. This strictly defines its functionality. Any JavaScript object is just an object, which is just an associative array in disguise. Prototypes can be used to emulate Java-style types in JavaScript, but the similarity is only skin deep.

These differences allow the language to be used in different ways and open up the possibility of a number of weird tricks worthy of a seasoned Lisp hacker. If you're a really clever, disciplined coder, you can take advantage of these tricks to do marvelous things, and you might even do so beyond a few hundred lines of code. If, on the other hand, you only *think* you're really clever and disciplined, you can quickly end up flat on your face.

I've tried it a few times and come to the conclusion that keeping things simple is generally a good thing. If you're working with a team, coding standards or guidelines should address these issues if the technical manager feels it is appropriate.

However, there is a second reason for knowing about these differences and tricks: the browser will use some of them internally, so understanding what is going on can save you much time and pain in debugging a badly behaved application. In particular, I've found it helpful to know where the code is not behaving like a Java object would, given that much of the apparent similarity is only apparent.

So read on, and find out what JavaScript objects really look like when the lights are out, how they are composed of member fields and functions, and what a JavaScript function is really capable of.

B.2 Objects in JavaScript

JavaScript doesn't require the use of objects or even functions. It is possible to write a JavaScript program as a single stream of text that is executed directly as it is read by the interpreter. As a program gets bigger, though, functions and objects become a tremendously useful way of organizing your code, and we recommend you use both.

The simplest way to create a new JavaScript object is to invoke the built-in constructor for the `Object` class:

```
var myObject=new Object();
```

We'll look at other approaches, and what the new keyword really does, in section B.2.2. Our object `myObject` is initially "empty," that is, it has no properties or methods. Adding them in is quite simple, so let's see how to do it now.

B.2.1 Building ad hoc objects

As already noted, the JavaScript object is essentially just an associative array, with fields and methods keyed by name. A C-like syntax is slapped on top to make it look familiar to C-family programmers, but the underlying implementation can be exploited in other ways, too. We can build up complex objects line by line, adding new variables and functions as we think of them.

There are two ways of building up objects in this ad hoc fashion. The first of these is to simply use JavaScript to create the object. The second is to use a special notation known as JSON. Let's start with the plain old JavaScript technique.

Using JavaScript statements

In the middle of a complicated piece of code, we may want to assign a value to some object's property. JavaScript object properties are read/write and can be assigned by the = operator. Let's add a property to our simple object:

```
myObject.shoeSize="12";
```

In a structured OO language, we would need to define a class that declared a property `shoeSize` or else suffer a compiler error. Not so with JavaScript. In fact, just to emphasize the array-like nature, we can also reference properties using array syntax:

```
myObject['shoeSize']="12";
```

This notation is clumsy for ordinary use but has the advantage that the array index is a JavaScript expression, offering a form of runtime reflection, which we'll return to in section B.2.4.

We can also add a new function to our object dynamically:

```
myObject.speakYourShoeSize=function(){
  alert("shoe size : "+this.shoeSize);
}
```

Or borrow a predefined function:

```
function sayHello(){
  alert('hello, my shoeSize is  '+this.shoeSize);
}
...
myObject.sayHello=sayHello;
```

Note that in assigning the predefined function, we omit the parentheses. If we were to write

```
myObject.sayHello=sayHello();
```

then we would execute the sayHello function and assign the return value, in this case null, to the sayHello property of `myObject`.

We can attach objects to other objects in order to build up complex data models and so on:

```
var myLibrary=new Object();
myLibrary.books=new Array();
myLibrary.books[0]=new Object();
myLibrary.books[0].title="Turnip Cultivation through the Ages";
myLibrary.books[0].authors=new Array();
var jim=new Object();
jim.name="Jim Brown";
jim.age=9;
myLibrary.books[0].authors[0]=jim;
```

This can quickly become tedious (often the case where turnips are involved, I'm afraid), and JavaScript offers a compact notation that we can use to assemble object graphs more quickly, known as JSON. Let's have a look at it now.

Using JSON

The JavaScript Object Notation (JSON) is a core feature of the language. It provides a concise mechanism for creating arrays and object graphs. In order to understand JSON, we need to know how JavaScript arrays work, so let's cover the basics of them first.

JavaScript has a built-in `Array` class that can be instantiated using the `new` keyword:

```
myLibrary.books=new Array();
```

Arrays can have values assigned to them by number, much like a conventional C or Java array:

```
myLibrary.books[4]=somePredefinedBook;
```

Or they can be associated with a key value, like a Java Map or Python Dictionary, or, indeed, any JavaScript Object:

```
myLibrary.books["BestSeller"]=somePredefinedBook;
```

This syntax is good for fine-tuning, but building a large array or object in the first place can be tedious. The shorthand for creating a numerically indexed array is to use square braces, with the entries being written as a comma-separated list of values, thus:

```
myLibrary.books=[predefinedBook1,predefinedBook2,predefinedBook3];
```

And to build a JavaScript Object, we use curly braces, with each value written as a key:value pair:

```
myLibrary.books={
  bestSeller   : predefinedBook1,
  cookbook     : predefinedBook2,
  spaceFiller  : predefinedBook3
};
```

In both notations, extra white space is ignored, allowing us to pretty-print for clarity. Keys can also have spaces in them, and can be quoted in the JSON notation, for example:

```
"Best Seller" : predefinedBook1,
```

We can nest JSON notations to create one-line definitions of complex object hierarchies (albeit rather a long line):

```
var myLibrary={
  location : "my house",
  keywords : [ "root vegetables", "turnip", "tedium" ],
  books: [
    {
      title : "Turnip Cultivation through the Ages",
      authors : [
        { name: "Jim Brown", age: 9 },
        { name: "Dick Turnip", age: 312 }
      ],
      publicationDate : "long ago"
    },
    {
      title : "Turnip Cultivation through the Ages, vol. 2",
```

```
      authors : [
        { name: "Jim Brown", age: 35 }
      ],
      publicationDate : new Date(1605,11,05)
    }
  ]
};
```

I have assigned three properties to the myLibrary object here: location is a simple string, keywords is a numerical list of strings, and books a numerically indexed list of objects, each with a title (a string), a publication date (a JavaScript Date object in one case and a string in the other), and a list of authors (an array). Each author is represented by a name and age parameter. JSON has provided us with a concise mechanism for creating this information in a single pass, something that would otherwise have taken many lines of code (and greater bandwidth).

Sharp-eyed readers will have noted that we populated the publication date for the second book using a JavaScript Date object. In assigning the value we can use any JavaScript code, in fact, even a function that we defined ourselves:

```
function gunpowderPlot(){
  return  new Date(1605,11,05);
}

var volNum=2;

var turnipVol2={
  title : "Turnip Cultivation through the Ages, vol. "
    +volNum,
  authors : [
    { name: "Jim Brown", age: 35 }
      ],
      publicationDate : gunpowderPlot()
    }
  ]
};
```

Here the title of the book is calculated dynamically by an inline expression, and the publicationDate is set to the return value from a predefined function.

In the previous example, we defined a function gunpowderPlot() that was evaluated at the time the object was created. We can also define member functions for our JSON-invoked objects, which can be invoked later by the object:

```
var turnipVol2={
  title : "Turnip Cultivation through the Ages, vol. "+volNum,
  authors : [
    { name: "Jim Brown", age: 35 }
      ],
```

```
        publicationDate : gunpowderPlot()
      }
    ],
    summarize:function(len){
      if (!len){ len=7; }
      var summary=this.title+" by "
        +this.authors[0].name
        +" and his cronies is very boring. Z";
      for (var i=0;i<len;i++){
        summary+="z";
      }
      alert(summary);
    }
  };

  ...

  turnipVol2.summarize(6);
```

The `summarize()` function has all the features of a standard JavaScript function, such as parameters and a context object identified by the keyword `this`. Indeed, once the object is created, it is just another JavaScript object, and we can mix and match the JavaScript and JSON notations as we please. We can use JavaScript to fine-tune an object declared in JSON:

```
var numbers={ one:1, two:2, three:3 };
numbers.five=5;
```

We initially define an object using JSON syntax and then add to it using plain JavaScript. Equally, we can extend our JavaScript-created objects using JSON:

```
var cookbook=new Object();
cookbook.pageCount=321;
cookbook.author={
  firstName: "Harry",
  secondName: "Christmas",
  birthdate: new Date(1900,2,29),
  interests: ["cheese","whistling",
    "history of lighthouse keeping"]
};
```

With the built-in JavaScript `Object` and `Array` classes and the JSON notation, we can build object hierarchies as complicated as we like, and we could get by with nothing else. JavaScript also offers a means for creating objects that provides a comforting resemblance to class definitions for OO programmers, so let's look at this next and see what it can offer us.

B.2.2 *Constructor functions, classes, and prototypes*

In OO programming, we generally create objects by stating the class from which we want them to be instantiated. Both Java and JavaScript support the new keyword, allowing us to create instances of a predefined kind of object. Here the similarity between the two ends.

In Java, everything (bar a few primitives) is an object, ultimately descended from the java.lang.Object class. The Java virtual machine has a built-in understanding of classes, fields, and methods, and when we declare in Java

```
MyObject myObj=new MyObject(arg1,arg2);
```

we first declare the type of the variable and then instantiate it using the relevant constructor. The prerequisite for success is that the class MyObject has been declared and offers a suitable constructor.

JavaScript, too, has a concept of objects and classes but no built-in concept of inheritance. In fact, every JavaScript object is really an instance of the same base class, a class that is capable of binding member fields and functions to itself at runtime. So, it is possible to assign arbitrary properties to an object on the fly:

```
MyJavaScriptObject.completelyNewProperty="something";
```

This free-for-all can be organized into something more familiar to the poor OO developer by using a prototype, which defines properties and functions that will automatically be bound to an object when it is constructed using a particular function. It is possible to write object-based JavaScript without the use of prototypes, but they offer a degree of regularity and familiarity to OO developers that is highly desirable when coding complex rich-client applications.

In JavaScript, then, we can write something that looks similar to the Java declaration

```
var myObj=new MyObject();
```

but we do not define a class MyObject, but rather a function with the same name. Here is a simple constructor:

```
function MyObject(name,size){
  this.name=name;
  this.size=size;
}
```

We can subsequently invoke it as follows:

```
var myObj=new MyObject("tiddles","7.5 meters");
alert("size of "+myObj.name+" is "+myObj.size);
```

Anything set as a property of this in the constructor is subsequently available as a member of the object. We might want to internalize the call to alert() as well, so that tiddles can take responsibility for telling us how big it is. One common idiom is to declare the function inside the constructor:

```
function MyObject(name,size){
  this.name=name;
  this.size=size;
  this.tellSize=function(){
    alert("size of "+this.name+" is "+this.size);
  }
}

var myObj=new Object("tiddles","7.5 meters");
myObj.tellSize();
```

This works, but is less than ideal in two respects. First, for every instance of MyObject that we create, we create a new function. As responsible Ajax programmers, memory leaks are never far from our minds (see chapter 7), and if we plan on creating many such objects, we should certainly avoid this idiom. Second, we have accidentally created a closure here—in this case a fairly harmless one—but as soon as we involve DOM nodes in our constructor, we can expect more serious problems. We'll look at closures in more detail later in this appendix. For now, let's look at the safer alternative, which is something known as a *prototype*.

A prototype is a property of JavaScript objects, for which no real equivalent exists in OO languages. Functions and properties can be associated with a constructor's prototype. The prototype and new keyword will then work together, and, when a function is invoked by new, all properties and methods of the prototype for the function are attached to the resulting object. That sounds a bit strange, but it's simple enough in action:

```
function MyObject(name,size){
  this.name=name;
  this.size=size;
}

MyObject.prototype.tellSize=function(){
  alert("size of "+this.name+" is "+this.size);
}

var myObj=new MyObject("tiddles","7.5 meters");
myObj.tellSize();
```

First, we declare the constructor as before, and then we add functions to the prototype. When we create an instance of the object, the function is attached. The keyword this resolves to the object instance at runtime, and all is well.

Note the ordering of events here. We can refer to the prototype only after the constructor function is declared, and objects will inherit from the prototype only what has already been added to it before the constructor is invoked. The prototype can be altered between invocations to the constructor, and we can attach anything to the prototype, not just a function:

```
MyObject.prototype.color="red";
var obj1=new MyObject();

MyObject.prototype.color="blue";
MyObject.prototype.soundEffect="boOOOoing!!";
var obj2=new MyObject();
```

`obj1` will be red, with no sound effect, and `obj2` will be blue with an annoyingly cheerful sound effect! There is generally little value in altering prototypes on the fly in this way. It's useful to know that such things can happen, but using the prototype to define class-like behavior for JavaScript objects is the safe and sure route.

Interestingly, the prototype of certain built-in classes (that is, those implemented by the browser and exposed through JavaScript, also known as *host objects*) can be extended, too. Let's have a look at how that works now.

B.2.3 *Extending built-in classes*

JavaScript is designed to be embedded in programs that can expose their own native objects, typically written in C++ or Java, to the scripting environment. These objects are usually described as built-in or host objects, and they differ in some regards to the user-defined objects that we have discussed so far. Nonetheless, the prototype mechanism can work with built-in classes, too. Within the web browser, DOM nodes cannot be extended in the Internet Explorer browser, but other core classes work across all major browsers. Let's take the `Array` class as an example and define a few useful helper functions:

```
Array.prototype.indexOf=function(obj){
  var result=-1;
  for (var i=0;i<this.length;i++){
    if (this[i]==obj){
      result=i;
      break;
    }
  }
  return result;
}
```

This provides an extra function to the `Array` object that returns the numerical index of an object in a given array, or -1 if the array doesn't contain the object. We can build on this further, writing a convenience method to check whether an array contains an object:

```
Array.prototype.contains=function(obj){
  return (this.indexOf(obj)>=0);
}
```

and then add another function for appending new members after optionally checking for duplicates:

```
Array.prototype.append=function(obj,nodup){
  if (!(nodup && this.contains(obj))){
    this[this.length]=obj;
  }
}
```

Any `Array` objects created after the declaration of these functions, whether by the new operator or as part of a JSON expression, will be able to use these functions:

```
var numbers=[1,2,3,4,5];
var got8=numbers.contains(8);
numbers.append("cheese",true);
```

As with the prototypes of user-defined objects, these can be manipulated in the midst of object creation, but I generally recommend that the prototype be modified once only at the outset of a program, to avoid unnecessary confusion, particularly if you're working with a team of programmers.

Prototypes can offer us a lot, then, when developing client-side object models for our Ajax applications. A meticulous object modeler used to C++, Java, or C# may not only want to define various object types but to implement inheritance between types. JavaScript doesn't offer this out of the box, but the prototype can come in useful here, too. Let's find out how.

B.2.4 *Inheritance of prototypes*

Object orientation provides not only support for distinct object classes but also a structured hierarchy of inheritance between them. The classic example is the Shape object, which defines methods for computing perimeter and area, on top of which we build concrete implementations for rectangles, squares, triangles, and circles.

With inheritance comes the concept of *scope*. The scope of an object's methods or properties determines who can use it—that is, whether it is public, private, or protected.

Scope and inheritance can be useful features when defining a domain model. Unfortunately, JavaScript doesn't support either natively. That hasn't stopped people from trying, however, and some fairly elegant solutions have developed.

Doug Crockford (see the Resources section at the end of this appendix) has developed some ingenious workarounds that enable both inheritance and scope in JavaScript objects. What he has accomplished is undoubtedly impressive and, unfortunately, too involved to merit a detailed treatment here. The syntax that his techniques require can be somewhat impenetrable to the casual reader, and in a team-based project, adopting such techniques should be considered similar to adopting a Java framework of the size and complexity of Struts or Tapestry—that is, either everybody uses it or nobody does. I urge anyone with an interest in this area to read the essays on Crockford's website.

Within the world of object orientation, there has been a gradual move away from complex use of inheritance and toward composition. With composition, common functionality is moved out into a helper class, which can be attached as a member of any class that needs it. In many scenarios, composition can provide similar benefits to inheritance, and JavaScript supports composition perfectly adequately.

The next stop in our brief tour of JavaScript objects is to look at reflection.

B.2.5 *Reflecting on JavaScript objects*

In the normal course of writing code, the programmer has a clear understanding of how the objects he is dealing with are composed, that is, what their properties and methods do. In some cases, though, we need to be able to deal with completely unknown objects and discover the nature of their properties and methods before dealing with them. For example, if we are writing a logging or debugging system, we may be required to handle arbitrary objects dumped on us from the outside world. This discovery process is known as *reflection*, and it should be familiar to most Java and .NET programmers.

If we want to find out whether a JavaScript object supports a certain property or method, we can simply test for it:

```
if (MyObject.someProperty){
  ...
}
```

This will fail, however, if `MyObject.someProperty` has been assigned the boolean value `false`, or a numerical `0`, or the special value `null`. A more rigorous test would be to write

```
if (typeof(MyObject.someProperty) != "undefined"){
```

If we are concerned about the type of the property, we can also use the `instanceof` operator. This recognizes a few basic built-in types:

```
if (myObj instanceof Array){
  ...
}else if (myObj instanceof Object){
  ...
}
```

as well as any class definitions that we define ourselves through constructors:

```
if (myObj instanceof MyObject){
  ...
}
```

If you do like using `instanceof` to test for custom classes, be aware of a couple of "gotchas." First, JSON doesn't support it—anything created with JSON is either a JavaScript `Object` or an `Array`. Second, built-in objects *do* support inheritance among themselves. `Function` and `Array`, for example, both inherit from `Object`, so the order of testing matters. If we write

```
function testType(myObj){
  if (myObj instanceof Array){
    alert("it's an array");
  }else if (myObj instanceof Object){
    alert("it's an object");
  }
}
testType([1,2,3,4]);
```

and pass an Array through the code, we will be told—correctly—that we have an Array. If, on the other hand, we write

```
function testType(myObj){
  if (myObj instanceof Object){
    alert("it's an object");
  }else if (myObj instanceof Array){
    alert("it's an array");
  }
}
testType([1,2,3,4]);
```

then we will be told that we have an Object, which is also technically correct but probably not what we intended.

Finally, there are times when we may want to exhaustively discover all of an object's properties and functions. We can do this using the simple for loop:

```
function MyObject(){
  this.color='red';
  this.flavor='strawberry';
```

```
    this.azimuth='45 degrees';
    this.favoriteDog='collie';
}

var myObj=new MyObject();
var debug="discovering...\n";
for (var i in myObj){
  debug+=i+" -> "+myObj[i]+"\n";
}
alert(debug);
```

This loop will execute four times, returning all the values set in the constructor. The `for` loop syntax works on built-in objects, too—the simple `debug` loop above produces very big alert boxes when pointed at DOM nodes! A more developed version of this technique is used in the examples in chapters 5 and 6 to develop the recursive ObjectViewer user interface.

There is one more feature of the conventional object-oriented language that we need to address—the virtual class or interface. Let's look at that now.

B.2.6 *Interfaces and duck typing*

There are many times in software development when we will want to specify how something behaves without providing a concrete implementation. In the case of our Shape object being subclassed by squares, circles, and so on, for example, we know that we will never hold a shape in our hands that is not a specific type of shape. The base concept of the Shape object is a convenient abstraction of common properties, without a real-world equivalent.

A C++ virtual class or a Java interface provides us with the necessary mechanism to define these concepts in code. We often speak of the interface defining a contract between the various components of the software. With the contract in place, the author of a Shape-processing library doesn't need to consider the specific implementations, and the author of a new implementation of Shape doesn't need to consider the internals of any library code or any other existing implementations of the interface.

Interfaces provide good separation of concerns and underpin many design patterns. If we're using design patterns in Ajax, we want to use interfaces. JavaScript has no formal concept of an interface, so how do we do it?

The simplest approach is to define the contract informally and simply rely on the developers at each side of the interface to know what they are doing. Dave Thomas has given this approach the engaging name of "duck typing"—if it walks like a duck and it quacks like a duck, then it is a duck. Similarly with our `Shape` interface, if it can compute an area and a perimeter, then it is a shape.

Let's suppose that we want to add the area of two shapes together. In Java, we could write

```
public double addAreas(Shape s1, Shape s2){
  return s1.getArea()+s2.getArea();
}
```

The method signature specifically forbids us from passing in anything other than a shape, so inside the method body, we know we're following the contract. In JavaScript, our method arguments aren't typed, so we have no such guarantees:

```
function addAreas(s1,s2){
  return s1.getArea()+s2.getArea();
}
```

If either object doesn't have a function `getArea()` attached to it, then we will get a JavaScript error. We can check for the presence of the function before we call it:

```
function hasArea(obj){
  return obj && obj.getArea && obj.getArea instanceof Function;
}
```

and modify our function to make use of the check:

```
function addAreas(s1,s2){
  var total=null;
  if (hasArea(s1) && hasArea(s2)){
    total=s1.getArea()+s2.getArea();
  }
  return total;
}
```

Using JavaScript reflection, in fact, we can write a generic function to check that an object has a function of a specific name:

```
function implements(obj,funcName){
  return obj && obj[funcName] && obj[funcName] instanceof Function;
}
```

Or, we can attach it to the prototype for the Object class:

```
Object.prototype.implements=function(funcName){
  return this && this[funcName] && this[funcName] instanceof Function;
}
```

That allows us to check specific functions by name:

```
function hasArea(obj){
  return obj.implements("getArea");
}
```

or even to test for compliance with an entire interface:

```
function isShape(obj){
  return obj.implements("getArea") && obj.implements("getPerimeter");
}
```

This gives us some degree of safety, although still not as much as we would get under Java. A rogue object might implement `getArea()` to return a string rather than a numerical value, for example. We have no way of knowing the return type of a JavaScript function unless we call it, because JavaScript functions have no predefined type. (Indeed, we could write a function that returns a number during the week and a string on weekends.) Writing a set of simple test functions to check return types is easy enough; for example:

```
function isNum(arg){
  return parseFloat(arg)!=NaN;
}
```

`NaN` is short for "not a number," a special JavaScript variable for handling number format errors. This function will actually return `true` for strings if they begin with a numeric portion, in fact. `parseFloat()` and its cousin `parseInt()` will try their best to extract a recognizable number where they can. `parseFloat("64 hectares")` will evaluate to `64`, not `NaN`.

We could firm up our `addAreas()` function a little further:

```
function addAreas(s1,s2){
  var total=null;
  if (hasArea(s1) && hasArea(s2)){
    var a1=s1.getArea();
    var a2=s2.getArea();
    if (isNum(a1) && isNum(a2)){
      total=parseFloat(a1)+parseFloat(a2);
    }
  }
  return total;
}
```

I call `parseFloat()` on both arguments to correctly handle strings that slip through the net. If `s1` returns a value of `32` and `s2` a value of `64 hectares`, then `addAreas()` will return `96`. If I didn't use `parseFloat`, I'd get a misleading value of `3264 hectares`!

In summary, duck typing keeps things simple but requires you to trust your development team to keep track of all the details. Duck typing is popular among the Ruby community, who are generally a very smart bunch. As one moves from a single author or small tightly bound team to larger projects involving separate subgroups, this trust inevitably weakens. If you want to add a few checks and balances to your code on top of duck typing, then perhaps this section will have shown you where to start.

We've looked at the language from the point of view of objects. Now let's drill down a little to look at these functions that we've been throwing around and see what they really are.

B.3   *Methods and functions*

We've been defining functions and calling them in the previous section and in the rest of this book. A Java or C# programmer might have assumed that they were something like a method, defined with a slightly funny-looking syntax. In this section, we'll take functions apart a bit more and see what we can do with them.

B.3.1   *Functions as first-class citizens*

Functions are a bit like Java methods in that they have arguments and return values when invoked, but there is a key difference. A Java method is inherently bound to the class that defined it and cannot exist apart from that class. A JavaScript function is a free-floating entity, a first-class object in its own right. (Static Java methods lie somewhere in between these two—they are not bound to any instance of an object but are still attached to a class definition.)

Programmers who have worked their way through the C family may think "Ah, so it's like a function pointer in C++, then." It is indeed, but that's not the end of it.

In JavaScript, Function is a type of built-in object. As expected, it contains executable code, and can be invoked, but it is also a descendant of Object, and can do everything that a JavaScript object can, such as storing properties by name. It is quite possible (and quite common) for a Function object to have other Function objects attached to it as methods.

We've already seen how to get a reference to a Function object. More usually, we would want to reference a function and invoke it in a single line, such as

```
var result=MyObject.doSomething(x,y,z)
```

However, the Function is a first-class object, and it can also be executed via the `call()` method (and its close cousin `apply()`):

```
var result=MyObject.doSomething.call(MyOtherObject,x,y,z)
```

or even

```
var result=MyObject['doSomething'].call(MyOtherObject,x,y,z)
```

The first argument of `Function.call()` is the object that will serve as the function context during the invocation, and subsequent arguments are treated as arguments to the function call. `apply()` works slightly differently in that the second argument is an array of arguments to pass to the function call, allowing greater flexibility in programmatically calling functions whose argument list length is undetermined.

It's worth pointing out here that the argument list to a JavaScript function is not of a fixed length. Calling a Java or C# method with more or fewer arguments than it declares would generate a compile-time error. JavaScript just ignores any extra args and assigns `undefined` to missing ones. A particularly clever function might query its own argument list through the `arguments` property and assign sensible defaults to missing values, throw an exception, or take any other remedial action. This can be exploited to combine a getter and setter method into a single function, for example:

```
function area(value){
  if (value){
    this.area=value;
  }
  return this.area;
}
```

If we simply call `area()`, then `value` is undefined, so no assignment takes place, and our function acts as a getter. If a value is passed in, our function acts as a setter. This technique is used extensively by Mike Foster's x library (see the Resources section at the end of this chapter, and also chapter 3), so if you plan on working with that, you'll soon be familiar with the idiom.

Functions become really interesting, though, when we take advantage of their independence as first-class objects.

B.3.2 *Attaching functions to objects*

As a functional language, JavaScript allows us to define functions in the absence of any object, for example:

```
function doSomething(x,y,z){ ... }
```

Functions can also be defined inline:

```
var doSomething=function(x,y,z){ ... }
```

As a concession to object-orientation, functions may be attached to objects, giving the semblance of a Java or C# method. There is more than one way of doing this.

and create an instance of our Dog class:

```
var Snowy=new Dog("snowy","wau! wau!");
```

Snowy wants to show us his bark, but, although we've defined it for him, he has no function through which to express it. He can, however, hijack the `Tree` class's function:

```
var tmpFunc=Beech.describe;
tmpFunc.call(Snowy);
```

Remember, the first argument to `function.call()` is the context object, that is, the object that the special variable `this` will resolve to. The previous code will generate an alert box displaying the text `Snowy: leaf=undefined, bark=wau! wau!`. Well, it's better than nothing for the poor dog.

So what's going on here? How can a dog call a function that really belongs to a tree? The answer is that the function doesn't belong to the tree. Despite being peppered with references to this, assigning the function to the `Tree` prototype binds it only inasmuch as it enables us to use the shorter `MyTree.describe()` notation. Internally, the function is stored as a piece of text that gets evaluated every time it is called, and that allows the meaning of `this` to differ from one invocation to the next.

Borrowing functions is a neat trick that we can use in our own code, but in production-quality code, we'd prefer to see someone implement a `bark()` method for Snowy of his very own. The real reason for discussing this behavior is that when you are writing event-handling code, the web browser will do it for you behind the scenes.

B.3.4 *Ajax event handling and function contexts*

Ajax event handlers are pretty much the same as most GUI toolkit languages, with specialized categories for mouse and keyboard events, as we saw in chapter 4. Our example uses the `onclick` handler, fired when a mouse is clicked on a visible element. A full discussion of DHTML event handling is beyond the scope of this book, but let's take the time here to highlight a particular issue that can often trip up the unwary.

Event handlers can be declared either as part of the HTML markup; for example

```
<div id='myDiv' onclick='alert(this.id)'></div>
```

or programmatically; for example:

and create an instance of our Dog class:

```
var Snowy=new Dog("snowy","wau! wau!");
```

Snowy wants to show us his bark, but, although we've defined it for him, he has no function through which to express it. He can, however, hijack the `Tree` class's function:

```
var tmpFunc=Beech.describe;
tmpFunc.call(Snowy);
```

Remember, the first argument to `function.call()` is the context object, that is, the object that the special variable `this` will resolve to. The previous code will generate an alert box displaying the text `Snowy: leaf=undefined, bark=wau! wau!`. Well, it's better than nothing for the poor dog.

So what's going on here? How can a dog call a function that really belongs to a tree? The answer is that the function doesn't belong to the tree. Despite being peppered with references to this, assigning the function to the `Tree` prototype binds it only inasmuch as it enables us to use the shorter `MyTree.describe()` notation. Internally, the function is stored as a piece of text that gets evaluated every time it is called, and that allows the meaning of `this` to differ from one invocation to the next.

Borrowing functions is a neat trick that we can use in our own code, but in production-quality code, we'd prefer to see someone implement a `bark()` method for Snowy of his very own. The real reason for discussing this behavior is that when you are writing event-handling code, the web browser will do it for you behind the scenes.

B.3.4 *Ajax event handling and function contexts*

Ajax event handlers are pretty much the same as most GUI toolkit languages, with specialized categories for mouse and keyboard events, as we saw in chapter 4. Our example uses the `onclick` handler, fired when a mouse is clicked on a visible element. A full discussion of DHTML event handling is beyond the scope of this book, but let's take the time here to highlight a particular issue that can often trip up the unwary.

Event handlers can be declared either as part of the HTML markup; for example

```
<div id='myDiv' onclick='alert:alert(this.id)'></div>
```

or programmatically; for example:

```
function clickHandler(){ alert(this.id); }
myDiv.onclick=clickHandler;
```

Note that in the programmatic case, we pass a reference to the Function object (that is no () after the clickHandler). When declaring the function in the HTML, we are effectively declaring an anonymous function inline, equivalent to

```
myDiv.onclick=function(){ alert(this.id); }
```

Note that in both cases, the function has no arguments assigned to it, nor is there any way for us to pass in arguments with the mouse click. However, when we click on the DOM element, the function is called with an Event object as the argument and the element itself as the context object. Knowing this can save a lot of grief and puzzlement, particularly when you're writing object-based code. The key source of confusion is that the DOM node is always passed as context, even if the function is attached to the prototype of a different object.

In the following example, we define a simple object with an event handler for a visible GUI element that it knows about. We can think of the object as the Model in MVC terms, with the event handler taking the role of Controller, and the DOM element being the View.

```
function myObj(id,div){
  this.id=id;
  this.div=div;

  this.div.onclick=this.clickHandler;
}
```

The constructor takes an internal ID and a DOM element, to which it assigns an onclick handler. We define the event handler as follows:

```
myObj.prototype.clickHandler=function(event){
  alert(this.id);
}
```

So, when we click on the GUI element, it will alert us to the ID of that object, right? In fact, it won't, because the myObj.clickHandler function will get borrowed by the browser (just as our wayward dog borrowed a method from the tree object in the previous section) and invoked in the context of the element, not the Model object. Since the element happens to have a built-in id property, it will show a value, and, depending on your naming conventions, it may even be the same as the Model object's ID, allowing the misunderstanding to continue for some time.

If we want the event handler to refer to the Model object that we've attached it to, we need another way of passing the reference to that object across. There are two idioms for doing this that I've commonly come across. One is clearly superior to the other, in my opinion, but I coded for years using the other one, and it works. One of the aims of this book is to give names to the patterns (and anti-patterns) that we have adopted by habit, so I will present both here.

Referencing the Model by name

In this solution, we assign a globally unique ID to each instance of our Model object and keep a global array of these objects referenced by the ID. Given a reference to a DOM element, we can then reference its Model object by using part of the ID as a key to the lookup array. Figure B.1 illustrates this strategy.

Generating a unique ID for every element is an overhead in this approach, but ID generation can be accomplished fairly automatically. We can use the array length as part of the key, for example, or a database key, if we're generating code on the web server.

As a simple example, we're creating an object of type myObj, which has a clickable title bar that invokes a function `myObj.foo()`.

Here is the global array:

```
var MyObjects=new Array();
```

And here is the constructor function, which registers the Model object with that array:

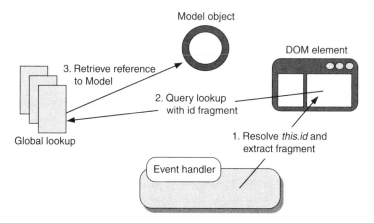

Figure B.1 Referencing the Model from an event handler function by name. The DOM element ID is parsed, and the parsed value used as a key to a global lookup array.

```
function myObj(id){
  this.uid=id;
  MyObjects[this.uid]=this;
  ...
  this.render();
}
```

Here is a method of the myObj object, which does something exciting. We want to invoke this when the title bar is clicked:

```
myObj.prototype.foo=function(){
  alert('foooo!!! '+this.uid);
}
```

Here is the object's render() method, which creates various DOM nodes:

```
myObj.prototype.render=function(){
  ...
  this.body=document.createElement("div");
  this.body.id=this.uid+"_body";
  ...
  this.titleBar=document.createElement("div");
  this.titleBar.id=this.uid+"_titleBar";
  this.titleBar.onclick=fooEventHandler;
  ...
}
```

When we construct any DOM nodes in the view for this Model object, we assign an ID value to them that contains the Model object ID.

Note that we refer to a function fooEventHandler() and set it as the onclick property of our title bar DOM element:

```
function fooEventHandler(event){
  var modelObj=getMyObj(this.id);
    if (modelObj){ modelObj.foo(); }
  }
}
```

The event handler function will need to find the instance of myObj in order to invoke its foo() method. We provide a finder method:

```
function getMyObj(id){
  var key=id.split("_")[0];
  return  MyObjects[key];
}
```

It has a reference to the DOM node and can use its id property to extract a key from which to retrieve the Model object from the global array.

And there it is. The *Reference Model By Name* method served me well for a few years, and it works, but there is a simpler, cleaner way that doesn't pepper your

DOM tree with lengthy IDs. (Actually, I never reached a decision as to whether that was good or bad. It was a waste of memory, for sure, but it also made debugging in the Mozilla DOM Inspector very easy.)

Attaching a Model to the DOM node

In this second approach to DOM event handling, everything is done with object references, not strings, and no global lookup array is needed. This is the approach that has been used throughout this book. Figure B.2 illustrates this approach.

This approach simplifies the event handler's job considerably. The constructor function for the Model object needs no specialized ID manipulation, and the `foo()` method is defined as before. When we construct DOM nodes, we exploit JavaScript's dynamic ability to attach arbitrary attributes to any object and clip the Model object directly onto the DOM node receiving the event:

```
myObj.prototype.createView=function(){
  ...
  this.body=document.createElement("div");
  this.body.modelObj=this;
  ...
  this.titleBar=document.createElement("div");
  this.titleBar.modelObj=this;
  this.titleBar.onclick=fooEventHandler;
  ...
}
```

When we write the event handler, we can then get a direct reference back to the Model:

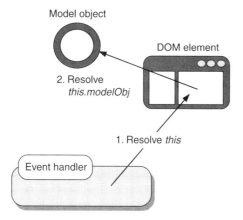

Figure B.2
Attaching a reference to the Model directly to a DOM node makes it easier for the event handler function to find the Model at runtime.

```
function fooEventHandler(event){
  var modelObj=this.modelObj;
    if (modelObj){ modelObj.foo(); }
  }
}
```

No finders, no global lookups—it's as simple as that.

One word of warning, however. When using this pattern, we create a cyclic reference between a DOM and a non-DOM variable, and web browser folklore has it that this is bad for garbage collection under certain popular browsers of the day. If this pattern is used correctly, memory overheads can be avoided, but I'd recommend you study chapter 7 before implementing the *Attach Model To* DOM *Node* pattern.

Understanding how a JavaScript function has defined its context has helped us to develop an elegant reusable solution for the browser event model, then. The ability of a function to switch between contexts can be confusing at first, but understanding the model behind us helps to work with it.

The final thing that we need to understand about JavaScript functions is the language's ability to create closures. Again, Java and C# lack the concept of closures, although some Java and .NET scripting languages, such as Groovy and Boo, support them, and C# 2.0 will support them, too. Let's look at what they are and how to work with them.

B.3.5 *Closures in JavaScript*

On its own, a Function object is incomplete—to invoke it, we need to pass in a context object and a set of arguments (possibly an empty set). At its simplest, a closure can be thought of as a Function bundled with all the resources that it needs to execute.

Closures are created in JavaScript implicitly, rather than explicitly. There is no constructor function `new Closure()` and no way to get a handle on a closure object. Creating a closure is as simple as declaring a function within a code block (such as another function) and making that function available outside the block.

Again, this sounds a bit weird conceptually but is simple enough when we look at an example. Let's define a simple object to represent a robot and record the system clock time at which each robot is created. We can write a constructor like this:

```
function Robot(){
  var createTime=new Date();
  this.getAge=function(){
    var now=new Date();
```

```
    var age=now-createTime;
    return age;
  }
}
```

(All the robots are identical, so we haven't bothered to assign names or anything else through constructor arguments.) Normally, we would record `createTime` as a member property, that is, write

```
this.createTime=new Date();
```

but here we've deliberately created it as a local variable, whose scope is limited to the block in which it is called, that is, the constructor. On the second line of the constructor, we define a function `getAge()`. Note here that we're defining a function inside another function and that the inner function uses the local variable createTime, belonging to the scope of the outer function. By doing this, and nothing else, we have in fact created a closure. If we define a robot and ask it how old it is once the page has loaded,

```
var robbie=new Robot();

window.onload=function(){
  alert(robbie.getAge());
}
```

then it works and gives us a value of around 10–50 milliseconds, the difference between the script first executing and the page loading up. Although we have declared createTime as being local to the constructor function scope, it cannot be garbage-collected so long as Robbie the robot is still referenced, because it has been bound up in a closure.

The closure works only if the inner function is created inside the outer one. If we refactor my code to predefine the `getAge` function and share it between all robot instances, like so

```
function Robot(){
  var createTime=new Date();
  this.getAge=roboAge;
}

function roboAge(){
  var now=new Date();
  var age=now-createTime;
  return age;
};
```

then the closure isn't created, and we get an error message telling me that createTime is not defined.

Closures are very easy to create and far too easy to create accidentally, because closures bind otherwise local variables and keep them from the garbage collector. If DOM nodes, for example, get caught up in this way, then inadvertently created closures can lead to significant memory leaks over time.

The most common situation in which to create closures is when binding an event-handler callback function to the source of the event. As we discussed in section B.3.4, the callback is invoked with a context and set of arguments that is sometimes not as useful as it might be. We presented a pattern for attaching additional references (the Model object) to the DOM element that generates the event, allowing us to retrieve the Model via the DOM element. Closures provide an alternative way of doing this, as illustrated here:

```
myObj.prototype.createView=function(){
  ...
  this.titleBar=document.createElement("div");
  var modelObj=this;
  this.titleBar.onclick=function(){
    fooEventHandler.call(modelObj);
  }
}
```

The anonymous `onclick` handler function that we define makes a reference to the locally declared variable `modelObj`, and so a closure is created around it, allowing `modelObj` to be resolved when the function is invoked. Note that closures will resolve only local variables, not those referenced through `this`.

We use this approach in the ContentLoader object that we introduced in chapter 2, because the `onreadystatechange` callback provided in Internet Explorer returns the window object as the function context. Since `window` is defined globally, we have no way of knowing which ContentLoader's readyState has changed, unless we pass a reference to the relevant loader object through a closure.

My recommendation to the average Ajax programmer is to avoid closures if there is an alternative. If you use the prototype to assign functions to your custom object types, then you don't duplicate the functions and you don't create closures. Let's rewrite our `Robot` class to follow this advice:

```
function Robot(){
  this.createTime=new Date();
}

Robot.prototype.getAge=function(){
  var now=new Date();
  var age=now-this.createTime;
  return age;
};
```

The function `getAge()` is defined only once, and, because it is attached to the prototype, it is accessible to every `Robot` that we create.

Closures have their uses, but we'd consider them an advanced topic. If you do want to explore closures in greater depth, then Jim Ley's article, listed in the Resources section, is a good place to start.

B.4 Conclusions

We've taken you through some of the stranger and more interesting features of the JavaScript language in this appendix, with two purposes in mind. The first was to show the expressive power of the language. The second was to point out several traps for the unwary, in which thinking in an OO style may result in suboptimal or even dangerous code.

We've looked at JavaScript's support for objects and at the similarities between the `Object` and `Array` classes. We've seen several ways of instantiating JavaScript objects, using JSON, constructor functions, and the prototype concept. Along the way, we've discussed how to tackle OO concepts such as inheritance and interfaces in JavaScript, in ways that work with rather than against the language.

In our exploration of JavaScript `Function` objects, we saw how functions can exist independently of any object to which they are assigned and even be borrowed or swapped between objects. We used this knowledge to get a better understanding of the JavaScript event model. Finally, we looked at closures and saw how some common programming idioms can create closures unintentionally, potentially resulting in memory leaks.

Compared to Java or C#, JavaScript offers a great deal of flexibility and scope for developing personal styles and approaches to the language. This can be liberating for the individual programmer, provided that you know what you are doing. It can also present problems when working in teams, but these problems can be alleviated by shared coding conventions or house styles.

JavaScript can be a very enjoyable language to work with, once you understand what makes it tick. If you're coming to Ajax from a structured OO background, we hope that this chapter has helped you to cross the gap.

B.5 Resources

There are very few books on JavaScript the language, as opposed to web browser programming. David Flanagan's *JavaScript: The Definitive Guide* (O'Reilly, 2001) is the definitive work. It's a bit old, but a new version is due out next year. A more recent book, Nicholas Zakas's *Professional JavaScript for Web Developers* (Wrox, 2004) offers a good language overview, too, and covers some more recent developments in the language.

On the Web, Doug Crockford discusses object-oriented approaches to JavaScript, such as creating private members for classes (www.crockford.com/javascript/private.html) and inheritance (www.crockford.com/javascript/private.html). Peter-Paul Koch's Quirksmode site (http://quirksmode.org) also discusses many of the finer points of the language. Jim Ley's discussion of closures in JavaScript can be found at http://jibbering.com/faq/faq_notes/closures.html.

Mike Foster's x library can be found at www.cross-browser.com.

Ajax frameworks
and libraries

The last year has seen a rapid proliferation of Ajax and JavaScript frameworks, from small cross-browser wrapper utilities to complete end-to-end client and server solutions. In this appendix, we attempt to take a snapshot of the current range of offerings, with apologies to any that we've omitted.

We, the authors of this book, haven't personally used all of these frameworks and toolkits in a production setting, and in many cases we've based our descriptions on the author or vendor's own claims for the toolkit. If you're reading this a year after publication, many of the descriptions will be wildly inaccurate or out of date, and many of the frameworks may have been abandoned or absorbed into other projects. The current state of play is unstable, in our opinions, and we would expect a few successful frameworks to predominate over the next 12 months.

So here, without any further ado, is our roundup of Ajax frameworks that you might encounter in the wild. We haven't attempted to categorize them beyond listing them alphabetically. Many thanks to Michael Mahemoff who collected much of this information on his site at www.ajaxpatterns.org. Happy coding!

Accesskey Underlining Library
Open source
www.gerv.net/software/aul/

Adds accesskey underlining to pages without requiring <u> tags in the source. Tag items with the `accesskey` attribute and JavaScript will create the appropriate underlining tags in the DOM.

ActiveWidgets
Commercial with free download
www.activewidgets.com

Rich client JavaScript widgets; current flagship product is a rich grid widget.

Ajax JavaServer Faces Framework
Open source (Apache)
http://smirnov.org.ru/en/ajax-jsf.html

The Ajax-JSF framework is designed to allow simple conversion of any existing JavaServer Faces application to Ajax functionality. Most of the existing components can be used as is or simply converted to Ajax support. Proposal to MyFaces project. Minimal differences from JSF specifications.

Ajax JSP Tag Library
Open source
http://ajaxtags.sourceforge.net/

The Ajax JSP Tag Library is a set of JSP tags that simplify the use of Asynchronous JavaScript and XML (Ajax) technology in JavaServer Pages. This tag library eases development by not forcing J2EE developers to write the necessary JavaScript to implement an Ajax-capable web form.

Autocomplete retrieves a list of values that matches the string entered in a text form field as the user types. Callout displays a callout or popup balloon, anchored to an HTML element with an onclick event. Select populates a second select field based on a selection within a drop-down field. Toggle switches a hidden form field between true and false and at the same time switches an image between two sources. Update Field updates one or more form field values based on the response to text entered in another field.

Ajax.NET
Michael Schwarz (2005)
Unspecified, free to use
http://weblogs.asp.net/mschwarz/

Ajax.NET is a library enabling various kinds of access from JavaScript to server-side .NET. Can pass calls from JavaScript into .NET methods and back out to Java-Script callbacks. Can access session data from JavaScript. Caches results. No source code change needed on server side; mark methods to expose with an attribute. Provides full class support for return values on client-side JavaScript, including DataTable, DataSet, DataView, Arrays, and Collections.

AjaxAC
Open source (Apache 2.0)
http://ajax.zervaas.com.au

AjaxAC encapsulates the entire application in a single PHP class. All application code is self-contained in a single class (plus any additional JavaScript libraries). The calling PHP file/HTML page is very clean. You simply create the application class, then reference the application JavaScript and attach any required HTML elements to the application. No messy JavaScript code clogging up the calling HTML code; all events are dynamically attached. Easy to integrate with templating engine, and to hook into existing PHP classes or MySQL database for returning data from subrequests. Extensible widget structure lets you easily create further JavaScript objects (this needs a bit of work, though, according to the author).

AjaxAspects
Free to use with source
http://ajaxaspects.blogspot.com

AjaxAspects is an engine that uses JavaScript proxies to call server-side Web Service methods. Standard SOAP and WSDL is reused for the communication between client and server. Simple types and XML objects are supported as parameters and return values. Supports caching and queuing of actions.

AjaxCaller
Michael Mahemoff (2005)
Open source
http://ajaxify.com/run/testAjaxCaller

AjaxCaller is a basic thread-safe wrapper around XMLHttpRequest mainly for Ajax newcomers; still raw alpha and under development and is only packaged with the AjaxPatterns live search demo for now. Follows REST principles.

AjaxFaces
Open source (ASF)
http://myfaces.apache.org/

Apache's JavaServer Faces implementation; currently experimenting with Ajax support.

BackBase
Commercial with community edition
http://www.backbase.com

BackBase is a comprehensive browser-side framework with support for rich browser functionality as well as .NET and Java integration. BackBase provides Rich Internet Application (RIA) software that radically improves the usability and effectiveness of online applications, and increases developer productivity. With BackBase you can build web applications with a richer and more responsive user interface. BackBase provides separation of presentation from logic through a custom XHTML namespace.

Behaviour

Ben Nolan (2005)
Open source
www.ripcord.co.nz/behaviour/

Behaviour works by using CSS selectors to add JavaScript code to DOM elements. You create a hash of CSS selectors and functions that take an element, and add JavaScript event handlers such as `onclick`. You then register these rules against a page and compare them against their matching DOM elements, and the JavaScript code is added. The code is designed in a way that you can treat these rule files just like stylesheets so that all the page using them needs is an include. Behaviour's goal is to remove the heavy use of `onclick` attributes and script nodes from pages so they aren't messing up content. It works well and can help make your JavaScript more reusable since it's more centralized.

Bindows

Commercial
www.bindows.net

Bindows is a software development kit (SDK) that generates highly interactive Internet applications with richness that rivals modern desktop applications using the strong combination of DHTML, JavaScript, CSS, and XML. Bindows applications require no downloads and no installation on the user's side; only a browser is required (no Java, Flash, or ActiveX is used). Bindows provides a range of widgets, as well as native XML, SOAP, and XML-RPC support.

BlueShoes

Commercial with free version
www.blueshoes.org

Rich component suite, including a WYSIWYG text editor and spreadsheet widget.

CakePHP

Open source
http://cakephp.org/

A comprehensive port of Ruby on Rails to PHP, including top-notch support for Ajax.

CL-Ajax

Richard Newman (2005)
Open source
http://cliki.net/cl-ajax

CL-Ajax directs JavaScript calls directly into server-side Lisp functions. Generates JavaScript stub with arguments. Can call back to JavaScript functions or DOM objects. May be integrated into SAJAX.

ComfortASP.NET

Pre-release commercial with free download
www.daniel-zeiss.de/ComfortASP/

ComfortASP.NET is an approach that lets developers rely on pure ASP.NET programming while offering Ajax-like features. ComfortASP.NET uses Ajax (DHTML, JavaScript, XMLHTTP) to implement these features, but the web developer only implements pure server-side ASP.NET.

Coolest DHTML Calendar

Open source with commercial support
www.dynarch.com/projects/calendar/

Configurable JavaScript calendar widget; can be wired up to form fields as a drop-down or pop-up, and styled using CSS.

CPAINT
(Cross-Platform Asynchronous Interface Toolkit)

Open source (GPL and LGPL)
http://cpaint.sourceforge.net

CPAINT is a true Ajax implementation and JSRS (JavaScript Remote Scripting) implementation that supports both PHP and ASP/VBScript. CPAINT provides you the code required to implement Ajax and JSRS on the back-end, while the returned data is manipulated, formatted, and displayed on the front-end in JavaScript. This allows you to build web applications that can provide near real-time feedback to the user.

Dojo
Alex Russell (2004)
Open source
http://dojotoolkit.org

Dojo provides several libraries for use with Ajax, including widgets, an event model, and messaging using XMLHttpRequest and other techniques. Aims to support JavaScript in a range of settings, including SVG and Netscape's Java-based Rhino engine, as well as in the web browser.

DWR (Direct Web Remoting)
Open source (Apache)
www.getahead.ltd.uk/dwr

Direct Web Remoting is a framework for calling Java methods directly from Java-Script code. Like SAJAX, it can pass calls from JavaScript into Java methods and back out to JavaScript callbacks. It can be used with any web framework—such as Struts or Tapestry—following a Spring-like KISS/POJO/orthogonality philosophy. Direct Web Remoting is due to be incorporated into the next release of the Open-Symphony WebWorks framework.

Echo 2
Open source (MPL or GPL)
www.nextapp.com/products/echo2

Echo 2 allows you to code Ajax apps in pure Java. Automatically generates HTML and JavaScript, and coordinates messages between the browser and the server. Offers messaging in XML. The developer can handwrite custom JavaScript components if desired.

f(m)
Open source
http://fm.dept-z.com/

The f(m) project is an ECMAScript Base Class Library, based on the .NET Framework, that was written to serve as the foundation for a new breed of browser-based web applications.

FCKEditor
Open source
www.fckeditor.net

Rich WYSIWYG editor widget; can be swapped in for an HTML textarea in one line of JavaScript code, allowing easy integration with existing web applications, CMS, wikis, and so forth. Very similar functionality to TinyMCE.

Flash JavaScript Integration Kit
Open source
www.osflash.org/doku.php?id=flashjs

The Flash JavaScript Integration Kit allows for the integration of JavaScript and Flash content. Enables JavaScript to invoke ActionScript functions, and vice versa. All major data types can be passed between the two environments.

Google AjaxSLT
Open source license (BSD)
http://goog-ajaxslt.sourceforge.net

AjaxSLT is offered by the innovative search solutions company that refers to itself as "Google." Google AjaxSLT is a JavaScript framework for performing XSLT transformations as well as XPath queries. Builds on Google Map work.

Guise
Commercial with free downloads
www.javaguise.com

Java-based server-side component model (similar in some ways to JSF, but simpler). Currently integrates Ajax functionality for greater responsiveness.

HTMLHttpRequest
Angus Turnbull (2005)
Open source (LGPL)
www.twinhelix.com/JavaScript/htmlhttprequest/

Simple remote scripting wrapper. Uses XMLHttpRequest and IFrames as well for improved compatibility.

Interactive Website Framework
Open source
http://sourceforge.net/projects/iwf/

Interactive Website Framework is a project whose aim is to support the various aspects of Ajax infrastructure in the browser. Describes itself as a framework for creating highly interactive websites using JavaScript, CSS, XML, and HTML. Includes a custom XML parser for highly readable JavaScript. Contains essentially all the plumbing for making Ajax-based websites, as well as other common scripts. Provides a thread-safe XMLHttpRequest implementation and a wrapper around the DOM, making for more readable code.

Jackbe
Commercial
www.jackbe.com/solutions/development.html

Ajax rich client widget suite; can be plugged into any middleware technology such as ASP, Java, .NET, or PHP.

JPSpan
Open source (PHP)
http://jpspan.sourceforge.net/wiki/doku.php

JPSpan passes JavaScript calls directly to PHP functions. Heavily unit-tested.

jsolait
Open source (LGPL)
http://jsolait.net

Set of open source JavaScript libraries, including cryptography, serialization and deserialization, XML-RPC, and JSON-RPC.

JSON
Open source; most implementations are LGPL
www.json-rpc.org/

JSON is a "fat-free XML alternative" and JSON-RPC is a remote procedure protocol, akin to XML-RPC, with strong support for JavaScript clients. Implementations exist for several server-side languages and platforms, including Java, Python, Ruby, and Perl.

JSRS (JavaScript Remote Scripting)

Brent Ashley (2000)
Open source
www.ashleyit.com/rs/jsrs/test.htm

JSRS routes calls directly from JavaScript into your server-side language and back out again. Known browsers: IE 4+, Netscape 4.*x*, Netscape 6.*x*, Mozilla, Opera 7, and Galeon. Server-side support: ASP, ColdFusion, PerlCGI, PHP, Python, and JSP (servlet).

LibXMLHttpRequest

Stephen W. Coate (2003)
Source available, protected by copyright
www.whitefrost.com/servlet/connector?file=reference/2003/06/17/libXml-Request.html

LibXMLHttpRequest is a thin wrapper around XMLHttpRequest.

Mochikit

Open source (MIT)
www.mochikit.com/

Mochikit is a set of libraries whose highlights include logging, visual effects, asynchronous task management, string and date/time formatting, and a "painless" DOM manipulation API that makes heavy use of JavaScript's built-in Array objects and JSON-like notation to represent the DOM.

netWindows

Open source
www.netwindows.org

Complete DHTML desktop/windowing environment inside the browser. Code is purely standards-based, with no browser hacks. Contains a "signals and slots" messaging implementation, modeled after Trolltech's Qt widgets and the Smalltalk language; also available as a standalone library.

Oddpost

Commercial
www.oddpost.com

JavaScript widget suite; includes fully functional rich e-mail client. Now part of Yahoo!.

OpenRico

Bill Scott, Darren James (2005)
Open source
http://openrico.org

A multipurpose framework with support for Ajax. Covers user interface issues such as animations, separation of content from logic through behaviors, drag and drop, and some prebuilt widgets, notably a data grid. Sponsored by Sabre Airline Solutions; has seen real-world use. Built on top of Prototype.

Pragmatic Objects

Open source
http://pragmaticobjects.com/products.html

Pragmatic Objects' WebControls is a set of JSP tag libraries designed as reusable controls or components to enrich Java-based web applications. As opposed to rich but fat web applications, a thin client web application, at the end of the day, consists of nothing but a series of HTML pages, containing JavaScript and CSS codes that are rendered by the browsers. Current offerings consist of an "outlook bar," a tree widget, and a control panel.

Prototype

Sam Stephenson (2004)
Open source
http://prototype.conio.net/

Prototype is a JavaScript framework designed for RIA development. It includes a solid Ajax library and a toolkit to simplify use. Prototype is the JavaScript engine for Ruby on Rails, Rico, and Scriptaculous, among others. Prototype's JavaScript code is generated from Ruby, but the generated JavaScript may be deployed in non-Ruby environments.

Qooxdoo

Open source (LGPL)
http://qooxdoo.sourceforge.net

This is an Ajax user interface library with a large range of prebuilt components and a well-thought-out design. Includes widgets, layout managers, and portable PNG transparency. Also provides development support such as timers for profiling and debugger support.

RSLite

Brent Ashley (pre-2000)
www.ashleyit.com/rs/main.htm

A simple component released as part of Brent Ashley's more comprehensive Remote Scripting work (see the JSRS entry earlier in this appendix).

Ruby on Rails

David Heinemeier Hansson (2004)
Open source (MIT)
www.rubyonrails.org

Ruby on Rails is a general web framework with strong Ajax support. Rails was still in its early days when the Ajax hype began, so Ajax may become increasingly core to the Rails framework. Generates most if not all of the JavaScript for widgets and animation in the browser. Support for calling server-side. Scheduling support. Current darling of the fashionable web development crowd, Ruby on Rails eschews the complex overdesigned, cover-all-bases strategy in favor of a straightforward, getting-the-job-done approach, with the help of a good deal of code generation. Has won over many Java developers for that reason. Our interest in Ruby on Rails for the purposes of this book is primarily its very good support for Ajax. Prototype, and most recently Scriptaculous, have been integrated into Rails.

Sack

Open source (modified MIT/X11)
http://twilightuniverse.com/2005/05/sack-of-ajax

Sack is a thin wrapper around XMLHttpRequest. The caller can specify a callback function or a callback DOM object. With a callback DOM, the response text is pushed directly into the DOM.

SAJAX

Open source
www.modernmethod.com/sajax

SAJAX routes calls directly from JavaScript into your server-side language and back out again. So, for example, calling a JavaScript method `x_calculateBudget()` will go the server and call a Java `calculateBudget()` method, then return the value in JavaScript to `x_calculateBudget_cb()`. Facilitates mapping from a JavaScript stub function to a back-end operation. Capable of stubbing calls to numerous server-side platforms: ASP, ColdFusion, Io, Lua, Perl, PHP, Python, and Ruby.

Sarissa
Open source (GPL and LGPL)
http://sarissa.sf.net

Sarissa is a JavaScript API that encapsulates XML functionality in browser-independent calls. Supports a variety of XML technologies, including XPath queries, XSLT, and serialization of JavaScript objects to XML, in a browser-neutral way.

Scriptaculous
Thomas Fuchs (2004)
Open source
http://script.aculo.us

Scriptaculous is a well-documented visual effects library built in JavaScript on top of Prototype. It includes demos, sample applications, and a drag-and-drop library.

SWATO...
Open source (ASF)
http://swato.dev.java.net

SWATO (Shift Web Application TO...) is a set of reusable and well-integrated Java/JavaScript libraries that give you an easier way to shift the interaction of your web apps through the Ajax way. The server-side Java library can be easily deployed in all Servlet 2.3+ compatible containers. The client-side JavaScript library can be worked in various browsers, as long as XMLHttpRequest is supported. SWATO uses JSON to marshal the data of your POJOs on the server side, so that you can access the remote data in any JavaScript environment (HTML, XUL, SVG) easily by either hard-coding or by integrating with mature JavaScript libraries. Comes with several reusable components (Auto-complete Textbox, Live Form, Live List, etc.) that help you develop your web apps rapidly.

Tibet
Commercial
www.technicalpursuit.com

Tibet aims to provide a highly portable and comprehensive JavaScript API, so that a great amount of client-side code is possible. Pitches itself as "Enterprise Ajax." Supports web service standards such as SOAP and XML-RPC, with prebuilt support for some popular web services such as Google, Amazon, and Jabber instant messaging. Includes an IDE written in JavaScript using the Tibet toolkit.

TinyMCE
Open source, with commercial backing and some proprietary plug-ins
http://tinymce.moxiecode.com/

Rich WYSIWYG editor widget; can be swapped in for an HTML textarea in one line of JavaScript code, allowing easy integration with existing web applications, CMS, wikis, etc. Very similar functionality to FCKEditor.

TrimPath Templates
Open source
http://trimpath.com/project/wiki/JavaScriptTemplates

JavaScript template engine for splicing together data and presentation on the browser.

Walter Zorn's DHTML Libraries
Open source
www.walterzorn.com/index.htm

DHTML libraries for drag-and-drop support, and for vector graphics drawing of lines and curves by using DIV elements as pixels.

WebORB for .NET
Commercial with free edition
www.themidnightcoders.com/weborb/aboutWeborb.htm

WebORB for .NET is a platform for developing Ajax and Flash-based rich client application and connecting them with .NET objects and XML web services.

WebORB for Java
Commercial with community/free edition
www.themidnightcoders.com/weborb/aboutWeborb.htm

WebORB for Java is a platform for developing Ajax and Flash-based rich client application and connecting them with Java objects and XML web services. Includes a client-side library called Rich Client System (www.themidnightcoders.com/rcs/index.htm). The Rich Client System provides a simple one-line API to bind to and invoke any method on any Java object, XML web service, or Enterprise JavaBean. Provides a special API for handling database query results; the server code can return DataSets or DataTables, and the client presents it as a special RecordSet JavaScript object. The object provides a way to retrieve column names as well as row data.

x

Mike Foster (2005)
Open source
www.cross-browser.com

Veteran DHTML library, providing cross-browser support for animation, styling, events, and other common functionality.

XAJAX

J. Max Wilson (2005)
Open source
http://xajax.sf.net

XAJAX passes JavaScript calls directly to PHP functions. Use a JavaScript stub to call a PHP script.

x-Desktop

Open source (GPL)
www.x-desktop.org/

This project comprises a library for developing thin client application front-ends using a browser. It helps developers to create GUI application interfaces for Internet, intranet, and extranet applications. x-Desktop features include the fact that it is browser based and that no plug-ins are required. It supports all operating systems that provide a DOM 2/JavaScript capable browser; offers a simple, well-documented object interface; and provides a customizable desktop and window skins.

XHConn

Brad Fults (2005)
http://xkr.us/code/JavaScript/XHConn

XHConn is a thin wrapper around XMLHttpRequest.

index